OUR
NATIONAL
PARKS

READER'S DIGEST

OUR NATIONAL PARKS

America's Spectacular Wilderness Heritage

The Reader's Digest Association, Inc.
Pleasantville, New York/Montreal

OUR NATIONAL PARKS

Project Editor: Susan J. Wernert
Project Art Editor: Evelyn S. Bauer
Senior Editor: Richard L. Scheffel
Associate Editor: James Dwyer
Associate Editor: Sharon Fass Yates
Art Associate: Roger Jones
Editorial Assistant: Melanie D. Hulse
Special Typesetting: Grace Del Bagno
Picture Editor: Robert J. Woodward
Associate Picture Editor: Richard Pasqual
Copy Editor: Patricia M. Godfrey

The Library of Congress has cataloged the
earlier edition as follows:

Our national parks: America's spectacular wilderness heritage.—
    Updated ed.
        p.   cm.
    At head of title: Reader's digest.
    Includes index.
    ISBN 0-89577-336-8
    1. National parks and reserves—United States.
I. Reader's digest.
E160.093   1989   89-3561
917.3—dc20   CIP

New Revised Edition ISBN 0-89577-941-2

Reader's Digest and the Pegasus logo are
registered trademarks of
The Reader's Digest Association, Inc.

Printed in the United States of America

Second Printing, August 2000

Contents

Where the Parks Are   6
Visitors' Guide   8
The Story of Our National Parks   10

Acadia, MAINE   16
*A rocky coast of cliffs and coves encircles a wilderness
of woodlands and ancient mountains.*

Arches, UTAH   24
*Dotting an austere yet hauntingly beautiful
desertscape is the world's largest concentration of
natural arches.*

Badlands, SOUTH DAKOTA   32
*From horizon to horizon, strangely eroded hills
and gullies are streaked with bands of color.*

Big Bend, TEXAS   38
*A scenic blend of river, mountains, and rugged
desert supports an unexpected explosion of life.*

Biscayne, FLORIDA   48
*In waters once prowled by pirates, an undersea
world of coral reefs swarms with exotic creatures.*

Bryce Canyon, UTAH   56
*Carved into rocky cliffs, squadrons of pink
pinnacles and spires stand guard over a maze of
twisting ravines.*

Canyonlands, UTAH   62
*Rushing rivers carved this labyrinth of brooding,
steep-walled desert chasms.*

Capitol Reef, UTAH   70
*To the Navajo these ramparts of multicolored
rock were the "Land of the Sleeping Rainbow."*

Carlsbad Caverns, NEW MEXICO   76
*Two spectaculars highlight the park — fantastic
caverns and nightly flights by clouds of bats.*

Channel Islands, CALIFORNIA   82
*Seabirds galore and six kinds of seals breed on the
islands — actually the tips of underwater mountains.*

Crater Lake, OREGON   90
*Cupped atop a collapsed volcano is the deepest,
clearest, bluest lake in all of the United States.*

Death Valley, CALIFORNIA-NEVADA   96
*Hottest, driest, lowest — the superb desert preserve
boasts a trio of superlatives.*

Denali, ALASKA   98
*Mount McKinley, North America's loftiest peak, is
the scenic centerpiece of a wildlife extravaganza.*

Dry Tortugas, FLORIDA   106
*At the farthest tip of the Florida Keys, the cluster
of islands seems afloat in a shimmering sea.*

Everglades, FLORIDA   108
*From alligators to zebra butterflies, the wetland
wonderland is teeming with life.*

Glacier, MONTANA 118
Glaciers sculpted these magnificent mountains, bejeweled with lakes and laced with waterfalls.

Grand Canyon, ARIZONA 126
From top to bottom and from rim to rim, the grandest of chasms is awesome to behold.

Grand Teton, WYOMING 136
Sky-piercing pinnacles and lowland valleys were once the haunts of mountain men.

Great Basin, NEVADA 146
Rising from the desert floor, snow-capped mountains offer marvelous surprises.

Great Smoky Mountains, 148
TENNESSEE-NORTH CAROLINA
Rank upon rank, the rolling mountain ridges are ever veiled in misty haze.

Guadalupe Mountains, TEXAS 154
In the midst of the desert, a vast undersea reef has risen to form a rugged, rocky mountain range.

Haleakala, HAWAII 160
The volcano's crater is a barren moonscape, but its slopes are lush and green with life.

Hawaii Volcanoes, HAWAII 166
Simmering still, the park's volcanoes periodically put on a spectacular show.

Hot Springs, ARKANSAS 174
Twin elixirs — soothing waters and wooded parklands — refresh and restore both body and soul.

Isle Royale, MICHIGAN 178
Lake Superior's natural ark, the island is home to wolves and moose and beavers and more.

Joshua Tree, CALIFORNIA 186
Intriguing trees, palm-fringed oases, and towering rock formations punctuate the desert wilderness.

Lassen Volcanic, CALIFORNIA 188
Boiling springs and bubbling mud pots are reminders that the great volcano is far from extinct.

Mammoth Cave, KENTUCKY 194
Hidden within a vast limestone plateau is the longest cave system in the world.

Mesa Verde, COLORADO 200
In a labor of lifetimes, vanished Indians built great dwellings in clefts high on canyon walls.

Mount Rainier, WASHINGTON 208
Great glaciers cloak the great volcano, towering high above Puget Sound.

North Cascades, WASHINGTON 216
Deer, bears, and mountain goats — all thrive in a magnificent medley of alpine scenery.

Olympic, WASHINGTON 222
Three worlds in one, the park boasts a seacoast, lush rain forests, and pristine mountain wilderness.

Petrified Forest, ARIZONA 232
In a colorful corner of the Painted Desert lie the remains of bygone forests that have been transformed into stone.

Redwood, CALIFORNIA 238
Towering trees — the tallest on earth — flourish in a splendid seaside sanctuary.

Rocky Mountain, COLORADO 246
From tundra on the peaks to forests on the slopes, a wondrous world of life abounds in this mountainous realm.

Saguaro, ARIZONA 256
Giant cactuses with upswept arms, stately saguaros hold center stage in an arid Eden.

Sequoia-Kings Canyon, CALIFORNIA 258
Ancient trees and dizzying chasms are twin hallmarks of a special wilderness domain.

Shenandoah, VIRGINIA 264
Superb in all seasons, the park is an ever-changing pageant of life.

Theodore Roosevelt, NORTH DAKOTA 272
From the moment he saw them, these badlands were good lands to the president-to-be.

Virgin Islands, U.S. VIRGIN ISLANDS 280
On land is the beauty of an idyllic isle, and offshore, the rainbow realm of the reef.

Voyageurs, MINNESOTA 288
This maze of bays and backwaters, islands and woodlands, is canoe country today just as it was in the past.

Wind Cave, SOUTH DAKOTA 294
Beneath rolling grasslands where bison still roam lies the secret world of a lovely cave.

Yellowstone, 300
WYOMING-MONTANA-IDAHO
Geysers and hot springs are only part of the allure of the superb and spectacular park.

Yosemite, CALIFORNIA 314
The picture-perfect scenic jewel is a matchless mix of mountains and valleys, wildlife and waterfalls.

Zion, UTAH 324
The canyon, lined with massive monoliths, is a peaceful haven in a harsh desert land

Our Special Alaskan Parks 332
From the golden dunes of Kobuk Valley to icebergs crashing endlessly into the sea at Glacier Bay, these seven Alaskan parks are filled with grand and glorious scenic spectacles.

Index 346
Acknowledgments and Credits 351

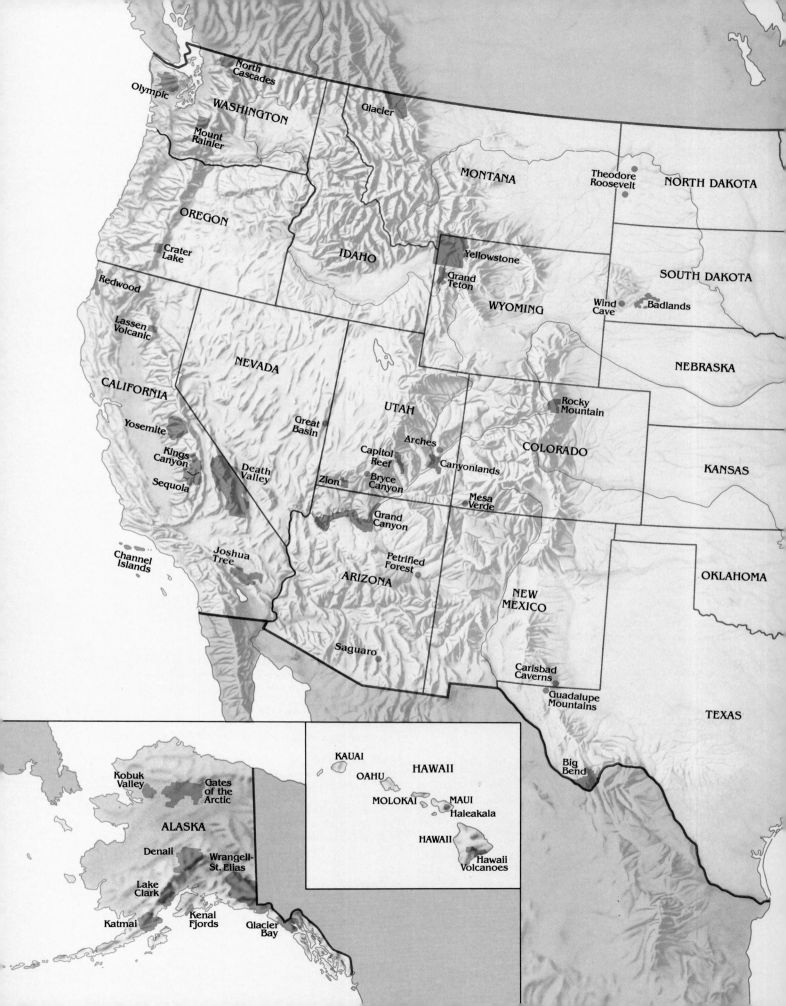

North
Cascades

Olympic

WASHINGTON

Glacier

Mount
Rainier

MONTANA

Theodore
Roosevelt

NORTH DAKOTA

OREGON

Crater
Lake

IDAHO

Yellowstone

SOUTH DAKOTA

Redwood

Grand
Teton

WYOMING

Wind
Cave

Badlands

Lassen
Volcanic

NEVADA

NEBRASKA

CALIFORNIA

Rocky
Mountain

Yosemite

Great
Basin

UTAH

Arches

COLORADO

KANSAS

Kings
Canyon

Capitol
Reef

Canyonlands

Death
Valley

Sequoia

Zion

Bryce
Canyon

Mesa
Verde

Grand
Canyon

Channel
Islands

Joshua
Tree

Petrified
Forest

OKLAHOMA

ARIZONA

NEW
MEXICO

Saguaro

Carlsbad
Caverns

Guadalupe
Mountains

TEXAS

Big
Bend

KAUAI

HAWAII

OAHU

Kobuk
Valley

Gates
of the
Arctic

MOLOKAI

MAUI

Haleakala

ALASKA

Denali

Wrangell-
St. Elias

HAWAII

Lake
Clark

Hawaii
Volcanoes

Katmai

Kenai
Fjords

Glacier
Bay

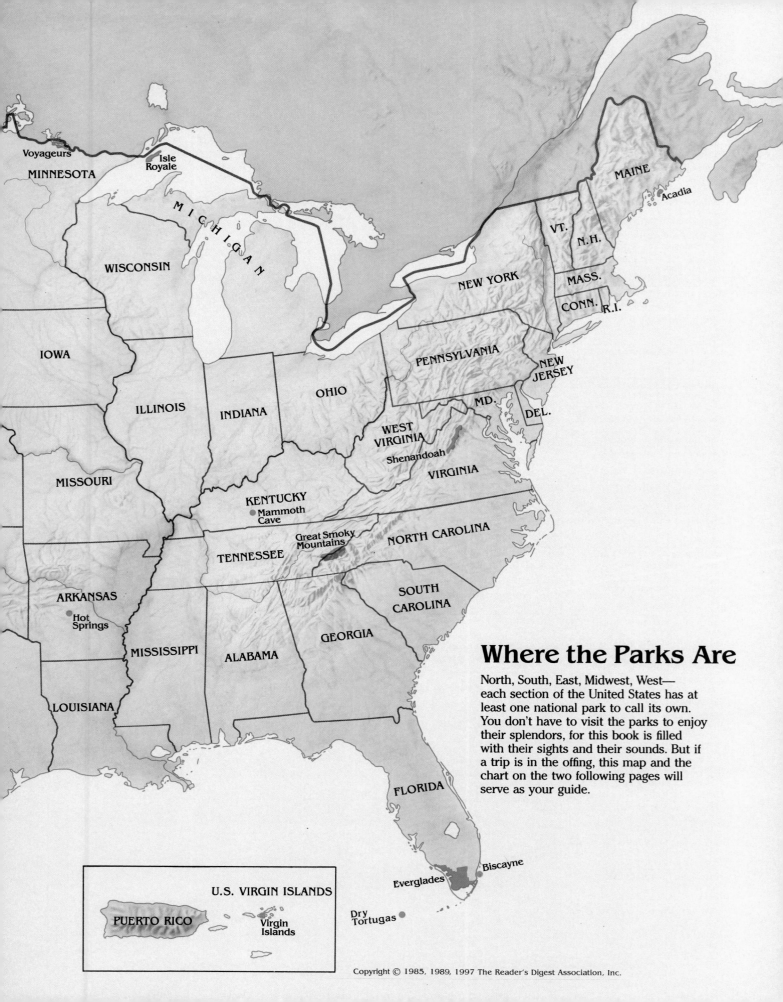

Voyageurs

MINNESOTA

Isle
Royale

WISCONSIN

M I C H I G A N

MAINE

Acadia

VT.

N.H.

IOWA

NEW YORK

MASS.

CONN.

R.I.

PENNSYLVANIA

NEW
JERSEY

ILLINOIS

INDIANA

OHIO

MD.

DEL.

WEST
VIRGINIA

Shenandoah

VIRGINIA

MISSOURI

KENTUCKY

Mammoth
Cave

Great Smoky
Mountains

NORTH CAROLINA

TENNESSEE

ARKANSAS

Hot
Springs

SOUTH
CAROLINA

MISSISSIPPI

ALABAMA

GEORGIA

Where the Parks Are

North, South, East, Midwest, West—
each section of the United States has at
least one national park to call its own.
You don't have to visit the parks to enjoy
their splendors, for this book is filled
with their sights and their sounds. But if
a trip is in the offing, this map and the
chart on the two following pages will
serve as your guide.

LOUISIANA

FLORIDA

Biscayne

U.S. VIRGIN ISLANDS

Everglades

PUERTO RICO

Virgin
Islands

Dry
Tortugas

Park	Entrance Fee	Visitor center	Museum	N.P.S. guided tour	Camping	Backcountry use permits	Hiking	Mountain climbing	Horseback riding	Swimming	Boat rental	Boat ramp	Fishing	Bicycling	Snowmobiling	Cross-country skiing	Cabin rental	Hotel, motel, lodge	Groceries, ice	Restaurants, snacks	Handicap: Visitor center	Handicap: Restrooms	Handicap: Campsites
Acadia National Park P.O. Box 177 Bar Harbor, Maine 04609	●	●	●	●	●		●	●	●		●	●	●	●				●	●	●	●	●	●
Arches National Park P.O. Box 907 Moab, Utah 84532	●	●	●	●	●	●	●	●													●	●	●
Badlands National Park P.O. Box 6 Interior, South Dakota 57750	●	●	●	●	●								●			●	●		●	●	●	●	●
Big Bend National Park Big Bend N.P., Texas 79834	●	●		●	●	●					●	●				●	●	●	●	●	●	●	
Biscayne National Park P.O. Box 1369 Homestead, Florida 33090-1369		●		●		●				●		●								●	●		
Bryce Canyon National Park Bryce Canyon, Utah 84717	●	●	●	●	●	●	●		●					●	●	●	●	●	●	●	●	●	●
Canyonlands National Park 2282 S. West Resource Blvd. Moab, Utah 54532	●	●		●	●	●							●								●	●	
Capitol Reef National Park HC 70 Box 15 Torrey, Utah 84775	●	●	●	●	●	●							●								●	●	●
Carlsbad Caverns National Park 3225 National Parks Highway Carlsbad, New Mexico 88220	●	●	●	●	●	●													●		●	●	
Channel Islands National Park 1901 Spinnaker Drive Ventura, California 93001		●	●	●	●		●			●											●	●	
Crater Lake National Park P.O. Box 7 Crater Lake, Oregon 97604	●	●	●	●	●	●	●						●			●		●	●	●	●	●	●
Death Valley National Park P.O. Box 579 Death Valley, California 92328	●	●	●	●	●	●	●	●	●	●			●				●	●	●	●	●	●	●
Denali National Park and Preserve P.O. Box 9 Denali Park, Alaska 99755	●	●		●	●	●	●	●					●			●		●	●	●	●	●	●
Dry Tortugas National Park 40001 State Road 9336 Homestead, Florida 33034-6733		●	●		●					●			●								●	●	
Everglades National Park 4001 State Road 9336 Homestead, Florida 33034-6733	●	●		●	●	●	●		●		●	●	●					●	●	●	●	●	●
Gates of the Arctic National Park P.O. Box 74680 Fairbanks, Alaska 99707				●	●			●		●			●			●							
Glacier National Park West Glacier, Montana 59936	●	●		●	●	●	●	●	●		●					●	●	●	●	●	●	●	●
Glacier Bay National Park and Preserve P.O. Box 140 Gustavus, Alaska 99826		●		●	●	●	●				●	●	●			●		●	●	●	●	●	
Grand Canyon National Park P.O. Box 129 Grand Canyon, Arizona 86023	●	●	●	●	●	●	●		●							●	●	●	●	●	●	●	●
Grand Teton National Park P.O. Drawer 170 Moose, Wyoming 83012	●	●	●	●	●	●	●	●	●	●	●	●	●	●		●	●	●	●	●	●	●	●
Great Basin National Park Baker, Nevada 89311		●		●	●		●						●			●		●		●	●	●	●
Great Smoky Mountains National Park 107 Park Headquarters Road Gatlinburg, Tennessee 37738		●	●	●	●	●	●		●				●				●				●	●	●
Guadalupe Mountains National Park HC 60, Box 400 Salt Flat, Texas 79847-9400		●	●	●	●	●	●														●	●	●
Haleakala National Park P.O. Box 369 Makawao, Maui, Hawaii 96768	●	●		●	●	●	●						●				●				●	●	●
Hawaii Volcanoes National Park P.O. Box 52 Hawaii, 96718	●	●	●	●	●	●	●						●				●	●	●	●	●	●	●
Hot Springs National Park P.O. Box 1860 Hot Springs N.P., Arkansas 71902-1860		●	●	●		●		●									●	●	●	●	●	●	●

Park	Entrance Fee	Visitor center	Museum	N.P.S. guided tour	Camping	Backcountry use permits	Hiking	Mountain climbing	Horseback riding	Swimming	Boat rental	Boat ramp	Fishing	Bicycling	Snowmobiling	Cross-country skiing	Cabin rental	Hotel, motel, lodge	Groceries, ice	Restaurants, snacks	Handicap access: Visitor center	Handicap access: Restrooms	Handicap access: Campsites
Isle Royale National Park 800 E. Lakeshore Drive Houghton, Michigan 49931		●	●	●	●	●	●				●		●				●	●	●	●	●	●	●
Joshua Tree National Park 74485 National Park Drive 29 Palms, California 92277	●	●	●	●	●	●	●	●	●					●				●	●	●	●	●	●
Katmai National Park P.O. Box 7 King Salmon, Alaska 99613		●		●	●	●	●	●			●	●	●		●	●	●	●		●	●	●	
Kenai Fjords National Park and Preserve P.O. Box 1727 Seward, Alaska 99664		●		●	●		●	●					●	●	●	●	●				●	●	
Kobuk Valley National Park P.O. Box 1029 Kotzebue, Alaska 99752														●		●							
Lake Clark National Park and Preserve 4230 University Drive, Suite 311 Anchorage, Alaska 99508		●		●	●		●	●		●	●		●		●	●	●	●		●			
Lassen Volcanic National Park P.O. Box 100 Mineral, California 96063	●	●		●	●	●	●		●	●		●	●	●		●	●		●	●	●	●	●
Mammoth Cave National Park Mammoth Cave, Kentucky 42259		●		●	●	●	●		●			●	●				●	●	●	●	●	●	●
Mesa Verde National Park P.O. Box 8 Mesa Verde N.P., Colorado 81330	●	●	●	●	●		●									●		●	●	●	●	●	●
Mount Ranier National Park Tahoma Woods, Star Route Ashford, Washington 98304-9751	●	●	●	●	●	●	●	●					●			●	●	●	●	●	●	●	●
North Cascades National Park 2105 State Route 20 Sedro Woolley, Washington 98284		●		●	●	●	●	●	●		●	●	●		●	●	●	●	●	●	●	●	●
Olympic National Park 600 East Park Avenue Port Angeles, Washington 98362	●	●	●	●	●	●	●	●	●	●	●	●	●	●	●	●	●	●	●	●	●	●	●
Petrified Forest National Park P.O. Box 2217 Petrified Forest, Arizona 86028	●	●	●			●	●													●	●	●	
Redwood National and State Parks 1111 Second Street Crescent City, California 95531		●		●	●	●	●		●	●		●	●					●	●	●	●	●	●
Rocky Mountain National Park Estes Park, Colorado 80517	●	●	●	●	●	●	●	●	●				●	●	●	●			●	●	●	●	●
Saguaro National Park 3693 South Old Spanish Trail Tucson, Arizona 85730	●	●	●	●	●	●	●		●					●							●	●	
Sequoia-Kings Canyon National Parks Three Rivers, California 93271	●	●	●	●	●	●	●	●	●	●			●			●	●	●	●	●	●	●	●
Shenandoah National Park Route 4 Box 34 Luray, Virginia 22835-9051	●	●		●	●	●	●	●	●				●			●	●	●	●	●	●	●	●
Theodore Roosevelt National Park P.O. Box 7 Medora, North Dakota 58645	●	●	●	●	●	●			●							●					●	●	●
Virgin Islands National Park 6310 Estate Nazareth # 1 St. Thomas, VI 00802		●	●	●	●		●			●			●				●	●	●	●	●	●	●
Voyageurs National Park 3131 Highway 53 International Falls, Minnesota 56649-8904		●		●	●		●			●	●	●	●		●	●	●	●	●	●	●	●	●
Wind Cave National Park RR 1, Box 190 Hot Springs, South Dakota 57747		●	●	●	●	●	●							●						●	●	●	●
Wrangell-St. Elias National Park P.O. Box 439 Cooper Center, Alaska 99573		●			●		●	●	●				●	●	●	●	●	●	●	●	●		
Yellowstone National Park P.O. Box 168 Yellowstone N.P., Wyoming 82190	●	●	●	●	●	●	●		●		●	●	●	●	●	●	●	●	●	●	●	●	●
Yosemite National Park P.O. Box 577 Yosemite, California 95389	●	●	●	●	●	●	●	●	●	●			●	●		●	●	●	●	●	●	●	●
Zion National Park Springdale, Utah 84767-1099	●	●	●	●	●	●	●	●	●					●		●	●	●	●	●	●	●	●

The Story of Our National Parks

May was a good time to be on the Great Plains, and 1832 was the best of years. The sky reached forever across a landscape flowing with lush young prairie grasses and vibrant with life. Great herds of bison fattened on the greening land—still virgin, untouched by the plow. Endless flocks of birds swept northward toward their nesting grounds, and prairie dogs yipped in the warm breezes.

Most Americans knew little of this landscape—the ever-encroaching frontier was still far to the east—but some were learning fast. One of these, an artist named George Catlin, who specialized in paintings of American Indians, was enjoying the experience immensely. On this particular day in May he was writing in his journal about what he had seen along the Missouri River in what is now South Dakota, slightly east of today's Badlands National Park. As he wrote of strange peoples and endless plains, an idea took shape—a unique and prophetic idea, one far ahead of its time.

"What a beautiful and thrilling specimen," he wrote, "for America to preserve and hold up to the view of her refined citizens and the world in future ages! A nation's Park, containing man and beast, in all the wild and freshness of their nature's beauty!"

A nation's park? In 1832 a park was a carefully cultivated landscape, an estate maintained by gardeners, with gentlefolk in residence—not a raw expanse populated by shaggy buffalo and wild Indians.

Explorers and dreamers

Almost forty years passed. The nation's border reached westward to California and Oregon, but it was a leapfrog expansion. Between the true frontier and the goldfields of California lay unmapped mountains, unknown canyons, and murderous deserts. It was a time for adventurers; among the greatest of them was Maj. John Wesley Powell. A scientist as well as an explorer, he spent the summer of 1869 navigating and mapping the Green and Colorado rivers as they sliced and raged through the mighty canyons of the Colorado Plateau.

In May of that same year, as Powell was preparing to embark on his momentous journey, a 31-year-old man, lanky, bearded, and full of life, walked eastward across the beautiful Central Valley of California. His name was

In the summer of 1871, the painter Thomas Moran viewed the Grand Canyon of the Yellowstone, which he later rendered in oil (above). The painting was an important part of the campaign for the first national park. Meanwhile, other explorers were discovering the wonders of the West; in 1869, as John Muir was reveling in the glories of the Sierra Nevada, Maj. John Wesley Powell was running the rapids in the Grand Canyon of the Colorado River (right).*

John Muir, and he was to become the most important single individual in the national park saga. He reveled in the vast meadowlands and scattered oak groves, the wildflower tapestries that touched the horizon ("bee pastures," he called them). Yet it was the great snowy range to the east that beckoned him—the Sierra Nevada, a mammoth, weathered block of granite that he would soon call the Range of Light. There, in the valley of the Yosemite, aroar with great waterfalls and rimmed by cliffs that framed the deep blue California sky, the young man was ecstatic. In the springtime of his life he had found pure delight.

During the next decade he was to immerse himself in the grandeur of the place, hiking the high country, climbing cliffs, almost freezing on mountains, testing the limits of endurance. Once he climbed a 10-story-tall Douglas fir during a winter gale and swayed for hours, exhilarating in "the passionate music of the storm."

Meanwhile, in September 1869, a week after Powell had emerged from the Grand Canyon, three men from Diamond City, Montana—David E. Folsom, Charles W. Cook, and William Peterson—gazed with awe at the wonders of a region known as Yellowstone. The three said little to others about their discoveries, but what they *did* say whetted people's appetites. For decades, tales of steaming fountains and petrified trees had been repeated over campfires. Confirmation awaited the word of more reputable and eloquent men.

A year later, in August of 1870, another group visited Yellowstone. This expedition bore the stamp of authority: a small detachment of U.S. cavalry served as escort, and the leader was Henry Washburn, surveyor general of Montana. For six weeks the men explored, crossing high snowy passes, gazing into the depths of the Grand Canyon of the Yellowstone, skirting the immensity of Yellowstone Lake, and finally setting up camp in the unique, steamy land of the geyser basins.

When they left Yellowstone, they carried with them the conviction that this magnificent wilderness should never fall prey to private exploitation: a national park *must* be established there. In the following months the expedition's members spoke often about their conviction, and the next summer a much larger party, led by the explorer-scientist Ferdinand V. Hayden, was sent to

In the 1830's and 1840's, adventurous painters such as John James Audubon and George Catlin roamed the wilderness, recording on canvas the continent's wildlife and native peoples. The red squirrels shown here, painted by Audubon in 1839, are a subspecies common in Glacier National Park.

11

In 1888, when this party posed on Yellowstone's Minerva Terrace, this part of the changeable Mammoth Hot Springs was inactive; today, as shown on pages 306–307, the steaming water flows freely, adding new limestone to the terraces. Visitors, delivered to the park's boundary by the Northern Pacific Railroad, toured in horse-drawn coaches.

Yellowstone. Hayden knew the value of documentation, so he took with him the photographer William Henry Jackson and the celebrated painter Thomas Moran. By the end of the summer, Jackson had produced the first photographs of Yellowstone and Moran had made sketches for a huge painting that was to hang for decades in the lobby of the U.S. Senate.

Soon every member of Congress knew about the wonders of Yellowstone. On March 1, 1872, after a short, vigorous lobbying campaign, the Yellowstone Park Act became law. The region was " . . . reserved and withdrawn from settlement, and dedicated and set apart as a public park or pleasuring-ground for the benefit and enjoyment of the people." The world's first national park had been born. Moreover, a precedent had been set; other parks would follow.

At the urging of friends, John Muir had begun to write about his beloved Yosemite, and his books and magazine articles rang with enthusiasm. At first he wrote only of beauty, but later a sense of mission was to seize him. In 1889, after a decade away from Yosemite, he returned, bringing with him Robert Underwood Johnson, an editor of *The Century,* one of the most widely read magazines of the time. The two were appalled that overgrazing by sheep had all but denuded the high country and the glorious valley. Even the area's groves of giant sequoias seemed threatened.

Johnson immediately began a campaign. At his urging, Muir wrote two articles for *The Century:* "The Treasures of the Yosemite" and "Features of the Proposed Yosemite National Park." Thomas Moran was hired to illustrate the articles. Having appealed to the public, Johnson then went personally before Congress.

America responded, Congress voted, and on October 1, 1890, the high country of Yosemite became a national park. Caught up in a wave of public opinion, Congress also voted that day to protect a magnificent grove of giant sequoia trees by establishing General Grant National Park (now part of Kings Canyon). A week earlier, other big trees had received protection through the establishment of Sequoia National Park.

Saving the wilderness
John Muir had become the father of our national park system. The later establishment of Mount Rainier, Petrified Forest, and Grand Canyon national parks was also due, in large measure, to his efforts. In 1903, after being guided by Muir on a four-day trek through Yosemite,

Perched 3,214 feet up on Yosemite's Overhanging Rock, William Henry Jackson prepared to take one of the pioneering scenic photos for which he became famous.

President Theodore Roosevelt was convinced that the park should be expanded; before his term in office ended, its boundaries included Yosemite Valley.

By the time of Roosevelt's presidency, the frontier was gone. No longer did bison roam the plains; never again would Indians follow their old ways. The thought bothered people. The challenge of new horizons had been a mighty force behind America's vitality; suddenly, the distant mountains and canyons that embodied that spirit took on new meaning.

Roosevelt's special love for the West had been born of tragedy and nurtured by personal renewal. On February 14, 1884, both his wife and his mother died, leaving him, at age 25, a man overwhelmed by sorrow. "The light has gone out of my life," he wrote in his diary. He soon went west to the Little Missouri River in Dakota Territory—a place that is now a national park bearing his name. There, astride his horse Manitou, he recovered from his sorrow by living the strenuous life of a working cowboy. The land gave him the gift of rebirth.

Later in his life, Roosevelt returned the gift. As president he worked diligently so that others could find vigor and health in the West he loved. Those were years in which such a man was needed. Magnificent groves of giant sequoias were being turned into shingles, and jewellike petrified trees were being blown to pieces by souvenir sellers. Something had to be done, and it was often Teddy Roosevelt who did it. Crater Lake, Mesa Verde, and Wind Cave became parks during his term of office, and he preserved other huge tracts of land—including the Grand Canyon, Mount Lassen, and Petrified Forest, later to become national parks.

The ranks of those who worked for the national parks were swelling rapidly. In Colorado, a writer named Enos Mills became the champion of the great soaring ridges and peaks of the Rocky Mountains in much the same way that Muir had been for Yosemite. In Oregon a judge named William Gladstone Steel fought for Crater Lake. The Grand Canyon had its champion in George Horace Lorimer, editor of *The Saturday Evening Post.* To remind him of the canyon's grandeur, he kept a huge Thomas Moran painting in his office. He even used it to judge the character of visitors; anyone who failed to appreciate the painting was in trouble. "I can tell 'em by that picture," he would say.

George Bird Grinnell, editor of *Forest and Stream,* argued for national parks as wildlife sanctuaries. First on his list of deserving places was a land of sharp-spined peaks and deep lakes in northern Montana. There grizzly bears and mountain goats found refuge, and a person could stand with one foot on the western edge of the Great Plains and the other on the front slopes of the Rockies. On May 11, 1910, after much work by Grinnell, the area became Glacier National Park.

Eastward ho!

Until 1919 all the national parks had been established in the West. There were reasons for that: the land was rich in magnificent scenery and natural wonders, and much of it already belonged to the government. But there were reasons for eastern parks too. The scenery, though not so grand, was certainly worth preserving, and the wildlife was even more endangered. Besides, only the wealthy had the leisure and the means to go west and stay for weeks at the great rustic hotels. Creating national parks closer to the people would help build the public support that was urgently needed.

The first eastern park, created in 1919, was along the rugged granite headlands of the Maine coast. Called Lafayette National Park, it later became Acadia. Farther south, the citizens of North Carolina and Tennessee made hundreds of thousands of small donations toward Great Smoky Mountains National Park. In much the same way, Shenandoah was born in the Blue Ridge Mountains of Virginia. Public donations were also important to Kentucky's Mammoth Cave.

At the same time, a new kind of park enthusiast was emerging—the philanthropist. A wealthy Bostonian, George B. Dorr, gave much of his fortune to Acadia. A tract of 5,000 acres near Carlsbad Caverns was given by William Pratt and his wife. When it came time to establish Grand Teton, Great Smoky Mountains, Acadia, and

Shenandoah, John D. Rockefeller, Jr., donated large tracts of land.

With each passing decade the story broadened. America was coming to value its wildlife, and so in 1934, for the first time, a national park was authorized for its preservation. This was Everglades, home to great flocks of elegant, endangered birds. In 1940, a rocky cluster of islands in the cold waters of Lake Superior became Isle Royale National Park, reachable only by boat.

Playgrounds or preserves?
After World War I, the parks became accessible by automobile, and the number of visitors soared. By the 1920's and 1930's, people were touring the nation's wonders and using them as playgrounds. It was just what friends of the national parks had most wanted. Signs went up identifying scenic features, museums were filled with mounted animals and geological specimens, and park rangers became teachers, interpreting the parks to crowds of visitors.

Sometimes education became amusement. In Sequoia, tunnels had already been cut through giant trees. Yosemite had one, too—and something else besides: during the summer, glowing coals were dumped over the cliffs of Glacier Point at dusk, creating a "firefall" that delighted visitors. In Yellowstone a spotlight was mounted atop the Old Faithful Inn to bathe nighttime eruptions of Old Faithful in colored light. Bear-feeding shows were held each evening, complete with grandstands and dozens of garbage-gobbling bears.

But the boom of those years was nothing compared with the explosion of visitors that began in the 1950's and continues today. Crowding became a problem. Tired vacationers were often faced by "Campground Full" signs; those who found accommodations were troubled by noise and lack of facilities. To answer the demand, more parks were established—Arches, Biscayne, Canyonlands, Capitol Reef, Channel Islands, Guadalupe Mountains, North Cascades, Redwood, and Voyageurs—and many others were expanded.

Still it had become clear by the mid 1970's that we had some tough choices to make: the national parks could not be, at once, wilderness sanctuaries and public playgrounds. Other kinds of parks and recreation areas must be used for sports and entertainment; the national parks must remain unique natural areas. To prevent overdevelopment, campsites were limited and reservation systems were introduced. To protect the backcountry, many roads were closed to private vehicles. To maintain the sense of wilderness, noise was curbed. To save our living heritage, a great deal of new thought was given to the management of wildlife.

The railroads played a large part in popularizing the national parks with ads like this one, from December 1910.

We have progressed a long way in our attitude toward widlife. The demands of conservation, we have found, are a great deal more complex than our grandparents ever imagined. When Steve Mather became the first director of the National Park Service in 1916, he ordered the killing of wolves, coyotes, and mountain lions so that deer and elk would flourish. Today we know that such predators are essential to healthy animal populations, and we value them: witness the equilibrium that has been struck between wolves and moose on Isle Royale.

There have been successes. Bison were almost extinct until a breeding program in Yellowstone brought them back. The graceful white trumpeter swans were saved by the protection given in Grand Teton and Yellowstone. Prairie dogs, which cattlemen had poisoned by the millions, dig their towns again beneath the grasslands of Badlands, Theodore Roosevelt, and Wind Cave, and badgers once more prowl after them. Roosevelt elk survive because of Olympic National Park, and Denali is a refuge for Dall sheep. Most of Shenandoah's deer are descendants of those brought in after hunters had eliminated the native population.

When natural fires were regularly extinguished, the sequoia groves of California became choked with small trees. Elsewhere, forests of lodgepole pines, dependent on fire for the release of seeds, began dying out. Today's solution is to let natural fires burn so that forests may renew themselves in the way nature intended.

New challenges
We are still a nation that looks forward, and our parks are continually threatened. In today's world an unprotected wilderness is doomed. Few living things can survive unless their total world is maintained.

The size of parks is important. They were seldom established with the needs of nature in mind. The elk of Yellowstone migrated down to Grand Teton each autumn, straight into hunters' gunfire, until the parks' borders were expanded to include the migration route. In Redwood, giant trees were toppling because logging just outside the park had created floods that undermined their roots. The park now includes a buffer zone.

In 1981 almost 44 million acres of Alaskan land became national parks, doubling the size of the system. Whole mountain ranges and river basins were preserved so that great herds of caribou could migrate unmolested, and grizzlies could prowl vast territories, as is their wont. Few people may visit these new parks in the near future, but that was true of Yellowstone, Glacier, Yosemite, and Grand Canyon once.

Dreams and memories

The national parks are an American triumph, a realized dream that has helped give us greatness. Though we may never see it, there will come a day when our children will remember a park they visited on a long-ago family trip. The memory will haunt them until they return. When they do, the cycle will be renewed; they will bring *their* children, perhaps even their grandchildren, to share the land.

For many of us, the memories span the continent and cross the years. Our minds are filled with snapshot images: a clear, sharp dawn from atop Acadia's Cadillac Mountain, the rising sun burnishing the Atlantic . . . the brooding mountains of Big Bend, lonely and silent in midwinter . . . the miracle of Crater Lake's blue, pure beyond reality . . . the endless sawgrass prairies of Everglades, and a huge alligator lying squarely across the trail . . . white plumes of beargrass against the turquoise of Glacier's Grinnell Lake, and a barefoot run across snowbanks on a hot July afternoon.

Different people hold different images: huge chunks of ice calving from glaciers, plunging deep into the leaden seawater of Glacier Bay . . . the Grand Canyon's immensity under a winter moon, even greater than by day . . . dawn in Grand Teton on the Fourth of July, the peaks lit by the rising sun . . . Newfound Gap on a gray February evening, the Great Smoky Mountains ahead coated with rime . . . the blue Pacific pounding itself into white spray against Hawaii Volcanoes' coastline of jagged black lava . . . a Rocky Mountain dawn, with sunlight filtering through the golden petals of countless alpine sunflowers . . . yellow lady's slippers on Shenandoah's Stony Man Mountain . . . great columns of steam billowing into Yellowstone's sharp morning air, mixing the pungence of hydrogen sulfide with the fragrance of spruce . . . Yosemite's sparkling waters and immutable granite, transcendent in purest light.

All our yesterdays and tomorrows are nourished by such subtleties and such grandeur. These are our national parks, a celebration of America. The dreams and memories they contain are in our care today; tomorrow's generations depend on us to keep them whole.

A VERY SPECIAL PARK: National Park of American Samoa

A ribbon of lush South Pacific islands surrounded by sparkling seas provides the idyllic setting for our only national park in the Southern Hemisphere. Rain—at a soggy 200-300 inches annually—nourishes the tropical forests that are home to a wide variety of plants and animals.

The mountaintops of Tutuila, the main island, boast a lush rain forest still largely undisturbed by man. Soaring overhead are fruit bats, called flying foxes, in search of the abundant fruit-bearing plants. Fruit bats are the park's most distinctive mammals; two species thrive here. The larger one, with wing spans of up to four feet, is among the few bats active during the day. In the forest's thick undergrowth are epiphytes, rootless plants that grow on other plants and live on rain, dust, and air.

Seabirds dwell on cliffs high above the shore: red-footed and brown boobies (so named because they sat still as sailors approached to kill them); petrels; blue-gray, brown, and black noddies; gray-backed and sooty terns; and great and lesser frigate birds—avian thieves that steal food from the beaks of other species. The reef heron, banded rail, and white-collared kingfisher inhabit the coastal areas along with several varieties of native doves, wattled and cardinal honey eaters, and Polynesian and Samoan starlings.

The waters off the island of Ofu boast a large section of coral reef undamaged by the predatory crown of thorns starfish. Here, schools of brilliantly colored tropical fish provide a spectacular underwater show for eager divers and snorkelers.

On the high slopes of Tau island lies a primeval rain forest. Enveloped in mist, moss-laden trees form a canopy over a dense tangle of ground vegetation. Lower on the slopes the coastal forest is the sole habitat of the only snake native to American Samoa, the Pacific boa. The beaches of Tau provide nesting grounds for two threatened species of sea turtles, the green and the hawksbill.

From forested summits to enchanting coral reefs, American Samoa is a land of splendor and surprise.

Luxuriant rain forests slope steeply to the shoreline in this park, 2,300 miles southwest of Hawaii.

Acadia

*". . . a world that is as old as the earth itself—
the primeval meeting place of the elements of
earth and water, a place of compromise
and conflict and eternal change."*

Rachel Carson

In September 1604, the French explorer Samuel de Champlain was sailing along the northeast coast of North America—mapping the borders of New France—when his ship crashed into a shoal. While the craft was under repair, Champlain investigated his surroundings, a mountainous island near what is now Maine. Up and down the shore, zigzagged with rocky coves and inlets, huge boulders rose from the sea, their stony faces pummeled by the rhythmic pounding of the Atlantic's foaming, frothy waves. Dense forests paraded down to the shore. Toward the interior of the island, broad, sloping mountains loomed, including one that clearly towered over the others.

On shore, Champlain encountered the Abnaki Indians, who occupied the island for most of the year and called it *Pemetic,* meaning "the sloping land." Champlain renamed it *L'Isle des Monts Déserts*, "The Isle of Bare Mountains," but only the pink-and-gray granite summits were barren. The rest of the island supported forests of evergreens and broad-leaved trees, flowering meadows, salt- and freshwater marshes, quiet lakes, rushing streams—and all with an abundance of life. Beavers, in particular, interested Champlain, for their pelts were highly valued in Europe.

Nine years after Champlain's stranding, the English attacked a French mission on the island, starting a series of wars between the two nations that lasted for just about 150 years. England finally triumphed in 1759, and this part of New France was renamed New England; Champlain's island became Mount Desert Island. Today much of this island, together with several smaller islands and part of the Schoodic Peninsula jutting out

Just as Bass Harbor Head Lighthouse, overlooking Blue Hill Bay, has been a beacon to sailors for more than a century, so has the bald eagle served to symbolize America's majesty and power.

from the mainland, makes up Acadia National Park.

Islands they are today, but millions of years ago they were part of the mainland. Then the Ice Age began, and a series of glaciers crept southward, slowly covering most of the continent with a frozen white blanket. Before they retreated, the glaciers would alter the landscape forever. The formidable Mount Desert ridge, an unbroken east-west granite barrier, was sliced by the force of the moving ice into 17 individual mountains, their peaks whittled down to rounded domes. Valleys in between were broadened. Lake basins were gouged in high mountain passes and rockbound gorges. South-facing slopes became steeper and were marked with jagged cliffs as downhill glaciers haphazardly plucked away chunks of rock. Boulders were carried across the land; some were left precariously perched on mountain ledges like oversized free-form sculptures displayed on too-small pedestals.

Even more dramatic was the effect of glacial meltwater: as it flowed into the ocean, the water level rose, flooding the land. Mountains became islands scattered in the water like so many gemstones; high ridges became peninsulas and rocky headlands jutting into the sea. Mount Desert Island was cut off from the mainland, but only by a narrow waterway, and the island was almost cut in half by a now-flooded valley—Somes Sound, the only fjord in the lower 48 states. (Fjords, which most people generally associate with Norway, are inlets of the sea bordered by steep slopes.) The ocean, a reservoir for meltwater from polar ice caps, continues to rise about two inches a century. Over time, more and more of Acadia's coast will be lost to the sea.

The ocean is a tireless sculptor, forever remodeling the shore, and though its designs are temporary, they are spectacular nonetheless. Thunder Hole, a narrow granite chasm on the southeast shore of Mount Desert Island, is a quiet place most of the time. But when just the right conditions of sea, wind, and tide occur, waves hurtle into the rocky gorge, compressing the air toward the back. For a moment, the water and air seem trapped. Then the air rises, escaping with the spray and foam, and expands with thunderous booms that can be heard miles away: the ocean's tremendous power has been transformed into sound.

Water quietly lapping onto the sand creates its own designs. Ceaselessly nibbling at the shore, waves dislodge rocks and pebbles and pile them up at a shallow place until a cobblestoned bar, or neck, is built like a bridge between two islands. (The town of Bar Harbor takes its name from a sandbar connecting Mount Desert and Bar islands.) Eventually, the ocean will dismantle the sandbar, but meanwhile herring gulls and other birds poke in the rocky rubble for clams, crabs, mussels, and fish. Over time, the ocean also builds sandy beaches, depositing finely ground grains of pulverized rock and seashells in protected coves. At Newport Cove, where Sand Beach stretches like a pale, narrow ribbon, the ocean washes away part of the beach each winter. Gentler currents rebuild it in summer, as is nature's way.

Life along the wave-whipped coast

Much of Acadia's marine life resides on the rocky coast in the area between high and low tides. Twice each day the sea rises and falls 9 to 14 feet, alternately flooding and exposing the shore. To survive here, plants and animals must be able to withstand not only continuously changing conditions (the amount of water, its temperature and salinity, and the sun's intensity are forever in flux) but also the effects of waves, storms, and winter frost. That any living thing can tolerate such extremes is remarkable indeed: that thousands of creatures thrive in this rigorous world is truly a marvel.

Like a high-rise building, the intertidal area is divided into horizontal bands, or floors. On the top floor, within reach of ocean spray but beyond the high-tide line, algae cover rocks with a blackish smudge. Representative of the oldest life-form on earth, these algae are covered with a slippery, gelatinlike covering that protects them from drying out. Periwinkles, snails with corkscrew-shaped shells, sometimes crawl up here from lower levels to graze on the algae. Only half an inch long, the periwinkle boasts a tonguelike structure called a radula that bristles with thousands of teeth.

Fog nearly obscures Cadillac Mountain's domed summit overlooking Otter Cove, a haven for lobster boats and other vessels. Such saltwater inlets are picturesquely framed by evergreens and autumn-painted maples, aspens, and birches.

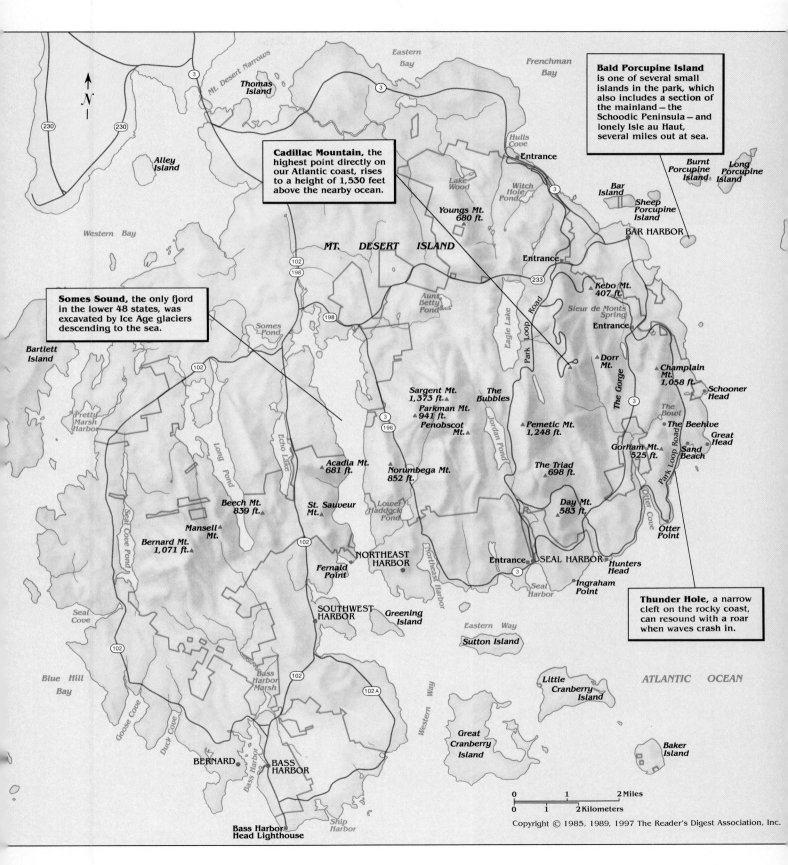

Cadillac Mountain, the highest point directly on our Atlantic coast, rises to a height of 1,530 feet above the nearby ocean.

Somes Sound, the only fjord in the lower 48 states, was excavated by Ice Age glaciers descending to the sea.

Thunder Hole, a narrow cleft on the rocky coast, can resound with a roar when waves crash in.

MT. DESERT ISLAND

N

Eastern Bay

Frenchman Bay

Mt. Desert Narrows

Thomas Island

Alley Island

Western Bay

Hulls Cove

Entrance

Lake Wood

Witch Hole Pond

Youngs Mt. 680 ft.

Bar Island

Burnt Porcupine Island

Long Porcupine Island

Sheep Porcupine Island

BAR HARBOR

Entrance

Kebo Mt. 407 ft.

Sieur de Monts Spring

Entrance

Eagle Lake

Park Loop Road

Aunt Betty Pond

Somes Pond

Dorr Mt.

The Gorge

Champlain Mt. 1,058 ft.

Schooner Head

Bartlett Island

Sargent Mt. 1,373 ft.

The Bubbles

Parkman Mt. 941 ft.

Penobscot Mt.

Pemetic Mt. 1,248 ft.

The Bowl

The Beehive

Pretty Marsh Harbor

Jordan Pond

Great Head

Acadia Mt. 681 ft.

Norumbega Mt. 852 ft.

The Triad 698 ft.

Gorham Mt. 525 ft.

Sand Beach

Long Pond

Echo Lake

Beech Mt. 839 ft.

St. Sauveur Mt.

Lower Haddock Pond

Day Mt. 583 ft.

Otter Cove

Mansell Mt.

Bernard Mt. 1,071 ft.

Seal Cove Pond

Fernald Point

NORTHEAST HARBOR

Entrance

SEAL HARBOR

Hunters Head

Otter Point

Seal Cove

Ingraham Point

Seal Harbor

Northeast Harbor

SOUTHWEST HARBOR

Greening Island

Eastern Way

Sutton Island

Blue Hill Bay

Bass Harbor Marsh

Little Cranberry Island

ATLANTIC OCEAN

Goose Cove

Duck Cove

Western Way

Bass Harbor

BERNARD

BASS HARBOR

Great Cranberry Island

Baker Island

Ship Harbor

Bass Harbor Head Lighthouse

0   1   2 Miles

0   1   2 Kilometers

Bullfrog

Green heron

River otter

Harbor seals

Sea stars

Atlantic rock crab

Dog whelks

Water is the music of Acadia, played by ocean waves as they rhythmically crash against the rocky, cliff-lined coast and then retreat, setting the tempo for shoreline life. When the tide recedes, sea stars find refuge in tide pools. Rock crabs and whelks, in contrast, must survive exposure to the air and escape detection by such winged predators as gulls—and so they hide under rocks and seaweed to await the sea's return. Harbor seals do just the opposite: at low tide they scramble atop rocks and loll lazily in the sun. After the waves roll back in, the seals jump into the water, frolicking and surface diving.

Inland, the melody is carried by running streams, where muskrats and playful river otters dig waterside dens and use their tails as rudders when they swim. Above the water, the green heron perches on a woody snag, occasionally sounding a harsh squawk. Loudest of all is the male bullfrog as he sings his deep-voiced solo, the notes reverberating through the forest like the music of a string bass.

Muskrat

Herring gull

The snail uses it as a sharp, serrated scraper to remove algae from the rocks. When the front end becomes dull, the creature simply pushes forward a freshly grown tooth-studded section of radula.

The stretch of rock below the periwinkles, exposed to the air for several hours twice each day and pounded in between by crashing waves, is perhaps the most difficult place in which to live—unless you are a barnacle. Barnacles are hardy creatures. With a superstrong glue, they cement themselves to rocks; with their volcano-shaped shells, they can withstand the force of waves exerting a ton and a half of pressure per square foot. Airtight plates at the top of the shells clamp shut at low tide, preserving moisture inside, and open at high tide, letting three pairs of feathery arms come out to net tiny bits of food in the water.

The stationary barnacles are an easy target for dog whelks, sea snails that force barnacles open and devour the animals inside. The color of the whelk's shell varies with its food. Those that feed mainly on barnacles are white; a diet of mussels may produce black, brown, or purplish shells. If a dog whelk alternates mussels and barnacles, its shell may develop stripes.

Whelks abound one zone down from the barnacles, where rockweed—a brown, rubbery seaweed—floats on the high tide, its stem branching out like antlers, and air bladders making it buoyant. Though this location is more hospitable than places higher on the shore, rockweed is still beaten about by the waves, and it must attach itself securely to rocks by means of a holdfast—a mass of strong rootlike structures. When the tide goes out, the plant becomes draped over the rocks, its slippery fronds affording protection to mussels, periwinkles, whelks, crabs, and other small life.

Irish moss, a slippery red seaweed, occupies the level below. Sea urchins and crabs can usually be found at this level, but at low tide they retreat to the lowest zone, which remains underwater nearly all the time. Here the long, leathery strands of kelp, another seaweed that uses a holdfast as an anchor, bend with the waves. Starfish, or sea stars, creep about in the kelp. They have miraculous powers of regener-

Warm sunny days bring out the incomparable beauty of the rose as it unfurls its luxuriant petals and scents the air with its sweet fragrance.

Brought to Acadia from the Pacific Northwest, lupines with their upright spikes of flowers have become familiar sights in fields and along grassy roads.

ation: an injury to one arm—most species have five—may result in two or more growing back to replace it.

Out beyond the tidal zone, lobsters scavenge in shallow waters, bewhiskered harbor seals lounge on surf-splashed rocks, and harbor porpoises cruise below the surface, frequently rising for air. Porpoises, members of the whale group, have a remarkable sensing ability: they can find prey by bouncing sounds off it. So accurate is this sonarlike system that it enables the porpoises to identify a creature by its echo and thus to pursue their favorite foods. Other whales, such as finbacks and humpbacks, also ply these waters, surfacing from time to time to blow misty sprays high into the air. Overhead, herring gulls swoop and soar on 4½-foot wingspans, adding their raucous calls to the sounds of the restless sea.

Forests by the sea
Unlike most other coasts, where the sea gradually gives way to sand dunes and high-grass marshes before forests take hold, Acadia changes directly from water to forest, with trees crowding close to the water. Conifer cones float in tide pools; tree squirrels scamper along ocean-sprayed cliffs; gnarled tree roots shade slick, algae-covered rocks; and seaside spruces, stunted and twisted by storm-whipped winds, guard the continent's edge. Farther inland, red spruce grow to 70-foot-high beauties and drop their sharp, stiff needles onto grassy bogs and swiftly flowing streams. Mixed in the red spruce forest are other kinds of spruce, several types of pine—white, red, pitch, and jack—and the sweet-smelling balsam fir. Most unusual is the tamarack, or eastern larch, which sheds its needles after they turn a dusty gold, adding an unexpected touch of glory to autumn's already magnificent show of color.

As if Jack Frost had been presented with a set of paints, in September hillsides covered with maples, birches, and aspens begin to sport tiny dabs of yellow and red. Soon the artist picks up a broader brush, and slaps colors across entire groves. By October the all-green slopes are a glowing patchwork of crimsons, golds, and burnt-oranges;

In this ocean-dominated park, autumn runs all the way down to the sea. Soon, winter's icy fingers will transform this colorful scene into a white wonderland; but the ocean will still be free, forever gnawing at the shore.

here and there unvarying firs provide a steady anchor of green. Beautiful but brief, the show is over all too soon, and the branches stretch out spindly and leafless. Once again the tall, stately dark green conifers dominate the landscape.

Acadia's autumn extravaganza was not always so extensive. Evergreens once covered a larger part of the park, but the vegetation changed dramatically after the Great Fire of October 1947 engulfed more than 17,000 acres. After the evergreens' deep shade was gone, quaking aspen, pin cherry, and gray and paper birch—all sun-loving trees—took root and thrived. The new trees, some in pure stands and others mixed with evergreens, afforded food and shelter for squirrels, deer, foxes, beavers (their fondness for aspens is legendary), and such birds as wood thrushes, woodcocks, and scarlet tanagers.

The oddest of these is the woodcock, a chunky, robin-sized member of the sandpiper clan whose sharply pointed bill is disproportionately long for its body. In the dusk of spring evenings, the male woodcock begins its acrobatic courtship. Landing in a clearing, he announces his arrival with a thin, nasal *peent*. Suddenly he takes off in a spiral, his wings producing a whistle-like sound. Circling higher and higher, he climbs until he is just a dark spot in the sky; then he tumbles down, warbling softly. Leveling off, he hovers just above ground and lands delicately on the same bare spot where he began. Then he starts the whole routine once

again. The musicale may continue for hours, long after a silvery moon has replaced the setting sun.

Beginning in April, wildflowers sprinkle their hues against spring's renewed green. In the forests, sweet-scented trailing arbutus is followed by pink lady's slipper and painted trillium, its "paint" a tinge of crimson atop the petals' whiteness. Bunchberry, a low-growing dogwood, covers the ground in June with bridal-white flower heads, which mature into clusters of brilliant red berries in August. On sunny slopes, lupine holds its stalk of pealike flowers erect while the harebell, a blue, bell-shaped flower, nods delicately on its stem. The single flower of the rose pogonia decorates bogs and wet shores, and jewelweed, also called touch-me-not, produces seedpods that explode at the faintest touch, sending seeds flying in all directions.

A system of carriage roads cuts through the forests and valleys, crosses quaint stone bridges, and winds past glassy lakes and bubbly streams. Other roads climb to the top of Cadillac Mountain, the highest point on North America's eastern coastline. From its summit you can see all the glory that is Acadia—from the rich expanse of evergreen forests, to the rugged shore dotted with fishing villages and elegant mansions, and to the sea beyond, where colorful lobster buoys bob in the water and dome-shaped islands stretch to the horizon. You can almost hear the sound of white-tipped waves as they roll rhythmically to shore, pounding like the eternal heartbeat of the earth.

Arches

"The finest workers in stone are not copper or steel tools, but the gentle touches of air and water working at their leisure with a liberal allowance of time."
Henry David Thoreau

Michelangelo said that statues are imprisoned in living stone; it was his job as a sculptor, working with hammer and chisel, to free them. Here in the broken desert landscape of Arches National Park, nature is the sculptor. Working at an infinitely slower pace than Michelangelo did, she has freed one of the world's great collections of abstract statuary from the grainy red rock in which it has long been locked.

In this vast outdoor gallery, many pieces are still emerging after tens of millions of years. Others have been worn away to stubs, which are themselves monumental forms. And some exist today at the peak of perfection, awesome in size, grandeur, and delicacy, each as individual as a fingerprint and each in a constant state of change.

The prime exhibits are, of course, the arches. More of them exist here than in any other place on earth—well over 2,000 by recent count—and they range in form and size from rounded windows only a yard or so wide, through walls of stone, to freestanding loops of ribbon-like rock as tall as apartment houses.

Delicate Arch, the park's symbol and star attraction, is a graceful hoop of salmon-colored sandstone about 65 feet high, with an opening nearly 35 feet wide. Cowboys used to call it the Schoolmarm's Bloomers for its distinctive silhouette, but today it is known by its more lyrical name because a spot on one leg has been worn nearly through. One day the arch will topple, but that day is probably long distant.

Landscape Arch, a span so thin it looks like ticker tape tossed from a high window, is 306 feet across, 106 feet high, and in one place perilously narrow. There is no engineering reason why it should stand, but there it is,

The crafty ringtail hunts at night along such sculpted cliffs and

canyons as these in Park Avenue. The central formation atop the right wall is known as both Queen Victoria and Whistler's Mother.

No stream or river ever ran beneath the ribbonlike span of Landscape Arch or any other of the park's arches. Unlike natural bridges, which are created by the cutting action of such waterways, arches are formed by weathering.

defying time and gravity. Although Zion National Park's Kolob Arch once was thought to be longer than Landscape Arch, more recent measurements have shown that Landscape is the world's longest natural arch. And it is still the most breathtaking. Like all arches, Landscape is not the same today as it was yesterday, nor will it be the same tomorrow. Its opening is ever growing, the span above ever diminishing. The day after tomorrow, it may be gone.

Occasionally the changes are that dramatic. Though few people have ever seen a great chunk of rock fall from an arch, such events occur, and their results are startling. Until November 1940, the structure that we now call Skyline Arch was known as Arch-in-the-Making because more than half of its opening was filled by a huge sandstone block that had been fractured all around. Sometime that month—probably during a cold night after a wet day, when a pocket of water froze and expanded—the block fell, more than doubling the arch's span to its present 71-foot measure.

For the most part, though, the changes are gradual, all but imperceptible. Winter snow and ice quietly gnaw at the stone. The water of spring rain soaks into its pores, accumulates in cracks and pockets, and dissolves the glue that holds grains of sand together. Windstorms whip the loose sand abrasively about, rounding corners and smoothing surfaces. Summer cloudbursts carry tons of silt and sand down normally dry washes toward the Colorado River, which flows along the park's southeastern boundary. It is a process that never ceases, and in this stark, naked landscape of eye-aching brilliance it is almost possible to hear and feel the geologic forces at their perpetual work.

There are also innumerable sculpted monoliths, spires, buttes, and cliffs—many the remnants of long-vanished arches. Some of them suggest the shapes of humans and animals, and people have given them appropriate names—the Three Gossips, the Parade of Elephants, the Marching Men, Queen Victoria, Dark Angel, Duck on the Rock, Sheep Rock, Eagle Rock. (The last is another example of dramatic change: in March 1941 the eagle-shaped rock that gave the formation its name fell off its high pedestal and broke into bits.)

Why are the arches here?

Before nature could set about freeing this immense collection of sculpted forms, she had to imprison them in a layer of sandstone some 500 feet thick. The rock had to be a subtle blend of many textures and densities so that it would erode away, not smoothly and evenly, but in odd ways. To accumulate the grainy materials that would form this layer—called the Entrada Sandstone by today's geologists—was the labor of more than 20 million years, and it required the creation and withdrawal of an entire ocean. Another 125 million years or more went into cementing the materials into solid rock, cracking the rock in special ways, lifting it, and exposing it to the gentle tools of erosion.

The world that gave birth to the Entrada existed along the shores of a big shallow sea that spread westward from this place. During the staggering stretch of time that this world lasted, there were many variations in the lay of the land. Each variation was to invest the future rock with a different blend of densities and textures.

At first the seashore itself came and went, so that some of the sand that was to be cemented into the Entrada was deposited beneath shallow water and some along the tide-washed shore. Sometimes there were tidal marshes and brief swampy stretches dense with life, and their thick, muddy substances add to the Entrada's complexity. Back from the shore, windswept dunes moved incessantly, accumulating to depths of hundreds of feet. Over the long ages, as the sea slowly withdrew, perpetually shifting winds piled the dunes high over the vanishing shoreline in capricious patterns, reflected in the cross-grained textures of the rock. At various times and in various places, streams and rivers made their way through the dunes to the sea; their courses left pockets of firm rock.

The Entrada was deposited atop the leavings of many other worlds—deserts, swamplands, ocean beds, and verdant valleys—that had existed earlier in this same place; and it was eventually covered by other, different layers whose weight turned the sand into rock. But it was one of the deepest layers, a 300-million-year-old bed of salt, left when another ancient landlocked sea had evaporated, that was to provide the stress that would eventually result in today's awesome display.

The power of oozing salt

Unlike the sand, silt, lime, and other materials that turn to stone under pressure, salt is an unstable substance. It becomes plastic under pressure, shifting and flowing like soft putty to places where the pressure is less. One such place was in this spot; because of fault lines in the underlying bedrock, the salt—set in motion by the weight of distant mountains—had been diverted upward here and had built to thicknesses of more than 3,000 feet. Over the course of tens of millions of years, as the weight of upper deposits increased, more and more salt was squeezed into this place. The salt bulged even farther upward, forming a long, slender dome. The land above it bulged, too, and sometimes cracked and was eroded away, so that the inequality of weight increased. Eventually the salt dome broke through the

The tough evening primrose produces its dramatic flowers in spring, bringing beauty to barren sites. In a good year it may blanket the landscape.

upper layers. When it breached the Entrada, the sandstone cracked in long parallel lines that were about 20 feet apart.

Meanwhile, even more massive geological forces had been at work. The continent itself had been moving, drifting thousands of miles westward and northward across the earth's molten mantle, and it had collided with the plate that lies beneath the Pacific Ocean. The force of the collision had fractured the western half of the continent and thrust mountain ranges upward. Wedged between them, a huge slab of land, which we now call the Colorado Plateau, began slowly to rise. It is rising still.

The Colorado Plateau includes much of Utah and parts of Colorado, New Mexico, and Arizona. It does not rise on a level but at an angle, south side first, and as it began its most recent surge about 15 million years ago, waters were set in motion that stripped away layer after layer of sediment. Hence, the farther south you go on the plateau, the more sediments have been removed, and the older are the rock layers that are revealed. Arches is the northernmost of the Colorado Plateau's eight national parks—the other seven are Bryce Canyon, Canyonlands, Capitol Reef, Grand Canyon, Mesa Verde, Petrified Forest, and Zion—and here the Entrada Sandstone is now being worn away.

Slanting through the northern part of the park is Salt Valley—the sand-covered top of the huge salt dome

Few humans have ever lived in Arches, though many have passed through over the ages. Ute Indians left these petroglyphs, perhaps commemorating a bighorn hunt, sometime after the Spanish had brought horses to the New World.

27

A graceful abstract sculpture freed by nature's patient toil
from the massive rock wall that had imprisoned it,
Delicate Arch stands in solitary splendor on the lip of
a deep sandstone bowl. Nothing else of the rock remains.

that fractured the Entrada. Flanking it on both sides are row after row of freestanding fins, or ribbons, of Entrada Sandstone. They are the slowly vanishing walls that separate canyons 300 and 400 feet deep, canyons that erosion has gouged along the parallel cracks in the sandstone. It is within these thin fins of beige, salmon, pink, and red that the arches and other sculptured pieces are imprisoned. As the fins are worn and weathered away, nature's immense statuary remains.

The process by which nature frees the sculptured forms is called differential erosion—which simply means that hard, dense places in the rock erode more slowly than soft, crumbly places. Moisture seeps into cracks and porous spots

A canyon treefrog spends its life in one of the few watery places that dot the desert. The small creature has a big voice, like the quack of a giant duck.

and dissolves the cement that holds the grains of sand together. In the winter, the moisture freezes and expands within the rock, cracking it, flaking it off, and allowing even more water to enter and do its work.

Sometimes a fin is pierced straight through—a cave becomes a window that gradually widens into an arch. At times, though, the slow process of arch making begins on the top surface of a fin. Rainwater collects in a pothole and gradually works its way down into the heart of the rock. Eventually the trapped water finds its way out through the side of the fin, creating a burrowlike tunnel, which then expands into a pothole arch. The base of the fin, where moisture tends to accumulate, is worn away beneath the exit hole, while the span above remains dry and firm. Still the span is whittled ever so slowly, down to its hardest core; eventually it falls, leaving a pinnacle, butte, or buttress on either side. These, too, continue to weather away.

The fins are in all stages of deterioration, the arches that emerge from them in all stages of creation and erosion. There are miles-long sandstone slabs containing caves not yet cut through, and there are dwarfish-looking spires, once joined at the top, now standing in isolated couples on the buff-colored sandstone that lies beneath the Entrada. Eventually water, freezing temperatures, wind, and gravity will reduce them all to sand and carry them, grain by grain, away.

Thorns and thirsty roots
Among these labyrinths of disintegrating stone, which rise like the bare ribs and knuckles of the earth, life is almost as stubborn and hard as the rock itself. Thin, clear air envelops a land of extremes, shimmering beneath the summer's hot sun, shivering in the cold winter's white light.

The plants and creatures that flourish here are endowed with special qualities. Perhaps we attribute to

them a character that is only a matter of natural selection and adaptation, but they *seem* more worthy of respect than plants that grow where soil is fertile, moisture is plentiful, and temperatures are benign. Each seems to outsmart the hard climate and stingy soil in its own way.

Some plants cling tenaciously to the rare damp places. Watercress, cattails, and marsh grasses survive around the edges of springs and in the few standing pools that endure along the beds of intermittent washes; when the streams flow, these plants soon inhabit them. In places where water seeps steadily through cracks and fissures in the Entrada Sandstone (places that may one day become the lower openings of infant pothole arches), maidenhair ferns, columbines, primroses, brilliant scarlet monkey flowers, and even wild orchids crowd together in hanging gardens. Here treefrogs live, and black-chinned hummingbirds hover, sipping the cool water and tasting the flowers' nectar.

Other plants survive on sandy flats because they have shallow, spreading roots that quickly soak up surface water after a brief shower, or long, fibrous roots that dig down to groundwater, no matter how deep. Nearly all have spines, needles, thorns, or other unpleasant protrusions that discourage browsing animals. Most bear very small leaves, diminishing the surface through which water can evaporate; and the leaf surfaces are usually hard or waxy to hold in moisture. Some drop their leaves in dry times and grow them back quickly when it rains. Cacti have no true leaves at all, but only hard spines that protect their stems, and fine hairs that gather morning dew.

Some survive by living quickly. In April and May of a good year, when rain does fall and temperatures are not yet killing, the park is carpeted by a colorful blend of bright wildflowers. Dozens of these plants—called, aptly enough, ephemerals—germinate, flower, and set seed like magic, almost overnight. The seeds may lie dormant for years until the right conditions return.

Pinyon pines, on the other hand, survive by living very slowly: they expend little moisture on unnecessary growth, conserving their energies for the long haul. A pinyon needs almost 200 years to reach full maturity, at which time it is a scraggly specimen about 20 feet tall. Many trees never reach such an age, however; the pinyon's worst enemy is the porcupine, which feeds on the moist inner bark, effectively banding a tree and cutting off its flow of nutrients. In company with the even more stunted Utah juniper, the pinyon forms scattered "pigmy forests" between fins and on rocky ridges and slopes. A juniper often looks more dead than alive, with a vital trunk growing from a mass of gnarled roots that have been exposed by erosion. The exquisitely sculptured forms of these twisted root masses, weathered to silvery gray, make the trees seem quite at home among the crafted rocks of Arches National Park.

Blackbrush, its stiff, spine-tipped branches sparsely covered by small, leathery leaves, is the principal plant that gives the open scrubland its scrubby character. It is joined by clumps of Mormon tea, with spindly greenish stems whose leaves are little more than scales, and by gray-green patches of perfumed sagebrush, its feathery branches bending with the western breezes.

Tough, woody cliffroses sprout out of crevices in the cliffs and may stand up to 10 feet tall in open, rocky, soil. They are not much to look at most of the time—their leaves are tiny and their bark is a rough, scaly brown—but in May each wears a glorious cloak of delicate white and yellow blossoms that brighten the landscape with airy specks of living sunlight.

Sand dunes, scattered in hummocky tracts about the park, are kept fairly stationary by the busy, meshing roots of buckwheat, fescue, ricegrass, sagebrush, and the fragrant and colorful little sand verbenas. Salt Valley is a broad swathe of mixed grasses. Cheatgrass, growing more than knee-high, is the most widespread; when pioneer cattlemen came into the area, the grass was so luxuriant that it could be cut and baled like hay. The slender, silvery stems caress the earth and etch lacy pictures against the sky; each pinhead-sized seed is encased in an almost white hull.

Creatures of the night

At night, when the lovely but ominous sacred datura (it contains a powerful narcotic) unfurls its fragrant white flowers, animals emerge from burrows and shady nooks to feed. Pugnacious collared lizards—their skins all bejeweled with dots of blue, green, and turquoise—hunt spiders, insects, snakes, and even other lizards. Giving chase, the foot-long reptiles can rear up on their hind legs and run like miniature tyrannosaurs.

Black-tailed jackrabbits and desert cottontails come out at dusk, and so do the gray foxes, kit foxes, bobcats, and coyotes that hunt them. Mule deer browse the brushy uplands and rest in secluded clumps of trees between the fins, their large ears constantly atwitch to catch the sounds of danger. Their greatest threat comes from the tawny mountain lion, stealthy and powerful. Each of the 200-pound cats kills and eats an average of one deer a week and supplements its diet with rodents and other small mammals.

Only after night has fallen does the skittish little ringtail emerge from the grass-lined rocky den or hollow tree where it spends the day. An agile cousin of the raccoon, with half its more than 2-foot length invested in its bushy, banded tail, it hunts rodents and lizards among the rocks where it lives, and climbs trees after roosting birds and their eggs. Well before the first gray light of dawn, it joins its mate in the darkness of its den.

Few creatures are abroad in the heat of the day. White-tailed antelope squirrels, rock squirrels, and Colorado chipmunks scurry after seeds while trying to avoid the watchful eyes of soaring golden eagles and red-tailed hawks. Raucous pinyon jays and busy little titmice flock among the branches of the pinyon and juniper woodlands, ravens scavenge everywhere for food, and common flickers pick for ants in dunes and for grubs beneath the bark of trees.

This vast gallery of nature's masterworks is home to these creatures, and they inhabit it comfortably, but their quick spirit is not the true heart of Arches. Here, where monolithic stone figures are born and flourish and die, their lives are but flickers—as are ours. It is the arches themselves that are this park's measure of time.

The Three Gossips, which stand several hundred feet high above the sand, have also been called the Three Graces. They are examples of hoodoos, odd rock forms that have been shaped for millions of years by nature's hand.

Badlands

"The hills are shadows, and they flow
From form to form, and nothing stands;
They melt like mist, the solid lands,
Like clouds they shape themselves and go."
Alfred, Lord Tennyson

There are badlands throughout the West, where treeless plains are being cut to pieces, shaped and reshaped by erosion. But jagged Badlands National Park is in *the* Badlands, the biggest and the baddest, from which all other badlands take their name. These Big Badlands actually cover about 6,000 square miles of South Dakota and Nebraska. Only about 13 percent of this land is contained in the national park.

When the Sioux coined the term *mako sica* (literally, "bad land"), they probably meant nothing more than to distinguish the austere clay spires and gullies from the surrounding grassy plains. The Indians most likely found the Badlands to be good hunting grounds. Bison and other wildlife drew hunters here as far back as 10,000 years ago. Badlands cliffs, often invisible when approached from the north and east, made ideal "buffalo jumps," where bison were stampeded to their deaths. About 500 of the great shaggy beasts can still be seen grazing in the Sage Creek Wilderness Area.

French fur traders called the region *mauvaises terres à traverser* (literally, and quite accurately, "bad lands to travel across"). For a traveler it is an apt description of this seemingly barren landscape—slashed and gouged by impossible gullies and ravines—that becomes a gaint mud pie when it rains.

Yet only 45 miles west of Badlands National Park are the Black Hills, a delightful island of forested "good lands" that helps the traveler appreciate by contrast the Badlands' hostile grandeur. Fairly recently, as geologists measure time, the Badlands flowed from these good lands. Beginning about 65 million years ago, when the Rockies began to form, the same pressures raised

Bands of muted color streak the tortured Badlandscape, testimony to the level plain that once covered it all. Despite the seeming sterility of the land, blazing life, such as the prairie golden pea, thrives in grasslands and moist pockets.

the land here, draining a shallow sea that had covered the region for 15 million years. Meanwhile, to the west, the surface warped into a blister, or dome, nearly 8,000 feet high—the Black Hills.

As the dome rose, it was slowly eroded. Streams became torrents, stripping rock from the hills and carrying it east to a broad, level valley where the sea had been. Here the torrents slowed to meandering streams and dropped the hills' debris. Over millions of years, the valley was filled with sediments up to 1,500 feet thick.

By the beginning of the Oligocene period, about 34 million years ago, the climate of the area resembled that of today's Gulf Coast. Rivers and streams made mud flats and marshes, then filled them with sediment to create forests and grasslands while beginning new swamps elsewhere. The sediments were by no means evenly distributed. The erratic routes of streams, the fluctuating rates of precipitation, the variety of debris from different sites in the Black Hills, the masses of volcanic ash that occasionally blew in from the west all contributed to the patchwork layering that gives today's Badlands their distinctive banded appearance. These layers are, for the most part, mudstone and siltstone: materials so insubstantial that it seems an exaggeration to call them stone at all.

Little sediment has been added over the last million years. Instead the whole place is falling apart, being carried away in rivulets that feed the White, Bad, and Cheyenne rivers. It is one of the world's most rapidly dissolving landscapes. In a few million years, the Badlands will very likely be gone.

Geologists speak matter-of-factly of a million years, but we short-lived human beings cannot really comprehend such time spans. In the Badlands, though, geologic events tear along at rates discernible to human eyes. In 1959 the U.S. Geological Survey set metal discs in concrete embedded atop hills near Dillon Pass. These were designed to be permanent reference points for mapmakers, but the hills eroded away at the rate of an inch a year. In a little over a decade, the "permanent" benchmarks and their concrete bases were embedded in nothing—which was just as well, for the elevations they recorded were now wrong by a foot.

Much of the clay eroded from the Badlands ends up in the White River, named for the chalky color imparted by its burden of sediment. This water is foul stuff. Each of the clay particles has the same electrical charge, and so they repel one another. They cannot clump together to settle out of the water. Perhaps the area should be called badwaters instead of badlands.

When the famed mountain man Jedediah Smith and his rugged band were scouring the West for beaver pelts in 1823, they drank from the White River, the only water available. They suffered severe diarrhea, followed by dehydration that could easily have killed them in such arid country. Two of the men were too weak to go on. Smith buried them up to their necks in sand to conserve body moisture until he could return with drinkable water. It is testimony to Smith's character and leadership that his men let themselves be buried alive, trusting that he both could find water and would bring it back. That night he did so and dug them out.

A chaos of cliffs

The source of much of the White River's sediment is a 200-foot-high chaos of cliffs, pinnacles, buttresses, and gorges known as the Wall. This desolate band, one-half to three miles wide, is the park's scenery belt. It divides the higher grasslands of the Bad and Cheyenne rivers from the lower grasslands of the White River. Primitive wagon trails once traversed the Wall through such passes as Dillon, Big Foot, Norbeck, and Cedar—passes that became impassable when rain turned the Badlands clay into soap-slick gumbo.

So slippery is the Wall's wet clay that it often cannot support itself. Masses of cliff face break loose and slide partway down to form slumps: hummocky green islands of life. A slump is green because it dams a drainage channel for a time, holding water for plants. Like all Badlands landmarks, though, slumps last only a few generations before the water drains away—and with it the life. Drainage begins when the clay dries out and cracks. The next rain enlarges the cracks into tunnels. These eventually collapse and form sinkholes, into which ever greater amounts of water drain. Finally all that remain are short-lived natural bridges marking the strongest parts of the tunnels. Equally temporary caves are formed where water emerges from the Wall. Usually they extend back only far enough to afford roosting areas for bats as well as cooling shade for rattlesnakes and for the bull snakes that eat them.

There are stable points amid all this land movement. When cracks in the clay were filled in with firmer material—usually volcanic ash—they formed clastic dikes. Today these show up as vertical greenish-white lines, from less than an inch to a foot wide, criss-crossing the Badlands. Sometimes the surrounding clay erodes away, leaving spinelike ridges of ash.

But though volcanic ash is solider than Badlands clay, it also melts away amazingly fast. Vampire Peak, a mountain of hardened ash that towered above Cedar Pass, was a well-known landmark to pioneers because of its fanglike twin spires. (It was named in 1915 by an artist, J. J. Peterkin, both for its dramatic appearance and for the many bats—not, in fact, vampires—that fluttered around it.) In a crashing thunderstorm on November 22, 1950, one of the twin spires fell. Today the artist would not recognize Vampire Peak, for it has averaged a loss of six inches per year since he named it.

By comparison, the nearby Millard Ridge erodes 3,000 times as slowly—at a rate of about one inch every 500 years. The difference is its caprock of sandstone. Throughout the Badlands such caprocks form ridges by protecting underlayers from erosion. Sometimes solitary sandstone slabs form the caps of "toadstools," supported by steadily diminishing "stems" of clay. Eventually, erosion from the sides eats away a stem, and the slab it supports tumbles to begin the process again. Some toadstools are 30 feet tall, while others are no bigger than the fungi for which they are named.

The intertwined roots of prairie grasses also hold back erosion for a while, but the sod only delays the inevitable. Patchy sod tables dot the Badlands, ephemeral remnants of vanished grassland. Gradually the soil is eaten away, and the roots on the edge are exposed and die. The table eventually falls, and seeds must take root below to begin the cycle again.

Preservation in stone

Among the most interesting erosion-resistant rocks in the Badlands are those known as concretions. Like pearls within oysters, they form within sedimentary layers when minerals adhere to foreign bodies. Often the foreign bodies are fossils: some large, some very small. In one study of 189 Badlands anthills, all but one contained tiny fossils that had been excavated by harvester ants from their deep burrows. These included lizard and fish parts, mammal teeth, and seeds—mostly from hackberry trees (they look like white BB's).

Where erosion has cut all the way down to bedrock, there appear fossils of animals that lived in the shallow ocean of 65 to 80 million years ago, including many marine turtles. One fossil turtle 12 feet long was found in the Badlands. The shells of these saltwater giants and of smaller, more numerous, and much more recent land turtles are the most noticeable animal fossils, though their shards are sometimes mistaken for broken pots. The shells have lasted millions of years but quickly disintegrate when finally exposed to the air.

The Badlands yield a wondrous number and variety of fossils from Oligocene times; they simply fall out of the fast-eroding landscape. None are larger than titanothere bones. Bigger than the average rhinoceros, this titanic creature had a pair of horns projecting from the

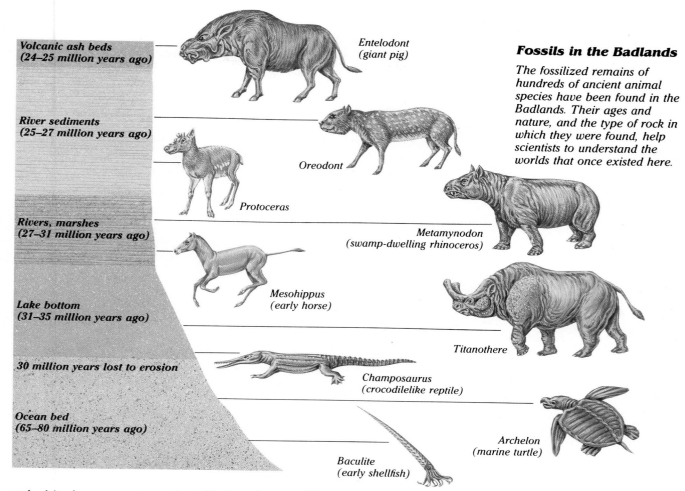

Volcanic ash beds
(24–25 million years ago)

River sediments
(25–27 million years ago)

Rivers, marshes
(27–31 million years ago)

Lake bottom
(31–35 million years ago)

30 million years lost to erosion

Ocean bed
(65–80 million years ago)

Enteledont
(giant pig)

Oreodont

Protoceras

Metamynodon
(swamp-dwelling rhinoceros)

Mesohippus
(early horse)

Titanothere

Champosaurus
(crocodilelike reptile)

Archelon
(marine turtle)

Baculite
(early shellfish)

Fossils in the Badlands

The fossilized remains of hundreds of ancient animal species have been found in the Badlands. Their ages and nature, and the type of rock in which they were found, help scientists to understand the worlds that once existed here.

end of its huge nose in a blunt, V-shaped prong. The horn was presumably for defense, but size alone must have protected healthy titanotheres, even from such fearsome predators as saber-toothed cats and the wolf-like *Hyaenodon horridus*.

The first titanotheres, about the size of a young calf, lived 50 million years ago. Gradually, bigger versions evolved, browsing on plentiful leaves and new-growth twigs. At last, their heads alone were three feet long and contained molars four inches square. But when the lush forests of the early Oligocene were replaced by grass-land, titanotheres died out, leaving no descendants. Coincidentally, three kinds of rhinoceros also roamed the area. These were unrelated to the titanotheres, although one kind did sport side-by-side nose horns. All Badlands rhinos, of course, are long extinct.

The commonest Oligocene mammals were the 22 species of oreodonts that ranged across the northern Great Plains. Their name refers to teeth shaped like mountains, but some of their teeth resembled those of cows, and their canines were short tusks. Their bodies varied in length from two to five feet, and all looked rather like pigs. (Speculating that they might have chewed cuds, scientists once called them ruminating pigs.) Each had an ecological niche in which it thrived: some were largely aquatic; some may have climbed

trees; one even had claws. Adaptable as they were, oreodonts also died out without descendants.

Another piglike animal, the enteledont, had wide, protruding cheekbones, a humped back, a small brain, and an assortment of teeth designed to eat just about anything. Up to 6 feet tall and 10 feet long, it is also called a giant pig, although it left no descendants when it went the way of the titanothere. True pigs originated in the Old World.

The protoceras—the name means "early horns"—was a sheep-sized beast whose lithe body was built for running and jumping. The male, with three pairs of knobby horns protruding from its head and face, may well have been the oddest-looking mammal of the Oli-gocene Badlands.

Horses, but not the modern version, also roamed the landscape. The two types that have been identified in Badlands National Park—*Mesohippus* and *Miohippus*—were about the size of collie dogs. They had three toes on each foot—the middle toe distinctly larger than the other two, forecasting the hoof of the modern horse.

Before 1850, petrified bones of these and many other now-extinct Oligocene mammals littered the land-scape. Indians invented a mythical thunderhorse to account for the largest of them. But in the mid-19th century scientists descended, hauling petrified bones

"Haystacks" punctuate fertile grasslands stretching to the distant Wall. These unique Badlands phenomena occur when

patches of rain-swollen clay clog drainage to lower layers, creating dry anchors in the slick sea of mud.

away by wagonloads for museums all over the world. Today it is rare to find a big fossil bone in the Badlands.

Much of this collecting was done on the run, for fear of hostile Indians. One collector, Ferdinand V. Hayden, was captured with the pockets of his frock coat full of fossils. The Indians assumed that anyone dressed so oddly who ran about picking up useless rocks had to be crazy. With their customary respect for the insane, they let him go to pursue a brilliant scientific career.

Grasslands reborn

In the Badlands, where the average annual precipitation is only 16 inches, most of the water comes in the form of spring downpours and runs quickly off the land. Temperatures are equally inhospitable, ranging from 115° F in summer to –30° F in winter. Woody plants have a hard time, but nearly 50 species of grass thrive, giving Badlands the largest native grasslands of any U.S. national park. The most important are buffalo grass, blue grama, western wheat grass, and needle-and-thread. They grow intermixed; when weather conditions are bad for some, others take over.

Wildflowers enliven the prosaic green of a grasslands spring. The clustered bayonetlike leaves of the abundant yuccas are accented by stalks of bell-like white flowers. Edible bulbs, such as textile onions and mariposa lilies, bloom alongside the poisonous grassy death camas. Blue narrowleaf penstemon hides among the grasses, and brazen yellow salsify and other tough competitors take over where grass has been destroyed.

When Badlands National Monument was established in 1939 (it was upgraded to park status in 1978), plows and livestock were banished, and the natural prairie grasses began to return. With them are returning the pronghorns, once nearly extinct. It is no longer unusual to see these unique North American animals grazing here, their tan and white coats blending into the background. You may notice their white rumps first, especially if one pronghorn becomes alarmed and raises its rump hairs as a signal. Their retreat will be rapid; the pronghorn is the fastest mammal on the continent, reaching speeds of 60 miles per hour and more.

In 1963 the Park Service reintroduced 53 bison to the Badlands. The herd is now held at 500. These shaggy symbols of the plains now beat out the only trails across 64,000 acres of rolling prairie in the park's Sage Creek Wilderness. Bison can be dangerous; so wise hikers on these trails give them the right-of-way and set up camp well off their routes.

Easily the most charming grassland animals are the black-tailed prairie dogs. Called dogs because of the two-syllable bark that alerts a colony to intruders, the animals are actually large ground squirrels. Prairie dogs dig complex systems of tunnels that include sleeping rooms, latrines, and storage rooms for such food as insects, grasses, and wildflower seeds. Together they form colonies, or towns, of hundreds of individuals, each burrow marked by a mound of earth. Surrounding vegetation is close-cropped, furnishing food for the prairie dogs and depriving potential predators of cover.

36

The towns are divided into neighborhoods called coteries. Within a coterie much time is spent kissing, cuddling, caressing, and grooming (strangers may be identified when they refuse to kiss resident dogs). Adults from other coteries are driven out, but young dogs seem free to wander wherever they want to go.

Not much can live on the rugged desolation of the Wall besides reptiles, bats, and rodents—including the least chipmunk, whose coloration blends into the drab setting. However, a small population of bighorn sheep dwells there, introduced in 1964 to replace a similar subspecies called Audubon's bighorn, which had been hunted to extinction.

Some trees and shrubs manage to survive along stream courses, on north-facing slopes protected from sun and wind, and in slumps. Plains cottonwoods, the largest trees in the park, line streambeds. Green ashes and elms shade sheltered areas. Although scraggly ponderosa pines perch picturesquely on cliff edges, the scrubby Rocky Mountain juniper is by far the commonest evergreen. Deer browse in gullies clogged with wild rose, chokeberry, and golden currant—all important food sources for birds and other wildlife. The big-eared mule deer outnumber whitetails by at least three to one, but both are common throughout the park. Coyotes and pronghorn antelope are among the other creatures that share the Badlands habitat.

The last battle

In 1876, after the Sioux were defeated by the U.S. Army, some Indians received federal subsidies for working the Badlands soil—though less than they had been promised. Much of their former hunting grounds was also given to white farmers. But the dream of creating an agricultural Utopia on this northern arm of the Great American Desert was an impossible one. Despite hard work, both Indian and white farmers failed tragically. The white homesteaders could retreat east or push on westward. The Indians had nowhere to go.

Frustrated, starving, and desperate, the Sioux looked back to the days when war and bison had created an exciting, satisfying life. In 1889 a new Ghost Dance religion arose, promising a miraculous world renewal, with all whites gone from the land. Some Sioux were attracted. A few angry warriors changed the original pacifism of the Ghost Dance to a war ritual centering on Ghost Shirts, supposedly impervious to "bluecoat" bullets. Abandoning their hopeless farms, they retreated to a steep mesa appropriately called the Stronghold (now in the southern section of the park).

In December 1890 Big Foot, chief of the Miniconjou Sioux (a band not involved with the Ghost Dancers), ushered his people through a tortuous Badlands pass that still bears his name. He hoped to keep his pugnacious young men separated from the soldiers until he could work out a settlement between the Ghost Dancers and the whites. But, dying from pneumonia, Big Foot surrendered to the cavalry at nearby Wounded Knee Creek. Neither side wanted a battle, but when the army began to disarm the Sioux, fighting exploded. The resulting carnage, the last major battle of the Indian Wars, saw most of Big Foot's band killed or wounded.

Today the protected Badlands more nearly resemble the *mako sica* where the Sioux hunted than they have for a century. Bison and pronghorn graze again on windy grassland ridges. Thunderheads still violently collide in endless skies to spill out brief torrents. The fearsomely cut-up land still dumps out fossils of the thunderhorse. And change is the only permanent thing, as it has always been in Badlands National Park.

Folklore has long held that prairie dogs and burrowing owls share living quarters. Lovely as the legend seems, it is not so—although the two creatures do mix freely on the surface and occasionally duck into the same hole when danger looms. The small owls nest and raise their young in abandoned prairie dog tunnels, not occupied ones.

Flowering yuccas highlight the spring season on Dagger Flat, where

Big Bend

"Big Bend is what Beethoven reached for in music; it is panorama without beginning or end."
Ludwig Bemelmans, *author and artist*

Long before you reach Big Bend National Park, it is clear that you are amid the wide open spaces of song and legend. You are, in fact, crossing the vast, seemingly empty land that Texans call Big Bend Country, an area about as large as Massachusetts and Connecticut combined. (The bend is the great southward loop that the Rio Grande makes on its long journey from the high Colorado Rockies to the Gulf of Mexico.) The park itself, about the size of Rhode Island, is nestled in a corner of this expanse.

You are also in the northern reaches of the great Chihuahuan desert, which extends from New Mexico far southward into old Mexico. About 98 percent of the park is true desert and desert grassland: the finest and most scenic stretch of Chihuahuan desert north of the border. But it is the interplay with the remaining 2 percent—the Chisos Mountains that loom at the heart of the park, and the Rio Grande that is its bulging southern boundary—that gives Big Bend its special character. Together these three environments, river, desert, and mountains, support a world of abundant life that is far greater than the sum of its parts.

Thanks largely to the Rio Grande, more kinds of birds—over 400 species by recent count—are found in Big Bend than in any other national park. Ducks and other water birds abound. Mourning doves and white-winged doves nest near the river, as do mockingbirds, summer tanagers, blue grosbeaks, painted buntings, and a host of other songsters. Peregrine falcons patrol the sky along canyon walls, alert for prey.

The Chisos Mountains are a moist island in a dry sea—one of the few places on earth where you can rest in the shade of a stately Douglas fir while enjoying the desert scent of creosote bush on the wind. Plant life that once flourished over a large area is now trapped here, often at the extreme edge of its range. An eastern tree, the chinquapin oak, grows in Pulliam Canyon, while a Mexican oak, Coahuila scrub, is found near Laguna Meadow. From the north and west come pon-

jackrabbits spread their large ears to release heat. In the background is the Sierra del Carmen, near the park's border.

derosa pine in Pine Canyon, Arizona cypress and Douglas fir in Boot Canyon, quaking aspen near Emory Peak, and bigtooth maples in several moist locations.

The lechuguilla, on the other hand, is an indicator plant of the Chihuahuan desert—if you see it growing anywhere else it has been introduced—and it thrives at almost all elevations in Big Bend. One of the park's two striking agave species (the other is the century plant), it blooms and dies after having lived for 10 to 15 years in the form of a rosette of tough, sword-shaped leaves. The needlelike spines on the end of each long blade can be painful to large animals and fatal to small ones; many a grasshopper has been skewered in midhop. The

insects are also put there by loggerhead shrikes, birds that habitually impale their prey on handy spikes. On desert slopes and in the grasslands that skirt the mountains, thickets of lechuguilla are often so dense that walking is difficult or impossible for man or beast.

In the 1880's, when great herds of cattle grazed the grasslands between the desert and the Chisos, ranchers considered the lechuguilla a curse. Today's grassland mammals don't mind it at all. Pronghorns (often miscalled American antelope) and the more abundant mule deer find good homes here, where the dry world slowly gives way to greenswards punctuated by shrubs and small trees; either animal, when hungry enough, will risk injury to browse on a lechuguilla's tender young shoots. A grassland animal that does so without risk is the tough-skinned javelina, or collared peccary. The possessor of vicious-looking tusks, a keen nose, poor eyesight, and a musk gland that leaves little doubt of its presence, the piglike javelina is a formidable creature that weighs in at 50 muscular pounds or so. They are also shy, traveling in bands of about a dozen and feeding in early morning or late evening on a largely vegetarian diet of lechuguilla, prickly pear, sotol, and mesquite beans, seasoned with a few insects.

Conflict and border wars

The land today is much the same as it was when prehistoric man arrived in Big Bend Country 10,000 or more years ago. Water is still carried across the desert to the Rio Grande by two natural drainage systems, Tornillo and Terlingua creeks. After heavy rains they are torrents, but more often their routes are dry. Here and there throughout the desert, seeps and springs still create green oases where horned toads are displaced by leopard frogs that splash among clumps of cattails.

The place has been inhabited to some extent for millennia. About A.D. 800 a band of hunters whose culture resembled that of the Plains tribes moved into the area. Big Bend's first farmers arrived around A.D. 1200; a Puebloan group moving south from New Mexico, they set to work tilling the floodplain by the river.

When the Spanish arrived in the 16th century, they called the area *el despoblado* ("the uninhabited land"), even though various Chisos Indian tribes lived and hunted there and the Puebloans still tilled the soil. The Spanish began capturing Indians to sell as slaves to mine operators in Mexico. When the Indians, essentially peaceful people, responded by raiding Spanish settlements, the Spanish virtually exterminated the Indians. Other, more warlike tribes from the north moved in to fill the void. First came the Mescalero Apaches, masters of desert survival. They conducted lightning raids on Spanish settlements and retreated into the desert, where they knew the edible plants and how to find the *tinajas*, or temporary water holes. Traveling light, they easily eluded their armored pursuers.

Later the fearsome Comanches followed, forced out of their homelands by advancing settlers. Accustomed to the more fertile plains, they found desert life hard, and turned to raiding on a large scale. Following a route south through Persimmon Gap (at what is today the park's main entrance), their war parties victimized Spanish and Apaches alike, taking slaves, livestock, and crops. Their route to the Rio Grande came to be known as the Comanche War Trail.

The Spanish were never able to master the Big Bend Country and relinquished it to newly independent Mexico in 1821. Fifteen years later, the territory became part of the Lone Star Republic of Texas. But neither the Mexicans nor the Texans were able to exercise any authority over the area; the Apaches and Comanches continued to rule by default.

Then, in 1848, the Treaty of Guadalupe Hidalgo defined the deepest channel of the Rio Grande as the U.S.–Mexican border, and the United States agreed to prevent Indian raids across the river. It was not until October 1880, however, when the renegade Apache leader Victorio was killed by Mexican troops, that the Indians were subdued. But that was by no means the end of border lawlessness.

With the coming of the railroad, the cattle industry blossomed in the grasslands, mercury mining became profitable, and small factories sprang up at such oases as Glenn Spring to extract wax from the candelilla plant. Rustlers and bandits plundered regularly, retreating to the mountains or into Mexico.

On the night of May 5, 1916, some 80 raiders crossed from Mexico and rode into Glenn Spring, guns ablaze. Leaving several dead behind, including three U.S. soldiers and a seven-year-old boy, they fled with all they could carry from the general store. They went to Boquillas, where they joined a smaller group that had raided Deemer's store. Together the looters took eight hostages, including Jesse Deemer and his store clerk, and the payroll of an American-managed silver mine.

What followed was one of the most peculiar chases in border history. Maj. George T. Langhorne of the U.S. 8th Cavalry came from El Paso in his chauffeur-driven Cadillac, followed by two Ford sedans carrying reporters, photographers, and a motion picture crew. The vehicles set off into the desert, along with a contingent of mounted troops. Unlikely as it seems, this odd caravan, after traveling more than 550 miles during 16 days in Mexico, succeeded. Deemer and the other hostages were freed, most of the loot was recaptured, several bandits were killed, and Langhorne lost no one.

After the raids, President Wilson ordered the National Guard units of Texas, New Mexico, and Arizona to active duty along the border. One guardsman, a cartoonist named Jodie P. Harris, had a drawing published in a supplement to the Fort Worth *Star Telegram*. It showed a soldier, ankle-deep in sand, declaring: "We have captured the Big Bend Country and have declared it a national park." Not until 1944, however, did his facetious suggestion become a reality.

The ribbon oasis

If you walk across the Big Bend desert in any direction except north, you'll eventually step into the big river. It could be a giant step: in some places the desert stops at the edge of a canyon overlooking a muddy stream hundreds of feet below. At other spots there are floodplains half a mile wide. For the most part, though, the change from desert creosote bush to riverbank cottonwood is instantaneous. The river is more than a political border: lush with life, the Rio Grande slices through the desert and changes it dramatically. Native species that have earned their right to the desert floor through

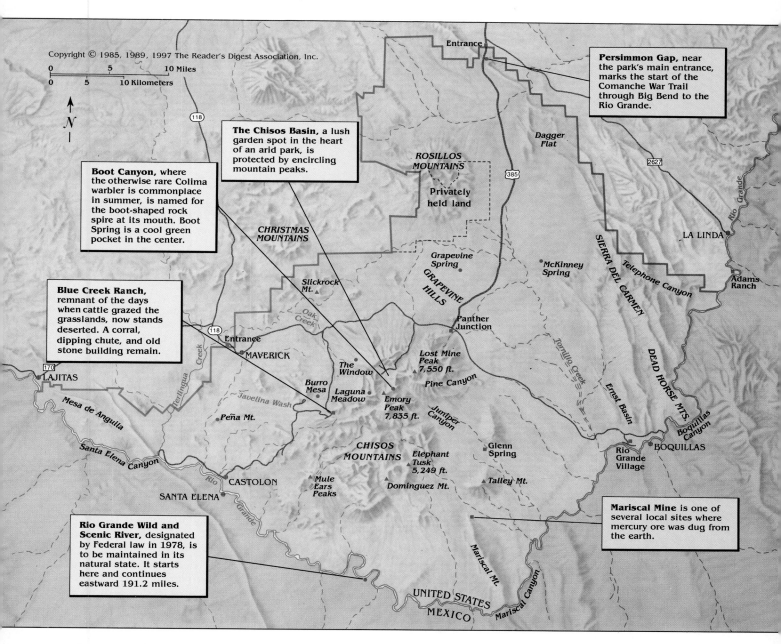

0   5   10 Miles
0   5   10 Kilometers

N

Persimmon Gap, near the park's main entrance, marks the start of the Comanche War Trail through Big Bend to the Rio Grande.

The Chisos Basin, a lush garden spot in the heart of an arid park, is protected by encircling mountain peaks.

Boot Canyon, where the otherwise rare Colima warbler is commonplace in summer, is named for the boot-shaped rock spire at its mouth. Boot Spring is a cool green pocket in the center.

Blue Creek Ranch, remnant of the days when cattle grazed the grasslands, now stands deserted. A corral, dipping chute, and old stone building remain.

Rio Grande Wild and Scenic River, designated by Federal law in 1978, is to be maintained in its natural state. It starts here and continues eastward 191.2 miles.

Mariscal Mine is one of several local sites where mercury ore was dug from the earth.

Entrance

ROSILLOS MOUNTAINS

Dagger Flat

Privately held land

CHRISTMAS MOUNTAINS

LA LINDA

Grapevine Spring

McKinney Spring

Slickrock Mt.

Adams Ranch

Oak Creek

GRAPEVINE HILLS

SIERRA DEL CARMEN

Panther Junction

Telephone Canyon

Entrance

MAVERICK

The Window

Lost Mine Peak 7,550 ft.

Pine Canyon

Tornillo Creek

DEAD HORSE MTS.

LAJITAS

Burro Mesa

Laguna Meadow

Ernst Basin

Boquillas Canyon

Mesa de Anguila

Javelina Wash

Emory Peak 7,835 ft.

Juniper Canyon

Peña Mt.

Santa Elena Canyon

CHISOS MOUNTAINS

Glenn Spring

Rio Grande Village

BOQUILLAS

CASTOLON

Mule Ears Peaks

Elephant Tusk 5,249 ft.

Talley Mt.

SANTA ELENA

Dominguez Mt.

Mariscal Mt.

Mariscal Canyon

UNITED STATES MEXICO

countless centuries of adaptation suddenly give way to life that has floated, swum, or hitchhiked with the flow. Beavers create wet worlds where frogs feed and turtles bask. Crayfish probe and scurry along rocky banks. Long-legged herons select their meals from an abundant variety of fish.

The river's waters teem with suckers, carp, and other typical river dwellers. Among the largest are the catfish—blue, channel, and flathead—that browse along the bottom. But it is one of the smallest fish, one that dwells not in the river but in pools near it, that has generated the most interest among the scientific community. The Big Bend gambusia is a top-water minnow, seldom longer than two inches, that exists nowhere else on earth. There are many species of gambusia, or mosquitofish, in and along the Rio Grande, but scientists are especially interested in the Big Bend gambusia

because it is a striking example of isolated change of a sort usually encountered only on small islands far from other land. Separated in the distant past from others of its kind, this distinct species gradually developed in pools (perhaps only one pool) of warm running water, able to survive only in its special habitat.

It was first discovered in 1928 by biologist Frederick M. Gaige, and it was for him that the species was named *Gambusia gaigei.* He described the place where he found it only as "a marshy cattail slough fed by springs located close to the Rio Grande at Boquillas." No one thought much more about the little fish or the place where it was found until 1954, when it turned up again in a small, warm pond. Two years after the rediscovery, predatory catfish and perch were also found in the pond, along with *Gambusia affinis,* a more common species that scientists felt might outcompete the Big

Shining only briefly in the narrow passage of Santa Elena Canyon, sunrise illuminates a tranquil Rio Grande. The eroded ridge along the canyon wall indicates the onetime level of the river in a rage.

Bend native. So the pond was seined, producing only 25 Big Bend gambusia. Twenty-one of these were distributed among three nearby springs and an artificial pond. All were dead within the year. Of the remaining four, held in an aquarium, one had also died, reducing the world population to three—two males and a lone female. These three fish were placed in a pool that had been specifically constructed for them (their home pond having ceased to exist), and the single female gave birth. Today her progeny seem to be flourishing near their historic home, with a backup population living in a fish hatchery.

Before dams were built on the Rio Grande, even eels passed through Big Bend Country on journeys from their birthplace in the Atlantic to the river's headwaters in Colorado. The park's three great canyons—Santa Elena, Mariscal, and Boquillas—made for some of the roughest white water in America, unnavigable by any but the hardiest adventurer. It was not until 1852 that wooden boats floated through Mariscal Canyon. Santa Elena Canyon was navigated in 1881, although the party's leader prudently took a dry route along the cliffs high above the river and met the boatmen at the canyon's mouth. Boquillas Canyon, the longest of the three, was conquered for the first time in 1899.

Today, because of dams that water the desert and provide power for communities both upstream and downstream, the river is less furious than it was. Most of the flow that passes by Big Bend comes not from the Rio Grande's historic drainage in the Rockies but from the Río Conchos out of Mexico. Were it not for this large tributary, which joins the Rio Grande about 60 miles upriver from the park, the big river would be very nearly dry here much of the year, as it is farther north. Instead, raft trips are regularly made through the canyons and only experienced canoeists dare to try it on their own. The ride may not be the life-threatening terror it used to be, but the water is still white enough to qualify a long stretch of the river for its protective designation as the Rio Grande Wild and Scenic River.

The flowering desert
The Chihuahuan desert is a paradox. Often described as inhospitable, hostile, harsh, drab, and forbidding, it can be all of those things. It can also be the most pleasant of places—serene, colorful, even magical. It all depends on your state of mind. If you can't handle the hard facts of solitude, searing heat, and scarce water, you are not likely to smell the flowers.

And flowers there are aplenty, both in the desert proper and in the desert grasslands that fringe the mountains. It is safe to say that somewhere, somehow, something is in bloom in the park every day of the year. Big Bend bluebonnets—the largest-flowered of several close cousins that have been declared the Texas state flower—are among the most dependable bloomers, washing hillsides with vibrant blue from midwinter on.

The century plant, an agave larger than the lechuguilla, grows in both the grasslands and the desert. For as long as 50 years it exists as a dense rosette of thick, spiny-edged leaves. Then one day its flowering mechanism is triggered, and an asparaguslike stalk shoots straight up to a height of as much as 15 feet. As the stalk grows, it extends side branches bearing platters of yellow flowers bigger than a man's hand. During this dramatic flowering period the plant serves as life support for dozens of creatures. The cactus wren makes the stalk—often the tallest thing around—its territorial perch. Several kinds of hummingbirds fuel their aerobatics with its nectar. In all, more than 20 bird species, including white-winged doves, sparrows, towhees, and finches, dine at the golden platters. So do a few kinds of bats, which pollinate the flowers as they hover before them, sipping nectar with their long tongues. Flycatchers and spiders wait for choice insects to come for their share of the copious nectar.

After the plant has set fruit and died, a ladder-backed woodpecker may excavate a nest in the stalk. And still the century plant's usefulness is not over. When after two or three years the stalk finally decays and falls, it shelters such diverse creatures as the Texas banded gecko lizard, the Mojave rattlesnake, and a small snail found only in Big Bend. Termites and other agents of decomposition finish off the remainder, generally in the shadow of a new plant, which has grown from seed or emerged from the roots of the dead one.

Throughout the desert from the riverbank to the foothills races the roadrunner, a fleet-footed member of the cuckoo family. An ungainly-looking creature at rest, all legs and neck and tail, it has little need to fly and does a poor job of it. But when, pursuing a juicy lizard or escaping a hungry hawk, it thrusts its head forward, levels its long tail, and sprints at up to 15 miles per hour, it becomes an image of streamlined beauty. All this speed burns much energy, and the roadrunner's gawky body is adapted to get rid of the resultant heat. Hence it has little substance in it to keep the bird warm; instead, the roadrunner relies on its own built-in solar energy collector. When the air turns chill, a roadrunner turns its back to the sun and raises its feathers, uncovering a patch of black skin that absorbs the sun's rays. When enough warmth has been soaked up, the feathers come down and the roadrunner is off again.

Waiting for rain

After spring rains or late summer thunderstorms, waves of flower colors sweep over the desert—the numbers and variety vary greatly from wet to dry years. Some seeds wait as long as a decade for rainfall to wash away chemicals that prevent them from sprouting. It takes a real storm to do the job; the seeds don't pop open after a trivial shower that would leave seedlings to wither in the sun. As quickly as they appear, the flowers fade, but the rain that woke them has brought pollinating insects

out too. Fresh seeds await nature's next caress.

Other life, too, awaits the rain. Every hollowed-out depression in the rocks along normally dry watercourses contains the eggs of tiny fairy shrimp. Add water and you have shrimp soup—with live shrimp. The life of these ephemeral crustaceans is a race against time; they must hatch, mature, mate, and lay eggs before the pool dries up—a few days at most.

The spadefoot toad survives by digging backward into the sand with its shovel-shaped hind feet. It may spend four-fifths of its life motionless underground. But after a big rainfall, the spadefoot goes on an energy-burning, pothole-hopping orgy, breeding and laying eggs. If water remains in a pothole for two days, the eggs become tadpoles. Give them 10 days and the tadpoles are adult enough to breathe on land.

To survive in the desert, plants and animals have developed elaborate and often bizarre devices for finding and storing water, for keeping other creatures from snatching it away, and for neutralizing the effects of the searing sun. While desert species have no monopoly on spines, thorns, poisons, foul odors, and thick leathery skins, they do seem to possess an inordinate number of these traits.

Gracing the park's more than 40 cactus species are blossoms that range in color from saffron yellow to deep maroon. Each kind of cactus is adapted to desert life in its own way. Questing roots soak up the slightest moisture. Water is stored in pulpy flesh and hoarded by thick skins. Spines turn stems into fortresses against thirsty animals; they also reflect the sun's rays and lose only enough moisture to air-condition the plants. The thorny coats of some kinds also protect such birds as cactus wrens, which nest under their aegis.

The ocotillo is a bare-bones shrub that could qualify

The quickest lizard is an easy meal for the fleet-footed roadrunner, but the bird is not a picky eater and will dine on spiders, rodents, centipedes, grasshoppers, scorpions, and anything else swallowable that it can catch.

A Big Bend Sunset

Day's end brings many creatures of the Big Bend desert and grasslands out of shady retreats to begin their nightly hunt for food. Others are finishing their day's activities. A pair of scaled quail (5)—also known as blue quail or cottontops—look for insects on the stems of a yellow-flowered prickly pear (11). High overhead, a lucifer hummingbird (2) hovers and sips sweet nectar from the fragrant blossoms of a century plant (1), while near the cluster of large, toothed leaves at the base of the treelike stalk, a black-tailed jackrabbit (6) cocks its large ears. It has heard the sudden sound of a tense encounter: a kangaroo rat (7), recently emerged from its burrow to forage seeds from a fallen yucca stalk, has surprised a scorpion (9) near a sotol's rosette of slender leaves (8). Neither creature is potential food for the other, so the standoff is likely to be brief and bloodless.

Nonetheless, the flurry of motion has startled a Texas banded gecko (10) from beneath the leaves of another nonflowering sotol, where it had been hunting for a fat beetle or spider to serve as its first meal of the night. Its quick movement has caught the attention of a black-tailed rattlesnake (12), basking in the waning light of the evening sun near a rosette of lechuguilla leaves. This encounter, too, should be without violence, for the snake's preferred diet is small rodents.

Overhead, among the protective spines of a cholla (16), a cactus wren (15)—the largest of the wrens—perches near its nest. A pair of wrens may maintain several such nests, raising as many as three different broods, each in a separate nest, over the course of a season. In the distance stretch the grasslands that skirt the Chisos Mountains, already purple with the shadows of dusk, and here mule deer (4) browse among flowering yuccas (3) and lechuguillas (14), surrounded by a bright carpet of Big Bend bluebonnets (13). The deer have been resting in shady nooks all day, sheltered from the ferocious sun, but now they will feed until dawn.

as a floral character in a Dr. Seuss book. Its unbranched stems, up to 20 feet long, seem dead most of the year. But a good rain during the growing season brings forth tiny leaves. They fall off when the moisture disappears and may sprout again with the next rain. In March and early April, the tips of the stems sport brilliant red flower spikes 4 to 10 inches long, looking from the distance as though someone has walked through with strips of red cloth, tying one to the top of each stem.

Displaying another strategy for survival, the mesquite bush, an oversized member of the pea family, makes itself independent of local rainfall. Its root system can delve as deep as 100 feet in search of groundwater; in drought years, when plants all around it are withering and browning, the mesquite's substantial plumbing keeps its tiny leaves green and glossy.

The surfaces of some desert plants are coated with resins and fatty substances to hold in water. One of the most abundant in Big Bend is the creosote bush, whose pungent smell most desert people eventually grow to enjoy. Its bitter resinous coat makes it palatable to few animals, and so it thrives unmolested; yet it does not become overcrowded. It produces a poison that kills its own seedlings when they sprout too close. Because of this infanticide, an expanse of creosote bush is as evenly spaced as a hand-planted urban park.

A thick coat of hard wax covers the fleshy stems of the nearly leafless candelilla shrub. The wax has long been used for candles; it has also served humans in much the same way it serves the plant—for waterproofing. Local inhabitants applied it to roof thatching and to walls of houses. During World War I it was harvested for coating munitions. It has also been used as an ingredi-

ent in chewing gum, phonograph records, and polishes for shoes, floors, and automobiles.

The refined wax formed the basis of a thriving industry in Big Bend Country for many years. Candelilla was pulled up by the roots, bundled, and taken by pack burros to rendering vats. There a boiling solution of water and sulfuric acid loosened the waxy coating; the resultant scum was skimmed off and cooled into hard cakes. Glenn Spring, where as many as 50 people were employed in 1916, was one of the many sites in Big Bend in which this process took place.

Among animals, the most frugal of water consumers is a little rodent with powerful hind legs, which can bound a foot and a half, kangaroo-style. Using its long tail as a rudder, the kangaroo rat can even make sharp turns in midair. It seldom hurries, however, unless pushed into action by the threat of a kit fox or other predator. After spending the day in its humid burrow, the entrance plugged to save moisture, the creature emerges at night to gather vast quantities of dry seeds, its staple food. Because of its uniquely efficient metabolism, a kangaroo rat can survive for weeks underground, quite content never to take a drink. Water is manufactured in its body as it digests the driest of food, and is hoarded and even recycled by a set of miserly kidneys. Even the rat's nasal anatomy helps, condensing and recapturing moisture from every breath.

The high garden
Once upon a time, when the land was lush and moist, ancient reptiles, including some dinosaurs, roamed what is now the park. Above them soared the largest creature ever to have flown. The reptile, dubbed the

Soaring over Big Bend more than 65 million years ago was the Texas pterosaur, the largest creature ever to have flown. Fossilized fragments of wing bones found in 1971 were pieced together to determine the great reptile's size, shown in comparison with that of a golden eagle.

The rock nettle's showy yellow blossoms open only in bright sunlight, livening the desert and dry mountain ledges. The leaves are covered with stinging hairs.

A claret cup, one of Big Bend's many cactus species, crowns this peak above Pine Canyon with a breathtaking display of scarlet.

Texas pterosaur, had a wingspan of about 36 feet, as wide as a modern jet fighter and half again the size of any pterosaur previously discovered. Its neck was long enough to probe a dinosaur carcass, and many scientists believe that the huge beast was a carrion eater who dined on dead dinosaurs.

Stupendous geologic changes have taken place since the pterosaur flew, not the least of which was the rise of the Chisos Mountains. Near the center of the park they stand, a sudden cluster of alpine peaks around a bowl-like garden spot known as the Chisos Basin. The Chisos Mountains were formed by volcanic activity near the end of the Cretaceous period, the same era of geologic tumult that saw the upthrust of the Rockies. Here, where flat layers of limestone had been left by ancient waters, molten rock pushed up from beneath, cooled, and hardened. Then weathering and erosion stripped away the fractured limestone, not only from the hard rock of the mountains but from the spaces around and between them, and created the rich sanctuary for varied life that is the Chisos Basin. It was within this sheltered bowl that Indians were to make their homes and it was in this refuge that outlaws of the Old West were to hide out.

The basin is a large part of the reason why many birds that winter in Mexico—including Big Bend's avian celebrity, the Colima warbler—spend their summers in Big Bend. This gray, white, and yellow songbird from the Mexican state of Colima is found nowhere else in the United States. No one knew it was here either, until a single bird was seen near Boot Spring by the same person who discovered the Big Bend gambusia—and in the same year. Four years later a scientific expedition, organized specifically for the purpose, located a warbler nest in the Chisos and reported the species to be quite common. Every year now, many birders travel to Big Bend with the singular hope of adding a Colima warbler to their lifetime lists.

The Chisos Basin's only drainage outlet, known as the Window, is at the end of a long canyon where a trickle called Oak Creek sometimes runs. Most of the time, the canyon is a tranquil setting where wildlife gathers to feast on the abundant vegetation. But like many intermittent Big Bend waterways, Oak Creek rages after a heavy rain, carrying boulders down the canyon like corks and hurling them through the Window to the bottom of a falls, 75 feet below.

Except on such stormy days, you can peek at the desert through the monumental rock bluffs that frame the Window. For a true overview, though, you must make your way to a summit such as 7,825-foot Emory Peak, the high point of the park. From this lofty perch you can see Big Bend as an eagle might, looking across the grassland that skirts the Chisos and the wide expanse of desert all the way to the zigzag course of the Rio Grande. It is an awesome vista, the more so when you know, as the eagle does, that it is not empty land you view but an arena filled with roiling life.

Biscayne

*"I remember . . .
. . . the sea tides tossing free;
And Spanish sailors with bearded lips,
And the beauty and mystery of the ships,
And the magic of the sea."*
Henry Wadsworth Longfellow

Stepping-stones to the horizon, Biscayne's islands separate the bay

Pirates once roamed these waters, seeking galleons laden with gold, and even today chests of their buried treasure are discovered now· and then. Ships that were surprised in the night by hidden reefs lie many fathoms deep, their secrets safe with the sharks, spiny lobsters, and crabs that live in Biscayne. Extending from the thick mangrove forests of the Florida mainland eastward across South Biscayne Bay, the park—the only underwater national park in the continental United States—reaches beyond a chain of islands to the coral reefs flourishing at the edge of the Gulf Stream. The Gulf Stream waters flow past the reefs like a gigantic river, their warmth enabling the coral to survive annual invasions of winter weather. Sea turtles, whales, and great schools of tuna ride the ocean river to new homes, and swept along with them are tremendous numbers of young animals from Caribbean spawning grounds, destined to grow into the adult fish, shellfish, and other marine creatures that populate the reefs of Biscayne.

Mighty stone fortresses besieged by the sea, coral reefs are actually living structures built by millions of soft-bodied, flowerlike animals called polyps. Each little polyp—most are scarcely an eighth of an inch across—nestles within a flower-shaped limestone cup. By day the fleshy polyps remain safely tucked inside their stony compartments, but at night they protrude to form a whitish fuzz over the surface of the colony, their tiny tentacles reaching out to snatch small bits of food from the water.

Small as they are, polyps are by no means simple creatures. The graceful dancing motions of their tentacles, the intricacy and symmetry of their bodies, their miraculous ability to take chemicals from the sea and turn them into stone—such complexities can astound those more accustomed to focusing on larger beings. Remarkably, each little polyp is itself host to other forms of life: a community of algae lives within its tissues, giving and receiving life. The minuscule green plants absorb carbon dioxide exhaled by the coral, and the coral breathes oxygen produced by the algae during photosynthesis. The relationship works only in shallow water, where sunlight can reach the algae—and only in shallow water will you find living coral.

(right) from the ocean; the mainland lies beyond the bay. Hidden from sight is the mysterious underwater world of the reef.

As new generations of polyps are born, they add layer after layer of limestone to the work of their ancestors, building a colony that may eventually contain millions of polyps. Each year, the colony lays down a ring of limestone, much as trees produce their annual growth rings. In good years, when there is plenty of food and sunlight and the temperature of the water remains above 68° F, the corals multiply rapidly and the rings are thick. In bad years they are thin.

How big a coral gets varies with the species. Some colonies grow to only a few feet tall; others rise hundreds of feet. Staghorn and elkhorn corals, their branching shapes reminiscent of the antlers of deer, sometimes grow so large that they shade out the smaller species, creating canyons beneath their "tines." Reaching these proportions is no short-term achievement: a massive brain coral—some colonies are 15 feet across—may take 30 years to add just an inch to its convoluted girth.

At Biscayne, elkhorns and staghorns form the sturdy backbone of the main reef, creating a barrier that protects the islands from the full force of the sea. Thousands of miniature reefs, called patch reefs, lie scattered in the shallow water between the outer reef and the islands. Ranging in size from several feet to several hundred, they consist mostly of rounded hills of star and brain corals and the leafy plates of lettuce coral. The elkhorns and staghorns, unable to tolerate the increased silt and shifting temperatures of the shallows, do not flourish in these quiet places.

Periodically hurricanes and severe winter storms kill part of a reef, leaving the white limestone skeleton to be colonized by barnacles, sponges, algae, and other marine life. Although this restores a living surface to the

49

coral, the new colonists break the skeleton into smaller chunks and pieces, some of which are ground into grains of sand by pounding surf. The reef illustrates a grand principle: no construction, whether of nature or of man, will last forever.

Pirates and shipwrecks

Hidden reefs were responsible for most of the wrecked ships that lie on Biscayne's sandy bottom, relics of a swashbuckling era when British, Spanish, French, and

Within Biscayne's watery world, some creatures look far more like plants than animals. The fernlike orange crinoid, kin to the starfish, seizes floating bits of food with its arms; the smooth-branched fire coral (below), like other coral species, has tiny tentacles that can sting.

American ships sailed these waters, vying for the rich Caribbean trade. One ship that fell victim to Biscayne's treachery was the H.M.S. *Fowey,* a British warship that in 1748 captured a Spanish trading vessel with a cargo of cocoa and indigo and a treasure in silver and gold. With her prize in tow, the *Fowey* set sail for Virginia, along with four British merchant ships. When one of the merchant ships ran aground (despite the fact she had not found bottom when sounding with 45 fathoms of line), the *Fowey* hastened to assist, carefully measuring the depths as she went. But suddenly she too ran into a jagged reef. The merchant ship floated free on the morning tide, but the *Fowey* had to be abandoned.

Though most of the treasures from various ship-wrecks were salvaged long ago, surprise caches are not unheard-of: in 1965 a chest containing silver pieces of eight turned up on Elliott Key when a tree was uprooted in a storm. But the true treasure of such discoveries lies more in their historical significance than in their cash value. Recovered artifacts reveal details never described in written records, such as the style of weapons, metal-casting techniques, and the like. Each proves an invaluable time capsule of life aboard ship in its day.

Perhaps even more dangerous than hidden reefs were the bloodthirsty pirates who preyed on richly laden ships in the Florida Keys. Black Caesar, one of the most notorious of all cutthroats, used what is now Biscayne National Park as his base of operations. (The deep channel between Elliott and Old Rhodes keys, believed by some to have been his headquarters, is called Caesar Creek.) Black Caesar would pretend to be adrift in an open boat while his crew waited behind a certain ledge (now known as Black Caesar's Rock), their ship heeled over to hide the mast. If a passing ship stopped to help the lone boater, the pirate ship was immediately righted for the surprise attack. Most of the captured crews were murdered; those spared were held prisoner until they agreed to join the pirates in their deadly deeds. Black Caesar, who joined forces with the infamous Blackbeard, was eventually caught and hanged on the gallows in Virginia.

Prowling the reef

From the mariner's point of view, reefs have always been dangerous places, capable of taking many a life. But from the naturalist's, their role is in fact *giving* life: for coral reefs are the houses, the forests, the hiding places of the sea. The orange and maroon tentacles of feather duster worms reach into the water to trap small living things; a passing shadow will cause them to bolt back into their leathery tubes. Hoary old loggerhead sea turtles sleep with the fronts of their barnacle-encrusted shells wedged tightly under coral rock. Hungry green moray eels, some 10 feet long, wait for unsuspecting octopuses to pass by their lairs. Arrow crabs balance on top of the coral, delicately bracing their tiny triangular bodies on pin-striped, spidery legs.

Damselfish and surgeonfish, among others, leave their hideaways every day (they feed on nearby algae and sea grass), but they never travel very far, and they soon return to the shelter of the coral. Their effect lingers far longer than they do: the intense foraging destroys the grass close to the reefs and creates a bare zone of sand and shell fragments—a "fish halo"—that surrounds the reef like a moat.

Shelter is not all a coral reef offers. During the day, schools of triggerfish, butterflyfish, angelfish, and other rainbow-hued swimmers dart about the coral, constantly on the prowl for food. Just about anything they can pluck out of a crevice is fair game—anything, that is, except inch-long cleaner shrimps. Standing brazenly out in the open, these peppermint-striped creatures sway back and forth as a signal that their cleaning business is open and that they are not frightened prey. Fish infected with parasites eagerly line up to await the shellfish's services. When the shrimp is ready, it crawls about on the fish's scales and into its gills and mouth, picking off the parasites with sharp little nippers. As soon as one fish is cleaned, it leaves, and the next swims into place.

When the last rays of sunlight filter into the water and darkness comes, nocturnal brittle stars—a type of starfish with five long, hairy arms winding out from a tiny round body—snake their way over the bottom. One brilliantly luminescent variety transmits waves of blue-green light when disturbed. Spiny lobsters, or Florida crayfish, test the water for smells and vibrations, waving long thorny antennae as they tiptoe over sand and grass, eagerly picking away at worms, sand dollars, and snails. (Though they lack the big, protective, crushing claws of their New England relatives, they make up for it in agility.) At daybreak, as many as 17 spiny lobsters crowd together under a rock ledge, their bristling antennae facing outward in defense.

Not even the deepest coral caves can offer total protection from an octopus. Changing into almost any color of the rainbow faster than a chameleon, this master of camouflage can blend into any background, even matching the texture of slippery brown seaweed. Blushing a dark red, then fading to gray or white as it moves agilely across the bottom, the eight-armed mollusk scans one coral cave after another, looking for prey. Using powerful suction discs on its arms, it drags a spiny lobster out of hiding. With one bite, it injects an immobilizing poison into the lobster; moments later, it spews out the remains.

Shoreward from this stony realm are gentler do-

Sailors who thought they were seeing a mermaid when this hulking mammal surfaced near their ships had probably been too long at sea. Measuring about 12 feet long and weighing up to a ton, the manatee is strictly vegetarian. The gentle, slow-moving beast uses its flippers to stuff sea grass into its mouth, and paddles with its tail. Limited to Florida, the entire manatee population of North America numbers only about a thousand.

Stoplight parrotfish

In the fast-paced world of the reef, predator can become prey with just the flip of a fin. Making sure that no one notices you is one way of staying out of trouble. Though the jackknife's stripes would seem to draw attention to it, they do just the opposite against the background of the reef. When in danger or about to rest, the fish sidles up to a branch of coral and aligns its vertical stripes with the edge, so that the jackknife appears to be part of the coral's silhouette. The dazzling pattern of the rock beauty serves much the same function.

Royal grammas—fairy basslet is another name—sport a round black spot on the upper fin. Masquerading as an eye, the dark spot deceives attackers, diverting them away from the head. If the gramma moves fast enough, the attacker may get a mouthful of water instead of a meal.

Color isn't always for camouflage: male stoplight parrotfish, for example, spruce themselves up (that is, change into their most vivid hues) to advertise their readiness to mate. Nor is color the only type of signal. When threatened, the bridled burrfish, or spiny boxfish, inflates itself with water and becomes a ball of prickly thorns—surely not the most vulnerable of prey.

Though fish are usually quiet creatures (they communicate more by sight than by sound), grunts and croakers are known for their noise. Grunts, the group that includes the cottonwick, are loudest when threatened or captured; the jackknife, a type of croaker, increases its chatter when spawning season comes round.

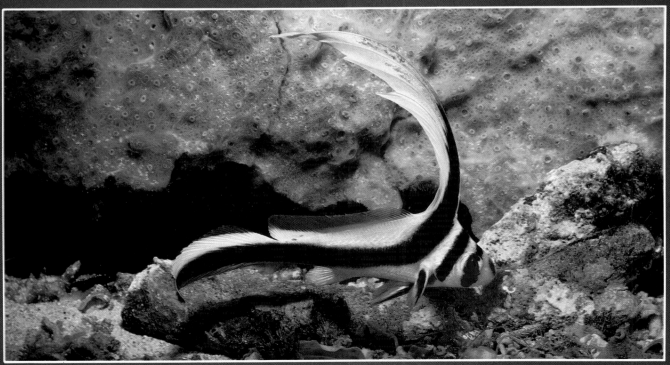

Jackknife fish

Royal gramma

Cottonwicks

Bridled burrfish

Rock beauty

mains, where sea whips, sea fans, and other soft corals replace their limestone cousins. Growing in colonies several feet high, they too are composed of tiny polyps, but their skeletons are far more flexible, gently swaying with the currents.

At night huge hammerhead sharks, some 10 or 12 feet long, cruise these shallows. On the alert for prey, the hammerhead uses sensory cells on the underside of its mallet-shaped head to detect electrical impulses from stingrays buried in the sand. Stingrays are famous—some would say infamous—for the venomous barbs on their lashing tails, but their weapons are useless against the sharks.

As the reef holds back the ocean's power, so another protective barrier—a chain of islands—creates shelter where underwater meadows can flourish. Horse-shaped

"Do not enter" is the message conveyed by mangroves, with their tangled roots and densely packed leaves. Though land-based predators cannot penetrate the swamps, such birds as herons and ibises use the trees as roosts.

seahorses, pipe-shaped pipefish, and star-shaped starfish all thrive in island-lined Biscayne Bay. Sea hares, mottled with purple and bearing rabbit-ear tentacles on their heads, nestle among the grass blades by day and gracefully undulate to the surface at night. If bothered, these snaillike creatures let out puffs of vivid purple ink—something that most other animals find it worth their while to avoid.

Looking for all the world like festive pink, white, and green pincushions, thousands of sea urchins graze on the algae that encrust the grasses. (Aside from the occasional manatee or green sea turtle, few creatures eat the leaves themselves.) Many of the sea urchins hold flat pieces of shell against their round bodies like shields, protecting themselves from ultraviolet light that penetrates the shallow water.

Nursery grounds

Carried on the currents that flow between the islands are enormous numbers of fish eggs, baby lobsters and shrimp, and the young of many other types of animals. When these tiny organisms reach the underwater meadows, they settle down, to grow up within the protection of the undulating grass. Between April and November, trillions of shrimp pour into the bay, where they grow rapidly—more than an inch a month—until they are six inches or bigger. Then they leave through the island passes, headed for the Atlantic to spawn and renew the cycle.

From birth to death, shrimp lead a precarious life. If currents carry them away from the nursery grounds before they are mature, their lives are swift to end. If not swept away by currents, they may be faced with another danger: being snapped up by a snapper, grouper, tarpon, snook, or other predatory fish. If they manage to dodge such enemies, the shrimp must still contend with schools of green-eyed opalescent squid. Hurling their jet-propelled bodies into hordes of shrimp, the squid lash out with their tentacles and draw the prey into their beaks. Many shrimp are lost this way every season—yet the sheer numbers born every year triumph over the losses.

By day, the shrimp fan their way to the bottom with their gills and cover themselves with a blanket of sand. At night they kick their way out and join the dance of other nocturnal creatures in the sea grass meadows, their stalked bulbous eyes glowing in the moonlight like hot red coals. Foraging about in the grass, the shrimp grasp bristle worms, clams, and other minute creatures in their tiny pincers.

Sponges don't dance about; nor do they forage. But though these plantlike animals lie seemingly inert on the meadow floor, they are constantly at work, pumping water through their bodies and straining out bits of food; to gain just one ounce, a sponge must filter a ton of water. Various creatures sponge off sponges. Stinging bristle worms crawl through their inner cavities, and thousands of transparent snapping shrimp, fully grown at less than an inch, live inside. Each shrimp has one relatively large claw, similar to a lobster's, that sounds a warning click when intruders venture too close. Stone crabs have claws too, but theirs are shovels, used to dig snug, hidden homes beneath the sponges.

Harvesting of sponges—now banned—was once a way of life on Biscayne Bay. Fishermen patrolled the bay in small skiffs, searching for the dark, round shapes. With poles ending in hooks, they jabbed at the base of a sponge until it broke loose from the bottom. The sponges were dried on webbed racks, then soaked in seawater to get rid of the "meat." The result was a sponge that far outlasts any synthetic product.

Worlds of green

Biscayne is predominantly an underwater park, but it has islands too—lumps that loom up from the horizon like the backs of enormous sea turtles, full of mystery and intrigue. Some, like the Arsenicker Keys, barely count as islands: they contain no dry land, and their greenery consists only of saltwater-loving mangroves. Throughout the Florida Keys, forests of these small trees perch like spiders above the silty mud and limestone rocks, supported by a crisscrossing web of arching roots. Unlike more conventional trees, with their subterranean roots, mangroves have their roots for the most part exposed to the air. They sprout out and downward from branches and trunks, forming a tangled maze and anchoring themselves in the mud. The trees' oval leaves make a dense green canopy, shielding fish and others in the shallows from the blazing sun. At high tide brown-spiraled periwinkle snails climb the roots, then creep back down as the water recedes. Male fiddler crabs wave their hefty claws from exposed mudbanks, trying to attract females into their lairs. With their graceful pink necks and long spindly legs, roseate spoonbills and an occasional flamingo stalk the fringes of the dense thickets; silvery bonefish search for worms, crabs, and other prey along the muddy roots.

Their tangled roots blocking access and acting like a natural fence, mangroves by and large keep bigger forms of life from the islands. Protected from nonflying creatures that might do them harm, thousands of birds flock about. Brown pelicans with their ungainly bodies and huge sacklike bills cruise along, diving headfirst into the sea when they spot a fish. Poised atop their nests, such birds of sea and shore as herons and frigate birds fill the air with screams and calls, their collective voices so loud that the noise is almost deafening.

Mangrove stands, once thought to be mere mosquito-

A lily of the forest rather than the field, the spider lily thrives in humid places. Other blossoms include butterfly orchids and wild poinsettias.

infested wastelands, are now known to make two very different—and two very valuable—contributions to life on earth. One concerns the ocean's food chain; the other, building up land. As mangrove leaves fall and pile up among the roots, bacteria and fungi attack them, turning them into nutrients needed by tiny forms of aquatic life. When storms surge into the tidal swamps, these nutrients are washed out to sea, nourishing plankton—the first link in the oceanic food chain. The roots, too, play a role in building land, trapping silt and debris. As the sediments settle out of the water, they build up the bottom. Though the increase in elevation is slight, it does make a difference (it holds back the tides), and so does the greater amount of soil. Plants less tolerant of saltwater, such as buttonwood, begin to take root. Over time the land will reclaim the swamp.

But not all of Biscayne's islands are amphibious places, swept throughout their entirety by the tides. Elliott and Adams keys are far more substantial, and they are among the ones with tropical hardwood forests. The most northern of such forests in the United States, they cover what is nearly the last of the undeveloped Florida Keys. Trees here tend to have crooked trunks, very hard wood, and evergreen leaves, which create a dense shade all year. Vines abound, twining their way toward the light. Spanish moss, among other plants, gets the sunlight it needs by growing perched on trees rather than in the ground. In the middle of the islands, hundreds of hermit crabs drag the snail shells in which they live over mossy green rocks, picking among the detritus for food. Giant land crabs dig deep, intricate tunnels through the soft stone.

Biscayne's forested islands, so vastly different from underwater reefs, are linked with them by time. Forming a loose chain five to seven miles from the mainland, the islands were once part of a line of coral reefs stretching from what is now Miami to Key West and beyond. But that was about 100,000 years ago; since then sea level has dropped about 25 feet, leaving the reefs high and dry. Trees on these former reefs do not stand securely in the ground, like mainland trees, but instead wrap their roots tightly around the ancient coral rock, seeking scarce patches of soil. Remarkably, the same types of coral that today flourish a mile or two offshore also sit in the forest, whitened and stony, supporting plant growth. A brain coral occupies precisely the same position as when it was alive and under water many thousands of years ago—but instead of fish, ferns and flowers are its modern-day companions.

Giant figures, delicately sculpted in brilliantly colored rock, line the Pink Cliffs of Bryce Canyon. Around and between them twists a

Bryce Canyon

*". . . the work of giant hands,
a race of genii once
rearing temples of rock,
but now chained up
in a spell of enchantment."*
Capt. C. E. Dutton,
19th-century surveyor

The Paiute Indians, who for centuries lived in and around Bryce Canyon, revered the place, with its colors that glow like pieces of a broken rainbow. They called it *Unka-timpe-wa-wince-pock-ich*. ("Red-rocks-many-standing-holes.")

The story they tell about how the canyon was formed begins in the Land Below, where the Paiutes used to live along with many godlike animal spirits. The most powerful of these, Coyote, was a constant troublemaker who one day stole the children of the great Water Monsters. In revenge, the Water Monsters flooded the land, driving all who dwelt there to the Land Above.

Disgusted with Coyote's antics, the Paiutes abandoned him. Only the Queer Ones—toads, lizards, bats, and insects—elected to stay with him in their new world. Coyote built a village for them in a canyon where they would be sheltered from the hot sun and desert winds. But the Queer Ones grew arrogant and lazy; they insulted Coyote, ignored his commands, and lay around all day instead of hunting for food. So Coyote called a council. The Queer Ones came in human form, dressed

bewildering maze of blind canyons and ravines.

57

in colorful clothing, and stood or sat in sullen silence, row upon row along the canyon walls. The more Coyote rebuked them the angrier he became, and he began to wave his arms wildly, throwing out a powerful magic. The Queer Ones remained silent; Coyote's medicine had turned them to stone. To this day, still colorfully clad, they line the walls of Bryce Canyon, mute and still.

Such stories satisfy a deep need in all people to understand the world around them. Our modern tale of how the canyon was formed is no less satisfying, though a good deal more complicated. Like the Paiute version, it begins in another land, at a time in the distant past, and it involves flooding on a grand scale.

The geologist's song

Once upon a time, 4½ billion years ago or so, all the continents of the world were one. Somehow, this great supercontinent broke apart. About 200 million years ago, the pieces slowly began to move, riding on mobile plates over the earth's molten mantle, propelled by currents that swelled and rolled like the surface of a thick, boiling pudding. The plate carrying North America migrated west and north, eventually crashing into the plate that underlies the Pacific Ocean.

By that time, Utah lay about where Guatemala is today. Its landscape was tropical, a broad coastal plain dotted with swamps and marshes just west of a warm, shallow sea. Meandering eastward across the plain on their way to the sea, wide, sluggish rivers dropped a thick residue of sand and gravel.

The stupendous, multimillion-year collision of the plates warped and buckled the land. Oceans, swamps, and deserts came and went, each leaving a distinctive layer of stone. The Rockies were thrust upward, and in time a series of shallow freshwater lakes formed in basins behind them. Spiraling down through the water were sediments that came to form the layers of soft stone: mud was compressed into mudstone, sand into sandstone, the limy remains of water life into lime-

stone, mixed materials into conglomerate. Various minerals added colors. Together, these contrasting layers make up Bryce Canyon's most distinctive feature—the multicolored Claron Formation.

Meanwhile, the continental plate was sliding westward over the edge of the oceanic plate and, as it continued to move northward, grinding upon it. By 15 million years ago, responding to the immense pressure of plate upon plate, the basin had begun gradually to rise. It was to become the Colorado Plateau, covering about 150,000 square miles of what is now Arizona, New Mexico, Colorado, and Utah. It began rising in the south, with the result that all the sedimentary layers that had been deposited by oceans, deserts, rivers, marshes, and lakes came to slope downward from south to north.

At the same time, stress was pulling the land apart. The Colorado Plateau fractured along clearly defined lines, or faults, into a series of individual plateaus, each rising as the whole did, south side first. As the rake of the land increased, sluggish streams became roaring agents of erosion, scouring canyons out of ravines and gullies, undercutting and stripping away whole layers of sediment, and eventually carving a series of cliffs that geologists call the Grand Staircase. On the face of each step are exposed deep layers of long-buried stone from a different period in the past. Because erosion began earlier in the south, more layers were lost there, and so on the southernmost plateau, called the Kaibab (from a Paiute word meaning "mountain lying down"), no rock younger than 225 million years remains. The northernmost and youngest step of the Grand Staircase we call the Paunsaugunt Plateau—also from the Paiute, for "home of the beaver." Bryce Canyon is cut into the Pink Cliffs on the eastern side of this step.

Bryce Canyon is actually not a single canyon, but a series of amphitheaters faced by countless little canyons. Each was cut by a trickle, stream, or rivulet as it sliced through the Pink Cliffs, joining the others at the base to make the Paria River. This river is constantly

The Grand Staircase

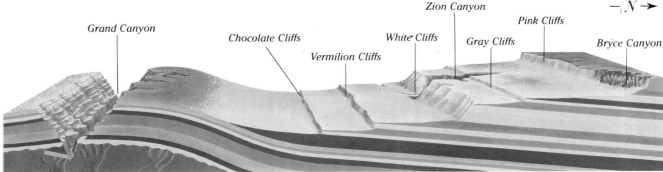

Although the beeline distance from Bryce Canyon's Pink Cliffs to the bottom of the Grand Canyon is only about 200 miles, the time span is more than 15 million centuries. As the Colorado Plateau was uplifted, south side first, streams became rushing rivers that sliced through its surface. Whole layers of rock were undercut and have been eroded away, leaving a series of south-facing cliffs— the Grand Staircase. Each row of cliffs reveals rock from a different distant age, and each is named for the distinctive color of the rock that it displays.

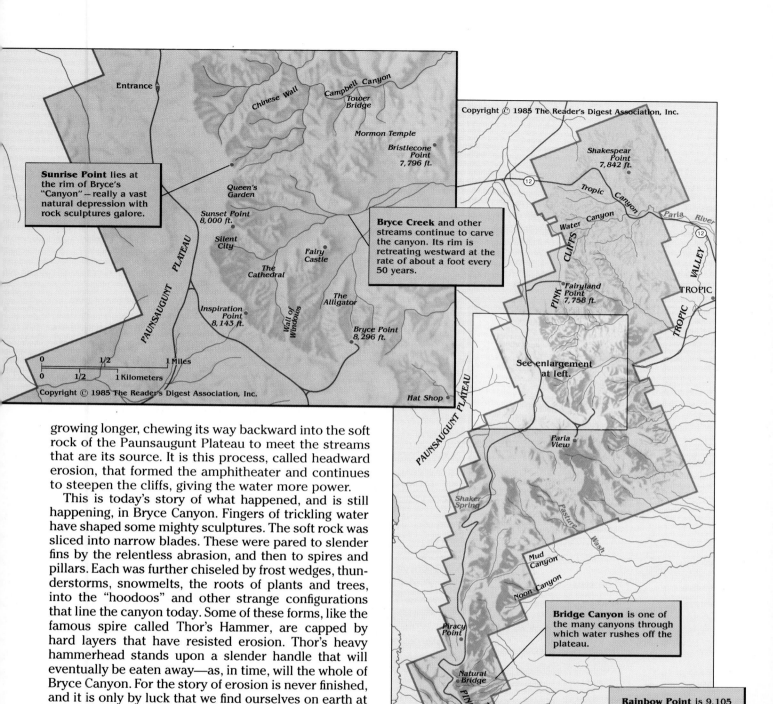

Sunrise Point lies at the rim of Bryce's "Canyon" – really a vast natural depression with rock sculptures galore.

Bryce Creek and other streams continue to carve the canyon. Its rim is retreating westward at the rate of about a foot every 50 years.

Bridge Canyon is one of the many canyons through which water rushes off the plateau.

Rainbow Point is 9,105 feet above sea level. As you go through the park from south to north, elevations decrease, for the entire Paunsaugunt Plateau is tilted.

growing longer, chewing its way backward into the soft rock of the Paunsaugunt Plateau to meet the streams that are its source. It is this process, called headward erosion, that formed the amphitheater and continues to steepen the cliffs, giving the water more power.

This is today's story of what happened, and is still happening, in Bryce Canyon. Fingers of trickling water have shaped some mighty sculptures. The soft rock was sliced into narrow blades. These were pared to slender fins by the relentless abrasion, and then to spires and pillars. Each was further chiseled by frost wedges, thunderstorms, snowmelts, the roots of plants and trees, into the "hoodoos" and other strange configurations that line the canyon today. Some of these forms, like the famous spire called Thor's Hammer, are capped by hard layers that have resisted erosion. Thor's heavy hammerhead stands upon a slender handle that will eventually be eaten away—as, in time, will the whole of Bryce Canyon. For the story of erosion is never finished, and it is only by luck that we find ourselves on earth at the right moment to see this remarkable place.

The forest world

It was atop the heavily forested Paunsaugunt Plateau that the nomadic Paiutes spent their summers, living in loosely organized family groups. Here they built brush shelters called wickiups, and hunted the abundant mule deer, along with rabbits and other small game. From the lush grasses growing in occasional meadows they gathered many kinds of seeds—a big item in their diet— which they winnowed in sturdy baskets.

The plateau, rising in a great dark lump off the desert floor, engenders rainclouds and milks them nearly dry. In summer, thunderheads stack up, sending vivid tentacles of lightning into the forests. From October to April,

The 96-foot-high Natural Bridge frames the beginning of the dense forest that blankets a large part of the southern Paunsaugunt Plateau. No river or stream ever ran beneath this bridge; instead, it was cut by the forces of weathering.

the snow is deep and wet—impossible to traverse without snowshoes. At the high south end of the plateau (at about 9,100 feet, the high point of the Grand Staircase) summer is but a brief pause between long, intense winters. Dark, shady forests of fir and spruce cover the land, similar to those found much farther north. Silver-barked aspens stand out in sharp contrast, their bright yellow leaves adding a brilliant dash of autumn color. In midsummer, mule deer browse on mountain lilac and other shade-tolerant shrubs; but for the most part, food resources are skimpy in these deep shadows, and fewer animals live here than at the lower elevations. When winter clamps down, and dark clouds glower, the canyon seems far away, and one feels like a castaway on a piece of Canadian terrain that by some weird magic has broken loose and drifted south to Utah.

Beyond the heavy forest, on desolate high ridges overlooking this end of the canyon, squat occasional bristlecone pines, as gnarled as gnomes. Some have clung there stubbornly for more than 1,000 years.

Farther north, as the plateau's elevation drops, ponderosa pines gradually come to dominate, growing to heights of 100 feet and more. A forest of ponderosa is a bright, spacious place; the lowest branches spread well overhead, and each tree's extensive root system efficiently drains moisture from surrounding soil, discouraging nearby competition. In the warm afternoon sun the air is scented with the subtle vanilla fragrance given off by the trees' scaly, orange-tinted bark. In autumn the ground is littered with prickly russet-brown cones, among which scurry chipmunks, marmots, ground squirrels, and their busy kin. Here and there the ponderosa forests are interrupted by grassy meadows, where elderberry, ceanothus, and creeping barberry

provide food for a large assortment of birds and other animals. Along occasional watercourses grow willows and cottonwoods, mixed with the distinctive water birches, their multiple trunks aglow with bronzy bark.

Throughout this diverse world are scattered blue-green Rocky Mountain juniper, manzanita, bitterbrush, and a richly varied selection of other shrubby growth upon which mule deer feed. Shy creatures with liquid eyes, they raise their heads when startled, fan their enormous ears out like radar screens, and stand perfectly still. Sensing danger, they disappear soundlessly, their tails pointing upward in alarm.

Mazes, fins, and hoodoos

As you approach the canyon rim, you get no hint of what's in store. The ponderosa forest grows more spacious as the soil gets drier; the earth tilts slightly upward underfoot as if toward the lip of a shallow bowl. Suddenly the ground falls away in countless gullies and ravines, and you gaze out upon one of the strangest landscapes you will ever see. It is as if a ferocious, taloned giant had raked the edge of the plateau, carving deep runnels and washes that bleed colors as they curve and slash their way down toward the desert floor. If the air is really clear, the rounded dome of Navajo Mountain, some 80 miles to the southeast, seems close enough to touch.

Descending the canyon walls is an ordeal. The slopes are steep, and any trail must double back upon itself in tight coils. The soft, crumbly materials of the Claron Formation give way easily underfoot. Close to the rim, the ponderosas are small and widely scattered, joined by pinyon pines, cliffroses, sagebrush, and desert scrub. Before long, the ponderosas are displaced altogether.

In a snowfall, the canyon seems mysteriously to vanish. The jutting rocks are obscured by gloomy clouds that spill over the rim like cotton from an overloaded bag. From down in the canyon, the same snowstorm is a marvel to behold. Puffy white flakes, spiraling slowly between reddish blades of rock, seem to take forever to land. Pinyon branches droop under the burdens that cling to every twig and needle.

Every autumn, before deep snows covered the plateau, the Paiutes took this route over the rim and through the canyon down to the desert valleys at its base. There they lived the hard life of desert foragers, digging sego lily bulbs and picking prickly pears and other cactus fruits. From such tough, sinewy plants as the yucca they made fiber for sandals and rope—to snare lizards, birds, and rabbits—as well as needles, soap, and other items. From pinyon pines they gathered nuts to mash and bake into nutritious little cakes.

Pinyons are plentiful out in the open reaches of the amphitheater, as are Utah junipers, small shaggy cousins of the Rocky Mountain juniper. Though less plentiful along the canyon walls and on the canyon floors, pinyons do survive there, sparse and stunted, among perfumed cliffroses and sharp-scented sagebrush. Pinyon nuts are the basis of a vital food chain. Ground squirrels and chipmunks devour the nuts, and in turn are preyed upon by hawks, eagles, bobcats, and ringtails—and sometimes by such larger animals as coyotes and mountain lions (although these mighty hunters prefer more substantial prey when they can find it).

Summers are long, hot, and arid in the canyon. Oven-like trails wind in mazes between sheer rock blades that hold in the heat, especially in the area known as Queens Garden, below Sunrise Point. Fracture lines are visible everywhere in the rock, and the litter of small chips and stones underfoot indicates the steady rate of disintegration. New colors and formations lurk around every turn. Many weirdly sculpted pinnacles, or hoo-doos, have been named: the Chinese Wall, Tower Bridge, Queen Victoria, The Pope. Others have no names, but in the late afternoon, when the light catches a lofty pedestal at a certain angle, a prominent nose may emerge, or the suggestion of an eye socket. The sight can send a shiver up your back; inside the rock you have seen one of the Paiutes' frozen Queer Ones.

The colors they wear come from minerals in rock layers. The Pink Cliffs at the top of the Claron Forma-tion are tinted by the oxidation of iron. In the yellow walls below, the iron oxide has rusted, becoming a substance called limonite. Blue and purple surfaces indicate traces of manganese oxide. The white layers are nearly pure beds of limestone and dolomite. These colors are often concealed under a reddish-brown clay, a natural "stucco" that covers the canyon walls.

But during early mornings and late afternoons in summer, when the slanting rays of the sun are almost palpable in the canyon, coating your flesh with a golden patina and seeming to soak through your pores like a liquid solution, it doesn't matter how the colors got there. What matters is the way the glowing light seems to radiate from the rocks—the way the living colors pulsate from within.

The Paiute way of life is gone now, replaced more than a century ago by the coming of settlers. (One of them, a carpenter named Ebenezer Bryce, gave his name to this canyon, which he described only as "a heck of a place to lose a cow.") But Paiutes still live, and many remember and still revere this monumental place, through which their ancestors made their way twice a year, overseen by spirits of the petrified dead.

Brightly tinted aspen leaves add their autumnal touch to the already colorful rock forms in Bryce Canyon. Many bizarre sculptures, like the hoodoos below, exist only because caprocks made of dolomite (limestone rich in magnesium) or some other hard substance protect the layers beneath from erosion.

Canyonlands

". . . the least inhabited, least inhibited, least developed, least improved, least civilized . . . most arid, most hostile, most lonesome, most grim bleak barren desolate and savage quarter of the state of Utah—the best part by far."

Edward Abbey, *writer*

At the heart of the arid stone wilderness that is Canyonlands National Park is a watery place called the Confluence. Here, between rock walls more than a thousand feet high, the waters of the Green River pour into those of the Colorado. From this point on, the Colorado—already a powerful force upon the land—becomes one of the great rivers of the world. Tumbling and raging in a white-water display that has weakened the resolve of many a boatman, it sets out through the echoing depths of Cataract Canyon on a long and tumultuous journey to the Gulf of California.

If the wide, rolling Mississippi is indeed this continent's Old Man River, and the cool, deep Hudson its mature Merchant Prince, then the hard-driving Colorado must be the Young Turk of American rivers. In the few million years since its birth, it has carried away the remains of solid rock nearly two miles thick, from an area almost the size of France. With the abrasive force of all this rocky sediment, it and its rushing tributaries have gouged out deep canyons and shaped stark landscapes, the likes of which exist nowhere else on earth.

Standing on Grand View Point, 2,300 feet above the Confluence, you survey one of the starkest of these landscapes. The view is grand indeed—especially at sunset. Orange mesas, red buttes, maroon towers and pinnacles, their intense colors made even more vivid by the last rays of a setting sun, create a strangely surreal scene, not unlike those amazing television transmissions from the surface of Mars. Softly rounded mounds of rock that look like melting ice cream add their own touch of otherworldliness. It seems to be a world just

Overseen by a twisted juniper, the Green River winds its way through Canyonlands' surreal landscape toward its meeting with the Colorado. The barren-seeming land is brightened by sego lilies and other flowers of the desert.

ending—or one just beginning. Long black shadows creep into the creases of the land, giving even greater relief to an already rugged terrain. No part of this awesome panorama is without steeply incised canyons; all converge grandly into the Y-shaped abyss that radiates from the Confluence.

The three great gorges that form the Y cut the park into three pieces, each with its own distinct character. Unless you descend into a canyon, cross the river at the bottom, and scale the wall on the other side, you can't get from one piece to another without leaving the park—without traveling, in fact, nearly 100 miles.

Grand View Point is in the northern piece, the aptly named Island in the Sky region between the arms of the Y. This is a land of high, flat-topped mesas that do indeed rise like islands from a sea of tortured rock. Averaging a mile or more above sea level, these tablelands are but remnants of the high plateau that was worn away ages ago by the Green and Colorado rivers and their tributaries. Although there are some grasslands here and "pygmy forests" of stunted pinyon pine and Utah juniper, this is mostly bare slickrock country, where your feet slip on naked stone, covered at most by a few inches of sand.

Still, those who look and watch carefully will discover much to marvel at in this land. The very soil can tell a fascinating story. In places the sand is covered by a dark gray crust that crunches audibly underfoot. This is cryptobiotic soil, a delicate entity in which a dramatic process is taking place. Colonies of cyanobacteria, mosses, and lichens are gradually creating nutritious, life-bearing soil. Growing amid sterile grains of sand, these organisms bind the tiny bits of rock together, retarding erosion; in the process, they add the organic matter without which plants cannot thrive. Because of cryptobiotic soil, an empty desert can one day support a diversity of life.

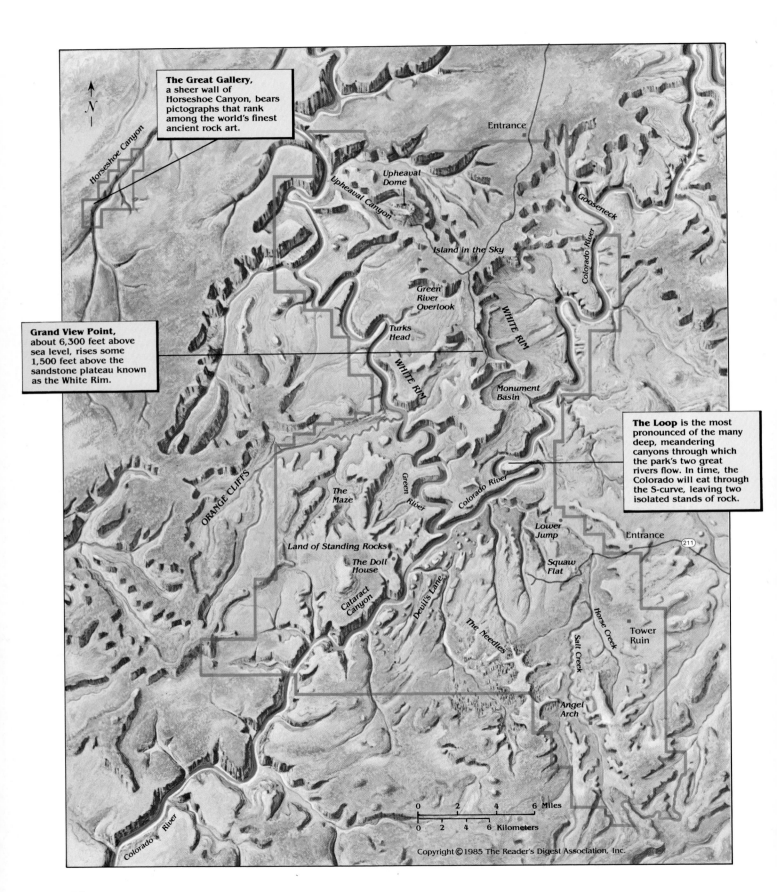

The Great Gallery, a sheer wall of Horseshoe Canyon, bears pictographs that rank among the world's finest ancient rock art.

Grand View Point, about 6,300 feet above sea level, rises some 1,500 feet above the sandstone plateau known as the White Rim.

The Loop is the most pronounced of the many deep, meandering canyons through which the park's two great rivers flow. In time, the Colorado will eat through the S-curve, leaving two isolated stands of rock.

Horseshoe Canyon

Entrance

Upheaval Dome

Upheaval Canyon

Gooseneck

Colorado River

Island in the Sky

Green River Overlook

WHITE RIM

Turks Head

WHITE RIM

Monument Basin

ORANGE CLIFFS

The Maze

Green River

Colorado River

Lower Jump

Entrance

211

Squaw Flat

Land of Standing Rocks

The Doll House

Devil's Lane

Horse Creek

Tower Ruin

Cataract Canyon

The Needles

Salt Creek

Angel Arch

Colorado River

0   2   4   6 Miles

0   2   4   6 Kilometers

Copyright ©1985 The Reader's Digest Association, Inc.

But the process is an extremely slow one. It may take 50 years or more for a small patch of soil to develop. And it is extremely delicate; with one footstep, a child can undo the accomplishment of decades.

Some areas sport luxuriant growths of stipa grass, tall and resilient. Each seed of this plant is a remarkable example of biological adaptation to a parched country, where the eight-inch annual rainfall often occurs in one or two drenching thunderstorms. Between storms, the saturated soil bakes and its surface hardens into another kind of crust, penetrable by the seeds of few plants. But the seeds of stipa grass, enclosed in hard, pointed shells, are equipped with threadlike tails up to 10 inches long. The tail has two functions. First, it allows the seed to travel a long way on the wind. (This is not unusual—the plumed seeds of many plants, such as dandelions and thistles, travel even farther.) More important, and far more special, is what the tail does after the seed lands: it coils tightly under the drying sun and uncurls with the moisture of morning dew, literally screwing the seed through the surface crust deep enough to sprout and grow when the rain falls again.

Creatures of the Maze
Westward across the Green River is a mysterious realm known to early Indians as *Toom-pin wu-near' tu-weap* ("Land of Standing Rocks"), and now also called the Maze. Either name fits perfectly. Eroded towers, slender fins of stone, and massive buttes stand among and above sheer canyons that twist and turn in every direction, dividing and subdividing into total confusion. More than anywhere else in the park, here you are aware that the extremes of climate in Canyonlands are just that: extreme. In any given year, the temperatures may range from 110°F to -20°F. These figures don't tell the full story, however; under the midday summer sun, the surface temperatures of rock and soil can exceed 150°F. Booted feet swelter; bare ones would fry.

Like the Island in the Sky, this forbidding and austere desert supports forms of life that can survive only in places like these, where salty sand, the constant presence of heat, and the nearly constant absence of water make survival all but impossible for most creatures.

The cornerstone of the desert scrub community here is a member of the rose family called blackbrush. Its dark gray branches, many tipped by sharp spikes, are nearly leafless during the long dry spells. But when moisture is available, the thick, paddle-shaped leaves appear, crowded into dense bundles along the stems. They act quickly, using the abundant energy of the sun to produce sugars, and as soon as the water supply diminishes, they fall. This fleeting greenery can appear not only after a summer thundershower, but also in midwinter, when a few warm days have melted enough snow to make the process worthwhile.

Most small mammals, such as kangaroo rats, lie in cool burrows during the day, emerging at night to forage. Darkness is also the time when the coyotes' haunting chorus can be heard. In the morning you may spot the tracks of a ringtail, a bobcat, or even a mountain lion. All three hunters prowl the park but are rarely seen because of their cautious, nocturnal habits.

As is true of most desert regions, the most conspicuous inhabitants of Canyonlands are reptiles—especially the lizards that scurry across open spaces and rustle among dry leaves in search of insects and spiders. Being cold-blooded, they are sluggish in the chill of night, most active in the daytime heat. Mornings, lizards may bask in direct sunlight, aligning themselves on rocks in just the right way to absorb the maximum solar energy. But later on, they must avoid too much direct sun or they will cook, and so they seek the shade of rocks or plants. Some long-legged types, such as the pale leopard lizard, are able to make fast forays across the hot sand because their bellies are held well away from the scorching surface. Others, such as the Utah banded gecko, stay in shaded nooks until evening.

Snakes are found here, too, though less frequently than in other deserts of the Southwest. If you happen upon a gopher snake, it may hiss loudly and vibrate its tail in apparent imitation of a rattlesnake, but its threat is an empty one. The nonpoisonous reptile preys on rodents, with an occasional snake—even a rattler—thrown in. The park's only really common rattlesnake, the midget faded rattler, is seldom met. Just as rattlesnakes terrify most people, so do people terrify most rattlesnakes. Given the opportunity, the venomous reptiles will try desperately to escape and hide. You may roam this land for a long time and never see one of them; and unless you were to step on one inadvertently, the chances of being bitten are minuscule. But the snakes are there, hiding from the sun in the heat of day, hunting rodents and other small mammals at nightfall.

Anasazi and the All-American Man
To the south and east of the Maze is the Needles district, bristling with towers and peaked spires of sandstone. In this piece of the park there is more diversity, both of terrain and of life, than in the other two pieces combined. There are water-cut canyons, the streams at their bases lined with lush green growth, and there are strange, straight canyons through which no stream has ever flowed. There are grassy swales where wildflowers bloom, mule deer and rabbits browse, and birds gather. There are the relics of ancient peoples who hunted or farmed the land here, and of more recent ranchers whose cattle grazed the grasslands.

The Needles district's surprising diversity of life is supported in large part by a mineral-laden stream called Salt Creek and its tributary, Horse Creek. In desert terms, Salt Creek is a bountiful water source—it flows *most* of the year. Entering the park from the south, it flows through steep-walled canyons and past strange landscapes of freestanding arches. (A particularly lovely one, Angel Arch, looks like a winged angel at rest, head bowed, leaning against a graceful harp.)

Basking in the early morning sun is a yellow-headed collared lizard, one of Canyonlands' many colorful reptile inhabitants. Able to stand on its hind legs and run like a tiny tyrannosaurus, it feeds on insects and on other lizards.

Where the Maze blends into the Land of Standing Rocks, eroded fins, banded with the colors of many sandstone layers, loom hundreds of feet above intricate canyons. Each name properly belongs to a specific area, but either may be used for the entire western region of the park.

Along the stream banks, especially in the vast canyon complex near the headwaters, large cottonwood trees grow, their leaves rustling at the slightest breeze. Cottonwoods are the classic example of opportunistic plant growth in the American deserts—if water exists, even deep beneath the sand, their roots find it and use it; if the water is at all plentiful, their growth is lush.

But lately, the cottonwood's dominance has been challenged by an even more opportunistic outsider. The tamarisk, or salt cedar tree, was imported to southern California from Egypt in the 19th century for use as a fast-growing ornamental. It was well chosen for the purpose; it grows quickly to 10 feet or more in height, and it is covered in spring with feathery blossoms of pink or lavender. But the lovely tree spreads by means of a deep, wide root system that soaks up available water with rapacious efficiency. Today tamarisk is the most profuse vegetation along much of the Colorado river system, dominating the banks of rivers and streams very nearly to the Rocky Mountain headwaters of the Colorado and the Green.

About 100 feet above Horse Canyon, perched in an alcove in a cliff face, is Tower Ruin. Not in fact a tower (the name is for the lofty height of the alcove where it sits), this squat, rectangular structure has been there for nearly a thousand years. It was built by the ancestors of the modern Pueblo people, who dwelt here from about A.D. 1000 to 1200, and it is minuscule compared with the magnificent cliff dwellings that the Ancestral Puebloans built on Mesa Verde. The park contains several such ruins as well as other remnants of these remarkable people.

In Upper Salt Creek Canyon in an alcove with several small structures is a pictograph, or painting, that was created about A.D. 1300 by ancestors of the modern Pueblo people. Known as the All-American Man, it has a nearly circular body decorated with blue, white, and red stripes, like the American flag. While this image is unique because of its bold color scheme, similar shield figures can be found on many of the region's canyon walls. Some have speculated that the circular figures represent shields and warfare, but their true meaning remains unknown.

Earlier peoples—the hunter-gatherers who lived in the area from about 7000 B.C. to A.D. 500—also left rock art on canyon walls. The most famous of their art sites is the Great Gallery in Horseshoe Canyon. It, along with the other sites in the canyon, features a distinctive style of rock art characterized by larger-than-life-size human figures. The figures are usually painted without arms or legs, and their only facial features are large, round, staring eyes, giving them a ghostlike appearance. These astonishing images have been preserved for thousands of years in the arid environment of canyon country. Treated with respect and care, they will continue to inspire Canyonlands' visitors.

Grasslands and flowers

Leaving its canyons, Salt Creek meanders in a slow curve around a place called Squaw Flat, where large pinyon pines and junipers offer welcome shade amid bare mounds and hummocks of smooth sandstone. The salt and alkali for which Salt Creek is named are made obvious here by white encrustations that edge the banks. Even footprints in the mud are outlined by white crystals when they dry.

Elsewhere in the Needles district, such broad grassy swales as Chesler Park and Virginia Park are more reminiscent of prairie than of desert. Many kinds of grass are intermixed: dense clumps of sand dropseed, broad-leaved and juicy; long, silky tufts of Indian ricegrass; patches of galleta, with its narrow, woolly blades; and tufts of blue grama, with slender, ribbonlike blades topped by sickle-shaped flower spikes on tall stalks.

Each spring these meadows—surrounded by tall, multicolored pinnacles that stand like encircling guards in fancy dress—are spangled with the vivid colors of wildflowers: orange globe mallows, yellow daisies, pink four-o'clocks, red skyrocket gilias and hummingbird trumpets, blue larkspurs and lupines. The abundant beavertail cactus and prickly pear display blossoms of bright yellow and maroon; those of the less abundant claret cup cactus are intensely red. All join under the bright desert sun with cliffroses, evening primroses, Indian paintbrushes, and a wealth of others to bedazzle the eye. But this spring revival is short. Soon the heat of summer shrivels everything, and all is brown and crackling, seemingly lifeless.

The seasonal verdure of Chesler Park is surrounded by places of brutal starkness. They say that in Devil's Kitchen you can fry an egg in midair on the Fourth of July. Close by are Devil's Lane, Devil's Pocket, and Devil's Horse Pasture. And there is the Joint Trail, an arrow-straight corridor, in places only the width of your body, between rock

Ghostlike pictographs, painted on a sheer stone wall in Horseshoe Canyon, are the 2,000-year-old work of hunter-gatherers who lived in this area in the Archaic period.

walls that rise vertically for 50 feet or more. It is one of the many canyons in the area that were not cut by running water. Long-ago stresses caused deep cracks in the sandstones, and eventually large blocks of rock separated slightly. The Joint Trail runs along the bottom of one such crack.

Devil's Lane is another "dry" canyon of a different kind. Geologists call it a graben (from the German for "ditch"), and it owes its existence to deep beds of salt about 300 million years old. At that distant time, this part of the continent was covered by a large, shallow inland sea. Partially isolated from the great ocean, hemmed in on the east by an abrupt range of mountains, the sea became gradually saltier as its waters evaporated. Since water can hold only so much salt, the crystals began sinking to the bottom; eventually the sea's bed was layered with salt more than 3,000 feet thick. As the nearby mountains were eroded away, silt and sand were carried to the sea and laid upon the salt. They were to become the first of more than 200 million years' worth of sandstone, siltstone, mudstone, and limestone that buried the salt some 6,000 feet deep.

Then, in comparatively recent times, after the Colorado Plateau had been uplifted by the tremendous pressures that shaped the western part of the continent, and after the rivers had done much of their canyon-cutting work across its face, the underlying salt in this place was dissolved by groundwater. Long blocks of overlying sandstones cracked and gradually settled into the voids thus created. The result is a nearly parallel series of sheer-walled grabens that, from above, look like furrows left by some monstrous rake.

Another, more dramatic variation on the same theme is found in the Island in the Sky region. It is called Upheaval Dome, although it does not look like a dome but like a huge crater marked by concentric circles of jagged rock—a three-mile-wide bull's-eye engraved in the landscape. Deep salt beds have led geologists to suspect that a large bubble of salt rose here to create an underground dome that, when overlying sediments were eroded away, exposed a craterlike depression. While the theory was popular for decades, scientists argued and brought forth other theories to explain its existence. Recent research suggests that the most plausible explanation is impact by a meteorite—either a comet or an asteroid. The meteorite, possibly 1,000 feet wide, slammed into the earth within the past 30 million years. In a complex sequence of events, the earth rebounded

Leaving the last of its long, looping canyons, the Green River joins the Colorado, running calmly from right to left in this aerial photo.

upward after the impact and subsequent erosion (which carried away all traces of the meteorite) exposed the craterlike structure. Although misnamed, the crater will always be an awesome sight, whether viewed up close or from the window of an airliner.

Raging waters

Salt Creek, the stream that wanders toward Squaw Flat, finally runs dry, its water sinking into desert sands just upstream from the Confluence. But after late-summer thunderstorms, the creek changes in character and empties into the Colorado. At Lower Jump it plunges over a 200-foot precipice into a steep canyon and becomes for the next several miles a spectacular torrent. It is as though the

waters were getting in practice for the gymnastics of Cataract Canyon, just a few miles downstream.

Many rapids in the Colorado River are formed where side canyons join it. Over millennia, boulders have been washed into the river, partly damming it and forcing its water to rush over and around them. The mightiest rapids of Cataract Canyon are created in this way. Huge blocks of rock, falling from overhead cliffs, also tumble regularly into the river. As the water battles against these jagged impediments, it is ripped into boiling waves—some up to 30 feet high— each marking the position of a mammoth rock on which a wooden boat can smash like an eggshell.

It is this stretch of wild river, where up to 40 million gallons of water per minute may be channeled between

In the distance is Spanish Bottom, where Cataract Canyon starts.

For the last several hundred feet, he and one other man inched their way up a narrow crevice "... as men would climb out of a well." Finally, overlooking the Confluence, he marveled: "And what a world of grandeur is spread before us!...From the northwest comes the Green in a narrow winding gorge. From the northeast comes the Grand, through a canyon that seems bottomless.... On the summit of the opposite wall of the canyon are rock forms that we do not understand."

Looking, as Powell did, toward the deep chasm of Cataract Canyon, you see an array of stone towers and pedestals lined up along the cliff, like petrified giants standing watch high above the roaring waters. This is the Doll House, the beginning of the Land of Standing Rocks. Beyond them is a silent desert valley populated by an army of these great totems, each made of many colorful layers of rock left by ancient waters. And beyond *them* are the bewildering canyons of the Maze.

Meandering canyon cutter
By contrast with knife-sharp Cataract Canyon, the snaky route of the Green River, which separates the Maze from the Island in the Sky, looks more like the path of a lazy stream on a flat plain than of a hardworking canyon cutter. And in fact, it is both. Geologists call the looping canyons through which it flows entrenched meanders—which means that the Green was once, indeed, a lazy river meandering across a flat plain. This was during a lull of a few million years in the gradual rise of the Colorado Plateau. Then the land began to rise again, at about the same speed that the river cut downward, so that over the ages the gentle-looking route was engraved hundreds of feet deep in stone.

On July 21, 1869, Powell and his party pushed off toward Cataract Canyon. They dared not risk running all the rapids. Instead they chose to portage—a slow, back-breaking task that entails unloading the boats, carrying them around the dangerous waters, then loading up again. After seven perilous days Powell and his men emerged from Cataract Canyon into the gentle waters of the incomparably beautiful Glen Canyon (now submerged by Lake Powell) on their way to "the great unknown" of Marble Gorge and the Grand Canyon.

In the decades following Powell's journeys, other explorers have come and gone. Prospectors have poked about in distant canyons looking for gold or silver, found little, and left. Cowboys have herded gaunt cattle across sparse, dry lands, seeking out the few permanent streams and water holes. It wasn't until the 1950's that the region experienced a boom of sorts. With the promise of riches created by the atomic age, uranium prospectors steered their jeeps and helicopters into the most remote and difficult places, listening for the rewarding rattle of their Geiger counters. Some uranium was mined in the region, but Canyonlands itself yielded few such riches. Instead there has come the gradual awareness that the real treasure of Canyonlands is the land itself, pure, harsh, and unspoiled.

sheer stone walls, that attracts most visitors to Canyonlands. They come from all over the world to experience the incomparable exhilaration of running the rapids in wooden boats, rubber rafts, even kayaks. All are following in the wake of one of the most famous of America's explorer-scientists: Maj. John Wesley Powell, who named Cataract Canyon during his epic 1869 journey down the Green and Colorado rivers.

At that time, the Confluence was considered the beginning of the Colorado River; upstream, the Colorado was known as the Grand River. Here, after nearly two months exploring the Green, he and his party camped for several days. Though one-armed—he had lost his right arm at the Battle of Shiloh seven years before—Powell made the difficult climb to the top of the cliffs.

Capitol Reef

*"Time, geologic time, looks out
at us from the rocks as from no other
objects in the landscape. The youth
of the earth is in the soil and in the trees
and verdure that spring from it;
its age is in the rocks . . ."*

John Burroughs

Something about the tough, dry world of Capitol Reef inspires odd and colorful names. Perhaps it is the very harshness of the land. This is a place that could have been designed to test human courage; and imaginative nicknames have always nourished courage by lending an air of familiarity, beauty, or absurdity to that which is alien, dire, and terrible.

The park's name is itself a combination of two picturesque images: "reef" is for the ridges of sharply jutting rock that interrupt the land, barriers as formidable as half-hidden reefs are in the ocean; and "capitol" describes the white, domed peaks of sandstone that dominate the reef's high horizon.

Those who have struggled to survive in this hot, rugged desert—Indians, grizzled prospectors, Mormon settlers, cowboys, pioneers, even early tourists—have put on the Capitol Reef map names that tell distinctive stories. The Navajos called the place "Land of the

Hauntingly expressive artwork up to 1,000 years old is found on

cliffs along the western face of Capitol Reef, where cottonwoods add autumn's passing color to ancient hues of layered stone.

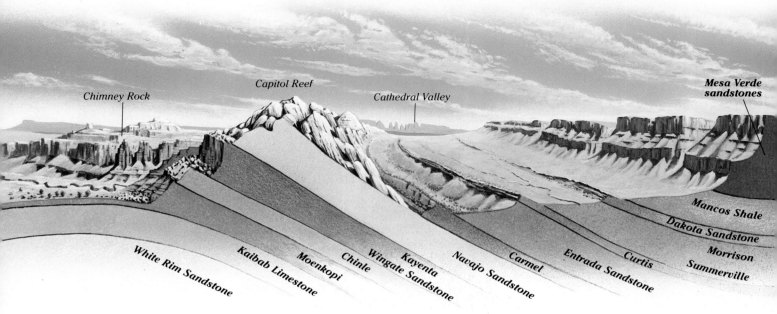

Chimney Rock

Capitol Reef

Cathedral Valley

Mesa Verde sandstones

Mancos Shale

Dakota Sandstone

Morrison

Summerville

Curtis

Entrada Sandstone

Carmel

Navajo Sandstone

Kayenta

Wingate Sandstone

Chinle

Moenkopi

Kaibab Limestone

White Rim Sandstone

Capitol Reef's topography, shown in exaggerated cross section, was caused by the geologic warpage called the Waterpocket Fold. Many upper layers of rock are gone, cracked by stress and stripped away by erosion.

Sleeping Rainbow," and indeed, its multicolored layers of tilted rock could be a rainbow that has curled up for a much-needed nap. Muley Twist Canyon is so narrow that pack mules had to slither like snakes to get through. Scratch Canyon is clogged with dense, thorny brush. Water from Bitter Creek tastes of alkali (Dogwater Creek is something else again). Polygamous Mormons hid in Cohab Canyon when the federal authorities came around. Travelers during Prohibition went on binges at Whiskey Flat; moonshiners used water from Whiskey Spring for their stills. Ford Hill is so steep that Model T's had to climb it in reverse so that gas could reach the carburetors. Other stories are contained in such names as Poverty Flat and Paradise Flats, Fern's Nipple, Tarantula Mesa, Onion Flats Seep, Cow Dung Wash, Dirty Devil River, and Bloody Hands Gap.

Even such a normally staid lot of wordsmiths as geologists have been inspired here, bestowing a mysterious name, Waterpocket Fold, upon the terrain. In the name lies the mystery's solution. The fold (actually more of a wrinkle) is a result of the monumental collision that occurred when the drifting continental plate beneath North America crashed into the plate that underlies the Pacific Ocean. It was the tremendous pressure generated by this event that, starting about 65 million years ago, gradually thrust the Rocky Mountains skyward, lifted the great Colorado Plateau, and set in motion the rushing waters that shaped—and are still shaping—such mighty canyons as Bryce, Zion, and the Grand Canyon itself. Here at Capitol Reef the land wrinkled, as a carpet might wrinkle if you were to push it against a wall. As thick layers of rock slowly flexed upward, they were ripped away, broken off in chunks, and worn down to pebbles and grains of sand. Only jagged stubs remain, raw wounds of rock in brilliantly contrasting colors. As you look east from atop the reef at ridge after broken ridge, oceanic imagery returns: long, low "waves" of rock seem to roll westward, cresting to crash at your feet.

Those imagined waves will never hit the reef. But the waterpockets that give the fold the rest of its name hold real water. The sandstone landscape is pockmarked with pits and depressions that fill with every rain. And every time a storm sends water and debris crashing across the arid land (water always *crashes* here), swirls and eddies make each pocket a little bigger.

Pockets of life

Minutes after a flash flood has passed, waterpockets teem with fairy shrimp and other small living things, hatched from waiting eggs. Some fairy shrimp become adults in less than a week, racing against the sure evaporation of their world. Swimming on their backs, propelled by scores of leaflike appendages that are also used for breathing and feeding, these tiny crustaceans writhe and mate. When the pool dries, the bed is strewn with corpses. But eggs lie dormant—sometimes for years—until water comes again.

Spadefoot toads, raised from their torpor beneath the sand, gather and mate amid loud croaking. Within a week, tadpoles feed. Those that make it to adulthood dig themselves backward into the sand, as their parents did, using their spade-shaped hind feet.

All this activity attracts salamanders, snakes, birds, badgers, coyotes, and other creatures that feed on the fleeting banquets and slake their thirst. Humans, too, are drawn to waterpockets, although the experience of drinking from one is not always pleasant. "We often had to sip our water through nearly clenched teeth in order to strain out either insects or coarse sediment," wrote Bob Hewitt, who explored southern Utah on horseback about 1940. Distasteful though inhabited water may be, the alternative is worse. Clear water devoid of any life may well be laced with either of two poisons, arsenic and selenium. For selenium, at least, nature has provided a warning sign: the yellow-flowered prince's plume. Its bright, feathery flower spikes are seen only where selenium is present. Because its tissues concentrate the deadly element, the plant is even more poisonous to eat than the water is to drink. Cooking negates the poison, however, and Indians ate the plant regularly.

Stories in stone

While the eastward slope of the reef is gentle—the name "whaleback" is often given to its profile—the western facade is brutal. Here layers of rock were torn off by the forces of erosion as one would rip away handfuls of pages from an open book. The remnant ridges, lying one atop another, form a series of cliffs more than a thousand feet high. Swifts and swallows swoop and swerve and sweep and swirl, while above, golden eagles glide through long, slow circles.

Though the pages of the book are gone, their ragged edges are quite thick and fairly easy to read. Each layer of rock has its own color, texture, name, and personality; each tells the story of what the world was like here during some long-ago epoch.

At the base of the cliff, piled up like layers of a chocolate cake, are the dark, ledgy slopes of the Moenkopi Formation: mudstones and siltstones left some 225 million years ago by tidal currents in the shallows of a slowly receding sea. Despite its massiveness, there is a fragility to the Moenkopi; thin slabs of "ripple rock" often break off, their surfaces still corrugated by the lapping of water upon a long-vanished shoreline. You can even see marks made by the fins of fish.

The sea's retreat left behind a coastal plain that changed constantly as the shore grew more distant.

These changes are reflected in the colorful and complex layering of the thick Chinle Formation, which lies atop the Moenkopi. Its bottom layer, the Shinarump, belongs in any list of expressive names—*shinar* means "wolf" in the Paiute tongue, and *rump*, of course, refers to an animal's upper hindquarters; the name comes from the humpish forms into which this hard, yellow-gray rock is often weathered. In recent decades the Shinarump has become a focus for prospectors. Uranium is found at points where logs, branches, leaves, and detritus had accumulated along the inner curves of meandering streams. Ages later, the fossil trees captured and held uranium-rich mineral solutions that trickled down from the porous layers above.

The upper beds of the Chinle make gracefully sculptured slopes tinted from a pastel palette. These are shales, sandstones, and limestones of red, brown, green, gray, pink, blue, purple, and white. They date from about 210 to 200 million years ago, when the land had become a shifting world of marshes, swamps, and open plains. (Volcanic ash is there, too, contributed by spewing mountains far to the west.)

Above the Chinle is a drastic change. A sheer orange wall, rising to 350 feet in height, blazes back at the late afternoon sun. This is the Wingate Sandstone, dense and fine-grained, that tells of several million years when the land had become desert, complete with howling Sahara-style sandstorms. The rock was named, in a very roundabout way, for a Civil War officer who would probably be amazed to know that he has been geologi-

Like a roadside cafeteria for giants, the landscape near Muley Twist Canyon offers a selection of oddly eroded "Hamburger Rocks." Some are up to four feet high.

Cathedral Valley's austere beauty became known only after World War II, as the result of a search for the wreckage of a lost military plane.

cally immortalized. Capt. Benjamin Wingate fell in 1862 at the battle of Valverde, New Mexico, and the Union Army honored his memory by giving his name to a fort. Later, when geologists needed a name for the orange rock that is displayed in cliffs near the fort, they chose Wingate—simply because Fort Wingate was nearby. Now the name belongs to all such rock, wherever it appears. (That is the usual way of naming rock. Moenkopi, Chinle, Kayenta, Navajo, Carmel, Entrada, Curtis, Summerville, Morrison, Dakota, Mancos, Mesa Verde, even Shinarump, were place-names first.)

The Wingate does not erode gradually, but fractures along smooth, straight planes; whole blocks topple, leaving sheer, open-faced cliffs. About a thousand years ago some of the finest rock art in the Americas was painted and chiseled on many of these cliffs: broad-shouldered, oversized human figures so strange and abstract—with their bucket heads and trapezoidal torsos—that some people believe them to be messages from ancient astronauts. They are the work of the Fremont people, who settled here about A.D. 950.

The Fremont people never built large dwellings, as their contemporaries the Anasazi did at Mesa Verde.

Long stripes of desert varnish coat the Wingate Sandstone of Tapestry Wall. No one is sure exactly how the process works, but it is believed that mineral deposits are slowly built up on the rock face with the help of microorganisms.

They lived in simple pit houses, often built into natural alcoves along the bases of cliffs. But these were no primitive cave dwellers. Besides the pictographs and petroglyphs (the first are painted; the second pecked into the rock with sharp instruments), they left sturdy pottery, attractive baskets, and beautiful clay figurines. They were accomplished leather workers as well—pieces of their well-tanned buckskin are still soft and pliable. They constructed a system of irrigation ditches that let them grow fields of maize, squash, and beans in this desert. But sometime around A.D. 1200, perhaps because a long drought had made life here impossible, the Fremont people left Capitol Reef forever.

Near the top of the Wingate cliffs on which the Fremont left their awesome artwork, the desert-born sandstone blends into another layer, the muddy red Kayenta. Its siltstones and sandstones were deposited on riverbeds and floodplains during another lush period about 190 million years ago. Dinosaurs roamed the landscape then, and their footprints can sometimes still be found in the Kayenta's weathered slopes.

But the desert returned, and with a vengeance. Tumultuous windstorms, stripping down mountains in the northwest, buried the land again—this time beneath fine grains of pure quartz. This was the great Navajo desert, a wilderness of huge white dunes continually shaped and reshaped for 10 to 15 million years by fickle winds that blew first one way, then another. This intricate cross-bedding produced a deep layer of hard, pale sandstone that erodes into humps, haystacks, or whatever the viewer wants to see. It is the stuff of Zion National Park's templed canyons, and it forms the skyscraping domes for which Capitol Reef is named.

Ironically, this desert-born formation is now a water source. On the long eastern slope, where it is the bedrock, the Navajo Sandstone holds pockets of pure water. It also feeds seeps and springs on the cliff face; moisture is filtered as it percolates down through the relatively porous sandstone, and when it works its way out, it is sweet to drink. Maidenhair ferns, wild orchids, monkey flowers, and other water-loving plants form verdant clumps around such places on the Navajo cliffs.

The land today
The ensuing 150 million years have seen the same story enacted over and over—oceans giving way to tidal flats, then to marshy lands, and finally to sandy worlds that were drowned beneath new oceans. The frozen waves that crest above the eastern slope's pale Navajo bedrock are not so easily read as are the thick pages of the western cliffs, but to a practiced eye the repetitive saga is clear. The dark, sharp ridges of the Carmel Formation were the bed of a sea that covered the Navajo desert. The broad expanse of dark red Entrada Sandstone is a legacy of the same sea's gradual filling in. The arches of Arches National Park were carved from this Entrada Sandstone, as were the "cathedrals" in Capitol Reef's Cathedral Valley—monoliths up to 500 feet high, har-

Fleecy clouds in the blue Utah sky are reflected on the surface of one of Capitol Reef's many waterpockets— guarantors of life in a dry land. Every rare rain turns this eroded sandstone channel into a wild cascade; afterward, each pocket is a little larger than it had been before. Some pockets can hold many gallons for a long time. Small ones may be dry in a few hours.

monious and symmetrical. They exist because they are capped by the firm Curtis Formation: gray sandstone from the bed of yet another sea.

And so it went. The chocolate-colored Summerville Formation, reminiscent of the tide-rippled Moenkopi, was left by this later sea's retreat. The soft Morrison Formation, its pale green and reddish gray bespeaking a swampy landscape, erodes into badlands. The Dakota Sandstone, studded with oyster shells, was the advancing beach of the area's last sea. The dark gray, almost black Mancos Shale was its bed, dense with stagnation. A large sandy spit of land became the flat-topped hills of the solid Mesa Verde sandstones.

Today, Capitol Reef is again desert. High plateaus to the west capture moisture, leaving only thunderstorms to rage and briefly flood the land. Then, walls of water roar down ravines, and blood-red cascades thunder over thousand-foot cliffs. But generally, cottonwoods, box elders, and willows must find the moisture they need along trickly streams and even in dry washes. Pioneers looked for cottonwoods to tell them water was at hand; the leaves seem to point to the sand and say: "Water is here, but you must dig for it."

Along the dry beds of intermittent streams, the loud quacking of a duck is sometimes heard where no duck lives. The big, raucous sound comes from the small throat of a canyon treefrog, more often heard than seen. Its toes equipped with sticky pads, the little green-spotted acrobat climbs out on branches to wait for flying insects. Leaping, it can catch one in midair, turn, and

The badger's black and white striped face is seldom seen in daytime. It hunts at night, digging after rodents with its powerful claws.

land securely on any surface, even upside down.

Across the open desert pungent sagebrush grows. Gnarled junipers endure, and pinyon pines bear nuts that draw scolding flocks of blue pinyon jays. Hummingbirds hang before tall spikes of brilliant scarlet bugler blossoms, sipping nectar through their long beaks. Waxy sego lilies rise from the desert sands, their large white petals often tinged with color. From canyons comes the most lyrical sound of the Colorado Plateau, the canyon wren's 8 to 14 descending notes: *tee-u, tee-u, tee-u, tew, tew, tew, tew, tew . . . .*

At night, the poisonous datura, or jimsonweed, offers up its white, sweet-scented flowers to the moon. (Its foliage, however, smells like a wet dog.) Great horned owls spread their wings, and ringtail cats leave their rocky dens in search of prey. Although it moves with feline grace, the agile ringtail is not a cat, but a close cousin to raccoons. The family resemblance is clearly seen in the dark mask across its foxlike face and the bands on its long, bushy tail.

To this harsh land, in the early 1880's, Mormons came. Along the Fremont River, near the then unnamed Cohab Canyon, they founded a village, which they called Fruita for the orchards they planted. The Mormons have long since gone, but the orchards remain and still bear fruit. Here, red-winged blackbirds send lingering calls across a meadow. And at sunset, when the hint of a cool breeze stirs the cottonwood leaves and a full moon begins to glow upon the Navajo domes, you can feel the promise of yet another, softer world again aborning.

Carlsbad Caverns

*"King Solomon in all his glory never had a room
in his palace that could compare with this
and the adjoining rooms on wonderful grandeur."*
Robert A. Holley,
early-20th-century mineral examiner

Standing atop a high point in Carlsbad Caverns National Park, you survey an arid land of purple shadows and gray-brown rock. Southwestward into Texas rise the Guadalupe Mountains, and your eye follows the line of the ancient seacoast that gave them birth. In steep-walled canyons, carved long ago by rushing water, deep rock layers are laid bare, a few so sharply tilted that you can almost feel the force of these mountains' upheaval. Northward, and all around, is the high New Mexico desert, a harsh landscape of mesquite and scrub, enlivened by agaves and abundantly varied cacti. Rock wrens flit through the low brush and into crevices; vultures, hawks, even golden eagles, glide and soar.

With the hot sun on your back, it is hard to realize you are standing over a deep, cool wonderland of stone, where the temperature varies little from 56° F, where the only light is man-made, where growth and change are measured in millimeters per century, where magnificently ornamented cliffs and canyons filled with surreal sculpture dwarf the outside landscape. It is harder still to see a correlation between the lively beauty around you and the silent, lifeless beauty far beneath your feet. Yet the changing nature of the aboveground world is responsible for the drama under way below.

Just as rushing water has the power to cut through stone, so can slow-moving water eat away solid rock. But slow water can also replace that rock, one drop at a

*Drop by patient drop, limestone-laden water has fashioned
such fragile intricacies as aragonite crystals and built
such mammoth columns as the awesome Temple of the Sun,
decorated with tier upon tier of flowstone.*

time, with equally solid new rock in shapes undreamed of by human sculptors. It is the results of this drama of water gradually replacing rock with rock that we see today in the vast underground theater of Carlsbad Cavern. The performance was majestic and incredibly graceful, more intricate than any ballet, with a grandeur that the grandest opera cannot touch.

We are late arrivals at the show, having come in partway through the third, and probably the final, act—an act that has been in progress for more than a million years. The play itself began perhaps 250 million years ago, long before birds flew, mammals walked, or flowers bloomed across the earth.

Act I—the building of a huge limestone reef along the edge of an ancient sea—was performed by tiny lime-secreting algae and other primitive marine creatures, many of whose bodies also became part of the reef. Generation after generation, these beings lived and died and added their substance. The sea itself added a limy mineral cement, and eventually the reef rose high enough to isolate a calm lagoon between the ocean and the shore. Before the act was over, the reef stood hundreds of feet high and up to four miles wide in places. The floor of the lagoon it protected, continuously fed sediments by streams and rivers, was rising steadily.

When the ocean eventually withdrew, leaving behind salty mineral deposits, the reef died. Its burial was slow. On the lagoon side, sediments continued to rise until the lagoon was no more. Then streams spilled over onto the seaward side and sediments built up there. The 100,000,000-year-long Act I had come to a close.

After another million centuries or so, during which

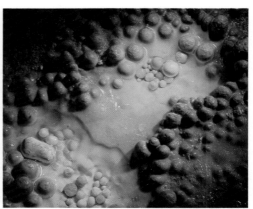

Among the seemingly infinite variety of forms found in Carlsbad Cavern are the slender soda straws, stalactites, and columns of the Doll's Theater (above). Rare cave pearls (upper right) are created when drops fall with just the right force into a shallow pool. Even rarer lily pads (right) were once dams around the rims of still pools.

sediments hundreds of feet thick accumulated above the limestone reef, Act II began. The plot was violent. The earth shuddered, and mountains arose. In a tremendous convulsion, part of the reef was broken off and thrust upward, to become the Guadalupe Mountains. This was no overnight occurrence; the action began here about 15 million years ago and has continued until quite recently, geologically speaking.

As the water level declined and the reef arose, groundwater seeped through cracks deep inside the limestone, softening and dissolving the rock. Water-weakened sections, unable to support their own weight, fell. The reef became honeycombed with chambers, varying in width from less than an inch to a thousand feet. Walls dissolved and disappeared, and water-filled rooms became caverns. When the water level dropped still farther, leaving spongy rock masses unsupported, great chunks fell. By a million years ago the upper caverns were dry, though seepage still continued below. Act II—unseen by any eyes—was at an end, and the underground stage was set for Act III, in which severe rock walls were to be adorned and decorated, transformed into the world's most beautiful cave.

The action

When rain falls and the drops seep through the soil, they combine with carbon dioxide to form a weak carbonic acid. Trickling down through cracks in the reef, this mild acid is strong enough to dissolve limestone, generally in the form of calcite, which it carries along. When a drop of this stone-in-solution reaches

the ceiling of an underground cavern, some of the carbon dioxide returns to the air, and crystals of limestone are released. More drops follow the same path, leaving their limestone loads, until a new rock formation—a stalactite—hangs from the roof.

Generally, the drop deposits a ring before it falls. Another drop adds its ring, and then another, building a tubular stalactite called a soda straw, through which drops of water run. This process may continue until, like hundreds of examples hanging from the level ceiling of Carlsbad's Soda Straw Forest, the tubes are several feet long. But when a prospective soda straw becomes plugged—probably because a droplet evaporated before it could fall—water starts to run down the outside of the formation, making a solid stalactite, usually in the familiar icicle shape.

Or the tube may become so constricted by lime deposits that drops no longer flow freely but are forced out by capillary action. The resultant helictite may seem to defy gravity, growing first to one side, then the other, even growing upward and then downward again. Not all helictites begin as soda straws: some arise from the floors of caves, some sprout from the walls, some grow from existing structures. There are many complex theories to explain why helictites behave as they do. Though none of them is entirely satisfactory, it seems certain that the irregular shapes of calcite crystals have a lot to do with it. Similarly, delicate epsomite needles owe their flimsy, hairlike forms to the needle-shaped epsomite crystals of which they are made. In Carlsbad Cavern some get to be 18 inches long, but this is exceptional: most break of their own weight first.

Sometimes water runs across the floor to form an "icing on the cake" called flowstone. Or a single droplet may run along a ridge or down a sloping wall, leaving a winding trail of stone behind. A million more droplets follow the trail, and a flowstone drapery is created, rock as soft-looking as velvet—or perhaps it becomes slabs of the intriguingly named cave bacon, hanging from the roof of a passage like meat on a hook.

Falling drops of calcite-laden water also leave their deposits on the cavern floor, and as they pile up, a stalagmite is born. Slowly, it grows upward toward the source of its substance. When a stalactite and a stalagmite meet, they form a column. Intricate layers of delicate dripstone may adorn its surface.

When drops fall onto limestone quickly enough and with enough force, they may carve out a nest, and then fill the nest with cave pearls. These opalescent balls form around tiny pebbles or grains of sand in puddles of heavily saturated water no more than an inch or so deep. Most are round; some, forming around bat bones or bits of debris, may be of any shape imaginable.

These forms are common to limestone caves all over the world. Indeed, some caves hold examples of one or another formation that Carlsbad cannot match. But in no cave yet discovered—a necessary qualification when speaking of caves, as people stumble regularly into new underground wonders—does such a variety of ornamentation come together with such symphonic beauty. In part this is because the easily dissolved limestone reef, with its myriad cracks and fissures, is ideal building material. In part, too, it is because of the way the climate in this region has changed over the ages since the Guadalupe Mountains arose.

A change of climate in the world above causes a change in the amount of water seeping down, and probably in the routes the water follows. It can also cause a change in the acid content of each drop: the less moisture in the soil, the less life; and because carbon dioxide is a by-product of the life process, less life means less carbon dioxide to form carbonic acid. Plentiful water, heavily saturated with calcite and running through clearly defined channels, can make for massive stalactites, stalagmites, and columns. Carlsbad has many of these, right up to the 60-foot Goliaths in the Hall of the Giants. A less plentiful supply might mean that stalactites grow long and slender, with no matching stalagmites, because droplets evaporate before they can fall. Other variations make for flowstone draperies, such as the graceful silken stone that cloaks the walls and throne of the Queen's Chamber.

Rarely, the stone-in-solution forms rounded, hollow shapes known as hydromagnesite balloons, their puffy form determined by the minerals mixed into the calcite. These structures may be a foot or more across. Carlsbad Cavern is one of only three caves in the United States where hydromagnesite balloons are found.

Gleaming in the light of a lantern like intricately cut diamonds, aragonite trees are probably the most beautiful of Carlsbad's strange formations. Like helictites, they may grow from walls, floors, ceilings, stalagmites, anywhere, and their spiny branches subdivide and twist and turn in all directions. When you come upon one of them unexpectedly, it is easy to see why they were once thought to be alive: plants made of stone.

Other minerals paint the normally beige or milk-white formations with a wide range of color. A structure may have been freshly washed (say, in the last 10,000 years) with the red of iron ore, streaked with the purple and blue of manganese oxide, or blotched and spangled with almost any other hue. Or the colors may be deep within, beneath recent layers of glossy white. Many dark, muddy-looking columns and stalagmites have been adorned with pigmented flowstone, then hung with jagged dripstone that looks like fine bone china, and finally crowned with crystalline aragonite jewelry.

The audience

For about a million years, until human beings began carrying light into the cavern depths, the growing stone itself was the nearest thing to life in this dark wonderland. About 17,000 years ago bats discovered the roomy ceiling of an upper chamber and moved in, but they do not venture far below the surface. At one time, as many as 12 million of these flying mammals made Bat Cave their summer home, migrating into Mexico for the winter, when insects are scarce. Today, largely because of the use of insecticides, the bat population has been reduced to about one million. Almost every summer night, each of these bats consumes about half its own body weight in insects. Since the average bat weighs about half an ounce, this adds up to more than three tons of insects eaten nightly by the bats of Carlsbad. (By comparison, 12 million bats could have eaten almost 100 tons a night.)

Mexican free-tailed bats make up more than 90 per-

Hanging densely clustered from the ceiling of Bat Cave, Mexican free-tailed bats await the evening, when they will emerge to hunt. In late summer, migrating bats from the north join Carlsbad's flock, and the population explodes.

The Lake of the Clouds, 1,037 feet below the cave's main entrance, is Carlsbad Cavern's lowest known point. Its level remains nearly constant, with water flowing neither in nor out, but it does not stagnate because it contains no life.

cent of Carlsbad's population. In early summer this community consists almost entirely of females and newborn young, most adult males having deserted the nurserylike cavern for the peace and quiet of another cave. When the females spread their 11-inch wings and take to the air, rising together like a great cloud from the cavern entrance, the babies are left hanging, crowded together to conserve body heat.

It was the spectacular flight of the bats that first led people to the entrance of Carlsbad Cavern. Like a dense black cloud they rise at the rate of up to 5,000 bats a minute, spiraling counterclockwise with a low, rustling roar of fluttering wings. The exodus is a popular attraction for park visitors—as many as 1,000 per night—who gather on stone bleachers to watch the spectacle and listen as park rangers describe the bats' many benefits to the environment. For reasons known only to bats, the nightly flight may begin as early as four o'clock or as late as nine—but nearly always at sunset. On rainy evenings the bats mill uncertainly at the entrance and then return to their cave, canceling the flight entirely.

Few see the bats come home. Before sunrise, they approach at great heights and simply fold their wings to plummet the last 200 feet, banking expertly into upside-down landings on their bedroom ceiling. A returning mother, nourished from her long feeding flight, locates and nurses her own bat cub. One midsummer day the nursing stops: a bat five or six weeks old must soon let go and join the nightly hunt. If it flies, it is a full-fledged adult. If not, it is food for the insects that inhabit guano on the cavern floor.

The hope of wealth from selling all the accumulated bat guano as fertilizer was what led to the cav-

erns' exploration. In 1883 a 12-year-old named Rolth Sublett was lowered by his father into the cave's main entrance at the end of a long rope. In the darkness, he went only to the end of the rope and turned back, his clearest impression the overpowering stench from the Bat Cave. Other reports of the living black whirlwind reached the ears of a clever man named Abijah Long, who filed a claim in 1903 on the cave entrance and surrounding lands. Over the next 20 years, about 100,000 tons of guano was taken from Bat Cave, mostly in large buckets lowered by cable into shafts that had been drilled down through the ceiling. Still, but for one man's exploratory itch Bat Cave might have remained the limit of human penetration into Carlsbad Cavern.

Jim White had found the cave entrance and had already done some investigating before the mines opened. He became a guano miner, and in his off-hours used his miner's lantern to delve deeper into the darkness. First alone and later with others, Jim White managed, over the years, to explore the main features of the cavern. His tales of what he saw were dismissed by most people as the ravings of a lunatic "as batty as his cave," but he persisted. Eventually he persuaded a photographer to lower his bulky equipment down a mining shaft and past the bat guano to the dangerous descent into the caverns below. By the early 1920's, when mining ended, adventurous visitors had begun making their way to the Guadalupe Mountains, to be lowered, two at a time, in mining buckets for the same difficult trek.

The largest of Carlsbad's public chambers exist at three levels—about 250 feet, 750 feet, and 830 feet beneath the surface. On the first level are Bat Cave, closed to all but bats, and in the opposite direction, a widening of the downward passage, where the Whale's Mouth gapes, its thin ribbons of dripstone looking like the baleen of a living whale. Just beyond, in the area known as the Devil's Den, among a maze of weirdly shaped gypsum rocks, are rounded, polished stones—evidence that a stream once ran through here, years after the cave formed.

The 750-foot level has most of Carlsbad's famous showpieces: Iceberg Rock, a 100,000-ton chunk of limestone that crashed down when water ceased to support it; the Boneyard, filled with structures that look more like sponges than bones; the Hall of the Giants, where the cavern's largest stalagmites—including the Giant Dome, the Twin Domes, and the Rock of Ages—tower, all adrip with stone decoration. At the 830-foot level are the King's Palace, where huge statuesque stalagmites are framed by flowstone draperies and cave bacon; the incredibly beautiful Queen's Chamber; and the eternally serene Green Lake, on whose calm waters reflected colors sparkle.

Awesome as all these are, they cannot prepare you for the experience of the Big Room. Covering 14 acres, with a ceiling so high that you could erect a 30-story building inside and still not touch it, the Big Room is the largest known underground chamber in the Americas. Within its vast space—populated by monstrous stone behemoths and glittering fantasies, overhung with jagged spikes and daggers that may weigh tons—you forget that there is a sunlit world above, where time passes in hours, days, and years. You have caught a whiff of the changeless air of eternity.

There are other levels at Carlsbad, unlit chambers that have been opened to the public. The Lower Cave, a mile-long section of the caverns located some 90 feet below the Big Room, for instance, attracts adventurous visitors. Elsewhere a narrow crevice, through which a park ranger first squirmed in 1966, leads to the Guadalupe Room: vast and echoing, dark and empty, it is the second largest room at Carlsbad Caverns.

For a fairly easy off-trail trip, visitors can also sign up for a tour of the Left Handed Tunnel. Or they can visit two other caves in the park—Slaughter Canyon Cave and Spider Cave—that are currently open to tourists.

More than 80 other caves have been explored within the park. One of them, Lechugilla Cave, a cavern located in Carlsbad's wilderness section, has in the past decade or so been explored from an original depth of 90 feet to its present known depth of more than 1,500 feet. Thus ranked as the deepest limestone cave in North America, Lechugilla Cave now boasts a grand total of 85 miles of surveyed passageways. As a wilderness cave, however, it will not be commercialized and will remain off-limits to the general public.

Certainly, within the dark heart of these mountains are more wonders yet unseen. The entrances to some are undiscovered; there are surely others—perhaps as magnificent as Carlsbad Cavern itself—which lack entry altogether to the sunlit world. But still the drama proceeds, oblivious to the absence of spectators. It will not be over until the ancient reef is again solid stone.

Prickly pear, yucca, agave, and other desert plants grow all around the cavern's huge natural entrance—the dividing point between the eerie, lifeless beauty that exists below ground and the living beauty on the surface. The flights of bats arising nightly from this great hole in the ground led to the discovery of the cave. Today, park visitors gather to await the dramatic exodus.

Anacapa is the first in a chain of mountaintops jutting up from the sea. On these islands the terrain is remarkably varied, with craggy

cliffs, rolling hills, and beaches prized by elephant seals.

CALIFORNIA

Channel Islands

"Today a little more land may belong to the sea, tomorrow a little less. Always the edge of the sea remains an elusive and indefinable boundary . . . a world that keeps alive the sense of continuing creation and of the relentless drive of life."
Rachel Carson

On misty winter days, they rise like grotesque forms from the sea, standing gaunt and forbidding against the darkened horizon. Calls of seabirds mingle with the incessant yelping of sea lions and the occasional song of the whale. Close to the shore, the chill of salt spray penetrates the soul as the Pacific surf pounds away against hard but yielding rock. These are the Channel Islands—eight mountainous islands that lie off the coast of California, interrupting the horizon with their big, hulking shapes. The four northernmost—Anacapa, Santa Cruz, Santa Rosa, and San Miguel—form an east-west chain. The distance between any two of them is not more than five miles, close enough for the wind on some days to carry the barking of sea lions and the squawk of birds from one to the next. Together with tiny Santa Barbara island 40 miles to the south, these four bits of land and the sea around them make up the national park.

It is not surprising that these islands look like mountains, because they are. Though only their tops are

83

visible, if the ocean were drained we would see the base of the mountains as well as smaller peaks, hills, and valleys—all strikingly similar to the mainland terrain. The similarity is more than superficial: the four northern islands are actually the seaward extension of the Santa Monica Mountains (part of the only east-west mountain belt in the lower 48 states), and they were formed by the same major geological events.

Solid as they are, mountains are not immutable. The northern islands, some scientists believe, were originally one big island (Santarosae, they call it) that became four separate pieces when glaciers melted, the level of the ocean rose, and water flowed into the low-lying areas. Over thousands of years the sea, along with winds and rains, beat down the islands to their present size and shape. By no means does "present" mean "final," for the erosion continues. Wind and water are like perfectionists, never completely satisfied with what they have done.

A triumphant arch

One spectacular example of nature's handiwork is Arch Rock, 40 feet high and standing straight up from the sea near Anacapa as if it were the grand entranceway to the park. At one time, this huge piece of rock may have been part of Anacapa, but now it lies apart, hollowed by the wind and sea into its intriguing, intricate shape. In other places along the islands' shores, a variety of landscapes bear witness to the power of the surf— narrow beaches, deep sea caves, and shallow tide pools that are marvelously accessible microcosms of the sea. Seaweeds weave a multihued carpet on the tide pool floor; sea anemones nestle together, their tentacles resembling flowers in bloom. Home to starfish, abalones, periwinkles, limpets, crabs, and other small crea-tures, tide pools offer mystery and magic and miracles too; even where ebb tides expose the inhabitants to the air, life survives.

Whales, wildflowers, and waterfalls

In deeper water, dense stands of kelp, which vies with bamboo for the title of the fastest-growing plant in the world, sway with the waves like palms battered by gale-force winds. Kelp are giant algae, attached to the ocean floor by suction feet called holdfasts. From there they rise more than a hundred feet to the surface, where the leathery yellow-brown fronds form a tangled floating mat. Just below the surface, air-filled bulbs serve as buoys, holding the tall vines upright.

Many sea animals find food and shelter in the great kelp forest. Mollusks and worms cling to the thick brown stalks. Tiny shrimp abound. Bronze-colored swordfish, blue-black bonitos, and red-gold garibaldis glide gracefully among the fronds; torpedo-shaped sharks and barracuda swim sleekly through the vines, alert to any unsuspecting prey.

Each December gray whales, migrating south from their summer feeding grounds in the Arctic, stop by the Channel Islands to partake of the bountiful harvest, to nourish themselves on the small forms of life. The warm lagoons of Baja California, some 5,000 miles from the Arctic, are their ultimate destination. There females bear their young, each usually giving birth to a single calf; sometimes mother and baby can be seen traveling back north together, especially when they venture near the islands' shores. Though by no means as large as their cousin the blue whale, the grays are no Little Leaguers. They weigh up to 20 tons, measure up to 45 feet in length, and spout a misty fountain an impressive 15 to 18 feet high when they come up for air.

CALIFORNIA

SANTA BARBARA

San Miguel, with no island to protect it on the west, has harsh weather.

Santa Rosa has bold mountains and, on the western side, magnificent beaches.

Santa Cruz, the largest island, is 21 miles long.

Anacapa is a chain of three little islands.

Santa Barbara lies some 40 miles from the others in the park.

The sea is one of nature's grandest sculptors, carving islands into such smaller forms as arches and sea stacks. Long ago

Arch Rock may have been connected to its neighbor; someday, the 40-foot-high arch may be no more.

Thousands of birds in raucous variety feed on the abundant food. Some, like double-crested cormorants, brown pelicans, and pigeon guillemots, dive for fish; surfbirds and oystercatchers prowl rocky shores for shellfish and other tasty morsels. And morsels there are in plenty—life here is superbly diverse, thanks to the convergence of cold currents from the north and warm ones from the south. Species usually found in separate climes thrive in this in-between world.

Most marine birds nest on the high, pockmarked cliffs of the islands, where they command a panoramic view of the sea, but western gulls—a snowy white and slate-black species—make their nests right on the flat-lands. Each spring, acre after acre of Santa Barbara's meadows is dotted with their nests. A female lays three eggs with dull mottled shells that blend in with the browns and greens of the landscape, hiding them from hungry marauders. Hatched by June, the chicks, like the shells they pecked their way out of, resemble the colors of the ground. Despite their camouflage, they are not left on their own to survive: the mother stays with the nest to defend her offspring while the father fishes near shore and brings back his catch. Two months later, the fledglings take their first flying lessons, quickly learning the flight patterns of the adults: sweeping those great circles in the sky and soaring on motionless wings. They also learn to pick up mollusks and other shellfish, drop them against rocks from on high, and scoop out the insides for a juicy snack.

Black storm petrels with their hooked beaks, rare Xantus' murrelets with their high-pitched cries, black oystercatchers with their brilliant red bills and long courtship flights—all enjoy the safety and seclusion of isolated Santa Barbara. The place is serene. Salt-laden breezes drift in from the sea, a girdle of bold cliffs surrounds a gentle grassy plateau, and the only disturbance is the birds' loud screeches and the sea's steady roar. Despite the fact that there is no year-round fresh-water on the island (which restricts vegetation to shrubs and low-growing plants), millions of wildflowers festoon Santa Barbara from winter through early spring. Acres of brilliant white morning glories, giant yellow coreopsis, goldfields, and pink-and-white–blossomed ice plants—their leaves always seem to glisten with frost—make it look as though Joseph's coat of many

Still at the "ugly duckling" stage, young brown pelicans waddle on webbed feet before learning to fly. These sociable birds are just beginning to molt their light-colored down.

Two gleaming white gulls keep watch in a cove on Santa Cruz, the largest island in the park, while a third perches on a loftier site. The brilliant yellow blooms are coreopsis, sunflowerlike plants that bedeck the islands in spring.

colors had been draped gently across the land.

Earlier in the year, during the rainy season, the focus of the island is not wildflowers or seabirds, but water. On occasion, heavy downpours turn dry gullies into aggressively raging brooks and streams. With no trees or large shrubs in the way to divert their path, torrents rush downhill, shooting off cliffs in roaring waterfalls that cascade 300 or more feet into the sea. When the rains stop, the falls slacken to a trickle and then are no more—until the next deluge.

A convention of seals

San Miguel, the westernmost island, is a moonscape populated by ghosts. An island that rises more gently from the sea than its sisters, San Miguel has its share of rolling hills and pretty places, but its uniqueness comes from its inland dunes. Scattered across the dunes are jagged white pillars that seem like apparitions or trees from some ancient petrified forest—which is not very different from what they are. The pillars are the molded casts of trees and other plants that once lived on this island. Wind-driven sand covered them completely, then hardened as a result of a chemical reaction between the vegetation and the sand. When the plants decayed, they left behind hollow sand sculptures of themselves, called caliche fossils (from the Spanish for

"lime")—a solid but empty record of their existence.

Such an eerie ghost forest seems an unlikely place for any activity except, perhaps, a horror movie. Yet San Miguel's beaches are host to thousands of noisy seals most of which come to the island specifically to mate. Six different kinds of pinnipeds (Latin for "fin-footed ones") gather here—the most varied seal convention in the world. For some species, such as the playful California sea lion and the gargantuan northern elephant seal, San Miguel is the birthplace they return to every year to give birth, rear their young, and mate again for the following year.

With their loud honking and barking, California sea lions, the most talkative type, can be heard all over the island. These sleek brown animals, the famous "performing seals" that do tricks at aquariums, circuses, and zoos, are equally entertaining offstage in their natural surroundings, where they chase after each other in the water, ride to shore on crashing waves, and toss fish back and forth in a game of catch. Young ones even play a game that looks a bit like leapfrog.

When sea lions climb out of the water, they turn their hind flippers forward, and so are able to walk on land: they waddle along the beach like ducks in oversized, floppy shoes. Suprisingly agile for animals with such a cumbersome gait, they rapidly clamber over sand dunes and slippery rocks and can conquer the shoreline cliffs.

Though sea lions spend much of their lives in water, the females give birth on land, usually to a single pup. Sea lions and their relatives have a remarkable biological clock that not only brings the adults together in the same place at the same time but also regulates when the pups are born. For sea lions migrating to San Miguel, that time is June. Soon after the young are born, the adults start mating. But whether the females become pregnant right away or not until a month or so later, the fertilized eggs stay at a suspended stage of development until September. The embryos all begin active growth at about the same time, and it is thus that the synchronized births of the following year are ensured.

Submerged arm over arm in a tide pool, starfish nestle together. Behind them is a colony of gooseneck barnacles, their shells open to feed.

California sea lions share San Miguel's beachfronts with harbor seals and also with such visiting relatives as the larger, paler Steller sea lion. Most Steller sea lions are northerly creatures, residents of Canada and Alaska, but about 200 sojourn here from time to time. A less frequent guest is the Guadalupe fur seal. Although most of its body is as sleek as a wet California sea lion's, the male Guadalupe has a thick, long-haired mane around its neck, making it look—with some imagination—as though a magician had put together the body of a seal and the head of a mole.

By far the strangest-looking creature on San Miguel's beaches is the northern elephant seal, with its enormous bulbous snout. Fur seals may remind some of moles, but elephant seals conjure up a very different image—a giant gray-brown sack of jelly beans tied together at either end. These animals may weigh 3 tons and measure some 20 feet long. Unlike a sea lion, an elephant seal cannot use its flippers to waddle on land. Instead, it wriggles up the beach on its belly like a gigantic, bloated inchworm. After reaching a comfortable spot, usually next to another elephant seal, this hulking creature stays put for most of its visit. (Perhaps too much effort is required to move all that bulk.) While on land, elephant seals are very clannish, nuzzling body to body on the beach even if there is plenty of room to spread out; if no other elephant seals are

Like a tongue of fire, the garibaldi flashes through watery canyons and forests of kelp. The fiery temper of this little fish keeps rivals at bay.

around, one of these endearingly ugly animals will accept substitutes and snuggle between several sea lions instead.

At the height of the mating season, when the elephant seal population swells to more than 10,000, San Miguel's beaches are packed from end to end—and the island resounds with a cacophonous symphony of bellows, grunts, and snorts. Using inflatable air chambers in its snout for amplification, a single elephant seal can be heard almost a mile away. The collective roar of so many musicians drowns out the sound of the surf.

Since the snouts of the adult males (bulls) are the biggest, it is they who are the loudest—and for a reason: bulls bellow to defend their harems from other amorous males. When challenged, a bull rears up on its flippers and bellows as loud as it can at its rival, who hollers back. Usually, the loudest wins, but if no clear winner is established, the two may come to blows. Each tries to strike the other with its head and sharp teeth, aiming for the opponent's neck or snout. After several blows, the loser will back away. Some older males boast scars on their necks, souvenirs of battles lost and won.

Around the turn of the century elephant seals were thought to be extinct. Then unexpectedly eight were sighted near Baja California. Museum specialists, thinking that the animals would surely die out, decided to have seven of them killed for research and display. The demise of the species was now complete—or so everyone thought. But 10 years later, a herd of 125 appeared, again near Baja, and this time these incredible creatures were put under government protection. Descendants of this herd now breed at San Miguel, their ancestral mating ground.

San Miguel isn't the only place in the park where seals congregate: smaller colonies of pinnipeds haul out on the beaches of the other islands, including Anacapa. Actually, Anacapa, the easternmost island, is three small islets—East, Middle, and West—joined beneath the surface. All three together occupy only about one square mile, but it is a grand and glorious mile: the islands' outlines are bold, with precipitous walls of jagged cliffs and sharply pointed rocks plunging to a network

In times gone by, this ghostly scene on San Miguel was lush and green. Wind-driven sand blanketed the vegetation, then hardened. As the plants decayed, casts that roughly mimicked their shapes were left behind.

of sea-sculpted caves, arches, blowholes, and stacks.

Depending on the weather, Anacapa can appear to slope gently into the sea. The Chumash Indians gave it the name *Anayapah*, meaning "deception" or "mirage," and many a navigator has been misled, especially when the cliffs and coasts have been shrouded in fog. Shipwrecks such as that of the *Winfield Scott*, a steamboat that sank in 1853, are proof that the place has continued to deceive. Today a lighthouse and a foghorn alert sailors to the treacherous shores.

For most of the year, Anacapa is a rather dull brown island, but in early spring the place glimmers with golden nuggets reaching toward the sky. The gold in these hills is coreopsis, kin to the sunflower. A stunted "tree" with stubby branches and a thick woody trunk, coreopsis in flower blankets the island with such an intense yellow that sailors say they can see it far out at sea, like a golden glow on the horizon.

Pelicans and the Painted Cave
By the time the coreopsis is blooming, brown pelicans have just about finished building nests on West Island—site of the only permanent colony of brown pelicans on the western coast of the United States. These aquatic birds (they can swim as well as fly) use updrafts on the windward side of the island to help lift their ponderous bodies into the air. Once airborne, its wings outstretched to seven feet, a brown pelican can soar gracefully for hours, alternating slow sweeping strokes with seemingly effortless glides. It usually spots prey while in flight, and then it nose-dives into the ocean with such a loud splash that it sounds like a huge rock smacking the water. Upon impact, the pelican's expandable lower bill opens and acts as a built-in net to catch fish close to the surface.

Members of one of the oldest families of birds on earth, dating back more than 20 million years, brown pelicans were almost reduced to a memory in this century. For years, practically no young brown pelicans were born, because the eggshells were too thin to support the parent's weight. Scientists traced the problem to small amounts of DDT in the fish the pelicans ate. After DDT was banned in the United States, the population of California brown pelicans swelled; but they are still an endangered species.

Anacapa is the most dramatically sculpted of the Channel Islands. A few black sand beaches show the stuff of which it is made: volcanic rock. The main forces of erosion—crashing waves, high winds, and heavy rains—have done their chiseling, and even the plant life has left its mark; acids in certain species eat away at the rock, turning it into particles of soil. When the rains come, carving gullies in the ground, the soil is washed over cliffs into the ocean. Each year the gullies deepen and widen, and more of the island is lost.

Not as bold, but nonetheless picturesque, are the changes wrought on another island, Santa Rosa. Its western tip is softly shaped by undulating dunes, some more than a hundred feet high, whose contours are continually redesigned by sweeping winds. In an endless cycle, sand blown out to sea later washes back ashore with the tides.

Santa Rosa, with at least one freshwater stream flowing through it, nurtures more than 350 different types of plants. Some, like the Torrey pine, are unique to the Channel Islands region. Forming a dwarf forest, the stooped, twisted, and stunted Torrey pine grows in the wild on Santa Rosa and at just one other place on earth—Del Mar, north of San Diego. Animals on the island are both plentiful and peculiar. Wild boar, sheep, deer, and elk, all introduced species, share the spotlight with native deer mice, spotted skunks, and foxes even smaller than domestic cats. The island fox, sociable and seemingly unafraid of visitors, eats mice and plants and lives in burrows away from the sea. Its only enemies are occasional hawks that prey upon the fox's young.

Along the shores of Santa Rosa's neighbor, Santa Cruz (the largest of the Channel Islands), more than a hundred sea caves beckon seals and other passersby to explore their secrets. Some are deep, vaulted caverns; others, only shallow chutes into which the surf slams with the force of a tumultuous gale. Painted Cave, with its 70-foot doorway shaped like a Gothic arch, is unquestionably the most spectacular. The bright colors splashed across its ceiling come from nature's palette: various minerals in the rock are gradually transformed by the salty air into gleaming yellows, muted browns, reds, greens, and, in places, a shining white.

Above the caves, Mount Diablo (Devil Peak) rises more than 2,400 feet high. On its steep slopes and elsewhere on the island thrive more than 450 different kinds of plants, including wild buckwheat, manzanita, ironwood, wild cherry, buckthorn—even two kinds of oak that are unique to Santa Cruz.

The oldest islanders

Long before Europeans discovered the Channel Islands, Indians lived here and harvested the sea. Clues to their life-style are revealed in more than a thousand middens (remnants of ancient kitchens) and other archeological finds from Santa Cruz. Expert fishermen, the Chumash Indians used 25-foot canoes of hand-hewn lumber in which to hunt fish, sea otters, and seals; accomplished artisans and builders, they constructed thatched houses supported by whalebone—the long baleen plates that hang in the mouths of gray whales and various other species. But the Chumash's peaceful paradise was not to last. Spanish settlers, the first white people on the Channel Islands, commissioned the Indians to hunt sea otters for the European fur trade. Soon, American settlers and Russian explorers began vying with the Spanish for pelts. When the Chumash could not keep up with the demand, Aleuts were brought from Alaska to hunt, but the Aleuts also attacked the Chumash. Those who were not killed fled to the mainland and were eventually absorbed into other groups. The sea otters, though, continued to be slaughtered—almost to extinction—and only recently have they begun to make a comeback.

But the Chumash were not the first pioneers on these rugged islands: apparently someone was here as far back as 30,000 years ago. On Santa Rosa archeologists discovered a kind of barbecue pit surrounded by ancient bones from a six-foot-tall dwarf mammoth. Moreover, some of the creature's bones had been burned. Some scientists speculate that early man may have dug the pit, started a fire, and roasted the mammoth; others are not sure the pit and the bones come from the same period of time. How man—and mammoth—got to Santa Rosa in the first place is even more puzzling. Were they swept out by a storm and did they survive by clinging to a log or something similar? Did they swim? And why haven't any *human* bones as ancient as these been found nearby?

While some people puzzle over these questions of the past, others contemplate the future of the Channel Islands and wonder how long the islands will hold out against the sea. We shall, of course, never know the answer in our lifetimes. But until the ocean captures these mountaintops, we can be sure that the birds and the flowers and the seals and the fish will bring birth and renewal to these ever-changing shores.

Sand and greenery might seem in endless struggle for space. But as the plants march up these gently undulating dunes, on the island of San Miguel, they anchor the sand, keeping it from being blown away by the wind.

Within the deep, blue waters of Crater Lake is not mystery but history: the lake lies atop a volcano that collapsed. Wizard Island is one of

Crater Lake

"A lake is the landscape's most beautiful and expressive feature. It is earth's eye, looking into which the beholder measures the depth of his own nature."
Henry David Thoreau

From any high point in the Pacific Northwest, volcanoes can be seen soaring well above the rest of the Cascade Range. One volcano, though, is not visible. The glory of this fallen giant lies not in its height but in what it cradles in its summit—Crater Lake, the clearest, deepest, bluest, most breathtakingly beautiful lake in the United States.

Hidden from view, the lake seems little more than a promise to first-time visitors. Roads climb slowly, offering no hint that they lead to one of the world's greatest natural wonders. Near the top, you expect the roads after rising 2,000 feet or so in 10 miles, to continue their gentle ascent. Instead of reaching toward the heavens, however, the mountain plunges earthward, disappearing into an immense bowl.

In a sense, Crater Lake offers an experience like that provided by the Grand Canyon—the jolt that comes with finding that you are at the edge of a precipice. In one lavish crescendo you are faced simultaneously with a lake six miles across, canyon-like depths, mountainous cliffs, and a natural amphi-

several volcanic features that rise above the surface.

theater where light and color play leading roles. Visitors seldom react indifferently. Some are astonished. Some step back, uncertain. Few can look away.

On all sides, the rim of the large bowl circles into the distance. Below the rim, steep slopes drop nearly 2,000 feet to the lake. A small island, Wizard Island, juts from the water: from its shores, the feeling of being inside a vast basin is awesome. Smooth slopes and jagged cliffs rise all around and up to the rim, creating a world that would seem harsh and forbidding were it not for the firs and hemlocks that soften the contours. The trees are proof that life exists.

Dawn's awakening

July and August are the only times when snow does not cover the entire rim. Although occasional storms sweeping in from the Pacific may disrupt the peace, this is the season of serenity at Crater Lake.

Imagine a summer dawn, crisp and still. A robin calls from somewhere, breaking the silence. Within a few moments the bird sounds are more insistent. An orange glow on Garfield Peak, along the southwestern rim, heralds the sunrise across the water, but the lake remains in shadow. In the stillness, the rim's reflection transforms the lake into a giant mirror. Steadily the sunshine moves down the wall until finally the reflection is lost.

With the shadows gone, the full glory of nature's colors bursts forth, proclaiming a new day with the clarity of a bugle. A breath of air stirs the evergreens and sets a clump of lupines asway. A pair of ravens whirls by, climbing and diving in aerobatic displays. Periodically, one does a roll while sounding a musical, bell-like note completely at odds with its usual hoarse cries. Then the performers exit the stage.

Another breeze rustles the branches of aspens and cottonwoods, sending a dusting of pollen into the air, which is beginning to warm. A ground squirrel scampers a few feet, stops, and waits; a rabbitlike pika squeaks a warning and scurries to safety. A Steller's jay utters a coarse cry, while a chickadee chatters anxiously in the trees. The watchers have awakened.

Furry guards

On a warm, sunny slope, a colony of yellow-bellied marmots goes about its routine. Familiar animals in the mountains of the West, these large members of the squirrel family average about eight pounds in weight and a foot or more in length. But their chunky size does not save them from being prey to foxes, martens, and golden eagles. Alert to this fact of life, marmots seem eternally vigilant. Never trusting to chance, they post sentinels instead.

Typically, marmots serving as guards rest on rocks high enough to afford a good view, while others forage for grasses and more succulent plants. Those not working lie lazily in the sun, and several youngsters romp playfully near the entrance to a burrow,

squeaking and squealing as they chase one another.

Suddenly a guard sits up for a better look at a movement it has seen in the trees—the shape of a minklike marten moving along a branch. Hesitating only an instant, the guard lets out a loud, shrill squeak. Within seconds every marmot in the colony has either disappeared into its burrow or is stationed at the entrance, ready to dive in. Then, for some unknown reason, the marten changes its mind and moves off. Gradually, the marmots emerge from their burrows and resume their activities.

The eye of eternity

Overhead, a fleet of large, puffy clouds moves across the summer sky. Breezes riffle the water, and the rim's tall peaks become shrouded in mist. Within an hour, a rumble of thunder reverberates from behind Mount Scott, the highest in the park. Suddenly the atmosphere is cold, damp, and most unfriendly. Before long, a veil of moisture begins to fall. The ground becomes soggy, and the only sounds are a steady plop, plop, plop. The rain seems settled in.

Toward late afternoon the rain tapers off to a drizzle and then stops. As the mist clears, the rim gradually reappears and the lake again becomes its usual sparkling blue, mirroring the color of the sky.

As with other lakes, when light enters the water, its rays are separated into the colors of the rainbow. All but blue are absorbed and lost from view. The deeper the lake, the purer the color—and with a depth of almost 2,000 feet, Crater Lake is the deepest lake in the United States and the seventh deepest in the world. In addition, the purer a lake, the bluer it is. Crater Lake is a self-contained bowl of rainwater, snowmelt, and nothing else. No water that might bring impurities flows in, and very little seeps out.

The crystal-clear water is so pure that sunlight can penetrate to great depths, with astonishing results. Moss grows 425 feet below the surface, probably a world record. Fishermen can watch their lures flash through deep water and are occasionally lucky enough to see a trout or a salmon strike at their lines. On very calm days, it is even possible to watch the bottom of the lake drop away from beneath your tour boat. In an instant you are suspended over the edge of an abyss, staring into the eye of eternity.

As twilight deepens, a last golden ray of sunlight touches Mount Scott and slowly fades into powder blue as the sun slips below the horizon. Soon nothing is visible except the jagged horizon and the dim reflection of the lake far below. A few stars appear, and then more. An owl hoots, perhaps well over a mile away, but the sound carries in the chill of night.

A wintry world

The great arbiter at Crater Lake is not sunshine but snow. Spring and summer merge; autumn is but an afterthought. Winter is the theme here for most of

Sparkling water nurtures such brilliant blossoms as western pasqueflowers (right), yellow arnicas, and purple fireweeds. In the Cascades the season of warmth and abundance is short: *winter barrels in early, bringing thick deposits of snow. Yellow-bellied marmots, so active and alert in summer, will hibernate until life is once again renewed.*

the year—a time of storms interrupted by an occasional brilliantly clear day when the intensely blue lake lies cupped in a bowl of white. At the rim, winds sculpt snow into giant overhanging cornices. In the forests, fierce winds whisk and mound the snow until in some places the ground may be nearly bare while at others there are swells as high as a house.

An average of 45 feet of snow falls on the park each year. For the Cascades, though, that is not an unusual amount. Paralleling the Pacific coast from northern California to southern British Columbia, the Cascade Range rises like a great wall and blocks the warm, wet winds blowing eastward from the ocean. As the air rises to pass over the mountain crests, it cools, and as it cools, it loses its ability to hold moisture, showering the mountains with rain and snow.

One might think that this part of the Cascades, with its long winters and great snows, would be extremely cold and that the lake would be frozen for much of the time. Neither is true. The same warm winds that bring moisture from the Pacific also keep temperatures at moderate levels. The surface temperature of the lake does not rise much above 55°F or fall to freezing with any regularity. Beneath the surface, the lake remains at a constant 39°F year-round.

A forest of needles

Nourished by all the rain and snow, the park's greenery displays an outstanding beauty and profusion. A forest of ponderosa pine is protected in a southern extension of the park. Evenly spaced and nearly 200 feet tall, these stately trees announce beyond doubt that an extraordinary landscape has been entered. Pine needles carpet the forest floor, gentle winds send dancing patterns of sunlight and shadow over the fallen needles, and black-tailed deer hide in the shadows. Quiet and solitude prevail.

Farther up the mountains, where the soil is thin

93

and the growing season usually dry, trees must be able to withstand periods without water. Here the forest trades the majesty of the ponderosa for the homelier but hardier lodgepole pine, which is sparsely needled, lean of girth, and less than 100 feet tall. In areas where the soil is even thinner and more porous, only such plants as manzanita and ceanothus, both flowering evergreens, take hold. These low-growing shrubs do well because of their leathery, waxy, water-conserving, small leaves.

Where creeks and springs furnish year-round water, the forest looks different—thicker, lusher, greener. Mountain hemlocks form dense stands, filtering sunlight onto the moist, mossy floor. Crowding in with them and in forests of their own are graceful subalpine firs and Shasta red firs, both bearing purple cones that grow upright on the topmost branches. Horsehair lichens trail from tree limbs, and huckleberry and currant bushes grow ripe with fruit.

At the crater's rim, the toughest of all the local trees sprawl, bent and twisted from the wind's fury but very much alive. They are whitebark pines, whose needles fill the air with a sweet aroma and whose soft limbs can bend like willows in the wind.

Often, the most interesting individuals are those that stand out from the crowd, and in a forest of conifers, those would have to be the broad-leaved trees—aspens, for instance, whose leaves quiver in the slightest breeze. Their light green foliage proclaims the new life of spring, then turns gold.

Woven into the forest tapestry are meadows, glades, and streamsides bright with blossoms. Many wildflowers, such as white corn lilies and pink western bleeding hearts, thrive only where the soil stays wet from snowmelt or near creeks and bogs. Some flowers, eager to blossom in early spring, don't wait for the snow to thaw; they use the warmth produced by their growth processes to melt their way through the snow. Fragrant yellow glacier lilies and white avalanche lilies are among the first to emerge. Where clear, ice-cold springs seep, pink monkey flowers and lavender to magenta shooting stars are plentiful, while various kinds of orchids, such as the rare phantom orchid, bloom in moist forests.

On the drier open meadows, the flowers are different—taller and not so prolific, yet no less colorful. Purple lupines, white sulphur flowers, red paintbrushes, and many others respond to the sun's warmth. In rocky areas, a bit of the desert even exists: yellow-flowering rabbitbrushes stand out against the azure sky.

And so the pattern goes: summer days with their hours of precious warmth compressed between winters that at times seem never to end. But if life here appears to hurry in those moments free of winter, it must be remembered that in geological terms, the world of Crater Lake is very young. Not so very long ago the land looked nothing like it does today.

What was once a mountaintop is now a lake. In the painting above, Mount Mazama spews a cloud of ash and lava into the sky. Then the volcano caved in, leaving an enormous basin that filled with water—today's Crater Lake.

A cataclysmic beginning

The story begins—and ends, some might say—7,700 years ago. Until then, Mount Mazama, the volcano in whose shattered crown Crater Lake lies, was between 10,000 and 12,000 feet high—one of the largest in a long row of volcanoes. Although no one knows exactly what it looked like, we do know that glaciers once covered its slopes. Advancing and retreating over thousands of years, they left scratch marks on the rocks in many places and, on the lower slopes, gouged out deep, U-shaped glacial valleys.

Eventually, the glaciers retreated for the last time, leaving a few behind as a white cloak on the volcano's shoulders. But even before that final retreat, Mount Mazama had begun its periodic habit of belching forth clouds of ash and small amounts of lava. As pressure built up deep within the volcano, molten rock and hot gases worked their way to the surface, to be released as thick flows of lava and clouds of ash. Then, abruptly, 1,000 years or more after the last glacial retreat, a larger eruption began. Liquid lava, gas-filled and frothy, erupted, cooled, and became a type of light, honeycombed rock called pumice. Clouds of ash billowed skyward and then rained down, blocking the sun. As day turned into night, lightning ripped through the ash clouds, now grown to colossal proportions. Glowing rocks and more ash soon burst from several vents in the volcano.

The pressure inside the mountain had become so

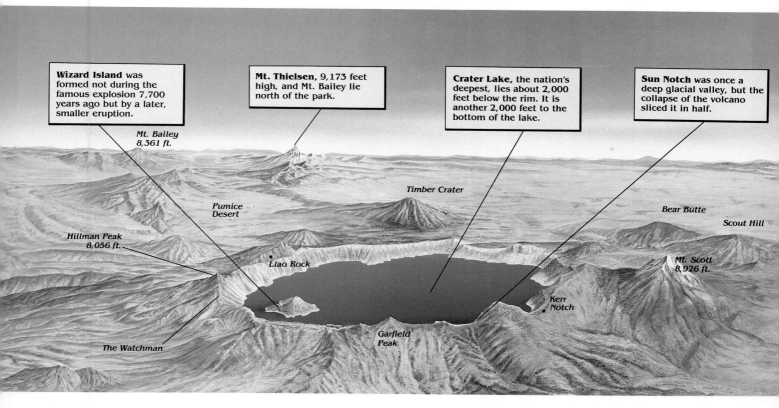

Wizard Island was formed not during the famous explosion 7,700 years ago but by a later, smaller eruption.

Mt. Thielsen, 9,173 feet high, and Mt. Bailey lie north of the park.

Crater Lake, the nation's deepest, lies about 2,000 feet below the rim. It is another 2,000 feet to the bottom of the lake.

Sun Notch was once a deep glacial valley, but the collapse of the volcano sliced it in half.

Mt. Bailey 8,361 ft.

Pumice Desert

Timber Crater

Bear Butte

Scout Hill

Hillman Peak 8,056 ft.

Llao Rock

Mt. Scott 8,926 ft.

Kerr Notch

The Watchman

Garfield Peak

great that the gas and lava mixture exploded into the atmosphere. To the Indians living nearby—believers in Skell, god of the heavens, and his enemy, Llao, god of the underworld—the climactic battle between the supernatural rulers had finally come.

The eruptions continued. The volcano was emptying its insides, blasting itself into oblivion in a mighty exhalation. There was no longer enough molten rock and hot gas inside the mountain to support its upper slopes, and so the mountaintop caved in, again sending up stupendous clouds of ash. There may have been one cataclysmic crash or perhaps several quick, successive crumplings. Along the edges of the cave-in, giant cracks opened; more rock, gases, and ash spewed out and cascaded down what remained of the mountain.

The mountain becomes a lake

After the cave-in, the ash clouds dissipated and the sky returned to its normal blue. But the landscape would never be the same; Mount Mazama would never again tower into the sky. Instead, marking the place where the summit had been was a giant pit (called a caldera, from the Spanish for "cauldron") measuring six miles across and 4,000 feet deep and still boiling with lava and steam. Valleys on the lower slopes were blanketed by thick layers of volcanic material. To the south, Annie Creek was buried under 400 feet of pumice; to the north, Pumice Desert was

created, and to this day it remains almost as barren as it was when it came into being. Ash lay 12 inches deep all the way to Idaho, and 6 inches deep in Montana. Hot gases hissed and boiled from holes in the ground—gas vents around which volcanic debris later solidified, forming spindly pinnacles.

The volcano cooled slowly, and the caldera remained a vast wasteland. Over the centuries, great quantities of water fell into the basin, only to steam off hot rocks or seep into its floor. Eventually, when enough water had fallen to cool the rocks, water began to collect. It took between 700 and 1,500 years more for the lake water to reach its present level.

Meanwhile, a small eruption of cinders had built a volcanic cone 1,300 feet high on the caldera's floor. This small volcano, Merriam Cone, is now totally submerged. Later eruptions built 12 other cones in the park. The most famous by far is Wizard Island, which rises 700 feet above the surface of Crater Lake. Like Merriam, Wizard Cone is a small volcano topped with a crater. A jumble of rocks surrounds the rim; a few trees survive on the dry, porous debris inside the crater. On the western side of the island, a lava flow from at least a thousand years ago marks the last major volcanic activity in the park. Until recently, it was thought that nothing remained of Mount Mazama's fire. Then, warm water was found deep in the lake—the first hint that heat still exists inside the volcano. The fires are banked, but a spark remains.

Death Valley

"The valley we call Death . . . is a land of illusion, a place in the mind, a shimmering mirage of riches and mystery."

Richard E. Lingenfelter

If ever a place has earned a reputation for brutal superlatives, surely it is Death Valley: the lowest, hottest, driest place in the United States. Still, the valley, which sprawls across more than 3.3 million acres in California and Nevada, is also a place of surprising tranquillity and beauty.

Death Valley itself is nearly 140 miles long, framed to the west by the Panamint Mountains, their peaks more than 11,000 feet high, and to the east by the somewhat lower Black and Amargosa ranges. More than 80 miles of the valley's basin lies below sea level; aptly named Badwater, where bitter, saline pools simmer beneath the sun, has an altitude of −282 feet, the lowest point in the Western Hemisphere.

As for temperatures, Death Valley in summer is a natural oven. Daytime highs in July average more than 115°F—*in the shade.* The highest air temperature ever recorded in the United States, 134°F, occurred at Furnace Creek in 1913. Not surprisingly, most visitors come to the park in winter, when days stay in the comfortable 70s. Rain is rarely a concern; on average, only an inch and a half falls here annually, and in some years there is none at all.

Sculpted and rawboned, this rugged landscape traces its beginnings back to a time, more than 500 million years ago, when a shallow sea covered the region. Over time, its silty bottom was transformed into layers of rock that buckled into mountains as the earth's vast crustal plates ground against each other. When the plates began to pull apart some 3 million years ago, great blocks of land shifted along fault lines, rising in some places, subsiding in others —lifting mountains like the Panamints higher, but also creating the trough that is Death Valley.

Moreover, volcanoes have boiled over many times in the past, painting the region with thick blankets of ash (the riotously colored badlands of Artist's Palette owe their hues to such deposits). Nor have such cataclysms ended. At Ubehebe in northern Death Valley, several clusters of craters—some half a mile across and 500 feet deep—mark the site of eruptions that took place just 3,000 years ago.

A world of unexpected life

On summer afternoons, little moves in Death Valley as the temperature inches steadily higher. Yet a remarkable array of living things has come to terms with the desert. Fleshy green pickleweed crowds the margins of Salt Creek and Badwater, growing in a medium so salty it would kill most other plants. Creosote bushes lard their tissues with a resinous sap that reduces evaporation and discourages nibbling by animals, while cacti store their meager ration of water inside their swollen spiny stems. In fact, thorns, bristles, and hairs are common on desert plants, both to ward off animals and to protect the leaves from the drying effects of wind and sun.

Other kinds of desert plants survive by cramming their lifetimes into a few short weeks. Waiting in the rocky, seemingly desolate soil are millions of seeds, shielded from the elements by tough, protective shells, biding their time, sometimes for years, for exactly the right combination of mild temperatures and sudden moisture. When Death Valley's hit-or-miss winter rains arrive, the seeds break their long dormancy and explode into growth, carpeting the desert with flowers in a kaleidoscope of colors.

In contrast to the arid lowlands, the mountains that rim Death Valley are much cooler and wetter, and so they harbor an even greater diversity of life. Starting at about 4,000 feet above sea level, the creosote bushes, mesquite, and desert hollies give way to sage, juniper, and pinyon pine; at about 8,500 feet, forests of mountain mahogany and juniper take over, sheltering mule deer and the mountain lions that hunt them. Higher still stand cold-tolerant bristlecone pines, some of them thousands of years old, their branches sheared and contorted by wind.

Of Death Valley's natural inhabitants, perhaps none is more surprising than its fish, or as dependent on tiny, fragile bits of habitat. The endangered Devil's Hole pupfish—electric blue and barely an inch long—for instance, has the smallest natural range of any vertebrate in the world. The entire pop-

Telescope Peak, reflected in the depths of Badwater, is home to mountain lions and a wide array of other wild creatures.

ulation, which numbers just a few hundred, is restricted to a shallow rock shelf along one side of Devil's Hole, a deep cavern flooded with 92°F water.

Wanderers and miners

People also have long inhabited Death Valley—Paleo-Indians during the Ice Age and, later, the ancestors of the Shoshone, who still live at Furnace Creek. Many of the whites who first passed this way came in search of riches, for despite its hardships, Death Valley offered chances for wealth as well. Its most famous resource, borax, set off a mining boom in the 1880s, which created an indelible image: the famous 20-mule team. Actually made up of 18 mules and two horses, the teams dragged massive wagons, each one laden with more than 36 tons of borax, on the arduous 165-mile trek from Furnace Creek to Mojave, a one-way journey of 10 to 12 days.

Gold and silver claims also attracted hordes of hopeful miners, spawning such short-lived towns as Ballarat, Skidoo, and Bullfrog. Panamint City, founded in 1873 and fed by a silver strike, enjoyed a brief boom. It was said to be "the toughest, rawest, most hard-boiled little hell hole that ever passed for a civilized town" before a flash flood wiped it out in 1876.

The park's most famous landmark, though, is still standing. Scotty's Castle, a Moorish-inspired fantasy of turrets, battlements, and red-tile roofs in northern Death Valley, is a monument to the unlikely friendship between Albert Johnson, a Chicago millionaire, and a flamboyant miner named Walter Scott—"Death Valley Scotty"—whose mine Johnson was underwriting. Although Johnson built the estate as a vacation home in the 1920s, Scott frequently passed it off as his own, supposedly built with riches culled from a secret mine. Today the castle is preserved in all its glory, silent but for the desert wind, moving across the land like a ghost.

Denali

"Not only had we been permitted to lift up eager eyes to these summits . . . but to enter boldly upon them . . . seeing all things as they spread out from the windows of heaven."

Hudson Stuck, Archdeacon, Alaska Episcopal Church

Bog blueberries darken and lowbush cranberries ripen to red as

The perpetual snow is deep atop Mount McKinley, and in midsummer the temperatures regularly plunge below 0°F, for at 20,320 feet above sea level, its south peak is the highest point in North America. But even this superlative does not do justice to the mountain called Denali ("the Great One") by native Alaskans. In terms of sheer rise from base to summit, it is the tallest mountain in the world, its awesome north face soaring some 18,000 feet above the wide tundra plain before it. The Alaska Range in which it stands contains other snowy summits that would dwarf the Colorado Rockies, but they seem no more than foothills beside Denali's majestic bulk.

Unlike mountains in the lower 48 states, those of the Alaska Range are clothed not in forests but only in ice and snow. Down their flanks flow vast, slow glaciers, gouging out deep, troughlike gorges and filling them with ice. Wet weather comes from the south here: dozens of feet of new snow are added yearly to the glaciers of the south face, and they grow deep and long from ice fields many miles across.

Though smaller, the north-face glaciers are better known because their snouts head into the accessible tundra, their meltwater feeding countless streams and rivers. Northward these waterways weave braid-ed paths along wide gravel beds before they dive down narrow canyons through the "outer hills," smaller mountains to the north of the Alaska Range. Occasionally, these streams, unleashed by warm weather or by sudden thunderstorms, become roaring torrents. But when they are not frozen, they are usually icy, ankle-deep trickles.

The timberline here is about 2,700 feet (in the Colorado Rockies it ranges from 11,000 to 12,000 feet), and so most of the park is treeless. Where trees do grow, they are often stunted, their top growth

Summer gives way to autumn on the tundra beneath the white-clad splendor of Mount McKinley, also called Denali—"the Great One."

sheared by winter winds. The landscape is open, exposed: the sense of space can be overwhelming.

Living things can be seen from afar. Along a distant ridge, a band of caribou moves gracefully and effortlessly. A movement in the low brush of a river bar reveals a grizzly sow and cubs. Dall sheep are easy to spot: tiny white dots against a brown hillside.

This is a raw wilderness, untamed and barely challenged. The ancient peoples who hunted here followed a pattern of life that was as firmly tied to the brief passage of summer as are the lives of the tun-

dra's plants and animals. Only in the past century have outsiders come: some to dig for gold beneath the outer hills, some to experience the wilderness itself, and many to challenge the mighty mountain.

The first ascent

There are those who, when confronted with a mountain, must stand on top of it. So it is small wonder that Denali has attracted adventurers since the day in 1897 that newspapers proclaimed the discovery of "America's rival to Everest."

From a barren ridge high on Denali's southern flank, a climber overlooks Mount Hunter, its 14,573-foot nose thrust through a sea of clouds. More than 3,500 people have stood atop Denali since the first ascent, in June 1913.

The approach to the mountain is easier than it used to be; ski-planes generally deliver climbers to the surface of a glacier at about 7,500 feet. But there is not, and never has been, anything easy about the climb. One must stand in awe of those early adventurers who attempted the first ascent.

Among them was Judge James Wickersham, who was appointed in 1900 to establish the rule of law on a gold-rush frontier. Covering his huge territory by riverboat, canoe, snowshoes, and dog team, he became as tough as any Alaskan of that era. In 1903 he set out, with four other men and two mules, on the first recorded assault on Denali's summit. They stopped at 8,000 feet but were hailed as heroes, having exceeded everyone's expectations.

Next came Dr. Frederick Cook, a famous polar explorer. After two well-publicized failures, he made a third trek in 1906. He and another man were gone 12 days and returned with photographs—including one that they said was the view from the summit of Mount McKinley. Many believed them, but some did not. In 1910 a group sent to test the claim found that the "summit" photo had actually been taken from a 5,300-foot ridge south of the mountain.

Meanwhile, in 1909 a group of Alaskans, alarmed that outsiders might be the first to climb "their"

mountain, had raised money to back a grizzled quartet of grizzled local miners. The four men, known ever after as "the sourdoughs," added a romantic and improbable chapter to the history of mountaineering. After arriving by dogsled from Fairbanks, 150 miles away, they followed the surface of the Muldrow Glacier partway up. On April 3, 1910, all but one left the 11,000-foot level for the final ascent, carrying an American flag, a 14-foot wooden flagpole, a thermos of hot chocolate, and a bag of doughnuts. They arrived back on the same day, claiming to have planted Old Glory on top of Mount McKinley. But no one could see the flag from Fairbanks, and the sourdoughs' story was generally dismissed. (Even today, climbers with modern equipment and no flagpoles allow at least two weeks for the same final ascent.)

After two more attempts failed, another Alaskan expedition was organized, by Archdeacon Hudson Stuck, a leader of the Episcopal Church in Alaska. Like Judge Wickersham, Stuck shared the life of those he served, traveling throughout his territory by the arduous means of the time and sleeping out along the trail in any temperature and in all weather, using whatever shelter was at hand.

To lead the expedition, he chose one Harry P. Karstens. Since leaving his Illinois home for the Klondike goldfields at age 17, Karstens had become the epitome of the early Alaskan sourdough: resourceful, self-reliant, tough, and adventurous. In later years, after his name had been given to Karsten's Ridge, the tortuous knife-edge route that flanks the upper Muldrow and Harper glaciers, he was to become the first superintendent of Mount McKinley National Park.

With two other men, Robert Tatum and Walter Harper, Stuck and Karstens succeeded in reaching South Peak, the mountain's true summit, on June 7, 1913. And to their surprise, atop North Peak, two miles away and only 850 feet lower, they saw the sourdoughs' flagpole, thus making their own expedition a double triumph for the people of Alaska.

Rivers of ice

The surface of the Muldrow Glacier was for many years the major route into the mountains. A 32-mile-long river of ice, it is fed by three large tributaries, each of which originates in a cirque, or huge, rounded bowl, high in the mountains. Here snow piled up for centuries, every foot of accumulation helping to compact the snow beneath into ice until, under the tremendous pressure, the bottom layer became puttylike and the entire mass began to move downhill.

For millennia the glaciers grew. The leading edges, or snouts, usually moved only as fast as they were forced to by the slow accumulation of snow at the glaciers' heads. But sometimes the action was more violent. The Muldrow, for instance, is a "surging" glacier, one of several in Alaska. Such a glacier creeps imperceptibly for many years, as most glaciers do, until, for reasons not clearly understood, it makes a convulsive forward lunge. During the winter of 1956-57 the Muldrow made a mighty surge, its snout pushing four miles forward. By late 1957, when the energy of the surge was spent, the surface of the lower end had fractured, great chunks and pinnacles of white ice had been exposed from within, and the upper end had sunk 200 feet. The Muldrow was no longer the easy route it had been.

The awakening tundra

Although winter is long and cold on the tundra—the land is locked under a cover of snow from October into May—the coming of spring is swift and dramatic. Brown earth appears, moist with melting snow, and is quickly covered by a spreading flush of green: lichens, mosses, fast-growing grasses and sedges, and low, matted perennials. Almost immediately, pinpoints and blotches of color—the blossoms of an array of wildflowers—punctuate the landscape.

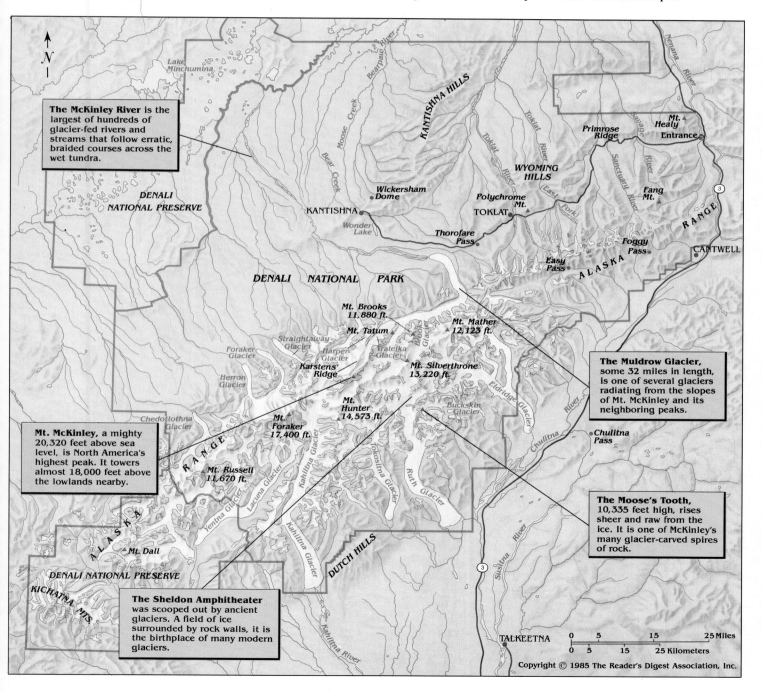

The McKinley River is the largest of hundreds of glacier-fed rivers and streams that follow erratic, braided courses across the wet tundra.

Mt. McKinley, a mighty 20,320 feet above sea level, is North America's highest peak. It towers almost 18,000 feet above the lowlands nearby.

The Sheldon Amphitheater was scooped out by ancient glaciers. A field of ice surrounded by rock walls, it is the birthplace of many modern glaciers.

The Muldrow Glacier, some 32 miles in length, is one of several glaciers radiating from the slopes of Mt. McKinley and its neighboring peaks.

The Moose's Tooth, 10,335 feet high, rises sheer and raw from the ice. It is one of McKinley's many glacier-carved spires of rock.

Copyright © 1985 The Reader's Digest Association, Inc.

Their distinctive white coats bright in the sun, a pair of male Dall sheep rests quietly on a high meadow. Like the annual rings on a tree, the dark lines on the rams' horns—which may spread to three feet across—indicate the animals' age.

In May, before the tundra grows soggy, bands of caribou set out through the valley toward their summer feeding grounds beyond the lower passes of the Alaska Range. The year's calves are born along the way and are almost immediately able to keep up with their mothers; those who cannot will probably fall victim to wolves.

Dall sheep, the only pure white wild sheep in North America, also make the hazardous trek across the lowlands. They move with urgency through this domain of wolves and grizzly bears to the rocky, windswept mountain heights, where they reign, sure-footed and supreme.

Grizzly bears roam the tundra unmolested and ravenous after their long winter sleep. They are for the most part vegetarians, digging the roots of pea vines and other plants in spring, and feeding on greens and flowers throughout the summer and on the plentiful fruits of autumn. But they do not scorn meat. Anything that a grizzly comes across in its travels it may eat—ground squirrels, caribou calves, even moose, are potential food. A grizzly that happens upon a wolf, or even a group of wolves, enjoying the outcome of a hunt will probably move in and take over. The wolves may object, but not for long. A grizzly bear does what it wants to do.

The long days of summer

From every corner of the globe, birds arrive to build nests and raise their young. Flocks of black and white snow buntings, often in the company of sparrowlike longspurs and redpolls, descend to feed while snow still lingers on meadows. From Southern Asia come the Arctic warbler and the wheatear, two tiny songbirds with large, lovely voices; and from South America, Australia, and Hawaii—as well as other islands of the South Seas—comes the beautiful golden plover, with its jet-black underside, yellow back and wings, and distinctive white-fringed face.

Near rivers and wild mountain lakes, the screams of gulls break the silence. Gray and white mew gulls nest in colonies in the gravel of river bars or on tundra close to lakes, often feeding on airborne swarms of insects. The small Bonaparte's gull, distinguished by its black head and bright red legs, nests in trees and dive-bombs everything that comes near.

Arctic terns arrive from Antarctica—the longest migration route of any bird. Light gray with a white breast and facial markings and a cap of black feathers, the tern flits and darts like a barn swallow on its long, gracefully pointed wings. It lays its two eggs directly on the ground, in a depression that may or may not be lined with leaves and grass.

During their northward journey, arctic terns may be accompanied —and harassed—by long-tailed jaegers, which winter on the high seas of the South Pacific. These formidable pirates survive during migration by robbing terns and other fishing birds of their catches. Ashore they become falconlike hunters, hovering motionless in the air, then diving with uncanny accuracy on their prey—a mouse, perhaps, or a pika or the young of another bird.

By June, as every day waxes noticeably longer than the day before, leaves suddenly pop out on shrubs and small, stunted trees. Wet tundra meadows grow lush with dwarf birch and bog blueberry, and fluffy catkins line willow branches. On the dry tundra of the high ground, bearberry and lowbush cranberry put forth their bell-like blossoms, the slender stems of white heather interweave into tight mats, and dense clumps of moss campion cover themselves over with pink blossoms.

Before long, Alaska cottongrass has spread a snowy mantle over bogs, lakeshores, and stream banks. The cloudberry's pulpy orange fruit has ripened. Blueberries are darkening; they will supply foragers with succulent food until frost. Late-melting snowdrifts make a continuous renewal of spring for small groups of wildflowers, which bloom around the edges of the drifts long after others of their kind have gone to seed.

Wandering caribou, back in the valley to graze on lichens and other greenery, stop to plunge their snouts into these snowdrifts, briefly escaping the harassment of botflies, which lay eggs in the great deer's nostrils. The bulls now sport towering racks with the shovellike scoops that are the caribou's trademark. Soft, dark velvet still covers the antlers; it will soon be shed, coming away in tatters. In October, when the bulls lock antlers in the serious business of competing for harems, the caribou bands will have gathered in the western part of the park, on the high tundra plateau.

Season's end

Autumn comes as suddenly as spring did. By August great beds of willow herb bury sections of the river bars beneath a rich magenta blanket. Soon the grasses of the marshy areas begin turning yellow and red, and then the foliage of countless low shrubs blends into the basic red of the tundra's fall garb. Willow and aspen add their bright yellow tones until the landscape glows in the waning light of the sun.

Ungainly-looking moose, the largest members of

Bright among the flowers of summer are arctic poppies, their fragrant blossoms rich with the sweet nectar that attracts pollinating bees.

the deer family, wade into tundra lakes and thrust their heads under the water to feed on succulent vegetation. The bulls are still antlered; soon they, too, will engage in the brutal competitions of the breeding season.

With the deepening of the autumn, migrating flocks throng the skies. Great V's of geese honk southward, and huge flocks of sandhill cranes issue their strange, haunting call overhead. The park's waterfowl slip away almost unnoticed. Suddenly they are gone. But not all the birds of the park depart. Tiny black-capped chickadees will remain all winter, busily pecking the seeds out of evergreen cones. Golden eagles will soar and hunt. Ravens and magpies will scavenge the remains of fallen creatures. Gray jays will eat anything remotely edible. And, dressed in white winter plumage, three species of ptarmigan will subsist on dry berries, leaves, and the buds of birches and willows.

The hush of winter spreads with the falling snows. Bears withdraw into their dens. Caribou, their antlers shed, seek open woodlands where the snow is less firmly packed and easier to brush aside with their broad hooves. Equally antlerless moose head for lower elevations, where they subsist on whatever dry browse they find. The snow line descends until lowlands and hills merge and the frozen surfaces of lakes disappear. Day by day, the sun retreats behind Denali's bulk until, in the long, ceaseless twilight of the Far North, the sterile breath of winter pervades all. Silently, the wilderness awaits another spring.

The collared pika, a busy denizen of rocky slopes, spends the summer gathering greenery, which it stores in piles among the rocks. It does not hibernate in winter but burrows beneath the snow to reach these tiny "haystacks."

The moon rises over the shoulder of Mount Brooks, glowing pink in the long sunset of an almost endless summer day. A mighty mountain in its own right, the 11,880-foot peak is dwarfed by its neighbor Denali.

Dry Tortugas

"The sea never changes, and its works, for all the talk of men, are wrapped in mystery."

Joseph Conrad

Curving southwest from land like a string of green-and-sand jewels, the Florida Keys stretch for nearly 180 miles across the limitless blue of the Gulf of Mexico. Most remote of all are the Dry Tortugas, a cluster of waterless islands that rise above dazzling coral reefs, where seabirds swarm like noisy insects and history lingers in the sunbaked walls of a mammoth fort.

In 1513 the Spaniard Juan Ponce de León found the seven tiny islands and named them *las Tortugas,* "the Turtles," after "the great amount of turtles which there do breed." His crew captured many of the loggerhead, hawksbill, and green sea turtles for their flesh, but they found no fresh water; in later years, maps showed the archipelago as the Dry Tortugas.

Remote as they are, the Dry Tortugas have gone through many incarnations over the years—they have been a pirates' hideaway in the 17th and 18th centuries, a lighthouse, fort, and prison in the 19th century, and a wildlife refuge, historical monument, and finally a national park in the 20th. Today's Dry Tortugas National Park encompasses nearly 100 square miles of ocean but less than 40 acres of dry land, a fitting ratio, as the natural wonders of this secluded park are largely hidden beneath the waves.

Almost 70 miles west of Key West and even farther

from the mainland, the park is accessible only by boat or seaplane. Visitors must rely wholly on themselves, carrying their own shelter, food, and drinking water. But the islands' splendid isolation is also one of their most powerful lures. Gaudy sunsets give way to nights that glow with vivid stars, undimmed by any artificial light; all day the flat horizon marks the unbroken seam between blue sky and azure water, where the only sound is the sea breeze and the shrieks of nesting terns.

Swarms of "sea swallows"

In 1825, just four years after Florida became part of the United States, a lighthouse was built on Garden Key, to alert ships to the treacherous shoals and reefs. Despite such warnings, hundreds of vessels went down in these waters over the years. In 1832 John James Audubon, drawn by the immense numbers of sooty terns and black noddy terns that crowded the low, salt-tolerant shrubs on the keys, sailed to the islands on a federal cutter. His pilot, describing the birds as black and white sea swallows, assured Audubon that "before we cast anchor, you will see them rise in swarms like those of bees when disturbed at their hive, and their cries will deafen you."

Audubon was there to paint birds; others came to profit from them. During his visit, Audubon noticed that commercial collectors were shipping tons of tern eggs to Cuba; even his own shipmates joined in the carnage, and everyone— Audubon included— feasted daily on "delicious" tern eggs.

Nearly a century of protection has allowed the vast breeding colony to regain its former proportions. On tiny Bush Key, more than 100,000 sooty terns jockey for position, dapper in their black-and-white plumage, long wings folded over their deeply forked tails. Pairs of birds scrape a shallow depression in the sand, into which the female lays a single egg, carefully shielding it from the grueling sun. Each night, when darkness protects them from predatory frigate birds, the parents change places at the nest. The colony never really sleeps; at all hours the air above the key seethes with terns, and the night is filled with the racket of their *wacky-wack* calls.

Failed fort, hellhole prison

Just across the narrow channel from Bush Key, on the site of the old lighthouse, sits the Dry Tortugas' most famous landmark, Fort Jefferson. The largest brick fortification in the world, it was begun in 1846 in an effort to protect the United States' vulnerable flank by controlling shipping in the Gulf of Mexico.

In 1861 the fort became a prison for Union Army deserters, who were punished with heat, humidity, disease, and an appalling diet. Doubtless, the prison's most famous inmate was Dr. Samuel Mudd, the Maryland physician sentenced to life behind bars

The harbor light towers above the massive brick walls of Fort Jefferson. Long since abandoned as a military installation, the fort is surrounded by an azure sea in which spiny lobsters and a wealth of other marine life flourish among colorful coral reefs.

polyps, organisms related to jellyfish that have traded freedom of movement for a life of cemented security. The colonies of polyps secrete calcium carbonate to form hard, stonelike structures that vary from species to species—round and corrugated in brain coral, delicate and branched in staghorn coral. It is a painfully slow process, one that may require a century or more to create a graceful candelabra and thousands of years to fashion the intricate, complex reefs that visitors see today.

Still, the rocklike fortress of the coral head is not an impregnable defense for the polyps. Foot-long fireworms, their sides bristling with feathery tufts that conceal sharp spines, browse on the living coral, leaving white, denuded areas in their wake. Parrotfish use their beaklike mouths to feed on the coral rock, swallowing grit and polyps alike.

Such natural predators pale, however, beside human threats. Even a careless touch by curious divers can damage living coral, to say nothing of the wreckage a dragging boat anchor can cause. Overuse, sediment, and pollutants have decimated many reefs in Florida and the Caribbean, but thanks to its isolation, the park has exceptionally clean, clear water and the healthiest reefs in the region. Day by sun-drenched day, the coral polyps of the Dry Tortugas slowly improve on their work of centuries, creating new marvels beneath the waves.

for setting the broken leg of fugitive Lincoln assassin John Wilkes Booth. Mudd tried to escape from the islands, and spent two years in chains for the attempt, but when a yellow fever epidemic broke out in 1867, he rose to the challenge. Mudd labored for three months to save the sick; two years later he earned a presidential pardon for his heroic efforts.

The military finally abandoned Fort Jefferson to the elements in 1873, and although it was used as a quarantine station and a naval refueling post around the turn of the century, it languished until President Franklin Roosevelt proclaimed it a national monument in 1935. In 1992 the Dry Tortugas became a national park, enjoying greater protection for its fragile environment, including one of the most pristine coral reefs in the United States.

Living cities of stone

Coral reefs are the marine equivalent of tropical rain forests—jammed with a diversity of life unequaled anywhere else at sea. Slip on a mask, fins, and a snorkel, and you enter a world where schools of multihued fish twist and dodge, gaudy fanworms blossom like red or orange flowers from the coral heads, and spiny lobsters wave their long, whiplike antennae at intruders. Angelfish and butterflyfish, adorned with neon colors, disappear among the culs-de-sac of coral, while squadrons of spotted eagle rays glide past majestically, their shadows playing catch-up across the undulating sandy bottom.

The foundation of the reef is millions of tiny coral

Built with more than 16 million bricks, Fort Jefferson has walls 8 feet thick and 50 feet high. It covers 11 of tiny Garden Key's 16 acres of land.

Everglades

"Where the grass and the water are, there is the heart, the current, the meaning of the Everglades. The truth of the river is the grass."
Marjorie Stoneman Douglas, *author-conservationist*

It is hard to remember, when you are in the Everglades, that the earth is round, for flatness is everywhere, as far as the eye can see. Miles and miles of shimmering saw grass stretch to the horizon in nearly infinite sameness, broken here and there by islands of tropical forest and ridges of Florida slash pine. This saw-grass prairie is rooted in the bed of a marshy, shallow river—it originally measured 100 miles long, 50 miles wide, and a mere 6 inches deep—that local Indians call *Pahayokee*, or "Grassy Water."

Creeping slowly southward to the sea, the river of grass carries the precious lifeblood of the Everglades. Without water, the 'Glades would be barren; with it, the place becomes a paradise splendidly crowded with life—bald eagles, wood storks, mosquitofish, raccoons, apple snails, alligators, crocodiles, wild orchids, and such tropical trees as gumbo-limbos, strangler figs, and royal palms. Day and night the air reverberates with the squawks of blackbirds, the hum of cicadas, the flapping of herons, and the cacophony of mewing, chirping, and croaking frogs.

Water is not always plentiful here. In winter, droughts reduce the river of grass to a soggy trickle and then dry it up completely. The parched land turns a brittle golden brown, and many animals breathe their last. When the summer rains come, the river again runs full; life is renewed. So it has been for centuries—the river's ebb and flow decreeing life and death in a delicate balance governed by the seasonal rhythms of nature.

The cycle of ebb and flow began long before the Everglades even existed, though then it was on a far larger scale. Ice Age glaciers never reached Florida, but

Water and grass, water and grass—these elements are the theme of the Everglades, their music punctuated by chords of palms and other lofty trees. The yellow "slippers" of the snowy egret add a golden note.

as they advanced and retreated, they alternately captured and released the seas; at least four times, southern Florida was flooded and then exposed. During the times when the land was submerged, generations of lime-producing plants and animals deposited thick layers of calcium carbonate, which hardened into limestone, the bare, white bedrock that is the floor of the Everglades. In some places, the lime rock forms higher ridges, on which today's pine groves and islands of trees—called hammocks—rest, but for the most part it is flat. Coated with a mixture of sand and peat from decayed vegetation (known as muck), the limestone serves as a vast, gently sloping tray over which the freshwater flows southward from Lake Okeechobee. It averages a foot a minute—surely not a fast flow, but a perceptible one.

Though a variety of plants grow in the muck, it is the tall saw grass that dominates, reaching beyond sight in every direction and changing color at the whim of the sun, the clouds, and the seasons. It starts out green, ages to yellow, and then, as the days shorten, shifts to brown. Barely ruffled by the wind sweeping above it, unswayed by the crystal-clear water whirling around its stems, saw grass thrusts its tufted heads as much as 10 feet toward the sky. Its blades have sharp, saw-toothed edges studded with glittering silica crystals that are, at best, difficult to chew. White-tailed deer, of a type smaller and daintier than their northern kin, feed on the bristly grass by jerking the wiry, stringy blades out by the roots, avoiding the dangerous edges and consuming the tender base.

Perching on blades of grass, such amphibians as leopard frogs, pig frogs, and narrow-mouthed toads exude their jelly-coated eggs into the water; after several days tadpoles will hatch out and join the prairie's watery world. Millions of little black grasshoppers ascend the stems, bunching together in such density that

they fool predators into thinking they are a gigantic seedpod. Whirligig beetles swim in circles on the water's surface, and tiny water boatmen—the insect equivalents of Venetian gondoliers—propel themselves with their two exaggerated "paddles" before bolting down into the muck. Around the roots, ram's horn snails, with round gray or chestnut-colored shells, edge aside thick mats of algae as they plow trails through the slimy muck.

Looking deceptively like algae are the bladderworts, flowering vinelike plants whose submerged leaves capture and devour small water animals. Concealed among the leaves are tiny but treacherous sacs—the bladders for which the plant is named. Each is armed with a hairlike trigger. Usually the bladder remains closed, having created a vacuum by expelling its water. When a wandering insect or water flea unsuspectingly touches the trigger, the bladder springs open and the prey is sucked in. Then the bladder closes, and a small pool of digestive enzymes dissolves the meal while excess water is pumped out, resetting the trap. If the victim is too big to be sucked in all at once, the plant takes successive "bites," holding it firmly until it is consumed.

Everglades escargots

Crawling ever so slowly among the aquatic plants are apple snails—golfball-sized mollusks that are able to breathe both underwater and in the air. (Unlike most other water-dwelling snails, apple snails have both gills and a simple type of lung.) At night, the brown-shelled snails climb up grass blades or other leaves and deposit their eggs just above the water. Although nature has designed the shells as protection, they don't always do

their job: a great many animals eat apple snails, and some have *only* this particular item on their menu. The Everglades kite, a crow-sized bird of prey, uses its sharp, curved bill as a snail fork to pry the snails from their shells. Circling over the wet prairies, its wings outstretched to 3½ feet, the kite scouts for its food. Spying a snail, it swoops down, snatches the creature with one claw, and flaps away. Then the kite settles on a high tree and, using its beak, removes the fleshy animal from the shell. Rare and endangered in the United States, the bird depends for its survival on the availability of apple snails. In years of prolonged drought, when the withered grass is littered with bleached and empty shells, kites fare poorly.

Another snail lover is the cranelike limpkin, a big brown and white speckled bird that has been nicknamed the crying bird because its call sounds like a grief-stricken human being. Hopping along the edges of watercourses on its long, thin legs, the limpkin repeatedly pecks at vegetation until it detects the apple snail's rounded shell. The bird swiftly plucks its quarry, flies to more solid ground, and drops the snail, waiting for it to relax and extend its soft body from the shell. Limpkins, found in the United States only in Florida and Louisiana, feed mainly at night.

River otters relish apple snails too, crunching the shells, with loud pops, in their powerful jaws. Alligators gorge on these mollusks, bullfrogs swallow them whole, and turtles grind them methodically, leaving shattered shells strewn behind them in an untidy trail. The leathery softshell turtle hunts snails furtively, raising its long, pointed head above water for a quick, spying glance before retreating below the surface. Like most other creatures, the turtle is itself prey, not only to alligators but also to humans, who savor it as a culinary treat. In the Everglades, where it plows down aquatic grasses in search of snails, fish, and anything else it can catch, it grows almost as big as a washtub.

Swimming along, the anhinga, or snakebird, looks more reptilian than avian when it sticks its long, S-shaped neck above the water. Periodically, it dives underwater and skewers a fish or small snake on its pointed beak; then it pops to the surface to gulp down its catch. When finished feeding, the anhinga climbs out of the water, finds a dry, elevated spot on which to perch, expands its tail into a fan, and spreads its wings, its glossy black feathers glistening in the bright sunlight. This display is not just for show. It used to be thought that, owing to the lack of a protective covering of oil, the anhinga's feathers became waterlogged and so had to be dried out before the birds could fly. It is now believed that they spread their wings as a means of controlling body temperature.

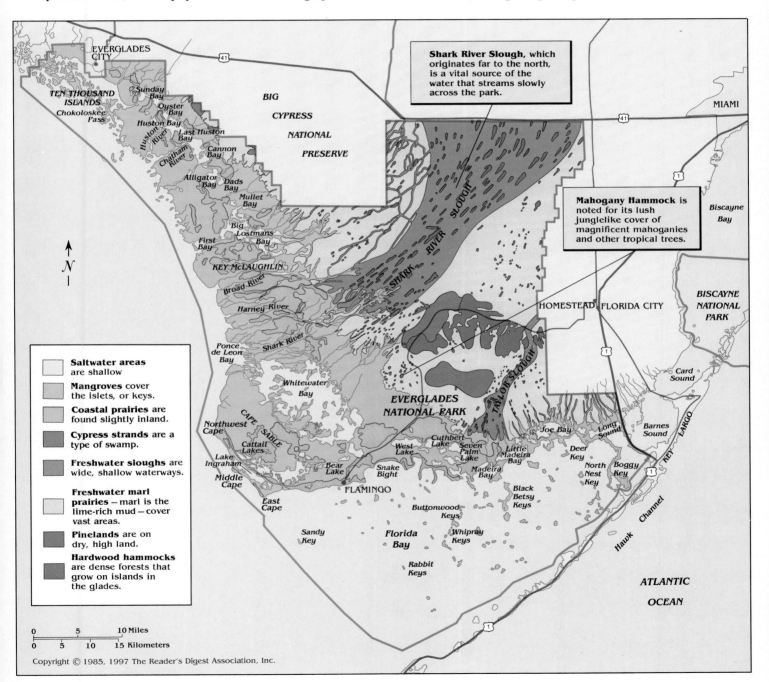

Shark River Slough, which originates far to the north, is a vital source of the water that streams slowly across the park.

Mahogany Hammock is noted for its lush junglelike cover of magnificent mahoganies and other tropical trees.

Saltwater areas are shallow

Mangroves cover the islets, or keys.

Coastal prairies are found slightly inland.

Cypress strands are a type of swamp.

Freshwater sloughs are wide, shallow waterways.

Freshwater marl prairies — marl is the lime-rich mud — cover vast areas.

Pinelands are on dry, high land.

Hardwood hammocks are dense forests that grow on islands in the glades.

0   5   10 Miles
0 5 10 15 Kilometers

Green treefrog

The pulse of the Everglades is not the silent river of grass running through it but the throbbing life deep within the heart of this watery wilderness. Here, anhingas dry their impressive wings, white ibises search the shallows for crayfish and crabs, spoonbills feed their unglamorous young, and pelicans ponder their next big catch. Peacefully, butterflies sip sugary nectar from tropical blossoms. In sharp contrast are predators large and small: awesome alligators more than 10 feet long and tiny, ¼-inch jumping spiders, which leap into the air to seize their prey. Turtles and treefrogs sun lazily—but if an intruder happens by, they will hurriedly disappear. The pulse of the Everglades may slow at night, but it never stops: such small mammals as raccoons, the masked bandits of the wild, remain on the prowl.

Zebra butterfly

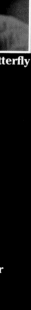

Brown pelican

Alligator

White ibises

Roseate spoonbills

Raccoons

Flood and famine

In the Everglades, the amount of water waxes and wanes with the seasons. Announced by spring rains, the wet season persists through summer, with fierce thunderstorms that roll across the landscape. Saw grass and hammocks alike gleam wetly in the late afternoon sun, and dry muds turn squishy as the river of grass begins its annual flow.

As if the rain-generated current were a signal, cypress trees, their leafless branches draped with shawls of Spanish moss, begin sprouting fresh green needlelike leaves; unusual for conifers, the leaves of these trees turn color in autumn and drop off, as do those of maples and other broad-leaved trees. Cypresses are members of the same family as the redwood, and like their California kin, some grow very tall. The bald cypress, for instance, towers more than a hundred feet above the riverbanks: in urban terms, one might call it the skyscraper of the swamp. In contrast, the aptly

In the brilliant sunlight of a freshwater marsh, the purple gallinule becomes a creature of particular beauty. The ducklike bird trots from one lily pad to another, its careful movements enhanced by its greatly elongated toes.

named dwarf cypress is only three or four feet tall.

Mosquitofish reproduce explosively to celebrate the spring and the coming of the rainy season. These rather drab little minnows, named for the food they eat, spread across the prairie so swiftly that farmers used to swear that minnows were raining down from heaven when they saw newly formed puddles filling up with mosquitofish. Other fish, such as bluegills, bass, and gars, soon leave their dry-season refuges and spread through the park—and the larger wildlife that feeds on them does the same. A good year for fish means a good year for herons, egrets, and other wading birds.

The rains culminate in gigantic midsummer downpours and sometimes in hurricanes that flatten the saw grass, turning the landscape gray and malevolent. Finally the storms subside. The land starts drying up, and by late autumn the *Pahayokee* is reduced to a trickle. By midwinter the flow may come to a halt and the water evaporate completely, leaving only puddles in the depressions. Some years are so dry the mud cracks, the land becomes parched, and the algae turn to wispy white dust.

Then alligators move out over the exposed and pitted limestone, seeking large holes filled with mud and the last of the water. Churning their bodies back and forth, the alligators shove the mud out with their blunt snouts and powerful tails, and the excavation fills slowly with water seeping in from underground. Here the alligators stay, the water a relief from the hot sun beating on their leathery black hides. The water holes created by the alligators become the swamp's salvation. Turtles, snakes, frogs, wading birds, raccoons, otters—an incredible variety of wildlife seeks out their cooling, life-giving waters.

As the sun beats down, fish may die by the millions, their skeletons rimming the shrinking pond. Gars—long-snouted, long-bodied fish—hold out longer than most, since the swim bladder acts as a lung and allows them to survive in warm, oxygen-depleted water by gulping air. Mosquitofish, too, can outlive others; their upturned mouths and flattened heads enable them to skim air from the thin film on the water's surface, where the amount of oxygen is highest.

Incredible as it may seem, the dry season encourages new life. Wading birds will mate only when food is plentiful at the proper time of year. Too much water, and mating does not occur, because the fish on which they depend are so spread out that the birds fail to congregate at the same holes. Too little water for too long, and the fish perish; then such birds as wood storks and herons refuse to breed.

But if the ponds and water holes are full, wood storks will walk slowly around the depressions, shuffling through the mud and stirring up hordes of wriggling fish. Wood storks hunt by touch, groping in the mud with their 10-inch-long bills. When the bill makes contact with a fish or with other prey, it snaps shut by reflex action, which is quick indeed: it takes a mere twenty-five thousandth of a second.

When disturbed, these black and white birds, the only storks native to North America, clack loudly and take to the air with difficulty—but once airborne they become the quintessence of grace. Their wings span an impressive five feet. Riding currents high in the sky, they may travel 40 miles a day in search of a well-stocked hole.

Gator mates

As the small holes dry out, alligators lumber across the limestone-whitened landscape looking for larger ones, where the water has not yet evaporated. To observe one of these sluggish reptiles trudging through the saw grass, the short legs thrusting the elongated body off the ground and only the tip of the tail dragging behind, is to enter the ancient time when mighty reptiles ruled the land. Kin of the dinosaurs, alligators have changed little in the last 60 million years: the animals are still mostly bone and muscle, and their brains make up less than 1 percent of their total weight.

The largest reptiles in North America, male alligators grow to 16 feet or longer; females, to 8 or 9. Together they fill the night with mating roars that shake the swamp with thunder. After they finish their noisy courting, a pair may bask languidly in the sun for days before mating. The female takes the leading role. When ready, she swims to the male, and they float together, sometimes with heads touching. Tenderly, the male may stroke her back with his forelimb before the two submerge and mate. Afterward, the male departs, and the female transforms into a busy mother to be.

The female alligator builds a large nest on an elevated riverbank, stacking vegetation high enough to not be flooded by summer's rising waters. The decaying vegetation generates warm, stable temperatures that will help to incubate the eggs. In the middle of the nest she lays from 20 to 60 oval, leathery eggs, each three inches long. Most nests are finished by mid-June; the eggs hatch about two months later, usually just before the river overflows. Sometimes, though, all the mother's precautions in building her nest high above the river are not enough to protect her unborn young; the nest is flooded and the eggs destroyed. But if it is an average year, the young alligators, sporting bright black and yellow stripes on their beaded hides, agilely crawl over each other to the water, where they hunt crayfish, insects, snakes, and frogs. Though the mother makes no effort to feed her charges, she does offer protection. When a predator threatens to attack, the young alligators grunt in alarm, and the mother rushes forward

The splendidly fragrant butterfly orchid, or palm poly, which grows perched on trees, reminds some of an insect; others, of a pale, leaping frog.

hissing, her mouth wide open—pink, cavernous, and studded with teeth. More than one careless raccoon has perished in a bone-shattering crunch. Even so, many baby alligators fall victim to the beak of the great blue heron, the otter's sharp incisors, and even the bullfrog's grasp.

Like all life in the Everglades, baby alligators are dependent on the unseen hand of the engineer. For a long time, the river was viewed as a wasteland to be drained and converted to farms, its water diverted to nourish nearby crops and cities. Eventually, the pioneers' zeal was tempered, and the Everglades was spared from further draining. Since the 1920's, however, a network of canals, pumps, and sluice gates built around the river of grass has artificially regulated its flow, sending water to the park only after urban and agricultural needs have been met. In dry years, the Everglades has been allowed to parch and burn; during wet periods, it became a floodway. Nature took thousands of years to develop the rhythms that control life in the Everglades. Whether government authorities and two Indian tribes, working together, can restore the natural water flow into the park remains to be seen.

Treetop ponds

During times of flood, the animals instinctively head for higher ground—the forested hammocks, which rise like dwarfed hills from the watery grasslands. Some hammocks are only knolls a few feet across, but others cover hundreds of acres, punctuating the landscape with thickets of such trees as the gumbo-limbo, nicknamed the "tourist tree" because its peeling shiny red bark resembles a sunburned bather. Majestic live oaks are heavily laden with glossy green leaves and with strands of Spanish moss, a flowering plant that takes its nourishment from the air instead of from the ground or the tree on which it hangs. Spanish moss has diminutive green flowers; other air plants explode with spectacular red blossoms like bright ribbons festooning the trees. The large ones with cup-shaped clusters of leaves create their own miniature world. The center of the leaf cluster fills with water, forming a treetop pond that attracts mosquitoes and other insects; warblers, treefrogs, lizards, and other animals come to feed.

Such air plants are givers of life. In contrast, the strangler fig takes it away. This tree begins life as a seed that becomes lodged in a tree, perhaps transferred there unwittingly by a bird. As it grows, it sends a profusion of roots down to the ground and wraps itself around the host's trunk in a series of bearlike hugs. It

Even a slight increase in elevation above the river of grass means a very different environment—a drier one where stands of such plants as paurotis palms and saw palmettos (a low-growing type of palm) can survive.

competes with its host for sunlight, water, and nutrients, and ultimately suffocates it, too. By the time the victim decays, the strangler has replaced it as a full-sized tree, adding a contorted, twisted beauty to the wooded islands.

In the late evening or early morning, when the hammocks are moist with dew and filled with rich smells from the fern-covered ground, tiny, colorful tree snails crawl ever so slowly on the bark of trees, decorating them like Christmas ornaments that have sprung to life. Some are orange, lavender, or vivid green; others are mottled, or banded in orange and white, or pale yellow

Few grasshoppers pause long enough to be admired, a fact to be regretted. They are magnificent creatures, with impressive eyes, prominent antennae, a sturdy outer coat, and strong hind legs that help them leap out of harm's way.

and rose. The color combinations are infinitely varied, but even more amazing is the fact that each variation is unique to a particular hammock, as though the jewel-like snails were living on solitary islands in the sea. With their antennae stretched out, the snails slide along on a carpet of self-made mucus, scraping off plant growths and retiring into their shelly houses when the sun is overhead. As soon as the annual drought arrives, these moisture-loving mollusks attach their shells to branches with adhesive and wait for the rains to return.

Fireproofed by nature

In the dry season, the slightest spark, such as one caused by a bolt of lightning, can turn the river of grass into a river of fire—fire that lasts for days or even weeks. Bright, crackling flames send billowing clouds of cream-colored smoke into the sky, and burn everything for miles around. Miraculously, the hammocks are saved. Each is protected by a watery moat, created by the hammock itself: acids from decomposing leaf litter leak out from the hammock, dissolving nearby limestone into a natural water-filled firebreak.

Fire is not only a scourge in the Everglades: it is a blessing too. So essential is it to the balance of life that park rangers sometimes start a fire intentionally, under well-controlled conditions and with a great deal of care. For fire consumes mats of dead leaves that prevent new sprouts from taking hold, and clears the way for saw grass to renew itself. Even the ashes help generate new life, by adding valuable minerals to the mud.

Were it not for fire, hardwood trees would crowd the highest ridges of the park, eliminating the last surviving groves of slash pine to flourish in south Florida. When a fiery storm reaches the ridges, the hardwoods, along with the smaller understory plants and the pine needles carpeting the forest floor, are natural tinder. Most of the vegetation is turned to ash—but the spindly-looking pines live on. Like the hammocks, the pines are endowed by nature with a fireproof shield: only the outer sheath of their multilayered bark is lost to the flames.

Although the ground is laid bare by burning, with uneven jags of exposed limestone turning the landscape into a tortuous terrain, life stirs anew beneath the surface. Saved by massive root systems, the plants in the pinelands resprout. Soon, the saw palmetto adds its long and graceful fan-shaped leaves to the forest, joined by the coontie, a foot-high fernlike plant that belongs to one of the oldest plant families on earth. Before too long, the ground is once again covered with greenery, and splashes of brilliantly colored flowers return the vibrancy of life to the land. Over all tower the pines, their bark splattered with rust and gray, their sparsely needled branches withholding only a small amount of light from the plants that spring eternal from the earth.

The steamy swamp

As the river of grass nears the ocean, freshwater begins to mix with the sea, and the hammocks and pinewoods give way to dense mangrove thickets. Symbols of a steamy world that is neither land nor sea, mangroves thrive in briny swamps where the air is heavy and moist and filled with buzzing mosquitoes and screeching tropical birds. Mangroves stand like natural barriers to the current, slowing it down and creating vast pools of stagnant water, stained brown from tannin in the trees. Mangrove roots, although anchored underwater in the mud, generally rise above the

Unlike their ground-dwelling kin, the intricately patterned tree snails cry out to be noticed as they crawl along the bark. They are about two inches long.

surface, arched like umbrella ribs and intertwined in an impenetrable maze. This arrangement is not accidental: the mud lacks oxygen, and the roots are able to breathe in the open air.

Red mangroves, the dominant species, have deep green waxy leaves that grow in a junglelike mass; the plants' delicate little yellow flowers bloom late in the summer, perfuming the air with a refreshing citrus fragrance. Hanging from the branches are podlike seeds, which sprout while still attached to the trees. Falling into the water, they are carried away along the winding creeks interlacing the swamps, eventually to settle down and take root.

For a long time people considered mangrove swamps to be little more than breeding places for mosquitoes, but now scientists realize that mangrove roots trap silt

and debris, building new land. Their leaves add valuable nutrients to the water, and the food and shelter they offer attract life from land and sea. Rainbow-colored fish flash through murky pools, the sun glinting off their backs. Rooted in the mud, sea anemones open their tentacles like flowers in full bloom. Crabs, snails, and other small animals crawl along the roots, picking for food among the waterlogged leaves. The diamond-back terrapin suns lazily on mud flats, its black shell etched with sets of concentric rings and its speckled face adorned with a clownlike grin. Local legend says that a terrapin's age can be calculated by counting the number of rings contained in one set; but when this works at all, it holds true only until the turtle is about 10 years old—and the diamondback can live to 40.

Female terrapins grow twice as big as the male. They dig sandy holes above the waterline, then deposit up to 18 eggs in the nest. Baby terrapins hatch from two to four months later—that is, if the eggs have not been snatched by gulls or other marauders.

Mangrove swamps, where the land oozes and shifts, are not for mammals that prefer firmer footing, but spectacular numbers of spectacular birds find such places safe and isolated havens. Snowy egrets and great white herons pierce the water with their long, pointed bills. Brown pelicans roost in the mangroves, fishing a short distance away in Florida Bay or the Gulf of Mexico. But by far the most magnificent feathered creature in the mangroves is the roseate spoonbill, a wading bird whose bright pink plumage brings a joyous glow to the swamp. The unique paddle-shaped bill differentiates this bird from the similarly hued flamingo, which occurs in the Everglades only sporadically.

If the roseate spoonbill is the queen of Florida Bay, surely the crocodile is the king. Roaming the mangrove creeks, its knobby, clay-colored back rising formidably above the water and its tapered snout studded with fangs, this reptile, when it wants to get other animals out of its way, needs only to give the water an angry slap with its tail. The crocodile rules its kingdom, confident and supreme, though its authority goes unnoticed by most human visitors. To catch a glimpse of one of these creatures surging ahead in the brackish waters of Florida Bay, the only place in the United States where they are found, is to feel fear and excitement rolled into one. Crocodiles are wild and wonderful, awesome and atavistic, mysterious and marvelous—superb symbols of the wilderness where they are king.

Far more beautiful than its name might imply, Glacier has deep green forests, flower-strewn meadows, and such pristine bodies of

Glacier

"Give a month at least to this precious reserve. The time will not be taken from the sum of your life. Instead of shortening, it will indefinitely lengthen it and make you truly immortal."
John Muir

water as Grinnell Lake. Beargrass is the floral emblem.

Y ou rest on a gnarled snag of fir, shoes off, feet touching a lake so cold it makes you shiver. Never-melting chunks of ice float in the frigid water. But the sun is high, warming the back of your neck, and the trail you have followed is blazed with blossoms. You are a summer visitor in a place that was shaped by the agents of winter, a landscape that owes its allegiance to ice.

More than 700 miles of trails traverse Glacier's million acres, but you do not have to tread on each and every one of them to know the park intimately. A shimmering expanse of prairie, evergreen forests with their stately boughs, glimmering lakes set into mountain crowns, high-meadow gardens, snowbanks blanketing the alpine tundra—your eyes can feast on all of these, and more, in a single day's hike. Every turn of the trail beckons you deeper into the heart of the wilderness; each discovery, whether of a glacier lily blooming in a snow patch or a sweeping vista of glistening mountaintops, propels you to the next. Even Glacier's peaks are attainable. Seldom more than 10,000 feet high, the mountains are almost human in scale when compared to the giant ice-clad peaks of Banff and Jasper a few hundred miles to the north.

Sheer grace is chiseled into this land, like poise into a

119

statue—the sharp spires, the toothed ridges, the abrupt cliffs that stand defiant in shadow and storm. All pay homage to glaciation, the most recent sculptor, for by its very name, Glacier celebrates the force that shaped it last. The signature of moving ice can be found everywhere in the park, and its creations are as yet unsoftened by time. Ending a scant 10,000 years ago, the last great ice age is a fresh memory to these peaks, but it is merely the newest chapter in the long, tumultuous history of the land.

The mountains' story begins a long, long time ago—more than a billion years back in time, when shallow seas alternately flooded and withdrew from the land. Each immersion left behind a characteristic layer of clay, lime, silt, or other sediments that settled on the seabed in the same way that sand sinks to the bottom of a pond. As the sediments built up over millions of years, they became compressed and cemented together, solidifying into rock layers thousands of feet thick. By the time the last sea retreated, lime had turned into limestone, sand into sandstone, mud into mudstone, and so on, creating the layer-cake look of the mountains we see today. Tiered with red, green, gray, and buff bands, Glacier's mountains rise in ancient splendor—the oldest sedimentary rocks on earth.

But not all the rock layers can be traced so evenly from peak to peak. In certain places, the layers are crumpled and stand on end; they look agonized, perhaps even tortured. In others, the layers are broken and stacked, with the older rocks on top. At Marias Pass, for example, billion-year-old, buff-colored limestone rests on 70-million-year-old dark gray sandstone—the result of a colossal upheaval. Over millions of years, geologic forces beneath the earth's surface gradually pushed up the layers of rock, forming the great Rocky Mountain system, of which Glacier's mountains are a part. Squeezed by uneven pressures, a massive block of Glacier's bedrock was thrust upward and over its eastern neighbors, buckling and cracking in the process. The mountains that we know today—chiseled and dramatic—thus stand as massive monuments to the earth's convulsive past.

Glacier's glaciers

After the rocks settled into place, the land gradually became eroded into soft contours. Pinnacled peaks were transformed into gentle domes, thickly wooded forests paraded up the slopes, and twisting streams etched V-shaped valleys into the mountain faces like wrinkles earned through time. Although these were peaceful times in the mountains, it was the proverbial calm before the storm. Over the next 3 million years, the land was gripped by tons of thick, steel-blue glaciers—groaning, thundering monsters so powerful that they slashed rounded peaks into razor-sharp ridges, barreled narrow troughs into wide, sloping valleys, and dug deep canyons where none had been before. At least four times glaciers overspread the land, and then re-

treated. Lakes and forests developed in each intermission, only to be destroyed in the next onslaught.

Great rivers of ice flowing downhill, glaciers claim and rearrange whatever lies in their way. The Ice Age glaciers followed the path of least resistance—the V-shaped glens—and widened them into graceful, U-shaped valleys. Where the ice was thickest, it gouged long, deep basins into the land. Glaciers are movers as well as bulldozers; they carry rocky debris as they forge along. When changes in climate caused the glaciers to halt, they dropped some of their load at their downstream ends. These massive piles of rock, technically known as terminal moraines, dammed meltwater from the glaciers, and the area became generously sprinkled with such sapphire-blue bodies of water as Lake McDonald, the park's largest lake. The ridges that line its sides are also moraines: lateral moraines.

Unfinished symphonies

Hundreds of smaller ice rivers—tributary glaciers—flowed into the main glaciers, and each etched the mountains it touched with a different hand; rather than being identical, the mountains lining the valleys are distinctly different in contour. Because the tributary glaciers could not excavate as deeply or as rapidly as the channels into which they flowed, some were stranded mid-mountain when the glaciers retreated—stopped in the act before they were finished with their work. Today these unfinished valleys, their heads usually cradling deep, bowl-shaped lakes called tarns, hang above the U-shaped valleys left by the larger glaciers. From the tarns, water flows down the hanging valleys and tumbles over stony staircased benches or falls free over sheer cliffs to reach the valley floor. Hidden Lake, an exquisite tarn tucked away in a crook of mountains near Logan Pass, is so snugly recessed in its rock setting that it looks like a jewel fitted to its mounting. Water leaving the neck of this narrow bowl plunges a breathtaking 2,600 feet into the Avalanche Creek basin. A drop of 500 feet more takes the roaring water to the McDonald Valley.

Sometimes more than one glacier formed on a mountain, and each traveled along a separate path. When two glaciers moved down opposite sides of the mountain, they nibbled away at the rock between them until only cleaver-sharp peaks and serrated ridges, called arêtes, remained. The Garden Wall is such a remnant. At other times, glaciers completely wore away the peaks and ridges, creating the graceful, saddle-shaped passes that connect many of Glacier's mountains.

When three or more glaciers attacked a mountain, they hewed a pyramidal or square-sided spire known as a horn. The park's mountains are a herd of such stony horns—from Ahearn to St. Nicholas, Wacheechee to Thunderbird, Kinnerly to Little Matterhorn. (The "big" Matterhorn, which straddles the border between Switzerland and Italy, was formed in the same way.)

In the park more than 50 glaciers are still at work

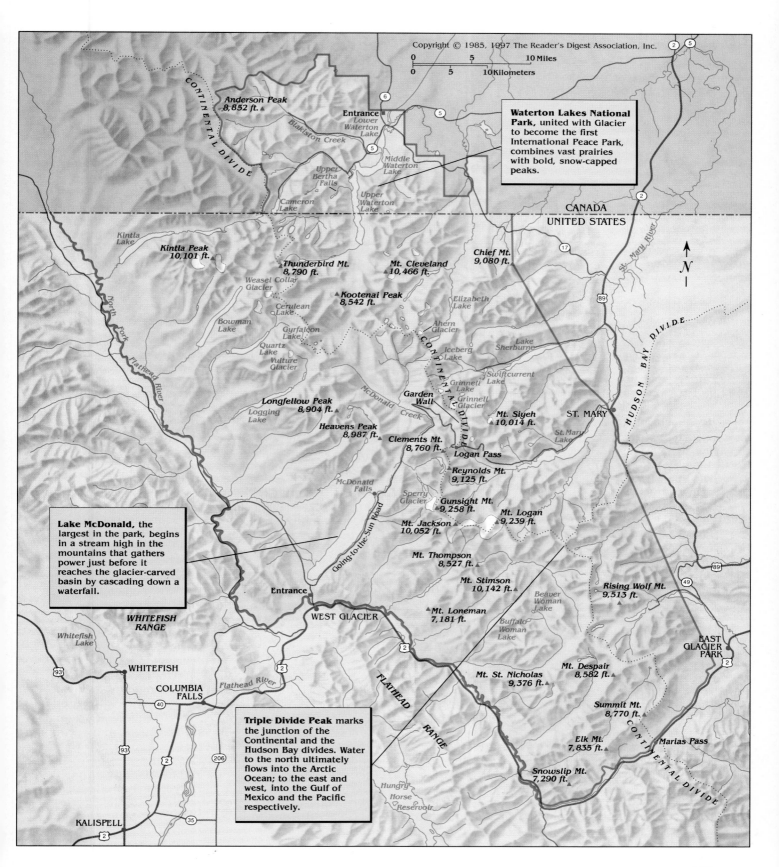

0   5   10 Miles
0   5   10 Kilometers

CONTINENTAL DIVIDE

Anderson Peak
8,852 ft.

Entrance
Lower Waterton Lake

Blakiston Creek

Upper Bertha Falls

Cameron Lake

Middle Waterton Lake

Upper Waterton Lake

Waterton Lakes National Park, united with Glacier to become the first International Peace Park, combines vast prairies with bold, snow-capped peaks.

CANADA
UNITED STATES

Kintla Lake

Kintla Peak
10,101 ft.

Thunderbird Mt.
8,790 ft.

Mt. Cleveland
10,466 ft.

Chief Mt.
9,080 ft.

Weasel Collar Glacier

Kootenai Peak
8,542 ft.

Cerulean Lake

Elizabeth Lake

Bowman Lake

Gyrfalcon Lake

Ahern Glacier

Iceberg Lake

Lake Sherburne

Quartz Lake

Vulture Glacier

McDonald Creek

Garden Wall

Grinnell Lake

Swiftcurrent Lake

Grinnell Glacier

North Fork Flathead River

Longfellow Peak
8,904 ft.

Logging Lake

Heavens Peak
8,987 ft.

Clements Mt.
8,760 ft.

Mt. Siyeh
10,014 ft.

ST. MARY

St. Mary Lake

HUDSON BAY DIVIDE

Logan Pass

Reynolds Mt.
9,125 ft.

McDonald Falls

Sperry Glacier

Gunsight Mt.
9,258 ft.

Mt. Logan
9,239 ft.

Mt. Jackson
10,052 ft.

Lake McDonald, the largest in the park, begins in a stream high in the mountains that gathers power just before it reaches the glacier-carved basin by cascading down a waterfall.

Going-to-the-Sun Road

Mt. Thompson
8,527 ft.

Mt. Stimson
10,142 ft.

Beaver Woman Lake

Rising Wolf Mt.
9,513 ft.

Entrance

WHITEFISH RANGE

WEST GLACIER

Mt. Loneman
7,181 ft.

Buffalo Woman Lake

Whitefish Lake

WHITEFISH

FLATHEAD RANGE

EAST GLACIER PARK

COLUMBIA FALLS

Flathead River

Mt. St. Nicholas
9,376 ft.

Mt. Despair
8,582 ft.

Summit Mt.
8,770 ft.

CONTINENTAL DIVIDE

Marias Pass

Triple Divide Peak marks the junction of the Continental and the Hudson Bay divides. Water to the north ultimately flows into the Arctic Ocean; to the east and west, into the Gulf of Mexico and the Pacific respectively.

Elk Mt.
7,835 ft.

Snowslip Mt.
7,290 ft.

Hungry Horse Reservoir

KALISPELL

121

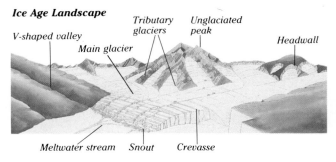

Ice Age Landscape

V-shaped valley
Tributary glaciers
Unglaciated peak
Main glacier
Headwall
Meltwater stream
Snout
Crevasse

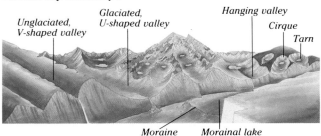

Present-day Landscape

Unglaciated, V-shaped valley
Glaciated, U-shaped valley
Hanging valley
Cirque
Tarn
Moraine
Morainal lake

Glaciers are giant bulldozers. During the ice ages, they flowed down the mountains and carved the land. Though today the park has far fewer glaciers, there are memories aplenty of those long-ago times. Hidden Lake (right) is a tarn—a lake that sits in a scooped-out basin, or cirque.

today, carving and shaping the landscape, like artisans who continually tinker with their work. But these are not the same sculptors that were active during the Ice Age; they are new ones, born about 4,000 years ago during a widespread cold snap. Inching along at a snaillike pace, our modern glaciers may take a year to accomplish what their ancestors easily managed in just a few hours. Sperry, the biggest glacier, progresses about 30 feet a year—token whittling compared to the heavy industry of the past. To visit one of the glaciers, however—to see the enormous crevasses that yawn open late in summer, to enter an ice cave spewing milky meltwater, to step on the living ice—is to bring alive the memory of those monsters that trod and tore the land so long ago.

Dwarfs and giants

As the last of the Ice Age glaciers melted, some of the water flowed east to the Missouri and Mississippi rivers and some went westward to the Pacific, for Glacier sits astride the Continental Divide. That line separates more than two different drainage systems; the two regions of the park, east and west, are as opposite as night and day. Blessed with warm, moisture-laden winds blowing inland from the Pacific, the western side of the Divide enjoys a climate that is wet and mild, much like Seattle's. But by the time the winds climb over the mountainous Divide, not much moisture is left, and the climate is drier—and harsher, too. Glacier's eastern prairies are blasted with frigid winters blown in on blustery Canadian winds, and parched in summer by hot air from the southern plains. Douglas firs, sheared and bent by the wind,

are stunted to half their usual size, while just a dozen miles to the west the species stands erect.

Nurtured by plentiful rain, the western valleys prosper with vegetation unusual for such an inland location. The lower half of the McDonald Valley, for instance, boasts a dense forest of red cedar and hemlock that looks very much like the rain forests along the Pacific coast. The aromatic red cedars and the smaller, gracefully branched hemlocks soar toward the sky, forming a closed canopy 200 feet above the valley floor. Sheltered in the palm of the valley, these forest giants thrive far beyond their usual range—and, in fact, are at their easternmost limit here.

Under the thick green canopy, perpetual dusk casts this wooded world into shadow. Without sunlight, the understory is scant. The forest is open, damp, and windless. Lichens droop unswaying from dead twigs and branches. Huge columns of fallen cedars, their red interiors fragrant even in death, lie in state, their trunks covered over with moss and clumps of hemlock seedlings and ferns. Moss claims everything, a serene, luminous shroud that softens boulders and unites the living and the dead in the pale light. A trillium with torchlike flowers is one of the early harbingers of spring, along with dainty violets and fragile-looking spring beauties. Twinflowers with their paired bells top the moss wherever the plants can twine, and here and there a diminutive calypso orchid sparkles with dew like an amethyst on a green velvet cushion. Through the cool, expansive hush of this cathedrallike forest, the varied thrush, its orange breast as bright as a beacon, sounds its haunting song.

Along the banks of wide, rushing streams, where

122

sunlight is allowed a narrow dominion, flash the leaves of the massive black cottonwood, its deeply contoured bark, with its ridges and valleys, resembling the land itself. Wherever the water runs fastest, the energetic, buoyant water ouzel, or dipper, makes its home. Marching along the edge of the torrent, this amazing bird pauses atop a rock to curtsy twice, slips off to fly underwater in search of insects, miraculously reappears upstream, and bobs like a cork for a time; then with a sudden rush it flies up and through a gush of waterfall. *Jigic, jigic,* cries the small, slate-gray bird, its stubby tail erect like a wren's, as it once again stands on a rock, its bill now lined with damselfly larvae. It heads for its nest, flying low above the stream. Four young—their mouths gaping open at the approach of the parent—crowd the entrance to the remarkable dome-shaped nest of moss, kept moist by incessant spray. Like the sound of the water itself, the bright, bubbling voice of the ouzel is seasonless, singing even in February when the rest of the forest is still and white.

The affairs of autumn

There are quieter waters in the McDonald Valley, small ponds and marshy backwaters where whirring dragonflies and deep-throated frogs in chorus offer background music for moose grazing languidly in shallow water. Wading slowly, water dripping from its pendulous muzzle, the moose appears placid and docile. In truth, though, this largest member of the deer family has formidable speed, strength, and agility, negotiating seemingly impenetrable terrain with ease. Every winter bull moose shed their antlers, but by autumn they have completely regrown their bony crowns—awesome weapons in the annual duels for mates. Reverberating in forests when leafy trees burn yellow against their needled companions, the bugle calls of the bulls announce the concerns of the season.

As if in response to the bellowing, thousands of kokanee salmon used to begin arriving at McDonald Creek for their annual spawning ritual; milling around in the shallow water, they provided an autumnal feast for both bald eagles and grizzly bears. In recent years, however, the salmon have suffered a disastrous population decline, and they no longer come in great numbers to the park.

But the bears are still there. The big humpbacked grizzlies simply must forage elsewhere in their final weeks of fattening themselves for their long winter sleep. These are creatures that combine sheer power with grace, and Glacier is one of the few wilderness areas in the United States where they can still be found roaming free.

Nor are bears the only big critters inhabiting these wilds: Glacier is the only place in the continental United States where grizzlies, wolves, and mountain lions all share the same turf. Gone from the area for 50 years, the wolves came back on their own, wandering south from Canada in the winter of 1985–86.

Researchers are excited by the opportunity to study interactions among this trio of heavyweights. And they have already come up with some surprises—wolves attacking grizzlies, for instance, and grizzlies poaching on leftover wolf kills.

High life in the mountains

Although Glacier's forests (and those of other western mountain parks, too) are dominated by evergreens, it would be a mistake to think they are all the same. From the long, slender cones of the western white pine to the little, round ones of the western hemlock, from the dark green scales of the western red cedar to the light blue-green needles of the subalpine larch, the looks of conifers are as varied as the mountains themselves. To those who know them, trees are like landmarks, telling you where you are.

Above the McDonald Valley, Douglas firs, lodgepole pines, and western larches march up the slopes; crowding the valleys are Englemann spruce and subalpine fir, the two most common trees in the park. The sweeping boughs of the spruces and the short, horizontal

Measuring as much as 10 feet wide and 60 feet deep, crevasses command caution and respect. Here a ranger-naturalist guides hikers past a yawning chasm in the Grinnell Glacier, a river of ice that is shrinking with time.

Not in the slightest is the nimble mountain goat fazed by dizzying heights. This surefooted mountaineer remains at high elevations throughout the year, relying on winter winds to uncover food plants buried beneath the snow.

branches of the firs create a thickly tangled forest offering coolness and shade. Farther north, some hardy subalpine firs cluster on rocky ledges above the treeline, where they manage to survive a growing season measured in weeks—but these individuals look very different from others of their kind. While those in the lower valleys stand 80 feet tall, the firs here have a prostrate existence; they are essentially straggly mats atop cold, bare boulders. Growth is painfully slow. From one year to the next, a twig seldom becomes more than a quarter-inch longer, and the appearance of a cone may represent a century of struggle.

This is the scrub forest—a rather prosaic name for the flower-rich growth mountains wear like leis around their necks. Whenever winter relaxes its grip, a mad succession of blossoms erupts at the edge of the retreating snow. Awash in meltwater, glacier lily and spring beauty emerge. Gentian, paintbrush, monkey flower, penstemon, and a profusion of others follow, each rushing to set seed before October sleet arrives. But even in the last days of September, when purple and yellow asters brave the growing chill, it remains June farther upslope: against the last ledge of sunken snow, spring's glacier lilies have at last appeared. Here beargrass, three feet tall and topped with tight clusters of creamy-white flowers, achieves its glory, growing in such numbers that the high slopes rival the snowfields in brilliance. Not a grass at all but a lily, this official park flower was given its name by Capt. William Clark—the Clark of Lewis and Clark—when he spotted some grizzlies in a beargrass field. While bears do in fact favor the new spring growth, it is the mule deer, which wander up into high meadows to spend the summer, that prize the big flower heads. All the plants on a mountainside may be decapitated by these relentless nibblers.

Sleeping sentries

The hoary marmot, largest of the rodent family, makes its home here, hibernating in burrows during the long winter. Draped over a sun-warmed boulder, this crafty mammal, with thick, grizzled yellowish fur, appears to be dozing, but it is acutely alert for any predator that might be near. As still as a statue, the marmot watches a golden eagle circle lazily overhead; if the eagle's wings were suddenly to fold, the marmot would be off the rock in a second, whistling a shrill alarm to be passed along from one marmot to the next. Cougars, wolverines, and grizzlies also haunt these slopes and can ambush the unwary with lightning speed.

Posing no threat to the marmots is the brief procession of bighorn sheep clattering past on the loose rocks above. Heads held high, their huge horns curled in a backward arc, the bighorn rams step with surefooted poise. The marmots will already be deep in their winter dens when autumn's first snowflakes signal the end of the rams' summer-long companionship and the start of their mating duels. Just as the lower valleys echo with moose calls, these high slopes will ring with the crash of horns during the weeks of battle among the males.

Alpine heights

From a distance, it seems that nothing grows at the very top of the peaks, which are alternately drenched in bright sunlight and cast in shadow by twilight and clouds. But in crevices, behind boulders, and between shards of fractured rock grow an amazing collection of hardy plants—an inches-high forest of flowers that survives intense sunlight, continual drying winds, and summer-long cycles of freeze and thaw.

The stems of the alpine pasqueflower, for instance, are thickly covered with soft hairs that protect them from being damaged by the sun. The matlike growth form of such plants as moss campion keeps them low and out of the wind while at the same time trapping precious grains of soil upon which they can build. Dryads—these roselike blossoms are named for the mythical wood nymphs—and others have evergreen leaves, which means they can photosynthesize just as soon as the snow around them has melted. The succulent-leaved stonecrop hoards water during the brief, wind-parched summer. Alpine buttercups burst into bloom while still in the snow, their waxy yellow petals helping to hurry the melt by capturing solar heat.

The only birds that remain on this alpine tundra year round are white-tailed ptarmigan, grouselike residents that grow new, differently colored feathers as the seasons change; so perfect is this chameleon trick that the ptarmigan might easily be mistaken for snow in winter or mottled brown rock in summer. Instead of flying south in autumn, female ptarmigan simply move down the mountain to the thickets of the scrub forest; the males remain high up despite fierce winds and blinding snows. During blizzard days they huddle together in snow dens, emerging after the storm to feed on wind-cleared slopes and doze in the meager warmth of the faint winter sun.

A plaintive bleat is sometimes heard in the thin, icy air—the voice of the pika, a small, tailless relative of the rabbit, scampering somewhere in sheltered tunnels beneath the snow. The provident pika sustains itself on miniature haystacks it has built under the rocks. Because it does not hibernate during the long alpine winter, it spends every waking hour of the growing season collecting and storing plants so that it will have enough to eat. Eventually a single individual may harvest a bushel or more of food—supplies with which to face the lean months ahead.

Glacier is in its essence a winter park. The summer gardens, brilliant but evanescent, are a flush of color and warmth in a land belonging to ice and snow. When winter overtakes the high canyons, the wind howls a victory from every crevice, and snow plumes swirl off cornices like clouds. Here the mountain goat, fearing little in this bleak, forbidding world, reigns supreme. With its specially designed hooves open for traction around nonslip pads, this marvelous animal moves as if weightless across spindle-thin ledges that seem far too steep and narrow to be traveled. Then it halts. Standing motionless, surrounded by an immensity of cold emptiness, its white, shaggy fur and long beard streaming in the wind, the mountain goat seems more a ghost from the Ice Age of long ago than a living, breathing mammal of our modern times. Perhaps its descendants will witness an awakening of the glaciers, a colder time when those thundering monsters will once again move across the land snuffing out flowers, felling forests, deepening meadows, and grinding mountains into valleys and peaks. Glaciers overran this land before, and they will do so again.

A turncoat with the turning of the seasons, the white-tailed ptarmigan sports snowy white plumage in winter and mottled browns in summer—the better to blend with its surroundings. Fringes of feathers on the toes form "snowshoes," another essential in the bird's winter wardrobe.

Only such winged creatures as the fulvia checkerspot butterfly, which lives on Indian paintbrush near both rims of the Grand Canyon,

Grand Canyon

"One cannot help but be in awe when he contemplates the mysteries of eternity, of life, of the marvelous structure of reality."
Albert Einstein

Mount Everest. The Sahara. The Amazon. The Grand Canyon. These are standards by which the earth's immense wonders are measured. They themselves defy human comprehension. Though people have mapped their surfaces and plumbed their depths, analyzed their climates, studied their histories, and catalogued the life they contain, they still numb the mind by the mere fact of their existence. The more you know about them, the more awesome they become.

The statistics about the Big Ditch (as Arizonans have been known to call their canyon) are stunning. To travel from end to end, including the narrow passageway called Marble Gorge, means a river journey of some 277 twisting miles, almost equal to the highway mileage from Chicago to Louisville, Kentucky. The distance between the walls ranges from 18 miles to less than ½ mile. In the awesome 10-mile-wide central section, the canyon averages a mile deep—4,700 feet from the South Rim, 5,700 from the North Rim. To travel from one rim to the other at this point, you must drive about 215 miles or walk at least 21 miles along steep trails; in the course of the arduous hike, you would experience at least four of the continent's seven life zones, the equivalent of a trek from the Mexican desert to the Canadian woods. Along the walls of the canyon, some 2,000,000,000 years of the earth's history have been laid bare by the driving, abrasive force of the Colorado River. To accomplish this erosive feat, the

can easily cross the vast expanse, seen here from the South Rim.

127

river has carried an average of 400,000 tons of silt per day through the canyon. (It would take 80,000 five-ton dump trucks to do the same job—that's nearly a truck a second.) There have been days on record when this incredible tonnage was multiplied almost seventyfold.

The Grand Canyon experience

All these numbers mean nothing at that moment when you find yourself abruptly at the canyon's rim. Without warning, the solid earth is gone, and reality crumbles beneath your feet. It is as though in a dream you have climbed a high mountain and you wake startled, teetering over empty space on the brim of a sheer cliff. You overlook a mountain range, but these are no ordinary peaks. Thrusting upward into the space before you, they shimmer and glow with colors from a surreal palette. Advancing into the hazy distance, they have the form and shape of architecture, of monumental sculpture. To name them, people have invoked the memories of ancient gods: Jupiter, Juno, Apollo, and Venus have temples here; and so do Vishnu, Deva, Shiva, and Brahma. There is an Isis Temple and an Osiris Temple, towers of Ra and of Set, Vulcan's Throne, Wotan's Throne, and the Freya Castle. There is no overstatement in these names. This grandest of canyons is the proper setting for the fearsome gods of old.

Small wonder that the first Europeans to view the mighty chasm, a group of Spanish conquistadores led by Don García López de Cárdenas, could not grasp its true magnitude. In search of golden cities, they had been led across the Painted Desert by Hopi Indian guides, who finally brought them to the canyon's steep South Rim. Like millions of visitors since that day in 1540, the Spaniards underestimated what they saw. After four fruitless days of trying to find a way down to the silvery ribbon of water flowing at the bottom, they gave up and left the canyon.

To look upon the canyon's immensity is to be awed, overwhelmed by unreality; to enter it is to be consumed by a very real world indeed. The way down is long and steep, not an afternoon's stroll. The lovely bands of color are sheer cliffs, or boulder-strewn talus slopes left by thousands of millennia of rockslides. The rocks are hard and sharp, and they sometimes give way underfoot. A delicate spire that you saw from the rim is, when you reach it, a towering monolith with automobile-sized boulders at its base. The deeper you go, the hotter and drier it gets. Tall ponderosa pines give way to twisted pinyon pines and junipers, and then to desert scrub. By the time you are deep enough to feel the horizons narrowing overhead, you have become just another small part of the canyon's vast totality.

The raging river

The easy way to reach the bottom of the canyon is to ride the force that is largely responsible for this vast wound in the face of the earth—the Colorado River. It is easy only by comparison, for the river is a great force

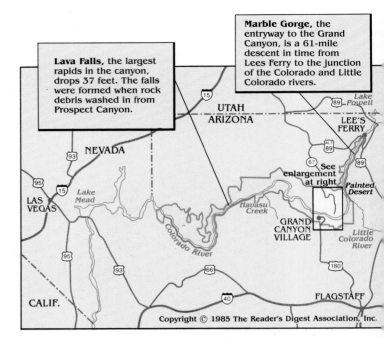

Lava Falls, the largest rapids in the canyon, drops 37 feet. The falls were formed when rock debris washed in from Prospect Canyon.

Marble Gorge, the entryway to the Grand Canyon, is a 61-mile descent in time from Lees Ferry to the junction of the Colorado and Little Colorado rivers.

indeed, and many rocky rapids fill its channel as it delves ever deeper into the bowels of the earth.

The Paiute Indians believed that, after the god Tavwoats had cut the canyon as a path to the joyous land beyond death, he filled the path with raging waters so that people could not flee the woes of the present world for the pleasures of the next. The Hualapai, however, who dwelt within the canyon, said that the river was the runoff from an earth-covering deluge like the one Noah knew; the canyon had begun, they said, when a hero named Packithaawi had struck deep into the earth with his knife to drain off the waters. The Havasupai, who still live in the canyon, also believed that the river was runoff from a giant flood, but they credited the river itself with cutting its own escape channel.

Until quite recently, scientists agreed with the Havasupai that the Colorado River—red and gritty with sand stripped from western Colorado and Wyoming, Utah, and much of New Mexico and Arizona—had cut like a rasp down into the Kaibab Plateau at the same speed that the land was being uplifted. That was the way that some of the river's gorges, including the looping canyons in Canyonlands National Park, came into being. But when scientists discovered that the Colorado has run through the Grand Canyon for only 5 to 10 million years, a problem was raised, because it was at least 65 million years ago that the Kaibab Plateau—the southernmost step of the Grand Staircase that starts with Bryce Canyon—began its slow, sporadic uplift. Thus, the canyon *cannot* have been cut solely by the erosive action of the Colorado. Many theories have been formulated to explain what really happened.

Currently popular is the theory of stream piracy that, like most of the Indian legends, also involves a great flood. This explanation supposes that, after its rise, the Kaibab Plateau separated two rivers. The one on the west drained into the Gulf of California, as the Colorado does today; the other, the ancestral Colorado, ran

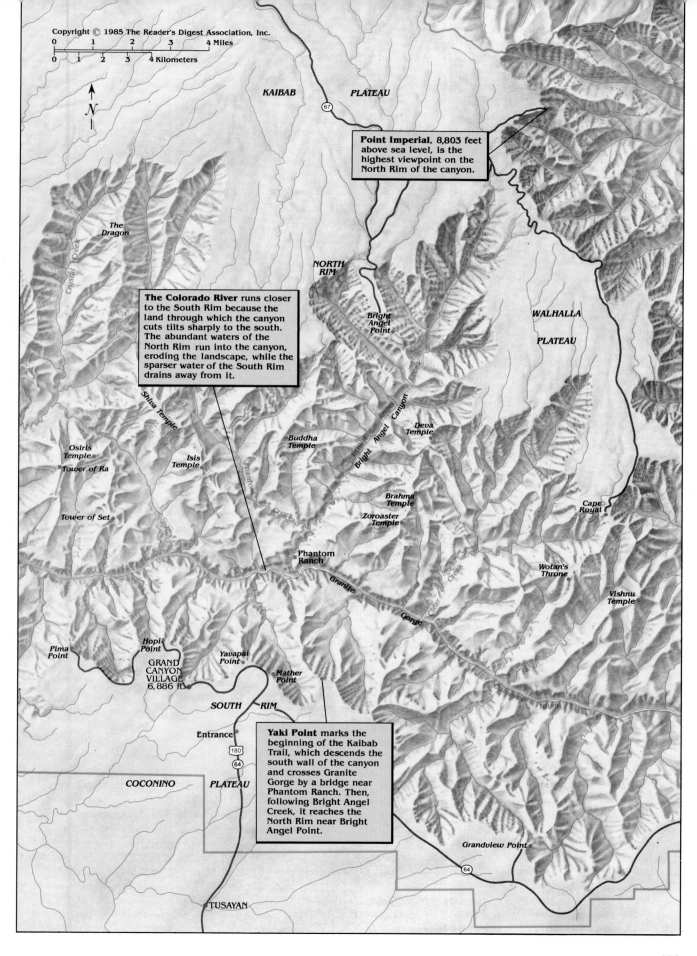

0 1 2 3 4 Miles
0 1 2 3 4 Kilometers

N

KAIBAB PLATEAU

67

Point Imperial, 8,803 feet above sea level, is the highest viewpoint on the North Rim of the canyon.

The Dragon

Crystal Creek

NORTH RIM

Bright Angel Point

WALHALLA PLATEAU

The Colorado River runs closer to the South Rim because the land through which the canyon cuts tilts sharply to the south. The abundant waters of the North Rim run into the canyon, eroding the landscape, while the sparser water of the South Rim drains away from it.

Shiva Temple

Bright Angel Canyon

Buddha Temple

Deva Temple

Osiris Temple

Tower of Ra

Isis Temple

Phantom Creek

Brahma Temple

Zoroaster Temple

Cape Royal

Tower of Set

Phantom Ranch

Granite

Gorge

Clear Creek

Wotan's Throne

Vishnu Temple

Pima Point

Hopi Point

Yavapai Point

GRAND CANYON VILLAGE 6,886 ft.

Mather Point

Colorado River

SOUTH RIM

Entrance

180

64

Yaki Point marks the beginning of the Kaibab Trail, which descends the south wall of the canyon and crosses Granite Gorge by a bridge near Phantom Ranch. Then, following Bright Angel Creek, it reaches the North Rim near Bright Angel Point.

COCONINO PLATEAU

Grandview Point

64

TUSAYAN

129

southeastward along the bed of today's Little Colorado, into the Rio Grande. A later uplift of land blocked the ancestral Colorado and formed a large lake. Meanwhile, the headwaters of the western river had been chewing backward through the Kaibab Plateau, as we see the Paria River doing today in Bryce Canyon. Finally, the plateau was breached and the Colorado was captured, to begin running through the canyon.

There are convincing arguments against this theory, and there are counterarguments to refine it. None of them add to or detract from the canyon's grandeur or the thrill of experiencing it from the river's perspective.

Backward in time

The river enters Marble Gorge, the Grand Canyon's magnificent foyer, from the north, diving between straight walls of grayish-tan Kaibab Limestone. Over the next 61 miles, the Colorado slices steadily southward and downward, its descent punctuated by sudden, sharp rapids. It also cuts backward in time through layer after layer of increasingly ancient stone, to a period more than half a billion years ago, before true fish swam in the sea. And faster than the river descends, the rock layers arise on either side, for the uplifted Kaibab Plateau bulges in a great hump toward the North Rim of the Grand Canyon, and Marble Gorge slices through this hump.

At about 225 million years of age, the Kaibab Limestone is the youngest rock in the Grand Canyon's walls. It is made of the remains of countless living things that rained to the floor of a sea that covered this place before dinosaurs walked, and it contains fossils of shellfish, corals, sponges, and sharks. It blends into an older limestone layer, called the Toroweap Formation, left by the life of an earlier sea.

As the river grinds its way down through the limestone, the walls rise straight and steep on both sides, channeling the sky ever tighter above. Before long, a dividing line appears at the water's edge. Below the line the walls are white, and though they rise as steeply as before, their texture is radically different. This is the Coconino Sandstone. It has no shellfish fossils, for it was left by a world of rolling dunes, where hot winds blew. Preserved in its textures are the tracks of reptiles, always scurrying uphill. (When one of them ran down a dune, its tracks were obliterated by sliding sand.)

Only about eight miles into the gorge, where Badger Creek joins the river, the steep white walls begin giving way to rubbly slopes, and the first serious rapids occur. This is no coincidence; here, the river has cut down to deep red Hermit Shale, made of mud and clay laid down on the floodplains of sluggish freshwater streams. Through this soft rock—colored by iron oxides, sprinkled with fossils of conifer needles, fern fronds, and giant dragonfly wings—the river slices a broad swath. The red slopes are littered with talus and boulders where the undercut sandstone and limestone have given way, and the narrow ribbon of sky spreads ever

wider above. Boulders, washed into the Colorado by Badger Creek, are the cause of the rapids; plugging the channel, they force the angry water to leap frothing over their backs. The red shale goes on for more than 16 miles, but only for half of that stretch does it form talus slopes. During the second half, the shale is interleaved with thin layers of sandstone and limestone that give it more firmness. This mixture is called the Supai Group, and here the canyon walls steepen again.

The Redwall

Near a furious place called 24½-mile Rapid, the gorge begins once more to close in. From here on, the river bucks and spews often, slicing down between hard, polished walls that arise fairly quickly, lifting the overlaying shale to a great height. They are of a strange stone, patterned and burnished, sometimes contorted by erosion into odd forms. It is the marble for which the whole of Marble Gorge was named by Maj. John Wesley Powell during his epic river journey. But the great explorer-scientist was mistaken; this is not marble but hard limestone some 300 to 345 million years old, the fossil accumulation from the bed of yet another shallow sea. Although the limestone is actually blue-gray, its surface is stained and mottled with runoff from the shales above, and so it is called Redwall Limestone.

It is in the firm, majestic corridors of the Redwall— shimmering with many tones of red, pink, and orange, underlain with brooding hints of deeper colors—that one begins to feel swallowed up, truly cut off from the flimsy world above, as much a part of the age-old interplay of rock and water as are the fossil seashells that the river has laid bare. There are caverns, caves, and occasional side canyons, and again and again there are rapids in the river. But the crashing white water no longer seems a foreign element; it is an integral part of the only reality that now exists, forever dashing itself into frothy spume against the seemingly eternal rock.

About halfway through Marble Gorge, where the Redwall cliffs are hundreds of feet high, is a spot that Powell described for all time: "The river turns sharply to the east," he wrote, "and seems enclosed by a wall, set with a million brilliant gems.... On coming nearer, we find fountains bursting from the rock, high overhead, and the spray in the sunshine forms the gems which bedeck the wall. The rocks below the fountain are covered with mosses, and ferns, and many beautiful flowering plants. We name it Vasey's Paradise, in honor of the botanist who traveled with us last year."

About 4,000 years ago, probably as part of a hunting ceremony, someone made figurines of animals—either deer or bighorn sheep—from split willow twigs, and then pierced them with miniature spears. The figurines were left buried under rocks in a deep cave near this place, 100 feet up the canyon walls, and there they remained until quite recently. They are the earliest signs yet found of humans in the canyon.

A short way downstream are niches 800 feet up in the

A redheaded western tanager refreshes himself in a small pool near the banks of the Colorado River. Though it regularly summers in the forests on and beneath the canyon's rims, like many birds in the park, it visits the river and its many small tributaries often. The great river, seen here from Toroweap Overlook on the canyon's North Rim, looks deceptively calm as it runs through the narrowest part of the Grand Canyon—the walls here are only a half-mile apart. The little riffles of white that seem, from 3,000 feet up, merely to brighten the water's surface are actually rapids.

Redwall cliff where the Anasazi of nine centuries ago stored grain. From about A.D. 500, their people—relatives of the "Ancient Ones" who built the great cliff dwellings at Mesa Verde—lived on both rims of the Grand Canyon. As the centuries passed and their civilization flourished, the population grew into the hundreds. They built homes and storehouses along the canyon walls. Crops of corn, beans, and squash filled every plantable plot. But sometime after A.D. 1150 they vanished from the Grand Canyon, as they did from dozens of places throughout the Colorado Plateau.

Lost eons

And still the river rushes onward, downward toward its junction with the Little Colorado—the beginning of the Grand Canyon proper. The base of the Redwall cliff rises from the riverbank atop another, older layer of sea-packed limestone, the Muav. Between the two limestones is a 150-million-year unconformity: a blank period when the land was above water and whole pages of the record were torn away by erosion. Something must have happened during all those millennia, but in Marble

Gorge the only signs that remain are a few pockets of lavender rock, called Temple Butte Limestone.

By the time the junction is reached, the Muav Limestone has itself risen, and the sloping walls of greenish-gray Bright Angel Shale, which holds fossils of crablike trilobites and other long-vanished creatures, have begun to blend into the underlying Tapeats Sandstone. Together, these three rock layers tell the story of a fishless ocean's long incursion from the west more than half a billion years ago: the sandstone was its invading beach and shallows, the shale its muddy offshore bed, and the limestone its depths. The changes from one layer to another are almost imperceptible. At the place where the Little Colorado adds its blue waters to the Colorado, the sandstone is still flaky with remnants of shale, and forms ledgy cliffs where tamarisks thrive.

If the geologists' theory of river piracy is true, then there must have been a precise moment just a few million years ago when the Little Colorado reversed its flow and, instead of filling the huge lake to the southeast, began to empty it. The process may have started with a trickle down a steep slope, but at some point the

131

trickle became a rush—a waterfall, perhaps, or a mighty cascade of rapids—that was to persist for a long time. It must have been a grand spectacle, this Niagara, cutting ever downward through layer upon layer of rock, diminishing itself by its own roaring power. If so, all sign is long since gone. There are not even rapids at the junction of the rivers now, only a sandbar where mingling sediments have settled.

It was near this junction, only two miles down the Colorado, that the Hopi Indians gathered sacred salt, which oozed from canyon walls and hung like stalactites. To reach it, they entered the canyon by way of the Little Colorado, past the great *sipapu*—a large mineral dome built up around a bubbling spring—through which they believed their ancestors had come into the world.

Today, the once-red Colorado River runs green through Marble Gorge, about 80 percent of its silt having settled to the bottom of Lake Powell, behind the Glen Canyon Dam that closed the tap upstream in 1964. It will only be a few centuries until the artificial lake that drowned Glen Canyon, that sedate and immensely beautiful chasm through which Powell passed on his way from Canyonlands to Marble Gorge, will be filled with silt. Then, red and abrasive again, the river will overflow the dam and resume its work. Meanwhile, the Little Colorado adds a small measure of cutting power before the river turns westward, to grind its narrow channel through the vast breadth of the central canyon.

After plunging for a few miles between firm walls of hard-packed sandstone, the river cuts through another unconformity, where the rock that would tell the story of the past is missing. Known as the Great Unconformity, it represents a staggering descent in time, a gap of 1,200 million years. During this vast span of eons, a complete mountain range arose and was worn back down to a plain, a sea advanced and laid down more than 12,000 feet of sedimentary rock upon that plain, those rocks were broken by earthquakes and reshaped into a landscape of low, rolling mountains and deep valleys, and *those* gentle peaks were eroded away. All that remains of the final mountains is a few isolated remnants of tilted stone wedged into the sharp dividing line between the ages.

There are no fossils in the black Vishnu schist below the Great Unconformity; although the first faint sparks of life had already been struck when this fire-twisted rock was formed, all record of it is gone here, destroyed by the immense heat that gave the rock its being. For nearly 200 miles, its primordial darkness lines Granite

Only among the ponderosa pines that grow on the North Rim of the Grand Canyon will you ever see a Kaibab squirrel, its ears lavishly tufted, its tail white, and its body black with undertones of gray and chestnut.

Gorge, rising to heights of 2,000 feet above the water, broken only by occasional veins of pink Zoroaster granite that boiled up from the earth's molten center when the planet was young and fierce.

Layers of life

Before the river makes its plunge into the earth's deep past, it crosses a stretch of tilted rock—called, aptly enough, the Grand Canyon Supergroup—left over from the last of the vanished mountains. Early in this interlude is a place where vistas open upon a rolling desert valley banked by low cliffs of sandstone. Atop these cliffs, slopes of greenish shale, interleaved with purple, flatten into a broad desert platform, where the Anasazi coaxed crops to grow near spotty springs. Beyond, wide bands of color rise in clear-cut layers along the sculptured temples and distant canyon walls.

The canyon's life is layered, too, though not with the precision of the bands of stone. As the elevation increases, so does the degree of moisture; and temperatures drop. The changing climate creates distinct zones, each a mesh of interwoven life where many plants and animals are confined by their needs and natures. The dividing lines are not sharp. The zones blend into each other, and many mammals and birds move freely back and forth. Differences in soil quality and exposure to the sun, and such vagaries as rising currents of warm air and invisible waterfalls of cool air, mean that the dividing lines are not constant either. But they are there, separating communities of trees and smaller plants, of insects, birds, and beasts.

The North Rim, the high point of the humped Kaibab Plateau, gets much more wet weather than any place else in the canyon—about 26 inches of precipitation per year, as against the South Rim's 16 inches. Summers are brief, but life is lush. A short distance back from the rim, mule deer browse in deep, still forests of spruce and fir. The spindly trunks of aspen trees grow arched and bent, in memory of the weight of 10-foot snows. Spotted coralroots and other wild orchids bloom amid dense stands of bracken fern on the mossy forest floor. Here and there, wild strawberries spread and white geraniums lift their delicately regal blossoms. Turkeys strut and porcupines waddle among blue columbines and larkspurs, and the hush is sometimes sweetened by the fluted song of a hermit thrush—or shattered by the strident chatter of a red squirrel, vehemently protesting the presence of a trespasser on its domain.

In places where the forests open onto broad mountain meadows, the yellow blossoms of mountain dandelions, owl clovers, buttercups, goldenrods, and salsifies make a brazen backdrop for the bright reds of Indian paintbrushes, skyrocket gilias, and scarlet buglers. Hummingbirds whir, and migrating monarch butterflies pause over fields of tall, orange butterfly weed to sip nectar and deposit eggs.

Near the rim itself, this verdant world blends into a drier, more open forest of ponderosa pines, much like the forest that covers the South Rim. Shrubby clumps of Gambel oak, mountain mahogany, locust, snowberry, and elderberry flourish among the copper-colored trunks of the tall, sedate ponderosas.

The ponderosa forests are home to two of the Grand Canyon's best-known animals: the Abert squirrel on the South Rim, and the Kaibab squirrel on the North. Both are striking tassel-eared squirrels—large tree-dwellers, with tufted ears and long, flowing tails—whose lives depend on ponderosa pines. They build their nests high in the great trees' crowns, and live largely on ponderosa seeds and twigs. Those on the South Rim look much like the tassel-eared squirrels found in ponderosa forests throughout the Southwest; though a few black ones appear, most are gray to dark reddish brown, with white bellies and salt-and-pepper tails. But the Kaibab

squirrels of the North Rim are quite different: black with pure white tails, they are the only squirrels of their kind in the world. They owe their unique qualities to their long isolation from their kin.

During the most recent Ice Age, when the climate in northern Arizona was much cooler and wetter than it is now, ponderosas grew deep in the canyon, and all the tassel-eared squirrels could mingle together and breed. But as the climate warmed and the land became more arid, the ponderosas were confined to higher elevations. The forests on the North Rim were isolated by the canyon to the south and by deserts in all other directions. Over the intervening 35,000 years or so, the tassel-eared squirrels in these forests, cut off from others of their kind, became a new kind of squirrel.

Beneath the rims
Below the lip of the canyon, the great trees, finding rootholds in crevices and on ledges, grow smaller, and the ponderosa forest itself is increasingly more sparse. By the time you reach the bottom of the thousand-foot cliffs of limestone and white sandstone that edge both rims of the canyon, you have entered a world where gnarled Utah junipers and pinyon pines clutch talus

Big-eared mule deer pick their way among pinyon pines and junipers along a limestone trail near the canyon's rim.

Although they prefer the forests near the rims, the gentle creatures may be seen almost anywhere in the park.

133

slopes of red shale. The pitchy, aromatic cones of the pinyons contain very large seeds called pinyon nuts, and when they ripen in late summer, the trees are aswarm all day with cackling squadrons of pinyon jays, gathering as many nuts as they can to store for the winter. Nervous pinyon mice, wearing their white feet like spats, take up the same task at nightfall, alert for the threat of a gray fox, kit fox, coyote, bobcat, or owl.

This pinyon-juniper woodland gradually diminishes as you descend the ledgy slopes toward the sheer Redwall cliffs. Brittle shrubs, such as the almost leafless Mormon tea and the desert thorn with its drooping flowers and knitting-needle spines, grow in shoulder-high clumps. Mule deer pick their way past shaley ledges, where mountain lions may lie in wait.

Although little seems to grow on the exposed face of the Redwall overlooking the desert platform hundreds of feet below, it is enough to support the bighorn sheep that live there. These regal creatures, crowned with massive, coiling horns, seldom leave the precipitous rock fastness where they alone can move with ease and grace. Their lives are a constant search for scraggly patches of pungent sagebrush, trailing four-o'clocks, white evening primroses, yellow-flowered cliffroses, and other bits of greenery on shelves and ledges.

The desert at the base of the cliffs is dry because it is hot—up to 35 Fahrenheit degrees hotter than the North Rim. Most of the rain that falls into the canyon evaporates before it hits the ground, and so only the river and its tributary streams support the kinds of life that need steady moisture. Away from these sanctuaries, plants are lean and mean, widely spaced, sparsely leaved, and often thorny. Tough blackbrush thrives, and so do

From its resting place on the branch of a juniper tree, a gray fox surveys the world. Found throughout the park, the lithe hunter lives mostly on such small prey as squirrels, mice, and rabbits, but also eats some fruit and berries.

shrubby catclaws, their grayish branches lined with the viciously hooked thorns for which they are named. Cactus wrens nest among the spines of chollas and other tall cacti. Grand Canyon rattlesnakes—found only here, where their pinkish scales blend into the colorful rock—wait patiently for cactus mice, jackrabbits, or lizards to venture within striking range.

At dawn, when the tang of creosote bush is strong in the air, pot-bellied chuckwallas—foot-long lizards whose blackish skin hangs like loose clothing—lumber from their hiding places to bask in the sun. When their body temperatures reach 100° F, they begin to look for buds, flowers, fruits, and juicy plant stems to eat. Although the vegetarian chuckwalla looks ferocious, it is a timid soul; if startled it scuttles into a rocky crevice and expands its body until it is wedged in tight. Coyotes have been known to defeat this strategy by thumping the lizards' noses until they back out of their nooks.

The living river

From the river's perspective, as it makes its brief passage across the broken rock between deep gorges, little of this life-and-death panorama can be seen. The flower stalks of century plants rise like distant flagpoles across the low valley, while the shorter stalks of yuccas, garlanded in white, look more like maypoles. And before very long, the entire vista is gone, shut out by the rising walls of the Inner Gorge.

Dropping a sudden 30 feet through some horrendous white water—Hance Rapids, rated 11 on a scale of severity that usually runs from 1 to 10—the river rushes headlong toward the dead black stone of Granite Gorge, where even greater rapids await. Though the Vishnu Schist of the gorge contains no remnant of ancient life, the river and its banks teem with the life of today. Ringtails hunt among patches of thorny mesquite, clumps of seep willows, and the ever-present pink-flowered tamarisk. River otters play and beavers build dugout dens along the bank (only in the calmest side streams are the busy, flat-tailed rodents likely to construct dams). Great blue herons stand among stretches of horsetail, patiently alert for the flash of fish or the twitching of frogs. Mallards, mergansers, and goldeneye ducks swim in stretches of calm water. Spotted sandpipers strut stiff-legged on the shore, and water ouzels bob and bow. Ospreys and red-winged blackbirds are among the other birds that stay near the water, but almost any bird in the park, from black-chinned hummingbirds to golden eagles, might be seen here. Chattering flocks of bushtits sometimes sweep in to pick for insects on shores and sandbars, and then are gone again in a nervous flurry.

But it is in the side canyons that the Grand Canyon's life is richest and most diverse. Each is different; all seem miraculous when the black depth of the gorge opens to them, as though life itself had suddenly been reinvented, fresh and new. Their freshness is made more poignant by the knowledge that, just beyond most

Idyllic in its setting between the Redwall Cliffs of Havasu Canyon, Havasu Falls splashes into a pool of turquoise water.

It is the second of lower Havasu Creek's three beautiful descents—Navajo Falls is above it, Mooney Falls below.

of them, rapids rage around and over rocks that were washed from these canyons.

The greatest of the side canyons, Havasu, is the home of the Havasupai, the last remaining Indian inhabitants of the Grand Canyon. Their village is a bit more than 10 miles south of the river on Havasu Creek, past a series of three waterfalls that tumble down the Redwall into pools of the most brilliant turquoise imaginable. *Havasupai* means "people of the blue-green water," and Havasu Creek is indeed blue-green like no other creek. It is the color of the sky, reflected and intensified by the hard white bed of the stream and by billions of white mineral particles suspended in the water. The minerals, contributed by the limestone through which the stream's water trickles before bursting from the Grand Canyon's south wall, build up on the bed in the same way that stalactites and stalagmites are built in such caves as Carlsbad Cavern.

Each of the three falls in lower Havasu Canyon is a glory. Together, they constitute a near-mystical experience. Their spray has created draperies of red stone, called travertine, on the adjacent Redwall cliffs. Around the blue pools into which they splash, amid maidenhair ferns, stream orchids, and a wealth of green, grow monkey flowers of red and yellow, stalks of blue monkshood and lupine, red columbines, and a rainbow of other blossoms. Bees bustle and butterflies glide and coast. Birds flash through the foliage like delicate fireworks: blue grosbeaks, goldfinches, orange orioles, red summer tanagers. The musical play of the falling water drowns out the memory of the Colorado's roar.

The fleeting life of Havasu Canyon is a bright counterpoint to the seemingly eternal blackness of the gorge into which its blue, blue waters run. The contrast is as much a part of the Grand Canyon experience as is the breathtaking view from the rim. The wonder of the Grand Canyon is that it is *not* eternal—not the forests of the North Rim nor the desert world of the canyon floor; certainly not the fragile pocket of beauty that lies nestled at the foot of Havasu Falls; nor even the black Vishnu Schist that the river carries, ever so slowly, away from the bottom of Granite Gorge. The Grand Canyon is a process. It is constantly growing wider as water eats at its rims, and its wondrous architecture is being relentlessly whittled away. If the process continues as it has, it will be only a few million years until the canyon has expanded to the point of nonexistence, leaving once more a level plain.

135

WYOMING

Grand Teton

"We would that you should stay here a while, . . . to solace yourselves with the good of these delectable Mountains."
John Bunyan, *17th-century author*

T o anyone who loves mountains, one name keeps coming to mind: the Tetons. The *grand* Tetons. For grand they are. While there are higher peaks elsewhere in the Rockies, none quite match the rugged majesty, the raw, wild beauty of this range. Bold, jagged spires of rock, the Tetons reach high into the Wyoming sky as if to snag the passing clouds.

The peaks are all the grander for their setting. To the east of the mountains lies Jackson Hole (fur trappers of the last century referred to mountain-rimmed valleys as "holes"). From this basin the Tetons rise abruptly, with no intervening foothills, to neck-craning heights—a solid mountain rampart towering some 7,000 feet above the valley floor. And then there are the lakes—Jackson Lake, Jenny Lake, and more. The mirrored images of the peaks in their waters seem to double the height of the mountain wall.

Winding through this lovely valley, like a silver thread of continuity, is the Snake River. A profusion of wildlife flourishes all along its course and throughout the park. Ospreys nest in the weathered skeletons of dead trees by the riverside, as do bald eagles. Otters

Rising like a wall from Jackson Hole, the craggy ramparts of the

Tetons seem to pierce the sky. A wealth of wildlife, from bears to bobcats, finds sanctuary in this mountain wilderness.

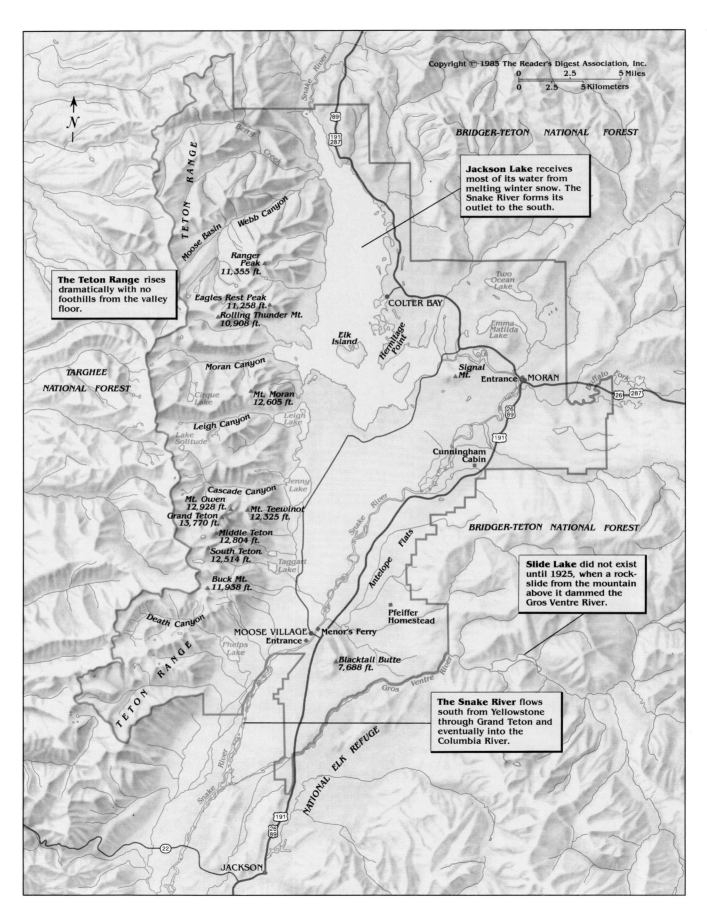

Copyright © 1985 The Reader's Digest Association, Inc.

0   2.5   5 Miles
0   2.5   5 Kilometers

N

TETON RANGE

BRIDGER-TETON NATIONAL FOREST

Jackson Lake receives most of its water from melting winter snow. The Snake River forms its outlet to the south.

Berry Creek

Moose Basin   Webb Canyon

Ranger Peak
11,355 ft.

The Teton Range rises dramatically with no foothills from the valley floor.

Eagles Rest Peak
11,258 ft.
Rolling Thunder Mt.
10,908 ft.

Elk Island

Hermitage Point

Two Ocean Lake

COLTER BAY

Emma Matilda Lake

Moran Canyon

TARGHEE NATIONAL FOREST

Cirque Lake

Mt. Moran
12,605 ft.

Leigh Lake

Signal Mt.

Entrance   MORAN

Buffalo Fork

26 287

Leigh Canyon

Lake Solitude

Cunningham Cabin

191

Jenny Lake

Cascade Canyon
Mt. Owen
12,928 ft.
Grand Teton
13,770 ft.   Mt. Teewinot
12,325 ft.
Middle Teton
12,804 ft.
South Teton
12,514 ft.

Snake River

Antelope Flats

BRIDGER-TETON NATIONAL FOREST

Buck Mt.
11,938 ft.

Taggart Lake

Slide Lake did not exist until 1925, when a rock-slide from the mountain above it dammed the Gros Ventre River.

Death Canyon

TETON RANGE

Phelps Lake

MOOSE VILLAGE
Entrance   Menor's Ferry

Pfeiffer Homestead

Blacktail Butte
7,688 ft.

Gros Ventre River

The Snake River flows south from Yellowstone through Grand Teton and eventually into the Columbia River.

Snake River

NATIONAL ELK REFUGE

191
26 89

22

JACKSON

138

With pinions spread against the icy air, a trumpeter swan wings across a winter-white landscape. Named for their booming trumpetlike calls, the big, graceful birds, once near extinction, have found sanctuary in several parks.

play on the riverbanks or glide gracefully through the water. Along tributary streams, the small ponds created by beavers are favored feeding spots for moose. The great beasts are often seen standing flank-deep—sometimes even neckdeep—in the ponds, munching on aquatic plants. The park's lodgepole pine forests are home to elk and mule deer, while the sagebrush flats of Jackson Hole are preferred by pronghorns. Black bears wander through the valley forests and on the lower mountain flanks, and grizzly bears are sometimes sighted in the northern reaches of the park. Coyotes, mountain lions, lynx, martens, bobcats, badgers, and a host of smaller animals also find refuge in this rugged wilderness. And above it all, always there, looming over the scene, sensed even when hidden within a shroud of clouds, are the Tetons, the newest of the many ranges that make up the Rocky Mountains. Less than 10 million years old, geologically the Tetons are mere babes; the rest of the Rockies average 60 million years in age.

Youthful mountains, ancient rocks
Five to nine million years ago there were no mountains on this spot. The landscape of what is now western Wyoming was a gently undulating plain, partly forested, partly covered with lush grasslands.

Though it must have seemed a peaceful scene, there was an ominous flaw: trending north-south across the countryside was a zone of weakness in the earth's crust, an area some 40 miles long. The birth of the mountains probably began with modest tremors that culminated in a violent earthquake, the result of a slippage of the rocks on either side of the fault. As the land shuddered in the quake, a great block of the earth's crust to the west of the fault tilted slightly upward. The land to the east simultaneously slipped down.

Birds and beasts no doubt fled in terror as the earth trembled and a great growling roar filled the air. Then when the quake ended and all was still again, a new feature marked the face of this land—a ridge. Even if a comprehending mind had been present to witness these events, however, it is doubtful that this relatively small disturbance of the earth's crust would have been recognized as the first stage in the creation of a massive mountain range.

Centuries may have passed before the earth quaked once again. There may have been days and weeks of nearly constant tremors, followed by decades or even centuries of quiescence. But with each new upheaval, the steep escarpment that was to become the eastern face of the Tetons rose higher into the sky, and the floor of the future Jackson Hole slipped slightly downward.

Neither the number nor the magnitude of each one of these mountain-building crustal movements is known, but the accumulated results over millions of years were truly staggering: scientists estimate that total vertical

Spring in a Teton Pond

While snow still clings to the rugged peaks, the warm sun and lengthening days of spring bring a burgeoning of life to the Tetons' wetlands. Like many other ponds in the high country, this one owes its existence to the activity of beavers, whose sturdy dams maintain the water level. A single beaver (1) is up and about on this bright day; the rest of the colony is probably dozing inside the big domed lodge, awaiting dusk to emerge and feed. Gnawed stumps of moisture-loving aspens all around the pond are evidence of their feeding forays.

Many kinds of animals move in to take advantage of the beaver-built ponds. A belted kingfisher (2) rests on a branch protruding from the beaver lodge, ready to plunge headfirst into the water if it spots a fish. The great blue heron (3), in contrast, stands immobile, waiting for fish or frogs to come within reach of its sharp beak. Nearby, a marsh hawk (4) glides slowly past, scanning the ground for frogs, mice, and other small prey. Another hunter, the mink (13), is an excellent swimmer that nabs its victims both underwater and on land.

Just as beaver kits are born in spring, so too are the young of the visitors to the pond. The moose and her calf (6) have ventured into the shallows to feed on water plants, while a common merganser (5), trailed by her fluffy ducklings, swims across the pond. Near the dam a spotted sandpiper (7) and its downy chick have left their nest to explore for insects and other morsels. A western toad (10) that has only recently changed from a fishlike tadpole to a creature with legs and no tail lurks among the plants.

A variety of other life adds color to the scene. The yellow warbler (14), a lover of damp places, pauses in its quest for insect food, which might include the common blue butterfly (8) resting near the yellow-flowered Oregon grape (9). At the edge of the stream, small-flowered woodland stars (11) and blue violets (12) supply colorful accents among the pervasive greens of spring.

141

displacement along the fault has been about 30,000 feet. Why, then, do the peaks rise only 7,000 feet above the valley floor today? This has happened because, though the upheavals were intermittent, erosion has been constant. Ever since that first little ridge appeared across the landscape, running water, seasonal freezing and thawing, and other forces of erosion have been grinding away the newly exposed rocks and depositing much of the debris on the subsiding valley floor. Over the eons, thousands of feet of sandstones, limestones, and volcanic rock layers have been stripped away. What remains today is primarily massive formations of granite, gneiss, and schist that once lay hidden deep beneath the surface of the earth. Born of intense heat and pressure in the earth's interior, these ancient basement rocks are about $2\frac{1}{2}$ billion years old.

Tough and resistant as this steel-hard bedrock may be, it too has succumbed to the forces of erosion, especially moving ice. Two times in the last quarter-million years, worldwide climatic changes have resulted in extensive glaciation over much of North America. During these glacial periods the summer sun no longer melted all of the winter's snow and gradually, over the centuries, large ice fields accumulated among the peaks and sent glaciers spilling down the slopes. Moving slowly but steadily under their own ponderous weight, the glaciers chipped and scoured and scraped away at the hard granitic rocks, sharpening and faceting the peaks into those jagged forms that are so familiar today: Mount Owen, Teewinot Mountain, Middle Teton, South Teton, and towering above all the rest, the majestic spire of Grand Teton.

The first visitors
Today only a few small reminders of those once massive glaciers are found in the Tetons, tucked here and there among the peaks. As the last glaciers receded back into their mountain refuges more than 10,000 years ago, it is possible, even likely, that human beings were on hand to observe their retreat. Within sight of the Tetons on the Snake River plain in Idaho, archeologists have discovered evidence of human habitation dating back about 10,000 years, to the very brink of the Ice Age. In more modern times the region has been home to such Indian tribes as the Shoshones, the Blackfeet, and the Gros Ventres. Like their counterparts on the plains, the Indians in the area were nomads, following the annual game migrations and establishing seasonal encampments. Jackson Hole was a buffer zone between territories claimed by the various tribes.

To the Shoshone these mountains, known as *Tee-win-ot* or "many pinnacles," were presumed to be the dwelling place of holy spirits. The modern name Tetons was bestowed by a party of fur trappers approaching the mountains from the west in 1819. Their first glimpse of the range revealed three prominent, pointed peaks, which caused some Frenchmen in the party to name them *Les Trois Tétons* ("The Three Breasts").

But the very first white man to visit the Teton country, it is said, was one John Colter. A bold adventurer, he was a member of the Lewis and Clark expedition, which had crossed the uncharted territory of the northern Rockies to the Pacific and back between 1804 and 1806. On the return journey, apparently still eager for adventure, Colter left the expedition to join two fur trappers bound for the unexplored upper reaches of the Yellowstone River. Subsequent wanderings apparently led him to Jackson Hole in 1807, where he no doubt gazed up in awe at these stupendous mountains, as impressed by their beauty as any visitor ever since.

The great beaver bonanza
Within a few years of Colter's discovery, other trappers followed in his footsteps, ushering in the fabulous era of the mountain men. The influx began slowly, dictated by a whim of fashion. In Europe and in the cities of the eastern United States, felt hats made of beaver fur had become the rage. Fortunes were to be made by those fearless enough to risk the dangers of the Rocky Mountain wilderness in order to trap the region's plentiful population of beavers. Luck played a role too, for many left the mountains the way they entered: broke.

An innocuous advertisement that appeared in a Missouri newspaper in 1822 did much to spark the invasion. A fledgling fur company, the ad announced, "wishes to engage one hundred young men to ascend the Missouri" to the Rocky Mountains, to be employed as hunters. Unmentioned were the incredible dangers and hardship the men would face.

The first to sign on were mostly greenhorns, but many would survive to become legends. There was Jedediah Smith, who would later buy out the trading company and still later pioneer new routes to California. Jim Bridger, an apprentice blacksmith when he joined up, became one of the toughest mountain men of all; wounded by a Blackfoot, he carried the offending arrowhead in his back for several years before a missionary finally removed it. Thomas "Broken Hand" Fitzpatrick was another; the crippling wound responsible for his nickname did nothing to impair his aim. And then there was David Jackson, who would leave his name on the valley he loved most, Jackson Hole. By the late 1820's several hundred of these indomitable mountain men were roaming this mountainous wilderness, some working on their own, others in the employ of the Rocky Mountain Fur Company, the Hudson's Bay Company, or John Jacob Astor's American Fur Company.

Theirs was a tough and dangerous business. Potential hazards lurked in ambush at every river crossing, every mountain pass, every bend in the trail. An unwary trapper might drown in a swollen river, freeze to death, or even, on occasion, starve. One trapper, Hugh Glass, was dreadfully mauled by a grizzly and left for dead by Jim Bridger and another companion. The victim recovered, and vowed vengeance on his former friends for abandoning him, but he never carried out his threat.

The greatest danger, however, came from Indians, the result of a tragic incident that occurred when Lewis and Clark were homeward-bound in 1806. A member of the expedition killed a Blackfoot Indian who was stealing rifles, and from that time on the Blackfeet and their allies became mortal enemies of all white men. More than a few trappers lost their scalps, sometimes while still alive. The trappers, in turn, reacted just as brutally. Most had a collection of topknots—Indian scalps—tied to their waistbands as evidence of their own cruel lust for revenge.

Forced to adapt to this wild and hostile environment, the mountain men developed skills that, at times, seemed to surpass even those of the Indians. They were a thousand miles from civilization and any mistake could be fatal—a rifle dropped in a river, a bone-breaking fall from a horse, or an overly smoky campfire that might tip off Indian raiders. The most successful mountain men—the ones who survived—seem to have developed a sixth sense, a fine attunement of body and mind to every wilderness sign and signal. Camped in Jackson Hole, a trapper learned to watch the game herds for any unusual movement that might warn of approaching Indians. While standing in a stream to set his traps, he took note if so much as a willow twig floated by: it might signal the presence of a hunting party nearby.

Like the Indians, the mountain men were nomads, seeking waterways where beavers were plentiful and moving out when the massive rodents were trapped out. Once a year they held an annual rendezvous, a month-long affair that was payday, trading mart, celebration, and three-ring circus all rolled into one. The wagons and pack trains of the various fur trading companies would arrive at the rendezvous site laden with whiskey, gunpowder, and such necessities as flour and bacon to be traded for the year's catch of furs. Friendly Indian tribes frequently joined the encampment and shared in the revelry. Even among rival fur companies there was camaraderie. The men raced horses. They drank. They played pranks. They vied with one another at telling the tallest tales. And in general they enjoyed high jinks to celebrate the survival of another year in the wilderness.

Tough and rowdy the mountain men undoubtedly were. But the few who could write recorded another side to these irrepressible adventurers. Warren Angus Ferris, a trapper for the American Fur Company, observed of his companions, "A strange, wild, terrible, romantic, hard and exciting life they lead, with alternate plenty and starvation, activity and repose, safety and alarm, and all the other adjuncts that belong to so vagrant a condition in a harsh, barren, untamed, and fearful region . . . . Yet so attached to it do they become that few ever leave it." Yet by the mid-1840's all the

A riot of color sweeps across mountains and meadowlands when the displays of wildflowers in Jackson Hole are at their peak. The parade of blossoming begins in the lowlands in early spring and continues until the first frosts of autumn. In addition to bright golden, daisylike mule ears and dainty wild geraniums, the park's wildflowers include Indian paintbrushes, monkey flowers, lupines, larkspurs, and scores of other species.

mountain men were gone, victims of another change in fashion and of their own success as trappers—the beavers were nearly gone as well.

Symbols of the season: cygnets and calves
Today the beavers have recovered and are once again splendidly plentiful in Teton country. The region's wild beauty continues to attract new generations of human visitors. The new breed, however, comes not as trappers but as hikers, as sightseers, and as lovers of untamed nature.

Time has done nothing to temper the magnificence of the mountains. And the climate, of course, remains as harsh and unrelenting as ever. "There ain't but two seasons around here, pardner," goes an old saying; "winter and a few muddy days of melting."

But if winter is indeed the longest season, spring is the most uncertain. As the sunlit days gradually grow longer, all life seems poised as if awaiting a signal to begin renewal. Flowers may be blooming elsewhere, but snow still swirls about the peaks and lies deep in Jackson Hole. There may be a week of warm and balmy weather, only to be followed by yet another snowstorm. Gradually, however, winter releases its icy grip. A meadow that was covered with snow one week becomes a swale of brown, matted grasses the next, and a few days later it has been transformed into a luxuriant carpet of fresh green growth.

Thousands of elk congregate at the southern end of Jackson Hole each winter to escape the deep mountain snows. Now, as the snow melts off the south-facing slopes, they begin their annual migration north into the high country, following the snow line as it recedes.

Abristle with quills, the porcupine is sluggish—but why should it hurry? Few predators dare meddle with this nocturnal, tree-climbing mammal.

Gathering in small bands, the cow elk, which are smaller than the bulls and have no antlers, seek out high mountainsides where there is a mix of open meadows for grazing and forest for cover. Here the gold-spotted calves are born in May and June. Spindly and awkward, the young are vulnerable to coyotes, mountain lions, and other predators during their first few weeks of life. For protection, the cows instinctively stay together in groups. Both bull and cow elk will remain in the high country until the deepening snows of late autumn drive them down to lower elevations once again.

As the color of renewed life spreads across the sagebrush flats and the bottomlands of the Snake River, birdlife becomes more prevalent. Sage grouse begin their noisy courtship dancing. Ducks and geese return from balmier winter quarters in the south. And trumpeter swans, which spend the winter in nearby streams and lakes with open water, prepare for another breeding season. Once on the verge of extinction, the big elegant birds found sanctuary in Grand Teton and Yellowstone national parks, and their numbers now seem secure. Pure white, with long, straight necks, the trumpeters are frequently seen gliding effortlessly over the surfaces of the many small ponds in the park. They build massive nests of dead vegetation and line them with down plucked from their breasts. The female lays five to seven eggs, usually in late May, and both parents share in the chore of incubation. Within hours of hatching, the young cygnets, pale gray and fluffy with down, follow the adults in search of aquatic plants and other food, awaiting the time when they will be able to take flight on their own in the fall.

The pace of life of the park's beavers also quickens in spring. Dependent on an abundance of aspens, the massive rodents generally build their dams across streams that are bordered by extensive stands of these slender, white-barked trees. They fell the trees by gnawing with their sharp, chisellike incisor teeth, then cut them into sections and make tangles of branches, tree trunks, and mud to block the flowing water. The beavers feed on the tender twigs and bark of aspens and willows and store larger branches underwater for a winter food supply. Out in the ponds the animals build large dome-shaped lodges with underwater exits and entrances. These impregnable fortresses protect the beavers from various predators and also provide snug, secure retreats during the long mountain winters.

Winter in summer
Summer in the Tetons is marked by an explosion of color as wildflowers burst into bloom: yellow mule ears and arnica, red Indian paintbrush, blue lupine. Eventually warm weather returns even to the high country. At places like Lake Solitude, perched high in the mountains on the North Fork of Cascade Canyon, spring finally arrives around the Fourth of July. Snowbanks may still rim the lake, but yellow glacier lilies are blooming within inches of the melting snow as though impatient to end their long winter's dormancy.

Even in summer there may be brief relapses into wintry weather. Storms sometimes swirl about the great mountain peaks and leave them mantled beneath a light dusting of snow. But always the weather breaks and bright sunshine quickly melts the snow, sending the accumulated trickles downward toward the valley.

The valley of Jackson Hole also endures the fury of occasional summer storms. At places like Leigh Lake, nestled near the base of Mount Moran, the morning may dawn clear, bright, and cloudless. The lake is a mirror—smooth, taut, unrippled—that perfectly reflects trees, mountain, and sky. By midmorning a few shreds of cloud may begin drifting over the peaks, and a light breeze ripples the lake. But the sun remains hot, and the sky gives no hint of trouble to come.

By early afternoon, puffy cumulus clouds begin to coalesce into huge, ominous thunderheads that tower above the peaks. Distant rumbles come down the canyons that crease the slopes, while the clouds change from white to forbidding black. Just before the onslaught the air turns still. Then as the storm approaches, winds roar down the canyons and blast lake and forest alike. Jagged forks of lightning streak in quick succession across the now darkened sky, and the thunder is no longer a distant rumble but a series of sharp nearby explosions. Fortunately these summer storms are usually quite brief, and within an hour or so the sun is shining once again. The clouds may cling to the peaks for a time, but by evening they become a tattered shroud that the setting sun illuminates with a dazzling burst of color.

From autumn gold to winter white

As autumn approaches, thunderstorms become less frequent, and the days are often clear from dawn to dusk. Now begin the annual courtship and mating rituals of the three local members of the deer family: mule deer, moose, and elk. All the males are fully antlered and regal in their autumn attire. One of the characteristic sounds of the season is the high-pitched trumpeting or bugling of the bull elk, a sound that serves as a warning or challenge to other bulls. Each male rounds up a herd of cows and vigorously defends his harem from rivals. Keeping the harem together is not always easy, however; the females seem to delight in running off and joining neighboring groups.

Autumn in Jackson Hole has other special qualities. Brilliant yellow aspens stand out boldly against the backdrop of the Tetons, which usually are already lightly dusted with snow. In some years the balmy days of Indian summer linger long after the leaves have turned and fallen from the trees. In other years heavy snows begin while the trees are in full color.

When winter comes, it brings a time of quietness and dormancy. Bears that grew fat on berries and other foods throughout the autumn now settle down for their long winter sleep in snug hollows beneath trees or in caves dug into hillsides. The elk return to the valley where the snow is not so deep as in the high country. Even in the lowlands, however, the snow may pile up to depths of three feet or more. Elk and deer alike must paw and dig for what meager forage they can find.

Frequently the mountains are hidden from view by dense clouds as storms assault the rocky crags. Occasionally there is the distant rumble of an avalanche thundering down the slopes. But normally it is quiet. Finally the clouds that have cloaked the peaks for days are dissipated. The dawn breaks on a crisp, cold winter morning and the jagged spires are there again—brilliant, fresh, clean, and pure white against a deep blue sky. As if in celebration of the sun, coyotes yelp and howl. A herd of elk, shaggier now than they were in summer, stand huddled in the valley, steam rising from their bodies in the warming rays. Patiently they wait, as if aware that soon the cycle of the seasons will come round once again to spring. And throughout it all, towering above Jackson Hole, there stand the mountains, the Teton Range, eternal monuments and monarchs of this precious wild place.

By early September, bull elk are resplendent in full racks of antlers. In this, the mating season, their resonant bugling calls announce the approach of winter.

Great Basin

"Life is not crowded upon life as in other places but scattered abroad in spareness and simplicity, with a generous gift of space for each herb and bush and tree."

Edward Abbey

A vast and lonely sunbaked land, the giant shallow bowl of the Great Basin extends across Nevada and reaches into five neighboring states. Far from uniform, the basin consists of desert flats punctuated by a series of north-south mountain ranges. Geologists call it the basin and range region. Most of the mountains rise high enough to catch moisture from the air, so that barren slopes are transformed into verdant oases with streams and lakes watered by the runoff from glistening snowcapped peaks.

The most spectacular part of the Great Basin, the South Snake Range, is the heart of this new national park. About 30 miles long and up to 14 miles wide, the range hosts a startling diversity of living things, arranged in varying horizontal layers, or life zones, and stacked high. A trip to the range's top, one observer noted, is like traveling from Arizona to Canada—from desert to alpine heights—all within 10 miles. Filled with such wonders as the world's oldest living tree species, huge underground natural sculptures, and Nevada's only glacier, this park offers surprises at every level.

Surviving where few other plants can, sagebrush covers the desert floor with a sea of gray-green leaves. The roots of this stubby evergreen grow wide and deep, searching for and absorbing any available water; silvery

gray hairs on the narrow leaves conserve moisture. The plant's rich, pungent aroma perfumes the air and lingers in the memory as a sharp remembrance of the West's desert wilderness.

Growing well into the foothills, where more moisture falls, sagebrush becomes luxuriant, with a silver-green color that contrasts with the dull hues of its lowland kin. Chipmunks, gophers, and jackrabbits seek shelter from coyotes and other predators under the intricately twisted branches.

Here, at 6,000 feet, larger plants are able to take root. Pinyon and juniper trees form a pygmy forest no higher than 40 feet, where long-eared mule deer browse on rabbitbrush in winter. Shoshone and Paiute Indians who lived in this region relied on the pinyon pine's sweet-tasting nuts as a source of food, and used its sap for waterproofing baskets and as glue for moccasins.

The pygmy forest stands guard outside a giant marvel: Lehman Caves, one of the most intimate and elaborately decorated caverns in the West. Narrow, twisting passageways connect spacious rooms that bear such fitting names as Grand Palace, Sunken Garden, and Gothic Palace. Filled with an incredible variety of stone sculptures, the cavern is a fantasy world created by nature—formed over thousands of years by untold drops of mineral-laden water.

As rain and meltwater from snow and ice seeped underground, they dissolved the underlying rock, hollowing out the cave. This seeping liquid was not, however, pure water; it was dilute carbonic acid (formed when water absorbs carbon dioxide from plant material near the surface), strong enough to dissolve the marble bedrock. You can still see patches of the blue-gray marble on the cave ceiling where it has not been covered by decorations. The acidic water carried the dissolved calcium carbonate (the mineral that makes up marble) into the cavern and deposited it as crystals, slowly building up the fantastic formations you see today. Still at work, nature continues to add to her creations and to begin new ones, ever changing her subterranean showcase, drop by drop.

Climbing to the top

Above the pygmy forest, at about 8,000 feet in elevation, you enter the realm of mountain mahogany, a shrub with hard, reddish wood. Climb just another 1,000 feet, and you find yourself in cooler air, surrounded by the sweet resinous smell of spruce-fir forests and aspen groves (their leaves turn the autumn hillsides a blazing gold). Fed by melting snows, ice-cold streams twist and tumble their way through the forests. You might even spot a bighorn sheep, a species reestablished here in the early 1980's.

Higher still, at about 11,000 feet, you approach the tree line. Stunted limber pines ring the shores of crisp blue alpine lakes nestled in beautifully carved glacial basins. Snow lies like a mantle on the mountains' shoulders. Yellow asters, lupines, and shooting stars grace

Sharp-shinned hawks swoop from the shoulders of Wheeler Peak, which presides over a contrasting world of desert and mountain.

unspoiled meadows during the brief summer, a crowning glory to the procession of color that has climbed up the slopes since spring.

At the very limit of the tree line, the park reveals its most prized treasure: three separate groves of bristlecone pines—the oldest living tree species on earth. Many bristlecones appear lifeless. Small, gnarled, and often mostly denuded of bark, the stunted branches reach upward as though clawing at the sky. Large areas of tree trunk have been baked by the sun and burnished by brutal winds, snow, and ice to a striking golden hue. Only on close inspection do you discover small patches of bark here and there and clusters of sharp green needles. Scanty clues, indeed, to the fact these trees are alive and growing—and some have been doing so for more than 4,000 years!

The secret of such longevity lies in the bristlecone's ability to adapt to a harsh and inconstant climate. During severe winter weather and prolonged annual droughts, most of the tree dies; just enough needles are left for photosynthesis to sustain life. (In warmer, wetter times, more needles develop.) Bristlecone needles survive some 15 to 30 years. This long duration is nature's method of conserving energy, since the tree does not have to grow as many new needles each year. In addition, the bristlecone's resinous wood protects the tree against disease. Even the arid alpine air is turned into a positive force: it helps preserve the trees from rotting.

Above the patriarch pines, you reach the snowy spires of the South Snake Range. Looking west from its highest pinnacle, Wheeler Peak (13,063 feet), you can view the almost endless march of desert and mountain, alternating across the basin, stretching into forever. In this wilderness, remote and rugged, nature proves once again that life is indomitable.

147

Great Smoky Mountains

"Nearly always there hovers over the high tops and around them, a tenuous mist, a dreamy blue haze . . . . Beyond is mystery, enchantment."

Horace Kephart, *folk historian*

Few mountains anywhere in the world are more aptly named than the Great Smokies. Rank upon rank of smoothly rounded ridges recede toward the horizon like shadowy silhouettes, their contours blurred during the summer months by an ever-present haze—the product of incalculable quantities of vapor exhaled into the air by the luxuriant mantle of forest that covers these well-watered slopes.

Time has gentled the ancient Smokies (they are among the oldest mountains on earth), softening their outlines as erosion works its magic. Yet the heights are still impressive: 20 peaks rise to elevations of more than 6,000 feet. Tallest of all is Clingmans Dome, near the very center of the park, at 6,642 feet.

On the heights are forests that seem strangely out of place in the South—a touch of Maine that is a remnant and reminder of the bygone Ice Age. During the thousands of years in which the northern part of the continent was locked in the grip of ice, the climate here was much cooler than today. As the glaciers advanced, cold-loving evergreens gradually extended their range farther and farther to the south. Then, as the Ice Age came to an end and the climate warmed, these forests receded toward the north—except on the mountain slopes, where they found the cool, moist growing conditions they require. And there they remain to this day, covering the ridgetops with the year-round greenery of red spruce and Fraser fir.

Rainbow Falls is one of many cascades that interrupt the descent of the Smokies' singing streams. Soggy nooks along their courses are often brightened by orange jewelweed and other water-loving plants.

Dampness is pervasive on these heights: showers are always imminent, fog a constant companion. Moss grows everywhere, and wood sorrel spreads its delightful blossoms over the forest floor. The calls of winter wrens and the scolding of red squirrels—wildlife more typical of Canada and New England than of the South—echo through the trees. Otherwise only the sighing of the wind interrupts the silence.

Spring on the summits is brief, summer is damp and cool, and autumn is almost nonexistent. By October the highest elevations have already felt frost, and the first icicles are forming on rocky cliff tops. Through November and early December the weather is indecisive: one day it is warm and hazy, the next day a howling wind pulls a shroud of clouds across the peaks, and on the third morning the trees glisten with a coating of rime. Finally the snows begin.

Even this far south, winter stakes out a claim—and often does so with force. Storms carry moisture hundreds of miles northward from the Gulf of Mexico and dump it on the Smokies. At lower elevations a cold, drizzly rain sometimes falls for days, feeding the streams until their roar fills every valley. On the ridges the moisture falls as snow, sometimes in big, wet flakes but often in fine, stinging, wind-driven granules. When the storms pass, warm Gulf air is replaced by frigid blasts howling their way southward from the interior of Canada. The trees moan under the assault of the wind. Clouds rip through the gaps, limbs snap in the gusts, and temperatures plummet, sometimes reaching –20° F in January. During these bursts of Arctic fury it seems as if the ice ages have once again returned, if only for several days or weeks. Finally toward mid-February

149

Rhododendrons are the crowning glory of the heights when they blossom in June and July. But they are only the icing on the cake; more than 1,500 species of flowering plants thrive in this mountain sanctuary.

warm spells become more frequent. But winter does not give up easily at these elevations. Though spring has been creeping up the slopes since late February or early March, it does not scale the summits until May.

Beauty and the bees
On a few high ridges, forests are interrupted by openings known as balds. In some, tangled shrubbery takes the place of trees; others are grassy. Both offer superb vistas, but only the grass ones are welcoming, their thick, luxuriant carpet creating the perfect resting place. Along the edges of the openings the forest begins hesitantly with a flowery fringe. Bees buzz around azalea and rhododendron shrubs, creating a subtle background music as they work the blooms for nectar. The fragrance of fir and of flowers drifts across the balds, mixing with the smell of warm, dry grass. Beyond, the mountains' hazy contours fade in the distance.

Despite the best efforts of science, the origins of these grass balds are still a mystery. Forest fires may be responsible for some of them; unusual conditions of wind, moisture, soil, and sunlight could account for others. What is certain, however, is that 200 years ago the mountains were balder than today, probably because grazing by herds of elk and bison—and later, by domestic stock—kept them free of trees. When the national park was established in the 1930's, the sheep and cattle were removed, and forests began to reclaim the openings. They have done their job well. Only a few balds remain, and whether these will survive can be answered only with the passage of time.

The woodland mosaic
As centuries passed and the climate warmed at the close of the Ice Age, rain replaced snow, and streams began dancing down the mountains, twisting their way between great gray boulders that had been cracked from the slopes by relentless freezing. In only a short time, perhaps a mere thousand years or so, the Smokies began to resemble the mountains we know today—mountains with a delightful array of forests of all different sorts. Oak and hickory, mixed together with pine, ungrudgingly contribute their gifts of acorns and nuts. In general such stands are confined to low elevations where thin soil and direct sun combine to rob the land of moisture. Quite different—but found just around the bend on the moist, cool, shady side of many a ridge—is another kind of forest, dominated by hemlocks. In mature forests these evergreens are huge, creating a moody sort of place where fog drifts among the branches and filters the morning sun into shafts of light and shadow. Little else grows within their world: the only shrubs that seem to thrive beneath the large old hemlocks are rhododendrons.

Growing from 2 to 20 feet in height, in some places rhododendrons form all but impenetrable thickets; stems and trunks are so intertwined that few creatures will attempt to pass through the tangled growth. This is especially true where rhododendrons and a few related shrubs grow not beneath taller plants but in solid stands of their own. Scientists know such places as heath balds; local people call them laurel slicks. From a distance, they look like open hilltop meadows where the grass is just right for resting. But this is pure illusion, as anyone who struggles up to one quickly realizes. The first few steps into the thicket, even one that is only chest-high, require the strength of an ox. In taller tangles, forward movement is all but impossible. The branches are tough: they grab, they scratch, they whip. Even the most persistent soon give up, realizing that a laurel slick is more prison than refuge.

Rhododendrons have their redeeming qualities, however: beauty and, in this park, abundance. In early summer the ridgetops are brightened by the great reddish-purple flower clusters of the catawba rhododendron. Each cluster is a bouquet some six inches in diameter, and each shrub bears dozens of bouquets. For generations people have made pilgrimages to these natural gardens, knowing that to see the rhododendrons in full bloom is to witness the wild glory of the high Appalachians at their best.

During July the thickets at lower elevations come into their own with the pinkish-white flowers of the rosebay rhododendron, by far more common in the park than the catawba rhododendron. In winter the long, waxy leaves of both species serve as natural thermometers, drooping as limp as the ears of a basset hound when the temperature nears zero. Nothing looks so forlorn as a rhododendron thicket in cold snow—yet no plants contribute more to the summer splendor than rhododendrons and their smaller relatives, azaleas and mountain laurel.

Dogwood and opossumwood

Of all the forests in the Great Smokies, one in particular seems to evoke a sense of awe: the broadleaf forest that claims the valleys and low mountain slopes with the richest soil, abundant sunshine, and just the right amount of rain. In those favored places, called coves, grow some of the largest trees, shrubs, and vines in the eastern United States. Among the astonishing variety of species, yellow poplars (or tulip trees), with trunks more than 20 feet around, are commonplace. Cucumber magnolias—the "cucumber" is the fruit—shade the woodland floor with leaves the size of platters. Wild cherries spread fruit-laden branches high above the forest floor, and scaly-barked old maples set the autumn air aglow with their gloriously colored leaves.

May is perhaps the finest time in the cove forest. As it awakens to returning warmth, green—pale, delicate, soft green—reclaims the forest from the browns and grays of winter. Dogwood and silverbell (opossumwood to those of a more zoological bent) come into their white-blossomed glory; lit up by the sun, they seem almost incandescent. On the forest floor, wildflowers weave lovely tapestries, with violets, white trilliums, and bluets randomly crowded between mossy logs and towering trees. Butterflies explore the various blooms, fragrances fill the air, and birdsong blends with the sound of water trickling from springs or cascading down creeks swollen with clear, sparkling snowmelt.

Farther up the slopes, where springtime arrives later, the trees are not so tall, straight, or widely spaced. Yellow birches, oaks, beeches, and buckeyes—trees typical of southern New England or the Midwest—mingle in this broadleaf forest. In the higher reaches the slopes sometimes appear covered with late snow as tiny white spring beauties bloom by the countless millions. Mixed with them are lemon-yellow trout lilies, large white trilliums, ruby-colored wake robins, and the tall green spires of false hellebore.

Of bears and boars

This green Eden once had wolves, elk, and bison roaming the slopes. Possibly gone now too is the cougar, or mountain lion, the great tawny cat that to many symbolizes the essence of wilderness. More than 50 years have passed since a cougar was killed, captured, or

"Beware" is the message of a mother bear as she places herself between her cub and any hint of danger. A diligent parent, she will tutor her offspring for the first two years of its life. Bears young and old climb trees.

even photographed in the Smokies. Yet reports of sightings persist. And some claim to have heard their blood-curdling screams in the night, a sound that once heard is never forgotten.

But if the cougar is more shadow than substance in these ancient hills, bears remain to beckon and reward. All the bears in the Smokies are black bears. Weighing up to 350 pounds, they have black fur, brown muzzles, and an unblinking gaze that seems to scrutinize everything. Bears are curious. Their greatest interest is in finding food, a job for which they depend on their highly sensitive noses. Shambling along, they look and they listen, but mainly they follow their noses, sniffing here, there, and everywhere. Anything that smells good to a bear, it wants to eat: honey, of course, but also berries, roots, and even carrion.

Most of the time bears move slowly, but if the need arises, even the slowest becomes a blur of fur. To see a fully grown individual shoot up a tree trunk with the agility of a squirrel is, to say the least, impressive. Bears learn at an early age to climb at their mother's command and to stay put until the all-clear signal is given. As adults, they use their tree-climbing skills to raid the hives of wild bees and to forage for fruits and nuts.

They take to the trees in winter too. Contrary to popular belief, bears in the Smokies most often den, not in a cave or hollow log but high in a cavity where a large old tree has lost a limb. They climb in, curl up, and settle down for a snooze that lasts from November until March. The bears do not actually hibernate. The heart rate does not slow down nor the body temperature drop as they do in woodchucks and other true hibernators. Bears simply sleep deeply, maintaining their life processes at only slightly reduced levels as they live on stored body fat.

Black bears mature at 2 years, and by the time a female is 3½ she is ready to mate. Cubs, usually twins, are born during the mother's winter sleep, normally in January or February. Blind, hairless creatures that weigh a mere eight ounces or so at birth, they grow steadily, nurtured by their mother's milk. By the time the mother is ready to leave the den, the cubs have grown to frolicsome, utterly appealing bundles of fur. They spend the next two years with the mother, learning the ways of the woods, and then finally are driven off to fend for themselves.

While bears are a natural part of the Great Smoky Mountain forest, European wild boars are another story: they were accidentally introduced into the park in the early 1920's, apparently when some escaped from a game preserve. Visitors are unlikely to see the boars; during the day they remain in hiding, alert for the slightest sound, testing the breezes for the scent of man. But evidence of their destructive activities is everywhere. Large, powerful animals with strong snouts and sharp tusks, these lanky, long-haired pigs wander the forests by night, wallowing in springs and streams and ripping up large tracts of land in search of food. As many as 2,000 of these bristly, animated bulldozers may be roaming the Great Smokies, but nobody really knows how many there are.

Memories of long ago

Man too has left his mark on the landscape. When the national park was established, humans had lived in these mountains for many centuries. First to come were the Indians and then, two centuries ago, the first white settlers arrived. The mountain people lived quietly, maintaining themselves on small farms and gathering what they could from the land. Later, timber companies removed vast tracts of the original forest.

In nature, however, such setbacks are only temporary. Trees have returned to the abandoned fields and cutover tracts, so that these areas now support vigorous young forests. In valleys and on rugged slopes that escaped the loggers, even some of the towering monarchs of the original forest remain.

Though the years have been few since this healing began, traces of man's handiwork have become cherished treasures rather than wounds. Embankments ascending wooded valleys are remnants of old roads or the railroad beds from logging days. Stone walls mark the boundaries of former croplands and pastures. Where apple trees cling stubbornly to life in the forest, they reveal the locations of vanished orchards. Here and there are the crumbled foundations of houses and barns, often surrounded by a few tenacious shrubs or garden flowers—especially daffodils—that speak of simple pride in home and hearth.

In a few park locations, however, it is possible to savor the rural landscape of pastures, farmhouses, churches, and country stores—and to imagine a way of life—as they existed two generations ago. Best known by far of several such historical areas is Cades Cove, a broad, fertile valley hemmed in by mountains. Pastures and croplands still stretch across the valley slopes, revealing broad vistas of farmlands and forested mountains. Cattle range over the pastures; log cabins and weathered barns, white churches and simple cemeteries, dot the roadsides.

At first glance Cades Cove seems to be a living community. But no one has lived here since the 1950's—though it is only at dusk that this becomes apparent. No lights appear in the cabins or barns. No conversations drift through the warm, still air. No gospel hymns sound from the churches. Except for the lowing of cattle, there are no sounds of rural life. The mood of the place is almost elegiac, yet there is joy in the confidence that its past will remain untouched. Elsewhere across the lowland, up the narrowing creek valleys, and on to the high ridges, the human past is disappearing. The returning forests are slowly, inevitably covering the tracks of man and returning the ancient mountains to the natural inhabitants.

Imagine Cades Cove as it might appear on a warm, muggy evening in July. In the distance, high above

With 27 different species, ranging in size from two-inch pygmy salamanders to grotesque two-foot hellbenders, the Smokies are the salamander capital of the country. The sleek red salamander (left) and the somewhat chunkier marbled salamander (above) are among those that can be found lurking in moist places throughout the park.

Thunderhead Mountain, sunlight is reflected—appropriately—from a lone thunderhead, creating a suffused glow that softens the features of everything it touches. It is the time of shadows, neither daylight nor darkness.

Along the edges of the forest a few quail continue their *bob-white* whistles. Insects hum in the still air; locusts buzz in the sweetgum trees. Occasionally the cloud trembles with lightning, and low rumbles reverberate across the valley. A crow caws from an old maple as if signaling for silence. Darkness thickens now; it is becoming difficult to make out the shapes of the black Angus cattle on the pastures. Bats fly past in endless, veering circles. Somewhere far off in the forest whippoorwills are beginning to call.

There are more shapes in the meadows now. Gradually, as if materializing from nothingness, dozens of deer are emerging from the forest to feed. Within the forest, too, activity increases. Soft sounds await those willing to stop and listen: raccoons and skunks exploring, foxes searching for mice, rabbits nibbling nervously in the starlight, opossums trundling through the undergrowth. Gradually the whippoorwills grow quiet, their plaintive calls replaced by the hooting of owls. Over the mountains the atmosphere is cooling, and the lightning finally flickers one last time.

After midnight and toward the small hours of the morning the mountains float on a sea of mist. In the darkness, fireflies drift through the undergrowth and across the fields, glowing like particles of primordial energy. There is an eternal quality about the night, an evocation of the wilderness heritage that endures. Sanctuary has been provided, and the great rounded ridges, softly luminous in the starlight, belong to the ages. Here a remnant of lost, wild America still lives on.

Guadalupe Mountains

"The hills and gulleys bore the appearance of having been created by some vast, fierce torrent . . . as if nature had saved all her ruggedness to pile it up in this colossal form."
Waterman Ormsby, *reporter, New York Herald, in 1858*

The Guadalupe Mountains are outlandish. It is hard to believe that a single gigantic piece of an ocean reef could have become stranded on the dry flats of west Texas; yet here the mountains stand, mile-high remnants of a vanished sea, thrust bodily upward from deep beneath the desert where they had lain buried for longer than 100 million years.

That this forbidding limestone outcrop supports a richly varied community of life is surprising. Yet wildflowers burst from rocky hillsides in springtime like bright pins from a pincushion. Chipmunks scurry among ferns and pines all summer, and the foliage of aspen, maple, oak, and ash colors the autumn. Deer browse and mountain lions stalk year-round, and an abundance of birds fills the air with song.

It is not so surprising, given the isolation of the place and the harshness of the desert around it, that the history of the Guadalupes is dominated by the sagas of desperate people. Foraging nomads, renegades, treasure hunters, bandits, outlaws—all have found refuge in this isolated bastion. Few, however, left enduring traces of their passage. There are signs of Indians who hunted bison and mammoth as long as 10,000 years ago, but so subtle are they, like the whisper of a moccasin on pine needles, that only a keen and knowing eye will find them. Even a comparatively recent stagecoach station,

once surrounded by stone walls, has been reduced to remnants. The Guadalupes hold their secrets well.

The range forms a great V, the arms extending northward into New Mexico (Carlsbad Cavern lies beneath one of them). Looking southward from the point of the V is the sheer face of El Capitán. At 8,085 feet (more than 2,000 of them straight up), this great ocean-built rock is not the highest mountain in Texas—that title belongs to nearby Guadalupe Peak—but it is certainly the most dramatic. For more than 50 miles you can see it shimmering in the desert heat, a monolithic landmark guiding travelers to a rich and rugged oasis.

The Capitán reef

Most of the fossil reef of which the Guadalupes are a visible part still lies buried thousands of feet deep. Seen on a geologist's map, the reef is a long, almost-complete oval defining the shoreline of a shallow sea that once covered 10,000 square miles of what is now Texas and New Mexico. That was some 230 to 280 million years ago, long before birds, mammals, or flowering plants had appeared on earth.

The climate was warm and humid. Low hills rimmed the horizon, but otherwise the land was flat, and water lapped gently along the shore. Lime-secreting algae flourished in the sea, and as they died, their remains were washed shoreward, where they accumulated. Living algae began to inhabit the limy mass, gluing it together with their own secretions. Other kinds of primitive ocean life lived on the reef, and with the help of minerals precipitated from the water, their bodies were incorporated in its fabric. With the infinite patience of

A beacon visible for 50 miles across the flat desert terrain of west Texas, the rugged face of El Capitán has guided travelers for centuries to the rich oasis of the Guadalupe Mountains, where the tawny mountain lion reigns supreme.

nature the structure grew upward and seaward until eventually it was more than a mile wide and hundreds of feet high, its top just below the water's surface.

The two sides were distinctly different. On the steep seaward side, where waves constantly tore at the reef, great chunks of limestone were broken off; they rolled down the slope into deeper water, creating a layer of rubble, or talus. On the shoreward side, where shallow lagoons formed, slow-moving streams deposited sediments, and so the lagoon floor remained almost level with the growing reef.

As the climate changed, the streams dried up and the sea level dropped. The lagoons became stagnant and salty; gypsum, salt, and other sediments built up at a faster and faster rate until they were completely filled in. Meanwhile, the sea itself had receded, leaving the reef high and dry, no longer alive, its steep slope coated with salt. After a few million years, the seabed, the lagoons, and the reef between them were all buried beneath a flat plain. And so they remained for more than 100 million years, entombed beneath layers of rock and soil that eventually reached a depth of thousands of feet.

Some 10 to 12 million years ago a great shifting of the earth's surface took place, part of the ongoing process that had begun with the upheaval of the Rocky Mountains. The basin that had held the ancient sea was tilted and uplifted. The Capitán reef was cracked and fractured in places, and one 40-mile-long piece of it—the part that we call the Guadalupe Mountains—was exposed. On the southeast, which had been the seaward side, the Guadalupe ridge marks the dividing line between the soft deposits of the seafloor and the harder limestone reef. On the west, where the reef was sharply broken in the upward thrust, limestone palisades rise almost a mile above broad salt flats.

The canyon oases
As the reef was being pushed up, cracks developed, and many of these, with the aid of erosion, became deeply incised canyons. These canyons are now the special wonder of the Guadalupes. In some, springs arise to feed streams that pause in limpid pools, forming cool and fragrant oases. Mosses cling to rocks, and flowering shrubs scent the air. Birds become intoxicated on the shrubs' overripe fruits and splash among watercress, valerian, and groundsel at the water's edge. Elsewhere, water seeps through cracks in sheer canyon walls to nourish hanging gardens, where mats of Venushair fern, wild orchids, and other delicate plants cling to moist limestone ledges, in glorious contrast to dry and rocky slopes that may be only 100 feet away.

In McKittrick Canyon, nearly five miles long and several thousand feet deep, there exists a blend of life unlike that found anywhere else on earth. Along its floor, in which you can see the bed of the 250-million-year-old sea, an underground stream surfaces from time to time, and where it flows, its banks are shaded by

a mixture of deciduous trees—velvety ash, bigtooth maple, oak, and walnut—that turn the canyon into a tunnel of red and gold in autumn. Bittersweet, chokecherry, striped coralroot, and wild roses compete for the patchy sun.

Along the limestone walls, pockmarked with caves, are hanging gardens that include species of mint, honeysuckle, and columbine unique to this place. Mingling with this lushness are yucca and cactus from the desert, as well as pines and firs that usually grow at higher elevations. Here, too, grows the odd and beautiful Texas madrone tree, its reddish bark looking like well-worked leather as it curls loose from the gnarled trunk, exposing young, pink bark beneath.

McKittrick Canyon was named for a Civil War veteran, Capt. Felix McKittrick, who moved to this area after the war and worked for a time in ranching. (He later moved on to Arizona, where another canyon was named after him.)

Much of the credit for protecting the canyon's pristine beauty goes to Wallace Pratt, a petroleum geologist who was smitten by its charms. Pratt first visited the canyon in 1921, escorted by a friend who had assured him that it was "the most beautiful spot in Texas." When he saw the place, Pratt enthusiastically agreed, and he eventually bought a sizable tract of land in the canyon.

Pratt built a rustic stone lodge in the canyon, where he and his family and friends found refuge from Houston's summer heat and humidity. Though he always referred to the building as the Stone Cabin, it is now known as Historic Pratt Lodge. It can be reached by a moderately strenuous hike along the creek that flows through McKittrick Canyon.

The Pratts later built a permanent home, Ship on the Desert, on a mountain slope outside the canyon. When they finally retired to Arizona, they turned their holdings over to the National Park Service, thus ensuring permanent protection for this uniquely beautiful treasure in the desert.

A blend of life
The canyons are by no means the only refuge of life in the Guadalupes. The range is a connecting link between the Rocky Mountains, the Chihuahuan desert of Mexico, the grasslands of the Great Plains, and the deciduous woodlands of the east. Dozens of plants and animals from all these diverse habitats mingle here, many at the edge of their natural ranges.

On rocky hillsides and mountain slopes, chickadees, grosbeaks, and finches dart from pinyon pine to Rocky Mountain juniper to Texas madrone. At higher elevations, where aspens light the slopes with clear yellow flames in autumn, red-shafted flickers shoot like arrows through forests of Douglas fir, limber pine, and ponderosa pine. Here, early on a spring morning, the wild tom turkey, iridescent in the sun, gobbles his brassy invitation to the hens of his harem to come from their treetop

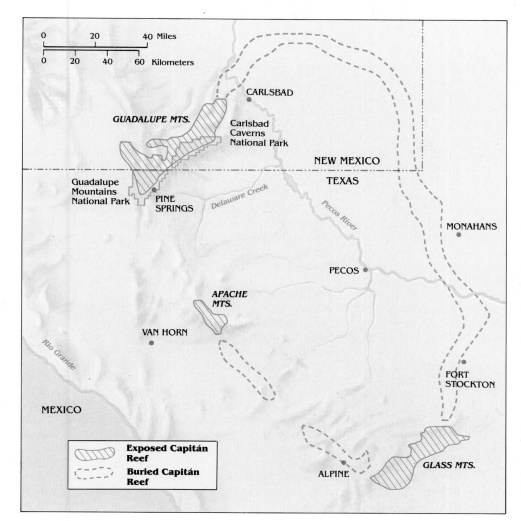

Such delicate fossils as this chambered nautilus, bespeaking the life of the ancient sea in which the Capitán Reef was formed, can be found throughout the Guadalupes, from the deepest canyons to the highest peaks. Most of the best-known fossil reef on earth still lies buried beneath the deserts of Texas and New Mexico. The Guadalupe Mountains, in which two national parks are located, is the largest exposed portion.

perches and join him in foraging for seeds and insects.

From the high desert to the south come spotted cactus wrens, and from the mountains come smaller, mottled rock wrens; both fly low to the ground, swooping up to alight on magenta-flowered chollas or clumps of prickly pear, with pink, orange, and yellow blossoms aglow like a captured sunrise. Scott's orioles can often be seen performing gymnastics to extract the nectar from cream-colored yucca blossoms. Although the bright yellow birds are drawn to the sweet yucca nectar, they play no part in pollinating the flowers; that job can be done only by a small white moth, performing one of nature's strangest rituals.

Emerging from their cocoons at the same time that yucca flowers open, the yucca moths mate. Then the female flies to a bell-shaped yucca blossom, where she rolls together a ball of sticky pollen. This she carries to another flower. After laying four or five eggs in the second flower's hidden heart, she forces the pollen ball down inside the blossom, ensuring cross-pollination. By the time the eggs hatch into caterpillars, the plant's seeds are developing. Each caterpillar eats about 20 seeds before the fruit matures, then they all burrow out, leaving about half the seed supply to produce more plants. The moths eat nothing else during their lives.

For centuries, the yucca supplied desert-dwelling Indians with food, drink, fiber, and soap. But it was the agave, also known as the century plant or mescal, that was the true staff of life. No part of the plant went to waste. The leaves yielded fiber for mats, sandals, baskets, and clothing; their hard, sharp points became needles and awls. The fruits and flowers were often eaten raw, and the milky juice was fermentated to produce a strong liquor. For the most part, though, flowers, stalks, roots, bulbs, and seeds were all roasted and stored for food. Hundreds of mescal-roasting pits have been found in the Guadalupes—some left by nomadic Basketmakers as early as 1000 B.C. and others by Mescalero Apaches (named for the plant that nourished them) beginning about A.D. 1400. The technique changed little over the centuries: first a shallow hole, 2 to 12 feet across, was lined with stones, and a fire built to heat the rocks; then the mescal was placed on the hot rocks, covered with sand, and allowed to roast.

King of the mountain

The undisputed ruler of this world is known by many names: cougar, panther, painter, puma, screamer, catamount (short for cat-of-the-mountains). All refer to the mountain lion. To hear its night call emerge from the forest like the scream of a woman in pain is to understand the meaning of primal fear. Few people hear its other call, a soft whistle, and fewer still are ever likely to see one of the great cats on the prowl.

Elusive and solitary, a mountain lion may cover 20 to 25 miles during a night's hunt, winter and summer. Mule deer are its preferred prey, although elk or bighorn sheep are not scorned. Hungry lions have also been known to dine on lesser prey, including skunks, raccoons, porcupines, rabbits, chipmunks, and squirrels—as well as such smaller predators as foxes, coyotes, bobcats, and even other mountain lions. Whatever the prey, a lion stalks carefully and patiently, keeping downwind and under cover until it is as close as possible, then making a sudden leap. Landing on a large animal's back, it breaks the neck with its powerful jaws or with a forepaw, then drags the carcass to cover. Though only about 5 feet long (not counting the black-tipped tail) and up to 200 pounds in weight, an adult lion is capable of carrying the body of an animal much

Spring and summer are sunny, lively seasons in McKittrick Canyon, but it is the autumn—when maples, oaks, and other deciduous trees brighten the air beneath towering pines and around spring-fed pools—that is the canyon's glory.

larger than itself—even of leaping upward several feet with a full-grown deer in its jaws.

Mountain lions are not monogamous. They meet and—after an athletic courtship ritual that involves chasing each other up and down trees and rolling about in mock battle—they mate. From that point on, the family is the female's problem; indeed, it is said that she must protect her cubs against hungry males. Three is the usual number of cubs in a litter, but anything from one to five is possible. Weighing only about a pound at birth, the furry kittens are blind for a few weeks and dependent on their mothers for almost two years. Then, when they have learned to hunt and are big enough to fend for themselves, they go off on their own, generally staking out territories many miles away.

The Pinery

In 1858, at the mouth of Pine Spring Canyon, where dense stands of ponderosa pines grew around a pure, fast-flowing spring, an entrepreneur named John Butterfield established a stagecoach station he called the Pinery. Built of the native limestone, it was almost as much a fort as it was a station. The 11-foot stone wall around it had only one entrance, and that was protected by a log stockade. A ditch brought water from the spring 300 feet away. A crew of six to eight men was kept on hand to serve as cooks, mechanics, blacksmiths, wranglers, and—in case of need—fighters.

The Pinery was only one of 140 such stations that Butterfield established along a brand-new stagecoach trail that ran from St. Louis to San Francisco, by way of Arkansas, Oklahoma, Texas, New Mexico, and Arizona. It became the most historic station of them all, for it was near here, under the brow of El Capitán, that an eastbound stage was to meet a westbound stage for the first time, marking the start of regular mail and passenger service across the North American continent.

The Butterfield Line's leather-lined coaches, pulled by four mules or horses, could carry nine passengers and 600 pounds of mail, but the only passenger on that first westbound stage, which left St. Louis on September 15, 1858, was a young reporter named Waterman Ormsby. In his dispatches back to the New York *Herald*, he described being bounced on a hard seat, even thrown against the sides and roof of the coach.

As Ormsby's stage approached the Pinery on September 28, the driver stood and blew a trumpet, a signal that was to become familiar at stage stations throughout the west. The station cook got a meal of venison steak, beans, and biscuits on the table, and while Ormsby and the crew ate, a fresh team of horses was hitched up. After dinner, the stage set out over Guadalupe Pass, just west of the station: "The road winds over some of the steepest and stoniest hills I have yet seen," Ormsby wrote, "studded with inextricable rocks, each one of which seems ready to jolt the wagon into the abyss below.... The great peak towers as if ready to fall at any moment." To add to Ormsby's apprehension, the

Seen across rolling dunes of white gypsum sand, the sheer western face of the Guadalupes glows in the sunset. Next to El Capitán, the mountain at the right of the escarpment, is 8,749-foot Guadalupe Peak, the highest point in Texas.

driver pointed out the grave of a Mexican guide who had been killed by Apaches.

Soon after darkness had fallen, Ormsby and the crew heard voices ahead. Their minds filled with thoughts of Apaches and bandits, they braced themselves for attack. Instead, they met the eastbound stage, which had left San Francisco on the day after they had left St. Louis. Surely the two relieved groups of men realized what a historic moment had just occurred, but they had deadlines to meet—Butterfield's contract depended on getting both loads of mail through in 25 days. And so, after brief congratulations, they hurried on their ways.

For 11 months the Pinery was a busy place. Four stages a week came through, two from each direction. Express riders stopped at all hours for fresh horses and quick meals. Pioneers, miners, and military men paused for shelter and food. Even after Butterfield had abandoned the route for a safer one 50 miles to the south,

travelers continued to use the station, until at last it fell into disrepair. Today, only one wall and some stone foundations remain, marked by a bronze plaque.

Even Pine Spring Canyon has a forsaken feeling; in 1931 an earthquake caused the spring to dry up. Now sun-loving penstemons, Indian paintbrushes, bright-flowered cacti, pinyon pines, junipers, and Texas madrone trees grow where water plants once flourished around clear, shady pools. Still, the soft call of the mourning dove wafts like a soothing benediction through the morning air, and at night the mockingbird turns the songs of the day into a lullaby. Here, among these great blue-gray crags, where the works of man are swallowed up like pesty intrusions, is the perfect expression of life's delicate, yet enduring balance. The Guadalupes show their gentle nature only to those plants and animals that belong here, and to the human who seeks and appreciates the blessing of solitude.

159

Haleakala

"It was a scene of vast bleakness and desolation, stern, forbidding, fascinating. . . . a workshop of nature cluttered with the raw beginnings of world-making."

Jack London

Sunrise comes early to the summit of Haleakala, the magnificent dome-shaped volcano towering over the island of Maui. Before the eastern sky has begun to lighten, sunrise watchers stand shivering in the cold, foggy air at the crater's rim after having driven up the twisty mountain road from the coast. Cold and drowsiness, however, are quickly forgotten when the first rays of the sun break through the sea of dawn-red clouds, illumining the mountain's splendor. As the shadows retreat, details in the dark recesses of the crater wall come into view, and a gigantic bowl, filled with strange and unearthly shapes, is unveiled. Dawn here is not just a new day but a whole new world.

Ancient Hawaiians named this mountain Haleakala (pronounced holly-ah-ka-lah), meaning "House of the Sun," and told a legend about how the mischievous demigod Maui tamed the sun. A long, long time ago, there were only three or four hours of daylight because the lazy sun hurried across the sky to return home for a long night's rest. Since the days were so short, Maui's mother could not dry her fabric, which came from plant fibers, in the sun. She appealed to her son for help. Maui studied the situation and observed that the sun rose over Haleakala by snaking one long beam and then another over the crater's rim, the same way a spider climbs onto a ledge. So one night Maui took a sack of rope snares and hid in a cave near the summit. As each of the sun's legs appeared over the edge, he threw a rope around it and tied them all to a wiliwili tree. The sun begged to be released, but Maui first made it promise that, if freed, it would always move slowly and steadily across the sky. And so it has done ever since.

Perhaps the sun has settled down, but the rain still needs a talking-to. Its handiwork is most uneven: one side of the mountain is drenched with rain, while the summit and the other side are virtual desert. Blowing from the northeast, moisture-laden trade winds water Haleakala's eastern flanks, pouring more than 250 inches of rain a year on the dense, junglelike forests of the Kipahulu Valley, which stretches like a swath of green velvet from the crater's rim to the shore. By the time the winds reach the peak and cross over to the west, they are nearly drained, offering only light sprinkles to the hardy plants that survive on the parched, arid slopes. Clouds circle the mountain from 4,000 to 7,000 feet like a thick, smoky ring. Above them, the weather is mercurial: the summit can be calm and brilliantly sunny or stormy with heavy winds and torrential rain. In winter, a dusting of snow sometimes gifts the heights with a thin, white carpet.

Inside the vast crater, which plunges more than 2,500 feet toward the heart of the mountain, the scene is starkly beautiful, a lunar landscape softened by cinder cones and lava sculptures streaked with reds, yellows, and browns. Age for the moment has turned this crater cold, but its contours are permanent reminders that it has been seared by fire and flame.

Volcanic islands, such as Maui and the others in the Hawaiian chain, begin life when magma—molten rock that forms in very hot places deep within the earth—rises and forces its way to the surface. Oozing through the earth's crust as lava that soon hardens, this volcanic rock accumulates on the sea bottom like a giant pile of candle drippings. After millions of years, the mound breaks through the ocean's surface. Continuing eruptions enlarge the island, heaping lava upon lava and building up a peak. Since much of an island volcano is underwater, there is more to it than meets the eye. Haleakala appears to be about 10,000 feet high when measured from sea to summit—a grand height to be

As clouds burn off inside Haleakala's crater, the undulating cinder cones glow like embers from the fires that brought them into being. The silversword, unique to this mountain, blooms just once in its lifetime, then dies.

How the Hawaiian Islands Came to Be

Like endless fountains, hot spots deep within the earth bubble up lava, building volcanoes that eventually emerge as islands from the sea. Remarkably, each of the Hawaiian Islands has been formed by the same hot spot —but at a different time. This part of the earth's surface is slowly drifting northwest, and for only a geological moment does an island linger over the hot spot.

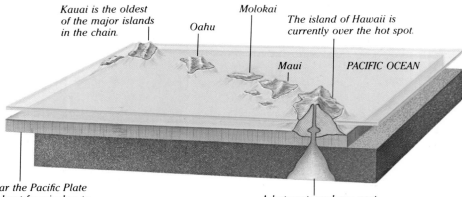

Kauai is the oldest of the major islands in the chain.

Oahu

Molokai

Maui

The island of Hawaii is currently over the hot spot.

PACIFIC OCEAN

Each year the Pacific Plate moves about four inches to the northwest.

A hot spot produces vast amounts of molten rock.

sure, but by no means exceptional. If the ocean were drained away, however, the mountain would measure 28,000 feet—putting it in the same class as the monumental Himalayan peaks.

Hot spots

For some unknown reason, about 125 areas beneath the earth's surface—"hot spots," scientists call them—generate more magma than others. The Hawaiian hot spot, which has produced molten rock for at least 70 million years (and is still going strong), is one of the largest in the world. Like a perpetual fountain continually bubbling up lava, it has, all by itself, created each and every one of the Hawaiian Islands, and even now it is in the process of giving birth once again.

Although a hot spot is stationary, the crust of the earth is not. Broken into about a dozen pieces like a cracked eggshell, the crust slides over the earth's mantle, one piece occasionally bumping into another. These pieces, called plates, support and pull along the material on top—the continents and the seas. Just as a cloud drifts lazily across the sky, the Pacific Plate moves over the hot spot, and an island is magically created from the molten rock. As the plate drifts northwestward at a speed of four inches a year, it pulls its new island away with it, and another part of the plate moves into place above the fiery fountain. This process has been taking place for millions of years, and the result is a chain of volcanic islands strung out like smoke signals from the island of Hawaii to Kure Island, more than 1,500 miles away.

But whatever Mother Nature builds, she eventually tears down. When it comes to permanence, a mountain or a volcano, for all its massive bulk, is as vulnerable as shifting sands. The older "islands" in the Hawaiian chain, those at the extreme northwest end, are greatly eroded—so much so that not even their peaks are visible above the waves. The islands get progressively younger toward the southeast end, where eight rise in various stages of youthful splendor. Kauai, about 5 million years old, and Oahu, 3 million years, are already weathered: erosion has worn away the volcanoes' top coats, exposing their inner flanks. The youngest island of all, Hawaii, less than a million years old, still has its youthful dome shape.

Older than Hawaii, the island of Maui began forming over the hot spot more than a million years ago. At that time, Maui was in the location now occupied by Hawaii, which did not yet exist. Since then, Maui has drifted about 100 miles to the northwest, and the eruptions of Haleakala, its biggest volcano, have waned as it slips from over the hot spot.

Youngsters are impetuous, often temperamental and volatile. But as the years pass, and youth turns into maturity, they eventually become subdued and cease to blow their tops. So it is with volcanoes. The youngest in the Hawaiian chain, Mauna Loa and Kilauea on the island of Hawaii, are still spitting fire; but as the island moves from the hot spot, its flames will become smoldering embers, as have those of its older neighbors.

It took scientists many years to figure out that the Hawaiian volcanoes have become progressively quieter, and to develop the hot spot theory. Hawaiians have understood the basics for generations: they told and retold stories of the goddess of fire, Pele, recounting her travels as she moved from Kauai to Oahu to Maui to Hawaii, her current home. Pele is easily angered. When she stamps her foot, the earth trembles; at her command, the mountaintop erupts.

Slumbering giant

Although Haleakala has been an active volcano for almost a million years, its most impressive feature, the enormous crater—7½ miles long, 2½ miles wide, and more than half a mile deep—was created not by a dramatic explosion but by the quieter, steadier forces of erosion. After the mountain was built, volcanic activity slowed, and wind, water, and ice began to take their toll. Streams flowing down the Kaupo and Keanae valleys swelled into raging rivers, deepening and lengthening the valleys until their heads met at the summit and the bowllike depression was formed. The distance from one side of the crater to the other is difficult to appreciate until you realize that the tiny black specks barely visible in the distance are people walking along trails around the crater wall.

After the crater was formed, volcanic activity increased once again, and Haleakala became even more explosive than during its days of creation. More gas was trapped in the magma, which erupted with a vengeance, creating incandescent lava fountains that danced high in the air. Fragments from these fiery fountains fell back around surface vents, building up the cinder cones that dot the crater floor today. Occasionally, fluid lava spilled out, swirling over the crater's floor and sliding down the volcano's two valleys as smooth, glossy, black lava. Some of the lava was thicker, and it inched along as a jumble of jagged hot rocks.

As time passed, the volcanic desert came alive with dancing colors. The hues intensified as the lava weathered. Iron changed from dark gray to reddish brown and then to bright red, dabbing its flame-colored pigments on the barren land. Sulfur added a cheery yellow note. Other minerals, once buried near the heart of the earth, now glisten in the sun, their crystals sparkling like diamonds. Here and there tufts of white lichen, sometimes called Hawaiian snow, are outlined against the coal-black lava—welcome signs of life in this otherwise bleak world.

No one knows precisely when Haleakala last erupted, but there is evidence—solid evidence, as it were—that gives us a fairly reliable approximation. Two European explorers, the Count de La Pérouse in 1786 and George Vancouver in 1793, each made a chart of Maui's southwest coast. The first chart shows a broad, shallow bay between two headlands; the later one, a distinct penin-sula in the bay, which was probably formed by lava that flowed into the sea and hardened. So it seems likely that the most recent eruption took place about 1790, and Hawaiian legends refer to an eruption of Haleakala about that time. But Haleakala will almost certainly erupt again: many people predict that this slumbering giant will once again breathe fire sometime in the next 100 or 200 years.

A late bloomer

Haleakala's crater is a dry, desolate place where the days can be scorchers and the nights cold as frost. A more inhospitable environment for plants would be hard to imagine. So explorers who first mapped the crater were astonished when they discovered the silversword, a plant whose dagger-shaped leaves curve inward and form a perfect rosette up to two feet around. From afar, the silversword is a shimmering sphere with an almost metallic sheen. Early Hawaiians, having no silver or other metals in their culture with which to compare the silversword, called the plant *ahinahina*—the word for gray said twice; others say, more poetically, that it is the color of moonlight.

When the silversword matures—sometimes it takes as much as 40 years—it sends up in summer a magnificent flower stalk that can be eight feet high, and

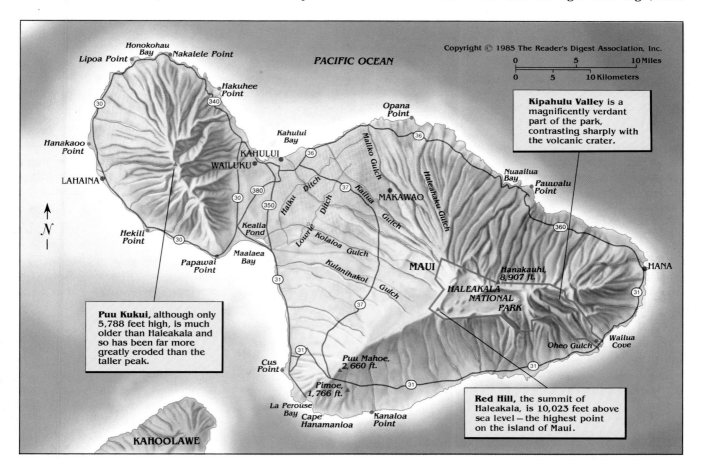

Kipahulu Valley is a magnificently verdant part of the park, contrasting sharply with the volcanic crater.

Puu Kukui, although only 5,788 feet high, is much older than Haleakala and so has been far more greatly eroded than the taller peak.

Red Hill, the summit of Haleakala, is 10,023 feet above sea level – the highest point on the island of Maui.

With winged grace, the white-tailed tropic bird soars from island to island, seemingly on beauty alone. Easily recognizable because of its distinctive black bands, long tail streamers, and raucous calls, this bird plunge-dives into the sea for fish and squid, carrying its catch back to nests tucked into the volcano's nooks and crannies.

hundreds of buds open into brilliant reddish-purple blossoms. After just a few weeks of glory, the flowers crumple and the plant dies, leaving its future progeny to the wind, which scatters the seeds.

Although a few of the silversword's close relatives live on two other Hawaiian islands, Haleakala is the only place in the world where these silvery treasures grow. The plants, descendants of a California tarweed whose seeds were probably carried to the island by birds, are marvels of adaptation. A special gelatinlike substance in the leaves fills the spaces between cells, allowing the silversword to store water—a mechanism found in few other plants anywhere in the world. The narrowness of the leaves helps to minimize moisture loss; each is densely covered with fine, silvery hairs that reflect the relentless sunlight and protect the plant from excessive ultraviolet rays. Even the curved shapes of the leaves serve a definite purpose—they shelter the silversword's growing tip, which is hidden deep in the plant's center.

Jungle birds and blossoms

Except for the silversword, Haleakala's crater is virtually bare of vegetation, but at its eastern end, where the lower crater wall slopes down, clouds spill over and rain falls in great quantities. The result is an isolated oasis, called Paliku (the Hawaiian word for "vertical cliff"), where such trees as the *mamane*, with its clusters of bright yellow, sweet pea–like flowers, add the magic and mystery of life. The ohia lehua, a rough-barked tree that grows anywhere from sea level to an elevation of 8,000 feet, is festooned with powder puffs—fluffy red flowers whose sweet nectar attracts the apapane. (A small, plumpish scarlet bird with black wings

At home in the isolation of Hawaiian mountain slopes, the nene is a better walker than swimmer—an adaptation to its lofty way of life.

and a black tail, the apapane makes a whirring noise as it flies from bloom to bloom.) The ohia lehua's crimson flowers, thought to be sacred to the goddess Pele, have been used for generations in fashioning the traditional Hawaiian garlands, or leis.

Poking around Paliku, the nene, or Hawaiian goose, searches for berries and leafy plants. Though geese are generally associated with water, the nene has become adapted to the arid environment of high lava flows sparsely punctuated with plants. The nene's feet have lost most of their webbing and are now better suited to walking on rocks than they are to swimming.

A ground-nesting bird that developed without natural enemies, the nene became easy prey for rats and other animals brought to the islands by man. By the middle of this century, the nene's soft honking could no longer be heard on Maui; the last survivors took refuge on the island of Hawaii, where they seemed destined for extinction. Since that time a special program has successfully reversed the decline, and the birds have been reintroduced on Maui. Now, from time to time, you can see these marvelous creatures flying low overhead, their necks extended and their broad wings flapping as they circle in the Hawaiian sky.

More likely to be heard than seen is the rare Hawaiian dark-rumped petrel, or u'au, whose call is often mistaken for the yipping of a small dog. A seabird that spends much of its time out at sea, the u'au arrives at Haleakala in March and nests in burrows in the cliff walls. After the females lay their eggs (each female lays only one) and the chicks hatch out, both parents share the responsibilities of the nestling's care. By the time October rolls around, the fledglings are ready to leave Haleakala on their own; the u'au's winter destination is unknown. Long ago, Hawaiians used to make the long, arduous climb up the mountain when the u'au came to nest in the cliffs, hunting the bird for its tasty flesh.

Contrasting sharply with the crater's dramatic starkness are the mountain's eastern slopes, blessed with the misty cliffs, rushing waterfalls, and lush tropical foliage of the Kipahulu Valley. The upper part is a jungle—a swampy, nearly impenetrable rain forest where such trees as the ohia lehua and the thick-trunked, yellow-flowering koa are clothed in velvety moss with lacy ferns dangling from their branches. The Palikea Stream cascades down this wild, six-mile-long valley, foaming and frothing in its rush to meet the sea. Just before reaching the ocean it tumbles down a series of wide ledges, creating sparkling blue pools surrounded by black lava, rimmed with green tropical foliage, and laced together by the foamy white water. Once called the Seven Sacred Pools (its true name is Oheo Gulch), these hollows are neither seven in number nor sacred—there are at least 24 and no group has ever worshipped them. The name matters not: they remain enchanting, delightful, and idyllic places in which to experience the special quality that is Hawaii's alone.

Only in Hawaii

Rising in splendid isolation 2,400 miles from the nearest continent, Hawaii's volcanic islands are among the remotest lands in the world and among the least likely for life to reach—much less flourish there. All of Hawaii's life-forms arrived by swimming or floating, by flying or drifting in the wind, by hitchhiking on migratory birds—or as stowaways on a boat with man. The odds against surviving such a long journey are immense. Scientists estimate that perhaps only one new life-form every 10,000 years was able to colonize the islands successfully. In Hawaii, as on other islands, colonization often leads to some rather strange developments in the plant and animal life. Certain beetles and other insects, for instance, no longer have the ability to fly, perhaps because the number of predators from which they have to escape is far fewer than on mainland areas. Hawaii's native fauna includes no lizards and only two mammals: a bat and a seal.

Nature dominated the Hawaiian Islands for several million years. Then man arrived—first the Polynesians about A.D. 400, followed some 1,400 years later by Europeans—bringing animals that destroyed native plants and introducing new plants that competed with the old. Soon, even small animals like dogs and rats were attacking ground-nesting birds, driving them to extinction or causing them to flee to places that were almost inaccessible, still wild—and safer, of course.

To this day, the Kipahulu Valley remains a primeval paradise, blessed with biological treasures. Exploring the valley for the first time in 1967, scientists were amazed to discover extremely rare birds of the Hawaiian honeycreeper family, such as the yellow and olive-green nukupuu and the Maui parrotbill, seen only once before in this century. Hawaiian honeycreepers are small birds, often brilliantly colored, and there are dozens of different kinds. Some, like the parrotbill, developed hooked bills with which to crack seeds; others have straight bills for plucking insects from crevices; and still others have long, curved bills that perfectly fit into the tube-shaped, nectar-rich lobelia flowers. Kipahulu Valley is also a stronghold of native Hawaiian plants.

Above this glorious rain forest, with its squawking birds and crashing waterfalls, lies the crater—spellbinding, silent, and stark. Looking across its immensity, as its undulating cones soften the desolation, one cannot help being captivated by the powerful and mysterious forces of the earth. At Haleakala the earth's deep, fiery heart is revealed.

Streams that race down Haleakala's eastern slopes, which are blessed with abundant rain (up to 250 inches a year), must descend thousands of feet within just a few miles. Spectacular waterfalls are the result.

Hawaii Volcanoes

"In violence the island lived, and in violence a great beauty was born."
James Michener

The eruption of a Hawaiian volcano is one of nature's grandest sound-and-light shows. Like the prelude to a main event, the ground begins to tremble with a series of tremors and earthquakes; then a long, narrow crack stretching across the volcano opens. Incandescent lava spurts out along the length of the crack, forming a curtain of fire that roars like the sound of a jet. After several hours, this dancing wall of flames coalesces into a single, giant fountain, shooting red-hot lava hundreds of feet high.

Suddenly the nighttime sky glows red-orange, as though a new day were dawning. For a mile or two around, it is so bright that one can read without a flashlight or a lamp. Uprushing sprays of lava create a pulsating roar; the tone is deep, like thunder, but more sustained, like a great waterfall's roar. Illuminated by the red light, the faces of human volcano watchers look devilish, and their bodies, silhouetted against the glow, become flat black cutouts. Heat radiating from the eruption can be felt a mile away; up close it is intolerable. Brimstone fumes, from burning sulfur, pervade the air, and the choking, acrid odor can be tasted as well as smelled. Every sense signals that some magnificent and colossal power is on the loose—a power that can create as well as destroy.

Eruptions like this are not uncommon on the Big Island (this name is used to distinguish the island of Hawaii from the state of Hawaii, which includes *all* the islands). Looming against the horizon like a pod of whales lolling in the sea, the Big Island is unmistakable because of its four hulking dome-shaped volcanoes:

Incandescent lava fountains, made possible by the very hot, fluid nature of the molten rock, spurt skyward at Kilauea. Lava temperatures may exceed 2000° F, but the surface soon cools enough for ferns and other plants to sprout.

Mauna Kea, Mauna Loa, Kohala, and Hualalai. A fifth, Kilauea, is growing on Mauna Loa's southeast flank, but it is not yet high enough to form a distinct dome. Two of the volcanoes—Mauna Loa and its companion, Kilauea—are within the boundaries of the national park, and both are still active.

Many people are surprised by their first view of a Hawaiian volcano. Instead of the steep, cone-shaped peaks of such majestic volcanoes as Washington State's Mount Rainier and Mount Fuji in Japan, Hawaiian volcanoes slope gently, rising to a pit rather than a point: the giant chasm—called a caldera, the Spanish word for cauldron—looks like a warrior's shield lying face up on the ground. Scientists call these domed mountains shield volcanoes. Their summits collapsed over a long period of time after repeated eruptions spewed out their insides.

Those who expect to see a high peak and find instead a gaping hole may be disappointed, but any disappointment is short-lived. Atop Kilauea, the most frequently visited volcano, the caldera is awesome. Two miles wide and three miles long, the oval pit is surrounded by jagged, inward-facing cliffs towering 400 feet high. Inside, swirling, bumpy lava rock stretches all about—an unearthly and surrealistic desert. Here and there wisps of steam rise from the ground, disappearing like puffs of smoke into the air. Crusts of yellow sulfur brighten the somber grays, red-browns, and blacks. But what makes the caldera all the more impressive is the sometimes fiery pit within the chasm—a circular crater, about 3,000 feet across and 250 feet deep, in the southern part of the caldera. Halemau-mau, this crater is called; it is the legendary home of Pele, goddess of fire, and the focal point of Kilauea's devastating power. It is here, scientists believe, that the main lava pipeline reaches the earth's surface.

Pele's future home

Most of the world's 500 or so active volcanoes are located where the oddly shaped pieces, or plates, that make up the earth's crust rub against each other. One such area, called the Ring of Fire, nearly encircles the Pacific. Mount St. Helens, Lassen, and Rainier are gemstones in this ring; so are Fuji and Argentina's Aconcagua, the highest mountain in the Western Hemisphere.

Restless and turbulent, the Ring of Fire is notorious for the number of earthquakes and eruptions occurring along its borders. In fact, since man began counting such things, more have been recorded along the Ring than anywhere else on earth. Its volcanoes are among the most violent in the world. Eruptions begin with deadly blasts of hot, solid lava fragments and volcanic ash that burst into the air with a vengeance, and end with thick, blocky lava hardening near the summit. After many, many eruptions, each heaping layers of lava and ash on one another, steep-sided conical peaks build up, towering toward the sky.

All this is what Hawaiian volcanoes are *not*. Mauna Loa, Kilauea, Haleakala on the neighboring island of Maui—these are built by quieter eruptions. The molten rock feeding them is much more fluid than that of the peaked volcanoes. Because the thicker, stiffer lava of the conical peaks inhibits the escape of gases, pressure builds up and they erupt violently. The thinner Hawaiian lava, in contrast, flows farther and gradually builds a mound with extensive, low slopes. The result is a long mountain, the very name Hawaiians gave to one of the volcanoes, Mauna Loa.

Since Hawaiian volcanoes fall not along the Ring of Fire, but in the middle of the area it circumscribes, the reasons for their occurence cannot be the same. Scientists now believe that Hawaii's fires are lit by a hot spot, buried deep beneath the sea in the earth's heart, that ceaselessly spews out magma—molten rock that rises to the surface, eventually breaks through, and hardens into lava. After millions of years, so much lava has built up on the seafloor that the outpourings have become taller than the sea is deep. An island is the result—an island that keeps growing. So long as the volcano is active, eruptions will continue to build up the mountain and enlarge the island.

About a million years ago Mauna Loa was born, its first eruptions occurring on the seafloor. These eruptions did not cause great explosions: the pressure of the overlying water was so great that steam could

Above an ancient rock carving, an ohia lehua tree displays its scarlet powder-puff blossoms. The most common tree in the park, the ohia lehua colonizes newly cooled lava flows.

Beneath the cooling silvery gray crust, a stream of red-hot lava cascades downslope at Kaena Point. Pahoehoe is the native Hawaiian name for this ropy, pillowy type of lava.

Brilliant yellow crystals of sulfur, deposited by acrid fumes emanating from inside the earth, rim a jagged vent on *Kilauea. Such deposits, colorful testimony to the continued activity of this volcano, may also be orange or white.*

not form, and piles of submarine lava quietly built their way upward. Tens of thousands of years later, the lava was piled so high that it approached sea level; this allowed steam to escape into the air and produced voluminous clouds of black volcanic ash and showers of hot but solidified lava. When enough volcanic material accumulated to block the sea from the active vents, Mauna Loa's island future was assured. Slowly but steadily—20 years for each new foot of height, 200 years for each new square mile of land—Mauna Loa became the giant volcano it is today. Having reached its apex, this volcano, like others before it, will slowly yield to erosion—and its ultimate destruction.

The Hawaiian hot spot is fixed. But the seafloor on top of it is moving slowly northwestward, pulling an island away from the hot spot and bringing a new area into position above it. Eventually another island is born. Over time a lengthy chain—the Hawaiian Islands—has been created, with the older, inactive volcanoes at the northwestern end and those still spouting fire at the southeastern. Since 1800, all of the chain's 100 or so eruptions have occurred on the Big Island—just where the hot spot is thought to be.

Early Hawaiians believed that the movements of Pele, goddess of fire, caused the eruptions to travel from one island to the next. Chased from her home on Kauai—the northernmost of the main Hawaiian islands—by her sister Namakaokahai, Pele fled first to Oahu, then to Maui, and finally to the Big Island, where she still makes her home. Easily provoked, she does not hesitate to show her displeasure. When her temper flared up in 1790, superheated gases and ash rained down Kilauea's slopes, trapping a small army of warriors who

opposed Kamehameha, the soldier-king who would later conquer and unite the islands of Hawaii. Many warriors were killed (which enhanced Kamehameha's reputation because Pele was perceived to be on his side), but the memory of their resistance has been preserved: footprints made in the volcano's outpourings are now cast in stone.

But is the Big Island Pele's permanent home? As the Pacific Ocean moves inexorably across the Hawaiian hot spot, another island should be forming to the southeast—and so it is. Twenty miles away, scientists have detected a submarine mountain extending from the ocean floor to less than 4,000 feet below the water's surface. This active and growing volcano, called Loihi, is destined to become Pele's home.

Stony trails and sandy beaches

Eruptions of Hawaiian volcanoes are usually much more spectacular than dangerous. The bright orange-red glow of the lava fountains is not from fire in the sense of burning but from lava that is about 2000°F. Some of the lava cools rapidly, hardening into a wall around the vent; hotter lava oozes downhill. Sometimes tiny droplets of molten lava are spun into fine strands, creating thin, brittle filaments called Pele's hair. If hot lava slips into the sea, it sizzles, steams, explodes, and fractures into tiny particles of black sand. Entire beaches are formed from such volcanic debris.

Although all the lava spewing from Hawaii's volcanoes comes from the same source, its ultimate appearance is determined by how hot it is and how fast it moves. Lava that is very hot, fluid, and fast-moving—some has sped along at 35 miles an hour—

creates long, tonguelike flows that are hundreds of feet wide and stretch out for miles. Called pahoehoe, this lava hardens to a smooth, high gloss, preserving the flowing swirls of the molten material in stone-sculpted waves. Sometimes pahoehoe hardens on the outside while the fluid lava underneath continues to stream. When the eruption ceases and all the lava has flowed out, a hollow tube remains, forming a long cave with walls of lava rock. (Visitors to the park can retrace the path of the glowing lava that once coursed through Thurston Lava Tube.) Thick lava that has cooled somewhat breaks up into a rubble of rough rocks, called aa, ranging from a few inches to several feet across. Not surprisingly, ancient Hawaiian trails followed the smooth pahoehoe and avoided the rough and tumble of aa where they could.

Long ago, Hawaiians had only Pele's whims on which to rely when they were worried that the volcanoes might erupt—reason enough to fear and placate the wrathful goddess. Today, with the help of sensitive instruments, scientists are more or less able to predict when Kilauea will erupt. Inside the volcano, a few miles below the summit, lies a chamber that stores magma from the hot spot. As the chamber fills up, the top of the mountain begins to inflate like a giant balloon. Although we cannot actually see this change, instruments called tiltmeters measure how much and how fast the volcano is enlarging. When the swelling has pushed the volcano a few feet higher than usual, or if the rate of expansion speeds up, scientists know there is enough magma in the chamber to cause an eruption. More clues are provided by seismographs, instruments that can detect and measure vibrations caused by earthquakes and even the tiniest underground tremors. Though we will never learn to prevent Pele's temperamental outbursts, at least we now know when she is working up to one.

Triumph of life
After the fury of an eruption has been spent, the volcano reigns over a new and different world—one that is silent, sterile, and still. Lava covers everything with a black shroud. But in just a few weeks or months, plants appear, brave souls in a lonely lava world, growing in cracks or crevices where some moisture has begun to accumulate.

Usually the first to gain a foothold are algae, soon followed by lichens, mosses, and ferns—all plants whose small spores are easily airborne. As soon as one plant becomes established, it creates a kind of welcome mat for others by trapping water and providing shade. Before too long, a miniature emerald colony is thriving on an otherwise bare, black rocky expanse, easing the way for the growth of such larger, woody plants as the ohia-lehua tree.

Most plant colonies begin life in the cracks and crevices and the innumerable nooks and crannies of the pahoehoe lava flows. But there is more to the story than this: some places magically sprout whole new forests while others remain barren and bleak. The secret is rain. Trade winds from the northeast cool as they rise up the windward slopes of Kilauea, their moisture condensing into dark cloud banks and heavy rain. Having shed their water, the clouds dissolve and vanish, and drier winds cross the summit and descend the leeward slopes. Annual rainfall on Kilauea's northern and eastern rims is about 100 inches, nurturing a lush tropical rain forest. On the southwest rim, where the trade winds have been partially robbed of their moisture, rainfall drops to less than 30 inches a year. Although this is enough rain to support plant life in most situations, the leeward flank of Kilauea, known as the Kau Desert, is virtually devoid of vegetation—a result of sulfuric-acid rainfall.

Strange and amazing creatures
Today's regeneration of plants on recent lava flows is just a small reminder of the larger miracle that took place here millions of years ago, when life first took hold on the newly formed islands. Like a handful of precious gems scattered in the sea, the Hawaiian Islands are isolated from the rest of the world—the nearest continent is 2,400 miles away—and they are not places easily found by living things. But plants and animals did arrive here, by accident: spores wafting on winds, seeds floating on waves or caught in a bird's foot or feathers, land snails rafting to shore on a log, and animals drifting with the ocean's currents. For any life-form to survive such a journey was, and still is, miraculous. On the average, approximately one new life-form colonized the islands every 25,000 years—a slow process to be sure, but one that eventually transformed empty volcanic islands into places that brim with greenery and echo with song.

Such an arduous trip was out of the question for many kinds of plants and animals. Only two mammals were successful in reaching the islands without human help: the monk seal and a small bat. The seal arrived by swimming and the bat by flying what must have been an extraordinary distance, with few, if any, rest stops. No reptiles, amphibians, or freshwater fish were able to make it to the islands by themselves, and only one palm can claim to be a true native. The life-forms that arrived in Hawaii—most are from places in the South and West Pacific—diversified dramatically: all of Hawaii's 2,500 different plants are derived from only 275 immigrants. But even more astounding is the fact that 10,000 species of insects and spiders evolved from as few as 150 original ancestors—and of these almost all are unique to the islands.

Once the plants and animals reached Hawaii, they gradually changed, and sometimes surprisingly so. Since there were no large animals to graze or browse on the vegetation, plants gradually lost most of their natural defense mechanisms: spines, thorns, repellent odors. Some, like the remarkable violets that grow more than eight feet tall, became woody and attained the height of trees. Lobelias, which are cultivated elsewhere as small, colorful, flowering ornamentals, grow an astonishing 40 feet tall here. No one is sure why ordinary plants have turned into giants. Perhaps it is because in this climate they can grow throughout the year; perhaps the densely packed plant life forces them to push skyward to capture the sun.

Found nowhere else on earth, the brilliantly colored Hawaiian honeycreepers developed unusual beaks. That of the akialoa is curved and so long it reminds one of Pinocchio's nose gone wild; the bird, which now lives only on the island of Kauai, uses its beak like a fishing hook to find and skewer insects hiding in bark. Tailored for tapping trees like a woodpecker's, the akiapolaau's lower bill, used for scraping bark, is straight; its curved upper bill spears insects dislodged by the lower one. Other honeycreepers have stout, parrotlike, seed-cracking beaks, and still other bills are shaped to match curving, tubular lobelia flowers, making accessible the nectar hidden deep inside. Two other nectar-eating honeycreepers, the iiwi and the apapane (each with a curved bill), dart from tree to tree in the ohia lehua forests. Both birds are small, plump, and bright scarlet

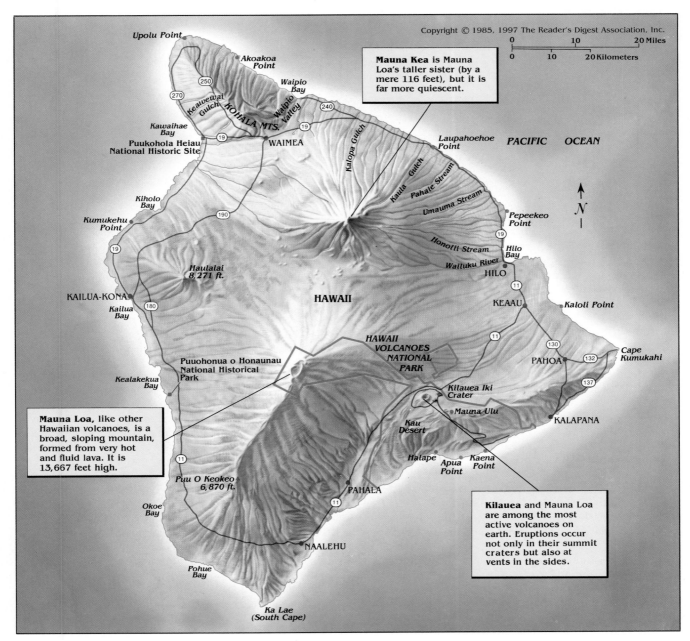

Mauna Kea is Mauna Loa's taller sister (by a mere 116 feet), but it is far more quiescent.

Mauna Loa, like other Hawaiian volcanoes, is a broad, sloping mountain, formed from very hot and fluid lava. It is 13,667 feet high.

Kilauea and Mauna Loa are among the most active volcanoes on earth. Eruptions occur not only in their summit craters but also at vents in the sides.

Relentless winds of high mountain slopes shaped this picturesquely twisted koa tree; at lower levels the koa may soar to heights of 100 feet. Ancient Hawaiians prized the hard, lustrous wood for surfboards and canoes.

marked with black, looking much like the ohia's sweet, round, red blossoms.

More bizarre are the changes that occurred among the insects. Crickets, beetles, and even moths became flightless; one type of caterpillar developed the ability to catch flies. Plant hoppers that took up residence in caves—they feed on roots dangling into the hollow chambers—lost the ability to see.

Ancient forests

The ohia lehua, which varies in form from straggly desert shrubs to handsome 100-foot rain forest giants, is definitely the most common and conspicuous tree on the Big Island. The branches of this gray-barked tree are usually gnarled and covered with small leaves that are sometimes red when young and dark gray-green when they mature. But its glory is the clusters of brilliant red pompons that decorate its branches, their deliciously fragrant nectar attracting many native birds.

In the wetter areas near Kilauea, a garden of tropical ferns, mosses, and flowers flourishes beneath the ohia's spreading branches, forming an almost impassable thicket. Wherever the uluhe, or false staghorn fern,

sends its creeping stems—even meandering up the trees themselves—gigantic fronds 10 to 15 feet long crochet the trees together into a sturdy green lace. Adding to the chaos are such smaller ferns as the amaumau, whose fanlike fronds, like the leaves of the ohia, gradually turn from red to green. Halemaumau, the fire pit atop Kilauea, takes its name from the amaumau, which supplied the Hawaiians with a reddish dye.

Above the ohia forests, where the climate is cooler, the majestic, moss-covered koa reigns, its yellow flowers like many small sunbursts brightening the day. These are handsome trees, with thick trunks, light-colored bark, and sickle-shaped foliage—not true leaves but flattened leafstalks—and they are giants, towering up to 100 feet high. The straight-growing koa furnished the best wood for surfboards, paddles, and house beams; canoes, all-important to Hawaiians, were often carved from just a single log.

The oldest ohia and koa trees stand guard in the kipuka, isolated oases of plants that are surrounded by hardened lava flows, some of which support younger trees and other plants. In the kipuka, one can luxuriate in the very forests that clothed these islands long before human colonists arrived. Kipuka Puaulu, or Bird Park—a kipuka much treasured on the island—shelters such rarities as the mamaki tree, whose inner bark was used to make clothing, and the papala, which burns with such a profusion of sparks that early Hawaiians used its branches for fireworks. Amid the ferns and vines of the understory, red berries on the ohelo bushes glisten like rubies. The shrub was considered sacred to Pele, and Hawaiians always dedicated the first fruit of the season to the goddess by tossing a handful of ohelo berries into the crater.

The sweet nectar of native flowering plants attracts and feeds such birds as the apapane, a tree-loving species of Hawaiian honeycreeper.

Sacred sites

The first humans to set foot on the Hawaiian Islands were Polynesians who had sailed more than 2,000 miles from their home in the Marquesas Islands in the South Pacific—a miraculous feat, considering that they had neither compass nor maps nor other navigational instruments. Such tools had not been invented by A.D. 400, when the Polynesians pulled their canoes onto Hawaii's black sand beaches and unloaded the chickens, pigs, coconuts, and other plants they had brought to begin their new life. In time more colonists came from the Marquesas, but it is thought that about A.D. 1200 a different group of Polynesians arrived—this time, from Tahiti. They quickly became the rulers of the islands, and their customs and culture have dominated the Hawaiian way of life ever since.

Although temples were built on the rim of Kilauea's crater, Pele's territory was considered too sacred for the humdrum activities of daily life. Most villages were established near the sea, where fish were plentiful, and in the lowlands, where the soil made for good farming. Along the seacoast are the ruins of several ancient fishing villages, marked by groves of tall coconut palms, or *niu*. These trees not only offered welcome shade to the new settlers but also supplied an incredible number of practical products. Both coconut meat and coconut milk were important foods. The empty shells made excellent storage containers or cups for drinking. Husks were turned into cord; fronds became baskets, mats, and thatching; and trunks ended up as the underpinnings of houses. In all, Hawaiians found more than a hundred differ-

A drabber cousin of the apapane, the insect- and nectar-eating amakihi is one of the few native Hawaiian birds that still occur in abundance.

ent uses for this tree—firm testimony to the creativity and resourcefulness of these islanders.

Along the coast is the remains of one of Hawaii's most sacred religious shrines, Wahaula Heiau, the Temple of the Red-Mouthed God. Constructed in the late 13th century, this temple was dedicated to the god of war, the bloodthirsty Kukailimoku. For five centuries Hawaiians passed through this hallowed place, paying homage to Kukailimoku and offering sacrifices.

From Wahaulu Heiau, an ancient footpath once led to another holy place. After crossing mile after mile of near-bare pahoehoe, bedecked with an occasional stunted ohia tree or tuft of grass, the trail suddenly enters a very special field where the grandest show of rock art, or petroglyphs, in all of Hawaii is on display. Although these rocks were once just as unadorned as the others around them, generations of Hawaiians believed this particular field—called Puuloa, after the Hill of Long Life at its center—to be sacred, and they carved pictures and symbols into the stone. Lacking metal tools, they used hard-edged rocks to chip away and carve into the softer ones. Elementary though this method may have been, it has stood the test of time: the oldest pictures are still visible despite a thousand years of weathering. Simple yet enigmatic, these carvings range in size from a few inches to six or more feet long, and in some places are so crowded that they overlap. Many of the early carvings are plain stick figures, but later ones are more fully developed, depicting a more detailed human form (sometimes in profile), outrigger canoes in full sail, and such creatures as dogs, turtles, and fish. Other petroglyphs are abstract symbols, precisely carved but indecipherable—their meaning locked in mystery.

Though we may never be able to interpret these drawings, we can still sit where the ancient artists sat, touching the same roughly textured rocks under the same blazing sun, and contemplate the same gentle sea as it dances its way to the horizon. No imagined paradise could be greener or sweeter or more peaceful, which makes it all the more difficult to remember that Hawaii owes its existence—and its future—to a volcano that breathes fire and brimstone.

Hot Springs

"As a reminder of his power to create good, the Great Spirit rent the earth, bringing forth pure, healing water. He asked that his favorite place be forever neutral ground, a place to partake of life and health."

Indian legend

Most national parks are wild places—places with primeval forests, surf-pounded shores, or deserts that stretch unpopulated for miles. Often encompassing tens of thousands of wilderness acres, they are sanctuaries where man is but a transient visitor. And then there is Hot Springs. With little more than a thousand acres, this park lies in the midst of a bustling city; and its focal point is not mountains or forests or glaciers or geysers but Bathhouse Row.

The bathhouses, built early in this century and elegantly replete with marble floors, elaborate fountains and even stained-glass windows, are monuments to the gilded age of this famous health spa. Here the faithful came, and continue to come, seeking cures for their afflictions in the steaming, naturally carbonated mineral water that issues from dozens of hot springs on a nearby slope. Whether bathed in or sipped, this shimmering, crystal-clear elixir supplies relaxation for the body and solace for the soul. Among the many notables who have visited the spa over the years are the boxers

Modeled after some of the finest spas in Europe, the palatial bathing

establishments of Bathhouse Row line Hot Springs' main thoroughfare. The splendors of this park are the creations of man.

First settled in the early 1800's, the community of Hot Springs grew rapidly. In 1886 the creek that had originally run through the wooded mountain glen was roofed over and its natural course replaced by a broad avenue.

"Gentleman Jim" Corbett and John L. Sullivan, the author Stephen Crane, and the evangelist Billy Sunday.

Of course there has not always been a city here, nestled among the folds of the Zig Zag Mountains: the narrow cleft through the mountains where Bathhouse Row now stands was once a wooded glen. Local Indians, the first to partake of the springs' healing waters, knew it as the Valley of the Vapors and considered it a sacred place. A stream gurgled through the glen, fed in part by overflow from the hot springs, which spilled from terraced hillside pools hemmed in by natural dams made up of mineral deposits. Dense forests covered the mountains, and bison, elk, deer, and bear roamed the land.

Today the forests remain, but much else has changed. The Spanish explorer Hernando de Soto wandered into modern-day Arkansas in 1541, searching for gold, and may have visited some of the springs. During the two centuries that followed, French trappers occasionally stopped by and bathed in the mineral waters. After the United States acquired the area as part of the Louisiana Purchase in 1803, President Jefferson sent a pair of scientists westward to examine the springs. Their enthusiastic report sparked the first influx of settlers and health seekers, who gradually transformed the region. The once pristine stream now flows through a tunnel beneath the broad avenue that fronts Bathhouse Row. And most of the springs have been enclosed and covered to ensure the remarkable purity of the water. (Since it is naturally sterile and free of contamination, the first rocks brought back from the moon were stored in water from the springs while scientists examined them for signs of life.) Nowadays the spring water is channeled to a central holding reservoir and then piped to the various bathhouses.

And plenty of water there is. The average daily flow from the springs is 850,000 gallons—enough to fill more than 20,000 bathtubs to the brim each day. Slightly laced with dissolved calcium, silica, bicarbonates, and other minerals, the water emerges from the earth with an average temperature of 143° F.

According to an Indian legend, the springs were the home of the Great Spirit, who warmed the water with his breath. Modern scientists have a different explanation for this remarkable outpouring of steaming liquid. The main source of the water is a broad valley to the north of the springs. Underlain by a deep formation of highly porous rock known as Bigfork Chert, the valley forms a natural catch basin. Over the eons, rainfall has been seeping slowly downward through pores and crevices in the chert to depths of 4,000 feet and more. There it becomes heated by contact with hot rocks of the earth's interior. The water escapes back to the surface through joints and fractures in surrounding deposits of Hot Springs Sandstone.

The downward journey of the water is slow—perhaps merely a foot each year. Scientists estimate that, on the average, water bubbling from the springs today fell as rain in the valley some 4,000 years ago. The return journey is much faster; once the heated water reaches the zone of joints and fractures, it surfaces in about a year. The minerals are dissolved from the rock as the water percolates slowly downward through the Bigfork Chert. The water also contains carbon dioxide and other gases, but these are held in solution by immense pressure in the depths. Once the water shoots to the surface, however, the carbon dioxide gas is released as sparkling bubbles.

Beyond the springs

No one has ever proved that the water actually has healing powers. Whatever benefits it may afford come from the combination of purity, warmth, minerals, and carbonation. Perhaps, too, part of the magic is in the surroundings. The gracious old bathhouses are set among parklike lawns traversed by a grand promenade and numerous paths for pensive strolls. In spring, when the dogwoods and redbuds are in bloom, and again in summer, when the giant magnolias come into flower, the lawns and gardens are at their fullest glory.

The mountains add to the beauty. Eighteen miles of trails for hiking and horseback riding lace the wooded slopes. For the less ambitious there are also several roadways punctuated by scenic overlooks that afford grand vistas of the hillsides, especially in autumn, when they become splashed with scarlet and gold.

Some of the trees in and around the park are champions of their kind. The biggest black cherry tree in Arkansas is a noted landmark in Sleepy Valley, and until recently the state's largest linden grew nearby. Many of the shortleaf pines on Sugarloaf Mountain—towering giants with spreading crowns and reddish-brown bark—are well over two centuries in age. The forests represent a crossroads between east and west, north and south. Cool northern slopes are dominated by stands of white oak, red maple, and hickory—trees typical of the east—with dogwoods, wild plums, ferns, trout lilies, and dwarf crested iris growing in their shade. Warm southern exposures, in contrast, are favored by pines of the same species that grow throughout the southeast. Dry, rocky outcrops are colonized by big bluestem grass, characteristic of midwestern prairies, and brightened in spring by birdfoot violets and firepinks. The southwest is represented here and there by prickly pear cacti and such animals as tarantulas and armadillos; occasionally, long-tailed roadrunners dart through the brush.

Most of the wildlife, however, is reminiscent of eastern forests. Though shy and scarce, deer and foxes are seen from time to time. Black bears, once hunted to extinction, have been reintroduced into the area, and several have been sighted in the park. But it is the smaller mammals—rabbits, raccoons, opossums—that are the most common. Both gray and fox squirrels scamper about in search of acorns. At night their dainty counterparts, flying squirrels, come out to forage.

Raccoons are especially adept at surviving near the city. Spending the daylight hours snoozing in hollow logs or trees, the masked mammals begin to prowl the creeks for crayfish, frogs, and fish at dusk; they also munch on fruits, insect grubs, and even garbage. At dawn they curtail their hunting and return to the privacy of their dens.

Wild turkeys also are fairly abundant at Hot Springs and roam freely throughout much of the area. The sound of their calls or, better still, the sight of the birds themselves is a special treat for visitors at the park. Turkeys can sometimes be spotted, especially among tangles of muscadine grapes in autumn and also along Sunset Trail, which skirts the western mountain ridges. The turkeys are skittish, but the males' courtship displays enthrall visitors who sit quietly in the woodlands in spring. To attract their harems, the toms fan their iridescent tails, strut pompously about shaking their bright, red-wattled heads, and fill the woods with their throaty gobbling calls.

The thrill of such experiences is, for many, the finest recreation this pocket-sized park has to offer: the renewal of the spirit that comes of close kinship with wild nature. But for others—the faithful—the mystique of the healing waters is the magnet that draws them irresistably to the age-old Valley of the Vapors. Each day a loyal clientele of residents, along with curious visitors, patronizes the thermal fountains of Bathhouse Row. Some are casual sippers, others patiently fill jug after jug with the sparkling brew; they drink no other water. For them the magic of the springs lives on.

The present-day spas of Hot Springs, built in the early decades of this century, are embellished with stained-glass windows, fountains, statuary, imported tiles, and gleaming marble floors. Still in use, the opulent bathhouses continue to attract visitors, some to partake of or bathe in the famous mineral waters and others to marvel at the beauty of these mementos of a bygone era.

Isle Royale

"The world . . . needs a place where wolves stalk the strand lines in the dark, because a land that can produce a wolf is a healthy, robust, and a perfect land."
Robert B. Weeden, *wildlife biologist*

I solated by the chill waters of the largest freshwater lake on earth is a richly forested island of volcanic rock that we call Isle Royale. It is a world apart, a uniquely secluded northern wilderness where the ruthless delicacy of nature's balance is an observable fact. This 45-mile-long refuge, some 15 to 18 miles from Canada and about 50 miles from the Michigan mainland, is one of the few places in the lower 48 states where wolves run free and unchallenged, playing—as they once did across much of the Northern Hemisphere—a vital role in maintaining the health and strength of the wildlife community they prey upon.

Some 9,000 springs and autumns have come and gone since glacial ice withdrew from the land around Lake Superior, leaving this scoured island. Always and dependably, spring has been a time of revival, when the many faces of nature have awakened fresh-eyed to new beginnings, and autumn a time of consolidation. Yet each seasonal cycle has been different from all the others, each a subtle variation on the long theme of nature's complex interweaving.

Winter's grip is still firm when the winter wren, that earliest herald of spring, begins pouring out a riotous

Dramatic bright-yellow lady's slippers, elegant white ladies' tresses,

song from upland thickets of beaked hazel and green alder. By mid-April, skunk cabbages, the first blooms of the new growing season, poke their tapered sheaths up through little melt holes in thinning crusts of swamp ice. Life is astir. Already great horned owls, ravens, and gray jays are feeding downy nestlings. Moose, having survived the winter on twigs and buds—even stripping the bark from trees—are discovering the leaves of wild strawberries, still green beneath the melting snow. The bulls' huge racks are gone now; swelling lumps high on

and dainty pink calypsos are among the many wild orchids that brighten the lush forest floor of Lake Superior's Isle Royale.

their foreheads show where new ones will soon grow. The common loon and its mysterious song once again invade the quiet and protected waters of this island wilderness. The sleek black-and-white birds busy themselves with courtship and with the seasonal rituals of nest building and rearing their young.

In the seclusion of a den, a wolf mother brings forth her litter, generally two to four pups. Den sites vary; this one is in an old beaver lodge concealed by a stand of alders. The meadow where the alders grow was once

a beaver pond, but the dam builders died or moved on, and now their lodge stands high and dry, a mound of tangled sticks, earth, rocks, and the roots of brushy overgrowth. On the raised platform of its inner chamber, the she-wolf nurses her brood. The pups pack together, whining and nuzzling in the cool gloom, and their warm body scent blends with the rich earth aura.

Most years, only one litter is born in a wolf pack, and that to the dominant female; the father is almost certainly the dominant male. The hierarchy of a wolf pack

179

is strict, and failure to observe its rules brings sharp retribution, not only from the leaders but from other members of the pack as well. A breeding pack generally has a pair of leaders and perhaps a second in command that scientists call the beta male. The dominant pair, which carry their tails raised like flags of authority, make strategic and tactical decisions; it is they who begin a hunt and, after choosing potential prey, make the first move against it. Other members of the pack, which may vary in number from 2 to 22, have their roles to play. As in any social structure, these vary from pack to pack and even from season to season, according to the skills and personalities of the wolves involved. In addition, most packs include one or two followers, usually males of low rank that tag along behind, scavenging the leftovers of a kill after the others have finished.

Isle Royale's other large inhabitants, the moose, lead solitary lives by comparison. They may feed in groups, even enjoying one another's company, but in matters of life and death each adult is on its own. The bond between a cow and her calf is strong, however; the two stay together for almost a year, the mother protecting her calf with all her considerable strength. But now it is time for an expectant cow to drive away her yearling calf in preparation for this spring's new responsibility.

Still unwise in the ways of wilderness survival, the yearling is likely to blunder about the forest, easy prey for wolves. It is a time for thinning out the generation, when those with undependable instincts are lost before they can reproduce. Many a yearling attaches itself to an older bull, from whose example it gradually gains competence in the many skills of moosehood.

Cycles of life

Spring's first awakenings on Isle Royale, back when the ice sheet was still withdrawing, probably aroused only algae and lichens, which had been carried from the mainland by the wind and water. But it cannot have been too many decades before mosses and a few higher plants—grasses and sedges, tangled mats of saxifrage, even dwarf birches and willows—began to gain footholds upon the thin, gravelly deposits left by the glacier. The seeds and spores of some of these tundra plants also came on the wind and water; others were carried by wandering birds. Once the tundra world was established, more birds must have started nesting here. Life attracts life, even to a remote island, and so further springtimes would have seen airborne insects swarm, spiders weave, hawks and owls soar.

Later, as the climate warmed, spruce trees, firs, and shrubs—which had earlier taken root in sheltered nooks and crevices—spread across the land in a dense forest, intermixed with aspens, birches, and pines. Beavers, lynx, muskrats, and martens, having walked across the winter ice, swum, or floated from the mainland, were among the inhabitants of this spruce-fir forest. Meanwhile, the island was growing. Its bedrock, relieved of the burden of mile-thick sheets of ice, was

rising slowly (as it is still doing, at the rate of about six inches a century), and the lake itself was changing; old shorelines and beach ridges exist now as much as 200 feet from the lakeshore.

By 5,000 years ago, under the influence of a long warming trend, hardwood forests of maple, yellow birch, and oak dominated the island. The spruce and fir were confined to wet lowlands and cool shorelines. But the warm trend did not last, and over the past few thousand years the spruce-fir forests have reclaimed all but the highlands.

Today Isle Royale's landscape is complex. Much of the northern coast is an unbroken wall of rock, incessantly pounded by the cold waters of Lake Superior; the remainder of the shoreline is a lacework tracery of narrow peninsulas and fiordlike inlets flanked by reefs, rock clusters, and smaller islands. Inland, the forests of spruce and fir surround cedar swamps, countless beaver ponds, some 27 named lakes ranging from a few hundred feet to seven miles long, and quavering acid bogs where the mire is deeply imprinted with the splay-toed tracks of mud-slogging moose.

In open meadows, most of which were once beaver ponds, the black soil is quickly covered by waving stands of goldenrod and pink-purple fireweed, as well as bright hawkweeds, pearly everlastings, and dainty-flowered asters of pink, blue, or white. Within a few years, brushy growth occupies these places in the sun; thimbleberries, blueberries, mountain ashes, red

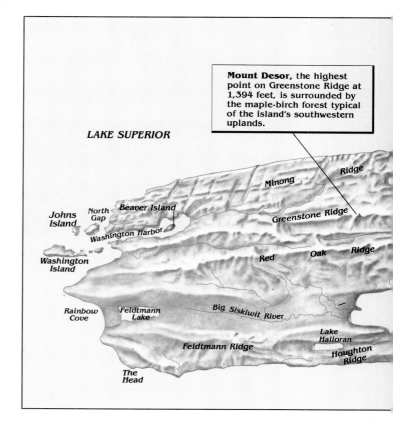

Mount Desor, the highest point on Greenstone Ridge at 1,394 feet, is surrounded by the maple-birch forest typical of the island's southwestern uplands.

LAKE SUPERIOR

Minong Ridge

Johns Island

North Gap

Beaver Island

Greenstone Ridge

Washington Harbor

Washington Island

Red Oak Ridge

Rainbow Cove

Feldtmann Lake

Big Siskiwit River

Lake Halloran

Feldtmann Ridge

Houghton Ridge

The Head

Open meadows and brushlands, where snowshoe hares and deer mice abound, are home to the red fox, whose hunting skill keeps these fast breeders in check. In summer the canny carnivore supplements its diet with fruit and berries; in winter it scavenges meat left by wolves.

Striking clusters of white-barked paper birch are often a sign that a part of the forest is well along the road to recovery after a fire. The fast-growing trees are, along with aspens, the favorite food of beavers, who weight whole branches down with stones to serve as winter food.

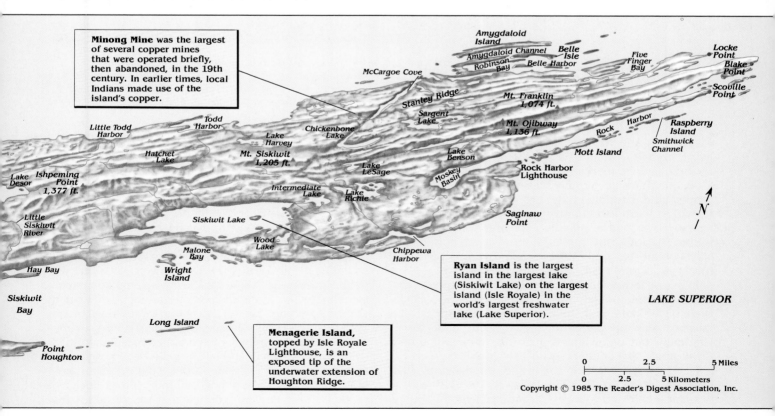

Minong Mine was the largest of several copper mines that were operated briefly, then abandoned, in the 19th century. In earlier times, local Indians made use of the island's copper.

Ryan Island is the largest island in the largest lake (Siskiwit Lake) on the largest island (Isle Royale) in the world's largest freshwater lake (Lake Superior).

Menagerie Island, topped by Isle Royale Lighthouse, is an exposed tip of the underwater extension of Houghton Ridge.

Amygdaloid Island
Amygdaloid Channel
Robinson Bay
Belle Isle
Belle Harbor
Five Finger Bay
Locke Point
Blake Point
McCargoe Cove
Scoville Point
Stanley Ridge
Mt. Franklin 1,074 ft.
Sargent Lake
Mt. Ojibway 1,136 ft.
Rock Harbor
Raspberry Island
Little Todd Harbor
Todd Harbor
Chickenbone Lake
Smithwick Channel
Lake Harvey
Mott Island
Hatchet Lake
Mt. Siskiwit 1,205 ft.
Lake LeSage
Lake Benson
Rock Harbor Lighthouse
Lake Desor
Ishpeming Point 1,377 ft.
Intermediate Lake
Lake Richie
Moskey Basin
Little Siskiwit River
Siskiwit Lake
Saginaw Point
Wood Lake
Malone Bay
Chippewa Harbor
Hay Bay
Wright Island
LAKE SUPERIOR
Siskiwit Bay
Long Island
Point Houghton

N

0   2.5   5 Miles
0   2.5   5 Kilometers
Copyright © 1985 The Reader's Digest Association, Inc.

The gray wolf was once the most widespread predator in the Northern Hemisphere, save only man himself. Today these animals run free in only a few places. Hunting packs in Canada, Alaska, and parts of Minnesota, Wisconsin, and Michigan have access to many kinds of prey. The wolves of Isle Royale, however, are almost totally dependent on moose and—in summer—on beavers as well.

raspberries, and fire cherries attract small birds and the avian predators that feed on them. Snowshoe hares abound, and so, therefore, do red foxes.

As the years go by, the area will be steadily over-topped and dominated by two kinds of trees well-known in the north country: paper birch and quaking aspen. For as long as a century, the area will be marked by the striking white trunks of these trees, both main-stays of the beaver, whose ponds are also home to muskrats, otters, mink, and various waterfowl.

In this orderly succession, the birches and aspens are but another temporary stage. They reproduce poorly in their own shade, and the more tolerant spruces and balsams grow up among them as a thrifty understory. Gradually the old white trunks lose their vigor and disintegrate; the conifers again take over.

On the western end of the island, the flanks of high open ridges are mantled with hardwood forests—mostly sugar maple and yellow birch, spiced with tall, rangy

pines. Here and there are stands of red maple, groves of sweet-scented balm of Gilead, and broad patches of the tree for which Red Oak Ridge is named.

The slow greening

By May Day, rose-tinged white hepaticas have begun to show on south slopes, and yellow clumps of marsh marigolds edge the brimming rivulets that stair-step down the drainageways. An advance guard of robins are sounding the first notes of the predawn chorus that will build up in weeks to come. Newly arrived song sparrows and white-throated sparrows announce that they are prospecting for territories in waterside brush. Somewhere among the aspens a mite of a bird, a ruby-crowned kinglet, bubbles forth a matchless melody.

Ice is gone from inland lakes, and it becomes evident that many winter residents and spring migrants have other plans for the coming summer. Mixed flocks of redpolls, siskins, and goldfinches are disappearing.

Small wedges of whistling swans stop over to spend the night; in the morning, after clamorous calling and beating of wings, they arise, pink-tinted in the early sun, to be on their way to some Arctic breeding ground. Deepwater ducks are leaving too—small flocks of scoters, goldeneyes, and oldsquaws that fished around shelf ice during the cold season. In the quiet of noonday, from a high shoulder of a ridge, comes a faint rasping cry: a wheeling bald eagle rides the thermals northward, a tiny fleck in the sky, white head and tail flashing momentarily against the blue.

About their 12th day of life, the wolf pups open their blue-gray eyes for the first time. In another week they will be moving about and venturing toward the sunlit world beyond the entrance of the den. Rearing the young is a communal affair with wolves, and in the early days of her parenthood the female is sustained by meat brought by other pack members, who carry it undigested in their stomachs. Sometimes the mother goes out to hunt with the pack, leaving another female in charge (baby-sitting comes naturally to any she-wolf, young or old). As the fuzzy, dark-furred pups develop, they make forays outside the den, romping, playing, exploring, already interacting as individuals.

In late May or early June a wise cow moose swims to an island in one of the inland lakes or makes her way to a heavy mat of sedge in a swampy area, where she gives birth to a spindly-legged youngster—or rarely two—weighing perhaps 25 pounds. The calf, covered with a woolly coat of brick-red hair, is able to stand almost immediately, but that is nearly the limit of its strength. After nudging her wobbly offspring to a sheltered place, the cow stands ferocious guard for three days or so, squatting or lying down from time to time so the calf can nurse. Then she begins moving away, coaxing the calf to follow, a little at a time. By the time the calf is a month old and weighs about 80 pounds, it can follow its mother almost anywhere, including deep water.

Water is the semiaquatic moose's best defense; and so during the few months when lakes and swamplands are not frozen over, the wolf pack must supplement its usual diet with other prey. At this same time of year, beavers are vulnerable. When the spring litter is about to be born in a beaver lodge, the male and all the older offspring move out. Most of them establish temporary dens along the banks of the pond or of nearby streams; others pair off and seek new territory, where they begin to set up housekeeping by building new dams. Many members of both groups fall prey to wolves.

Blossom time

Summer comes in a rush, beginning in June. The air is alive with mosquitoes, blackflies, and midges, all aswarm around the heads and flanks of adult moose (the calves are well protected by their woolly coats). Dainty clusters of diminutive calypso orchids—the most elegant of Isle Royale's 34 wild orchid species—have sprung up from the rich mold of shady woodlands,

and the fiddleheads of ferns have unfurled. Iris and clumps of yellow lady's slipper orchids edge the bogs where, among thick mats of tawny sphagnum and the spare vinery of cranberry, insect-eating pitcher plants rear their nodding flower heads and spread their leafy traps. Deciduous trees and shrubs are in full leaf, and the island is a feasting ground for moose.

Sometime near the last of June the wolf family abandons the natal den and moves by night to another location, usually the edge of an open wood near water and, if possible, a grassy meadow. Here the pups establish beds, trails, and digs; they exercise, contest for dominance among themselves, and even begin to hunt the moving insects or other small creatures that show themselves. No longer dependent on mother's milk, they joyously greet the return of the adults from a hunt, nipping and licking at their jaws. This is more than an affectionate gesture; it is a biological trigger guaranteed to produce a semisolid meal of regurgitated food.

In the course of the summer there may be three or four more of these child-care centers, or rendezvous areas, where the pack is temporarily headquartered and from which the young begin to venture out with the adults to travel and hunt. During their first year—one of learning by trial and many errors—the pups will have extraordinary privileges in dealing with their tolerant elders. Then they will be on their own as responsible adults and must conform to the pack's precise relationships of dominance and submission.

Tagging along behind its long-legged mother, the moose calf bleats from time to time for food and rest; it will not be completely weaned until August. It has grown into an odd, gnomish creature. Although its body is clearly becoming that of a moose, the most massive member of the deer family, its head remains small and stubby. Not until fall will it begin to develop the long moose face, complete with the characteristically bulbous snout. At that time, too, round velvety knobs will begin to sprout on the foreheads of bull calves—rudimentary indications of future antlers.

Season's end

By late August, the leaves of maple, aspen, oak, and birch have begun to turn. Blueberries and thimbleberries are heavy with juicy fruit to welcome migrant birds back from the north. Wolves have given up their rendezvous sites; the pups of summer are now able to run with the pack over its territory of many square miles, and have learned the fundamentals of the hunt.

Although she sets a strenuous pace for her calf to follow, the cow moose remains solicitous and protective. Making her way through heavy brush or tall grass, she keeps up a grunting monologue so the calf always knows where she is, and any sudden sound or movement is likely to bring her snorting to the youngster's side, ready for battle. Alone or with other youngsters, calves are energetic and playful. While their mothers feed, they spend much time literally kicking up their

In his second summer of adulthood a young bull moose's stubby antlers merely hint at the great racks to come; as a yearling, he wore antlers that were little more than spikes.

heels, an exuberant action that in adulthood will be their most forceful defense. All four feet of an adult moose are razor-edged bludgeons, but it is the rear hooves that are the most lethal. In reflexive response to a touch, they lash out to the side or rear with devastating power. Many an overeager young wolf has suffered broken ribs or worse in learning this fact.

Bull moose are becoming cantankerous. They spend much time scraping their majestic antlers against tree trunks to remove the itchy velvet. By late September, when the island's glowing cap of red, orange, and yellow foliage has begun to thin, the bull's racks—measuring up to six feet from tip to tip—are hard and tough, ready for the competitions of the breeding season. The bulls are ready, too; for the past month wolves have avoided them, concentrating on beavers and the gangly calves of unwary cows, because the bulls are as likely to attack a pack of wolves as they are to run.

Now, in response to the cows' echoing moans, the bulls emit thunderous basso hoots and come crashing through the brush—and woe betide anything that stands in their way. When two bulls meet, the larger lowers his head and dips his antlers from side to side in a display of strength that usually ends the confrontation. When combat does occur, it is as much a contest of skill as of power, not unlike a good arm wrestling match. After much sparring for position and leverage, the warriors stand head to head, antlers locked, bodies arched, and push with all their strength. When one must give ground, the contest is usually over, but meetings between well-matched bulls can end in death.

After the breeding season, bulls shed their weapons and the island prepares for winter. Beavers, having

spent the fall storing toothsome twigs and branches, retreat to their lodges—soon to be safely ensconced beneath ice and snow. When the snows come, especially if accumulations are deep, moose concentrate in lowland areas where evergreens are dense, browsing first on the balsam firs that they prefer. The wolf packs of Isle Royale have no prey but moose during the long winter and have honed their hunting skills accordingly. Following single file the trail a moose plows through the snow, they run their quarry down and test it for weakness. Those that fail the test do not see spring.

Striking the balance

The story of wolves, moose, and beavers is a recent one on Isle Royale, even in terms of the island's relatively short history. At the beginning of this century, neither moose nor wolf was here at all, and beavers were rare at best. In fact, few of the mammals of the past were to be found here. Some had died out in the natural course of events. Others were victims of human exploitation.

Copper miners in the late 1800's had burned off much of the forest cover. Loggers took most of what was left, so that life became impossible for large mammals. Fur trappers had found the island a rich source of beaver, lynx, and marten pelts and had trapped the animals and taken their skins. But the copper mines did not pay off, and the loggers and trappers, having used up the available resources, lost interest in Isle Royale; thus the devastated land was well into the early stages of recovery when the first moose arrived, sometime after the turn of the century.

They probably swam from the Canadian mainland—the trip is well within a moose's range. What they found was moose heaven: lakes full of water plants, vast stretches of fairly recent burns still in the brush and sapling stages, other areas of pristine young forest with an understory of American yew—choice year-round browse—and no predators at all. Their numbers doubled and redoubled and continued to grow so fast that, by the early 1920's, weed beds in lakes and bays were being depleted. The American yew was well-nigh wiped out, and a browse line, below which no branches grew, marked the balsam firs as high as a moose could reach.

What was happening to the moose's food supply did not interest most of the people who came by boat in summer and fall to see the cows with their calves and the great antlered bulls standing in picture-postcard groups along the shores. At its peak, the island's moose population probably numbered 2,000 to 3,000; their proliferation was regarded by many as a landmark success story. Michigan game biologists, however, predicted a catastrophic die-off. And that is what happened. In the early 1930's, beset by malnutrition and disease, the moose died back to a few hundred.

The 1930's brought the most famous drought in history. During the summer of 1936, about 20 percent of the forest of the island was destroyed by fire. It seemed another disaster. But events proved otherwise.

With plentiful rainfall in the 1940's, the burn area became a thriving brushland. It was what the moose needed, and they responded with another buildup of numbers that threatened another population crisis. Meanwhile, the beaver too had made a comeback. Their presence was already conspicuous by the 1920's, and the succession of birch and aspen on burned ground gave them an ideal world in which to multiply.

That was the situation in the winter of 1948–49, when a breeding pack of wolves made it across an ice bridge from Canada and brought a new dimension to life on Isle Royale. When their presence was discovered, many people feared that it was the beginning of the end for the moose, that the predators would run rampant through the population and destroy it. But many people had a great deal to learn from the wolves of Isle Royale.

The pack grew quickly, and within a decade numbered about a dozen and a half. In addition there were a handful of nonbreeding males who ran alone or in small groups. (These are generally low-status followers who are driven away from the pack.) Wolves have a built-in method of population control, whereby the number of each year's young is related to the size of the pack's territory and the available food it contains. During the 1960's a second small pack branched off from the first and established its own territory; since then the number of packs has ranged from one to five.

Wolves do not kill except to eat, and they are selective about their prey. A pack may pass by a dozen or more likely-looking moose before launching an attack, and only a small percentage of attacks result in kills—most are tests, during which the leader looks for signs of weakness. A healthy bull that stands its ground, a cow adept at staying between the attackers and her calf, a yearling that quickly wades into water—all are likely to survive many such tests. Only rarely do moose in their prime—adults between two and eight years of age—fall prey to wolves. For the most part it is the aged, the diseased, the injured, the weak, and the foolish that are successfully dispatched.

Wolves, moose, and beavers have varied widely in number over the decades. However, as the forest matures, it is losing its capacity to support all three of them. In part, this has happened because people have regarded fires—commonly started by lightning during dry seasons—as catastrophic and have extinguished them. Now the master plan for the park includes a prescribed "natural-fire-management policy," in the hope that ecological diversity will return. In times and patterns unpredictable, areas of mature spruce and fir will be lost so that a renewal of aspen, birch, and brush can sustain new generations of the island's wildlife.

Chance happenings have made this park what it is. Mankind's footsteps have been heavy and destructive at times, and only slowly has nature's fragile equilibrium begun to reestablish itself. Today, our challenge is to tread lightly and allow the events that come naturally to shape the future of this island wilderness.

The delicate blossoms of gaywings, or fringed polygala, less than an inch long, arise in early summer from the rich forest floor. When a bee lands on the blossom's fringe in search of nectar, its weight opens the flower a little.

Isle Royale's many lakes, beaver ponds, bogs, and swamplands support a varied wealth of aquatic and waterside plants, such as this cluster of marsh marigolds, and are ideal habitats for ducks, kingfishers, loons, herons, and many other water birds.

185

Joshua Tree

"Love me or hate me, the desert seems to say, this is what I am and this is what I shall remain."
Joseph Wood Krutch

In the shadow of California's Transverse Ranges lies an arid sanctuary of almost unearthly beauty—a wilderness of exotic desert plants and sunblazed boulders, of craggy mountains and boundless shimmering plains, of sun and wind and stone. In this unforgiving clime, stillness and solitude reign. Stop and listen, and only the wind fills your ears; look about, and you will behold a land where nothing seems to move except the clouds, scudding across a sky of endless cobalt blue. Rugged though they may be, these 793,000 acres of southern California desert wilderness—Joshua Tree National Park—are nothing if not mesmerizing.

The park is named for the fantastical Joshua tree, without a doubt its most fascinating resident. Growing to a height of 40 feet, this huge yucca (which, technically, is not a tree at all) seems to assume as many poses as a runway model. Its trunk bristles with a grizzled bark; from its twisted branches sprout clusters of fibrous green leaves, as pointed as paring knives, and in spring, fat white blossoms. The oldest among these trees were, at 800 years, already ancient when the Pilgrims landed. Explorer John Fremont called them "stiff and ungraceful . . . the most repulsive trees in the vegetable kingdom." But not all the reviews have been so negative.

Crossing this region en route from Utah in 1851, some Mormon pioneers are said to have seen a grove of these twisted giants and found in their shape a hopeful beckoning—an image of the prophet Joshua, raising his arms to lead them to a promised land. The story is fanciful, but the name has stuck.

The desert, high and low
In fact, Joshua Tree National Park comprises portions of not one desert but two. The differences are many, but boil down to elevation. The northern and western parts of the park lie in the southern range of the Mojave, or high desert, which extends all the way to Nevada. It is here that one finds Joshua trees, which thrive on the extremes of temperature and the hard winter freezes between 3,000 and 5,000 feet.

Here, the land is also littered with astonishing rock formations. Exposed to the forces of erosion, masses of ancient granite have been splintered into shapes of all descriptions and polished to a fine finish. Rising like islands from the pebbly desert floor, they are as plump as marshmallows. Whether as small as a grapefruit or as big as a stadium, standing alone or massed in improbable piles, they are especially breathtaking at sunset, when their polished faces seem to reflect all the colors of the sky.

Many a visitor has detected in the rocks weathered surfaces the images of long-lost relatives, and some of the more intriguing formations are named for their evocative shapes. Skull Rock, in the Jumbo Rocks area, looks just as you'd expect, while Southern California's legion of rock climbers flocks to Hidden Valley to scale the slickened heights of Trojan Head, Rock Hudson, and Old Woman.

Because of its greater elevation, the Mojave is generally cooler and wetter than the low-lying, eastern portion of the park. An average of four to seven inches of rain falls each year (usually in a few quick bursts), and there are occasional snowfalls in winter; summertime temperatures, although hardly mild, are at least endurable, usually in the 90s. (At the highest elevations, above 5,000 feet, things get downright chilly even in summer; the vegetation is dominated not by Joshua trees but by pinyon pines, common throughout the West.)

Moving southeast, the land tips like a ramp toward the Pinto Basin, briefly passing through a transitional zone known as the Wilson Canyon. In this area, roughly between 3,000 and 4,000 feet, it is not uncommon to see creosote bushes and palm trees—both natives of the low desert—growing beside high-country junipers and Joshua trees.

Below 3,000 feet, the Colorado Desert officially takes the stage. This arid expanse, a subdivision of the Great Sonoran Desert, is considerably bleaker and more foreboding than its upcountry cousin. Seared by the sun and blasted by scorching winds, its rocky washes and cactus fields recede to a shimmering horizon. Less than three inches of rain fall here each year, and summertime temperatures routinely hit 110°F. But looks can be deceiving. Ravaged though it may appear, the park's low desert region supports an array of plants that in many ways surpass those of the high desert. Creosote bush, smoke tree, mesquite, ironwood, ocotillo, paloverde, and cacti (dozens of types) are among the many hardy plants that have adapted to this torturous clime.

Islands of green, an abundance of life
Water, in general, runs deep underground at Joshua Tree, but here and there it emerges at the surface, where it nurtures life. Five such oases can be found within the park, although only two actually have water flowing at the surface: Cottonwood Springs, in the low desert near the park's southern entrance, and 49 Palms Oasis, accessed by a steep trail off Highway 62. Ringed by lush banks of cottonwoods, colorful barrel cacti, rustling fanpalms—even cattails—these miniature gardens are virtual terraria

compared with the surrounding desert, and they attract birds and animals from miles around, including the park's population of rare peninsular bighorn sheep. (49 Palms Oasis is considered the best spot to see one; try to visit in the early morning or late afternoon, when desert wildlife is most active.)

Life, however, is by no means limited to these scattered islands of green. Although at times it may seem the stillest, most forbidding place on Earth, the desert fairly hums with activity. Mountain lions and bobcats pace the rocky ledges of the high desert; roadrunners dart from underfoot, chasing snakes and lizards to feed upon; from atop the outstretched limbs of the spiny Joshua tree, red-tailed hawks coolly survey the landscape, then launch themselves with a flurry of wings to dive and seize their prey. The spring rains come, and then one day the desert is abloom with color, as all the wildflowers seem to burst open at once. Like a delicate web, life in the desert endures, each strand connected to the others and forming a magnificent whole.

Adorned with clusters of big white blossoms, Joshua trees punctuate the landscape near the Split Rock area of Joshua *Tree National Park, an arid Eden where cactus wrens and other creatures are undaunted by adversity.*

CALIFORNIA

Lassen Volcanic

*" . . . Is this the scene
Where the old Earthquake-daemon
       taught her young
Ruin? Were these their toys? or did a sea
Of fire envelop once this silent snow?"*
                           Percy Bysshe Shelley

I magine, for a moment, that from time immemorial a magical camera has been taking pictures of Lassen Volcanic National Park. Imagine, too, that by pressing a button on the camera you are able to speed up the sequence of photos showing the distant past and watch as Lassen's explosive life unfolds. In quick motion, a 10,000-foot volcano blows off its top, spewing a mushroom cloud of steam and ash high into the air; simultaneously, a wall of fiery lava gushes from deep within the mountain and plunges down its slopes, destroying everything in its path. Within minutes the once green countryside lies entombed beneath a blanket of black lava rock. New volcanoes begin to erupt. Pure white snow soon masks the destruction. Then glaciers come down from the North, crushing the mountains that lie in their way, grinding the rock into soil. Almost as fast as it came, the ice withdraws, leaving behind a new and ravaged landscape. But the ground quickly thaws, rivers flow, and forests spring to life.

You watch, fascinated, as parts of this drama are repeated, with variations, over the eons—new volcanoes erupt, new glaciers intrude, new life takes hold

Intricate sulfur crystals, the rolling Painted Dunes, and brooding

and greens the land. Suddenly, only seconds after an explosive eruption, the replay stops short. You have arrived at the present, and although nature's cycle of ruin and renewal is still in progress and will continue far into the future, it will do so only at an all but imperceptible pace.

Lassen Park owes its turbulent history to its position astride the Ring of Fire, a chain of about 300 volcanoes that nearly encircles the Pacific Ocean. The volcanoes line the edges of the Pacific Plate, one of the many oddly shaped sections that make up the

Cinder Cone are among the products of the intense heat that rages beneath the peaceful surface of Lassen Volcanic National Park.

earth's crust. As the Pacific Plate grinds against its neighboring plates, the friction produces intense heat deep inside the earth, melting stone into a liquid called magma that works its way up through fissures in the subterranean rock until it bursts forth as lava. This bursting forth can happen in many ways, depending on the nature of the channel that the magma finds and of the place where it emerges. The remains of many of these volcanic variations are among the outstanding landscape features to be seen at Lassen Volcanic National Park.

Lassen Peak, 10,457 feet in elevation, is quiescent now; perhaps it is resting from its last mighty eruption, which continued from 1914 until 1917. Still, Lassen is only the latest volcanic mountain to reign here. Not long before the Ice Age, it emerged from the northernmost flank of an even more impressive volcano, Mount Tehama. Much later, Tehama's summit collapsed, leaving a giant pit, or caldera, surrounded by a crown of jagged remains. These remnants—Brokeoff Mountain, Mount Conard, Pilot Pinnacle, Mount Diller—form a steepled circle south of Lassen, like a stony monument to Mount Tehama's past glory.

Just north of Lassen Peak lies Chaos Jumbles, a 4¹/₂-square-mile rubble of shattered boulders and broken stones partly overgrown by a young evergreen forest. The jumbled mass of rock is the result of explosions that occurred about 300 years ago from Chaos Crags, six volcanic domes near Lassen's northern foot. Like Lassen itself, they are known as plug-dome volcanoes. A long time ago, solidified magma stopped up their main vents. Pressure from inside the earth mounted until finally the mountains blew up, setting off a series of avalanches that came to rest as Chaos Jumbles.

A different process created Cinder Cone, an 800-foot-high pile of volcanic debris near the park's northeastern border. Since Cinder Cone's vent was not blocked, red-hot lava was able to erupt freely, sometimes sending pillars of fire hundreds of feet high. During these eruptions, fragments of charred lava fell back around the vent, accumulating as the huge anthill-shaped cone we see today. Finer ash, rising thousands of feet high, was winnowed by the wind and fell in a blanket all around the base of the cone. These barren deposits, later piled into dunes by winds and weathered by volcanic gases into earthen reds, yellows, and browns, have formed the Painted Dunes. During the last such eruption, some 200 to 250 years ago, rivers of molten lava also flowed from the vent. As it cooled, the lava formed low ridges and gave birth to two lakes: Butte Lake and Snag Lake. The bare branches of a drowned forest jut from the water of Snag Lake, the larger of the two.

Roundabout route

Visible from 50 miles away, snow-cloaked Mount Lassen was a prominent landmark for explorers and early settlers in northern California. Known by a variety of names over the years, the mountain eventually came to be called Lassen's Peak—in wry honor of one of the region's favorite pioneers, the resourceful rancher and trail guide Peter Lassen.

A Danish-born blacksmith, Lassen came to California just before the gold rush. After persuading the Mexican government to give him a large tract of land east of the Sacramento River in 1844, he established a ranch. His plan was to build a town; and so, in need of settlers to populate the town, he set himself up as a guide, leading immigrants through the mountains by a winding route that he called Lassen's Trail. A better promoter than pathfinder, Lassen

The snow plant's scarlet flower head, poking through the late winter snow, is often the first sign of new life to appear on Lassen's forest floor.

sometimes confused Mount Shasta to the north with Lassen Peak—a mistake that complicated the already roundabout trek and occasionally led him and his followers thoroughly astray. Many groups became outraged when they realized they were lost. Some almost starved. One group even forced their leader at gunpoint to climb to the top of Lassen Peak so that he could figure out where they were. But Lassen was quite a charming man, and when his charges eventually reached the comfort and safety of his ranch, they forgave him—usually.

Thump, bubble, and boil

If you knew nothing of Lassen Park's stormy past, you could still deduce it from such place names as Bumpass Hell, Devil's Kitchen, Vulcan's Castle, and Boiling Springs Lake. These are part of the park's network of thermal areas—hissing steam jets, boiling springs, and thumping mud pots. Even in winter, when the park is wearing its 20-foot-deep mantle of snow, these thermal features go full blast, heated by underground pools and rivulets of magma. Hot streams melt the snowpack, and 630-foot-long Boiling Springs Lake remains scalding hot through Lassen's bitterest winters.

Surrounding this lake is a fringe of mud pots—holes full of churning, bubbling hot mud. Other holes, called fumaroles, emit a wide variety of sounds, from hisses to roars, as jets of steam escape and spread into giant, smelly ground clouds.

The biggest of the thermal areas is the mile-wide valley called Bumpass Hell—a well-named place with all manner of steamy, sulfurous features. An ominous note is struck by a red-topped sign warning visitors to stay on the trails. And well they might: in 1864 settler Kendall Bumpass took a wrong step on the crust of a boiling mud pot, broke through into scalding mud, and had to have a leg amputated.

Inhospitable though Bumpass Hell may be, a few shallow-rooted grasses and shrubs manage to survive near its streams and pools, and despite temperatures that range from 125°F to 196°F, tiny algae flourish in the waters. Most algae are green, but these come in a variety of colors—red, yellow, brown, and even black—that form brilliant films, or blooms, on lakes and streams.

Flowers and flying squirrels

Considering the harshness of this landscape, one wonders how it supports so much plant life. The secret is nature's power of regeneration. Almost as soon as lava hardens into rock, it begins to erode into soil. The process is a slow one, but eventually enough soil accumulates to nurture life.

Magnificent stands of conifers cast deep shade over wildflowers and tangled shrubs. The first forest flower to thrust above ground in spring is usually the snow plant, which pokes up like a fat, red asparagus spear even before the snow has melted. Soon fawn lilies raise their creamy pinkish flowers on long stems. By June, bumblebees are forcing their way into the deep blue blossoms of Columbia monkshood, and hummingbirds hover before crimson columbines.

More dabs of color are added by thickets of the hardy shrub called manzanita, its leathery-leafed branches festooned with the berries for which the plant is named—*manzanita* is Spanish for "little apple." Eagerly eaten by deer and by such birds as robins and chipping sparrows, these pulpy fruits were also favorites of local Indians, who crushed them to make cider. Even the tough twigs are useful; California pioneers made pegs and nails from them.

With the onrush of high summer, the full range of Lassen's floral beauty fills the meadows with fragrance and color: alpine shooting stars, star-shaped skyrocket gilias, sunflowerlike mule-ears, purple larkspurs, spiky lupines, and Indian paintbrushes.

Such a wide variety of plants and habitats supplies ample food and shelter for Lassen's animal life, which ranges from raccoons and coyotes to wood ducks, tree frogs, and June bugs. Mule deer are common, spending their winters in the foothill country and moving upland in spring to browse amid the new greenery. But the park's most noticeable animals are the lodgepole chipmunks—cute, darting creatures that swarm over trees and trails, shamelessly begging visitors for scraps of food—and chattering chickarees, also known as Douglas squirrels.

Few ever glimpse the flying squirrel, a shy, diminutive creature of the night. Extending from its forelegs to its rear paws are flight skins, which function almost like a pair of wings. When traveling from tree to tree, the little rodent flings wide its legs—thus deploying its "wings"—and launches itself from a high branch, gliding as far as 150 feet while steering with its bushy tail. It finally lands by rearing back to an upright position, so that its "wings" catch the air and slow it down.

Furry, gray-brown pikas, also known as rock rabbits, scurry about, letting out squeaks and squawks that keep them in touch with others of their kind (hence the nickname "whistling hare"). Their favorite foods are green things—grasses, flower stems, and leaves. They don't hibernate in winter

Creating a zigzag pattern on the grass of the hot-springs area near Mount Diller, shallow pools are dyed a striking hue by red algae in the water. Pigments in the algae mask its green. Although the groundwater can become quite hot—heated by molten rock coursing near the earth's surface—the park supports rich and varied habitats: flowering meadows, dense forests, and cool, limpid lakes, as well as boiling springs, hot lakes and streams, and other thermal features.

As an autumn mist retreats, the graceful spires of a forest of red fir, rising from a dense growth of shrubby manzanita, *come into sharp focus. Come next summer, the manzanita will once again be adorned with edible berries.*

but remain active beneath the snow, so they collect grass all summer, dry it in the sun, and stash it under rocks for winter fare. One four-ounce pika can, in a single season, accumulate a cache of hay weighing as much as 50 pounds.

The last survivor

Long before European settlers reached California, four Indian tribes—the Yana, Yahi, Maidu, and Atsugewi—lived in relative harmony under the shadow of Lassen Peak. Until the mid-19th century, Indians in the region had encountered little trouble with European settlers; they had ignored—and been largely ignored by—the Spanish, who had been in California for many decades. But by 1850, gold fever was sweeping America, and prospectors intent on making big strikes were pouring into California. Some found gold. Many found rich lands for farming, and new waves of immigrants followed from the East.

Most of the Indians who lived on these lands were killed or sent to reservations. Others withdrew into inaccessible wilderness places like Lassen Peak, where they competed with the tribes who were already there, living uneasily and vulnerably in tiny pockets within white-dominated territories.

By the early 1900's only seven Yahi Indians were still alive in the region. By 1911 just one Yahi remained. We know him as Ishi, the Yahi word for "man." Exhausted and half starved, speaking a language no one understood, Ishi caused a sensation when he appeared in the California gold-mining town of Oroville. Happily, feelings toward Indians had changed over the years—Ishi's father had been lynched in the 1880's by white settlers—and, instead of killing their visitor, the townspeople called in anthropologists from the University of California. The scientists befriended Ishi and learned to talk with him in an Indian dialect related to Yahi. Whisked off to a university museum near San Francisco, Ishi was given a porter's job to pay for his keep and was eagerly questioned about his vanished people and his spartan wilderness life.

In 1913 Ishi returned to Lassen Peak with several anthropologists. The group lived for several weeks as the Indians once had. Ishi showed the scientists the locations of secret caves, ancient burial sites, old trails and campgrounds, and ceremonial hot springs. He taught them how to make stone arrowheads and other weapons, and how to survive on wild plants. Like most of his ancestors, Ishi had never been to the top of Lassen—the Indians had considered it too sacred for humans—but Ishi joined the scientists in their ascent.

The mountain, which could shake the ground when displeased or send up puffs of smoke with indecipherable messages, was at the heart of the Indians' world. Ishi's tribe had explained the mountain's fearsome powers in a legend. An ill-tempered god was especially distrustful of strangers, they said, and the sound of any language other than Yana roused him to such fury that he would stamp his foot, making the earth shudder and tremble.

Ishi's onetime neighbors, the Atsugewi, or Hat Creek, tribe, told different stories—tales of smoke spirits who lived in Lassen's caves. One legend recounted a chieftain's attempt to rescue a lovely maiden who had been kidnapped by the spirits and sequestered deep within the mountain. Impressed by the chieftain's determined efforts to free his love, the spirits allowed the couple to marry and dwell forever with them inside the mountain. The puffs of smoke emerging from Lassen Peak came, the Hat Creeks said, from the peace pipe that was passed back and forth between the chieftain and the spirits.

Lassen blows its top
Ishi was safely ensconced in his San Francisco home in the spring of 1914 when Lassen began to erupt. For about 200 years the volcano's inner channel had been plugged with cooled magma, but even this massive block could not contain Lassen's subterranean sea of molten rock. Eventually, the magma forced its way through a small fissure in the peak, and plumes of steam and black ash began venting almost two miles into the air. Ishi may well have wondered at his own responsibility in having accompanied English speakers to the sacred peak.

In the following year, some 200 steam explosions shot out of Lassen, tearing the peak wide open. Now the vent yawned about 1,000 feet across and lava flowed. For days molten rock spilled out, melting Lassen's snow cover. Water and volcanic ash

A parasol-topped mushroom stands at the height of its maturity, but its neighbor, a hemlock seedling, will one day surpass 100 feet in height.

churned together till they formed thick mudflows that overspread the region, pouring through valleys for up to 30 miles and burying the countryside under a sea of gray-black goo.

Dramatic as these eruptions were, Lassen Peak was merely clearing its throat. On May 22, 1915, the mighty volcano grumbled, thundered, and then shot up a black-brown mushroom-shaped cloud fully seven miles high. Red-hot boulders 12 feet across were hurled great distances; eight days later they were still hot to the touch. Fish trapped in burning mudflows were done to a turn. As steam and pumice surged up through the mushroom's stem, the cap widened spectacularly, like a slowly opening umbrella. Not long afterward, a rain of ash and other debris began to fall.

In the midst of this inferno, a superheated head of gas and steam burst out of Lassen Peak and slashed across the land like a tornado, leaving a three-mile swath in its wake. Whole forests were knocked flat by the withering blast; the devastated trail can still be seen today.

Ishi died in 1916 while Mount Lassen, still engorged with hot lava, continued to grumble and cough up smoke. The eruptions went on well into 1917 before Lassen lapsed into its present slumber. But, as our speeded-up photos of all the violence and all the peace at Lassen Park have shown, this slumber is doubtless temporary, a passing phase in the ongoing drama of destruction and rebirth.

When courting, a blue grouse proudly shows off his mating colors by raising his ruff and fanning his tail. His booming, ventriloquistic song is amplified by the inflatable air sacs that bulge beneath the yellow patches on his neck.

Mammoth Cave

"Beneath, the distant torrent's rushing sound
Tells where the volumed cataract doth roll
Between those hanging rocks, that shock yet
please the soul." George Gordon, Lord Byron

Local Indians knew about Mammoth Cave long ago. It was about 2000 B.C. when, no doubt impelled by normal human curiosity, they first ventured through the entrance, a gaping hole on a forested hillside, overlooking the Green River far below.

To find their way as they penetrated this dark and silent underground world, the Indians fashioned crude torches from bundles of giant cane, a tall, tough relative of bamboo that still grows in dense stands beside the river. (Scorched remnants of their torches have been found in many passageways inside the cave.) Probing the unknown depths must have been an awesome experience for these first adventurous explorers. In the hushed interior of the cave, their normally muted footsteps must have echoed distinctly, even ominously. In the flickering torchlight, their own shadows probably danced like giant ghosts across the cavern walls.

Advancing ever deeper into the labyrinth, the Indians found many wonders to reward their curiosity: rivers that flowed underground; massive rock piles where cave ceilings had collapsed; stone formations that looked like icicles, columns, and billowing windblown drapery. Most wonderful of all were scattered chambers lined with deposits of gypsum crystals, some of them glittering and white like snow—gypsum in fluffy cottonlike masses, in fragile needles that shattered at the slightest touch, even in the shape of startlingly realistic flowers that sprouted from the walls. These were the prizes that kept the Indians returning to the cave for centuries:

Great chambers and fantastical formations await all who venture into Mammoth Cave, an eerie yet awesome underground world that shelters creatures as varied as bats and blind fish.

they mined the gypsum, which they are believed to have used for ceremonial purposes. (It probably was a valued trade commodity as well.)

Signs of the Indians' comings and goings are plentiful in the cave. In some places their footprints have survived in the soil, undisturbed by wind or weather for thousands of years; long-forgotten sandals and other articles of clothing, finely woven from local plant fibers, have been retrieved from the depths. But the most impressive discovery was made in 1935, when the mummified body of an Indian gypsum miner was found about two miles from the cave entrance. Killed about 420 B.C., he had been crushed by a five-ton boulder dislodged by his own digging. His body, his clothing, even the remnants of the last meal in his stomach—all were perfectly preserved. The body of "Lost John," as he was dubbed, remains in the cave.

Then, for unknown reasons, the Indians abandoned Mammoth Cave about 1,000 years ago. It was not rediscovered until the 1790's when, according to legend, a hunter named Houchins stumbled upon the entrance while tracking a wounded bear. Whatever may have been the case, settlers soon found a new use for the cave. During the War of 1812 they began to mine its extensive deposits of nitrate, which was used to make saltpeter, a major ingredient of gunpowder. (Foreign supplies of both saltpeter and gunpowder had been cut off by the British blockade of shipping.) Visitors can still see the miners' leaching vats, wooden pipes, and other paraphernalia that remind us of Mammoth's brief but crucial role in the nation's history.

Modern exploration of the cave began in earnest in 1838 when a local lawyer bought the property for development as a tourist attraction. For the role of guide he chose his 17-year-old black slave, Stephen Bishop. The choice was an ideal one, for Bishop seems to have been afflicted immediately with a case of cave fever. Insatiable in his curiosity to know what lay around the next bend and beyond the next rockfall, he threw himself enthusiastically into the task of unraveling the cave's mysteries. By the time he died in 1857, he had discovered some 10 miles of major passageways and earned an unrivaled reputation as Mammoth's greatest explorer.

Yet even Bishop's work was only a beginning. Over the years, intrepid explorers added mile after mile to the known extent of the cave. Inching their way through cramped passages, enduring agony and fatigue, these mud-caked adventurers probed ever deeper into the labyrinth. And in time there came the realization that Mammoth Cave is mammoth indeed.

Its size keeps growing—not only because the forces that created it are still at work, but also because the underground world is by no means fully explored. In recent decades the focus has shifted from unraveling the mysteries of Mammoth's maze of corridors to finding links between Mammoth and the other cave systems that riddle the surrounding plateau. The enormous Flint Ridge system a little to the north of Mammoth was a particularly tantalizing target. For years explorers tried to find a connection between the two, but met with only dead ends and disappointment. The payoff for their efforts finally came in 1972 when, working south from Flint Ridge, a young woman, Patricia Crowther, wormed her small body through yet another

muddy hole, which was later to be named the Tight Spot. A short distance beyond, she and her companions soon spotted a metal handrail: they were in Mammoth Cave. The two systems in fact were one, a single cave with a total of 144 miles of interconnected tunnels and passageways.

More discoveries followed. In 1979, cavers found a link between Mammoth and Proctor Cave, to the southwest. Then in 1983—crawling, squeezing, climbing, wading neck-deep through water—they discovered a connection with Roppel Cave, beyond the boundaries of the park. That brought the total mapped length of the Mammoth Cave system to 294 miles, by far the longest cave in the world. (Its nearest rival, in the U.S.S.R., is only about one-third as long.) And no one knows what the future may reveal as cavers continue to probe the secrets of this realm of eternal darkness.

The powerful work of water

Echo River, a waterway that flows through the lowermost depths of Mammoth Cave, offers a key to understanding the origins of this subterranean wonderland. For water is the subtle sculptor that carved—and is still carving—Mammoth's seemingly endless labyrinth of chambers and passageways. Rain falling through the air and then seeping through decaying vegetation on the ground picks up enough carbon dioxide to become a mild solution of carbonic acid—and given enough time, this acidic water is capable of dissolving solid limestone and opening passageways in the rock.

Such was the origin of Echo River's channel and,

How Water Carves Caves in Limestone

Acidic water flowing down through surface sinkholes dissolves limestone as it seeps through cracks and fissures in the rock. It gradually enlarges them into an interconnected maze of vertical shafts and horizontal galleries. In time

the water table (the top of the saturated zone in the limestone) may drop. Water then drains from the upper passageways, leaving them high and dry, and new openings are hollowed out at lower levels in the rock.

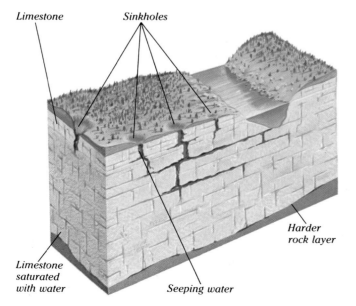

Limestone   Sinkholes

Harder rock layer

Limestone saturated with water

Seeping water

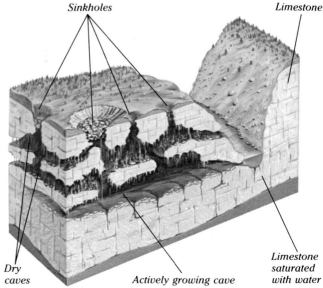

Sinkholes   Limestone

Dry caves

Actively growing cave

Limestone saturated with water

Flowing through lovely, gently rolling woodlands, the Green River traces a lazy course across Mammoth Cave National Park. Encom-

passing more than 50,000 acres, the above-ground areas of the park offer splendid opportunities for camping, hiking, and canoeing.

indeed, of every other passageway in the cave network. Eons ago, what is now the river's course was probably marked by the minutest of fractures in the limestone that makes up the Mammoth Cave Plateau. Bit by bit, seeping water gradually dissolved the rock. Now the calm, greenish river flows along a channel that averages 20 feet in width and in some places is as much as 25 feet deep.

The story of the cave began about 300 million years ago, when the region was flooded by a shallow inland sea. For millions of years, the limy shells and skeletons of sea creatures, many of them microscopic in size, settled to the floor of the sea and accumulated into layers of limestone hundreds of feet thick. Mud and sand later washed in and were transformed into layers of shale and sandstone atop the limestone.

When the land began to rise and the sea retreated, about 280 million years ago, countless cracks and fissures developed in the limestone, and erosion began to attack the caprock. On the plains southeast of the park—the source of most of the water that carved the cave—the protective layers of shale and sandstone have disappeared entirely. Here the land is pockmarked with sinkholes, huge circular pits that were eroded into the limestone where surface water plunges underground. (Sinkholes can also be formed or enlarged by the collapse of cave ceilings.)

Flowing through fissures in the limestone, the water

gradually enlarged them into mighty passageways where underground rivers rushed toward their outlets, the springs along the Green River. Then, as the Green River deepened its valley, upper passages were left high and dry and the water began carving new channels at lower levels in the rock. At the lowest levels—along Echo River some 360 feet below ground level, for instance—the process still goes on. A living cave, Mammoth continues to grow.

Fantasies in stone

The acidic water that carves cave passageways can also fill them with all sorts of fanciful decorations. Seeping through pores and crevices in the limestone, the water becomes saturated with dissolved calcium carbonate. When it trickles into open chambers and tunnels, it deposits its cargo of dissolved minerals in a variety of intriguing forms.

Most familiar are the stalactites that dangle like icicles from cave ceilings and the stalagmites that grow upward where water drips on the floor. (Stalactites and stalagmites sometimes unite to form columns.) But Mammoth Cave boasts many other formations as well, some of them snowy white, others tinted in tones of yellow, orange, brown, or even black by mineral impurities in the calcium carbonate.

Translucent draperies, for instance, form where the mineralized water drips from cracks in the ceiling.

Dripping with tier upon tier of gracefully fluid flowstone, Mammoth's Frozen Niagara is a wintry-looking cascade of solid rock that stands some 75 feet high. The delicate gypsum flowers that decorate the walls of many of the cave's drier areas, in contrast, are seldom more than six inches in diameter. These and all the other formations that are found in many parts of the cave were deposited over the eons by mineral-laden water seeping from pores and fissures in the cavern's walls and ceilings.

Flowstone is deposited where the water flows across a wall or other surface instead of dripping. If it flows across a jumbled heap of rocks, the result is likely to resemble a waterfall. That was the origin of Mammoth's Frozen Niagara, one of the most elaborate formations in the cave. Cave popcorn grows in grapelike clusters on the walls, the product of the splattering of real waterfalls or of water seeping from microscopic pores in the limestone. Strangest of all are the bizarre-looking helictites, gnarled fingers of stone that wildly twist and turn in all directions.

In caves, even running streams can be decorated with deposits. Where the water flows over an irregularity on the streambed, calcium carbonate gradually builds up to form a crusty-looking rimstone dam, creating a pool or even a sizable lake. Sometimes a steplike series of such dams fills a passage, resulting in a lovely sight as the water spills over the dams from one pool to the next.

And then there are the wondrous gypsum formations that continue to grow in some of the dry galleries. As gypsum-bearing water escapes from microscopic pores in the limestone, the water evaporates and the spar-kling white or sometimes brownish gypsum crystals are left behind. The gypsum may collect in cracks or accumulate beneath the surface of the limestone until it wedges off flakes or even large chunks of rock. But usually the gypsum forms a crust on the cave walls. As more gypsum crystals form beneath the crust, they force it to swell outward in blisters known as gypsum snowballs. Finally the snowballs burst open to form wonderfully lifelike gypsum flowers, complete with curving "petals" that are sometimes as much as six inches long. A visit to Mammoth's famous Snowball Room or Alice's Grotto will reveal these wintry fantasies in all their fragile splendor.

Dwellers in darkness

Strange creatures lurk in the stygian depths of Mammoth Cave. Gliding slowly through the water of Echo River, as pale and silent as ghosts, are little cave fish—eyeless, colorless, no longer than a finger. It was Stephen Bishop, the pioneering guide-explorer, who first introduced the world to Mammoth's eyeless fish. Ever since, the unearthly forms that life takes in coping with an utterly lightless environment have been a source of endless fascination for the scientists who study them.

Slender little eyeless crayfish, as smooth and white as alabaster, also inhabit Mammoth's waterways, where they move slowly about, waving their extralong, supersensitive antennae through the water in search of bits of food. Among the other animals that live their entire lives in the cave and never venture into sunlight are endangered Kentucky cave shrimp, tiny white snails, flatworms, spiders, mites, and six kinds of beetles. In all, Mammoth harbors nearly 30 species of permanent cave dwellers. These full-time residents, which can survive only in caves, are known as troglobites.

Other animals—the troglophiles, or cave lovers—are less particular about their surroundings: they frequently live in caves but can get along just as well in cool, damp, dark places in the outside world. The most colorful by far of these opportunists are cave salamanders. Bright orange spotted with black, they are sometimes seen near cave entrances.

Least dependent on caves are the part-time visitors, or trogloxenes. Phoebes, for example, occasionally build their nests and raise their young on ledges near the dimly lit cave entrances, but never fly farther into the deepening gloom. Much more numerous are the four species of bats that congregate in Mammoth to hibernate each winter. Some kinds dangle from cave ceilings, isolated from their neighbors; others form dense furry mats where throngs of them cling to the limestone overhead.

The biggest problem for all cave dwellers is finding enough to eat. Unlike the sunlit outside world, the inky darkness of the cave cannot support green plants. Yet green plants are the first link in every food chain. In caves this need is provided for by imports from above ground. Spring floods regularly raise the water level in Mammoth Cave by as much as 30 or 40 feet. And with this huge influx of water, a great deal of organic material—the dead and dying remains of plants and animals from the surface world—is washed into the cave. Scavengers from worms to snails feed on this decaying debris and are eaten in turn by the cave fish and various other predators.

Cave crickets are another major importer of food at Mammoth. Each night when the weather is right, hordes of crickets leave the cave on feeding forays to the surface. Back in the cave their droppings—and eventually their own dead bodies—are a significant food source for other cave creatures. Even their eggs are eaten. One kind of cave beetle, only about a quarter of an inch long, is constantly on the lookout for cricket eggs. A single egg provides all the nourishment it needs for a week.

Food, nonetheless, is very scarce in Mammoth Cave, and this scarcity, scientists theorize, has had much to do with the development of the cave dwellers' unusual adaptations. Since eyes, for example, are useless structures in a world of total darkness, it would be advantageous to a developing embryo to conserve energy by

not producing them. In an environment where nothing can see or be seen, producing pigment cells for camouflage or to attract a mate likewise would be a waste of energy. And so, over time, most of Mammoth's troglobites have become colorless and blind.

They conserve energy in other ways too. In addition to its two species of eyeless cave fish, Mammoth is sometimes home to the closely related springfish, a species that is neither eyeless nor white. In contrast to these brown and white and sighted creatures, which swim with jerky, erratic movements, the cave fish glide through the water with calm deliberation. With each smooth stroke of their oversized fins, they move twice as far as the springfish do with each stroke. Cave fish also lay fewer eggs at a time, live many years longer than the springfish do, and generally get by with a much lower metabolic rate.

Perhaps most astonishing of all is the cave fish's ability to "see" in the perpetual gloom of their underground rivers. Grouped in short rows on their heads and bodies are multitudes of highly developed sense organs that detect the faintest changes in water movement. Even the feeble swimming motions of a tiny crustacean—a tasty morsel to a cave fish—furnish the blind hunters with clues enough to pinpoint its location. Springfish, which have far fewer, less sensitive, ranks of these vibration receptors, must come within one inch to detect prey that cave fish can "see" while still three inches away.

Such are the kinds of adaptations that creatures must develop if they are to succeed in carrying life's banner in this strange and hostile netherworld. That anything at all can live in this place of perpetual night seems wondrous in itself. That such a wide variety of animals can manage to survive in Mammoth Cave seems a miracle that in its own way is even more awesome than the spectacle of inanimate gypsum mimicking the delicate beauty of living flowers.

Eyeless and colorless like most of Mammoth Cave's permanent residents, the dainty little cave crayfish relies on its long and sensitive antennae to locate prey in the underworld's never-ending night.

Mesa Verde

"I saw a little city of stone asleep . . . . That village sat looking down into the canyon with the calmness of eternity . . . preserved in the dry air and almost perpetual sunlight like a fly in amber, guarded by the cliffs and the river and the desert."
Willa Cather

Ghosts walk much of the American Southwest, and nowhere is their silent presence more strongly felt than along the steep walls of the many canyons that slice the high tablelands of Mesa Verde. Although nearly 700 years have passed since the last of the people known to the Navajos as *Anasazi*, or "Ancient Ones," left the complex community they had built here, something of their vital spirit remains to resonate in the souls of modern visitors.

Standing in the courtyard of Cliff Palace or Long House, the two largest cliff dwellings, one can imagine the shrill sound of children at play, sense the murmur of sandaled feet, envision a group of women grinding corn, and catch the echo of drums and chanting voices from a kiva's depth. But to do so is to touch only the most recent history of this place. For the magnificent cliff dwellings that are the park's main attraction are but the capstone of a culture that grew and flourished here over a span of about 750 years. The true spirit that inhabits Mesa Verde is the legacy of a civilization—the accumulated experience, hope, skill, faith, and understanding of all the generations who built that society, lifetime upon lifetime.

Those who first came here, about A.D. 550, were descendants of nomadic peoples who had roamed the Southwest for thousands of years, hunting with stone-tipped spears, gathering wild plants where they found them, and occasionally growing a little squash. Their immediate ancestors—beginning about the time of Christ—are known as Basketmakers because of their skill at weaving the fibers of the yucca. So finely woven were many of the baskets they made that they could be

The only U.S. national park devoted to the works of early man, Mesa Verde holds mysteries yet unsolved about the artisans who made cities on canyon walls with tools of stone and fashioned exquisite pottery from coils of clay.

used for carrying water and even for cooking: hot rocks were dropped into baskets of water.

By the time the offspring of these early people came to Mesa Verde, they had entered a stage of development that today's scientists call the Modified Basketmaker Period. They knew how to grow corn, a grain that does not seed itself in the wild, and so they had a good reason to stay in one place. This dependable food supply had given them time and energy for improving tools, weapons, and other utensils. Families were larger and so were overall populations. Thus they came looking, not merely for good hunting grounds, but for a place to settle down, till the soil, and create a community.

They found the land atop the great mesa much as it is today. Forests of pinyon pine and Utah juniper promised a good supply of wood for homes, fires, tools, and weapons. Broad mesa tops offered a wide array of plants, especially yucca, and supported a healthy population of mule deer, wild turkeys, and other game. Seeps and springs were a steady source of water; and the thunderstorms of summer—the result of the mesa's abrupt rise above the surrounding valley—were ideal for growing corn in the deep, rich, reddish soil that had been dropped here, a dry grain at a time, by southwest winds.

The simple pit houses built by these first permanent inhabitants of Mesa Verde began as shallow holes in the ground, circular pits a few feet deep dug with crude wooden tools. The soil was carried away in baskets. Then the men went out and cut four straight poles of pinyon pine, which they set into four evenly spaced holes within the pit so that the tops were about head high. Four smaller poles became crossbeams to support a roof of additional poles, sticks, and bark. The walls, leaning from the edge of the pit to the crossbeams, were of the same materials. The whole structure was then covered with mud, which baked in the hot sun to a hard, stuccolike finish. The entrance to this weatherproof mound was by ladder through a hole in the center of the roof; in the winter, when a fire was built, the smoke escaped through the same hole. Dug into one end of some of these houses was a storage room, or anteroom, and occasionally this was designed to serve as an burrowlike second entrance.

They were small, sturdy people—few stood as tall as five and a half feet—who worked hard to stay alive. Although the small patches of corn and squash that they grew near their pit houses gave a measure of security, they still looked to the wild for most of life's necessities. The bulbs of sego lilies, the spring shoots of

The Spanish-speaking people who named Mesa Verde—the name means "green table"—never saw it from the air, as in this view looking northward over Chapin Mesa. Had they done so, the name would certainly still be the same.

Rocky Mountain bee plants, the leaves of Mormon tea, and the seeds of pinyon pines were among the myriad treasures to be gleaned from forest and mesa top, but none was as vital as the yucca. The petals of its bell-shaped flowers, the pith of its stout flower stalks, and the juicy meat of its fruits were eaten. Part of its heavy root was made into soap. Its stiff, swordlike leaves were softened by soaking in water, then pounded with stones to loosen the strong fibers within. From these were made baskets, bags, cords, nets, snares, and sandals. The sharp points of the leaves were used to make holes in rabbit skins and rawhide, and other parts of the leaf were used as paintbrushes.

A great advantage of staying in one place was that traders, who regularly traveled among the Indian peoples of the Southwest and Mexico, knew where the Mesa Verde Anasazi were and included them among their customers. We don't know how or when pottery was first introduced. Perhaps a trader arrived from the south with a vessel of fired clay. It was strong, it was beautiful, and it could hold water far better than the best baskets. Perhaps he left it in trade for baskets, or perhaps he simply answered questions about how it was made. In any case, there must have been great excitement afterward, as the women began to experiment with this new material. They learned to mix clay from the soil beneath their feet, to roll it between their palms into long ropelike strands, and to coil these, one atop another, into the shapes of dishes, bowls, and larger vessels. They smoothed these creations inside and out, and they decorated them.

When meat was needed, the men took their stone-tipped spears and spear throwers, or atlatls, and went hunting. Surely they sought help through chanting and prayer, for the atlatl was not an accurate weapon. It was merely a short piece of wood, cupped at one end to hold the base of a spear; but properly used it lengthened the thrower's arm, adding a joint to it and greatly increasing the power of a throw. Rabbits were the usual game. The skins were sewn together to make blankets; tools were made from the bones. On those occasions when a mule deer was brought down, the clan set to work on the carcass. The fresh meat was stripped and allowed to dry for winter rations. The skin became rawhide leather, some of which was sliced into thongs for binding stone blades to wooden handles. Sinews became a tough thread. Bones were broken and fashioned into such tools as awls, punches, needles, and fleshers for removing meat from hides. Antlers were used as pressure tools in making stone blades or spearheads.

The first pueblos

During the two centuries after the Basketmakers had settled in Mesa Verde, they acquired a new and very important item: the bow and arrow. This made hunting easier and much more efficient, and so more time could be spent tending crops. Beans were added to the staple crops of corn and squash. With a stable

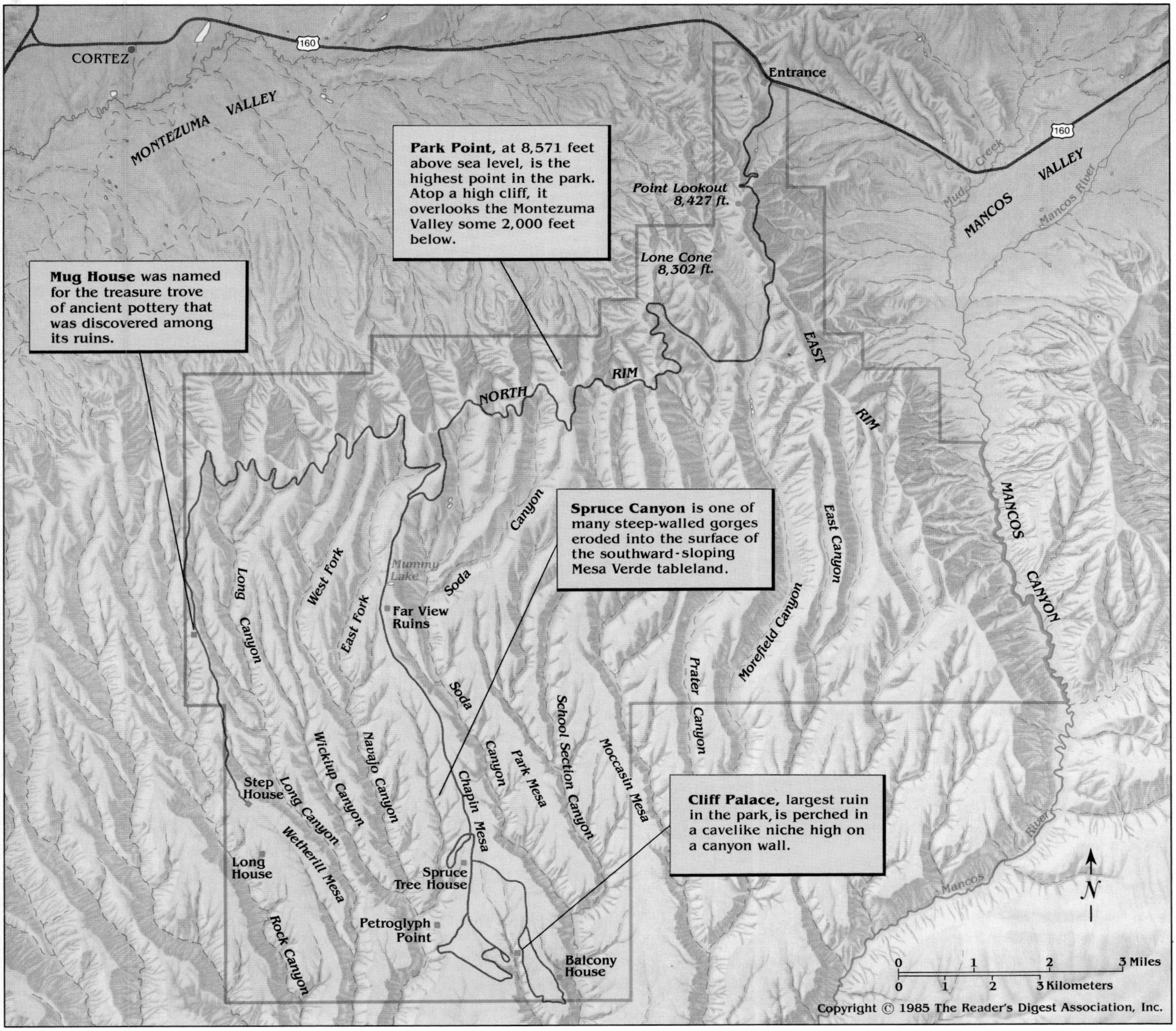
CORTEZ
160
MONTEZUMA VALLEY
Entrance
160
MANCOS VALLEY
Mud Creek
Mancos River
Park Point, at 8,571 feet above sea level, is the highest point in the park. Atop a high cliff, it overlooks the Montezuma Valley some 2,000 feet below.
Point Lookout 8,427 ft.
Lone Cone 8,302 ft.
Mug House was named for the treasure trove of ancient pottery that was discovered among its ruins.
NORTH RIM
EAST RIM
Spruce Canyon is one of many steep-walled gorges eroded into the surface of the southward-sloping Mesa Verde tableland.
MANCOS CANYON
East Canyon
Morefield Canyon
Prater Canyon
Moccasin Mesa
School Section Canyon
Park Mesa
Soda Canyon
Mummy Lake
Far View Ruins
West Fork
East Fork
Long Canyon
Wickiup Canyon
Navajo Canyon
Chapin Mesa
Step House
Long Canyon
Wetherill Mesa
Long House
Rock Canyon
Spruce Tree House
Petroglyph Point
Balcony House
Cliff Palace, largest ruin in the park, is perched in a cavelike niche high on a canyon wall.
Mancos River
N
0 1 2 3 Miles
0 1 2 3 Kilometers
Copyright © 1985 The Reader's Digest Association, Inc.

food supply their way of life changed, as farming gradually replaced hunting. By the middle of the eighth century, the Anasazi began to congregate in larger settlements and to build structures above ground. With this act they entered a period that scientists call Developmental Pueblo.

The boxy frameworks of these houses were wooden poles, and the substance of the walls was a mixture of sticks, stones, and lots of mud. From these materials were created large houses that were one story high and many rooms long—some stretched on for 150 feet. When a new room was needed, it was simply built onto the end of the line. Rapidly developing their extraordinary skills as masons, their construction technique advanced from mud plastered over a wood frame to finely constructed stone masonry with blocks shaped to corners and curved walls.

The old ways were not entirely forgotten, however; some became tradition. Near its long rowhouse each clan dug a pit room, similar to the old pit houses but deeper and more solidly built. To allow for air movement, each included a small tunnel at floor level which connected to a vertical air shaft. These pit rooms were workshops and meeting rooms for members of the clan, and it was in them that religious activities took place.

In the springtime, when food reserves were dwindling after long and sometimes snowy winters, it was important to get crops started early. The farmers found through experimentation that, by building small dams of stones across intermittent watercourses, they could hold the moisture of the melting snow in the soil. These were places where early corn could survive until summer rains began to fall, and over the years hundreds of these check dams were built.

More and more land came to be devoted to agriculture, and the population spread out over many of the long, slender mesas that make up Mesa Verde. All summer long, farmers went daily to the fields carrying their digging sticks—oblong pieces of juniper wood that were sharpened at one end and rounded at the other. Most extensive farming was done on the mesa tops, which the Indians cleared by cutting pinyon and juniper for wood. Some land was also cleared by forest fires. Dogs and turkeys had been domesticated, and turkey feathers were twisted around yucca cordage to make blankets for the winter. Traders brought cotton from the south, and the weaving of cloth was added to the list of crafts.

Pottery making all but replaced basketry. It was a time-consuming process. Clay had to be gathered, mixed with temper so it would not crack when it was fired, carefully shaped one coil at a time, smoothed, decorated, and fired. A fresh, developing craft, pottery making was open to self-expression, and potters experimented with shapes, sizes, and forms. There were large mugs, narrow-necked jugs, shallow bowls and dishes, animal-shaped vessels, and small whimsical pieces that may have been the work of youngsters learning the art.

Most of all, it was the decoration—black designs on a white background—that marked a piece as a product of the Mesa Verde Anasazi. The work of some potters was distinguished by the figures of lizards, centipedes, birds, and mammals, but geometric patterns were by far the commonest. For centuries, most potters made their black paint from minerals, such as hematite and other ochers, but early in the 11th century someone tried boiling plants to make a thick paint. This worked better, and so after A.D. 1050 plants became a far more popular source—the Rocky Mountain bee plant yielded a particularly good black. One type of pottery, however, used mostly for cooking, was left unpainted. We call it corrugated ware because of its rough outer surface, made by pinching the soft clay coils before firing.

Community action

The blessings of civilization are not unmixed, and in a growing population social tensions are bound to increase. Each clan required more and more land for agriculture, and the success of each year's crop became increasingly vital. The periodic droughts that are a fact of life in this part of the world were no longer simply hard times to be endured; they loomed as threats to the very fabric of society, to survival itself.

As the families of the clans joined their rooms to live together, complex social and religious organizations that focused on nature and agriculture developed. The earlier pit houses evolved into subterranean ceremonial and communal chambers—the kiva as it is called today by Hopi Indians, one of the modern Pueblo tribes who are descendants of the ancient Anasazi. It was here that special ceremonies and dances, many designed to bring rain, ensure crop fertility, and ward off natural disasters, were held. The kiva's form was almost identical to some of today's kivas: a deep, round pit lined with masonry blocks, the roof supported by pilasters of masonry. Ringing the wall was a bench or shelf of masonry, and a masonry deflector shielded the central fire pit from air entering through the ventilator shaft. In the floor was a small hole, called a *sipapu*—symbolic of the Great Sipapu, through which it was believed mankind had entered the world.

By A.D. 1100 some 2,500 people lived in Mesa Verde. Clans began working together as they never had done before. At least two great kivas were built that were more than twice the size of the average clan kiva and unconnected to any clan house. The Anasazi became expert at conserving local water supplies. On Chapin Mesa, a reservoir about 90 feet across with high, artificial banks on two sides, was dug; we call its dry remains Mummy Lake. The stone-lined reservoir was filled through a series of ditches and some archeologists think it served several nearby communities, attesting to cooperation among hundreds of villagers in work projects essential for survival.

About A.D. 1075 the Anasazi farmers began to build round towers of stone about 15 feet high near their houses and kivas; some were connected to kivas by tunnels. Others were freestanding, near no other structures. We don't know why these towers were built; it is presumed that they served some religious purpose, although some of them may have been lookout posts.

Villages of stone

A series of droughts blighted the end of the 11th century, and during this time the people began abandoning their clan houses and moving farther north on the mesas, where rainfall was heavier. Here they no longer built the rowhouses of the past, but erected stone buildings three and four stories high, and they built them in groups—planned communities where several clans coexisted. As the years went on and these villages grew, the stonework became more sophisticated, careful, and precise. Rather than using great dollops of mud to mortar the spaces between

Looking at the well-preserved ruins of Cliff Palace, Mesa Verde's largest cliff dwelling, on a sunny summer afternoon, you can easily populate the scene in your mind's eye with the life of seven centuries ago. The rooms in front were living quarters; storage rooms were behind them. The open court was a busy place. While most of the men were away hunting, gathering wood, and tending crops, the women ground corn with hand-held stones called manos, cooked and prepared food for storage, and did dozens of other jobs in preparation for winter. Building was a continuous process.

random-sized stones, masons invented a technique of chipping large stones into rectangular blocks. Their tools were stone hammers, and the resultant dimpled surface is another hallmark of the Mesa Verde culture.

Although we have found no evidence of warfare between communities or large-scale raids by outsiders, the villages became decidedly fortresslike. Their outer walls were doorless, windowless, and sometimes of double thickness. The houses they enclosed faced open courtyards where kivas were still the central focus.

In the kivas—formalized echos of the distant past—farmers prayed for rain when there was none. When rain fell, they prayed that it would be enough to nourish their corn, beans, and squash, and that there would be an overflow to run into the reservoirs begun by their forebears. Check dams were built on the mesas in increasing numbers, and seeps and springs along canyon walls were cleaned and enlarged.

In many important ways, the Anasazi of Mesa Verde were not unlike the Anasazi who built communities in other areas of the Colorado Plateau over the course of

Like the Anasazi of 700 years ago, today's visitors reach the upper levels of Long House by climbing rough wooden ladders. Second in size only to Cliff Palace, Long House is located in the largest alcove ever occupied on the mesa.

these same centuries. But in the late 12th century, they came to a group decision that sets them apart. They began to build intricate cities of stone in alcoves along the steep walls of the canyons that slice between the tablelands where they had lived for so long.

The cliff houses

For their new home sites, many of the Mesa Verde residents moved from open areas on the mesa tops to sheltered areas in the cliffs below. They took advantage of whatever alcove was available regardless of its orientation. Perhaps the most sought-after alcoves faced south-southwest. The low winter sun would shine in, but not the overhead rays of summer. East-facing alcoves might have been second choices, since they received morning light in winter. Most of the alcoves are near the 7,000-foot level, several hundred feet above the canyon floors and a hundred feet or more below the mesa rim. Some of them could be reached only by means of handholds that the Anasazi painstakingly carved into sheer rock walls.

We may never know why so many of the Anasazi moved to the cliffs. They never developed a written language, and so nothing remains of personal thoughts and feelings. We can only imagine what political upheavals, religious promptings, social tensions, or outside threats might have caused such a group decision to be taken. But we *do* know what a tremendous effort must have been involved in bringing about this relocation.

The sloping floors of the alcoves had to be leveled. Stones had to be gathered and lowered from mesa rims or raised from canyon floors. Water had to be brought, a jug at a time, from springs and seeps to make mud for mortar. The dirt itself had to be carried, and so did the large logs that were used in construction. It was a labor of lifetimes—we know that Cliff Palace was under construction for more than 70 years—and all the while food had to be grown as before, meat had to be hunted, pottery had to be made, children had to be raised, and winter had to be survived.

Only slowly, as new quarters were completed, did the population, numbering perhaps 3,000 souls by now, move to the cliffs. By A.D. 1250 there were about a dozen large cliff dwellings—varying in room count from 40 to 217—as well as several hundred one-family houses with 6 to 8 rooms and a kiva. Among the Anasazi, there were no palaces or special buildings set aside for the powerful or wealthy. All lived alike—the religious leaders, the farmers, the pottery makers, hunters, and weavers.

During the warm summers, when men wore only loincloths and women small aprons, the multilevel courtyards of the cliff houses must have been busy, noisy places, the activities of many families overlapping. Children, dogs, and turkeys were everywhere. Some boys might be mixing mortar or plaster to cover walls that needed repair. Women were working outdoors at their many tasks, and men were coming and going with building materials, game from hunting expeditions,

The importance of the sacred kiva to the cliff dwellers of Mesa Verde is clearly seen by the amount of space it commanded and the work that went into its construction. Note the opening of the ventilation shaft in the foreground.

crops from the fields above, and firewood from the canyons below.

Life was more complicated than ever. Every year it took more work and more land to produce the same crops from soil that was depleted after centuries of use. Many of the strongest and ablest workers were involved in construction. Wood gatherers had to go farther and farther from home to find winter fuel. Toward the end of the period, some architecture became more slapdash, the rocks irregular and rough-hewn, their surfaces less carefully dimpled, as though the builders were wearying of their long task.

Pottery—still the Anasazi's primary craft—had become more diverse. Attractive and functional, it was a good trade item. One community, Mug House, gets its name from a form of pottery common in Mesa Verde, the heavy handled mug. In addition, shallow bowls, large narrow-necked jars, spoonlike ladles—all decorated with intricate geometric patterns in the traditional Mesa Verde black on white—have been found over a wide area in the ruins of many cultures.

By winter, when tremendous piles of dry wood stood in front of houses, if enough materials of all types had been gathered and stored, there would be little reason to venture out into the deep snow. Mornings were cold, but afternoons, when the sun's rays showered down on the houses and courtyards, were probably pleasant. Men gathered in kivas, trying to ensure next season's success. But hard times were coming.

In the summer of A.D. 1276 it quit raining, and no appreciable rain fell during the next 23 summers. Depleted soil became dust in the hot wind, and wild plants withered along with the crops. Nothing that could be done in the kivas seemed to help. By A.D. 1300, when the rain began to fall again, the canyons and tablelands were deserted.

We can only speculate why the people of Mesa Verde left the homeland of their ancestors. Part of it might have been the drought. After hundreds of years of intensive use the land and its resources could have been depleted. Perhaps the climate became cooler, shortening the growing season and interfering with successful harvests. Their trade with Mexico could have evaporated. Because they left no written history, there is much we cannot know about them. But we know that they were human beings, like ourselves, who dreamed and worked to make their dreams reality. And knowing this, we marvel at their accomplishments.

Mount Rainier

" 'Midst broken rocks, a rugged scene,
With green and grassy dales between,
. . . Where nature seems to sit alone,
Majestic on a craggy throne."
Joseph Warton, *18th-century poet*

When at day's end the last of the light washes across Mount Rainier, its snow-crowned summit is suffused with a glowing pink, as though a piece of the sunset had somehow settled to earth. The icy old volcano is so high—14,411 feet—that as much as 20 minutes sometimes passes before lowland shadows climb to the mountaintop and the rosy glow at last gives way to a ghostly white, looming against the nighttime sky.

The spectacle is visible from afar, for Rainier rises head and shoulders above any nearby peaks. Towering over the shores of Puget Sound like a splendid beacon, it has few rivals for vertical contrast between foot and summit. In all of the country south of Alaska, only Telescope Peak, bordering Death Valley, California, rises higher above its immediate surroundings.

Fire and ice are the improbable twins that shaped this majestic peak. Volcanism built the cone; glaciers are wearing it away. Any mountaineer who ascends Rainier's steep slopes can experience both of these forces. Indeed, the first documented summit climb, in 1870, would have ended in disaster if the two climbers, P. B. Van Trump and Hazard Stevens, had not found one

Abroad in all seasons, the red fox is but one of many wild creatures

that roam the rugged slopes of Mount Rainier, a peak so tall and massive that it completely dominates its lowland surroundings.

of the many caves that penetrate beneath the ice on Rainier's crater rim—caves that were hollowed out by steam escaping from volcanic vents.

It was just before dusk when the weary climbers reached the mountaintop and stumbled into one of these unexpected shelters. There they spent a miserable night trying to warm themselves beside the sulfurous steam vents. The heat that issued from the vents was unbearable for more than a few minutes at a time, the fumes were nauseating, and the steam quickly saturated their clothing. Yet whenever they crept away from the infernal vents, bitter cold instantly froze their trousers and sleeves. Eventually the long night passed, however, and in the morning the pair managed to climb back down the mountain to safety.

Ninety years later, scientists recognized that Rai-

nier's summit was a uniquely suitable site for experiments preparatory to our first moon probe. Anxious to learn how it feels, mentally and physically, to survive in a hostile environment, totally cut off from other human beings and the events of daily life, they spent more than a month living in the same place where those early climbers had bivouacked.

The scientists soon found that they had chosen a hostile site indeed. Rocks surrounding the steam vents reached temperatures of 170° F—almost hot enough to boil water at these high elevations. A yard or two away from the hot rocks, in contrast, their thermometers recorded winter air temperatures as low as 0° F inside the caves, and outside the mercury dropped to −80° F at night. This temperature range of 250 degrees is greater than that recorded almost anywhere else on earth—

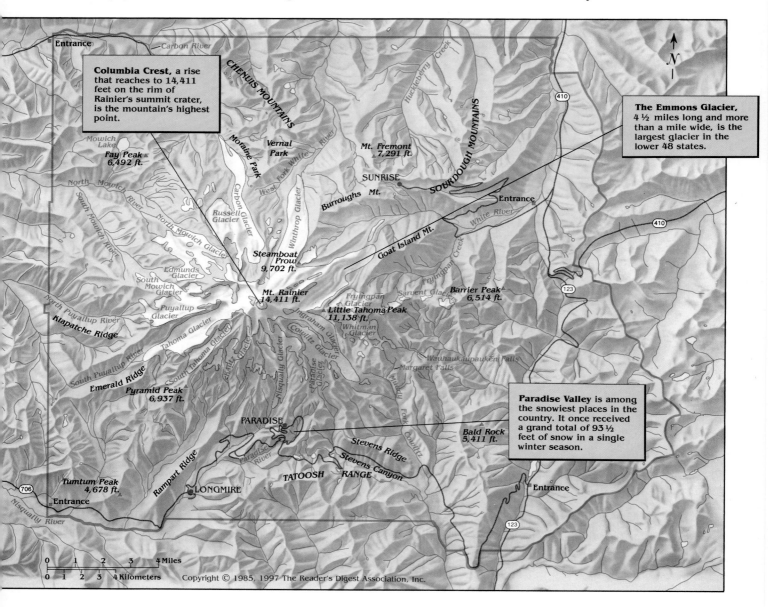

Columbia Crest, a rise that reaches to 14,411 feet on the rim of Rainier's summit crater, is the mountain's highest point.

The Emmons Glacier, 4 ½ miles long and more than a mile wide, is the largest glacier in the lower 48 states.

Paradise Valley is among the snowiest places in the country. It once received a grand total of 93 ½ feet of snow in a single winter season.

Dwarfed by the immensity of the mountain, a line of climbers approaches Rainier's lofty summit crater. The snow-filled basin, some 1,400 feet in diameter, was created when the volcano last erupted about 2,500 years ago. The Liberty Cap, rising to the rear, is actually about 300 feet lower than the crater's rim.

Seemingly oblivious of his surroundings—that's Rainier in the background—a climber assaults a peak in the Tatoosh Range, just south of the mighty volcano.

ideal for experiencing the kind of temperature extremes that might be encountered on the moon.

Austere, in fact, is the only word for the summit of Rainier. Permanently covered with ice and snow, it is ringed with glaciers that spill down the slopes on all sides. Fierce winds howl almost constantly, and blizzards may blind climbers even in midsummer. Few who reach the top have enough energy left to explore the whole broad crown of the mountain. Instead, they cross the small crater left by Rainier's most recent eruption in order to reach Columbia Crest, the highest point on its rim, then seek a spot where they can sit and relax. And there, if the day is clear, they exult in the astonishing view and rest up for the descent. This peak, so serene at sunset or when seen floating above Seattle like an anchored white cloud, demands real stamina to climb—but the magic and euphoria that come with the accomplishment are unmatched.

The ascent to the summit takes two days. On the first day, climbers make their way to a permanent camp located about two-thirds of the way up the mountain. They get an early start the next morning, setting out while the sky is still dark and street lights are still gleaming in sleeping communities far below. The idea is to make it to the top of the mountain and come back down again before the heat of the day softens the snow's surface and creates other hazards.

Even with the help of ice axes and steel spikes on your boots, the climb is tough, especially in the oxygen-poor air at these high elevations. The route, moreover, goes across the jagged surface of a living glacier, threading its way between crevasses that split the ice into a maze of miniature canyons; some must be jumped, others crossed on bridges of ice and snow. The crevasses are caused by stresses that develop as the glacier inches downslope over uneven bedrock. Their walls are sculpted with ledges that lead nowhere; icicles that weigh tons hang from their lips, melting by day, freezing again at night. Although the crevasses look bottomless, few are more than 100 feet deep. But they certainly add to the excitement of the climb.

Ice in action

Great expanses of this year-round ice descend like rough white tongues from all sides of Rainier's summit. Few lone peaks anywhere, in fact, can match Rainier for the extent of its glaciers, which blanket nearly 34 square miles. In all, the mountain boasts at least 25 living, moving glaciers and about 15 stagnant remnants of glaciers that are no longer actively advancing.

Glacial ice can form in any place where, year after year, more snow falls in winter than melts in summer. Fresh snow is fluffy, but as it settles, air is forced out and the snow gradually is compacted into ice as more and more drifts accumulate on the surface. When the ice is finally thick enough, it starts to spread out under the stress of its own weight and begins to flow downslope like a river in slow motion.

It is the dynamic quality of this moving ice that fascinates us with glaciers: they do something. Cre-

Backed by a cloudless sky of the purest blue, a pair of climbers pauses in their exploration of the Cowlitz Glacier, one of many

vasses open and close; the size and shape of inner ledges and dropoffs change constantly. Pinnacles, called seracs, heave upward, then fall with a crash as the glacier cascades over cliffs.

A glacier's surface may be so black with rubble torn from the mountainsides that it looks like rock instead of ice. Insulated by this overburden of debris, detached remnants of such a glacier can take centuries to melt. Water raging through channels beneath a glacier also is laden with pulverized rock and other debris.

Great beauty can mark the thinning edge of the ice where a glacier is melting back. Caves along the margin, walls and ceilings of melting glaciers may glow with an extraordinary aquamarine hue as blue light penetrates the ice. The caves beneath Rainier's summit ice cap are dark because of thick ice and snow overhead. Lower down, the Paradise Ice Caves were exceptionally lovely for years until the stagnant lobe of ice in which the caves were located melted away.

Life on ice, life on land
Cold and forbidding as the glaciers may seem, they are far from lifeless. Focus your binoculars on one, and

that radiate from Mount Rainier's snow-clad summit.

lives in this winter-white world. So do ice worms, threadlike relatives of earthworms that measure about one inch in length. At times, the ice worms are numerous enough to form dark patches on a glacier's surface; at other times there are none. The little creatures feed on windblown pollen and minute one-celled algae that live exclusively in snow. In most years, these algae flourish so well that by August they streak depressions in the snow with watermelon pink—and even, oddly enough, cause the snow to smell like watermelon.

Below the glaciers and snowfields, at the 4,500- to 6,500-foot level, Mount Rainier is garlanded with meadows that burst into sudden bloom every summer. A parade of color marches up the slopes, following the line of melting snow as lupines, asters, paintbrushes, and many others rush to flower and set seed before the brief mountain summer ends. As if impatient to get started, some even send out new shoots while still blanketed with snow. White avalanche lilies, for example, routinely poke their flower stalks up through crusts of snow two to four inches thick.

Birds and mammals react quickly to spring's renewed plant growth. The nutritious new shoots of sedges, which begin to sprout while snow-covered soil remains a degree or two below freezing, supply voles with the first fresh food of the season. Inquisitive golden-mantled ground squirrels, looking like the familiar chipmunk but without its facial stripes, emerge from hibernation and frisk about the meadows, nibbling on tender new growth. Mountain goats head for windward ridges blown relatively free of snow and there find the summer's first grazing. Gray-crowned rosy finches nest on rocky slopes above the flower meadows while blizzards are still raging; by the time their nestlings hatch, a plentiful supply of heather buds and emerging insects is available as food.

Throughout the summer, waves of color—red of paintbrush, pink-purple of fireweed, blue of asters and lupines, yellow of arnica and mountain goldenrod—brighten the high country. By late August the blossoming of purple gentians signals the conclusion of the display.

As fall takes over, a final spectacle closes the season of growth: the leaves of willow and mountain ash turn bright chrome-yellow, and huckleberry bushes bathe the slopes in crimson. By this time, hoary marmots have already vanished into their burrows and slowed into torpid hibernation; but black bears are still up and about, gorging on incredible quantities of huckleberries before denning up for the winter. With teeth and claws, they literally rake the fruit into their mouths. Pikas, miniature cousins of rabbits that live in loose rock piles, finish drying the mounds of grass that they store for winter food.

Throngs of robins, thrushes, bluebirds, flickers, and grouse also convene on the huckleberry slopes for a last feast. Red-tailed and Swainson's hawks and northern harriers pass through the park on their southward migration and for a few weeks join the golden eagles as

what at first seemed to be a rock turns out on rare occasions to be a mountain goat slowly picking its way across the jagged surface. Birds also visit from time to time. Wind blows so many insects onto glaciers and snowfields that pine siskins and rosy finches routinely feed there, supplementing their usual diet of seeds. Water pipits, which choose Rainier's high slopes for nesting, also stalk the snowfields in July when their eggs have hatched, constantly wagging their long dark tails as they search for stranded insects.

In contrast, pinhead-sized snow fleas—tiny insects that hop for astonishing distances—spend their entire they circle above the meadows, hunting for chipmunks, ground squirrels, and small birds.

Before long, however, snow begins to stay on the ground between storms. Lowland hemlock and fir forests are transformed into great expanses of giant white plumes as snow piles up on the branches. In the high country, meadows are locked beneath a deepening blanket of white, not to reappear until summer. By March the snow sometimes reaches to the third-story dormers of the inn at Paradise Valley, one of the snowiest spots in the entire United States. But eventually the days grow warmer as the sun climbs higher in the sky. And eventually the snow line begins to recede up the mountainsides, pursued, as it has always been, by the springtime miracle of rebirth and renewal.

Birth of a volcano
Rainier's impressive height, reaching nearly three miles above sea level, is testimony to the awesome mountain-building power of volcanic forces. And the sulfurous fumes still issuing from its summit vents are reminders that its internal fires continue to smolder; for though Rainier seems dormant, it is by no means dead. On the contrary, geologists speculate that sputterings of renewed volcanic life could conceivably occur within the next few years, most likely in the form of small ash eruptions and ocasional mudflows. Nor can the possibility of a catastrophic outburst be discounted. Mount Rainier's volcanic pulse seems to beat in a 3,000-year cycle—and the last major eruption occurred approximately 2,500 years ago.

But that was only the most recent in a long chain of events, for the mountain's enormous bulk took a long time to build. Geologists believe it first began to form about 12 million years ago, when a mass of molten rock welled up from the earth's interior and, for the most part, cooled without breaking through to the surface. This rock forms the foundation for the cone itself.

Sometime within the last million years, new upwellings began bursting through the surface and spewing out streams of lava. Periodically, too, violent explosions shot out masses of pumice—molten rock made frothy by trapped gas bubbles. Layer upon layer, the lava and debris piled up, building a great volcanic cone. By the time the major eruptions had ceased, Rainier stood as the highest peak in the Pacific Northwest.

In fact, it was even higher than it is today. Instead of the classic pointed top of a volcanic cone, Rainier's summit is a broad dome. Judging from the angle of lava flows preserved on upper rock ledges, and from various other clues, scientists estimate that Rainier is missing at least 1,000 feet, compared with its height immediately after the main cone finished building.

Geologists used to think that the summit blew off in a

With the return of warm weather in early summer, black-tailed deer migrate up the slopes and give birth to speckled *fawns. They are a common sight along most park roads and trails, especially in the early morning and evening hours.*

spectacular eruption such as the one that in May 1980 demolished the top of Mount St. Helens, 50 miles southwest of Rainier. Now they believe the former summit was lost in a massive mudflow. Changes in Mount Rainier's interior volcanic "plumbing" probably set events in motion. About 5,000 years ago the mountain's slumbering fires apparently stirred to life, and their increased heat melted summit ice and weakened the volcanic rock. A minor eruption then shook the mountain and sent the unstable summit sliding down on the surrounding lowlands. As the muddy torrent swept down the slopes, it carried along tons of silt and rubble as well as the previously solid rock that had been softened by hot gases and superheated water. Snow and ice torn from the glaciers added to the flow, boulders rode the moving mass, and cliffs undercut by the force of the flowing mud collapsed into it. When the cataclysm ended, the land at the base of Rainier lay buried beneath an apron of viscous mud and debris some 20 miles long and up to 10 miles wide. And the old mountaintop was gone forever.

Dippers haunt the mountain streams, enchanting all with their antics—they plunge into the water in search of food —and their cheery, bubbling songs.

When the mud flows
Though that ancient catastrophe was the worst, it is by no means the only mudflow that has shaped Rainier's slopes. Geologists have traced the courses of 55 individual flows down the mountainsides. The water that fuels them comes from Rainier's numerous glaciers, which contain vast amounts of it, both as liquid and as ice. Melt-streams rage as unseen torrents beneath the glaciers and through channels within the ice itself. The water sometimes collects in enormous impoundments, invisible from the surface. When this water breaks free, it gathers rock rubble and gravel that were worn from the mountains by glacial action and carried along by the slow conveyor-belt movement of the ice, and the entire mass goes roaring down the slopes.

The volume of water available for such outburst floods is stupendous; an estimated one cubic mile of ice makes up Rainier's mantle of perpetual white. Given this potential for disaster, Rainier's frequent mudflows and landslides should come as no surprise. Several occurred in the 1940's and 1960's, and more are certain in the future. In October 1947, for example, a large quantity of ice suddenly vanished from the lower Kautz Glacier, as a mixture of water, ice, rock, and mud surged down the slopes. Tremendous boulders rode along with the churning mass, which easily snapped off the trunks of trees three feet in diameter. When the muddy avalanche finally came to a halt, the road to Longmire was buried beneath 20 feet of debris, and vast areas of the forest's green carpet of ferns and mosses had been replaced by the lifeless gray of cementlike mud.

For more than a decade, things remained relatively stable on Rainier. Then in the fall of 1960, mudflows from the lower Nisqually Glacier wiped out a bridge spanning the Nisqually River. Three years later, a cliff 1,500 feet high fell from the face of the peak called Little Tahoma (in Indian legend the "son" of Mount Rainier). Rock debris 50 feet thick tumbled onto the Emmons Glacier directly below, and huge boulders hurtled several miles down the slopes, apparently riding on cushions of air at speeds of up to 300 miles an hour. The cause, geologists surmise, may have been a small steam explosion that loosened unstable rock layers. The Tahoma Glacier gave birth to sizable mudflows, beginning in August 1967 and continuing into the 1990's. Water from within the glacier mixed with loose material downstream, unleashing a torrent of mud and rock that swamped a small campground below and, more recently, obliterated a portion of Westside Road.

The glaciers, too, are subject to sudden changes as a result of the underlying volcanic fires. In 1969 the normally smooth surface of the upper part of the Emmons Glacier rumbled up with huge upheavals in the ice. It was also split by dizzying crevasses that in some places reached all the way through the glacier to the bedrock below. An abrupt warming of the ice by subsurface heat may have triggered this unexpected surge of activity.

Scientists, of course, wish they could fully understand Rainier's volcanic pulse and so learn to predict such catastrophes. Seismometers and thermal recorders now read the snores of the volcano's awesome slumbering; aerial photographs made on infrared film help experts pinpoint the hot spots. For all their monitoring of data, however, volcanologists cannot say what will happen or when. Although they see no immediate threat of a lava eruption, they do expect at least a steam explosion or perhaps a minor venting of ash sometime within the next few decades or centuries. And mudflows are almost a certainty; for changes in the old volcano are inevitable. The lofty offspring of fire and ice, Rainier is very much a living mountain, a work of art still in the process of completion.

North Cascades

"Whoever wishes to see nature in all its primitive glory and grandeur, in its almost ferocious wildness, must go and visit these mountain regions." Henry Custer, *19th-century topographer*

Although Sourdough Mountain is far from the tallest peak in North Cascades National Park—it is only 6,106 feet high—its summit seems like the top of the world. That is only partly because you must make a steep five-mile climb to reach its crowning snowfields, rocky ridges, and meadows open to the sun. Mostly it is because of the view. Located near the center of the park, Sourdough is completely surrounded by jagged peaks. Glaciers glisten in the bright sunshine, contrasting sharply with the gray rocks that cradle them. Below the craggy pinnacles, dark green forests cover the slopes like a rough-textured blanket.

Sourdough's summit, in fact, overlooks nearly all of the park, which includes hundreds of peaks, each with its own distinctive character. Sourdough, with its flower-filled meadows, for instance, is parklike and inviting. At Sourdough's foot, little Pumpkin Mountain, forested from top to bottom, seems meek and insignificant. To the south, Forbidden Peak—rocky and rimmed with several immense glaciers—looks every bit as cold and threatening as its name implies.

In the valley bottoms far below, streams and rivers streak like twisted ribbons. To the north of Sourdough the stretch of blue extending like a crooked finger toward the Canadian border is Ross Lake. The lake fills the bottom of the Skagit River valley, one of the deep, wide Cascade valleys that were carved out long ago by massive glaciers.

Splendid in all seasons, the North Cascades attract climbers even in the depths of winter. Among the wild creatures that survive the frigid wintry weather are snowshoe hares, mountain goats, and a host of others.

Even today, many Cascades peaks remain garlanded by glaciers. Though small compared with the giants of old, still the sparkling masses of ice are a major feature of this awesome landscape. Scientists count a total of 318 glaciers in the park—nearly one-third of all the glaciers in the United States south of Alaska.

As the glaciers melt, tiny rivulets form at their margins and begin their long journey from the barren highlands to lush lowland valleys. A spectacular example of the birth of a mountain stream can be seen below Mount Shuksan's Sulfide Glacier. Rivulets emerging all along the edge of the ice intertwine and merge, forming a lacy network of white water cascading down the mountain's stark, gray, rocky face. Just above the timberline all the rivulets unite to form a single stream that hurtles down a gigantic roaring waterfall.

This single stream rushes through the forest, growing ever larger as it is joined by similar streams flowing down from Shuksan's glaciers. When it enters a pool, the frothy white water slows down momentarily and turns light green. Then the brush-covered banks close in again, and the water speeds through, churning white once more. At the valley bottom several streams converge to form Sulfide Creek, which roars as it rushes down the slope. Dull *thunks* punctuate the din as the current tumbles big rocks against one another.

Almost anywhere along the way a water ouzel, or dipper, may appear and supply a delightful sign of life. Flitting to a rock, the little bird sings a few staccato notes that resound above the roaring water and does a curious, curtsylike jig before plunging into the stream, where it walks along the bottom in search of food.

Finally Sulfide Creek merges with the Baker River,

which carries Shuksan's meltwater, through the Skagit, to Puget Sound. During the transformation from rivulet to river, Sulfide Creek speeds through a varied landscape, the result of the Cascades' high landmass and steep slopes. Here, as on mountains everywhere, the climate grows harsher with increasing elevation. Thus the tall Douglas firs and hemlocks of the lowland forests gradually give way to smaller trees, such as Pacific silver fir, at middle elevations. Still farther up the slopes, scattered groves of hardy subalpine and alpine trees—mountain hemlock is an example—take over, then yield in turn to flowered meadows. Finally, in the high country where it is so cold that snow remains on the ground most of the year, only a few scattered patches of moss campion and other ground-hugging little alpine plants are able to maintain a hold on life.

The mountain range as a whole creates an even more startling climatic contrast. Moist prevailing winds from the Pacific flow up over the western slopes, cooling as they rise and releasing their moisture as rain and snow. Beyond the crest, the air descends and warms, dropping relatively little precipitation.

As a result, the west side of the range wears a lush, green mantle of tall trees and tangled undergrowth. Forests on the eastern slopes are more diminutive, with far scantier vegetation. The Douglas fir, which grows to towering heights on the west side of the Cascades, for instance, may grow only half as tall on the east side. And the moisture-loving hemlocks of western slopes are replaced in the east by ponderosas and other pines that tolerate much drier conditions.

Time and change

At first glance the dim, serene forests of the North Cascades seem permanent, unchanging. But the reality is constant flux, an ebb and flow of destruction and rebirth that affects every living thing. The cycle may begin when disease or insects kill a few trees. Years later lightning strikes, and their tinder-dry skeletons burst into flame. The fire may consume only a few acres or it may last for months, charring thousands of acres. Such was the Big Beaver fire, which started on July 4, 1926, in the Big Beaver Valley near Sourdough Mountain; burning until October snow doused the last sparks, it devastated 40,000 acres.

When the snow melted the next spring, the scene was one of utter desolation. Charred trees littered the ground; those still standing were dead and bare. But tiny green sprouts soon rose from the blackened soil. The process of succession—the change from bare land to mature forest—had begun.

Succession follows no single set of rules. Elevation, soil, weather—all may cause variations in the sequence. But there is a pattern, too. The healing process begins with the so-called pioneers, sun-loving plants that are the first to colonize a devastated land. Often the earliest pioneer is the aptly named fireweed, which thrives nearly anywhere it can get full sunlight. Growing up to six feet tall and topped by spires of lovely purple-rose flowers, by midsummer it may brighten the charred landscape with a riot of color. Soon the fireweed is joined by other pioneers—delicate ferns, for example, and fragrant blue lupines.

This land has mountains, and it has ice. Many of the peaks, sculpted long ago—during the ice ages—by massive glaciers, still have glaciers clinging to the slopes. Their survival depends on moisture-laden winds blowing in from the Pacific, which supply the snow needed to maintain these slow-moving rivers of ice. Here, looming beyond Cascade Pass in the southern part of the park, is the craggy, barren summit of Magic Mountain.

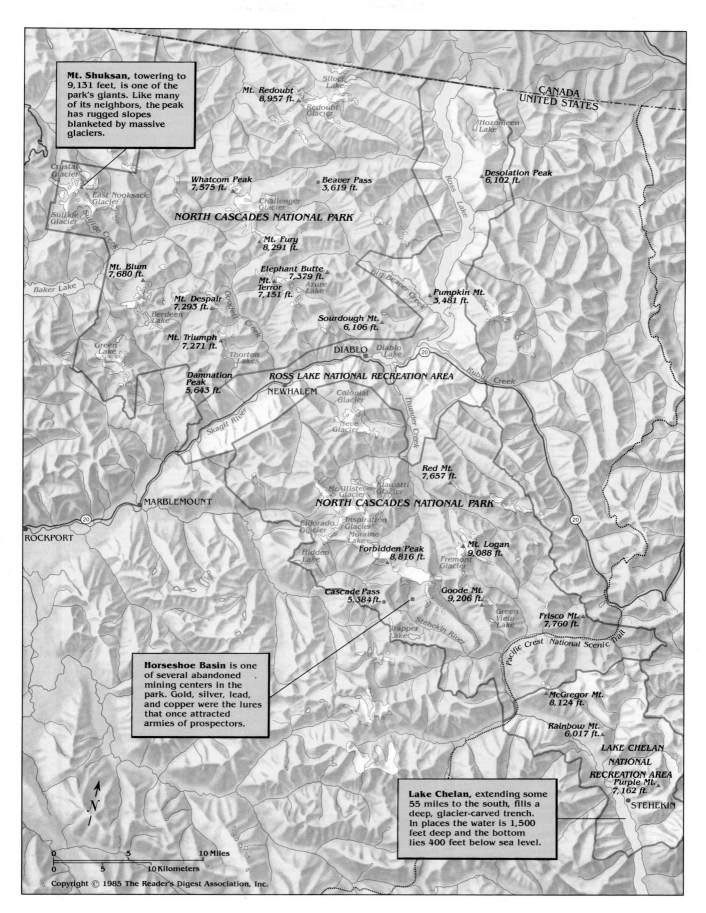

Mt. Shuksan, towering to 9,131 feet, is one of the park's giants. Like many of its neighbors, the peak has rugged slopes blanketed by massive glaciers.

Crystal Glacier

East Nooksack Glacier

Sulfide Glacier

Sulfide Creek

Mt. Redoubt
8,957 ft.

Silver Lake

Redoubt Glacier

CANADA
UNITED STATES

Hozomeen Lake

Whatcom Peak
7,575 ft.

Beaver Pass
3,619 ft.

Desolation Peak
6,102 ft.

Challenger Glacier

NORTH CASCADES NATIONAL PARK

Mt. Fury
8,291 ft.

Mt. Blum
7,680 ft.

Elephant Butte
7,379 ft.

Mt.
Terror
7,151 ft.

Azure Lake

Pumpkin Mt.
3,481 ft.

Baker Lake

Goodell Creek

Mt. Despair
7,293 ft.

Berdeen Lake

Sourdough Mt.
6,106 ft.

Big Beaver Creek

Green Lake

Mt. Triumph
7,271 ft.

Thorton Lakes

DIABLO

Diablo Lake

20

Ruby Creek

Damnation Peak
5,643 ft.

ROSS LAKE NATIONAL RECREATION AREA

Ross Lake

NEWHALEM

Colonial Glacier

Skagit River

Neve Glacier

Thunder Creek

Red Mt.
7,657 ft.

MARBLEMOUNT

McAllister Glacier

Klawatti Glacier

NORTH CASCADES NATIONAL PARK

20

Eldorado Glacier

Inspiration Glacier
Moraine Lake

20

ROCKPORT

Hidden Lake

Forbidden Peak
8,816 ft.

Mt. Logan
9,088 ft.

Fremont Glacier

Cascade Pass
5,384 ft.

Goode Mt.
9,206 ft.

Green View Lake

Frisco Mt.
7,760 ft.

Trapper Lake

Stehekin River

Pacific Crest National Scenic Trail

Horseshoe Basin is one of several abandoned mining centers in the park. Gold, silver, lead, and copper were the lures that once attracted armies of prospectors.

McGregor Mt.
8,124 ft.

Rainbow Mt.
6,017 ft.

LAKE CHELAN

NATIONAL

RECREATION AREA
Purple Mt.
7,162 ft.

N

Lake Chelan, extending some 55 miles to the south, fills a deep, glacier-carved trench. In places the water is 1,500 feet deep and the bottom lies 400 feet below sea level.

STEHEKIN

| 0 | | 5 | | 10 Miles |
| 0 | 5 | | 10 Kilometers |

Eventually the pioneers are crowded out by woodier plants. The newcomers are almost certain to include huckleberries, small shrubs that grow throughout the Cascades. Sometimes red, sometimes deep blue, their tangy pea-sized fruits are prized by a variety of creatures, including human trailside snackers. Briery salmonberry and thimbleberry are among the other plants making up this second stage in forest succession.

Deer soon move in to browse on all the succulent new growth. (In the North Cascades they are either the Columbia black-tailed deer or the closely related mule deer.) The brushy thickets may also attract black bears. They come to gobble up the plentiful supply of berries, but also dine on almost anything else that is edible.

Although the tangles of new growth seem almost impenetrable, young trees eventually poke through, starting the third stage of succession. Curiously, though the Cascades' forests are dominated by evergreens, those first saplings to appear are likely to be broadleaf trees—bigleaf maple, for instance, or black cottonwood, or western red alder. The red alder, clad with smooth gray bark, rarely grows more than 100 feet tall, but it grows quickly, crowding out the smaller, sunloving shrubs that preceded it.

The final phase in succession begins whenever a break occurs in the canopy of broadleaf trees. A few alders may die from disease or be toppled in a windstorm. Sunlight streams through the opening, and stunted young evergreens that had been struggling for existence in the dim light on the forest floor suddenly gain a new lease on life. Taking advantage of the opening to reach for the sun, they begin to grow rapidly and soon overtop their broadleaf neighbors.

The prime benefactor of such openings is usually the Douglas fir, an adaptable tree that thrives in most Cascade environments. Able to survive drought and insulated against minor fires by foot-thick bark, it may live for 1,000 years and reach heights of 300 feet. Thus it is that the skyscraping Douglas fir dominates most Cascade forests— but not all of them. In many cases other trees win out in the battle for survival and bring a welcome note of variety. On wet sites, western red cedars may crowd out the Douglas firs and dominate the forest. The smaller, hardier Pacific silver firs often take over at higher elevations where the climate is more severe. Another successful competitor is the western hemlock. Tolerant of dense shade, its seedlings may grow slowly but tenaciously for decades in dark, damp glens beneath the Douglas firs. When a tree of the older forest topples, the hemlocks quickly fill the breach in the canopy. And when the hemlocks in turn die of old age, there is nothing on the forest floor to replace them except more of the shade-tolerant young hemlocks. And so the mature forest remains a stand of hemlocks, self-perpetuating until fire, flood, or storm destroys it, and the process of succession begins anew.

Life among the evergreens

As the coniferous forest crowds out the last of the broadleaf trees, the cast of wildlife characters gradually changes. Black bears may remain, but most of the deer move on, and true forest-lovers move in. Among the most conspicuous are Douglas' squirrels, little scamps that loudly scold all intruders in "their" forest. Fond of the seeds of evergreens, they tear the cones apart and litter the ground beneath their favorite perches with deep piles of cone scales. Nearby there may be Townsend's chipmunks or tiny Pacific jumping mice that escape enemies by leaping six feet in a single bound. The Trowbridge shrew, a miniature bundle of energy, moves constantly and frantically in its endless search for small prey.

As the forest ages, carpenter ants may burrow into older trees, sprinkling the ground below with sawdust as they excavate their tunnels. The carpenters' burrows in turn are an invitation to the pileated woodpecker; the ants are its principal food. The big bird chips away the wood until it can reach the ants inside their burrows with its long, sticky tongue. It uses a similar technique to make its nest. Choosing a likely tree in a stand of evergreens, both male and female hack out a hole where the female lays her clutch of three to five eggs.

The spotted owl, a nocturnal hunter with a taste for small animals, also haunts the evergreen forest. Relying on keen eyesight and extremely sensitive ears to locate prey in the dark, it swoops down on feathers softened for silent flight and snatches its victims with powerful talons.

The stealthy, secretive mountain lion ranges through nearly every part of the park—including the deepest, darkest forest. A sleek, silent, tawny-gray wanderer and an efficient killer, it slips, graceful and unseen, from one hiding place to the next, waiting to pounce on unsuspecting prey. It takes chiefly deer and eats every part of a kill, gorging until its belly bloats, then hiding the remainder until it is ready for more.

The dainty blossoms of the lovely crimson columbine, dangling from the tips of delicate stems, dance in response to the slightest of breezes.

"Steep and precipitous"— that is the meaning of the Indian word Shuksan. *And clearly it is a fitting description for Mount* Shuksan, *one of the most impressive of the towering, glacier-capped peaks in this mountain wilderness.*

Of marmots and mountain goats

In sharp contrast to the evergreen forests are the open meadows of higher elevations. White with snow in winter, in spring and summer they are aglow with color as wildflowers come into bloom. Several kinds of paintbrushes grow there, including a whitish variety found only in the North Cascades. Other paintbrushes range from yellow to brilliant crimson, with much of the color supplied by modified leaves, called bracts, that grow among the clusters of flowers.

Bistort, another prominent meadow flower, produces elongated flower heads at the tips of long stalks; they look like fluffy white caterpillars swaying in the breeze. Tall asters contribute a pink-purple hue, and heathers brighten the scene with white or purple flowers that dangle from the branches like miniature bells.

The meadow flowers supply a rich menu for such high-country animals as hoary marmots, which munch on the greenery all summer long and then hibernate through the winter. In contrast, their smaller companions, pikas, provide for winter by storing sun-dried plants in rock crannies.

Mountain goats are the nimblest residents of the heights. Relying on soft, cupped hoof pads for traction, they leap from one precarious perch to the next with seeming unconcern. Thanks to a woolly winter under-coat beneath their shaggy outer fur, they are pretty much unfazed by fierce winter weather.

Another high-country survivor, the snowshoe hare, changes from brown to white when winter approaches, and develops the dense furry footpads that give it its name. Hopping about on their snowshoes, the hares actually benefit as the snow cover deepens: each new snowfall brings them within range of twigs and buds that had previously been beyond their reach.

Pocket gophers also remain active through the winter, but seldom do they venture out into the weather. Instead, they burrow through the snow, pushing loose dirt into the tunnel behind them as they dig for roots and tubers. When the snow melts, the dirt settles to the ground in long, twisting heaps that mark their winter-time comings and goings. During the summer they burrow underground and get at surface plants by pulling them into their burrows from below.

Like every creature large and small, like every plant from the tiniest moss to the tallest tree, the little pocket gophers survive because they are attuned to their environment and to the unending cycle of the seasons in the North Cascades. Here they are at home—here in these magnificent mountains that are regularly watered by wet winds off the Pacific, warmed by the sun's bright rays, and governed by laws as ancient as life itself.

221

Olympic

*"This is the forest primeval. . . .
Loud from its rocky caverns, the deep-voiced
neighboring ocean
Speaks, and in accents disconsolate answers the
wail of the forest."* Henry Wadsworth Longfellow

It is summer, early in the morning, with a full moon setting over the Pacific Ocean just as a low, damp bank of clouds drifts shoreward. Far out at sea, where the ocean rises and falls endlessly in long waves of deep, grayish water, a pod of whales break the surface, blowing columns of spray as they exhale. Four cormorants, their long wings beating almost in unison, fly in close formation, low to the water. Quickly they become specks among the swells, and then disappear into the mist.

Just offshore, sea stacks—some of them small, others substantial islands—rise steeply from the surf like great chunks of rock broken free from the mainland. In the mist they seem threatening, even evil, as if they existed for just one purpose—to cause shipwrecks. And indeed many of them have done so. But they serve benign ends as well: seabirds nest on them, safe from land predators, and colonies of seals and sea lions take shelter from direct pounding by the surf.

The surf, of course, is relentless here. Where there are headlands, waves crash into the cliffs, booming as they explode against unyielding rock. Where there are beaches, breakers thunder ashore in a frenzy of foam, and then, their energy spent, quietly recede, sucking and swirling sullenly across the sand. Gulls circle overhead, and sandpipers and black oystercatchers explore the wave edges for food. Beyond the reach of the surf, the beach slopes up gradually, then abruptly ends, hemmed in by a bluff that rises steeply to a forest-fringed summit half lost in the mist.

This is the coastal strip of Olympic National Park—over 60 miles of brooding beauty, restless seas, fragmented

In the lush, moss-draped world of the Olympic rain forest, life seems to flourish everywhere. From the yellow fungus clinging to an ancient stump to ferns on the forest floor, myriads of life-forms add to the beauty of the scene.

shoreline, and teeming wildlife. Each winter, storms rearrange this coast a little, wrenching land from resistant cliffs and headlands and depositing the rubble on intervening stretches of protected beach. The result is a coastline that is constantly changing.

Perhaps the most fascinating of all its realms is the ever-changing world between the limits of high and low tide. When the tide comes in, attention turns toward the limit of the highest storm tides, where the bleached skeletons of innumerable dead trees line the upper beach. In times of storm and flood the trees are washed from riverbanks and then out to sea; returned by the storms, they remain beached until an even more powerful storm rearranges them. Where the highest waves wash ashore, the sea leaves other bits of debris: shell fragments, pieces of seaweed, chunks of wet, tannish wood that dries to a bony gray. The ocean is not choosy about what it moves; the energy is there, and whatever can be washed ashore will be.

Slowly the tide begins to recede. The change is imperceptible at first, but gradually the high-tide line becomes evident: on the beaches strands of kelp and eelgrass lie undisturbed just beyond the reach of the waves, and on the cliffs a line of periwinkles and limpets—both small snails—begins to show above the water where they are clinging to the rocks. On its way out, the tide reveals an entirely new world, a place where creatures live in endless alternation between saltwater and sea wind. The area between the tidelines is a slippery, squishy, yet crunchy world of seaweed and seashell. Strands of rockweed pop underfoot, shore crabs scuttle for cover, and shellfish cluster densely wherever there is rock.

And then there are the tide pools. When the tide is out, each water-filled nook and cranny among the rocks shelters an amazing variety of life: bright orange star-

These sea stacks, standing like sturdy offshore sentinels, originally were part of the Olympic mainland; they are the eroded remnants of headlands that once projected out to sea. Eventually, they too will be demolished by the surf.

fish that prey on brownish-gray snails, fluorescent-green sea anemones, crimson sea urchins, throngs of mussels and barnacles, and small fish called tide-pool sculpins that hide among the shelled residents and occasionally dart about in search of food. The color and variety, the natural interactions and patterns of mutual dependence, in the tide pools are a never-ending source of delight.

On sandy beaches, low tide abandons heaps and curving windrows of giant kelp, a seaweed usually anchored to the bottom, but sometimes torn loose by waves. The tracks of deer, elk, and raccoons mark the aimless wanderings and purposeful travels of wild creatures that have ventured out of the forest. Flocks of gulls stand at the water's edge, watching the waves; an occasional bald eagle flaps by, scouting for stranded fish.

In the distance, headlands interrupt the beaches with cliffs and forested slopes that add much to the magic of the scene. By blocking the view, they seem to stand guard over discoveries imagined—surely there, just around the bend—and waiting to be confirmed. For anyone willing to explore and make those discoveries, the shoreline is a place of exhilaration and intensity. Sound piles upon sound, both restful and exciting: the surf serves as background music, individual waves thud against sand and rock, outgo-

Black oystercatchers, year-round residents of Olympic coasts, specialize in a diet of mollusks but settle for occasional worms and crabs as well.

ing backwash hisses as it rolls grains of sand, and bird cries pierce even the loudest surges of the surf.

The enchanted forest

Beyond the pounding of the surf, forest stretches away toward the interior of the Olympic Peninsula, uninterrupted except by rivers and lakes. The growth is healthy and heavy, a response to moderate temperatures and an annual rainfall of more than 100 inches. Great conifers compete with each other for light and space, often reaching well over 100 feet in height, while cottonwoods and alders thrive along the edges of rivers. Grouse drum their mating tattoos from atop fallen logs in the forest, woodpeckers hammer stumps apart, and juncos flit quietly through the underbrush. In most places such a woodland would be cause enough for a visit, but in Olympic National Park there is something even more unusual. In four ocean-facing river valleys—the Queets, the Quinault, the Hoh, and the Bogachiel—the annual rainfall increases to 140 inches, and the soil is rich and deep. The result is a unique botanical treasure—the Olympic rain forest.

Within the deepest part of the rain forest the light is dim, with a greenish glow, for these trees are so tall—they average at least 200 feet and tower to 300 feet in places—and so densely branched that little sunlight filters through to the ground. The dominant trees are Sitka spruce and western hemlock, many of them ancient monarchs perhaps 250 years old or more. Rising like columns, their stout trunks are spattered with mosses, lichens, and ferns. Breezes sigh through the uppermost boughs and a few small birds move quietly through the branches; down below, the feeling is one of repose.

Fallen trees are scattered throughout the forest, decaying by degrees into a carpet of mosses, mushrooms, and ferns. The cycle of life and death, decay and rebirth, that perpetuates the forest is evident everywhere, in many shapes and forms. Among the agents of decay, the most noticeable are the many kinds of mushrooms and other fungi. The moist Olympic forest has them in abundance, bracketing the sides of rotting logs like scalloped sculptures and springing up overnight from the ground. Fallen trees also become nurseries for seedlings, which respond well to the moisture and nutrients in the rotting wood. By the time the logs decay and crumble to nothing, the seedlings have matured into young trees ranked in rows and supported on stiltlike roots that once gripped the parent log. "Nurse logs" the fallen trees are called, in reference to their ability to nurture life.

At first the forest seems uniform and unchanging, but it is not. Just where the evergreens seem to be thickest, the scene unexpectedly takes on an entirely different character. Bigleaf maples festooned with living plants, vine maples curving over into arches, and, along the riverbanks, huge old black cottonwoods suddenly dominate, relegating the evergreens to a subordinate role. Growing to heights of 100 feet or more, these broadleaf trees, strong limbed and thick bodied, stretch skyward to form canopies that catch the summer sunlight and in autumn paint the forest with touches of crimson and broad splashes of gold.

Where the bigleaf and vine maples grow, the rain forest is as much a place for admiring the plants *on* the trees as it is for enjoying the maples themselves. The outstretched limbs are so upholstered and draped with greenery that they seem to have grown only as support for lush aerial gardens. It is as if the rain forest plants had finally lost control of themselves and, finding no more space on the ground, had taken to the trees in one huge, collective leap; the trees, not quite prepared, seem bowed down under the added weight of the festoons and curtains spilling over their limbs.

The silence of a place so padded with mosses, fringed by ferns, and flanked by giant trees would seem to be almost complete. Yet there are sounds aplenty, some of them as hushed as the wind rustling through the leaves, others as loud and persistent as the frequent rains. In heavy downpours the rain creates a tremendous roar as countless raindrops pelt millions of leaves, each hitting with a splat, then dripping to the ground.

The largest and the least of living things in the rain forest thrive on the constant dampness. Consider the lowly slug, that snail without a shell, a creature always, it seems, just there, scarcely more than a few paces away, slowly gliding along on a silvery trail of its own mucus. There is nothing fancy about a slug—no sleek fur, no colorful, water-repellent feathers—just a pale, slimy body a little longer than your index finger, with a pair of eyes periscoping up and down on retractable stalks. For the slug, wetness is essential to its way of life, and in the rain forest water is everywhere. The result is a perfect match, with slugs on trees, slugs on stems, slugs on the ground—slugs everywhere.

The richness of life in the rain forest does not come about by chance. It can exist only if certain strict requirements are met. Moisture, first and foremost, must be superabundant, and even when it is not raining, the air should be humid or even foggy. In addition, temperatures must be mild, since too much heat withers the plants and too little freezes them. In the rain forest, summer temperatures rarely surpass 80° F, and below-freezing winter weather is usually brief. Helping fulfill both of these requirements—abundant rainfall and moderate temperatures—is the nearby ocean. Winds blowing in from the Pacific are heated by contact

Low tide reveals a wealth of life on these rugged shores, including festoons of the seaweed called sea cabbage, sea urchins abristle with spines, colorful starfish of several species, and sponges that cover the rocks with a crustlike growth.

with the water, and when they reach the Olympic shore they bring the breath of the warm, moist sea with them. The air flows eastward through the forest like a powerful upwelling current and releases its load of moisture in seemingly endless showers.

The other basic need of the rain forest, a deep, mineral-laden soil, was fulfilled during the ice ages, when these westward-facing valleys were occupied by glaciers. As the ice moved down from the mountains and then retreated, unloading its cargo of debris, it filled the valley bottoms with deep deposits of soil, perfect for supporting the largest, lushest vegetation.

In summer and autumn the Olympic Peninsula belies its soggy reputation, for little rain falls and the mountains are not hidden in thick clouds. Instead the sky is faultlessly blue, and the only water in the rivers is the runoff from melting snowfields and glaciers. Yet the rain forest plants easily survive these warm sunny weeks. Their salvation comes in the form of fog. Each night, cool streamers of mist, invisible in the dark but easily felt, blow in from the Pacific and bathe the forest in moisture. Along the beach the fog comes with a surge of wind, but deep in the rain forest it merely steals through the trees, laying its moist breath down on whatever it touches. By morning the trees, their cushions of plants, wildflowers on the forest floor—everything—are laden with dew, refreshed, and ready to endure the heat of the afternoon.

Beyond the rain forest

Where the land begins to rise toward the mountains it does so abruptly, without any hesitation. The slopes are steep and difficult to climb: huge moss-covered logs lie tumbled across each other, and streams fed by melting snow sluice down the mountainsides, daring anyone to cross their icy waters and slippery boulders. In some places huge western red cedars rise into the foggy air, their cordovan-colored bark contrasting with the delicate green of maple leaves. Elsewhere Douglas firs, some of them even larger, grow together with Pacific madrones, which have shiny evergreen leaves and in early spring are decorated with clusters of little white urn-shaped flowers.

As elevations increase above 1,000 feet, then past 2,000, the air becomes perceptibly cooler, and forest patterns begin to change: no longer are there any moss-hung limbs, nurse logs, or giant spruce. Pacific silver fir, western white pine, western hemlock, and Douglas fir instead become the dominant trees. Beyond 3,000 feet, the lush green of the lowland forest gives way to a grayish gloom beneath dense stands of firs. Still higher up, on the crests of ridges that rise like shoulders from the forested valleys, more changes occur as subalpine fir, mountain hemlock, and Alaska cedars begin to appear. These are tough trees, strong enough to survive 10-foot snowfalls and winds that whip the ridges with hurricane force. Finally, as elevations edge toward 5,000 feet, another change, one of the most dramatic in

the Olympics, takes place. Beyond the last windfalls, beyond the dense stands of firs, the forest seems brighter, as if the land beyond might be open to the sun. Suddenly the confining world of the forest falls away to reveal the subalpine meadows of Olympic.

There is a great sense of harmony and undeniable beauty in these upland meadows. Caught between the clouds below and the barren peaks above, they are a special Eden where furry Olympic marmots cautiously search for succulent stems, black-tailed deer graze quietly along gentle slopes, and elk laze in the warmth of the summer sun. In the early morning, wisps of fog may touch the meadows, moistening the flowers and grasses, but soon the sun burns through, splitting into distinct rays as it sifts through scattered groves of spirelike firs.

In response to the light and warmth of early summer, wildflowers seem to leap from the ground. Studding the ground like stars, pale white avalanche lilies take over on slopes only recently vacated by snowfields. Elsewhere, among lingering snowdrifts, the grasses are greening and myriads of other wildflowers—magenta paintbrush, blue lupine, and western pasqueflower—make their seasonal debuts. On clear, bright summer days the Olympic meadows even smell warm: an earthy pungency combines with the fragrance of firs and flowers to confirm the power of the sun to awaken life.

The odyssey of the elk

Into this setting Olympic's elk migrate each summer. About 5,000 of the oversized deer live in the park, all of them a subspecies of the North American elk called Roosevelt elk in honor of Theodore Roosevelt. Slightly heavier and darker than elk living in the Rockies, these majestic animals weigh in at 700 pounds or more and stand about 5 feet tall at the shoulder.

As spring warms the mountains, some of the elk work their way slowly up the valleys and ridges, foraging on tender new grasses as they go. Eventually many of them climb as far as the subalpine meadows, where they spend the summer among green pastures and cool breezes. Usually they are up and about at dawn, feeding on the dewy grasses. Bulls graze quietly in small groups or by themselves, ignoring each other. Later, when the sun is higher, the elk retire to secluded resting places and chew their cud. Then, toward evening, they move back out on the meadows to graze some more. It is a peaceful routine, easy and undemanding.

Calves are born soon after the elk arrive in the highlands—June, usually. Vulnerable and completely dependent on their mothers, the young rest close by or nurse hungrily. At first the cows are patient and attentive, but as the calves grow bigger and learn to graze, they are often pushed away. By late summer the calves are so large they must kneel to nurse—but by that time they are given few chances.

During the summer months, the bulls grow new racks of antlers. For young bulls these are spikes perhaps a foot long, but on mature bulls full-size sets of antlers usually span 2½ feet, weigh 20 pounds or more, and have 6 tines, or points, on each rack. As the new antlers grow each summer, they take shape and harden under a soft protective layer of skin called velvet. When the antlers have hardened, the bulls scrape off the velvet, usually by rubbing against a tree scarcely larger than the antlers themselves.

By summer's end the bulls' personalities change dramatically. There is a menace in them now: hooves and antlers suddenly become weapons, spears that slash and jab. Driven by instinct, the bulls focus all their energy on domination—mastering and mating with groups of females called harems. For the time being, even food is ignored.

Once a bull acquires a harem, he challenges any other male who ventures near. Most often, challengers are driven off with little effort. If supremacy is seriously questioned, however, the adversaries lunge viciously at each other, their antlers swinging through the air, their laboring breath and sweating bodies sending wisps of steam into the cold autumn air. Dirt flies as they struggle for footing and leverage. Antlers rake across ribs, hooves gouge legs. Blood is drawn. If the match is uneven, the loser trots off quickly; otherwise the fight continues, sometimes even ending in death.

Throughout the mating season, the dominant bulls patrol restlessly. If females try to leave the harems they are herded back with antler jabs. Territory, strength, and power are proclaimed with long wailing cries and grunts, a sound called bugling. By October, however, all of the cows have been bred, and the harems begin to dissolve. Forgetting their need for supremacy, the weary bulls wander off into the forest to heal their wounds and regain their strength.

The elk leave the higher ridges before the snows arrive. Urged on by cold winds and lack of new plant growth, they drift down through the forest, heading lower with each passing day. Instinctively they seem to know that the forested slopes along the base of the

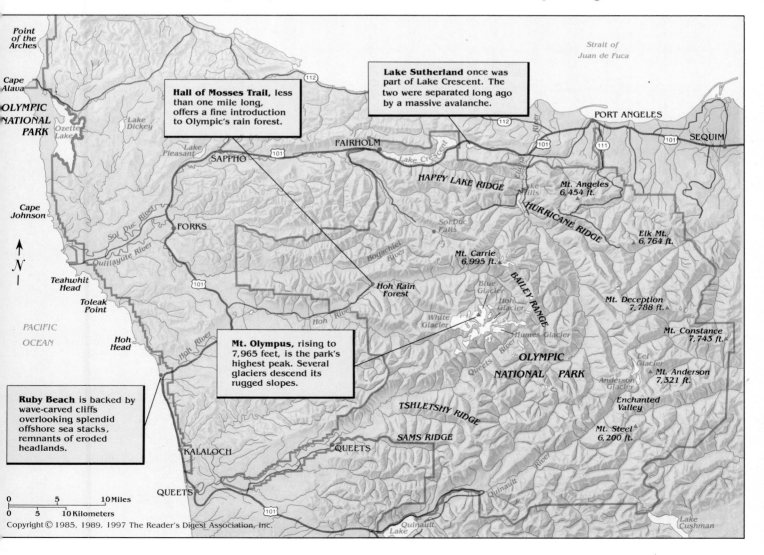

Hall of Mosses Trail, less than one mile long, offers a fine introduction to Olympic's rain forest.

Lake Sutherland once was part of Lake Crescent. The two were separated long ago by a massive avalanche.

Mt. Olympus, rising to 7,965 feet, is the park's highest peak. Several glaciers descend its rugged slopes.

Ruby Beach is backed by wave-carved cliffs overlooking splendid offshore sea stacks, remnants of eroded headlands.

A Lush Green World

Step into the Olympic rain forest and you will sense both the flow of time and the interdependence of life. Moss-upholstered trees, already ancient when American settlers first came west, still stand in cathedrallike splendor. Sitka spruce (18) grow larger here than anywhere else on earth, and beneath their somber heights vine maple (4) spreads a lacy green canopy. On most days, mist filters through the forest, closing it in upon itself, but occasionally sunlight streams through foliage and spotlights the forest floor.

Give yourself to this forest for even an hour and you will begin to appreciate the wealth of life that flourishes here, for a forest is far more than trees—it is a whole community of living things. The snowshoe hare (17) watching from its secret hiding place, the Douglas' squirrel (16) poised by a patch of turkey tail (15), the minute fluff of a kinglet (19) or a winter wren (1)— these, too, are part of the forest. So are the lowly millipede (5) and the oversized banana slug (11).

Surprisingly, Roosevelt elk (2) serve as landscape architects: their browsing determines where various plants can live. Sword fern (3) manages to survive despite heavy pruning by elk; but logs quickly disintegrate as elk paw them to feast on obscure fungi that they locate by smell, ignoring the more accessible kinds that humans regard as delicious—such as the chanterelle (12)—or deadly—such as the amanita (9). Bead-ruby (7), vanilla leaf (10), lady fern (14), and maidenhair fern (6) suffer trampling but no significant browsing.

Visit here and a multitude of sensory memories will be yours forever. There is the wind rustling the trees and brushing across your cheek; the beauty of a spiderweb clearly visible against shadow; the silent green flash of a surprised treefrog (8) hopping to safety; and the white flick of outer tail feathers and annoyed *chit* of a junco (13) taking sudden flight. All this—and more—make up the verdant realm of the Olympic rain forest.

mountains, especially those protected from the wind and facing south, are the best places to find food and shelter. In these favored areas and throughout the lowland forests the herds take refuge during the long winter months of snow and rain.

Whatever the location, however, food becomes a problem, especially as winter wears on and the snow deepens. For aged, sick, and weakened animals, this is the most dangerous time of year, for mountain lions are never far away. The great cats do not hurry; instead they examine, eyeing the young, evaluating the amount

Constantly replenished by frequent rains and melting snow, streams and rivers in the Olympics rush headlong from the heights to the sea, sometimes making spectacular leaps along the way, like this one at lovely Sol Duc Falls.

of protection each mother might be able to provide. Large animals in good health are left alone, but any elk that stumbles from weakness is quickly targeted. Thus the predators help assure that the fittest survive—and that the weakest do not. As a species, or even as herds, the elk will see spring again, but for individual animals winter is often the time of final defeat.

The clouds remain heavy well into spring, and the budding of tender shoots and grasses seems interminably delayed. For the elk the first break comes when enough snow melts to make food easier to find. Finally, as the forest and meadows turn again from brown to green, the season of privation ends. Inside the cows new life stirs; soon another generation of calves will be born. In the meadows and along forest paths, the bulls have dropped their old antlers, which now serve only as relics of battles past. For them—for all members of the herds—all that is forgotten. The present is what matters, and the elk are once again heading toward the ridges and meadows of the high country, there to begin anew the cycle of life.

On icebound summits

Toward 7,000 feet the forest posts its last sentinels, low-lying firs that seem to crouch against the wind. At these elevations the best strategy for survival is to lie low, where snow and wind are less able to crush and contort. The result is a stunted forest of twisted trees that sprawl along the ground. "Krummholz" the botanists call it, from the German words meaning "crooked wood." Beyond these elfin forests a few patches of tough perennial plants persist, but the land is mostly lost to hard rocks and heavy snow.

In this steep, serrated world the jagged horizon tumbles chaotically in every direction, seeming almost to grip and lunge at the sky. Snow falls for months on end, blowing off the windward crags in howling streamers and piling up in other places to thicken upon itself until its very weight makes it unstable. Accumulating to depths of perhaps 30 to 40 feet, laden with moisture as summer sun warms the snow and causes it to settle, the weighty masses of white eventually become a menace: avalanche energy lurks within them, poised, waiting for the moment of release.

Potential becomes reality with a sound, sometimes a dull boom that seems to come from deep inside something. Overhanging cornices—huge curls of snow shelving out from cliff tops—collapse as if shrugging off the burden of their own weight. Broad snowfields suddenly slump forward, usually in response to warm temperatures but sometimes for no apparent reason. These are the beginnings of avalanches, white death for anything in their paths. From a distance the process looks deceptively slow, even ponderous, but the snow gathers speed quickly as it is propelled downslope by its own momentum and the countless tons of weight behind it. The leading edge broadens rapidly and turns to a white fog—a hissing surge of snow, rock, and bits of debris. In a large avalanche a shock wave develops as air is pushed out ahead of the snow. The wave swirls across the slope ahead of the main weight, sometimes even toppling trees. And then, as suddenly as it started, the avalanche is over.

In places where a great deal of snow collects, so much may accumulate that the summer sun does not melt it. Year after year, season after season, it is buried ever deeper, until the weight of the ages is upon it. The result is glaciers, over 60 of them lying scattered across the Olympic peaks. Most are captives of the high mountain basins in which they form, but on high peaks facing the sea wind, where the snowfall is greatest, a few of the glaciers are strong enough to move ponderously down into distant valleys. The best known of these moving rivers of ice is the Blue Glacier, 3 miles long and 900 feet thick in places. The breeding ground for the Blue Glacier, along with its two companions, the Hoh and White glaciers, is Mount Olympus, the highest mountain in the entire park.

Mount Olympus and the other taller peaks in the park form a jumble of crags without apparent order—knife-edged ridges, jagged summits, and deep valleys that seem to twist randomly toward the horizon. Seen in their entirety, the Olympic Mountains occupy a more or less circular area about 40 miles in diameter, with their center near the commanding, 7,976-foot summit of Mount Olympus. On the north and east, the mountains slope steeply downward toward the waters of the Strait of Juan de Fuca and the Hood Canal, an arm of Puget Sound; to the south and west the slopes descend more gradually.

In absolute terms the mountains and glaciers of Olympic National Park may not seem particularly impressive—after all, the mightiest peaks reach to less than 8,000 feet and the largest glacier covers only 3 square miles. Yet for anyone who ventures into the high country, such figures are deceiving, for the mountains seem much taller than they really are. In the far distance the ocean curves toward the hazy blue horizon—like the edge of the earth seen from space. Nearer at hand, the view is from a place where the air is sparkling clean and clear onto lowlands that are partially obscured in haze. On days when the lowlands are completely covered by clouds, the impression of height and the feeling of isolation are even greater. This is true wilderness, worthy of all the sacrifices made and the struggles endured to reach it. In their own way these alpine heights of the Olympics are the realm of giants, shared only with Rainier and a few

Beating its wings, a ruffed grouse celebrates spring with a loud drumming that echoes through the woods.

other great mountains in the Pacific Northwest.

On the summits there are occasional sounds: wind moans across jagged rocks, snow hisses in winter gales, glaciers boom sullenly, avalanches now and then crack into life. But all these are the exceptions: the high Olympic wilderness is normally frozen in silence.

Here the months pass slowly, marking the depths of winter, until one evening late in March a hint of clearing shows in the western sky. By midnight all but a few clouds have vanished, and before dawn the mountains are bathed in starlight. Toward daybreak the eastern horizon brightens, glowing an ember red that melts away the fading night sky. Against the rising sun, Rainier casts a long shadow toward the west; nearby the snowbound high country tumbles away in all directions, its rocky ridges superbly defined as they descend beyond the snow line. By midmorning the deep green of the lowland forests contrasts sharply with the nearby peaks, looking almost black to eyes narrowed against the strong sunlight reflecting off the snow. The sun feels warm and the day is peaceful and still— except for a sound long absent and eagerly awaited. It is the sound of flowing water. In a thousand places throughout the park—high on Mount Steel, at the edges of Humes Glacier, along the snowfields on Mount Angeles—the snow is beginning to melt.

By early afternoon the temperature has reached 55° F. The valleys below are filled with the fragrance of sun-warmed spruce and fir and vibrant with the sound of running water. Ribbons of it trail over cliffs or wash down valley walls, dripping from the snowfields above. Trapped by the rock walls, the sounds fill the valleys to their very edges. These are the first hours of a new season. The day has become a vibrant celebration of spring, and the rivers announce its arrival.

The rivers rush swiftly down the slopes, passing through scenes that capture the essence of this place— the blur of a kingfisher diving for a minnow along the Bogachiel, the stab of a great blue heron catching a tadpole in the Quinault, the early morning fog in the dense rain forests of the lower valleys—before the final slow merging of their waters with the sea. In terms of what it contains, Olympic National Park is huge. Few areas span so many life zones, packing everything from mountain marmots to sea urchins into a distance of 40 miles or less, or offer so much to those who know their seasons and places. Here is a wilderness so splendid and so varied that its gift to all is an opportunity for the endless discovery of life itself.

Petrified Forest

"Chips of carnelian, onyx, agate, and jasper were strewn . . . in exotic and intricate patterns like a kaleidoscope fashioned by God's hand."
John Muir

Beneath the endless sky of northeastern Arizona spreads an arid rainbow wilderness called the Painted Desert, where streaks and bands of bright colors twist across a tortured landscape that bears the signature of unimaginable time. It is a magical and mysterious land, and nowhere is the mystery more intriguing or the magic more enthralling than in the swatch of blistered badlands along its southwestern edge—the Petrified Forest.

Here erosion eats away at a high, grassy plateau, creating a barren disarray of tinted cones and buttes, hills and gullies—reshaped and redefined by every rare rainstorm. When water turns sunbaked clay to slippery ooze, only those ridges, peaks, and spires that are protected by resistant caprocks are likely to hold firm. Regularly emerging from this convoluted chaos are wonders from the distant past: the bones of long-extinct animals, the delicate fossils of ferns, and—above all—the colorful remains of mighty fallen conifers now turned to stone.

In a region where vegetation is reduced to a few twisted junipers, low shrubs, sparse cacti, bunched grasses, and ephemeral wildflowers, the huge, shattered tree trunks seem strangely out of place. The Paiutes said that they were the arrow shafts of Shinauv, their thunder god. The Navajos thought of them as the bones of Yietso, a great mythological giant. Each piece is a unique creation that blazes with the colors of the land itself—a wild patchwork of rust-reds, slate-blues, tobacco-yellows, smoked purples, burnt oranges, antique whites, and all shades between. Mixed into their substance are rare pockets of semiprecious stones: rose quartz, smoky quartz, jasper, amethyst.

You can still read the life histories of a few of the trees in their annual rings. The surfaces of many are pockmarked with dimples left by a wood-destroying fungus. In the remains of some you can see the tunnels of prehistoric insect larvae. But, though the logs resemble wood, they no longer have its soft, spongy texture. They are dry and brittle, hard enough to scratch glass, and they weigh 150 to 200 pounds per cubic foot.

The name "Petrified Forest" is really a misnomer, for most of the petrified trees that are found here grew some distance away and were washed to this burial ground by rivers and streams. There are few standing stumps, and even fewer trunks that have roots or branches. Agate Bridge, a 100-foot log, spans a shallow arroyo like a stone footbridge, but the other huge trunks were broken to firewood lengths by long-ago quakes and stresses in the earth. Now they lie scattered as though strewn by some giant hand. Some bright chunks cap pedestals of clay, their stony hardness having long protected the softer material from erosion.

Legacy of a lush world

Some 200 million years ago this was a subtropical land. It was a vast, low-lying floodplain fringed on the south and west by active volcanoes—a swampy world overgrown with lush tangles of green and populated by an assortment of giant reptiles and amphibians. Across the floodplain spread an emerald shag of dainty club moss. Spreading ginkgo trees, palmlike cycads, tree ferns and their low-growing cousins, all crowded the banks of

Beneath the desert sky, where once lush forests grew and giant reptiles walked, the massive trunks of trees dead 200,000,000 years lie stone-hard and glistening. Above the patchy grasslands horned larks sing their tinkling melodies.

After every rain, the broken terrain gives up new pieces of petrified wood, its organic substance long since replaced by bright fantasies of stone, gem-studded and intershot with infinite colors. The park holds the largest and brightest collection of petrified wood ever discovered.

Shattered trunks, neatly sliced rounds, and flinty chips accumulate like a jumble of petrified firewood at the base of wrinkled mounds of earth on Blue Mesa. Atop the bluff, chunks of wood stand poised on shrinking pedestals of clay.

rivers that meandered northward toward a sea that has long since vanished. Giant ancestors of the modern horsetail rose 30 to 40 feet above the mud-clouded waters of marshes. Tall conifers dotted the highlands and mantled the slopes of distant mountains.

The titan of these upland forests was an extinct relative of the Norfolk Island pine. When it lived, there were no humans to give it a name; today's scientists call it *Araucarioxylon arizonicum*. A mushroom-shaped tree, it commonly topped out at 100 feet and attained a diameter of 6 to 8 feet—some grew to double that size. The species accounts for about 90 percent of the petrified wood in the park, and nearly all of the most brightly colored specimens. The remainder of the wood comes from two other extinct trees: the pinelike *Woodworthia* and the water-loving *Schilderia*, with a slender trunk that was fluted and buttressed at the base like that of a modern bald cypress. Neither grew much taller than 50 to 75 feet.

Some of the trees died of old age; fire, flood, and disease probably killed many others. Whatever the cause of death, the conifers periodically fell where they stood, and most of them rotted away—but not all. Intermittent floods carried some of the toppled giants along rain-swollen rivers and through swirling rapids—an arduous journey that stripped them clean of bark, branches, and roots. When at last the naked trunks

arrived on the lowlands, many lodged at bends in stream banks; others came to rest atop sandbars or in shallow pools. Logjams formed and were quickly covered by thick layers of mud, sand, and volcanic ash that cut off oxygen and retarded decomposition.

Beneath their airless shroud, the logs began to change. Water leached silica from the volcanic ash and carried it down through the sediments, picking up traces of other minerals along the way. As the solution soaked into the wood, molecules of silica were drawn inside the cell walls, where they crystallized in the form of quartz. Gradually the trees became stone. Sometimes the process culminated in exact look-alikes, in which the wood's cellular structure was preserved in microscopic detail. More often, the mineral simply replaced woody matter and formed gigantic chunks of quartz that masqueraded as trees. In wide cracks and hollows, where the quartz crystals were unconfined by the structures of woody cells, they were able to assume their natural hexagonal shape, and here they crystallized as jewels. Some logs became warehouses in which multitudes of semiprecious gems were hidden.

Other minerals in the silica-laden waters gave the petrifying trees their colors. Pure quartz resulted in white and gray; iron supplied reds, yellows, browns, blues, and greens; carbon and manganese produced black. At times the colors were true and well defined. At other times, shades swirled and blended into tints without names and patterns without edges—blurred color wheels frozen in time.

As the transformations continued, flood after flood, logjam upon logjam, the strange burial ground reached a depth of hundreds of feet. The climate changed. Deep waters and dry landscapes came and went, and for millions of years new sediments piled up, thousands of feet thick, on top of the prehistoric graveyard. Beneath the great weight, the mud, ash, silt, and sand of that vanished world hardened into the layers of shale and sandstone that geologists call the Chinle Formation. There it remained until, beginning about 65 million years ago, a series of slow geologic convulsions split much of the Southwest asunder. Over tens of millions of years, the Rocky Mountains were thrust skyward, the Colorado Plateau was uplifted, and the buried floodplain rose at least a mile. As it did so, the younger sediments were peeled away by erosion and sluiced to the Colorado River. Eons after their soggy interment, the ancient trees were once again exposed to the sky.

Dinosaurs' ancestors

Though the transformed trees are the most obvious and startling fossils that this part of the Painted Desert brings forth, they are not the only stone legacy from that distant time. Equally beautiful in their delicate way are the preserved replicas of leaves, seeds, cones, and fern fronds; equally dramatic are the long-entombed remains of animals, ranging from freshwater clams and fish to giant amphibians and reptiles, and including some of the earliest forerunners of the dinosaurs.

The masters of the swamps and waterways were the phytosaurs, crocodilelike creatures whose long slender snouts were studded with knife-sharp teeth. Averaging 12 to 20 feet in length (some exceeded 30 feet), they may have weighed several tons. Propelled by strong hind legs and powerful tails, they sculled through the swamps with only eyes and snorkling nostrils exposed—ever on the hunt.

Among their prey may have been salamanderlike metoposaurs, some of the largest amphibians of all time. These fish eaters were about 10 feet long and weighed up to half a ton, but their legs were very short; they probably wallowed in shallow water like the modern hippopotamus. They had massive skulls, often as long as two feet, equipped with needlelike teeth and large lower-jaw fangs.

The aetosaurs were heavily armored vegetarians—a sort of reptilian armadillo—whose large bodies made eating a full-time occupation. Covered with hard, protective plates, the creatures ranged from the size of a house cat to 15 feet long. Despite their armor plating, which sometimes included long shoulder spikes or rows of sharp spines along their sides, all must have been high-priority cuisine for the several kinds of great meat eaters that roamed the land.

Outstanding among these was the fast and fearful predator called *Lythrodynastes,* or "gore lord," the bane of the floodplain, with its horrendous claws and daggerlike teeth. Capable of walking on all fours or rearing up on its hind legs like the much later and larger tyrannosaurs, it was 14 to 20 feet long and weighed up to a ton.

Its largest prey was *Placerias,* an odd, three-eyed reptile that looked a bit like today's rhinoceros. The third eye on its forehead, less developed than the other two, was probably a simple light-sensing organ. Up to 12 feet long and weighing 2 to 3 tons, the ponderous barrel-shaped vegetarian traveled in herds and sported large tusks for digging up roots and plants.

Although many different kinds of long-vanished reptiles and amphibians have recently been found, and more are coming to light every year, complete skeletons are rare. In part, this is because the raging waters of the primal floodplain tore many of the bodies apart before they were buried, leaving the bones scattered and broken. Another reason is that the petrified bones, though they have endured for millions of centuries beneath the surface, last but a short time once they are exposed to the elements. The material of bones is replaced by a process that leaves them light and porous—unlike the steel-hard petrified wood—and they simply fall apart after a few rains. Even so, Petrified Forest is one of the world's best fossil locations from this period—a wonderland where scientists can find the clues, preserved in fragile, powdery stone, that help them to solve the mysteries of ancient life.

Prehistoric melting pot

Less ancient, but equally mysterious, are the vestiges of prehistoric Indian peoples that dot the hills and knolls. Although Petrified Forest was never a major cultural center, as Mesa Verde was, these high grasslands became a sort of melting pot where three great prehistoric cultures—the Anasazi from the north and east, the Mogollon from the south, and the Sinagua from the west—overlapped, and their people intermingled. Little is known of how these folk resolved their differences, but no evidence has been found of warfare between them, and some sites contain artifacts from two or three cultures, suggesting that peaceful coexistence was the rule.

The sites of several communities have been found. The remarkable Agate House, for example, is an eight-room pueblo built from chunks of petrified wood. It may have been occupied for only a short time between about A.D. 1050, and 1300. The Puerco Pueblo, the largest and most recently inhabited of the park's ancient buildings, had nearly 100 rooms of sandstone and mortar in which 60 to 75 people survived the drought that brought an end to many other communities in the Southwest. It was erected on a bluff overlooking the Puerco River, which continued to run sporadically during the late 13th century, when the drought was at its height. Farming collectively, its people raised beans, corn, and squash along the river's natural terraces. The pueblo was occupied until about A.D. 1400, but all that remains of it today are hints of sandstone walls, a ceremonial kiva, some shallow depressions in the earth, and hundreds of petroglyphs carved into low-lying cliffs.

Calendars in stone

It is the mystery contained in the petroglyphs, far more than any of the sites, that piques the curiosity of modern viewers. The rock carvings, dating back nearly to the beginning of human habitation, are everywhere in the park. Painstakingly carved into desert varnish—the thin, dark patina that slowly forms on sandstone surfaces throughout the Southwest—they range from childlike stick figures of humans and animals to intricate geometric masterpieces.

Some viewers have said that the carvings have no meaning, that they are aimless doodles left for the sake of leaving marks. Others profess to find religious significance in them or puzzle over them to decipher the sounds of unknown languages. Any or all of these things may be true of some of the petroglyphs. The only certainty is that they are haunting works of art whose significance, for the most part, remains mysterious. However, there are a few petroglyphs in the park whose functions, if not their precise meanings, have recently been learned: they are stone calendars that mark the cycle of the seasons with astonishing accuracy.

One small cave, known as the Cave of Life, though strictly off-limits to visitors, has been shown to be a particularly dramatic example of the way in which these calendars work. The cave has an entrance that faces west, and through that entrance, and through many chinks between the boulders that en-

Tiny kangaroo rats survive the heat of the day by plugging the entrances to their burrows from within, sealing in humidity. They never drink, but get all the water they need from the many small seeds that they gather at night.

close it, the setting sun sends its rays; and as the season progresses toward midwinter and the sun sets daily a little farther southward, the resultant patterns of light move gradually across the opposite wall of the cave. This wall is adorned with many petroglyphs. One of the chinks shapes the light into a thin dagger, and just before sunset about one-eighth of a year, or 45 days, before the winter solstice, the point of this dagger approaches a complex pattern of petroglyphs. Slowly, as the sun descends toward the horizon, the dagger moves across this pattern, its point touching first one symbol, then another, until—precisely at sunset—the dagger's point comes to rest in the center of an elaborate cross. There it fades to darkness. (The Hopi Indians, believed to be direct descendants of the Anasazi, have a ceremony called *Wuwuchim*, celebrating the beginning of creation, that starts at that moment.)

Another set of petroglyphs on the cave wall has at its heart a circle, out of which a spiral, like the fiddlehead of a fern, seems to sprout sideways. At the autumnal equinox, and again on the first day of spring, the light of the setting sun floods through the cave entrance to perfectly frame the conjoined figures. (These equinoxes are also ceremonially observed by the Hopi.)

Coincidence? Perhaps. But throughout the park, more than a dozen other such coincidences have been found in recent years. The changing seasons are marked by shafts of light that dart and disappear, flow liquidly down rock faces to end at the centers of intricate spirals, or intersect with lizardlike shapes. Some of the petroglyphs that mark the summer solstice are particularly eerie in their accuracy, for they adorn the faces of rocks that stand alone in the open, and are touched only once a year—either at dawn or at sunset of the longest day—by the shadows of nearby hills and bluffs, or by slivers of light that slip through cracks between distant cliffs.

Thus, the land itself was made to serve as a solar almanac, by means of which ancient farmers knew when to sow, when to reap, when to prepare for winter, and when to renew their faith that summer would return. It is an awesome phenomenon—a testimony to the creativity of a people who devised a method of atuning their lives to the eternal order of the universe.

The land today

Though the details of the Petrified Forest's landscape are constantly changing, the character of the land itself is much the same as it was when the first humans walked its haunting panoramas. It is still a pristine world of solitude and space—a place where, beneath the golden fury of the sun, turkey vultures sailplane the updrafts, and small whirlwinds known as dust devils pirouette across the color-streaked flats. Horizons are lost in purple haze; and in the evening, when the sun's slanting rays sharpen the textures and contours of the land, yipping choirs of coyotes orchestrate vermilion sunsets. The cooling air wears a heady perfume, and

Even on the barren, convoluted moonscape of the Painted Desert, where the brightest colors are often displayed in the banded dunes and long-dead trees, life persists. Sparse grasses and brush support a wide range of birds and beasts.

from nooks and crannies comes the soprano counterpoint of crickets heralding the end of day.

This is the hour when the desert, silent and sweltering beneath the hot sun all day, comes to life. Creatures emerge from their dens, nests, and burrows. Tiny, buff-colored canyon mice dart from shaded rock crevices; larger, big-eared pinyon mice scurry from hollow logs. Kangaroo rats remove the plugs from their underground homes and hop forth in search of seeds; they will be busy all night stuffing their external cheek pouches with food to carry back to their burrows. A single kangaroo rat, weighing barely an ounce, has been known to amass a 12-pound cache of seeds.

Another collector, the white-throated woodrat, or packrat, has much more eclectic tastes. It fills its nest of sticks, stones, shredded bark, and spiny cactus joints with little bits of almost anything that catches its attention. As much as 10 bushels of material has been excavated from one packrat's home, including a pawn-shop inventory of junk: scraps of colored cloth, shiny buttons, pieces of metal (including coins), plastic toys, and even false teeth. The long-tailed puffball always seems to be carrying something, and since it has no pouches, it can only carry one item at a time. Therefore, to pick up a new treasure it must drop an old one. It may make several such swaps before it arrives home, a practice that has earned it the nickname trade rat. More than one backpacker has awakened to discover a possession replaced by a stone or a bit of petrified wood.

In search of the park's prolific rodent population are the many predators that stalk the starlit blackness of a desert night. Rattlesnakes slither along the badlands dunes. Coyotes and bobcats pad silently across the shortgrass plains. Badgers waddle through the brush, and tiny kit foxes sniff along the scrub, their large, scooplike ears swiveling to catch the sounds of dinner swishing in and out of hiding places.

Every so often, phantom mists seem to cloak the forms of ancient people walking across the land, and now and again whistling winds carry the sounds of forgotten voices. There are times in this arid land when thunderstorms reverberate with the howls of primordial beasts, and rain-frenzied streams seem to respond with the cracks and thuds of mammoth water-tumbled trees. But even when the day is clear, even when the moisture of spring spreads bright floral carpets over sandy flats, and freckles sunburned mesas with green, the Petrified Forest is a mysterious realm. Where else but in the land of the stone rainbows can you stub your toe on a jeweled piece of eternity?

Redwood

*"From their mute forms there flows a poise, in silence,
a lovely sound and motion in response to wind. What peace
comes to those aware of the voice and bearing of trees!"*
Cedric Wright, *20th-century author*

Everywhere among the redwoods there is overwhelming immensity, a gigantism that leaves mere mortals slack-jawed and unbelieving. Kings of their race, the redwoods are mighty titans whose straight, massive trunks soar 300 feet toward the sky—higher than any other tree on earth. Accentuating the redwoods' unparalleled height is the fact that their furrowed, auburn trunks are often bare of branches for the first 100 or 200 feet. High overhead, the branches seem to sweep the clouds, their delicate, feathery foliage forming a celestial canopy far above the forest floor.

Although each tree is wondrous in itself, these giants derive their full power from being part of a pure redwood forest where their massed beauty becomes awesome, inspirational—and a bit intimidating. Such redwood forests are found only along California's northern coast, in a strip bounded on one side by mountains and on the other by the Pacific Ocean. Dependent on warm, moist air, the redwood empire stretches nearly 500 miles in length, from Big Sur, south of San Francisco, to just over the Oregon border, and varies in width from 5 to 20 miles, depending on how far the ocean's wet fog fingers creep inland.

Height is not the coast redwoods' only impressive characteristic. In the redwood realm, as in the world of people, there is no correlation between an individual's age and its height and girth. Even when trees receive the same amount of sun, moisture, and nutrients, the tallest is not necessarily the oldest; the oldest is not always the bulkiest; the shortest or slimmest is not inevitably the youngest. Why this should be so for the redwoods, and not other types of trees, remains a

As though to brush the sky with their delicate foliage, California's redwood trees, the tallest living things on earth, stretch upward. Centuries old, these giants can not only survive fires, but heal themselves with hardly a scar.

mystery locked deep inside these stately monarchs.

A breath away from immortality, the redwoods have an astonishingly long life span—a millennium or two is not unusual—earning them the nickname "the everlasting." They have few natural enemies and are stubbornly persistent in the face of adversity, triumphing over all but the most radical assaults on their well-being. Even when all upper growth is destroyed, the tenacious trees have a backup plan: they clone themselves. Coast redwoods have a regenerative ability rare in conifers, enabling them to produce sprouts from the many knobby burls that form along the bases of mature trees. When a parent tree is cut or damaged, the clones vigorously spring to life. In just a few weeks, the whole stump is awash with hundreds of hopeful new shoots; those receiving the best light and moisture will form a ring or "family circle" around the parent. Although redwoods can also reproduce by seed, sprouts grow faster and have a greater chance of survival—for sprouts are not new lives, like seedlings, but the same life in continuation, fed by established roots.

Despite the tree's gargantuan proportions, its cones are surprisingly small, hardly bigger than a human thumbnail. The seeds contained in these cones are minute; an astounding 125,000 of them are needed to make a pound. Each season, a tree releases millions of seeds, but anywhere from one-half to three-quarters are nonviable, and the remainder face terrible odds. Although winds sometimes carry the lucky ones far afield, most seeds fall within 200 to 400 feet of the parent—not a favorable place to be. To grow, a seed requires open soil, some sunshine, and adequate moisture—all difficult to obtain beneath the dense canopy of an already established redwood forest. Even the seeds that land in desirable places must survive still other perils—hungry wildlife, root rot, insufficient rain, sudden cold spells, drying hot winds. The mortality rate is astronomical. Only about one seedling out of a million lives to become a mature tree.

Once a redwood is tall enough to add its feathery boughs to the celestial canopy, it is almost indestructible—a formidable fortress that is able to protect itself against the ravages of fire and disease. Remarkably fire-resistant, a redwood will be killed only by the most savage inferno. It is saved by three things: its heavy layer of insulating bark, often more than a foot thick on a mature tree; the considerable water in the wood itself; and the absence of pitch—the flammable substance that ignites readily in other conifers. When flames do damage a coast redwood, leaving a hollowed-out or blackened trunk, the tree's cambium, or growth layer, will cover up the wound so completely that all evidence of the fire is gone. If just a fraction of a tree remains intact after a fire, the redwood will not die; instead it will heal and rejuvenate itself, eventually becoming the flourishing Olympian it once was.

While most other trees are vulnerable to fungus attacks and insect invasions, the coast redwood is not. Its bark and heartwood are well endowed with tannin, an astringent substance that not only gives the tree its rich, red color but also inhibits decay and repels insects: most dislike tannin's bitter taste.

Floods are a more formidable enemy: they can and do contribute to a redwood's demise by attacking its most vulnerable spot—the roots. One might imagine these forest skyscrapers to have taproots stretching almost to the center of the earth, but in fact the world's tallest trees have no taproots at all. Instead, they have shallow root systems that reach only 6 to 10 feet down, though they spread as much

The lovely but deadly Amanita muscaria, *or fly agaric, is among the many mushrooms that grow in the shade of the mighty redwoods.*

as 50 feet across. Because the whole network lies so close to the surface, floods can erode the soil from beneath the giant's base, leaving the hulking tower precariously perched atop a gaping hole. In such instances the verdict is nearly always the same—death by windfall.

More frequently, though, floods have just the opposite effect: instead of washing away soil, they bring new layers, burying the roots under deep mounds. In these cases, the redwoods must adjust or smother. So with typical redwood panache, the trees simply grow new roots at the higher level and carry on with their lives. One coast redwood is known to have survived as many as seven major floods and several minor ones, each time sprouting a new root layer. Not only had this patriarch's life begun 1,200 years earlier; it had started more than 11 feet deeper.

There are redwoods alive today that grew at the time of Christ; the species itself dates back some 20 million years; but the family from which it springs goes back even further, to a time when clumsy-footed dinosaurs dominated the animal kingdom. Cone-bearing evergreens then covered vast areas of the earth with what must have been an infinitude of green. Exactly when the first redwoods became a part of this scene is uncertain, although fossil leaves and cones embedded in ancient rock indicate that the ancestors of today's giant conifers existed at least 160 million years ago. They began in what may seem to us a very strange place—Greenland. Far too cold for redwoods today, this frigid frontier was, in eons past, a subtropical Eden of river deltas and floodplains.

The family proliferated, and at its zenith stretched across much of what is now Europe, Asia, and North America. But then geological forces reshaped the face of the earth and its climate. Mountains pushing skyward blocked humid sea winds, causing a drying trend across the Northern Hemisphere. The Arctic froze, and glaciers moved southward like bulldozers, crunching and flattening everything in their path. When the destruction ended, after the glaciers had melted, most of the giant trees were gone.

But not all; three kinds of redwoods survived. Two are native to California—the coast redwood and the sierra redwood (better known as the giant sequoia), which grows along the Sierra Nevada's western slopes. The third species, the dawn redwood, is native to the other side of the world, flourishing in China's remote interior provinces.

Because the two Californians look alike, they are often taken for the same tree. But the differences are many: the coast redwoods are taller; the giant sequoias are wider, with more wood relative to their height, and they are older, outliving their coast relatives by almost 1,000 years. Compared with its colossal cousins, the dawn redwood is a midget, seldom exceeding a height of 140 feet. Unlike the Californian trees, it is deciduous, scattering its needlelike leaves in amber drifts each fall.

The Emerald Mile

When pioneers first came to live along the California coast, the towering redwoods covered almost 2 million acres. Since the giants were nearly impossible to fell with equipment designed for normal-sized trees, the early settlers had little impact on the virgin forest. A few hardy souls managed to clear some land for pastures and crops, but only the most determined were able to maintain their acreage, for where one redwood came down, hundreds of sprouts grew back. Superstitious settlers took to cutting out sprouts "in the dark of the moon," hoping that this might rid them of the trees forever. It did not.

By the 1830's and 1840's, a few enterprising individuals had figured out how to handle the unwieldy conifers, and a scattering of sawmills went into operation. But it was the gold rush in 1849 that drastically changed the redwoods' fate. Cities and towns sprang up, seemingly overnight, and the swelling population made increasing demands on the coast redwood forests—a great green storehouse that offered cheap and accessible lumber. To their own detriment, the giant trees consistently produced wood that was straight-grained, durable, and resistant to rot, fire, and termites. Within two decades after the Mother Lode had been discovered, the redwood belt's southern hills lay denuded. More efficient mechanization permitted even greater advances into redwood territory, and by 1964 only 250,000 acres of the original forest was left, sheltered in the coast's more remote and rugged regions.

Safe among them is one of the earth's greatest treasures—the world's tallest tree, a colossus nearly 370 feet high. Not far away stand the second, third, and sixth tallest trees. This magnificent stretch of record-breaking redwoods, called Tall Trees Grove, is part of a long corridor known as the Emerald Mile. It is an incomparable place, both statistically and in terms of mood. Under its vaulted canopy, sunshine is splintered into slivers of light that dance along the forest floor. When fog floats through, wrapping the trees in mystery, the columns seem to recede into the eerie darkness, looming ghostlike in the mist, their presence felt rather than seen. Whether bright or shadowy, cheerful or otherwordly, the redwood forest is always silent, a wilderness cathedral where every sound is muffled to a soft, worshipful hush.

At the giants' feet

Along hillsides and ridges the pure redwood groves of streamside flats give way to mixed forests where the Gulliver-like giants rule over Lilliputian conifers and deciduous trees, shrubs and shaggy ferns, miniature groundcovers, and filigreed mosses. A world removed from the silent majesty of pure redwood stands, these slope forests are filled with skittering sounds, cheery flowers, and sun-filled, airy spaces. The most flamboyant blossoms are those of the California rosebay and western azalea; both are rhododendrons. For most of the year these loosely branched, leather-leaved shrubs blend into the forests' greens and browns, but from June through July they put on a dazzling show. The rosebay blooms in brilliant hues, ranging from a rosy to a purplish pink marked by patches of olive-green to orange; the deliciously scented azaleas are somewhat less pretentious, their delicate pinks and whites gently tinged with hints of yellow.

In a world filled with giants and show-offs, one hardly notices the demure maidenhair fern, which overspills stream banks and decorates mossy seeps with clouds of lacy foliage, or the sword fern, a denizen of every shady nook and cranny, where its long slender fronds hold aloft sword-shaped leaflets. Sprinkling the giants' feet from late March to early summer are trilliums, members of the lily family whose blossoms slowly turn from white to a dusty rose. The various parts of this plant, such as its petals and leaves, come in threes—hence its name, from the Latin for "three." Spread

A full-grown California black-tailed deer looks like a miniature among the immense redwoods. Despite the trees' size (it would take a dozen people, arms outstretched, to encircle some of them), they have shallow roots.

everywhere are verdant mats of redwood sorrel bearing cloverlike leaves that open wide in the shade and furl tightly at dusk. Each spring the sorrel's leaves serve as little umbrellas for the plant's pinkish-lavender flowers.

For year-round beauty nothing surpasses two prolific, viny shrubs: vine maple and poison oak. Vine maple sends tough, octopuslike limbs throughout the understory, rooting anew wherever its tentacles touch the earth; poison oak twines around the redwoods, gracing unimagined heights with spiraling foliage. The leaves of both species grow parallel to the sky, catching, reflecting, and diffusing the light, saturating everything below with a seasonal glow that is either summer-green or autumn-red.

From their roots to the tops of their leafy crowns, the slope forests afford homes for animal life. Decaying logs house the mouselike shrew, a beady-eyed creature with a long, whiskery snout and sleek, dark brown fur. Active day and night, this small bundle of energy must maintain its high body temperature in order to survive, and so it is always in search of food. In any 24-hour period the hyperactive animal consumes twice its own weight in insects, earthworms, and other invertebrates—quite an accomplishment considering that the shrew's eyesight is so poor that all tasty tidbits must first be sniffed out with its extremely pointed nose. Shrews seem to be born skittish—even a change in the weather can cause the young to respond with fear. Grabbing the tail of a sibling in its mouth, each youngster links up behind the

The Steller's jay, a raucous denizen of conifer forests throughout the West, is a notorious pilferer. It steals food and eggs from the nests of other birds, and has even been known to snatch tasty morsels from campers' tables.

mother, forming a chain that slithers along the ground seeking a safer situation. Shrews do not outgrow this nervousness; their hearts may beat so fast that they can literally be scared—or excited—to death.

The mountain beaver, contrary to its name, is not a beaver: it does not build dams, fell trees, or construct lodges in water. But like the more famous and widespread aquatic architect, the mountain beaver—found only along the Pacific coast of North America—has consummate engineering skills. It digs elaborate underground tunnels and burrows in moist forests, usually near a river or stream whose path it may divert to supply its labyrinthine lodgings with water. Although this short, chunky, tailless animal is not especially adept at tree climbing, it may occasionally scale a trunk to obtain choice, tender leaves or to gnaw off twigs or branches—another beaverlike talent—with which to carpet its home. A fastidious housekeeper, the mountain beaver maintains separate rooms for nesting or sleeping and for storing food. It uses fist-sized stones as movable doors for rooms and tunnels and as whetstones on which to sharpen its teeth. Since it does not hibernate in winter, the mountain beaver stashes away bits of bark and summer-greened ferns and grasses that it has painstakingly cut, piled into little haystacks, and dried—just as the rabbitlike pikas do. When snows cover the ground, the mountain beaver will not starve, even if its pantry is bare: it can excavate new tunnels under the snowpack to reach the trees.

While most forest creatures keep a low profile, a few are bold and bossy. Ravens squabble in treetops, and crows caw from limb to limb. The prize loudmouth, however, is an energetic blue bird called the Steller's jay. This black-crested bandit is both beautiful and brash, endlessly flirting and posturing, yet ready at a moment's notice to rob a nest of eggs or newly hatched young. Regarding its own nest, though, the robin-sized daredevil is remarkably discreet, coming and going with shadowy stillness to conceal the nest's location. But the silence is short-lived, for the babies are as sassy as the parents, and before long the forest is filled with the whole family's raucous scoldings.

Beachcombers and seasonal visitors

The park's soul is in its forests, but its life is not limited to the great trees and the creatures that live among them. It boasts a 33-mile coastline, an untamed place where wind-whipped waves smash against rocky headlands, pummeling boulders into polished cobblestones. Rain, wind, and waves wear away the shore, sculpting stony arches that eventually erode and collapse into the sea, becoming craggy, offshore isles that are ghostly reminders of the land's former edge. Keen-eyed gulls sailplane the updrafts, soaring high above the saw-toothed shore. Marbled murrelets, robin-sized birds, float on the waves from dawn to dusk, diving below the surface for fish. When darkness falls, the chubby birds take off and fly toward shore; where they go, however,

In Fern Canyon, too shady for trees and most flowers, conditions are just right for sword ferns, lady ferns, deer ferns, five-fingered ferns, and many others. Mingled fronds create a wonderland of subtly contrasting color and texture.

was a mystery for many years. Only recently has it been discovered that their nighttime retreat is high in the branches of virgin redwoods.

Between the highest surf-splashed rock and the lowest algae-carpeted tide pool is a ribbon where only special forms of life can survive. Alternately, twice a day, this intertidal zone is first buffeted by frothy, foaming waves that tumble over each other in their rush to shore, and then left high and dry as tides suck the water out to sea. Yet an astonishing variety of plants and animals are perfectly suited to this in-again, out-again existence, making their homes in pools that the outgoing tide leaves behind. Sea urchins bristle their needles, sometimes hiding under leafy kelp or other algae; crabs scurry from one rocky crevice to another; snails and worms slink along the sand; and starfish, more properly called sea stars, walk on their suction-cupped feet in search of food. Acorn barnacles attach their volcano-shaped shells to algae or rocks, reaching out with barbed, feathery arms to strain tiny bits of food from the water. When ebb tides leave them high and dry, the shrimplike creatures retreat inside their shells, closing the rooftop flaps against the perils of heat, dryness, and predators.

Sea anemones, looking more like colorful carnations than marine animals, most often adhere to rocks or plants; on occasion they burrow into mud or sand. Their innocent-looking, petallike tentacles are armed with stingers that immobilize small prey. Some types of anemones build dense colonies, covering rocks with a squishy fuzz. Should danger approach, the colony releases a chemical that discourages any further advance.

In deeper water just offshore, harbor seals poke their bewhiskered faces above the waves, easily treading water with their flippers. Frequent visitors to bays and estuaries where the fishing is good, these dappled mammals also spend a good deal of time basking on land. They haul themselves onto beaches and rocky ledges when tides are low, but—better suited to a watery environment than to dry land—they are rather awkward; their flippers are of little value as legs, and so they must lurch forward on their bellies, wriggling like overinflated eels. Unlike their noisy sea lion cousins, harbor seals voice only occasional squeals. If threatened, they will return to the sea for safety; they can stay underwater for almost half an hour without coming up for air.

The largest aquatic animal that can be seen from the park is the gray whale, a 45-foot-long mammal that makes an annual 5,000-mile journey from its Arctic summer feeding grounds to its warm-water calving lagoons in Baja California. Traveling in groups called pods, the whales parade past California's northern coast on their way south in December. They are usually close enough to shore for whale watchers to see them blow misty sprays high into the air.

Seagoing animals are not the only travelers to visit the rocky coast. The Pacific Flyway is a popular avian highway between the Arctic and Mexico, and hundreds of birds that are making the annual journey pause for seasonal stopovers. Sanderlings, plump members of the sandpiper clan, arrive in droves to spend their winters on the beach far from their tundra homes. These shorebirds tend to remain in flocks even when dining, stretching out in single file along the water's edge; with chorus-line precision, they advance and retreat with each breaking wave—avian choreography performed on spindly legs.

The long-billed curlew, another sandpiper, also winters along the shore, feeding on mollusks, crustaceans, and lugworms—quite a change in menu for a bird that spends the rest of the year in high, dry grasslands. This marbled buff and black bird, the largest shorebird in North America, is most renowned for its large bill—a nearly nine-inch-long, down-curved stiletto that serves admirably for probing into the tunnels of aquatic worms. Though useless as a weapon, the bizarre bill serves the creature well as an instrument of intimidation against predators.

Lazy summers find brown pelicans gliding along the shoreline and flapping from one rocky islet to another. Despite its large, bulky body, this bird is an elegant flier with powerful wings that span up to seven feet. The scoop-beaked fisherman is an expert diver, often plunging headfirst into the water from as high as 30 feet in order to net a pouchful of fish. After surfacing, the pelican will float for a minute or two, until the water-filled pouch drains, before swallowing its catch.

Prairies near the sea

Beyond the sandy beachfront lies a patchwork of dunes, wetlands, thickets, and grassy bluffs. Each is a tightly knit community; each influences its neighboring communities. Rivers meet the sea's backwash, creating saltwater marshes and estuaries; pulsing currents push river-delta sands seaward, building new beaches; a

The grass at the edge of the continent seems to run all the way down to meet the sea. California's northern coast is both rugged and peaceful—a place where harbor seals bask atop surf-pounded rocks. Just inland, the mighty redwoods tower; the titans of the seas, gray whales, can sometimes be seen not far offshore.

storm-stirred ocean overspills its bounds, flooding lowlands and turning them into lazy lagoons; winds and waves whip up sands, moving and remolding the dunes one particle at a time.

In these interdependent communities, populations sometimes overlap. Where freshwater intermingles with saltwater, fish from both worlds coexist. Salmon spend most of their lives in the ocean, but spawn in upstream river riffles; youngsters abound in the salty estuaries that lie between. Egrets and great blue herons move easily between freshwater marshes and saltwater flats, feeding on fish, frogs, and snakes. Striped skunks hunt insects and mice along open beaches as well as in knotty thickets. Raccoons are not at all particular about where they dine, leaving their babylike footprints as telltale evidence of forays into tidal mud flats and sandy stream banks. Preferring to hunt under cover of darkness, these masked raiders of the wild are amazingly adept at snatching turtle eggs, nestling birds, small mammals, frogs, fish, and even such fleet-footed insects as grasshoppers; they also nibble on nuts, berries, grapes, and other fruits when they become ripe for the picking.

Seven miles inland rise the Bald Hills, a haphazard collection of grasslands, treeless knolls, and oak woodlands—terrain that seems more suited to South Dakota than to the California coast. One almost expects to see bison making their way across the tawny-grassed slopes. This 2,000-acre prairie has never been home to these shaggy beasts, but it has long been the domain of the California black-tailed deer—a delicate subspecies of mule deer—and the mighty Roosevelt elk.

The second largest member of the deer family (only the moose is bigger), weighing up to 1,000 pounds, these massive animals once roamed throughout North America, but now their number is greatly reduced. Roosevelt elk—they are named after Theodore Roosevelt—can be found only along the coast of the Pacific Northwest, in places like Redwood and Olympic national parks. Several herds graze in Redwood's amber meadows, munching grasses and other plants, straying only occasionally to nearby woodlands for shade or shelter. The groups seldom intermingle, even where territories are not separated by fields or dense forests. Many elk spend their days reclining in the tall, strawlike grass, so well camouflaged that only limpid eyes and twitching ears show. Sometimes an impudent blackbird may land atop an elk's back, using the smooth, broad surface as a pedestal from which it can survey the scene; the elk seeems not to care. Despite their weight, their size, and the male's huge, unwieldy antlers, elk are

Among the tough yet delicate-looking flowers that flourish along the seashore are beach morning glories and sand verbenas.

sleek, powerful animals that move with a fluid grace and, when necessary, with surprising speed—some can gallop 35 miles an hour.

Each spring, bull elk grow new antlers in anticipation of the time when they will have to defend their harems against amorous challengers. Throughout the summer the massive, towering racks are covered with soft velvet; but autumn brings the mating season, and the spiked weapons are unsheathed. For many days the prairies reverberate with the bellowing and trumpeting of the bulls, and at times the clash of antlers can be heard as they battle for dominion over their cows. The long-legged, spotted calves are born the following spring and the cycle begins anew.

Here in the Bald Hills, where the sun is hot, the soil is thin, and trees are scattered into deciduous fringes, California black-tailed deer make their way up shallow draws; black bears lope ponderously along oak-dotted hills; and California voles, mouselike creatures, scamper in secret burrows. Kestrels—also known as sparrow hawks—and red-tailed hawks circle above the clearings, their screams almost an intrusion on the lazy peacefulness of the prairies. The loud, cackling calls of California quail echo across the land; their black teardrop-shaped head plumes make them easy to identify. More melodious is the joyful, flutelike song of the western meadowlark; this colorful bird, its bright yellow underside marked with a distinctive V-shaped black bib, sings almost constantly, but during courtship the males sing even more lustily, as though they were competing for prizes in a contest.

Spring turns the prairie lands into an explosion of color as wildflowers bloom with such brilliance it would seem a rainbow had splintered and fallen to earth. Shrubby forests of blueblossoms, or California lilacs, are wrapped in bluish-purple clouds; occasional Indian paintbrushes dot the landscape with dabs of orange, scarlet, maroon, and all shades between; wild irises nod gracefully on hillsides; and along the banks of streams, buttercups bear lemon-yellow saucers of sweet nectar where bees hum.

Here in Redwood National Park, the day's first light falls on these high prairies. It is a golden mantle that dispels the ocean's billowing fog and dries the dew-shimmering grass. Looking westward from the steep ridgetops, one has an overview of verdant valleys where coast redwoods loom like dark towers along serpentine waters, standing guard at the edge of the continent. In the distance, where the sky melts into the sea, lies the azure horizon. In every direction there is a clear-eyed sweep across the grandeur that is Redwood.

Rocky Mountain

"Climb the mountains and get their good tidings.
Nature's peace will flow into you as sunshine
flows into trees."
                                                    John Muir

Winter winds scream at more than 200 miles an hour through gaps in the rocks high atop Tombstone Ridge. It seems impossible that anything could survive in so inhospitable a spot. Yet heroic limber pines, their roots sunk deep into cracks in the rock ridge, continue to wave the banner of life here at the timberline. Majestic in their tortured poses, they are battered, twisted, and sandblasted by the wind—a sculptor that shapes them into its own violent self-portrait.

The timberline, undulating between elevations of 11,000 and 11,500 feet here in Rocky Mountain National Park, is the most dramatic battlefront in life's long struggle to clothe the mountains—a struggle that is the spiritual core of the Rockies. With almost geological deliberation, one seed at a time, the forest creeps upslope.

Although Engelmann spruce and subalpine firs, less pliant than the limber pines, cannot survive by bending with the murderous wind, they have their own way of letting its power shape them into elfin-wood, or krummholz (German for "twisted wood"). Some mild, moist summer, a seed may germinate in the shelter of a rock, and a tree may sprout. Any shoots that peek above the rock are sucked dry; but the tree must grow or die, and so it extends itself sideways. Huddled behind the rock, season after season, its trunk and cowering branches add girth; and as it becomes increasingly dwarfish, its own wood begins to shelter new

growth. Very gradually, it expands beyond the protection of the rock and joins with other hardy pioneers to form a low front wall that protects the trees behind it and lets them grow a little taller. Someday, another generation of seeds may take root behind other rocks and advance the timberline again.

Dramatic though the timberline struggle is, it is not the true front line of life in the park. Above it are the treeless peaks of more than 60 mountains, as well as several long ridges; during the brief growing season, all but the highest summits are bestrewn with bright wildflowers and carpeted with broad swathes of green. This is the alpine tundra, a rolling, rocky expanse bounded only by the sky above and by dramatic vistas of glacier-sliced cliffs all round about. Here, as on the vast Arctic tundra that covers much of Alaska and northern Canada, plants must be tough if they are to survive. They must tolerate drying winds that would quickly wilt a rose, and temperature shifts that would brown a violet. And yet they are very fragile—any extra stress, even the tramp of one person's foot in the same place as another's, can kill.

The plants grow low to the ground, out of the main force of the desiccating wind. Like desert plants, they conserve moisture. Many cut their water losses and hold in warmth by wearing furry coats; others, such as the yellow stonecrop, have hard, waxy leaf surfaces. Because plants have but a short time to flourish and bloom on the tundra—late June and part of July—more than one growing season is generally needed to complete a life cycle; annuals have little chance of survival. Snow buttercups, the first blossoms to appear, do not even wait for the snow to melt. By the heat of their own

Snow is permanent atop the peaks of the Never Summer range, part of the Great Divide. Bright high-elevation flowers attract such pollinators as the tiger swallowtail butterfly, seen resting here on a clump of ponderosa pine needles.

247

Aptly named Dream Lake, nestled calm and blue at the foot of 12,713-foot Hallett Peak, is one of the park's many idyllic settings where, in the clear mountain air, hushed conifer forests surround grassy meadows.

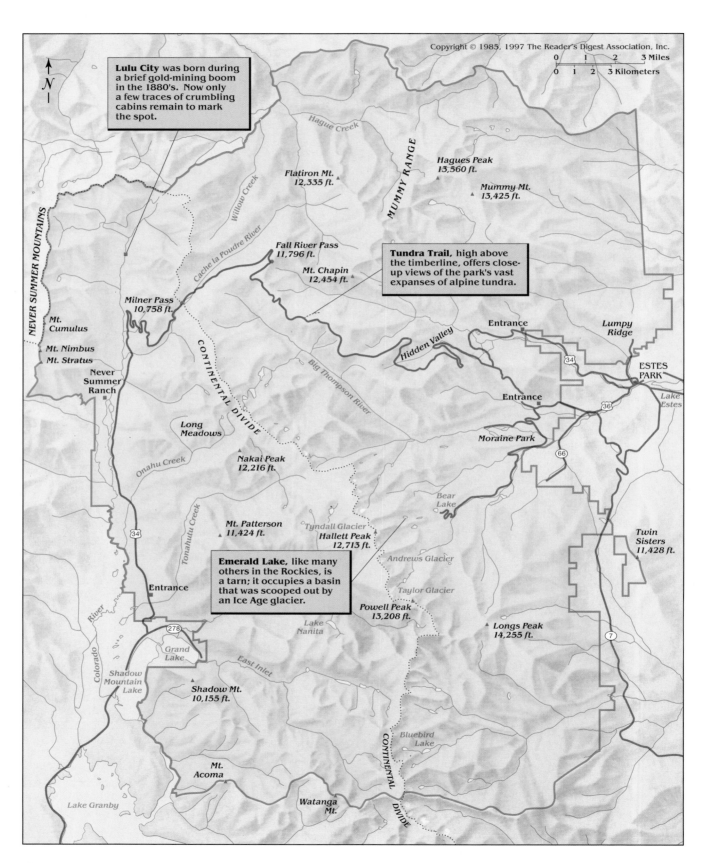

0   1   2   3 Miles
0   1   2   3 Kilometers

Lulu City was born during a brief gold-mining boom in the 1880's. Now only a few traces of crumbling cabins remain to mark the spot.

Hague Creek

NEVER SUMMER MOUNTAINS

Flatiron Mt. 12,335 ft.

MUMMY RANGE

Hagues Peak 13,560 ft.

Mummy Mt. 13,425 ft.

Willow Creek

Fall River Pass 11,796 ft.

Mt. Chapin 12,454 ft.

Tundra Trail, high above the timberline, offers close-up views of the park's vast expanses of alpine tundra.

Cache la Poudre River

Milner Pass 10,758 ft.

Mt. Cumulus

Entrance

Lumpy Ridge

Mt. Nimbus
Mt. Stratus

Hidden Valley

34

ESTES PARK

Never Summer Ranch

CONTINENTAL DIVIDE

Big Thompson River

Entrance

36

Lake Estes

Long Meadows

Moraine Park

66

Onahu Creek

Nakai Peak 12,216 ft.

Bear Lake

34

Mt. Patterson 11,424 ft.

Tyndall Glacier

Hallett Peak 12,713 ft.

Twin Sisters 11,428 ft.

Tonahutu Creek

Emerald Lake, like many others in the Rockies, is a tarn; it occupies a basin that was scooped out by an Ice Age glacier.

Andrews Glacier

Taylor Glacier

Entrance

278

Lake Nanita

Powell Peak 13,208 ft.

Longs Peak 14,255 ft.

7

Colorado River

Grand Lake

East Inlet

Shadow Mountain Lake

Shadow Mt. 10,155 ft.

Bluebird Lake

CONTINENTAL

Mt. Acoma

DIVIDE

Watanga Mt.

Lake Granby

At all elevations below the timberline, groves of quaking aspens quickly cover moist ground that has been cleared by fire. In the shade of these groves, taller, longer-lived conifers slowly grow, eventually shading the aspens out.

growth, they shove their way up through snowbanks. And though the plants are small, most of them bear large, bright flowers, for they must attract pollinating insects quickly if their seeds are to be spread before August, when winter returns. The tundra's largest blossoms, two to four inches across, are borne by alpine sunflowers; blooming is their last act, after years of storing energy in long, fleshy taproots.

Scurrying among the rocks of the tundra are pikas and yellow-bellied marmots, two creatures with markedly different life-styles. The hyperactive little pikas—short-eared cousins to hares and rabbits—do not hibernate in winter, and so they must spend long, busy summer days gathering food. They spread great quantities of greenery to dry, then store it among the rocks. (Hikers entering pika territory often hear a high-pitched bark of warning; pikas are cranky because they must guard their hay piles against the thievery of their own kind.) Adding to the stress of their existence are the threats of ermine, which can follow pikas through rocky passageways, and prairie falcons, which strike from the sky with great speed and no warning.

The roly-poly, buck-toothed marmots, however, with their quizzical faces and waddling gait, are *never* busy. Rising sometime after the sun comes up, they stuff themselves at their leisure on the foods they like, sunbathe on warm rocks, take shelter from afternoon thunderstorms, and come out again in the evening to eat more good green herbage. They need not store up anything but fat, for they hibernate all winter—generally losing as much as half of their body weight by spring. Marmots are not much concerned about human intruders, but their sharp whistles warn of serious trouble when a golden eagle soars overhead.

The vertical landscape

Tenuous as it is on the summits, life's hold is firm below the timberline—on mountain slopes, in deep valleys, and across the broad lowland glades called parks. Because every 1,000-foot rise in elevation is the equivalent of about 600 miles of northward travel, the 1¼-mile drop from the park's highest mountaintop to its deepest valley is like an overland trek of more than 2,000 miles. Along the way—as though all that geography had been compressed and stood on end—one passes through several zones of life that band the mountains. Each imposes its own requirements for survival and each, therefore, is home to different kinds of living things. Cutting through these zones are lush watercourses, dry rockslides, stripes of destruction where fire has licked from below or avalanches have slashed from above, and other variations that make a patchwork of life's neatly layered pattern.

Downward from the timberline to about 9,000 feet is a mountain-slope world, where the spruce, fir, and pine species that grow dwarfish and stunted in the krumm-

Indian paintbrush

Blue columbine

Alpine buttercup

From the high tundra to shady river valleys, the Rockies are graced with a wealth of wildflowers. Colorado's state flower, the blue columbine, grows at nearly every elevation in the vertical landscape. So does the dramatic shooting star, though only in moist areas. Indian paintbrushes flourish everywhere too; those on the tundra are yellow, those of the lowlands are deep red, and those of the mountain-slope world vary. Confined to the tundra are the early-blooming alpine buttercups, dwarf clovers, and alpine forget-me-nots, as well as the big-rooted spring beauties, whose roots delve as deep as six feet for water. Penstemons and yellow violets are common flowers of the mountain slopes, while wood lilies and tansy asters are found growing in the wet, open meadows of the lowland parks.

Alpine forget-me-not and dwarf clover

Shooting star

Big-rooted spring beauty

Tansy aster

Wood lily

Yellow violet

Tall one-sided penstemon

holz stand tall and erect in cool, shady forests. Snow, blown from the mountaintops, accumulates among them, and some deep piles do not melt away until late July. These snowbanks, marked by the large tracks of snowshoe hares, are the reservoirs of the mountain slopes, the fountains of life for things below. Slowly melting, they feed clear mountain streams that tumble laughingly down into lakes and rushing valley rivers.

Some drops of this water will eventually reach the Pacific Ocean, by way of the Colorado River; others will be carried eastward to the Mississippi and thence to the Gulf of Mexico. The boundary is the Great Divide—the high spine of the continent—that winds northward along the park's peaks and ridges. Air comes from the west and, as it rises toward the divide, its moisture condenses; hence the western slopes get much more rain and snow than those on the east.

Interspersed among the forests of spruce and fir are stands of lodgepole pine, so named because Indians came up from the plains to cut the straight, slender trunks for use as tepee poles. On upper slopes, the lodgepoles are a sign that a forest fire raged in the not too distant past. An integral part of the lodgepole life cycle, fire sweeps easily through the thin-barked trees, killing most of them. But immolation is the means by which the lodgepoles proliferate. Their cones open only in the presence of such intense heat; and so, not long after a fire has reduced a lodgepole stand to a waste-land of blackened trunks, a seed storm rains down. A new stand is begun before the ruin cools.

Eventually, on moist upper slopes, the shade-loving spruces and subalpine firs take root beneath the shel-tering lodgepoles. Over the decades they gain height, finally overtopping the lodgepoles and shading them out. But lower down, on drier slopes near the 9,000-foot level, the lodgepoles dominate, waiting like living tinder piles for lightning to set off new life-giving fires. Licking upslope into the spruce-fir forests, the fires clear fresh land for temporary lodgepole incursions.

Diminutive red squirrels chatter in the branches of

all the forests in this mountain-slope zone, roundly cursing hikers and other trespassers. More easily heard than seen, they reveal their presence by "squirrel kitchens," piles of cone scales that accumulate beneath the branches where they have ripped cones apart to get the seeds. Sometimes they store unopened cones in the cool, damp interiors of such piles to preserve them; lodgepole cones, however, are just dumped on the ground, for they remain closed without special storage.

Parks and valleys

The word "park" has a special meaning in Colorado: it describes a low, open pocket of land surrounded by protective peaks. Because it is level, it has water—a lake, a stream, a swampy patch—fed by mountain rills; and because it has water, it is a focal point for life. Mule deer and elk feed in parks when higher elevations are winter-locked. Mountain bluebirds and broad-tailed hummingbirds arrive to nest in early spring and linger well into autumn, among evening grosbeaks, pygmy

The bighorn sheep, symbol of Rocky Mountain National Park, is at home on the grassy tundra slopes above the timberline, taking refuge when necessary on cliffs and rocky crags where predators cannot navigate.

At 14,255 feet elevation, Longs Peak is the park's highest mountain. The mighty glaciers that carved this rugged landscape did not come from the north, but were born atop the peaks whose granite sides they sheared away.

nuthatches, and other permanent inhabitants. Scurrying through the summer, chipmunks and the larger Wyoming ground squirrels may fall prey to plummeting golden eagles that soar sharp-eyed high above the summits.

Flourishing around the parks, and on other lowland slopes on the comparatively dry eastern side of the Great Divide, are ponderosa forests, spacious and sunny because each tree's thirsty, spreading roots allow little nearby competition for moisture. The underbrush that does manage to become established is periodically cleared out by low ground fires, from which the mature trees are themselves protected by the armor plating of their thick, russet bark. The bright, grassy floors of these forests are carpeted in summer with multicolored mosaics of wildflowers; the branches above are the year-round home of North America's showiest squirrels, the tassel-eared Aberts. Nearly housecat-sized, with flowing tails and large, tufted ears, Abert squirrels have glossy coats that may range in color from solid black to dark rusty brown, or they may wear any of several elegant variations. They rarely venture far from the stately ponderosas, living on the seeds in summer and on new-growth twigs in winter.

When forest fires burn fiercely enough to wipe out the ponderosas—or the denser forests of Douglas fir that flourish on north-facing slopes and in valleys west of the Great Divide—the desolated land is soon covered over with such pioneering wildflowers as fireweed and goldenrod. Close behind come quaking aspens.

Wherever a stand of aspen grows, beavers are likely to find it. The layer beneath the white bark is one of their favorite foods, and the soft trunks their preferred building material. Entire aspen stands can be leveled in a few beaver generations; sometimes the industrious rodents build canals to float the fallen trees where they want them. But aspens grow very quickly from their roots, and each cut trunk is soon replaced by two or three new ones.

One reason that aspens grow so fast is that they are extremely efficient gatherers of solar energy. Unlike the leaves of most trees, an aspen leaf is equipped on both sides with chlorophyll factories that use the energy of the sun to manufacture food. And because the leafstalks are flat, the leaves turn from side to side with every change of the breeze, always presenting a working surface to the sun. The resultant quivering rustle is the reason that the trees are called quaking aspens.

In the fall, when the chlorophyll factories shut down and the leaves' natural pigments of yellow, red, and orange are no longer masked by green, the aspens become resplendent. The color may last only a few days before it is stripped by winds from the mountain heights, but while it lasts, the aspen gold—in combination with the incomparably beautiful Colorado blue spruce that crowds the banks of streams and lakes, its perfectly conical form ashimmer all year round with the color of the sky—is the glory of the Rockies.

Saguaro

"What good is a desert? It's good because it's so starkly, stubbornly beautiful, a respite to the eye."

Ann Zwinger

Blasted and bewitching, the Sonoran desert of Mexico and the American Southwest has long stirred the imagination. Perhaps it is because, amid its arid plains and rocky arroyos, this dry, rugged land seems so indifferent to the needs of human life. Perhaps, too, it is the landscape's very harshness, its ceaseless challenge to the ingenuity of all living things, that so attracts us. And perhaps it is the cactus.

Certainly no plant is so closely linked to the desert Southwest as the giant saguaro, the second largest of 2,000 known species of cacti. (It is surpassed only by the cardon cactus of southern Mexico.) Oddly human in form, the saguaro has plump green arms that, outstretched and uplifted, seem to wave—although whether in greeting or warning, it is hard to say. And, unless you travel to Sonora, Mexico, nowhere else on Earth will you find a more stately assemblage of the prickly giants than here, in Saguaro National Park.

Saguaro East

Bracketing booming Tucson to the east and west, Saguaro National Park consists of two separate units: Saguaro East and Saguaro West. Saguaro East, also known as the Rincon Mountain District, is the larger of the two. Its 104 square miles include not only the great forests of aging saguaros but also the high-country wilderness of the Rincon Range, a majestic, brooding presence that looms to the east.

As you enter the district from Tucson, you encounter a landscape of awesome bleakness: an arid, rolling plain of boulders and sand, dry washes and arroyos, slender canyons and fan-shaped bajadas. The climate is undeniably harsh; in winter the temperature may dip into the 40s, but summertime highs routinely top 100°F, and months may pass without a drop of rain. (The desert receives, on average, just 12 inches of rain per year, most of it in the fall and winter, when violent downpours can quickly fill arroyos and create dangerous flash floods.)

Untamable as it may appear, however, this is the land that the saguaro loves. And the saguaros of the Rincon Mountain District are some of the oldest and largest in the world. Reaching heights of 50 feet, the largest of these giants weigh in at eight tons. A great deal of its mass is actually water, as the saguaro is, in effect, a living storage tank. By means of a system of shallow roots that form a kind of catch-basin, it can collect as much as 200 gallons of water in a single downpour. This moisture is then stored in the spongy flesh of the cactus's limbs and trunk. Accordionlike pleats expand and contract according to the amount of water the plant has stored; the fatter a saguaro's limbs and trunk, the more water it contains inside.

The giant saguaros of the Rincon Mountain District are even more remarkable when you consider the odds against their existence. Although a single saguaro produces some 40 million seeds in its lifetime, perhaps one will take hold and grow to maturity. The lucky survivors are generally those that sprout in the shadow of a "nurse tree," such as a paloverde or a mesquite, which shades the young plant from the summer sun, protects it during winter cold spells, and conceals it from grazers.

Growth is slow and hard-won; a 10-year-old plant may be no taller than an inch. Those that survive the first decade of life grow roughly a foot every 15 years, mostly in spurts that closely follow the rhythms of seasonal rainfall. Thirty years pass before the plant produces its first flower; 75 years, before its first branches appear. Not until a century has come and gone does the plant reach a height of 25 feet and assume its familiar waving profile.

Even the most established of saguaros remain vulnerable. If the temperature dips below the freezing point for 36 hours, many will succumb to the cold. Lightning is another threat: it strikes and kills many of the oldest, tallest specimens.

Standing apart from others of its kind, the saquaro may seem to be nature's ultimate loner, a solitary survivor superbly adapted to the extreme conditions of desert life. But look more closely and you will see that the saguaro does not dwell alone. It is frequently described as a living apartment complex, since at every level there is evidence that the saguaro nurtures its fellow desert residents. Gila woodpeckers and gilded flickers carve nest holes in its trunk and branches; providing cool shade in summer and insulated warmth in winter, these cavities, when abandoned, are soon adopted by other birds, including screech owls, purple martins, and sparrow hawks, and by insects, such as honeybees.

The cactus's flowers—trumpet-shaped blossoms that appear on spring evenings and fade by the following afternoon—produce juicy red fruits that are relished by coyotes, foxes, and a number of other desert mammals. Humans, too, have put the saguaro to use. For centuries, local Indians have gathered the fruits to make wine, jams, and jellies, and have harvested the long ribs of the plant's skeleton for both fuel and building material.

Looking west

As indomitable as they appear, the saguaros of the Rincon Mountain District were once thought to be endangered. Poaching, grazing, urban growth, and old age had all taken their toll, and so the area now known as Saguaro West or the Tucson Mountain District was set aside to safeguard this living treasure. Saguaro West is considerably smaller than Saguaro East—at 34 square miles, just one third its size. Nestled against the Tucson Mountains, its dimensions are tidier, more manageable, perhaps, for the casual observer. (An air-conditioned visitor center with a shaded terrace makes it possible to survey the landscape without so much as setting foot on the desert floor.) The saguaros here are younger—not the aged titans that are found in Saguaro East but 100-year-old youngsters, marching in prickly profusion across the dusty bajadas and sun-seared hillsides.

Smaller and younger though it may be, Saguaro West is every bit as compelling as its larger partner to the east. The desert is the desert, after all—wild and untamable, a realm where nature's will, not human resourcefulness, is in command. And in the last analysis, perhaps this is the message of the saguaro, in whose upraised arms one may see not a wave of welcome or warning but of stoic triumph: we're here to stay.

Adorned in season with white blossoms that give way to red fruits, armies of saguaros stand guard in the Arizona desert.

Sequoia-Kings Canyon

"Beautiful and impressive contrasts meet you everywhere: the colors of tree and flower, rock and sky, light and shade, strength and frailty, endurance and evanescence."
John Muir

Storms are born without warning above the sharply tilted slopes of the Sierra Nevada as masses of fluffy clouds merge into blue-black thunderheads. In October 1905 one such thunderhead rolled through a Sierra canyon. Booms echoed up and down the rocky gorge, and lightning lit up the canyon walls. One lightning bolt shot up into the sky, another down to earth. When a third sliced into the 16-foot-wide trunk of a giant sequoia, the tree's midsection instantly exploded, sending clots of wood and bark flying. Daylight momentarily showed through the gap between the top half of the tree, seemingly suspended in midair, and the bottom half of the trunk. Then the upper half crashed straight down, wedging itself into the grip of the still-living trunk. The sequoia did not die. It kept on growing, adding new wood each year, and it shows every intention of remaining alive for another thousand years.

Kings Canyon, the deepest in the nation, was cut by a combination o

...water power and glaciers. High above, Clark's nutcrackers store thousands of seeds a year—and manage to find most of them again.

The world's third-largest tree, the General Grant was officially decreed "the Nation's Christmas Tree" by Congress and is honored every year by celebrators who gather under its snow-topped branches for special Yuletide services.

This will to live, typical of the mighty sequoias, is evident in other living things throughout these two adjacent parks, Sequoia and Kings Canyon. From the plants that bloom in the dry foothills of the Sierra to the tiny plants that cling bravely to windswept alpine peaks, endurance is the key to life.

The Giant Forest

The lightning-split tree was unusual. The sequoia's bark is such a poor conductor of electricity that lightning rarely affects it, and the tree's dense coat—sometimes almost two feet thick—enables it to shrug off most electrical storms, brush fires, and insect invasions and to return to work.

For giant sequoias, "work" is growing to a gargantuan size. The most successful worker has been the General Sherman tree, which towers to a height of more than 270 feet. Although it is not the world's tallest or widest living thing, it is by far the most massive in bulk. Weighing approximately $4\frac{1}{2}$ million pounds, it contains enough wood to build more than 40 five-room houses. And it keeps on growing. An indefatigable worker despite its age—between 2,300 and 2,700 years—the General Sherman adds enough wood every year to equal a 60-foot-tall tree.

In contrast to their staggering size, giant sequoias produce cones that are tiny—hardly as large as a hen's eggs. Although the cones mature after two years, they can remain tightly closed, hoarding their seeds for 20 years or more, until they are forced open. Yet each autumn the air flickers with reflected light from a glistening rain of sequoia seeds, so miniscule that it takes 91,000 of them to make a pound. Sometimes the seeds fall because they have been freed by the larvae of wood-boring beetles, which munch through the cones' sap-filled veins. Severed from their lifeblood, the cones shrivel and release their seeds, which flutter to the ground.

Other seeds are unlocked by chattering chickarees that harvest the cones for the sake of their fleshy scales. While these squirrels eat the seeds of other evergreens, they ignore those of the sequoias, leaving them to rot or to take root at the giants' feet.

Once the seeds reach the ground, they need special conditions in order to grow—the nearly bare, mineral-rich earth that is exposed after forest fires. Such fires, usually sparked when electrical storms ignite the scrub and leaf litter on the forest floor, reduce the thick overhead cover of fir, allowing sunlight to nurture the seedlings.

The most famous sequoia grove, the Giant Forest, was named by John Muir. Its northern edge is guarded by General Sherman and several of his ancient troops. Other groves are scattered throughout the two parks, but all of the sequoias are limited to elevations of between 3,500 and 7,500 feet on the Sierra Nevada's western slopes, where the air is crisp, water is plentiful, and winters are mild.

King of canyons

Immense as they are, the sequoias are dwarfed by the snowcapped sweep of the Sierra Nevada, the most recent of three mountain ranges that have occupied this part of California. The present Sierra Nevada, the longest single continuous mountain range in the lower 48 states, began to form some 25 million years ago, when a slow uplift forced the land upward in a long, domed block of solid granite. Then, about 3 million years ago, when the highest peaks towered nearly three miles above sea level, the Sierra's eastern face cracked along fault lines and began to rise upward—a continu-

Despite its sweet face, the nocturnal pine marten is a swift and deadly hunter, stalking chipmunks and tiny chickarees along tree branches.

ing process that accounts for the Sierra's wedgelike appearance. The raw granite of the eastern escarpment drops off dramatically, while the heavily forested western slope climbs gently upward.

Rushing rivers eventually added a sculptured touch, scoring the Sierra with narrow V-shaped canyons. During the ice ages, glaciers advanced down the slopes—scooping out lake basins, crushing hills into rubble, polishing the granite, and gouging steep river gorges into broader U-shaped canyons. Some canyons bear the mark of both rivers and glaciers. Kings Canyon, for example, is V-shaped for most of its course but broadens into a U in places like the long, peaceful Zumwalt Meadow.

Kings Canyon, deeper than the Grand Canyon—in fact, the deepest in North America—plunges at one place more than 8,000 feet from ridge to river. Other canyons in the park are almost as compelling: Kern Canyon is nearly 6,000 feet deep, and several others exceed 3,000 feet.

Wildcats, weasels, and wolverines

Although much of the Sierra's foothill area is dry, it is well wooded with blue oak, manzanita, yucca, and other hard-leafed plants that flourish despite droughts and occasional scorching temperatures. Mild winters drift into spring, producing a long growing season filled with a succession of wildflowers that splash colorful patches across the landscape.

Stealthily padding about in the brush and jumbled boulders is the bobcat, the nation's most common wildcat. Named for its tail's short, chopped-off look, this tawny feline has a spotted belly, tufted ears, and legs that seem too long for its body. A nocturnal stalker of hares and rabbits, the bobcat also hunts rodents, reptiles, birds, and deer, pursuing its prey, if necessary, all the way up to the dizzying heights of the alpine meadows.

For most of the year the bobcat is a loner; it seeks companionship only during the winter mating season. Then its throaty growls—punctuated by bloodcurdling screams—tear through the nighttime silence. Despite the chilling nature of the sounds, this is a song of romance, a courting duet sung as the male circles slowly around the female, with both shrieking and snarling through the night.

As the foothills blend into the mountains, the terrain becomes a patchwork of forests and meadows, white-water rivers, lakes, and canyons. The western slopes are so thickly forested that sun-loving species cannot take root; instead, shade-tolerant ferns wave their lacy fronds over moss-covered rocks and mushrooms cluster around tree trunks.

Prominent among the denizens of these forests are several members of the weasel family: long-tailed weasels, badgers, striped and spotted skunks, pine martens, fishers, and wolverines. All have scent glands that can release an obnoxious odor—the skunks' are the most powerful—and all except the wolverines have lithe, serpentine bodies. Most are nighttime hunters, although when hungry enough, some will venture forth in daylight.

A master Houdini, the long-tailed weasel slithers with lightning speed in and out of the smallest spaces, especially the tunnels of mice, its favorite food. It is a determined hunter and will rarely give up a chase, even if that means climbing a tree.

The chickaree, or Douglas squirrel, helps conifers to reproduce by cutting down their cones. Some seeds scatter in the wind and take root, eventually growing into the tall, stately evergreens that grace the Sierra slopes.

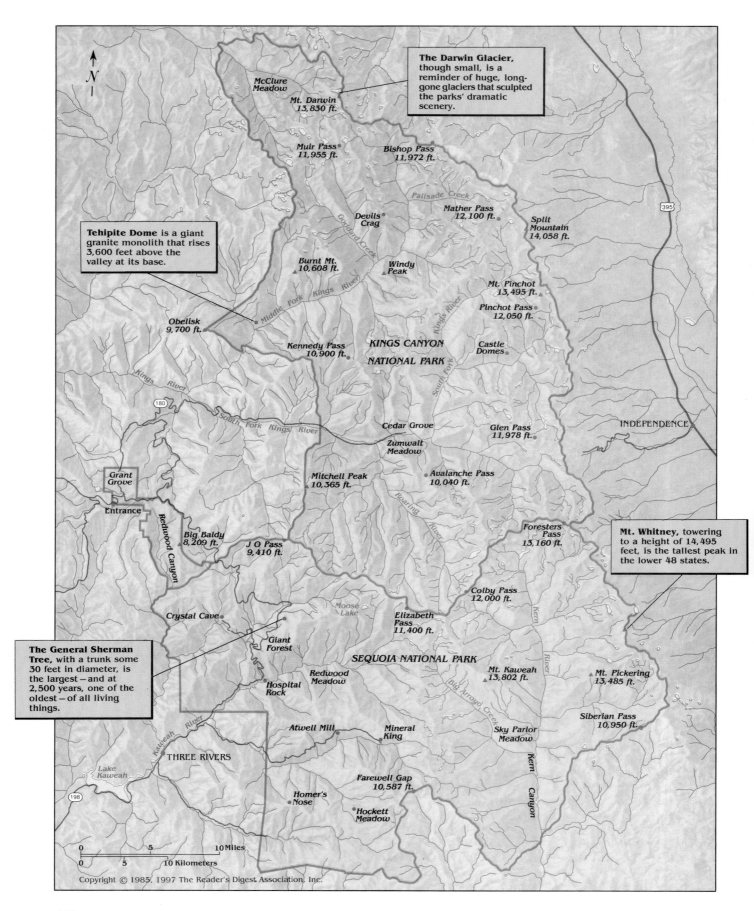

N

The Darwin Glacier, though small, is a reminder of huge, long-gone glaciers that sculpted the parks' dramatic scenery.

McClure Meadow

Mt. Darwin 13,830 ft.

Muir Pass 11,955 ft.

Bishop Pass 11,972 ft.

Palisade Creek

Mather Pass 12,100 ft.

Split Mountain 14,058 ft.

Devils Crag

Goddard Creek

Tehipite Dome is a giant granite monolith that rises 3,600 feet above the valley at its base.

Burnt Mt. 10,608 ft.

Windy Peak

Middle Fork Kings River

Mt. Pinchot 13,495 ft.

Pinchot Pass 12,050 ft.

Obelisk 9,700 ft.

Kennedy Pass 10,900 ft.

KINGS CANYON NATIONAL PARK

Castle Domes

Kings River

Kings River

395

180

South Fork Kings River

Cedar Grove

Zumwalt Meadow

Glen Pass 11,978 ft.

INDEPENDENCE

Grant Grove

Mitchell Peak 10,365 ft.

Avalanche Pass 10,040 ft.

Roaring River

Entrance

Redwood Canyon

Big Baldy 8,209 ft.

J O Pass 9,410 ft.

Foresters Pass 13,160 ft.

Mt. Whitney, towering to a height of 14,495 feet, is the tallest peak in the lower 48 states.

Colby Pass 12,000 ft.

Kern River

Crystal Cave

Moose Lake

Elizabeth Pass 11,400 ft.

Giant Forest

The General Sherman Tree, with a trunk some 30 feet in diameter, is the largest—and at 2,500 years, one of the oldest—of all living things.

SEQUOIA NATIONAL PARK

Redwood Meadow

Hospital Rock

Mt. Kaweah 13,802 ft.

Mt. Pickering 13,485 ft.

Big Arroyo Creek

Kaweah River

Atwell Mill

Mineral King

Sky Parlor Meadow

Siberian Pass 10,950 ft.

Kern Canyon

THREE RIVERS

Lake Kaweah

Farewell Gap 10,587 ft.

198

Homer's Nose

Hockett Meadow

0   5   10 Miles
0   5   10 Kilometers

Copyright © 1985, 1997 The Reader's Digest Association, Inc.

262

The pine marten, a brown, almost three-foot-long creature with a foxlike face and a bushy tail, also takes to the trees. Although it usually tracks its prey along the ground, the pine marten frequently chases chickarees, chipmunks, and birds up trees and down. Unfortunately for its prey, the pine marten is very quick and can move with amazing agility from one tree to the next.

Even quicker than the pine marten—in fact, the fastest tree climber in North America—is the fisher, a larger version of the marten. Despite its name, the fisher's favorite foods are not fish but fleet-footed snowshoe hares and slow-moving porcupines. Undaunted by the porcupine's quills, the fisher bites the animal on the nose, flips it onto its back, and chews into its soft, unprotected belly.

The weasel with the meanest reputation by far is the wolverine, a shaggy creature that looks like a bear and smells like a skunk. It is difficult to imagine why this powerful animal would need a repulsive spray as a defense. Although at its largest a wolverine weighs only about 35 pounds, it is capable of conquering animals as big as elk and of chasing coyotes, mountain lions, and even bears away from their kills. A voracious eater, the wolverine's legendary appetite has earned it a nickname—glutton.

Aquatic gymnasts

Beneath the Sierra's snowy summits, sparkling streams twist and slip down the mountains, gaining momentum as they cascade from cliff to cliff, merging with rivers as they squeeze through canyons, racing downslope to become foaming, unstoppable forces. Along the way, the water slices through thick evergreen forests where many of the trees, like the giant sequoias, react to the mild winters and long growing season by achieving record heights.

These forests are home to Clark's nutcracker, a gray bird with black wings and tail. In autumn, when pinecones are ripening, the nutcracker gathers the seeds and stores them temporarily in an expandable pouch under its tongue. When the bird has collected enough seeds—it can carry as many as 180 whitebark pine seeds at one time—it will fly to a south-facing slope or to another place where winter snows usually do not get very deep. Once a suitable spot is found, the nutcracker pecks at the hard ground with its sturdy bill to loosen the soil. After inserting some of the seeds into the hole, it covers the spot with dirt and debris, then places a small stone on top to complete the camouflage.

Endowed with a superb memory, the nutcracker then scrutinizes surrounding landmarks in order to remember exactly where its seeds are stashed—a prodigious feat, considering that the bird buries up to 30,000 seeds in a season. The system, moreover, is quite successful: the nutcracker is able to find most of its stashes even if several months have passed and the hiding places are buried under snow.

Throughout this forested mountain-slope world the loud, melodic song of the dipper, or water ouzel, accents the sounds of streams and waterfalls. This stocky slate-gray bird hatches near streams and rivers—its nest is often built on the rocks behind a waterfall—and spends the rest of its life close to water. Dippers are lively and energetic. They dive into streams and scour the bottom for aquatic insects and other food; they swim beneath the surface by beating their wings rapidly, as though they were flying under water.

Equally adept at aquatic gymnastics is the water shrew, a molelike mammal that can actually walk on water. Its hind feet are equipped with hairs that trap air, giving it enough buoyancy to skitter across the water's surface, usually in pursuit of insect prey. An expert underwater swimmer as well, the water shrew dives to the bottom of streams and slow-moving rivers, where it searches for tadpoles and other aquatic food. Air bubbles that lodge in the shrew's water-resistant fur help it bob back to the surface.

The Sierra's crowning glory

Above the timberline, where winter has a long, bitter reign, the cold and windswept High Sierra spreads all around, like waves of granite rising from an immense evergreen sea. At lower elevations light is softened by moisture and dust in the air; here the air is so clear that shadows seem to have a cutting edge, and the sky deepens from blue to purple. The clarity also intensifies the sunlight, which unexpectedly warms the peaks as it reflects off glacier-polished granite. If you sit in the same place for too long, you may be sunburned on one side while on the other your muscles may ache from the cold.

Although this is a granite world, it is far from a moonscape. Green meadows are tucked away behind cliffs, and hardy little plants flourish on the most unpromising rock surfaces. Smallness is nature's secret of survival at these heights, for it is the diminutive size of alpine plants that protects them from the wind's killing force. Just four inches tall, an alpine willow, for example, is in its entirety smaller than a single leaf of some of its lowland kin.

Not until August does summer arrive at the highest elevations, and the growing season here is no more than a brief six weeks. But, as if by magic, a host of tiny alpine flowers—blue-violet sky pilots, red and yellow columbines, and fuchsia primroses—manage to transform the snowy heights into a living rainbow. Even on the windy summit of Mount Whitney, the tallest peak in the lower 48 states, tiny plants eke out a living. And during the brief blooming season, these tenacious little champions wave their bright bouquets in triumph, proving that life, given even less than half a chance, will not only endure but prevail.

Shenandoah

"And still a new succession sings and flies;
Fresh groves grow up, and their green branches shoot
Towards the old and still enduring skies,
While the low violet thrives at their root."

Henry Vaughan, *17th-century Welsh poet*

Stretching north to south in western Virginia, the Blue Ridge Mountains loom like a wall against the sky. Although not especially high, their summits offer splendid views in all directions. Westward the panorama includes not only the Shenandoah Valley with its patchwork of towns and farmlands, but often two or three ridges of the distant Appalachian ranges as well; to the east the view encompasses the rolling uplands of the Piedmont Plateau and, occasionally, glimpses of the Tidewater lowlands beyond; and to the north and south there is peak after rounded peak of the Blue Ridge itself, rich green nearby, misty blue in the middle ground, and in the distance fading into the clouds.

These are the glory spots of Shenandoah National Park, these time-worn peaks that drop away to heavily forested slopes laced with streams and singing waterfalls. Here visitors from the lowlands find solace in an island of wilderness that seems as ancient as the mountains themselves. Strangely, though, this wilderness at Shenandoah is testimony to the vitality of nature for, not so long ago, these slopes were largely bare of trees. Generations of mountain folk lived here, clearing the forests for croplands and tending their sheep and cattle on upland pastures. Loggers moved in after the Civil War, removing timber to rebuild structures that had been destroyed in the valley. And forest fires were frequent.

Then, early in this century, declining resources forced many of the mountain people to leave the Blue Ridge and seek their livelihoods elsewhere. Shrubs moved in on the abandoned fields and pastures, then thickets of saplings took over, and before long the

Forests, lush and green throughout the summer, blanket the slopes at Shenandoah. The tulip tree, named for its lovely flowers, is but one of about 100 different kinds of trees to be found in the park's exceptionally varied woodlands.

forest had returned. So successful was nature's reclamation, in fact, that more than 95 percent of the park is now completely reforested.

When spring sneaks in

Just as the look of the Blue Ridge has changed over recent decades, so it continues to change with the passing seasons. Each is punctuated by its own special events and permeated by a distinctive mood. Spring, for example, is the sneaky season at Shenandoah. It creeps up the mountains with a subtle wave of color as buds expand on winter-bare twigs and new leaves gradually unfurl. The tones, pale pastels at first, eventually deepen to bold, bright green by the time the leaves are fully formed. One rule of thumb has spring climbing the slopes at a rate of 100 feet a day, with the trees finally leafing out on the highest peaks late in May.

But anyone waiting for the greening of the forest canopy misses half the show, for much of the drama of the annual reawakening takes place underfoot. As the soil warms with each lengthening day, wildflowers spring to life everywhere and in many cases rush to blossom and set seed before the full-blown canopy overhead blots out the warming sun. Among the earliest of the seasonal performers is the dainty little hepatica. As if impatient to get started, its fuzzy gray buds rise above dead leaves littering the forest floor and open to delicate pink or lavender blossoms even before the ice has melted from nearby waterfalls. Another, coltsfoot—yellow and looking much like a leafless dandelion—pops up in clusters along the roadsides as treefrogs begin their nightly choruses from the edges of half-frozen puddles of melting snow.

Once the blossoming starts, it bursts through the woods like wildfire. Trilliums, neatly symmetrical lilies with three petals, three sepals, and three leaves, open their stately flowers everywhere. Bloodroots, as white, bright, and cheerful as daisies, spangle the forest floor. Elsewhere, among the unfurling fiddleheads of ferns, the woodlands are brightened with violets, wild geraniums, dainty, ground-hugging hepaticas, pink and yellow lady's slippers, and hosts of others, while the edges of wet places are accented with the golden yellow blooms of marsh marigolds. Another special favorite, the wonderfully fragrant trailing arbutus, garlands the slopes with clusters of tiny pink and white, trumpetlike flowers tucked among its evergreen leaves.

Flowering trees and shrubs add to the spectacle. Redbuds proclaim their identity even from afar; every twig on the little trees is covered with clusters of shocking-pink flowers that resemble miniature sweet peas. Hawthorns and wild cherries follow a few days later, along with serviceberries, which are for a time transformed into billowing clouds as the petals unfold on thousands of delicate white blooms. The dogwoods soon take over with yet another display of sparkling white, and wild azaleas explode into splashes of pink while the trees all around them are still leafless.

And throughout it all, animal life is reawakening too. Black bears, lean and hungry after their long winter rest, begin to roam the woods in search of food.

Opossums, North America's only marsupials, carry their developing young kangaroo-style in a pouch. Active all year round, these agile climbers sometimes use their prehensile tails as extra legs as they move from branch to branch.

Butterflies burst from pupal cases and spread their wings. Salamanders emerge from hibernation and begin their silent mating rituals. And the birds return, warblers and thrushes, wrens and vireos, throngs and throngs of them, some just to pass through on their way to nesting grounds farther north, others to stay and sing and raise their broods here in the Blue Ridge.

One of the first arrivals—and for many, one of the most welcome signs of spring—is the woodcock. Early in March the chunky, mottled brown birds return to Big Meadows, a grassy tableland high on the ridges where they spend the summer. And there for several weeks they put on a nightly show for anyone willing to spend an hour or so standing quietly in the evening chill.

Just after sunset, in the deepening twilight, the male emerges from the brushy area where he has hidden by day, and claims an open space for his stage. There he struts about for a minute or two, making a sound between a squeak and a buzz. Then suddenly he bursts into the air and spirals up to a height of 300 feet or so, with the wind causing a soft twittering sound as it passes between his outer wing feathers; there he circles a few times, then zigzags back to the ground, warbling all the way.

Back on the ground he resumes his strutting and then, without warning, flashes upward on another of his dizzying flights. After a few repetitions of these maneuvers, he may be joined by a female who has been hiding quietly among the grasses and consents to be his mate. If so, that marks the end of the show for the evening. Otherwise he will continue until full darkness falls, and on moonlit nights he may never quit until dawn.

Summer rambles

Spring, which began to be noticeable in late February, is essentially over by early June. The mountain laurel and many kinds of wildflowers are still blooming or are yet to bloom, but the frenzied activity of early spring has slowed down to a more deliberate pace. Birds and mammals, busy with the tasks of bearing and rearing their young, have grown wary. And the dense foliage helps keep them hidden from view.

Visitors throng to Shenandoah now to tour the Skyline Drive, the famous scenic roadway that runs the length of the park, threading along the crest of the Blue Ridge and offering breathtaking views at every turn. For more intimate views, they hike the park's many woodland trails including, more or less parallel to the Skyline Drive, 101 miles of the Appalachian Trail, the continuous footpath that extends all the way from Maine to Georgia. Numerous side trails branch from it, some leading up to the high peaks, others down into the ravines known as "hollows" in this area.

The forest is at its richest in the broad hollows, cool and moist with deep, fertile soil. Growing side by side with sturdy white pines and lacy hemlocks are maples, hickories, basswoods, black walnuts, and many others. Tulip trees rise straight toward the sky to heights of 120 feet or more, and umbrella magnolias are covered with leaves up to 2 feet long.

These are the haunts of pileated woodpeckers, almost as big as crows, and smaller birds such as scarlet tanagers, rose-breasted grosbeaks, and reclusive wood thrushes. Wild turkeys wander through from time to time, and deer are a common sight. Bears live here too and leave signs of their presence—large rocks, for instance, that they have overturned in search of salamanders and other morsels to supplement their mainly vegetarian diets.

Just when the sense of wilderness seems most complete, the mood may be broken by signs of past human life—an old stone wall encrusted with century-old lichens, a stone chimney wrapped in wild vines where a log cabin once stood, or rotting pickets enclosing the weathered gravestones of a burial plot. It seems difficult to believe that generations of mountain folk lived and died here. But now they are gone, and the forest has reclaimed the slopes and hollows.

Another favorite destination for hikers is the Limberlost, a grove of giant hemlocks untouched by time and perhaps 500 years old. In the dim light here, the mood is one of mystery. Partridgeberries embroider the brown carpet of fallen needles with traceries of tiny green leaves and even smaller red fruits. Here and there are patches of ferns, colorful elfin-looking mushrooms, and the ghostly white stalks of Indian pipes. The place has the look of a far northern forest, and in fact the birds flitting through the foliage are typically northern species—Blackburnian warblers (aptly named "fire throats"), pert little kinglets, red-breasted nuthatches.

Many of the trails leading down from the ridges follow streams, and most sooner or later pass beside waterfalls that are at their exuberant best in spring but still a photographer's delight through the summer months. The best known is Dark Hollow Falls, near Big Meadows; the 70-foot cascade, gurgling over crumbling rocks, was admired long ago by Thomas Jefferson, who was fond of exploring the Blue Ridge. His home, Monticello, to the east of the park near Charlottesville, overlooks a superb panorama of the mountains.

Away from the waterfalls, where the streams slow down in deep pools, water striders dimple the surface with their outspread legs; brook trout, as elusive as shadows, lurk beside fallen logs; and crayfish creep across the rocky bottoms. Waterthrushes nest near the creeks, flit from boulder to wet boulder, and sing in quick, sharp rhythms. Kingfishers perch above the pools by day and swoop down on their prey, and barred owls patrol the streams at night, hunting for crayfish and frogs. The streams are also favorite foraging places for raccoons, which like the owls feed on crayfish.

Wind-down toward winter

In late summer the brilliant spires of cardinal flowers come into bloom along soggy stream banks, and by early September, witch hazels are brightening damp

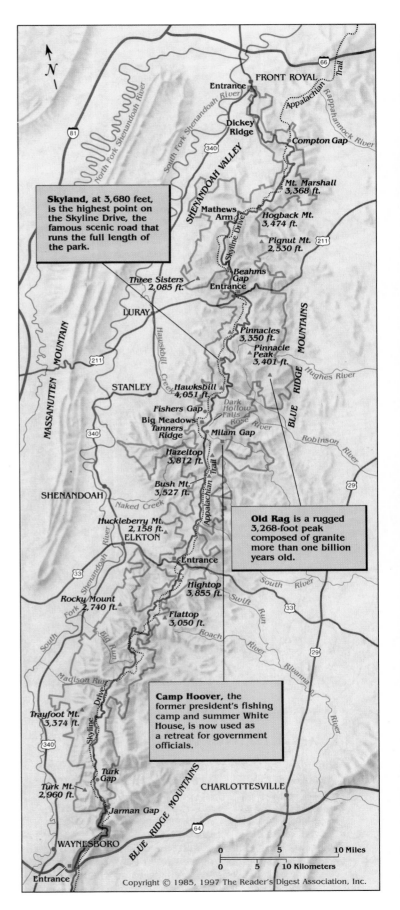

Skyland, at 3,680 feet, is the highest point on the Skyline Drive, the famous scenic road that runs the full length of the park.

Old Rag is a rugged 3,268-foot peak composed of granite more than one billion years old.

Camp Hoover, the former president's fishing camp and summer White House, is now used as a retreat for government officials.

267

J.DAWSON

Blossom Time in the Blue Ridge

Spring comes to Shenandoah with a burst of bloom. Throughout the Blue Ridge Mountains, such flowering shrubs as pink azaleas (1) and mountain laurel (4) supply bold masses of color, while dainty wildflowers brighten the forest floor. In this sunny glade, a broad-winged katydid (9) pauses on the leaf of a Virginia spiderwort (8), as if to admire the blooms. The showy orchis (11), a member of the orchid family, thrives in the cool, moist woodland environment, as do clumps of common blue violets (12). Nearby, the dangling flowers of

wild columbine (13) attract a tiger swallowtail butterfly (14). With their long tongues, butterflies can reach nectar hidden deep in the bright red spurs of the columbine, pollinating the flowers as they feed.

The trees are fully clothed in their spring greenery, from the northern red oak (2) with its intricately lobed leaves to the tulip tree (16) with its characteristically blunt-lobed ones. Loose, curling strips of bark identify a shagbark hickory (5), which like the oak produces a plentiful supply of nuts that afford fall and winter food for a host of wildlife. Many of the nuts buried by squirrels survive to sprout the following spring.

All sorts of woodland creatures are up for the day. A striped forest snail (10) creeps along a fallen branch, and

an eastern box turtle (15) basks on a sunlit boulder in the middle of the glade. Alerted by some forest sound, a gray fox (7) pricks up its ears and sniffs the still air. In the distance a turkey vulture (3) soars in lazy spirals above the mountain slopes, taking advantage of the updrafts created by the sun's warmth. The colorful little chestnut-sided warbler (6), which nests in the park, is indefatigable as it flits through the foliage in its search for insects. Nearby a pileated woodpecker (17), a year-round resident at Shenandoah, pauses to inspect a stump; chips will fly from the hammering of its sharp bill if it finds signs of carpenter ants, its favorite food. Surveying the entire scene is a black bear (18), up and abroad once again after its long winter snooze.

269

glades with their lacy yellow flowers. (One of the last holdouts against winter, the witch hazels keep right on blossoming into early December.) As the autumn days grow shorter and the night air takes on a noticeable chill, other changes become apparent. Those mushroom oddities, giant puffballs, spring up in grassy areas beside the Skyline Drive. Asters, gentians, and the little orchids known as ladies' tresses are still in bloom, but as frosts become more frequent, most of the other weeds and wildflowers shrivel to withered browns.

Chipmunks disappear into their burrows for the winter. Ladybugs, bright orange-red and dotted with black, begin to congregate in sheltered rock crannies where they will endure the months of cold in huddled masses. Bucks have scraped the velvety covering from their new, fully formed antlers and on all the deer the ruddy tan of summer is giving way to thicker winter coats of sandy gray.

Migratory monarch butterflies pass through the park, heading south toward warmer regions, and throngs of migrant birds join in the procession. Most impressive are the south-bound hawks, especially the broadwinged hawks; in late September, when the winds are right, they glide above the ridges, en route to South America, in seemingly endless parades.

And the forest itself is transformed as the deciduous trees shut down operations for the winter. Over a period of several weeks the leaves stop producing the green chlorophyll essential to photosynthesis, and other pigments are revealed, some that were present in the leaves all along, others that are produced by chemical reactions taking place as the weather grows colder. Then, after a week or two of glorious color, the leaves flutter to the ground.

Each species has its own particular mix of pigments, and so each tree and shrub puts on its own distinctive colors, from the silvery yellow of striped maples to the deep crimson of blackgums. The brilliance of the display varies from year to year, depending on weather conditions. Mild cloudy days followed by heavy frosts can turn the leaves almost directly from summer green to withered brown. But normally the slopes are, for a time, awash with a sea of color that, just as spring crept upward, flows down the mountainsides at a rate of about 100 feet a day. The peak of the show usually occurs about the middle of October, when the color is most vivid and pervasive. These are the weeks of autumn at its rainbow best.

Winter wildlife

As with all the seasons, there is no sharp demarcation between the crisp clear days of autumn and the onset of winter. Often the first light snows arrive while the trees are still brilliant with color, then melt away within a day or two. But eventually the leaves drift down, and then become matted beneath a blanket of white as more snowstorms arrive.

The air is clearer now, for the trees are no longer

exhaling the vapor that creates the characteristic haze responsible for the Blue Ridge's name, and the forest is much quieter than it was in spring and summer. The woodchucks have holed up for the deep slumber of hibernation; chipmunks are asleep in their burrows, rousing only occasionally to feed on their stores of nuts and seeds; the black bears are curled up in their dens, emerging only during occasional brief warm spells. And all the migratory birds have long since disappeared from the mountainsides.

Even so, the stillness is punctuated by occasional sounds. The year-round birds, foraging through the trees in search of seeds and insect life, give their characteristic call notes from time to time. The *dee-dee-dee* of chickadees, the nasal double notes of nuthatches, the staccato hammering of woodpeckers—all carry well in the clear, cold air.

Some mammals, too, are up and about, becoming bolder in the urgency of their quest for food. Or perhaps they only seem less cautious because they are easier to spot now that all the leaves have fallen. Even when they go into hiding you can read the record of their comings and goings on dustings of new-fallen snow. Faint trails of tiny tracks like stitches across the snow mark the scurrying of voles, and four-pawed sets

Woodcocks, lovers of moist places, probe in the damp soil with their long slender bills as they search for earthworms, their principal food. A flexible tip on the bill enables the bird to grasp its elusive underground prey.

Among the springtime glories of Shenandoah is the blossoming of large white trilliums. As the flowers age the petals turn to pink, then wither away, and the blossoms eventually are replaced by bright red berries.

of prints resembling miniature squirrel tracks record the leaps of deer mice. Gray foxes, bobcats, skunks, raccoons, deer—all remain active, embroidering the pristine surface of the snow with their own distinctive, telltale signatures of tracks and trails.

Winter is also a good time for observing ravens and their aerobatic antics. (Shenandoah is one of many places in the Appalachians with a resident population of the big black birds, which like to nest on the park's inaccessible rocky cliffs.) When a stiff wind is blowing in from the west and forming an updraft along steep western slopes, it is not at all unusual to see a pair of ravens tumbling against the blue backdrop of the sky, much like puppies frolicking on a lawn. They make sudden sharp turns, they roll to fly upside-down for a few seconds, they stall and spiral downward like daredevil pilots at an air show—and always they perform with such seeming exuberance that it is difficult not to believe they are doing it just for fun.

The weather, too, is interesting to watch. Some days are crystal clear, but fogs are frequent as low-lying clouds envelop the mountaintops. On other days the fog fills the lowlands but does not reach all the way up the slopes, and the summits become sunlit islands afloat in an ocean of white froth.

When conditions are just right, the fog can transform the heights. Blowing against obstacles, tiny droplets of supercooled moisture in the air freeze into crystals of ice. Over the course of several hours, six or eight inches of these frost crystals, called rime, can accumulate on the upwind side of every twig and blade of grass, and decorate the sides of buildings with delicate frosting until they resemble gingerbread houses. Then, when the fog clears and the sun shines, the forest for a time becomes a glittering fairyland.

Winter weather is not always so benign. Long cold spells and heavy snowfalls can take their toll on wildlife. Most must forage widely to find enough food, and when deep snow makes travel difficult or severe cold makes prolonged exposure dangerous, casualties are common. Even the plants, despite their dormancy, can suffer, especially in times of freezing rain.

When temperatures are at or just below 32° F, misty drizzle freezes instantly on any surface it touches. Layer upon layer the ice builds up until every plant large and small, every twig and bit of bark, every boulder and blade of grass, is locked beneath a transparent armor. The tiniest details such as buds show through, their colors delicately enhanced, and if the sun then shines, the entire forest scintillates. But if the rain continues for several hours, damage begins; for unlike the fragile rime of freezing fog, this ice is heavy. Before long, branches begin to break under the strain of its added weight. Oaks, with their strong but brittle wood, are especially vulnerable, while birch saplings, despite their seeming fragility, are flexible enough to bend under the burden, then spring back when the ice melts.

As the rain continues to fall and freeze, the forest is enveloped in a somber silence that is broken only by a faint tinkling as icy branches brush against each other in the breeze. Then suddenly a booming crack is followed by a sound like a crystal chandelier crashing to the floor and shattering into a heap of shards. The first branch has broken. Other great limbs begin to bow down and finally snap, and even whole trees sometimes topple to the ground.

The scars from a severe ice storm remain for years. Yet eventually the broken but still-living trees produce new limbs, often growing at odd angles or in strange curves. It is this pruning by the ice and subsequent regeneration that accounts for the bizarrely contorted forms of so many of the oaks that can be seen throughout the park. A bit monstrous perhaps, yet their very grotesqueness testifies to an admirable endurance.

So it is with every plant and animal of the forest. Watching the winter wildlife at Shenandoah and experiencing the rigors of the weather yourself, you come to respect the adaptability and toughness of all that lives here. There may be individual casualties, but the forest itself lives on. Soon the gentle seasons, spring and summer, will return; soon the birds, the burgeoning wildflowers, and all other forms of life will reenact their roles in the unending cycle of renewal and rebirth.

Theodore Roosevelt

". . . the loneliness and the vastness of the country seemed as unbroken as if the old vanished days had returned—the days of the wild wilderness wanderers, and the teeming myriads of game they followed. . . ."

Theodore Roosevelt

Only one U.S. national park is named after a U.S. president. It is fitting that the person should be Theodore Roosevelt, and that the park bearing his name should be in the badlands of North Dakota. Roosevelt chose these badlands as his own. They also chose *him*—captured his spirit and dominated his outlook for the rest of his life.

He was not quite 25 years old when he first stepped from a Northern Pacific train onto the wooden platform of Little Missouri, Dakota Territory—a ramshackle frontier village that was known locally as "Little Misery." It was 3 o'clock in the morning of September 8, 1883, and as the train chugged off westward under the starry sky, Roosevelt stood alone in the sage-scented autumn chill.

He had come to shoot a bison. Not many of the great shaggy beasts remained since the railroad had stretched its tracks across the area, making it possible for commercial hunters to ship the heavy hides east by the carload. That very week, the Sioux from the Standing Rock Reservation, allowed one final hunt, were preparing to finish off the last big herd of 10,000. But Roosevelt—among the first eastern sportsmen to respond to recent publicity about this paradise for big game hunters—was determined to bag one for himself.

Joe Ferris, the guide at the log army barracks that had lately been converted into a hunting lodge, tried to

Slicing northward through the grassy prairie, its rugged banks brightened by yellow prickly pears, the Little Missouri River unites the three sections of Theodore Roosevelt National Park, one of the nation's few divided parks.

explain the situation to the undersized, bespectacled young dude. It was like talking to the wind. So, since Roosevelt was willing to pay well for the hunt, the two men soon headed southwest in a wagon.

It would have been fairly easy in the wagon to cross the miles-wide stretches of grassland, where western wheat grass, blue grama, little bluestem, needle-and-thread, and buffalo grass grew intermixed with yuccas, prickly pears, and short yellow Indian paintbrushes—except that it would have involved descending or climbing occasional cliffs, and crossing broad canyons filled with tortuous badlands terrain. So they bumped along through the twisting gorges that border the bed of the Little Missouri River. These, too, were badlands—rugged, colorful mazes of canyons, cliffs, and pyramidal buttes that the river had carved out of the otherwise featureless plain—and it took several hours to cover a distance of about eight miles.

Though the steep-sided defiles made travel difficult, they brought variety to a monotonous sea of grass; and variety of terrain supported a variety of animal life. Besides the pronghorns and bison of the open plain, there were shy white-tailed deer in brushy gullies and riverside thickets, big-eared mule deer on sage-spangled hillsides, and Audubon's bighorn sheep—a subspecies that was to become extinct at the turn of the century.

It was growing dark when the wagon arrived at the log cabin of the Maltese Cross Ranch, where the two men spent the night. In the morning Roosevelt bought a horse and accompanied the wagon to another ranch house that was to serve as headquarters for the hunt.

273

A sharp-eyed prairie falcon, high atop a badlands butte, watches intently for a sign of small prey.

Rust-colored badlands scoria, a kind of natural red brick baked by the heat of burning lignite, resembles true scoria, which is a volcanic rock. Exposed slabs slow the constant force of erosion.

During the night foul weather arose, turning the badlands clay to slick gumbo; rain was to continue for many days, hampering Teddy's hunt but never dampening his ebullient spirits. Every morning Ferris protested that the weather was too bad for hunting, and every morning his client overruled him. Every evening they came back from long, hard, and often dangerous rides through deep badlands mud without having seen any sign of bison. Every night, while his exhausted guide slept, Teddy sat up talking with the ranch manager. Their conversations covered a wide variety of subjects, but Roosevelt kept bringing the focus back to the cattle business. He managed to learn a great deal.

He and Ferris *did* come upon some bison near the end of the sixth day. Not only did they fail to kill any, but one full-grown bull, over six feet tall and weighing more than a ton, came close to killing the hunters. There followed a miserable night on the soggy, naked plain—a night that became a grotesque nightmare when the horses ran away. After the mounts had been recaptured, the "four-eyed dude" earned his exhausted guide's everlasting respect and friendship when, with utter sincerity, he exclaimed through the broad, toothy grin that seemed a permanent feature of his mud-stained face: "By Godfrey, but this is fun!"

The changing land

On September 20, Roosevelt finally got his bison. Surely he was proud of the achievement, but from the hunt he also gained an insight into the plight of the huge beasts. His was among the last wild bison to be shot by sportsmen. The man who brought it down would, 22 years later, become the honorary president of the American Bison Society, an organization that did much to save the shaggy symbol of America from extinction.

It is estimated that at one time North America supported a population of about 60 million bison. Vast, dusty oceans of them had surged over the prairies, constantly on the move, cropping broad swathes clean of grass and leaving behind the natural fertilizer that would allow dense root systems to renew green growth. Wolves and other predators had kept the herds strong by culling weak and unhealthy animals. Indians had sometimes killed entire herds by stampeding them over cliffs, but even this wholesale hunting procedure had had little effect on the total bison populaton. The only real limitations to their numbers had been disease and weather. In summers of drought or in hard winters, the herds had shrunk; in good years they had grown.

In 1883, when Roosevelt discovered the badlands, cattle were fast replacing bison. A young French nobleman, the marquis de Mores, had arrived the spring before, intent on making enough money to buy control of the French Army and seize the throne of France. His plan was to build a meat-packing plant in the badlands; by slaughtering cattle where they were raised and shipping the beef in refrigerator cars, he could save the cost of transporting live cattle to eastern stockyards. An accomplished duellist, he had quickly established his frontier credentials by killing a man. Then he had set about creating his new industry, the success of which depended on the growth of cattle ranching.

The plan seemed reasonable. Moreover, Roosevelt had fallen in love with the land. And so, before returning to his political career in New York, he bought a part interest in the Maltese Cross Ranch, where he and Ferris had spent the first night of their hunt. Like other cattlemen, he and his two partners did not actually own the land. They bought the cabin, cattle, brands, and squatter's rights. There were no fences, and the cattle grazed as freely as bison had once done, on open range that belonged either to the Northern Pacific Railroad or to the federal government.

That fall, a herd of longhorns arrived, having been driven all the way from Texas to fatten on free northern grass. It was the first of many such outside herds that were eventually to deplete the land, but few people yet imagined that there could be a limit to the wealth that could be taken from this bountiful range.

The delicate badlands

Despite the seemingly endless vistas of grass, despite the implacably rugged badlands that slash through them, despite the calm quality of eternal sameness that the Little Missouri lends as it winds northward toward its junction with the Missouri, despite all the elements that create the illusion of immutable toughness, this is a delicate, fragile, and ever-changing world. It is a landscape of limited water and shallow soil, altered by every rainstorm, remade with every spring thaw.

The gray clay that is largely responsible for the variable topography is called bentonite. It is the product of volcanic ash, which began settling over this land about 60 million years ago as the result of vast eruptions in the Yellowstone region, and continued to do so for tens of millions of years. Thick layers of it, intermixed with other sediments, lie beneath the topsoil, holding water for the roots of grasses and blocking the growth of most larger plants. Only the tough roots of the ubiquitous sagebrush, delving many feet deep for

water, seem able to break easily through the barrier.

Each tiny particle of bentonite soaks up water and swells, doubling and redoubling its volume. When rain falls or snow melts, the top bentonite particles squeeze together into a slick shield through which water cannot seep. When this impermeable layer has absorbed as much water as it can hold, the rest runs off, cutting channels as it goes down through underlying layers of sandstone, mudstone, and clay. Soil that overlies the bentonite in these channels is eventually washed away, and the channels deepen into gullies and ravines.

Sometimes large masses of grassland slowly slide downhill, their paths lubricated by the slick bentonite beneath them. These are not landslides, broken and tumbling, but slump blocks: intact masses of soil held together by interwoven grass roots. They fill up low spots, leaving new slopes exposed; here the gray clay hardens, shrinks, and splits as it dries, forming deep cracks that will erode into new badlandscapes.

In many places the clay is protected from erosion by level patches of sod or by caprocks, including steel-hard pieces of petrified wood. The resultant pillars, cones, and castellated bluffs seem to grow ever taller as the gullies between them are eaten away, and their sides are striped and banded with the bright colors of underlying sediments—brighter than in Badlands National Park because they came from the mineral-rich Rockies, rather than the Black Hills of South Dakota.

Contrasting with the bright badlands sediments are thick, black veins of lignite, or soft coal—the partly rotted, partly petrified remains of palms, tree ferns, and other lush semitropical vegetation that flourished here some 60 to 70 million years ago. One sign of the coal's

Deep layers of lignite, or soft coal, may sometimes be accidentally ignited and may smolder for decades. This pocket of flame, exposed by the collapse of a patch of soil, was part of a vein that burned between 1951 and 1977.

Protected by hard caprocks and sod mats, the buttes and columns of the badlands form a fantasy landscape. The canyons that twist among these contorted towers, spires, and turrets are the easiest avenues of travel.

Its noble head and massive shoulders cloaked by a thick coat of dense hair, the bison is ideally suited to its life on the open plains, where fierce winter winds are the rule.

presence is black dust that sometimes peppers the pelts of prairie dogs when they emerge from their burrows. Another may be a horizontal band of Rocky Mountain junipers on a hillside; the trees' roots, blocked by clay beneath much of the badlands' dry, shallow soil, take moisture from the water-permeable lignite when they can reach it.

When the junipers take the shape of narrow columns, rather than spreading into graceful pyramids, it means that a nearby lignite vein has smoldered underground in the not too distant past. Such veins, ignited by lightning, grass fires, or even spontaneous combustion, may burn for decades. One vein, about 30 feet below the surface of the nearby Little Missouri National Grassland, is said to have been alight since before the first fur traders arrived. Heat from the burning lignite bakes the sediments above into a natural brick known as scoria.

At one time, the columnar junipers growing near these underground ovens were thought to be a separate species, but when such trees were transplanted away from the burning coal, they resumed their normal shapes. Exactly why the fumes cause junipers to grow

this way no one knows, but the phenomenon has occurred elsewhere, downwind from coal-fired industries.

Today the land once again supports a rich and varied wildlife community. Bison graze the plains again; pronghorns—North America's fleetest land animals—feed largely on sage and wildflowers. Both white-tailed and mule deer are common, the whitetails leaping like ballet dancers through brushy thickets, the mulies bouncing stiff-legged across open hillsides. Some 30 prairie dog towns—one covering 106 acres—support such predators as badgers, coyotes, and golden eagles.

The cattleman

The year 1884 was devastating to Teddy Roosevelt. His wife and his mother died on the same day in February. In June a disastrous confrontation at the Republican Convention left his promising political career in ruins. Disheartened, defeated, and grieving, he retired from public life and returned to the badlands, intent on making a new life for himself as an outdoorsman and cattle rancher. As it turned out, he was to live this new life for only two years, but they were crucial years in his development as a man—and through him, in America's development as a nation.

Roosevelt bought a second ranch, the Elkhorn. Faced with new challenges, he quickly regained the joyous self-confidence that was his lifelong hallmark. At first, with his owlish spectacles and eastern mannerisms, Teddy was an object of derision to the rough-edged cowboys who worked for him. During one of his first roundups, when he ordered a cowboy to "hasten forward quickly there!" every man within earshot was convulsed with laughter. So hilarious did the westerners find the phrase that they began to use it themselves, and it remained for years a badlands idiom.

It was not long before the pluck that had made a friend of Joe Ferris on that first bison hunt began to impress others. Teddy earned the respect of his men with hard, dirty labor. At least once, he had to earn the respect of strangers with his fists. Told and retold around bars and campfires was the story of his barefisted knockout of a drunken bully with a revolver in each hand who had tried to intimidate "Four-eyes."

Another tale—one you can still hear from old-timers whose grandparents claimed they were witnesses—has to do with Teddy's capture of three rustlers who had stolen his boat to escape the law. He and two friends chased the desperadoes for 100 miles amid crushing blocks of ice during the spring thaw on the Little Missouri. Then, instead of hanging the thieves from the handiest tree as was the custom, Teddy brought them back for the law to deal with. The journey to the nearest jail involved guarding the prisoners night and day for a week on the river, followed by a 45-mile wagon trek through ankle-deep mud. (The tied-up prisoners rode; Roosevelt walked, rifle at the ready.) When he arrived, caked with mud, his clothes were in shreds and his feet a mass of blisters. But he had upheld the law.

Rocky Mountain junipers and sagebrush dot the hills and upland plains of the Little Missouri Valley, while cottonwoods and willows thrive along the riverbanks. The junipers, along with an occasional ash tree, grow mostly on north slopes where water is slow to evaporate. The deep-rooted sage colors the whole land with its blue-green foliage.

Such rigorous displays of integrity earned the respect of the frontier community as a whole. Willy-nilly, Roosevelt found himself a public figure again. He was elected to lead area-wide roundups, to chair the Little Missouri Stockmen's Association, and to represent badlands cattlemen in regional meetings.

The ranchers had real problems to take to such meetings. They knew that the ever-increasing influx of outside herds would destroy the range through overgrazing. But there was no legal remedy; they did not own the land and no laws existed for its protection. That the end had to come was obvious. It came sooner than anyone expected. In 1886 a cyclical dry summer destroyed the depleted pastures. It was followed by a bitterly cold winter, when deep snows melted and refroze into ice many inches thick. The starving cattle had little resistance to the fierce, cold winds, and when spring arrived 75 percent of them were dead. The marquis's slaughterhouse closed, and although Roosevelt tried to rebuild his herds, the loss was too great.

Meanwhile, eastern politics had beckoned; Roosevelt had been asked to run for mayor of New York. Though he lost the election, he found himself again in the thick of the political wars that he loved. Thanks to his time in the badlands he entered the fray with renewed vigor and a new depth of commitment.

He never forgot the badlands, and returned to them often. Nor did he ever forget the sights of dwindling brown grass or of frozen cattle; nor the bitter fact of vanishing wildlife. He had learned the hard way the cost of abusive exploitation. A skilled writer, he published several books that made the public more aware of the need to preserve the wilderness and its creatures.

As president of the United States, Theodore Roosevelt approved 5 national parks, 16 national monuments, and 51 national wildlife refuges. He set aside over 86 million acres of national mineral reserves and 125 million acres of national forests. His stated goal, to manage the nation's limited resources in a wise way for the public good, marked a turning point in the history of the United States—indeed, in the history of the world. Nothing could have pleased him more than to know that the ravines and prairies he loved are now preserved in memory of his name.

Virgin Islands

*"To see a World in a grain of sand
And a Heaven in a Wild Flower,
Hold Infinity in the palm of your hand
And Eternity in an hour."* **William Blake**

The Caribbean. For many, a mere mention of that far-off sea conjures up visions of lush tropical islands and bright sun-drenched beaches lined with graceful palms that rustle in the breeze, beaches where lovely turquoise water, warm and soothing, laps gently at the shore. And what comfort we find in the knowledge that such places do exist! There are, for instance, the U.S. Virgin Islands—St. Croix, St. Thomas, and St. John, together with many smaller islands and islets—scattered across the deep blue sea just east of Puerto Rico. And on one of them is found a uniquely beautiful natural treasure, Virgin Islands National Park.

Comprising more than half of the island of St. John and 5,650 acres of adjacent waters, it totals only about 15,000 acres, and so is one of the very smallest of our national parks. But size alone is no measure of the special quality of a place. Here we have an island rich in natural beauty and with a varied human heritage. (No other national park can boast a direct historical link with Christopher Columbus.) Even more intriguing is the under-water portion of the park, a marine preserve where all can explore the mysteries of the secret realm beneath the sea: coral reefs, broad expanses of white sand, underwater grasslands—each of them teeming with incredibly colorful creatures.

Like most of the other islands of the Lesser Antilles,

curving southward like an emerald necklace toward the shoulder of South America, this earthly Eden was born of volcanic fires. The first eruptions, beginning perhaps 100 million years ago, took place far beneath the sea. With the weight of thousands of feet of overlying water suppressing explosive activity, lava flowed smoothly from an opening in the earth's crust and solidified to form the foundation of the island-to-be.

Then about 70 million years ago, a general uplifting of the ocean floor set the stage for the next episode of island building—violent eruptions above the surface of the sea. By the time they ended, a substantial island had risen above the Caribbean. Parts of the island's flanks were covered by a veneer of sedimentary rocks—some of them limestone formed from the calcareous remains of marine plants and animals, others apparently formed from debris deposited there by submarine landslides.

The greening of St. John no doubt began not long after the island was formed. Modern observations at such volcanic sites as Mount St. Helens and the island of Surtsey in the North Atlantic have shown that plants become established very soon after the eruptions quiet down: seeds blown in by the wind or washed up on the shore quickly take root and begin to flourish. So it must have been on St. John. And as soon as plants gained a foothold, animals also colonized the island. Some, such as birds, insects, and bats (St. John's only native mammals) flew in; others, including the island's several kinds of lizards, probably landed there by accident, perhaps after long journeys adrift at sea on floating logs or other vegetation.

A world of wonder awaits all who don diving gear and explore Virgin Islands' underwater realm, where the creatures of the reef range from colorful corals and flashing swarms of fish to the timid, tentacled octopus.

Creatures of the Reef

Corals, creating fantasies in stone, are the master builders of the reef. Their limestone fortresses—each one the work of a colony of countless tiny animals—come in an amazing variety of shapes and sizes, from the convoluted masses of brain coral (19), often several feet in diameter, and the great mounds of star coral (8) to the aptly named staghorn coral (22) and elkhorn coral (6). Their close relatives the common gorgonian (3) and the sea fan (16), also composed of many individuals, have leathery rather than stony skeletons and so are able to sway with passing currents.

Lurking among the corals are hordes of other animals as well. The hawksbill turtle (2), once common in these waters but now becoming scarce, is seen occasionally. The banded coral shrimp (10), skulking near a purple vase sponge (11), sometimes earns its keep by picking parasites from the mouths of moray eels. Two of the more deceptive denizens of the reef should be admired for their beauty, but only from afar: the bristles of the bristleworm (13) and the stiletto spines of the long-spined sea urchin (4) cause great pain if touched.

And then there are the fish, swarms of them, supplying flashes of brilliant color. Among the most common—they often form huge schools—are yellowtail snappers (1) and French grunts (5), named for the noises they make. Less sociable, sharknose gobies (18), which glean

parasites from other fish, and foureye butterflyfish (17) usually travel in pairs. The smooth trunkfish (20) uncovers burrowing prey by spitting streams of water into the sand. The sand diver (12) finds protection there; it sometimes buries itself so deeply in the sand that only its eyes are exposed. Also common are squirrelfish (14) and sergeant majors (21), feisty little fighters who nip at other fish intruding on their territories. Completing the rainbow of the reef are the fish that change their colors. In its youth, the male bluehead wrasse (15) was yellow with dark side-stripes. Similarly, mature males of the stoplight parrotfish (7) change from the reddish of the female to bluish green, and blue tangs (9) gradually turn from yellow to blue.

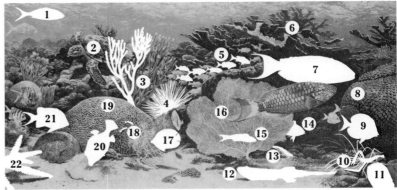

Humans, too, eventually found their way to St. John, presumably by island-hopping northward from the coast of South America. Such a feat would not have been especially difficult, even in the crudest of boats: as modern-day sailors know, it is possible to cruise the full length of the Lesser Antilles and seldom be out of sight of one island or another. By the second century A.D., a peaceful people, the Tainos, had established settlements on St. John. There they remained for more than a thousand years, fishing in the bountiful offshore waters and practicing a crude form of agriculture. In the 1300's, however, their tranquil lives were shattered forever by

Trunk Bay is but one of many that indent St. John's tortuous coastline. Like most, it is edged with lovely white sand beaches composed primarily of pulverized coral from the fringing reef just a short distance offshore.

the arrival of aggressive, seafaring Caribs, who had also migrated up the island chain from South America. It was probably these fierce warriors who exterminated the Tainos on St. John.

The greatest human impact on the island, however, was yet to come. In 1493, Christopher Columbus set out on his second voyage to the New World, taking settlers to his recent discovery, Hispaniola, in a fleet of 17 ships; making his landfall on the island of Dominica, well to the south of his goal, he sailed north and discovered other islands along the way—Guadeloupe, Montserrat, Antigua, St. Kitts, and more. Then, with the persistent force of the trade winds in his sails, Columbus swung westward and chanced upon a cluster of islands and islets of particular charm and beauty. These he named *Las Once Mil Virgines* ("The 11,000 Virgins") after the legendary Virgins of St. Ursula.

Though he was clearly impressed by their pristine beauty, Columbus never returned to the Virgin Islands. He claimed them as Spanish territory, but for almost 200 years they were rarely visited by any Europeans, save for occasional pirates. (Caves on nearby Norman Island served as pirates' dens, and a smaller island, Deadman's Cay, was frequented by that most infamous of freebooters, Blackbeard.)

The islands changed hands in 1672 with the establishment of a permanent Danish settlement, and before long St. John was transformed. With the discovery that the balmy climate was just right for growing sugarcane and cotton, several plantations were established; and with the help of slaves imported from Africa, large tracts of forest were cleared for cane and cotton fields. Then in 1848, with rumblings of revolt in the air, the Danish governor declared an end to slavery. And with emancipation, sugar and cotton production declined abruptly. By 1909 all the plantations had been abandoned and left to the encroaching forest. In 1917 the United States purchased the Virgin Islands from Denmark, and eventually they found new prosperity as a tourist destination.

From forest to sea
St. John's green forested peaks and valleys are always a delight to explore. Of several trails in the park, the Reef Bay Trail offers an especially fascinating look at both the natural and the human history of the island. The walk begins on Centerline Road near Mamey Peak, one of the highest points on St. John, and heads south to Reef Bay. Hikers are invariably impressed by the lushness of the vegetation, for the first part of the trail passes through a zone of the moist tropical forest that once predominated on much of St. John. Elevation and exposure both influence the kinds of plants that grow on the island. Higher land receives more rainfall because the moist trade winds, when forced upward by the terrain, are cooled and release their moisture; lower slopes on the south side of the island are dry and even desertlike. The several kinds of cacti that grow there

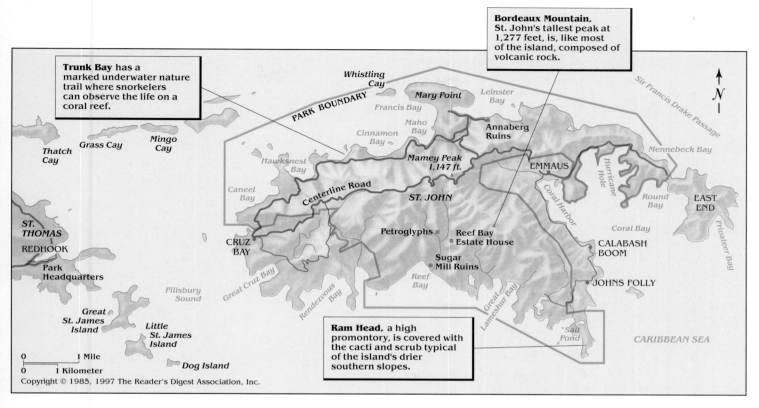

Trunk Bay has a marked underwater nature trail where snorkelers can observe the life on a coral reef.

Bordeaux Mountain, St. John's tallest peak at 1,277 feet, is, like most of the island, composed of volcanic rock.

Ram Head, a high promontory, is covered with the cacti and scrub typical of the island's drier southern slopes.

always come as a surprise to visitors, who expect to find luxuriant rain forest everywhere.

The forest is still in the process of recovery from plantation days, and here and there you can see old stone walls—reminders of that bygone era—being overgrown by thick tangles of vegetation. Walking in the cool shade beneath the leafy canopy, strollers are likely to hear the mournful call of Zenaida doves and the melodic song of the pearly-eyed thrasher, just 2 of 125 species of birds found in the park. Land-dwelling hermit crabs rustle through the fallen leaves, each one carrying its own portable home, the shell of a whelk or other sea snail. Anoles, small lizards related to iguanas, skitter about. Some are green, others brown, still others mottled in appearance for, like chameleons, they can change their colors to match their surroundings. Another creature to watch for is the rust-colored, ferretlike mongoose, which is often seen scooting through the undergrowth. Introduced by the Danes in an unsuccessful effort to control marauding rodents in the fields, mongooses have proliferated because they have few natural predators.

About a mile and a half from the start of the trip, a side trail leads to some lovely pools nestled at the base of a 40-foot cliff. And on the rocks rimming one of the pools is found one of the park's unanswered mysteries—a series of strange petroglyphs. Who made these rock carvings, and when? Although they were originally thought to be of pre-Columbian origin, recent studies have shown that some of them are similar to designs produced by certain African cultures, and so they may date from early slave days on the island.

Near the end of the trail, where the forest becomes

drier, there stands another remnant of the past, the crumbling ruins of a sugar mill. And just beyond is the blue water of Reef Bay itself with, a short distance offshore, the coral reef that gives the bay its name—an ideal place to respond to the island's other invitation to enchantment, the sea.

Castles of stone

Throughout the park the sea is never far from sight or mind. Sometimes during the winter months, surf caused by swells from distant Atlantic storms pounds the northern and eastern shorelines with waves up to eight feet high, but such fury occurs infrequently and lasts only a day or two. Normally, these waters are calm and quiet, with tidal ranges averaging only a foot or less. Warm, placid, and crystal clear, the sea is ideal for snorkeling or scuba diving. And anyone who tries either sport soon discovers that these Caribbean waters contain a fascinating and stunningly beautiful world, the realm of the coral reef.

People often have the mistaken impression that reefs are merely rocks, but in fact they contain and are constructed by living creatures. The individual coral animal, called a polyp, is small (generally a fraction of an inch in size) and usually tubular in shape, with a ring of tentacles resembling those of its larger relatives, sea anemones. Equipped with stinging capsules, the tentacles sway about, gathering the tiny drifting animals that are the coral's food. But that is only part of the story, for certain species of algae grow inside the coral itself. Numbering in the thousands in a single polyp, these minute plants are responsible for the great variety of vivid colors among the corals. More important, the

Now overgrown with rampant vegetation, the ruins at one of St. John's many former plantations stand as mute reminders of the bygone era when sugarcane was king on this idyllic island in the Caribbean.

algae absorb carbon dioxide and through the process of photosynthesis produce oxygen and certain nutrients vital to both the coral and themselves.

The coral animal protects its soft, vulnerable body from predators in two ways: it secretes calcium carbonate, the substance that forms limestone, to create a hard shell around itself, and it finds safety in numbers by living in colonies of thousands—sometimes millions—of its kind that grow into large, formidable rocky masses. What we see, then, beneath these waters are complex and colorful fortresses created by a simple animal. They are, however, castles that take a long time to build; a brain coral just a few feet in diameter may be centuries in age.

Not all corals form such hard, rocky masses. Polyps of the type known as gorgonians—sea fans, sea whips, and the like—secrete only small amounts of carbonate and are instead connected together by a flexible horny material that allows them to sway rhythmically with the undersea currents like grasses in the wind.

The rainbow realm

Corals in all their varieties, shapes, and sizes are the very foundation for survival of a host of other animals and plants that live on the reef. For some, such as parrotfish, corals are a source of both food and protection. Crevices, overhangs, and caves in the reefs allow the fish to hide from predators; for food the parrotfish eats algae growing on dead corals, which it takes with its sharp, parrotlike beak. In the process the fish crush-

es the limestone and converts it into fine sand, and so contributes to the building of the island's lovely white beaches.

The ideal way to explore this fascinating world is by donning face mask and fins or, for the more adventurous, scuba gear. Regardless of choice, entering this realm is a little like being an astronaut landing on a strange new planet. The strongest first impression is one of color—astonishing, vivid colors of every hue. Your gaze is torn between the bright orange "antlers" of elkhorn coral; the green and yellow forms of brain corals; the white to yellow staghorn coral that lies in tangled masses on the bottom; the purple sea fans swaying gently in the undersea currents; and the brown pillar coral growing in tall, cylindrical columns whose soft, furry look belies their rocky hardness (the "fur" is actually the tentacles of thousands of coral polyps).

When you move closer, the color becomes even more astounding. Sponges with an incredible array of hues make their home among the corals. Intense red, orange, green, yellow, and blue forms of these simple animals can often be found growing within inches of each other. Adding to the chromatic explosion are the fish—blue and green wrasses; red-striped squirrelfish; bright yellow juvenile tangs and the fluorescent blue adults; multicolored angelfish and butterflyfish. The variety is overwhelming.

And that is what usually makes the next-strongest impression on the novice reef visitor—life. Teeming life. Swimming among or living amid the corals is an incredible richness of life-forms, plant and animal, vertebrate and invertebrate. Under a shelf of coral a spiny lobster may sit quietly, only its spiked antennae protruding and probing for food or signs of danger. Delicate fairy shrimp scavenge the nooks and crannies, looking for the leftover morsels of another's meal. Orange-spotted flamingo-tongue cowries and other equally colorful snails cling to sea fans and sea whips. Attached to the surfaces of star corals and brain corals are numerous tube worms topped with feathery plumes that sway in the current to capture plankton. The most common types are Christmas trees and feather dusters, both aptly named for their shapes.

And there is more. Black sea urchins are everywhere, their long, slender spines waving menacingly as though to warn that contact can be painful. A three-foot-long moray eel slithers snakelike past a brain coral. Despite an evil reputation, it presents no danger to divers or snorkelers if left undisturbed. The same is true of the octopus, a gentle, timid reef dweller that is rarely seen. A master at hiding, it can ooze its soft, fluid body into the most improbable crevices, emerging only to stalk its favorite prey—such mollusks as conchs or whelks. Using its parrotlike beak, it can open or chip away the hardest of shells to get at the animal inside.

Although such creatures sometimes frighten newcomers to the reef, in reality few things here are harmful to humans. True, a person foolish enough to thrust a hand blindly into a dark crevice might be bitten by a moray eel, but such occurrences are rare. Nor is there much danger from sharks, since these predators of the open sea seldom venture into the shallows near shore.

Beyond the reef

Not all of the sea bottom is covered with coral formations. If the reefs can be compared to forests rich in life, other areas are analogous to deserts and grasslands. In some places great expanses of pure white sand seem at first glance to be totally uninhabited. Like our terrestrial deserts, however, they are far from being wastelands. The many mounds and depressions in the sand hint of the secretive, subterranean activities of the sea worms and burrowing varieties of crabs, shrimps, and mollusks that make their home there.

Extensive undersea grasslands also dot the shallows. Like our Great Plains, these "prairies" are a fertile habitat for many kinds of creatures. Swimming over such a grassland, snorkelers are likely to spot a "herd" of large, slowly moving, conical snails—the queen conchs that are familiar to many for their lovely pink shells. True grazers, the conchs range over large areas, feeding not only on grasses, but on algae as well. Though seemingly protected by their hard shells, the conchs are preyed upon by spiny lobsters, octopuses, and stingrays. The first two are rarely seen because of their secretive nature, but the big kite-shaped rays—some of them six feet or more from "wingtip" to "wingtip"—are often observed gliding effortlessly above the grassy plains. Timid and fearful of man, they swim off rapidly when approached—a thrilling sight to behold, for few other creatures move with such exquisite grace and beauty.

It never seems to grow tiresome, this exploration of the sea. There is always some new wonder to be revealed, some new encounter bound to enchant and enthrall. Resting on a snow-white beach, we might never suspect that the very sand beneath our feet is the result of a chain of events starting with a tiny animal, the coral polyp. Similarly, the migrating humpbacked whales occasionally seen offshore and the playful dolphins that sometimes frolic near Reef Bay are part of this complex scheme of life, with their own well-being inextricably entwined with the existence of myriads of other creatures of the sea. Virgin Islands National Park provides a unique "window" for observing this incredibly rich array of ocean life, offering visitors endless opportunities for the delight of discovery and the discovery of delight.

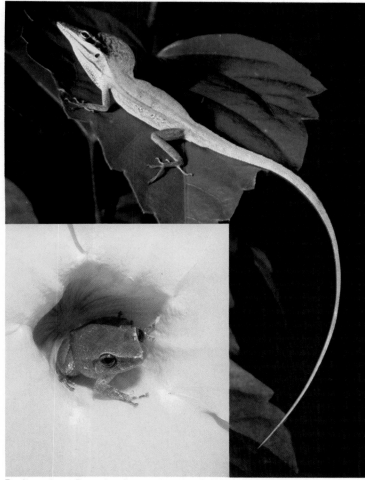

Radiant in reflected color, a tiny treefrog nestles in the blossom of an allamanda. Anoles, small lizards, can also be found clambering through trees and shrubs.

Voyageurs

*"Land of the silver birch, home of the beaver,
Where still the mighty moose wanders at will.
Blue lake and rocky shore, I will return once more."*
Canadian folk song

The wild 25-mile-long Kabetogama Peninsula, the heart of Voyageurs National Park, is robust canoe country. Nestled in the watery embrace of Rainy Lake and Kabetogama Lake, with their myriad bays and backwaters, and dotted with small lakes, ponds, and swamps that bear such intriguing names as War Club, Beast, Quill, and Little Shoepack, it holds some of the last remnants of the great forested wilderness that once spread across most of this part of the North American continent.

Here, and southward in the mainland section of the park, bald eagles still pose regally on snag-limbed pines. Great blue herons stalk aristocratically along swamp shores, and mallard ducks cautiously guide flotillas of precious puffballs through the water. Ospreys hover over beaches, peering for fish. Over and under the driftwood that edges the lakes and coves, where stands of wild rice flex gently in the breeze, shiny mink scamper and sniff out their suppers. Otters swim lazily through the dark amber water, diving from time to time after crayfish or perch, then hoisting themselves onto rocks for leisurely lunches.

To the Native Americans, these wetlands were treasure troves of fish, furs, and fowl. They gathered ruby-red wild cranberries that glowed in the noonday sun of muskeg bogs. In autumn they harvested the heavy-headed wild rice, beating the grains into their bark canoes with flailing sticks. Their spirit and presence is still strong in the land.

But it is the spirit of quite another group of canoeists that is commemorated in this park. The voyageurs were tough, muscular French Canadians who paddled the length of Rainy Lake every summer during the late 18th

In the woodlands that border the lakes and waterways of Voyageurs National Park, the pileated woodpecker makes its nest. A pair of birds spends weeks digging the deep nesting hole. Then both parents take turns incubating the eggs.

and early 19th centuries, straining to move tons of furs and trade goods 3,000 miles along intricate waterways before winter set in. Canoe life was even more rigorous in those years than it is today, and the strength and stamina of these canoeists was legendary. They seldom stood more than 5½ feet tall or weighed over 150 pounds—such uniformity of size made it easier both to paddle in unison and to carry canoes upside down when portaging—yet they could shoulder two or more packs of 90 pounds each, using tumplines, or portage straps, across their foreheads, and could paddle or carry their large canoes for hours at a stretch.

Every year in early May, two groups of voyageurs started paddling toward each other, one from Montreal, the other from Fort Chipewyan in northwestern Canada. Their object was a mid-July rendezvous at trading posts in what is now Minnesota. The men leaving from Montreal stored boxes and barrels of food, firearms, ammunition, tobacco, cloth, blankets, rum, and brandy in "work canoes" that were up to 40 feet long and carried about 5 tons. Other paddlers, 3,000 miles to the west and north, lashed bales of animal pelts into smaller "north canoes." These were roughly 26 feet long and carried 2 to 3 tons apiece.

Work canoes carried crews of 12 men; north canoes, 6 to 8. Each team was led by an experienced bowman; in boiling rapids and storm-tossed waters, lives depended on his sharp vision and quick commands. Equally important was the swift response of the sternman, whose paddle was the rudder that steered the craft. The paddlers sat amidships, their red-painted blades flashing in the sun as, like well-oiled machines, they kept up a steady rhythm of 40 strokes a minute for 10, 12, even 14 hours. More often than not, as they paddled they sang. The old French folk songs helped them work in unison; the camaraderie of singing lightened their labors, eased their monotony, and fed the

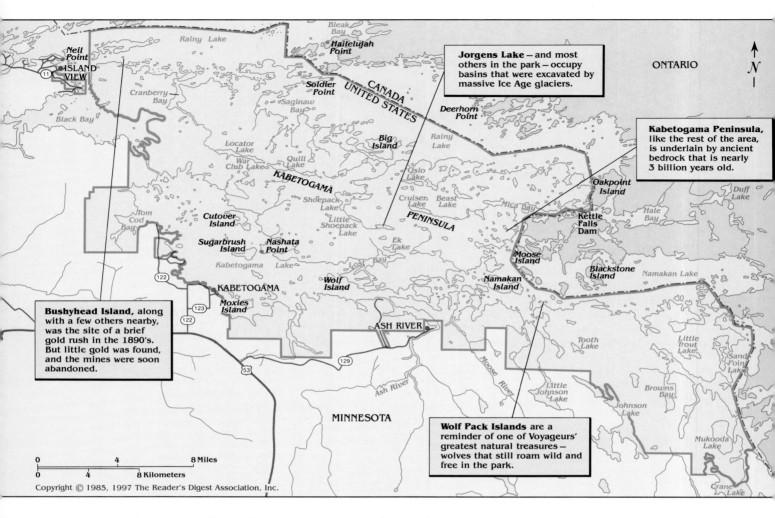

Map labels:

Neil Point · ISLAND VIEW · Black Bay · Cranberry Bay · Rainy Lake · Bleak Bay · Hailelujah Point · Soldier Point · CANADA · UNITED STATES · ONTARIO · N

Jorgens Lake — and most others in the park — occupy basins that were excavated by massive Ice Age glaciers.

Deerhorn Point · Big Island · Rainy Lake · Oslo Lake · Locator Lake · War Club Lakes · Quill Lake · KABETOGAMA · Shoepack Lake · Cruisen Lake · Beast Lake · PENINSULA

Kabetogama Peninsula, like the rest of the area, is underlain by ancient bedrock that is nearly 3 billion years old.

Oakpoint Island · Duff Lake · Mica Bay · Hale Bay · Kettle Falls Dam · Jtom Cod Bay · Cutover Island · Little Shoepack Lake · Ek Lake · Lost Bay · Moose Island · Blackstone Island · Namakan Lake · Sugarbrush Island · Nashata Point · Kabetogama Lake · Wolf Island · Namakan Island · KABETOGAMA · Moxies Island

Bushyhead Island, along with a few others nearby, was the site of a brief gold rush in the 1890's. But little gold was found, and the mines were soon abandoned.

ASH RIVER · Tooth Lake · Little Trout Lake · Sand Point Lake · Little Johnson Lake · Browns Bay · Ash River · Moose River · Johnson Lake · MINNESOTA

Wolf Pack Islands are a reminder of one of Voyageurs' greatest natural treasures — wolves that still roam wild and free in the park.

Mukooda Lake · Crane Lake

0   4   8 Miles
0   4   8 Kilometers

---

courage that was needed to face the dangers and discomforts that waited along the way.

Singing and smoking were the two main pleasures in the lives of these hardworking men; indeed, the distance across large lakes was figured not by miles, but by the number of pipes. On ordinary daytime travels, a stop was called every hour, and then the men would loosen their bright waist sashes, take the red wool stocking caps from their perspiring heads, and pull clay pipes from deerskin pouches. Soon the air was heavy with strong tobacco.

But there were times when black-boweled thunderclouds bore down, or strong headwinds blew. Big Rainy Lake could be lashed into mighty waves, though they were as nothing compared to the heavy waters that the work canoes faced in Lake Superior. In such times of emergency, the paddle tempo increased to 60 or more strokes a minute. (The most common "emergency," however, was a challenge by another brigade; such races might last a day and night, so proud were the voyageurs of their strength and endurance.)

On hot, humid evenings, when lakes lay as flat and gray as slate and hills faded away in folds of blue denim, the voyageurs might keep paddling rather than sleep in the stifling woods where mosquitoes whined unmercifully. The setting sun, a flattened orange ball, would throw a brassy bar across the water; as canoes passed, it would be smudged by mother-of-pearl ripples. Then darkness would fall, and the bowmen, navigating by night sight and memory, would depend on silhouetted trees and peninsulas to stay on course. Distinctive trees, called "lob pines," helped them find their way. These were huge white pines, 150 to 200 feet high, that were clearly visible against the skyline. To make them even more distinctive, a man was often sent aloft with an ax to lop off branches, leaving pronounced topknots. (Although forest fires and loggers have all but eliminated these big signposts, a few old lob pines still stand.)

Portaging, when the canoes and all the gear they held had to be carried overland, was the hardest part of any voyageur's life. In all, the voyageurs' route included 120 portages; the toughest of all was Grand Portage, a nine-mile trek over tendon-straining hills and shoe-sucking swamps between the large rendezvous post on the shore of Lake Superior and the Pigeon River, which led westward toward Rainy Lake. While carrying, the men made two or three rest stops, or *posés,* per mile. The voyageurs tucked the bows of their canoes snugly into tree crotches, slid out from beneath, dumped their packs on the ground, straightened their aching backs, and lit up their precious pipes.

The birch-bark craft required constant attention and

mending—they were often damaged on rocks and stumps—but they were sturdy and roomy. It seems incredible that soft and graceful, chalk-white birch trees could have supplied the thin, tough bark for these shell-like craft. Actually, a trio of trees went into the canoes. The wood of the white cedar, a tree of damp, lowland areas, was easily carved into canoe ribs, paddles, and other essential parts. Black spruce yielded root fibers, for sewing together bark sections, and pitch, for sealing the seams.

At suppertime, the cook would serve one of two menus: pea stew or corn stew. Into this mush, laced with bacon grease, was thrown anything resembling meat. Canoeists from Montreal carried salt pork. Those from the remote Canadian outposts had to catch fish, gulls, deer, or beavers. If a canoe paddle stood straight up in the stew, it was perfect. Every meal was washed down with strong brown tea, but after an extra-grueling day's work, a ration of rum or brandy would also be handed out. On these occasions, the men were certain to break into song, their voices echoing through the woods and ringing for miles across the water.

After supper, the voyageurs simply rolled up in heavy wool blankets to lie on the ground. Often as they drifted off to sleep, the *whap!* of a beaver's tail hitting the still water might startle them for a moment, or the eerie wail of a loon would echo over the campsite. Shafts of green polar light sometimes flared up beyond the shoreline, silhouetting wind-flagged pines, while peach-colored veils tinged the lake with pink. But northern lights and loon calls could not stir those weary paddlers. At the first light of dawn they jerked awake and set off, stopping after a few hours to wolf down some stew.

Loons were the voyageurs' constant companions on

The pads and fragrant blossoms of waterlilies float on lakes and ponds throughout the park. The stems curve down to roots as starchy as potatoes.

Rainy Lake. On mist-shrouded mornings, the regal black and white birds floated as still as decoys, only their low chuckles and the occasional blink of a morocco-red eye giving proof of life. But if a pair were caring for young, as they generally are during the summer in these northern waters, and if the canoeists came a little too close, the adults would swim quickly away, hoping to distract the intruders, while the loonlets skulked off to hide near shore. If, by chance, a chick were captured by canoeists, the frantic parents would perform a formidable threat display, racing around the canoe, rearing up and beating the water with their large wings, and filling the air with their high-pitched wails.

Loons never go ashore except to nest. They can hardly walk on land, but they are graceful and quick both upon and beneath the water. Expert fishermen, they dive effortlessly, leaving barely a ripple, and they often eat their catches—fish, crustaceans, frogs, or aquatic insects—before they surface. At dusk, they regularly join together in rowdy chases, yodeling as they fly in giant circles. Before the first ice skims out from shore, the loons patter ponderously across the cold lakes, their wings slapping the water until they finally gain the air. Then they circle for height and head south.

The living wilderness

Along the voyageurs' routes, wildlife was plentiful. The men saw moose munching pondweeds, heard lynx and bobcats caterwauling at night, and glimpsed the reflections of their own campfires in the yellow-green eyes of timber wolves. Virgin forests of enormous white and red pines dominated the landscape; and in the dry upland woods, red spruces, birches, jack pines, aspens,

The noble loon embodies the very spirit of the north woods as no other creature does. A pair mate for life, and once their eggs hatch in spring, the young remain with their look-alike parents for 12 weeks or more. One parent or the other is always in attendance, escorting the chicks around their watery nursery, bringing them tasty tidbits from beneath the surface, and sometimes cradling them piggyback between its wings.

Beaver ponds are important to the life of the north country, creating habitats for creatures of pond and marsh, and for those that prey upon them. Once nearly extinct, the sleek rodents are once again plentiful; in the lodges they build in the water of their ponds, a pair may raise as many as eight kits a season, each with a life span of up to 15 years.

red maples, and balsam firs added variety. Caribou pawed at reindeer moss, deer rubbed their antlers against aspens, wolverines slinked after prey, and beavers labored over their dams and lodges.

The caribou and wolverines are gone now, and you seldom see a moose; but black bears and white-tailed deer are plentiful. So are foxes, mink, and fishers, as well as the squirrels, chipmunks, snowshoe hares, and water creatures on which they feed. On a winter night you can still hear the melancholy sound of a wolf's full-throated howl, and sometimes, in the blue December dusk, you may be lucky enough to witness the thrilling sight of a silent pack, cruising like charcoal gray smudges against the snow.

In place of the magnificent mature forest, thousands of acres of pale green aspens and birches now shimmer in the summer breeze. Come springtime, their fresh

color is a fairytale backdrop for the bright blue lakes, and their aromatic scent lends a spicy tang to the air. Both trees are pioneers—nature's way of healing old scars. They take hold early on land that has been disturbed and hold the soil with their roots while they replenish it with their leaves and their soft, fast-growing substance. They serve the land's renewal, too, by being the beaver's favorite food and building material.

Nature's master builders

Master architects, these sleek, flat-tailed rodents build dams on winding creeks and other waterways, creating ponds in which to live their aquatic lives. The tools they work with are their incisors and forepaws. Constant gnawing keeps the teeth as sharp as axes, and the paws can easily grip rocks, mud, and branches.

The impounded water is soon filled with waterlilies,

292

duckweed, cattails, water arums, and other aquatic plants. Along the shores grow moisture-loving poplars, willows, and alders. Thus the vegetarian beaver surrounds itself with food, and in the process creates an excellent habitat for fish, frogs, mink, otters, moose, waterfowl, and many songbirds. Eventually the ponds fill in, but it is a slow process, and by the time it is complete the land is rich and lush.

Dam building is only the beginning of the beavers' constructive labors. In the pond that collects, they build strong, durable lodges in which to raise their young and survive the winter. Most shelters rise 4 to 5 feet above the water surface and measure roughly 12 to 15 feet around, although some may rise to 8 feet with a circumference of more than 20 feet. Generally, there is one room, accessible only by underwater entrances, in which a beaver family dines and dozes during the day.

A canoeist paddling quietly by a beaver lodge can often hear the mewing and whining of youngsters within. One pair of beavers can produce two to eight kits a year, and they are mostly kept inside until they are able to swim and dive well. During most of this time the adult males are banished from the lodge and set up bachelor quarters in dens along the shore.

Though clumsy on land, beavers are marvels of underwater adaptation. Transparent membranes over their eyes allow them to see, almost as a face mask aids a skin diver. Their blood supply and lung capacity are so good that they can remain submerged for 15 minutes and swim half a mile, propelled by hind feet that splay out into seven-inch-wide paddles. (These hind feet also serve as grooming aids; claws on the second and third toes are split, rather like little combs.)

Beavers' tails are both rudders and signaling devices. When a big male slaps the lake with this thick, flat appendage it means, "Pay attention!" Fat is also stored in the scaled tail—that's why it may be twice as large in fall as in spring. For this reason, Indians and voyageurs alike prized roast beaver tail.

Most prized, however, were the dense fur coats that allow beavers to withstand the chilly northern waters. A short, fine, gray underfur keeps the animals well insulated; the long, coarse, shiny-brown guard hairs keep them waterproof. It was for the sake of this fur—known to the trade as "brown gold"—that the animals were trapped almost to the point of extinction, and beaver pelts made up a large part of the load that the voyageurs carried eastward to Montreal.

Journey's end

Two large trading posts—one at Grand Portage on the shore of Lake Superior, and the other on Rainy Lake—were the principal sites where east met west. Here voyageurs renewed old friendships and enmities, as they bragged and boasted of their prowess and adventures. Clerks frantically tallied the bales and bundles that daily poured in from brigade after brigade of canoes, then repacked and redirected the goods.

Each July at Grand Portage a great ball was held. It was the closest thing to a formal affair for hundreds of miles around. Voyageurs appeared in clean colored shirts with their holiday-best sashes, moccasins, and caps. Clerks wore freshly ironed white shirts and trousers. Indian women, their cheeks and the parts in their hair dabbed with vermilion, came in their softest doeskins and fanciest beadwork. Braves sported showy buckskins and face paint. The great hall blazed with the light of dozens upon dozens of candles; tables were laden with venison, trout, moose, buffalo, whitefish, sturgeon roe, fresh bread, butter, and maple syrup; fiddles, flutes, and bagpipes played chansons, Virginia reels, square dances, and Highland flings. A marvelous and exhausting time was had by all.

Then, the annual gala over, canoes were reladen with new freight. The large work canoes were filled with furs for Montreal; the north canoes with trade goods and supplies for points westward. And once again the tough, adventurous voyageurs set off to complete their round-trip journey before winter.

Do any tokens remain of these gallant travelers? Very few. Their boats have long since disintegrated, their muskets and ax heads rusted and mixed with earth. Their graves, marked with stones or simple wooden crosses, cannot be found.

Their memory endures in the many old French place-names in Canada and the northern United States, in the traditional water routes now in use by modern-day canoeists, in the lilting echoes of voyageur songs, in the whisper of sweet-scented waterlilies brushing against a skimming craft, in the liquid evening chant of a white-throated sparrow, in the sight of mist drifting across dawn water, in the sound of blue waves crashing on low cliffs—and in Voyageurs National Park.

Each purple-veined leaf of the northern pitcher plant—common in the park's marshy areas—is a trap for crawling insects. Their bodies supply the nitrogen that the plant's roots cannot get from the boggy soil in which they grow.

A mosaic of grasslands and woodlands, Wind Cave has creatures as diverse as bison and mountain bluebirds. And beneath the rolling

Wind Cave

*"It's a warm wind, the west wind,
full of birds' cries;
I never hear the west wind
but tears are in my eyes."*
John Masefield

To be alive on the western fringes of the Great Plains is to be on terms with the wind. The wind is a messenger, foretelling storms; it is an explorer, searching shadowy ravines; and it is a musician, swishing through grasses and rustling the cottonwood leaves. When it hesitates, the plains are not themselves: the stillness seems alien to this place.

Yet it is in such moments of quiet that another wind can be heard at its best—an echo from within the earth itself. This wind *shooshes* through a small vent in a rocky ravine, sometimes inhaling, and then hours or days later exhaling in response to the changes in atmospheric pressure that mark the eternal rhythms of storm and sunshine.

Winds have whistled through that vent for eons, but its presence was unknown to local settlers until a calm spring day in 1881 when, it is said, two brothers tracking a wounded deer heard the sound of wind and, turning around, saw a patch of grass waving violently in the still air. Moving closer, they found a hole in the rock and when they knelt to peer inside, the force of the wind blew off one of their hats. One of the men returned later to show some friends the strange "blowhole," but

prairie it has a hidden world as well, the secret realm of the cave.

295

Alert for signs of danger, a prairie dog pauses on the mound at the entrance to its burrow. Its network of tunnels—a miniature, animal-excavated cave system—sometimes extends as far as 10 or 12 feet underground.

to his astonishment, the air that day was being drawn in—so violently, in fact, that it sucked the hat from his hands as easily as a bison inhales a gnat.

Although the brothers did not realize it, under them was a cave so large that it must breathe in order to equalize the air pressure inside with that on the outside. The extent of the labyrinth is remarkable: more than 78 miles of passages have been charted so far in this maze of rooms and passageways tiered in many interlocking levels that span a vertical distance of 650 feet. Even today, almost a century after a 17-year-old named Alvin McDonald became the first person to explore the cave in earnest, its innermost secrets have not been revealed.

Seas of grass, islands of trees

The landscape above the hidden cavern, on the other hand, is an open book for all to read. Most pervasive are the grasslands, washing up across the rolling hills of the eastern regions of the park like the swells on a seemingly endless sea. This is mixed-grass prairie, part of a vast north-south belt of prairie with grasses of medium height—not as verdant as the famed tallgrass prairies far to the east, but not as harsh as the shortgrass prairie farther west. Responding to the warm sunshine of early summer, the grasses—blue grama, western wheatgrass, little bluestem—grow lush, green, and as much as three feet tall, bearing seeds in their turn and ripening into a golden sea. Wildflowers—lavender horse-mint, purplish pasqueflowers, blue spiderworts, white sego lilies, and many others—splash the prairie with color. Meadowlarks sing in the warm summer light, celebrating life by claiming patches of land as their own individual territories.

The park is more than grasslands, however. Here on the southeastern shoulder of the densely forested Black Hills, pines venture tentatively into the open lands, the vanguard of a slow invasion that nature once kept in check with prairie fire. These are ponderosa pines, deep-rooted trees that, once established, can endure the drought of the prairie. Pure stands of pines crowd the higher, rocky western areas of the park, while isolated groves dot the grass-covered eastern regions.

Other trees find refuge at Wind Cave too, but are restricted to a few areas with just the right growing conditions. Lacing through the park, in deep, steep ravines where moisture is not so scarce, are woodlands made up of broadleaf trees and shrubs. Their presence in a region mostly given over to prairies and ponderosa pines tells botanists something that the casual visitor might not notice: because of its location and varied topography, Wind Cave is both meeting ground and range limit for strikingly different plant and animal communities. Here the bur oak and American elm reach the westernmost limits of their range—both within a stone's throw of ponderosa pines and Rocky Mountain junipers, growing at their eastern frontier. Paper birches, normally at home in cool northern forests, also hide in isolated pockets along the shaded watercourses, while on dry, south-facing slopes, prickly pear cacti and yuccas—plants associated with southwestern deserts—find suitable terrain.

To people attuned to the avian world, the park's mosaic of contrasting life zones is immediately apparent. Rock wrens, denizens of drier regions of the park, sometimes exchange songs with house wrens, inhabitants of the moist woodlands. The flutelike gurgling of the meadowlark, resounding from the grasslands, occasionally can be heard competing with the long, loud warbling of the Townsend's solitaire, a bird of the coniferous forests. It is even possible to spot such birds of the plains as a prairie falcon or sharp-tailed grouse within minutes of sighting woodland birds like a white-breasted nuthatch or redheaded woodpecker—all from the same vantage point.

With luck a visitor might also get to see some of the larger creatures that live mainly in the wooded areas— a bobcat, perhaps, or a wild turkey. Mule deer are almost certain to put in an appearance; they quickly lose their fear of humans when not hunted. The park's 350 or so elk are more elusive, retiring to the cover of deeper woods during daylight hours. At dawn and again at dusk, however, they can often be seen in moist meadows, since they come out at night to graze on succulent grasses and herbs.

Pageantry of the plains

What visitors to the surface park remember most, however, is the grassland. Gazing across the prairie dog town on Bison Flats, out beyond the ridge where a band of pronghorn graze, and far south to the horizon that is Nebraska, you can still imagine what the Great Plains used to be: home to one of the greatest assemblages of wildlife the world has ever known. From Texas all the way to Canada, the plains were honeycombed with the burrows of prairie dog towns that sheltered some 5 *billion* individuals. Timeworn trails traveled by 60 million bison knitted together an area stretching from the Appalachians in the east to the Rocky Mountains in the west. Clouds of migrating waterfowl, cranes, shorebirds, and passenger pigeons darkened the sky as they passed overhead.

In Wind Cave National Park, a remnant of this lost pageant lives on. Bison still roam the grasslands, persevering through brute strength and bulk, and pronghorns graze watchfully, ready to sprint from sight at the least hint of danger. Prairie dogs stand warily near their burrows, ignoring the grazers while scanning the skies for hungry hawks and eagles.

All of these animals once played important roles in ensuring the health of the prairie, and they continue to do so in the park. Consider the bison. Surely such large animals must devastate the grasslands with their con-

Bands of grazing pronghorns are a common sight at Wind Cave. Fleet of foot and endowed with keen eyesight, they *usually spot potential predators long before they pose any threat but, if pressed, can easily outrun most pursuers.*

Snowdrift Avenue, in the northeastern part of the Wind Cave labyrinth, was named for its extensive displays of frostwork, fragile tufts of snow-white aragonite crystals that cover large areas of its walls and ceilings. Not included on the usual routes for guided tours of the cave, it retains in full measure the sense of mystery and unexpected discovery that greeted the first intrepid explorers of Wind Cave's hidden maze of winding tunnels and passageways.

stant grazing, trampling, and wallowing—or so it would seem. But bison also create fertilizer, which eventually becomes a source of vital nutrients for the grasses. Burrowing rodents, especially prairie dogs, keep the soil open to moisture and air. Digging far deeper than any plow, they have aerated, mixed, and moved the earth for untold centuries. In its own way, each species helps enrich and maintain the grasslands, even as it perpetuates its own kind.

Of all the animals on the plains, few seem better adapted to their surroundings than the pronghorn. A marvel of grace and speed, it can escape danger by covering the ground in 20-foot leaps that add up to running rates of 60 miles an hour. Unlike most other fast runners, moreover, it can maintain high speeds for long distances, its endurance made possible in large part by its oversized heart, windpipe, and lungs.

Although flight is its primary defense, the pronghorn usually spots danger long before it can pose a threat. The placement of its eyes on the sides of its head gives the animal a wide-angle view of the world, and its eyesight is as keen as that of a person using eight-power binoculars. Even the newborn young are not without protection. Lying motionless on the ground, they rely on protective coloration for camouflage. They also are completely odorless: dogs have frequently been observed passing within a few feet of day-old pronghorns and never noticing them.

Like the bison and prairie dog, the pronghorn is a social animal, and like them it has various means of communication. Most obvious is the patch of white hairs on the animal's rump—hairs that can be raised when danger is sighted. Passing from animal to animal, this flashing white alarm note quickly spreads the warning throughout the pronghorn band. In addition to this visual signal the animals emit a special odor, again a silent and compelling alert.

Admirably adapted to the harsh extremes of the Great Plains climate, the pronghorn is undaunted by both searing heat and freezing cold. Like the prairie dog and kangaroo rat, it is even independent of a source of water, for it can get all it needs from the plants it eats. In times of drought, pronghorns sometimes survive entirely on the moisture found in the fleshy pads of prickly pear cacti.

Billions of animals. How was it possible, the first white settlers wondered, that so many animals could exist in such a barren land? The secret was in the highly nutritious grasses that licked about their knees. Grasses grow from the bases rather than the tips of their leaves, a significant trait that allows them to be severely grazed without suffering permanent damage. They can go dormant during times of drought, and they rejuvenate quickly after fires. And grasslands contain far more living plant material than one might expect. On every square foot of ground, many square feet of leaves are turned toward the sun, converting its energy to food—more than enough to support the wealth of wildlife that once flooded across the Great Plains and still survives in places like Wind Cave.

Temple of darkness
But if light and life and limitless space are the hallmarks of the prairie world, Wind Cave has its darker side, too—its underground realm. It is anything but a feeling of spaciousness that greets the visitor when the cave's entry door is opened and the descent begins. Even with modern conveniences—staircases, handrails, electric lights—a certain sense of apprehension descends as the narrow stairway steepens and turns, leaving day-

light and sound behind as it enters the confining rock.

To understand the tunnellike passages, it is necessary to go back in time. The thick beds of limestone that contain the cave were deposited some 345 to 360 million years ago, when this region lay beneath the sea. Later, beginning about 65 million years ago, the Black Hills were formed when a huge subterranean mass of molten rock welled upward, bulging the overlying sedimentary rocks into a great dome. On the high central part of the dome, the soft upper layers of limestone were quickly eroded away, leaving the harder rocks underneath to form the major peaks of the Black Hills. Around the margins of the uplift, where Wind Cave is located, the limestone was not completely stripped away by erosion. During the formation of the dome, however, the limestone was subjected to great stress, and it became riddled with cracks and fissures. Over the eons, surface water percolated through the cracks, slowly dissolving the limestone and enlarging the fissures into the narrow passageways we find today.

Deep inside the cave, wandering through these subterranean tunnels, most visitors tend to speak in hushed tones, sensing that sound is unwelcome here. Even the voice of the guide seems out of place. And then for a few moments the guide, too, falls silent as he turns off the lights. Darkness and a profound, eerie stillness engulf the cave. This is not mere gloom or hush; it is utter void. Close the eyes; open them; strain the ears—nothing makes any difference. Light and sound have vanished. Mercifully the lights are turned on again, but the cave no longer seems quite the same. It has become an ancient, alien temple of utter darkness.

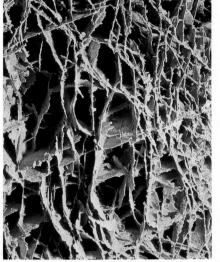

Boxwork, formed of thin, protruding blades of calcite, is Wind Cave's signature formation.

Even so, it is a beautifully adorned temple. Above ground, water can be a savage sculptor, wild and continental in scale; here below it is an artisan, invariably patient, steady, and controlled. Among the formations in Wind Cave are some with names that describe their appearance: popcorn, frostwork, mule-ear drapery, and dogtooth spar. But Wind Cave is best known for its boxwork. This too was named for its appearance: its grids of thin, protruding blades reminded early cavers of the boxes found in old-fashioned post offices. Indeed, the large room in which they first encountered boxwork was named the Post Office.

Boxwork is Wind Cave's most widespread and distinctive structure. Nowhere else is it found in such abundance or variety. Large forms up to three feet deep are called cratework; smaller forms are known as lacework. Whatever the size, boxwork was created by

groundwater seeping into the interlocking networks of cracks and fissures in the limestone. The water carried dissolved calcium carbonate that slowly crystallized into calcite in the cracks. Harder than the surrounding limestone, the blades of calcite were left behind in bold relief when the limestone between them eventually dissolved away.

The boxwork and other cave features still look much as they did when the water table dropped about 40 million years ago. Some water still seeps through pores and crevices in the limestone, but it is not enough to noticeably alter the contours of the cave. The scarcity of water and nutrients entering from the surface also means that Wind Cave is relatively devoid of life. Bushy-tailed woodrats may wander in from time to time and a few bats roost in the cave, but the only known permanent residents are a few springtails and cave crickets.

The cave, however, has its other attractions, all of them casting their own magical spell. Visitors here walk in a world magnificent with mystery, old beyond measure, and more extensive than charts can yet show. They seem to regain their speech only at tour's end, as they await the elevator that will return them to a familiar world of light, sound, and seasons.

Prairie song

After an hour in the cave, the contrast of the outside world is instantly appreciated. Even the cloudiest day seems radiant. The call of a meadowlark is impossibly loud, the scents of pine and wild plum unexpectedly pungent. The strange medley of whistles and squawks of a yellow-breasted chat, the warbler that lays claim to the ravine along the trail, erases the last residue of cave hush, beckoning the senses back to the complex world of wind and sun.

Toward evening, elk steal out of the pine forest to graze on the open prairie. From the pines, owls hoot in the gathering dimness and seem to be answered by nighthawks veering across the dark sky. The prairie wind quiets at dusk, rustling the grasses only furtively, but sometimes in the night it gathers strength.

The wind makes many sounds in many places, but if it ever makes music it is here on the Great Plains. "Prairie song" we might call it, this wind in the grasses mingled with the joyous melody of the meadowlark. Prairie song—it is the chant of the vanished Sioux and the thunder of the herds they hunted long ago. And in one place it is also a lone note: the moan of air gushing from a vast cave that has innermost secrets it shares only with the wind.

Yellowstone

*"It is a fabulous country, the only fabulous country;
it is the one place where miracles not only happen, but
where they happen all the time."*
Thomas Wolfe

There are many Yellowstones. Each in its own way is something of a miracle. That they should all exist together—here in this one place, at this moment in time—is among the major miracles of this truly fabulous country of ours.

There is the historian's Yellowstone: the world's first national park—indeed, the place where the very idea of national parks was given shape. There is the tourist's Yellowstone: a unique landscape of overwhelming scenic splendor and natural wonders. There is the scientist's Yellowstone: an immense volcanic cauldron where a bubble of fire from deep inside the earth fuels the world's greatest concentration of geysers. There is the naturalist's Yellowstone: a rich and varied wilderness of forests, lakes, rivers, mountains, plains, and canyons, inhabited by every animal species (including the gray wolf) that was here when the first pioneers ventured into the place. And there is the Yellowstone that belongs to these creatures of the wild: not miraculous to their eyes, simply a place where life goes on as nature intended.

On the coldest and clearest of winter nights, when the temperature falls far below zero for the first time in the season and the sky is aglitter with brittle starlight, vast stretches of this last, wildlings' Yellowstone are locked in snowy silence. Nothing moves; the stillness seems unbreakable, eternal.

Then strange noises begin. The forest cracks with sounds like rifle fire. Across the icy expanses of the lakes the silence itself grows taut—and then seems to moan and sing. In the primeval unseen, the atmosphere echoes and reverberates with chords struck from the

Old Faithful, the crown jewel of Yellowstone, erupts in a cloud of steam. The water from thousands of geysers and hot springs keeps parts of the Firehole River from freezing, and so elk graze on its banks when snow is on the ground.

very sinews of the earth. (Explanations exist: the sap in the trees is freezing, splitting the wood; the ice is straining as it freezes and expands. But explanations matter little on such nights.)

Yet on this same night, in another part of this huge park, the sounds of flowing water, gabbling waterfowl, and snorting animals can be heard. In and around the waters of the geyser basins near the Firehole River—even though the steam above hot springs shatters into ice crystals as it meets the air—plant life grows and insects continue their activities. Elk and bison paw the ground, still warm enough to melt the falling snow. Just enough warm water flows into the Firehole River to keep it from freezing, and so ducks and geese swim through the winter.

Here, too, strange sounds disturb the darkness: hissing, burping, splashing, and lapping in the night. The air seems to breathe, first with exhalations—warm, moist, and foul smelling—and then with inrushes of cold night air. From time to time there is the shriek of a distant fumarole venting steam. And then a soft rumble comes from deep within the earth, the clearing of a monstrously powerful throat, and Old Faithful itself spews and splashes.

The queen of geysers

Old Faithful, the symbol of Yellowstone Park, is an impresario: its eruptions are pure showmanship. Each begins, as though to gather an audience, with a few spurts and splashes that go on intermittently for as long as half an hour. Occasionally a series of splashes seems to be reaching for a crescendo, and a spurt shoots 10, 20, even 30 feet into the air; but such tantalizing displays are mere overtures to the main show. The eruption, when it finally happens, gives little warning. A splash simply swells into a column of water that rises higher and higher, becoming a great steaming fountain well over 100 feet high—sometimes nearly 200.

The spectacle is awesome. During the 1½ to 5 minutes that the geyser "plays," hurling as much as 8,400 gallons of water high into the air, it is a thing of tremendous power. It is also a thing of great beauty—graceful, symmetrical, and never entirely predictable.

Contrary to popular opinion, Old Faithful does not go off every hour on the hour, nor by any other clockwork schedule. It keeps its own time, following a complex set of rules. Once you understand these rules, however, you find that Old Faithful really *is* faithful in its fashion. It announces its future plans by varying the size, duration, and intensity of its eruptions.

The intervals between eruptions average 79 minutes, but they have been known to range from about half an hour to a full two hours. In general, a powerful, long-lasting eruption is followed by a long rest period, and a brief eruption by a shorter one; but there are so many variations on this simple formula that books have been written on the subject. After each eruption, a park ranger—who has timed the play with a stopwatch and estimated the height, volume, and temperature of the water—posts a sign telling when the next eruption is likely to occur. The ranger is seldom more than 10 minutes or so off the mark.

The ground around the geyser's mouth is covered by a broad, gently sloping cone of pearly gray rock. The rock has two names: it is called either sinter or geyserite. It is made largely of silica, dissolved by hot water from stone deep beneath the ground, then carried up to harden upon the surface. Other minerals, especially sulfur and iron, sometimes add hushed tones of yellow, purple, rose, lavender, and other colors.

Tremendous quantities are involved; each time Old Faithful erupts, 65 pounds of silica spew up from its vent. At the same time, each eruption adds a thin coat to the inner walls of the underground plumbing. Someday even this most dependable of geysers will become clogged, and the water will have to find a new route upward. Perhaps a new geyser will be born, or perhaps the flow will be added to an existing pool or geyser.

Old Faithful is one of nearly 350 geysers in Yellowstone National Park. This is the world's largest collec-

In the early autumn chill, as wisps of morning mist suffuse the Hayden Valley, a young bull moose feeds on marshy growth along the meandering Yellowstone River. Solitary in the distance, a bison grazes on a river-bracketed meadow.

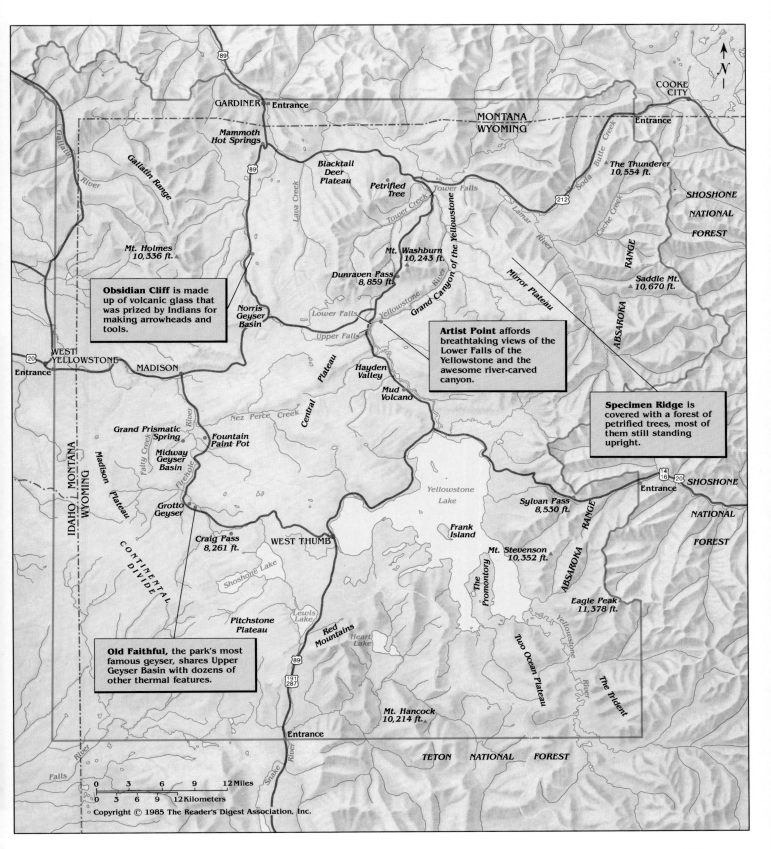

N

COOKE CITY

GARDINER Entrance

MONTANA
WYOMING

Entrance

Mammoth
Hot Springs

The Thunderer
10,554 ft.

Blacktail
Deer
Plateau

Petrified
Tree

Tower Falls

SHOSHONE

NATIONAL

FOREST

Gallatin Range

Gallatin River

Lava Creek

Tower Creek

212

Soda Butte Creek

Lamar River

Cache Creek

ABSAROKA RANGE

Mt. Holmes
10,336 ft.

Mt. Washburn
10,243 ft.

Grand Canyon of the Yellowstone

Mirror Plateau

Saddle Mt.
10,670 ft.

Obsidian Cliff is made up of volcanic glass that was prized by Indians for making arrowheads and tools.

Dunraven Pass
8,859 ft.

Yellowstone River

Norris
Geyser
Basin

Lower Falls

Upper Falls

Artist Point affords breathtaking views of the Lower Falls of the Yellowstone and the awesome river-carved canyon.

WEST
YELLOWSTONE

20

Entrance

MADISON

Central Plateau

Hayden
Valley

Mud
Volcano

Specimen Ridge is covered with a forest of petrified trees, most of them still standing upright.

Nez Perce Creek

Grand Prismatic
Spring

Fountain
Paint Pot

Fairy Creek

Firehole River

Madison Plateau

Midway
Geyser
Basin

IDAHO MONTANA
MONTANA WYOMING

Yellowstone
Lake

14
16 20 SHOSHONE

Entrance

NATIONAL

FOREST

Grotto
Geyser

Sylvan Pass
8,530 ft.

Frank
Island

CONTINENTAL DIVIDE

Craig Pass
8,261 ft.

WEST THUMB

Mt. Stevenson
10,352 ft.

The Promontory

ABSAROKA RANGE

Eagle Peak
11,378 ft.

Shoshone Lake

Old Faithful, the park's most famous geyser, shares Upper Geyser Basin with dozens of other thermal features.

Pitchstone
Plateau

Lewis
Lake

Red
Mountains

Heart
Lake

89

191
287

Two Ocean Plateau

Yellowstone River

The Trident

Mt. Hancock
10,214 ft.

Entrance

TETON NATIONAL FOREST

Snake River

Falls

0   3   6   9   12 Miles

0   3   6   9   12 Kilometers

Copyright © 1985 The Reader's Digest Association, Inc.

tion, and it includes some that are bigger than Old Faithful, several that are more regular, and a few that are more spectacular—but none that combines the three elements in quite the same way. Although its pattern of behavior changed little for at least a century, making Old Faithful unique among geysers, it has shown signs of change in recent years.

The waters of Excelsior Geyser, once the largest in the park, used to shoot periodically more than 300 feet high. Its last eruption was in 1985, however; since then it has behaved like a hot spring, placidly pouring about 5.8 million gallons of scalding water every day from its gaping, steam-shrouded crater into the nearby Firehole River. Even so, no one can state with certainty that Excelsior will not resume its violent activity at any moment. Only a fool tries to second-guess a geyser.

Riverside Geyser, on the east bank of the Firehole, is at present more dependable than Old Faithful, but its main claim to fame is that it does not shoot straight up, as most geysers do. For about 20 minutes every 7 hours, it sends a beautiful 75-foot plume of water arching gracefully over the river.

Grotto Geyser is irregular but consistent; it plays about half the time, day in and day out, but you can never be sure exactly when it will do so. Though its steaming waters shoot only about 20 to 30 feet high, the eruptions are spectacular because of the fantastic, dwarfish shapes through which the water spurts. The geyser's cone is slowly building up around the twisted remains of trees that once grew in this spot; now,

encased in geyserite deposits, they are bowed and bent over the mouth of the geyser, forming the eerie grotto for which it is named.

Some geysers are named for the distinctive cones that have built up around their vents. Beehive Geyser is one such; at irregular and unpredictable intervals a powerful stream of water squirts through the small hole in the top of its big, rounded cone, sometimes reaching heights of 200 feet. Castle Geyser, possibly the oldest in the park, has an architectural-looking cone that measures 120 feet around and is still growing. Its eruptions have two phases; first water is lifted about 80 feet high for as long as 20 minutes, then a jet of steam roars forth for about an hour.

Others, known as fountain geysers, have no cones. Great Fountain Geyser is the most spectacular of these; every nine hours or so several powerful bursts break the surface of the broad pool that covers its vent— scalding columns that may reach 200 feet in height.

Fire and ice

All of Yellowstone's geysers have one thing in common: they result from a link between ancient volcanism beneath the earth and water that falls from above. The same is true of all the water that bubbles, boils, spurts, and hisses from the ground in whatever form throughout the park. It is all surface water—rain and snow— that has trickled down thousands of feet through areas of weakness, or faults, in the earth's crust.

These faults date far back into time, as does the

Hot springs are deep channels through which water flows with deceptive calm from the molten interior of the planet—closer to the surface in Yellowstone than anywhere else on earth. So Yellowstone has hot springs galore. Grand Prismatic Spring (left), a colorful medallion of light and living things, measures 370 feet wide; for scale, note the tiny people on the boardwalk.

How Thermal Features Work

Hot springs, fumaroles, and geysers occur because surface water seeps steadily downward to meet the heat of the earth's molten interior, only three miles below Yellowstone's surface.

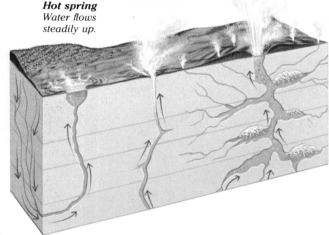

Geyser
Pockets of steam create great pressure.

Fumarole
Only enough water enters to form steam.

Hot spring
Water flows steadily up.

bubble of volcanic fire that heats the water. Some 65 million years ago, when the upthrust of the Rocky Mountains began, this area was a point of great stress. Molten rock, or magma, was forced upward from deep within the earth and—starting about 50 million years ago—erupted in the form of great volcanoes. The massive eruptions continued off and on for another 10 million years or more, building mountainous cones and spewing ash over vast stretches of the Great Plains.

One of the legacies of this long period of intermittent volcanic activity can be seen on the steep face of Specimen Ridge, in the northern part of the park. Here erosion has exposed entire petrified forests—27 of them, one atop the other—of standing redwoods, walnuts, sycamores, magnolias, hickories, persimmons, maples, dogwoods, and other warm-climate trees that grew in the broad, gentle valleys of that era.

Each forest grew for several hundred years, spreading at the feet of seemingly dormant volcanoes. Then, when the volcanoes returned to violent life for months, years, even decades at a time, each forest was buried to depths of up to 15 feet by a constant rain of debris, ranging from fine ash to boulder-sized cinders to viscous mud. Leaves, branches, and bark were stripped away; the tops of the trees snapped off or decayed; but beneath the ash many roots were firm and many trunks still stood. Between eruptions, as the devastation was slowly covered by soil and new forests, water seeped down through the ash and leached silica from it; and gradually this silica replaced the living tissue of the

trees with quartz, beautifully patterned and bronzed by oxides of iron. The petrified trees had passed a boundary rarely crossed, moving from the organic to the geologic, from the temporal to the eternal.

After dwindling and sputtering for many millions of years, those ancient volcanoes finally died out. Over the eons, most of their cones were eroded away; further destruction took place under the crushing weight of glaciers that pushed down from the Beartooth Mountains to the north some 2½ million years ago.

But the volcanism of ancient times was not dead, merely trapped. Two giant pockets of molten rock and superheated gas were less than a mile below the surface. Between further periods of glaciation, when heavy rivers of ice gouged the land and weighed it down, there were times when the tightly capped pressure had to be released. Then the ground bulged, stretched, and cracked like the unvented crust of a bubbling fruit pie. Finally and suddenly, in giant explosions similar to those that formed Crater Lake, but hundreds of times larger—perhaps the largest explosions the world has ever known—the trapped material burst through the surface. Ash, rocks, and fire spewed across the continent. Three times this happened—2,000,000 years ago, 1,300,000 years ago, and 600,000 years ago. It was the third explosion that created today's landscape.

Hollowed out, the land collapsed into itself, creating a vast pit, or caldera—the word is Spanish for "cauldron"—nearly a mile deep and up to 50 miles across. Still the volcanic fury continued. Over the next 500,000

Storm clouds gather over Mammoth Hot Springs in the northwest corner of the park. Here, where hot water rises through limestone rather than lava, it has shaped balconies and terraces of porcelainlike travertine.

Lazing in the winter sun, a young bobcat awaits nightfall, when it will begin to prowl after rabbits, snowshoe hares, squirrels, woodrats, and other small prey. On a good night, it may make many kills, most of which it will hide for harder times.

Many regard the view from Artist Point, looking up the Grand Canyon of the Yellowstone toward the 308-foot Lower Falls, as the park's most spectacular vista. The volcanic rock of the canyon walls, naturally gray or pinkish, was given its brilliant yellow stain by minerals in seeping hot water.

years, at least 30 lava flows filled the caldera, erasing all but the largest traces of it, such as the fragmented mountains that outline parts of its rim.

These lava flows are the dark gray, pink, and brown rocks seen almost everywhere in Yellowstone today; most of it is rhyolite, a rough-textured rock built up by layers of flowing lava. Earlier volcanism left basalt, the harder, purer rock seen in the columns of the cliffs near Tower Falls. The glassy black face of Obsidian Cliff, in the northwestern part of the park, is a rare result of silica-rich lava's having pushed upward and cooled so quickly that few minerals could crystallize in its substance. Indian peoples made regular journeys to gather the brittle black obsidian, hard enough to scratch glass.

Long after the main caldera collapsed, yet another, smaller explosion and collapse formed the depression that was to become the West Thumb of Yellowstone Lake. Meanwhile, glaciers came and went—the last one melted here 10,000 to 15,000 years ago—and earthquakes and other violent phenomena cracked the comparatively thin shell of lava-born rock that lies between the surface and the primal heat of the planet.

Subterranean pressure cooker

As water trickles down through the cracks and nears molten rock, it becomes extremely hot—much hotter than it ever could on the surface. This is because it is under pressure, and—as anyone who has ever used a pressure cooker probably knows—pressure raises the boiling point of water. At Yellowstone's elevations, water normally boils at about 199° F, but, trapped in the deep passageways beneath geysers, it can reach temperatures of 400° F and more without boiling. Yet although it cannot boil, it can circulate. The hottest water rises to a point where the pressure is less intense, and then begins to bubble.

As the bubbles move up through passages in the earth, they push water before them, and it leaps out of the ground in small spurts. Sometimes this is all there is to a geyser: it spurts continuously. The big geysers, such as Old Faithful, are another story. When water spurts out of them, it is as though the lid were taken off the pressure cooker. Instantly, the deep mass of superheated water boils and roars from the earth.

Spectacular as they are, geysers are but a small part

of Yellowstone's incredible range of thermal features. In all, there are about 10,000 such features in the park, ranging from fumaroles—roaring hillside vents or small whistling holes from which no water emerges, only live steam—to beautifully tinted, placid-looking hot lakes. There are bubbling mud pots, caused when fumaroles emerge into subterranean basins, sending acid groundwater up to melt rock into clay. In an area known as the Fountain Paint Pot, hot gases belch up through such mud-filled pits, staining the mud with colored minerals to create a rainbowed moonscape of foot-high cones and plate-sized craters that *ploop* and *pop* and reshape themselves like the work of some demented medieval alchemist. Elsewhere are ominous acid lakes and cauldrons aboil with a sulfurous black broth.

Hot pools, into which water does not erupt but flows steadily, are often delicately colored, both by minerals and by tiny living creatures that thrive in an unlikely world of water that is too cool to boil yet too hot to be touched. Most of these algae and bacteria form thick green clumps in water that ranges from 122° to 140° F. As the water temperature rises, however, different kinds of algae are able to thrive. Their colors are a guide to the heat of the water. First the green life is replaced by orange, and then—at 163° to 167° F—the orange gives way to yellow. There is even life in the water that approaches the boiling point, but it is tiny, colorless, invisible to our eyes.

In combination with the minerals in the water and in the geyserite beneath it, the living organisms turn hot pools into amazingly patterned palettes of color. In the depths of large springs the water shades to a deep, cobalt blue; but if the geyserite on the bottom contains much sulfur, the mineral's intense yellow combines with the blue of the water to create luminous and variable shades of green. Around the edges, depending on the heat of the water and its acidity, algae add tones of yellow, bright green, orange, brown, and even purple.

A misty landscape

Most of the park's thermal features are concentrated in the geyser basins of the west-central part of the park. This rare and unpredictable landscape—threatening, powerful, and touched with subtle beauty—occupies much of the great lava-filled caldera that is now, for the most part, a broad broken plateau.

In the channels where water flows out of pools, the temperature patterns show plainly; the main flows are often too hot for visible life, but along the edges filaments of colored algae undulate slowly in the current. The channels themselves are beds of pearly geyserite, shot with colored minerals and lumpy with the coated shapes of sticks, pine cones, bones—anything that has fallen into the water. Along the borders grow dense clumps of yellow monkey flowers; nurtured by the warm soil and steamy air, they bloom early, and their bright blossoms continue all through the summer.

Hot water flows across much of the ground. Running

down glistening slopes or terraces of mineral-stained geyserite, it blends into a landscape that is both sinister and beautiful. Steam drifts out of the ground in small wisps, venting through unseen cracks and jarring the senses with the smell of hydrogen sulfide. Here and there, reedy plants tolerate beds of warm mud. The hoofprints of bison and elk can endure for weeks in places where the sulfur-scented mud has dried.

Distant pines are hazy through the mist. In front of them stand the bleached trunks of a forest of dead trees, barkless and branchless, testimony that the pattern of underground heat is sometimes restless. A few dead trunks have fallen, and their pale color blends into the barren earth. Yet all is not dead in the geyser basins.

Along the marshy banks of the Firehole River—misty with the steam of nearby hot springs, fumaroles, and geysers—a flock of sandhill cranes settles to feed. Moving slowly on their long, spindly legs, they poke with daggerlike beaks for the roots of marsh plants, and occasionally make quick jabs after tadpoles, frogs, or fish. Later in the season, when the marsh grasses bear seeds, the cranes will feed almost exclusively on the wild grain, forgoing meaty tidbits.

In the pines nearby, cow elk laze in the shade, and in the broad meadow through which the river meanders, a coyote is on the prowl. Searching the meadow, it covers a large area without much more than a pause. Abruptly it stops; it looks intently at something, waits, and then leaps soundlessly forward in a single bound. For a few seconds nothing can be seen above the grass but its tail, tense with excitement. The head reappears and the routing resumes. The prey, perhaps a mouse, was apparently faster than the coyote.

From somewhere among the sparse forests that cover the Twin Buttes—two rounded gray hills on the far side of the meadows—come two loud sounds. One is a low beating that begins slowly and within a second or two speeds up, like someone gaining momentum upon an Indian drum, and then quits. The other sound is that of wood being ripped apart by something powerful. The first sound is easy to identify: it is the courtship drumming of a male grouse. The other may be the sound of a bear, perhaps even a grizzly, looking under fallen logs for insects, grubs, ground squirrels, and mice.

A tapestry of green

Northeastward, hazy in the distance, looms 10,243-foot Mount Washburn, the northern part of a 50-million-year-old volcano that lost much of its bulk in the collapse of the great Yellowstone Caldera. Despite that cataclysm, the summit is still almost 3,000 feet above the surrounding wilderness. It is only a few miles north of the center of the park, and the view from the top is panoramic, encompassing most of the park.

About five percent of Yellowstone is covered by water, most of which is in Yellowstone Lake. Another 80 percent is forested, and 80 percent of *that* is dominated by one kind of tree—the lodgepole pine. The lodgepoles do well here because they can survive on poor soil, and the rhyolite rock—born of the lava that filled the great caldera—breaks down into coarse, sandy soil that is poor indeed in many mineral nutrients. On hillsides, lakeshores, lower mountain slopes, and around the edges of meadows, the lodgepoles' slender, upright trunks, covered with thin, scalelike bark of brown or gray, crowd together, bearing their sparse crowns 50 feet or more above the forest floor.

In the clear mountain air the trees do not fade into distant haze as they seem to when viewed from lower elevations. Instead they gradually lose their individual identities, weaving themselves into a gently textured carpet. Stands of quaking aspens stipple the landscape, their soft green foliage creating a subtle, summer-long mosaic with the deeper tones of the conifers—a contrast that intensifies to high drama when the aspen leaves are touched with autumn color.

On higher slopes—perhaps beginning at about 8,000 feet—Englemann spruce and subalpine fir mix with the

A solitary black bear, prowling through the early summer, is always looking for something to eat—and it will eat almost anything. By late autumn, when it retires into a restless semihibernation, it may have gained 250 pounds.

lodgepole pines. There is no strict cutoff, but as elevations increase, the rock of older volcanoes stands above the rhyolite, and it breaks down into richer soil. Hence, the yellowish-green lodgepole tapestry gradually incorporates the deep blue-greens of fir and spruce, until finally only the dark tones remain.

During the summer of 1988, drought and unprecedented winds caused intense fires in Yellowstone and surrounding areas. The face of the park changed drastically. Fortunately, vast sections of the dense forest survived, and losses to wildlife were surprisingly light. After the fire, regeneration began on a grand scale. Burned areas turned green, and meadows resprouted. In just a few years' time, most of Yellowstone will have attained a new splendor.

The mountaintop world

On the flanks of nearby mountains, the tapestry diminishes, grows ragged, and finally disappears. The peaks look bald and dead. But here on Mount Washburn grow the gnarled whitebark pines that survive on all but a few of the highest peaks. Built to withstand wind, dryness, and heavy snows, they shelter one another from wintry blasts. Between and above them is the alpine tundra, where pikas scurry among rocks, gathering greenery to live on in winter, and where regal bighorn sheep move confidently on windswept ridges; every summer, a herd makes its home on Mount Washburn's slopes, the males holding their heads high to bear up the weight of their massive crowns of horns. Here, too—tenacious, but fragile enough to be erased by footsteps—are the lichens, grasses, and miniature flowering plants of the alpine tundra. For a few weeks in July, the tundra blooms with alpine buttercups, clover, forget-me-nots, phlox, and other tiny blossoms.

Distant mountain ranges meet the horizon in all directions. Northward are the snaggled, snowy Beartooths; to the west, the Gallatins; far to the south are the white-capped Tetons; and stretching along the park's eastern boundary is a range of barren peaks called the Absarokas. They, like Mount Washburn, are remnants of ancient volcanoes that now mark a rim of the Yellowstone Caldera; they form a wall between the pocket in which Yellowstone lies and the Great Plains that stretch eastward to the Mississippi.

At the foot of the Absarokas is the shining expanse of Yellowstone Lake. Measuring 20 miles long, with a surface area of 136 square miles, it is almost an inland sea. It is a cold lake, its depths never warming to 40° F. Cutthroat trout thrive in its clear waters. Water birds ride the winds above—including many kinds that one associates with the ocean. Cormorants range the waves, terns wheel and soar, and gulls hang motionless on the wind. White pelicans fly low over the water, their long wings sweeping rhythmically in slow, powerful strokes. Ducks bob in large flotillas, and flocks of geese fly purposefully along the shore, honking as they go.

Like any large body of water, Yellowstone Lake has

Though it was once a living thing, this petrified tree trunk, standing high atop Specimen Ridge, is now a rock relic of unimaginably distant times, when volcanic eruptions buried forest upon forest under deep layers of ash.

many moods. On calm summer nights it can reflect the moon and stars flawlessly. But when gales churn its surface, whitecaps 10 feet high can smash against the gravelly shorelines or eat away at bluffs until trees lose their footing and fall into the churning waters. In winter, it is a vast Arctic tableland, and sweeping winds pile 20-foot snowdrifts over islands and along the shoreline.

Landscape of the sky

Because of Yellowstone's elevation—generally between 7,000 and 8,500 feet—the air tends to be clear and dry during the summer: pleasantly warm in the sun, sharply cool in the shadows, often chilly at night. Puffy white cumulus clouds, beautiful against the deep blue sky, drift eastward overhead. But because Yellowstone is in a pocket surrounded by high peaks, its weather can change in odd ways.

Sometimes, in the middle levels of the atmosphere above the gentle cumulus, strange, lens-shaped white clouds ride invisible winds. These are mountain wave clouds, formed as air flows up over westward peaks, cools, and condenses into saucer shapes. Often they presage nothing, simply forming and dissipating for hours in the undulating atmosphere. But on other days they are the forerunners of thunderclouds that boil quickly upward into the clear western sky.

If the evening is warm, a luminous wall of thunderheads may even form over the *eastern* edge of the park, fed by hot air that rises along the front range of the Rockies. Then Yellowstone Lake is bathed in shadowless white light reflected from the billowing clouds, and everything becomes perfectly still. For long, hushed, breathless moments the park waits while thunder rolls and lightning flickers through the towers and battlements that seethe in the east. Often the storm remains only a distant and dramatic presence; but often, too, in apparent contradiction to the normal scheme of things, the thunderhead spreads backward, westward, over the park, and the air turns violent.

From whatever direction they come, Yellowstone's

thunderstorms possess a stunning power to mix the summer air, lifting it and then pushing it earthward again. Rain is sucked high into the atmosphere, where the air is below freezing, and then flung down in the form of sleet, or hail, or even snow. Temperatures can drop from 75° F to the low 30's in less than an hour, transforming a warm, dry afternoon into a cold, wet evening. By morning the temperature, even in July or August, is likely to be below freezing, and snow may cover the ground. In early June or late August, such storms sometimes dump several inches of it.

Marshes and grassland
Northward from the lake flows the Yellowstone River, quietly meandering at first through a flatulent, sulfurous landscape of mud volcanoes—where the seething thermal features have such apt names as Mud Caldron, Sizzling Basin, Black Dragon's Caldron, Sour Lake, and Sulphur Caldron—and then into the broad, beautiful Hayden Valley. This flat, sandy saucer of land, the bottom of a lake during the last ice age, is now among the largest and loveliest of the park's many peaceful pockets of green.

When spring comes to the valley in late May or June, and patches of snow—thick, dirty, and strewn with pine needles—slowly melt into the soggy soil, vibrant green grasses surge from the warming earth and delicate

white spring beauties seem to leap out of the ground by the thousands. Soon tall spikes of crimson paintbrush and stalks of deep blue lupine wave in the gentle air. Flowers in all colors and sizes swell to garland the surrounding ridges and caress the meadows. Great herds of elk, drifting as quietly as wisps of steam, move from the forests to join mule deer, pronghorns, and other grazing beasts on the open meadows.

Summer, once it begins, comes quickly. During the warm, lazy days, a circling red-tailed hawk rides a column of warm air above the valley on motionless wings, its sharp eyes scanning the riverside marshes, the meadows, the sage-studded rolling rangeland, and the distant forest fringes. Directly below, almost hidden by reeds, a Canada goose and her six downy goslings feed on aquatic growth, floating downstream on the broad, clear Yellowstone River as they nibble. A little farther downriver a group of white pelicans circle and settle onto the water with military precision. Forming a line, the birds begin to fish cooperatively, slapping the water with their wings as they herd their prey toward the shallows.

Along the marshy banks two moose methodically browse, dipping their long snouts deeply to pull up water plants. Some distance from the river a few bison move along a hillside, grazing as they go; their great chocolate-brown bodies look almost like boulders or

A female Wilson's warbler (it lacks the male's black cap) hunts insects on branches chilled by summer snow. The bird builds its cuplike nest of grass in thickets near such streams as Soda Butte Creek. In the distance are peaks of the Absaroka Range.

tree stumps. Near the edge of a pine forest about a half mile beyond, another large, brown thing moves—a bear, exploring the hillside, pawing up roots and sampling its finds. The large brown beasts are of no interest to the circling hawk. But not far from the bear, it sees the quick movement of a Uinta chipmunk, the white stripes on its back flashing in the sun. With a scream, the hawk stoops, talons first, upon its lunch.

Canyon of light

The Yellowstone River meanders northward across the open, rolling landscape until, at the fringe of the valley, the land begins to change. The forest no longer keeps its distance; lodgepole pines crowd the banks. The banks themselves are higher, and outcroppings of dull gray rock seem to cramp the water's passage. The river runs deeper now and darker; its channel narrows and straightens. No longer a nursery for goslings, it flows with urgency, power, and resolve.

A roar is heard in the distance. Between its banks—now hundred-foot walls of steep, dark rock—the river dives onward at an ever-increasing rate. The very rocks resonate with the tempo of its passage. And then, in a burst of sound and spume, the water curls over a ledge to fall 109 feet into a deeper, darker chasm. This is the Upper Falls, and it is only a prelude. Ahead is the Lower Falls—and the Grand Canyon of the Yellowstone.

After roaring onward for half a mile or so between walls of dark stone, the river seems to hesitate at the brink of another precipice, and then it thunders over and down, into the canyon 308 feet below. The foot of the falls—indeed, its bottom third—is lost in the spray that washes the sides of the canyon and nurtures a broad swathe of low green mosses.

During the day, when rainbows ride the spray, the entire Grand Canyon of the Yellowstone is bathed in sunlight and suffused with a glow that reflects from its walls—the rich, yellow stone for which the river and the park itself are named. Through geologic time these rocks have taken on the colors of minerals in the hot water that seeps through their substance. Now it is as though the canyon were itself a source of light; one half expects the yellow glow to linger into night.

Approached from either side, the canyon is a sudden surprise. There is little in the relatively level, glacier-scoured landscape to suggest that this steep gorge, as much as 1,200 feet deep, lies just ahead. To one who knows the glacial history of the area, the V-shaped canyon is even more of a surprise.

It is a basic rule of geology that glaciers transform such narrow, V-shaped, river-cut canyons into broad, U-shaped valleys. As it happened here, however, the glacier flowed *across* the canyon, not down its length. It buried the land beneath ice up to 3,000 feet thick, crushed and rearranged the surface, scraped the canyon's rim, but did not carve its depths. The result is a sharp-edged gash in the earth, whose walls drop so precipitously that its depth is hard to judge.

The long-tailed weasel's sinuous body is built for moving easily through tight places. The voracious little hunter lives on mice, chipmunks, rabbits, birds, and anything else it can catch. In winter, its two-toned coat turns white.

When, from the rim, you watch an osprey, with a wingspan of five feet, dive and slowly diminish to a tiny dot, you begin to appreciate the scale of the scene before you. Standing on bare rock, astride a shallow scar left by a wall of glacial ice more than 10,000 years ago, you look down into a far deeper, older scar—the glowing chasm that was cut by rushing water through stone that once gushed molten from the fiery heart of the earth. For just a moment, you are on intimate terms with nature's most awesome forces.

It is the intimacy that is the essence of Yellowstone's many miracles. To walk on wooden boards a yard or less above a sea of boiling mud as a thunderstorm is born; to feel the air grow still and chill as steam billows; and then, through the warm, enveloping cloud, to feel the nips of a thousand sleety bits of ice upon your face—this is an experience of the soul. Many such experiences are here. In this park, the ancient elements of fire, water, air, and earth are all infused with the immense power of nature in her wildest dress, and their violent potential—like that of the lumbering bear of the forest or the moose that solemnly grazes in the shallows of a river—is a real and constant presence. Chaos threatens to erupt from every geyser, to bubble forth from cauldrons of seething mud, to crash down from sudden thunderclouds; and yet the powerful potential seldom overwhelms. Rather, it encloses, embraces, touches the visitor in ways that can never be forgotten.

It is our good fortune that those who came before us were so moved by the miracle of Yellowstone in all its facets that they took steps to keep it whole, to protect it as no land had ever been protected before. It is our responsibility to ensure that those who follow shall also inherit this place that nature and humankind, working in harmony, have preserved.

Yosemite

*"Things frail and fleeting . . . meeting here
and blending in countless forms, as if into this
one mountain mansion Nature had gathered
her choicest treasures."*   John Muir

Stretching for almost 400 miles near California's eastern border, the Sierra Nevada is a saw-toothed spine of blue-gray ridges and alabaster peaks—the longest and highest unbroken mountain range in the lower 48 states. At its stony heart lies Yosemite National Park, a spectacular showcase where wooded groves boast some of the world's largest trees, pageants of wildflowers strew color over ice-sculpted canyons, alpine gardens nestle at the foot of glaciers, and roaring waterfalls leap from the shoulders of enormous granite cliffs.

Unlike the Rockies and Cascades, the Sierra Nevada is not a chain of individual mountains but a single block of solid granite, ranging from 50 to 80 miles wide. A massive piece of the earth's crust that was thrust upward as a whole and then tilted by powerful geological forces deep within the earth, the Sierra rises more than 14,000 feet from low foothills on the west and culminates in a nearly perpendicular wall on the east. En masse, the great snow-topped range looks like an immense ocean wave surging mightily toward the east.

As the Sierra gradually tilted upward, the steeper incline turned mountain rivers into torrents that created V-shaped valleys as they sliced downward through the rock. The higher the peaks were thrust, the colder they became. More snow fell in winter than could melt in summer, building up an accumulation thousands of feet deep. Under this pressure, the snow hardened into glacial ice, and when the frozen fingers began creeping downslope, they followed the paths of least resistance: the valleys. The glaciers' great weight dramatically altered the landscape, broadening valleys, shearing mountaintops, and scooping out canyons and basins.

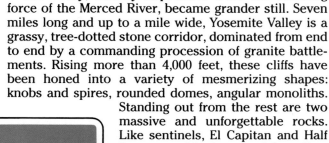

Neither snow nor dreamlike mists can totally obscure Half Dome's sheared face and hulking shape at the eastern end of Yosemite Valley. High above the stately evergreens, golden eagles nest on perilous cliffs.

One valley, already impressive from the chiseling force of the Merced River, became grander still. Seven miles long and up to a mile wide, Yosemite Valley is a grassy, tree-dotted stone corridor, dominated from end to end by a commanding procession of granite battlements. Rising more than 4,000 feet, these cliffs have been honed into a variety of mesmerizing shapes: knobs and spires, rounded domes, angular monoliths.

Standing out from the rest are two massive and unforgettable rocks. Like sentinels, El Capitan and Half Dome guard both ends of the valley. Throughout the world, their bold, vaulting silhouettes are symbols of this park.

Of the two, El Capitan—its name in Spanish means "The Captain"—most crowds the valley floor, its broad shoulders flanking the western gateway. It is the world's largest solid granite rock, and its substance is so strong that its base is nearly free of broken boulders and other rocky debris. With its sleek, nearly vertical profile rising 3,604 feet above the Merced like the prow of an ocean liner above the sea, El Capitan is unquestionably Yosemite's most precipitous rock.

At the opposite end of the valley is Half Dome, its huge, hulking shape looming like a monk's hooded head. Although its northwestern face looks as if a sharp cleaver had cut straight through, the prominent dome has never known a glacier's touch. Even during the fiercest glacial onslaught, when ice nearly filled the valley rim to rim, Half Dome's top 700 feet remained uncovered, like a rocky islet in a frozen sea. But glaciers affected Half Dome's summit nonetheless. As the ice moved down the valley, it undercut the mountain's base, causing the unsupported upper layers to break and fall atop the glacier. The face of the mountain has been sheared ever since.

There are many other domes in the park—Basket Dome, Sentinel Dome, Liberty Cap, Turtleback Dome, Mount Watkins, Mount Starr King. Each is a solid gran-

315

ite block, smoothly rounded like a new helmet and as barren as the Sahara. Contrary to popular belief, glaciers did not rub these enormous blocks into smooth domes. Rather, their roundness is the result of a process called exfoliation, by which granite sheds its outer layers as an onion sheds its skins. As temperatures change, the granite expands and contracts; this causes horizontal cracks to form and layers to develop in the rock. (Some of the granite layers are immense: Half Dome's measure 6 to 10 feet, and Royal Arches' may surpass 100.) Gradually, the granite's top layer rises, breaks apart, and peels off, relieving the pressure on the layer beneath and giving it room to rise. Over the course of eons, after many successive peelings, a dome could smooth itself right out of existence—as some undoubtedly have done. Solid granite is the only type of rock to form domes in this way, and such domes are relatively rare; Yosemite, in fact, has the world's largest collection.

Dancing waters

Before the Sierra was lifted, the Merced's tributaries joined the river with scarcely a ripple. But as the mountains rose higher and tilted more abruptly, the Merced cut deeper, abandoning the side streams that were unable to match its cutting edge. Stranded atop steep, jagged slopes, the streams cascaded from ledge to ledge on their way to the river. When the glaciers advanced on the valley, they sheared the slopes into nearly perpendicular walls, truncating the side streams even more. Now they were free-falling cataracts whose colossal heights punctuated the valley walls like watery exclamation points.

Known as "the place of dancing waters," Yosemite Valley is the perfect stage for an aquatic ballet of rainbowed waterfalls leaping, twirling, prancing from lofty chutes, and pirouetting from cliff to cliff. In spring, the performance becomes a full-blown extravaganza as snowmelt enlivens hundreds of streams that rush to join the regular cast in a magnificent aerial display. To be sure that their show does not pass unnoticed, the performers send up a thunderous roar that resounds throughout the valley. Unfortunately, the dance ends all too soon. By mid-August, most of the falls are bone-dry. Autumn rains renew some to wispy tendrils, and sunny winter days may start a bit of meltwater flowing; but frosty nights ice the ledges and turn the falls into frozen columns. One must wait for the melting waters of the next spring thaw for an encore.

More than half of America's highest waterfalls occur in this park, but because you generally see them from afar, it is difficult to tell how big they truly are. Trying to estimate their height or width is like guessing a star's size in the vastness of the heavens. Snow Creek and Sentinel falls are 2,000-foot cascades that tumble down ridged granite; Ribbon Fall, the park's highest single waterfall, is a white-water rocket dropping 1,612 feet. Bridalveil Fall, which never runs dry, plunges 620 feet,

and a grand and graceful rainbow often sweeps across its diaphanous mists. Even the 300-foot midgets are impressive. In any other place they would undoubtedly reign as monarchs, but here everything is measured against the champion—Yosemite Falls, highest in North America and second highest in the world. The 2,425-foot waterfall, equal in height to 13 Niagaras, descends in two thunderous phases: the Upper Fall drops 1,430 feet; the Lower Fall, 320. In between is a series of cascades that leap from one level to the next, whipping the water into a frenzy, splashing and spraying the sides of a quarter-mile gorge. From below, Yosemite Falls seems like one continuous waterfall, mighty and magnificent, a symbol of nature's power unleashed.

The falls eventually feed into a sometimes placid, sometimes stormy waterway that Spanish explorers named El Río de Nuestra Señora de la Merced, meaning "The River of Our Lady of Mercy." Beginning as a swift creek, the Merced first tumbles haphazardly down the Giant Stairway, a mountain slope with glacially carved steps. But after it roars down Nevada Fall, it becomes a river dashed to foam—a wild, aquatic avalanche that surges toward yet another swelling cascade, Vernal Fall. In just a half-mile stretch, the Merced drops 1,200 feet. Once the river levels out on the valley floor, it becomes little more than a lazy meander with riffled edges and deep, quiet pools—a sparkling blue thread winding its way down the long-forgotten corridor of ancient Lake Yosemite.

A vanished lake

The prehistoric lake had come and gone many times: meltwater from glacial withdrawals gave it life; glacial advances dried it up. When the climate finally warmed and the last glacier retreated upslope, meltwater once again filled the valley, re-creating ancient Lake Yosemite in all its glory. Stretching from wall to wall and almost seven miles in length, the lake was impounded on the east by Half Dome and on the west by a pile of rocky debris left by the glacier.

If time and the river had not obliterated Lake Yosemite, it would have been a world-class contender—a sapphire mirror reflecting majestic mountain walls, the play of light on granite, and ragged-edged clouds skimming the heights. But Lake Yosemite was not to last, for the very forces that gave it life insured its demise. As the two major watercourses, the Merced River and Tenaya Creek, dumped tons of sand and gravel into the lake, deltas began to form, and these gradually expanded, merged, and spread down the valley. The lake grew shallower and shallower and eventually began to shrink. Water-loving plants colonized the borders, gradually building up the soil so that meadow grasses and wildflowers could take up residence. The lake dried up and disappeared. With a solid earthen base firmly established, trees put down roots and became permanent settlers.

Nature is not quite finished with her long transforma-

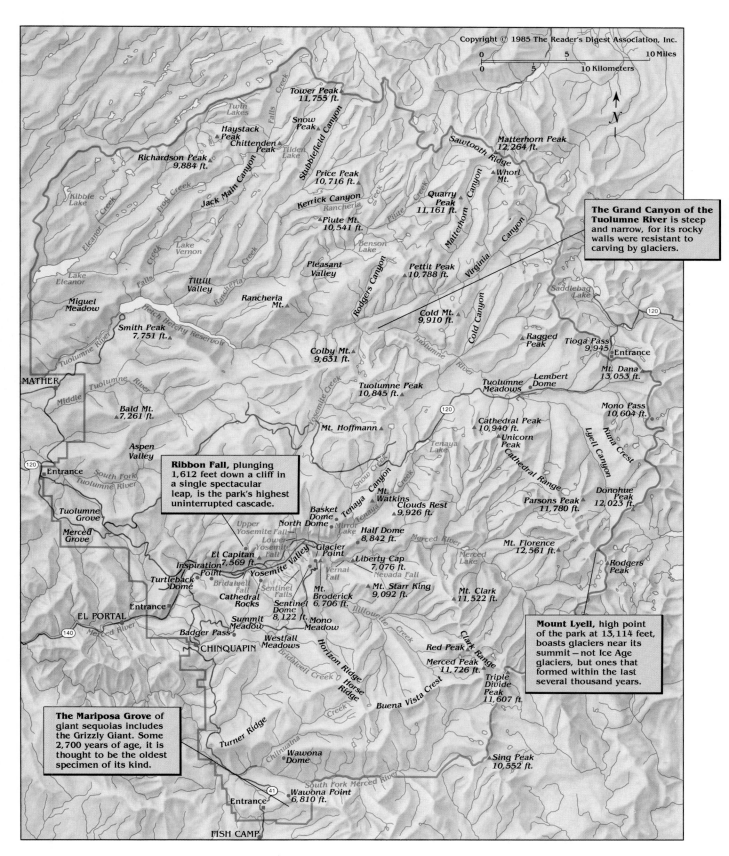

Copyright © 1985 The Reader's Digest Association, Inc.

0   5   10 Miles
0   5   10 Kilometers

N

The Grand Canyon of the Tuolumne River is steep and narrow, for its rocky walls were resistant to carving by glaciers.

Tower Peak
11,755 ft.

Snow Peak

Haystack Peak
Chittenden Peak

Stubblefield Canyon

Matterhorn Peak
12,264 ft.

Sawtooth Ridge

Whorl Mt.

Richardson Peak
9,884 ft.

Twin Lakes

Tilden Lake

Price Peak
10,716 ft.

Quarry Peak
11,161 ft.

Jack Main Canyon

Kibbie Lake

Rancheria Creek

Kerrick Canyon

Piute Mt.
10,541 ft.

Piute Creek

Matterhorn Canyon

Virginia Canyon

Lake Vernon

Benson Lake

Pleasant Valley

Rodgers Canyon

Pettit Peak
10,788 ft.

Cold Canyon

Saddlebag Lake

Lake Eleanor

Tiltill Valley

Rancheria Mt.

Cold Mt.
9,910 ft.

Tuolumne River

Ragged Peak

Tioga Pass
9,945 ft.

Entrance

120

Miguel Meadow

Smith Peak
7,751 ft.

Hetch Hetchy Reservoir

Colby Mt.
9,631 ft.

Mt. Dana
13,053 ft.

Mono Pass
10,604 ft.

MATHER

Tuolumne River

Middle

Tuolumne Peak
10,845 ft.

Tuolumne Meadows

Lembert Dome

Bald Mt.
7,261 ft.

Yosemite Creek

Mt. Hoffmann

120

Cathedral Peak
10,940 ft.

Unicorn Peak

Lyell Canyon

Tuna Crest

Aspen Valley

120

Entrance

South Fork Tuolumne River

Ribbon Fall, plunging 1,612 feet down a cliff in a single spectacular leap, is the park's highest uninterrupted cascade.

Tenaya Lake

Snow Creek

Tenaya Canyon

Tenaya Creek

Cathedral Range

Parsons Peak
11,780 ft.

Donohue Peak
12,023 ft.

Tuolumne Grove

Merced Grove

Mt. Watkins

Clouds Rest
9,926 ft.

Mt. Florence
12,561 ft.

Rodgers Peak

Basket Dome

North Dome

Mirror Lake

Half Dome
8,842 ft.

Merced River

Upper Yosemite Fall

Lower Yosemite Fall

Glacier Point

El Capitan
7,569 ft.

Yosemite Valley

Liberty Cap
7,076 ft.

Merced Lake

Inspiration Point

Vernal Fall

Nevada Fall

Mt. Starr King
9,092 ft.

Mt. Clark
11,522 ft.

Bridalveil Fall

Turtleback Dome

Sentinel Falls

Mt. Broderick
6,706 ft.

Cathedral Rocks

Sentinel Dome
8,122 ft.

Mono Meadow

Clark Range

Entrance

EL PORTAL

Merced River

140

Summit Meadow

Badger Pass

Westfall Meadows

CHINQUAPIN

Bridalveil Creek

Horizon Ridge

Horse Ridge

Illilouette Creek

Red Peak

Merced Peak
11,726 ft.

Mount Lyell, high point of the park at 13,114 feet, boasts glaciers near its summit—not Ice Age glaciers, but ones that formed within the last several thousand years.

Buena Vista Crest

Triple Divide Peak
11,607 ft.

The Mariposa Grove of giant sequoias includes the Grizzly Giant. Some 2,700 years of age, it is thought to be the oldest specimen of its kind.

Turner Ridge

Chilnualna Creek

Wawona Dome

South Fork Merced River

Sing Peak
10,552 ft.

41

Wawona Point
6,810 ft.

Entrance

FISH CAMP

The highest waterfall in North America, Yosemite Falls catapults into the valley with a thunderous roar. Fueled by snowmelt, the cascade is grandest in spring; then it slows to a trickle until it is renewed the following year.

tion. There are still a few grassy meadows holding out against the ever-encroaching forest. Trees continue to inch forward, but they are held in abeyance by the flooding of low-lying pockets each spring. A similar process is reclaiming Mirror Lake in Tenaya Canyon, northeast of Yosemite Valley, and one day this beautiful, gemlike lake, too, will be only a memory.

Feathered carpenters

Each season paints a different picture in Yosemite Valley. Summer dabs cheerful wildflowers in the long grass and draws leafy shadows atop rocks; autumn blazes through the hardwoods with intense yellows, oranges, and reds; winter is an opalescent masterpiece of iced twigs, glazed branches, and frosted evergreens; and spring is a moving picture with snowmelt rushing down thousands of irised streams, waterfalls roaring at their fullest, and dogwood and azalea blossoms bobbing in gentle breezes.

The Pacific dogwood, a slender-trunked tree no more than 50 feet tall, is one of the few hardwoods that can grow in dense shade. Every May it produces such a profusion of creamy white blossoms that it stands out like a resplendent bride against the somber dark-green background of evergreens. By September the big blooms have formed clusters of bright red berries, eagerly consumed by robins and band-tailed pigeons.

The incense cedar has a more constant beauty. Visitors often mistake the tree's reddish-brown bark, buttressed trunk, and lacelike foliage for those of the giant sequoia, a colossus that grows in pure groves on higher slopes. Unlike the sequoia, the incense cedar is seldom

found in pure stands, and it reaches only 150 feet high—a mere midget by sequoia standards. Mischievous winds, funneling along the valley's rock-walled corridor, carry aloft the incense cedar's seeds, helping this prolific species to homestead countless nooks and crannies and to spread its pungent fragrance throughout the valley.

The California black oak grows in nearly pure stands along meadow edges, creating a sun-dappled woodland. In spring its bristle-tipped, 10-inch-long leaves are not light green, as one would expect, but a wild array of velvety reds. By late spring they have turned a traditional green, which deepens into emerald as summer progresses; by autumn they are a tawny gold, and countless chestnut-colored acorns hide in the shadows. The Ahwahneechee Indians used to harvest the abundant black oak acorn crop while they summered in the valley. Each family consumed about 500 pounds of acorns a year, all painstakingly gathered, shelled, ground into meal, leached of tannic acid, and baked into mush or bread.

Today's harvest belongs to wildlife—chief among them the acorn woodpecker, a noisy black and white bird with a bright red cap. Like most other woodpeckers, this one flits from tree to tree, boring neat little holes into branches and trunks with a drumlike rat-a-tat rhythm. But the acorn woodpecker is not usually searching for insects; rather, it is making holes in which to store its acorn cache for the winter. Early Spanish settlers called the bird *carpintero,* and it is a skilled carpenter indeed. It can estimate the size of an acorn, drill a hole to precise specifications, maneuver the acorn's small end into the hole, and then hammer with its beak until the acorn is flush with the tree. Sometimes an overzealous individual stores cherry or date pits, but for the most part the holes serve as an acorn pantry, and one that is used season after season. In lean years when the acorn crop was meager, the Ahwahneechee used to search the forest, ferreting out the woodpeckers' caches. Today's would-be thieves are mostly squirrels and jays—neither of which are very successful at dislodging the tightly fitted stash: bands of cheeky woodpeckers vigilantly defend the trees.

A more casual acorn consumer is the mule deer, which pokes along in the woodland, munching acorns the woodpeckers have overlooked. The most abundant of the park's large mammals, mule deer can usually be seen in the valley in early morning and late afternoon when they come out of hiding to forage the meadows for berries, mushrooms, flowers, leaves, and grasses. In autumn the females wander in the latticed shadows of the valley's apple orchards—planted by early pioneers—showing their young where to find the crunchy red fruits.

The mule deer has ears like a mule's, five- to six-inch-long structures that flip forward and back as the ever-alert creature listens for sounds of danger. If it detects a bobcat, coyote, black bear, or human—all possible

Red-winged blackbirds perch under the tall-stalked, umbrella-shaped blossoms of cow parsnips during spring and summer. When autumn comes, the birds gather in flocks and head south for the winter.

The fleeting beauty of such butterflies as the California sister stands in stark contrast to the solid, ostensibly permanent nature of rocks. Yet this boulder-strewn alpine meadow nestled in the High Sierra bears testimony to the tumultuous time when glaciers redesigned the landscape, flattening some mountains and slicing others, scooping out precipitously walled canyons, widening valleys, and scattering odd-shaped rocks all the way to the Sierra's foothills.

predators—the deer will run for cover; its peculiar gait, called a stott, is a series of stiff-legged jumps, with all four feet hitting the ground simultaneously. Though less graceful than others in the antlered group, the mule deer can still clock an impressive 35 miles an hour and jump as far as 25 feet in a single bound.

Black bears and the Grizzly Giant

Toward late spring, the deer begin following the retreating snow line upslope, stopping to browse in one or more of Yosemite's three giant sequoia groves—glorious galleries where the world's largest living things dominate the landscape. The cinnamon-colored sequoias are monuments of antiquity, living as long as 3,000 years—a record that is surpassed only by bristlecone pines, some of which are more than 4,000 years old. The giant sequoias form stands that are shadowy corridors so steeped in silence you can hear the rustle of treetops and the soft thud of a pine cone as it lands on the thickly cushioned forest floor.

One Yosemite sequoia, the 2-million-pound Grizzly Giant, is the world's fifth largest tree (the largest, at 4½ million pounds, is in Sequoia National Park). The Grizzly Giant is so big that its branches are the size of some tree trunks; its lowest limb is six feet across. Despite

having been gnarled by innumerable fires and struck by lightning many times, the tree still lifts its lofty crown more than 200 feet high. This venerable elder, which leans 17° out of plumb, continues to thrive after 2,700 years—the oldest sequoia known today.

Yosemite's giant sequoia groves are far apart from each other, separated by mixed evergreen forests and sun-flooded meadows. White firs are abundant, their Christmas-tree shapes gracing knolls and stream banks; Jeffrey pines on windy outcroppings are often battered into wizened dwarfs; ponderosa pines grow as straight as sentinels, averaging 200 feet in height. Throughout the forests, mistletoe nests in crooks of branches, producing tangles of long, forked, brittle stems and rubbery leaves. Its greenish-white flowers develop into sticky white berries greedily gobbled by birds. (Mistletoe is a parasite, and a persistent one at that: it sends hairlike suckers into the sap-bearing layers of its host to siphon off water and nutrients.) Lupine carpets hills and meadows, overspilling fallen timber with a profusion of blue; groundsel spreads lemon-yellow along shady rills and boggy flats; and penstemon thrusts its purple head up ramrod-straight, thriving on bedrock that has barely a thimbleful of soil.

Some of the creatures in these woods and meadows

sleep or hide out during daylight. Small and vulnerable, the deer mouse ventures out only on the darkest nights lest moonlight reveal its presence; the weak-eyed pocket gopher seldom goes out at all, remaining underground, where it tunnels for roots and bulbs. Even larger animals sometimes shun the sun. The gray fox sleeps away the day in a well-hidden den, preferring to stalk through the night like a ghost. The bobcat also prowls under cover of darkness, but it may occasionally spend a sunny day outside, snoozing on a ledge or relaxing under a shady bush. The black bear, another night wanderer, sometimes lumbers through forests and into alpine meadows during the day.

Despite its name, the black bear is just as often brown, cinnamon-colored, or tan. It is the smallest of the three North American bears (the others are the grizzly and the polar bear), averaging about 300 pounds. With so much weight to carry around, the bears usually shuffle along at a leisurely pace, but when necessary they can run 30 miles an hour and scamper up trees with lightning speed. Basically unsocial, males and females mingle together only during the midsummer mating period. When winter approaches, the female looks for a den in which to sleep and give birth. Although the black bear does not hibernate—its body temperature and heart rate are not greatly reduced as they are in true hibernators—the bear does enter a deep sleep from which it wakes from time to time.

Usually one or two cubs are born about January, in the den. At this early point in life they are far from the shaggy beasts they grow up to be; they are born blind, toothless, and nearly hairless, and they weigh a mere eight ounces. But by the time they emerge from the den in early spring, the cubs have gained sight, teeth, fur, and several pounds. Playful and mischievous, they are trained by their mother to obey her at all times. The

El Capitan's sheer face presents an overwhelming but not impossible challenge to climbers. Conquering it is a thrill for even the most experienced mountaineers.

Clear, crisp mornings double nature's beauty when the mirrorlike water reflects the majestic Cathedral Rocks, across the valley from El Capitan.

father does not take part in cub rearing, and given the opportunity, may even kill and eat them. So the mother is always on the alert. Should danger threaten, she will send the cubs up a tree, turn on the predator, and overpower it, even if it is a much larger male.

Black bears will eat almost anything, but mostly they stuff themselves with nuts, berries, grasses, and other plants. When an anthill is discovered, the bears will scratch it open; the ants swarm all over the offending paws only to be licked up by the long, pink tongue. Honey remains a bear's delight, and a black bear will attack a hive, consuming the honey, honeycomb, bees, and all—regardless of the pain. With their frightful teeth, their strength, and their surprising speed, one might assume that black bears are formidable hunters, but in fact the pigeon-toed hulks are usually too lazy to chase anything of substantial size.

The high heartland

Above the sequoia range is a colder and harsher world, a place of pristine beauty dominated by rock. It was here that the glaciers were born. Yosemite's highest peak, 13,114-foot Mount Lyell, spawned several, each moving away from the parent at about the same time. One flowed east toward what is now a high desert; another crept down Mount Lyell's west side to Yosemite Valley; the largest pushed north, dropping a big block at Tuolumne Meadows, and then went on to fill the Grand Canyon of the Tuolumne River and Hetch Hetchy Valley with an ice sheet 60 miles long and 4,000 feet deep—the largest single glacier in the entire range.

Although it has been at least 10,000 years since the last great glaciers retreated upslope, little has happened to alter the scene. The high heartland is still mostly a slate-gray world gouged and chiseled by the ice. It is littered with boulders that were dropped by melting glaciers, and its walls are polished to a high sheen—a sort of granitic mirror created when ice-trapped sand and stone scoured the bedrock.

Yet wherever rock is covered by soil, evergreen forests, interrupted by azure lakelets and flowering meadows, alleviate the starkness of this rooftop world. Largest of all the Sierra's alpine meadows is Tuolumne, its lawnlike expanse sliced by the Tuolumne River and framed by peaks both jagged and round. From June to mid-August, wildflowers embroider the meadow with color. Like Yosemite Valley and other Sierra meadows, Tuolumne is only a temporary phase in the process by which glacial lakes yield to meadows and then to full-grown forests. This transition is incredibly slow, and in the High Sierra it is hindered by interminable winters and brief summers, so the luster of this Sierran valley

To survive the High Sierra's cold, frosty winters, the Yosemite toad hibernates in burrows. The males serenade the females after they all emerge in spring.

should not be dimmed for thousands of years.

Romping through the meadows during the warmer seasons is Belding's ground squirrel, a prairie dog look-alike that often sits on its hind legs, neck craned and paws folded across its paunchy stomach. It hibernates longer than most other North American mammals, remaining underground eight months of the year. To prepare for such an extended hibernation, the rodent eats from the time it emerges from its burrow until the time it returns—and by the end of summer it is nearly too fat to run.

Etched against the horizon, on rocky outcroppings, stands the twisted form of the Sierra, or western, juniper, a stout, heavy-limbed evergreen. Its branches reach out toward the sky like living driftwood; its roots curl around the granite like claws, keeping the tree in place despite brutal winds and storms. Corkscrewed and weathered by the elements, the picturesque tree is the patriarch of the highlands—a Methuselah that can live as long as 2,000 years.

Above the tree line, the gray-crowned rosy finch summers on windy ridges and rocky slopes that are shunned by other highland birds. This finch is sometimes called the refrigerator bird because it builds its nests at elevations above 10,000 feet. Flying from one snowfield to another, it eats insects that have been blown upward from lower elevations and immobilized by the cold. When the days grow short, the finch descends to lower slopes for the winter.

Just as spring creeps into this high country a blossom at a time, so autumn trickles downward leaf by leaf—a foliage shower of claret, amber, and brass that drenches fawn-hued meadows and forested slopes. Later in the season, dark, ominous clouds hover in brooding silence, their gunmetal gray matching the granite's tones until all of the Sierra is a monochrome world. Winter's unleashed fury blazes a wild path across the Sierran crest, then whips savagely down Yosemite Valley. When the screaming winds stop, the land lies smooth and quiet and white; snow blankets all. Evergreens bow under the weight of miniature avalanches, hardwood branches are wrapped in thin icy coats, and bubbling streams are frozen silent.

From the loftiest outpost to the lowest foothill, it is a scene of lonely grandeur. In time the snowmelt will once again thunder downward in great, exuberant leaps, and rainbows will stretch from Yosemite Valley's crest to the grassy floor. The snow will melt from El Capitan and run in tiny rivulets down Half Dome's head. This is Yosemite—a place so incomparable that Mark Twain once suggested it must be where God cast all His remaining treasures after creating the rest of the world.

Zion

"The wilderness and the solitary place shall be glad for them; and the desert shall rejoice, and blossom as the rose."   **Isaiah 35:1**

Angels Landing, the Altar of Sacrifice, the East Temple, the great White Throne—the names of Zion's landmarks reflect the mood of awe and reverence that so impressed early settlers and visitors to this wondrous canyon, carved through solid rock by the North Fork of the Virgin River. Nowadays that mood of tranquility is sometimes tarnished by traffic jams and throngs of visitors. But with proper planning—early-morning, late-evening, and off-season tours—visitors can still experience the Zion of old.

Occasional sounds then interrupt the silence: birds sing from the cottonwoods that line the river; leaves rustle in the breeze; here and there water trickles down the canyon cliffs and splashes into tranquil pools. But mostly there is an all-pervasive hush, a serene silence that provokes grand thoughts and the contemplation of eternity. Hemmed in by sheer walls that soar straight upward for 2,000 feet or more, mere humans gain a new sense of perspective as they stand beside the stream that carved such wonders.

Water colors all of our perceptions of Zion, for in addition to creating the canyon itself, it is water that brings the park to life. The streamside woodlands along the Virgin River and its tributaries cover only a small fraction of Zion's total acreage. Yet the cottonwoods, box elders, and ash trees beside the watercourses shelter the park's greatest wealth of wildlife. Cool and shady, the woodlands are also favored by humans as

Encircled by the curve of the river that carved it, the Organ towers

above the floor of Zion Canyon. Gambel's quail are but one of the many kinds of birds that enliven the park's spectacular scenery.

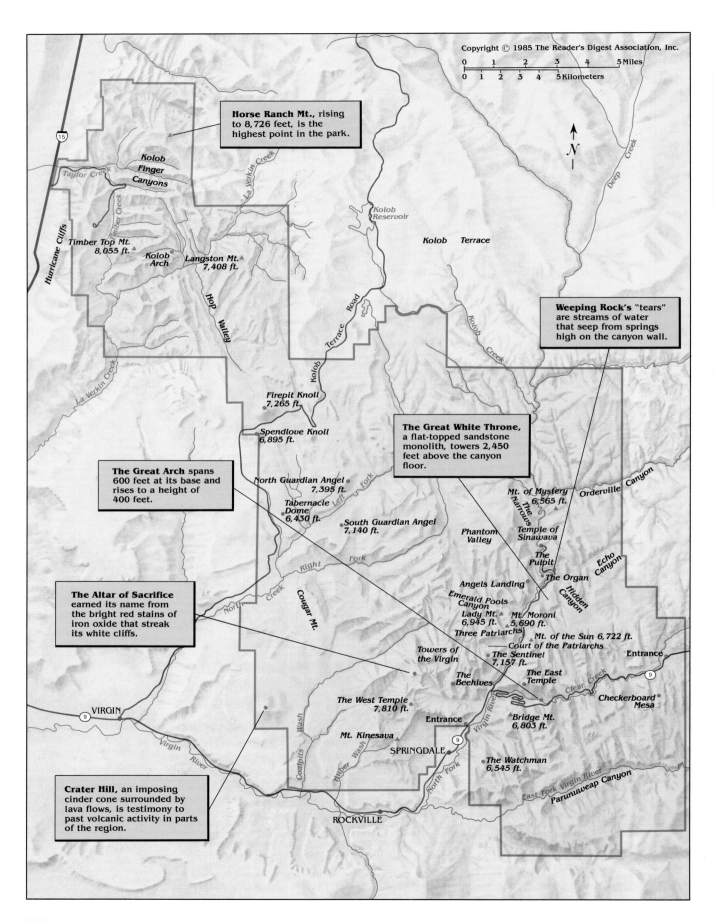

Copyright © 1985 The Reader's Digest Association, Inc.

0   1   2   3   4   5 Miles
0 1 2 3 4 5 Kilometers

N

Horse Ranch Mt., rising to 8,726 feet, is the highest point in the park.

Kolob Finger Canyons

Taylor Creek

La Verkin Creek

Kolob Reservoir

Kolob Terrace

Deep Creek

Timber Top Mt. 8,055 ft.

Kolob Arch

Langston Mt. 7,408 ft.

Hop Valley

Kolob Terrace Road

Kolob Creek

Weeping Rock's "tears" are streams of water that seep from springs high on the canyon wall.

Hurricane Cliffs

Timber Creek

Firepit Knoll 7,265 ft.

Spendlove Knoll 6,895 ft.

The Great Arch spans 600 feet at its base and rises to a height of 400 feet.

North Guardian Angel 7,395 ft.

Tabernacle Dome 6,430 ft.

South Guardian Angel 7,140 ft.

The Great White Throne, a flat-topped sandstone monolith, towers 2,450 feet above the canyon floor.

Mt. of Mystery 6,565 ft.

Orderville Canyon

The Narrows

Temple of Sinawava

Phantom Valley

Echo Canyon

The Pulpit

The Organ

Left Fork

Right Fork

North Creek

Cougar Mt.

The Altar of Sacrifice earned its name from the bright red stains of iron oxide that streak its white cliffs.

Angels Landing

Emerald Pools Canyon

Lady Mt. 6,945 ft.

Mt. Moroni 5,690 ft.

Three Patriarchs

Mt. of the Sun 6,722 ft.

Court of the Patriarchs

Hidden Canyon

Towers of the Virgin

The Sentinel 7,157 ft.

Entrance

The Beehives

The East Temple

Clear Creek

Checkerboard Mesa

9

The West Temple 7,810 ft.

VIRGIN

9

Virgin River

Entrance

Bridge Mt. 6,803 ft.

Mt. Kinesava

Coalpits Wash

Huber Wash

SPRINGDALE

9

North Fork

The Watchman 6,545 ft.

East Fork Virgin River

Parunuweap Canyon

Crater Hill, an imposing cinder cone surrounded by lava flows, is testimony to past volcanic activity in parts of the region.

Virgin River

ROCKVILLE

326

Checkerboard Mesa, one of Zion's most extraordinary landmarks, clearly reveals the overlapping contours of the petrified dunes that make up the park's most prominent rock, the 2,000-foot-thick layer of Navajo Sandstone. Weathering along the lines of the ancient dunes and in the intersecting vertical cracks in the rock accounts for the mesa's strikingly symmetrical checkered appearance.

vantage points for viewing the park's rock formations. In spring and summer we see the red sandstone cliffs within frames of brilliant green cottonwood leaves. Later the golden leaves of autumn accent the colors of the rocky walls, and in winter we see them through the twisting tracery of bare but living twigs and branches.

Water, surprisingly, is present too on the cliffs themselves, trickling down from innumerable seeps and springs high on the canyon walls. The moisture is the outflow from a vast invisible reservoir held in pore spaces in the 2,000-foot-thick Navajo Sandstone that makes up much of the canyon walls. Water from rain and snow that fall on Zion's uplands seeps slowly down through openings in the sandstone until it reaches a layer of impermeable shale at the base, then flows sideways atop the shale to emerge at the so-called spring line found along much of Zion's walls.

Many of these seepage points support lush green oases of ferns and wildflowers, inhabited by all sorts of water-loving animals. At dripping springs on sheer walls along the Narrows, for instance, lives the Zion snail, a species that developed in this moist haven in the desert and is found nowhere else in the world.

The best-known oasis, however, is Weeping Rock, so named for the multiple little streams of water that sprinkle like tears from the overhanging rock. The short hike to Weeping Rock—a favorite destination for many park visitors—affords a seemingly endless variety of experiences. Along the way you can marvel at the myriad hues of wildflowers, sample the flavor of a canyon wild grape, listen to the surprisingly goatlike bleats of canyon treefrogs, and savor the refreshing coolness of the rock's dripping tears.

Because of all this unexpected dampness within the confines of the canyons, we tend to think of Zion as much more lush and alive than it really is. The effect is heightened because we must travel across broad expanses of sparsely vegetated desert to reach the sanctuary of the well-watered canyon floor. By contrast with the desert, the springs and streamside woodlands seem all the more verdant and inviting.

Festoons of flowers

Away from the river and on ledges along the canyon walls are stands of pinyon pines and junipers, trees more typical of the arid Southwest. On the highlands beyond the canyon rims, the common trees are ponderosa pine, Douglas fir, white fir, and quaking aspen. But you don't have to climb all the way to the top to see them: the pines and firs also find suitable living conditions in some of the cool, damp side canyons. There too you can look for the bright blossoms of such moisture-loving plants as monkey flowers and the brilliant red spikes of cardinal flowers.

The park's summer-long parade of wildflowers, in fact, frequently competes with the rocks themselves for the visitor's attention. Even iron-stained Navajo Sandstone seems dull compared to a scarlet slickrock paintbrush growing from a pocket of sandy soil that has accumulated in a crack on the canyon wall. The same crevice might also contain a clump of desert phlox covered with dainty pink blooms or a cluster of puccoon topped with an explosion of yellow trumpets.

Rugged-looking most of the year, the cacti of Zion also have their season of special beauty; beginning in April they put on a splendid show of color. The very names of claret cup and purple torch describe the brilliance of their blooms, while sprawling mounds of

Contained by natural dams, the three Emerald Pools in one of Zion's side canyons stand as oases of serenity. Fringing

this one with greenery are ponderosa pines, trees normally found at higher elevations in the park.

the closely related beavertail cactus are often nearly covered with rosy pink blossoms.

All the cacti are succulents, plants that survive drought by storing water in their fleshy stems. They have no normal leaves (their pores would permit too much water to escape from the plants), and instead manufacture food in chlorophyll-bearing cells in their

From soggy stream banks to crevices high on the cliffs, wildflowers of many kinds flourish throughout Zion. The several species of monkey flowers found in the park supply colorful accents from May through the summer months.

stems. Most, however, are amply armed with spines, structures that help to reduce water evaporation and also discourage animals from eating them.

Among the park's other prominent plants are sego lilies, the state flower of Utah; the edible bulbs of this lovely white lily saved the Mormon pioneers from starvation in 1848. Another, sacred datura, found throughout the canyons, produces spectacular white trumpets several inches long. An eerily beautiful sight by the light of a full moon, the short-lived flowers open late in the afternoon and wither the following morning. Depending on the season, yarrows, wild marigolds, asters, pentemons, and a host of others accent the scenery with splashes of color.

Birth of a canyon

The centerpiece of the scenery, however, inevitably remains the canyon itself. The main architect of that masterpiece in stone, the North Fork of the Virgin River, is not an especially large river, but it does flow fast, dropping as much as 160 feet per mile in some sections. And after thunderstorms, water rushing off the bare rock of the surrounding uplands can transform it into a raging torrent—one that sweeps along a load of more than a million tons of sand, grit, and even thumping boulders every year. Armed with all this water-borne debris, the Virgin has been likened to an endless belt of sandpaper that scours ceaselessly away at the rocks of the canyon floor.

But if the river is the carving tool, the rocks of Zion are the raw material from which it has created its breathtaking sculptures. The oldest in the canyon, exposed in multicolored bands along the lower levels of the cliffs, began to form some 250 million years ago. Alternating layers of limestone, sandstone, shale, volcanic ash, and other kinds of rock, they tell a tale of changing conditions over the course of the past 35 million years. Some of the rocks were deposited as sediments on the floor of a shallow sea, others on coastal plains and mud flats, in vanished lakes, and in the backwaters of bygone rivers. Fossils of clams that lived in those ancient seas, and footprints left where dinosaurs walked across streamside mud, are reminders that even then there was life in this place.

A few of the rock layers also contain chunks and pieces—even whole logs—of petrified wood. Washed in by rivers flowing from highlands far to the south long before there was a Grand Canyon to block the way, the battered trees came to rest here and were covered with silt before they had time to rot. Gradually, silica in groundwater seeping through the wood replaced the organic matter in individual cells and transformed them into stone. Today in places like Huber Wash, some of the gray stone logs have been exposed and look very much like slowly disintegrating tree trunks.

By 190 million years ago, the climate had become so dry that there was practically no precipitation at all. The entire region, in fact, became a Sahara-like sea of windblown, shifting sand dunes. Eventually piling up to a thickness of 3,000 feet or so, they would in time be transformed into the Navajo Sandstone now exposed on the upper canyon walls. The contours of the wind-shaped dunes, piled one on top of the other, are still visible in the rock.

The dunes were consolidated into sandstone when the sea once again invaded the area, about 175 million years ago. Red iron oxide and calcium carbonate in water seeping through the drowned dunes cemented the individual sand grains into a solid mass. Over the ensuing eons, as the sea came and went, layer upon layer of additional sediments—some 2,800 feet in all—was deposited on top of the Navajo Sandstone, though most of these younger rocks have since been eroded away in the Zion area.

The actual carving of Zion and the park's other canyons came about with the long, slow uplift of the Colorado Plateau, the final phase in a period of tremendous turmoil that began about 65 million years ago and continued in fits and starts that spanned millions of years. Volcanoes erupted during these periods of crustal instability, and their signatures—basaltic lava flows—are common in Zion. (Crater Hill and other well-preserved volcanic cones along the western edge of the park are products of much more recent eruptions.)

A phase of vigorous uplift, beginning some 15 million years ago, dramatically steepened the gradient of the Virgin River, and the increased water supplies during the Ice Age climate of the past million years further heightened its cutting power. During the course of the uplift, the great mass of Navajo Sandstone was riddled with networks of cracks, called joints. These formed a path of least resistance to erosion and so determined Zion's basic pattern: precipitous canyons walled in by massive blocks of sandstone.

The most dramatic of the park's erosion-enlarged

An early explorer of Zion's Narrows described it as "the most wonderful defile it has been my fortune to behold." Most visitors to the chasm—2,000 feet deep and in places only 20 feet wide—heartily agree with his enthusiastic judgment.

fractures is the Narrows at the head of Zion Canyon. In some places along this 12-mile route, the slotlike defile is 2,000 feet deep and only 30 feet wide. Walking and wading through the remarkable gorge, which normally contains only a small stream of water, is a popular trek with park visitors—as long as weather forecasts are favorable. But beware if there is any possibility of thunderstorms: within minutes the rapid runoff of water from many square miles of bare rock can transform the usual flow into a wall-to-wall flash flood up to 30 feet deep.

The Narrows remains so deep and constricted because the river has not yet eroded its course all the way down through the Navajo Sandstone to the layer of impermeable shale at its base. Farther downstream, where the river *has* sliced its way down to the shale, the canyon is much wider. The shale is very soft and easily washes away—and when it washes away, the sandstone above it loses its support and caves in. The cement between individual grains in the sandstone just above the impermeable shale dissolves, and that also contributes to the undermining of the canyon walls. And so

over time they have retreated as the rocks come tumbling down, sometimes in massive slabs but more often in bits and pieces that rapidly disintegrate and are washed away by the river.

Occasionally, as the rocks are undermined by erosion at their base, the entire cliff face does not collapse. Instead, only the lower section gives way while the top of the cliff remains intact. The result is a natural arch, sometimes of massive proportions. Most of the arches in Zion are so-called blind arches—alcoves in the faces of cliffs—but there are also a few freestanding arches. One of them, the Kolob Arch, spans 310 feet and is the largest freestanding arch in the world.

And so, bit by bit, Zion is falling apart: its beauty is the handiwork of forces of destruction. Occasionally we can see the changes while they are occurring, as on August 1, 1968, when 5,000 tons of rock fell on the Riverside Walk. But normally the course of change is unimaginably slow—at least in human terms. To the transient visitor, the majestic walls of Zion Canyon seem immutable.

Seeking shelter from the burning glare of the midday sun, a mountain lion and two of her cubs loll in the cool comfort of a rock shelter. Though fairly common at Zion, the big cats are as elusive as shadows and rarely seen.

Paiutes and pioneers

The soaring cliffs and streamside woodlands of Zion have long been known to humans. From A.D. 500 until about A.D. 1200, small bands of Anasazi Indians, the "Ancient Ones" of the Navajos, dwelt in the canyon, where they lived by hunting game, gathering wild foods, and tending small garden plots. Relics of their presence—scattered petroglyphs, storage bins, the crumbling remains of cliff dwellings, and other artifacts—speak of the simple, peaceful way of life of these vanished people.

After the Anasazi, for unknown reasons, abandoned the Zion area, groups of Paiute Indians visited from time to time. *Ioogoon,* "the arrow quiver," is what the Paiutes called the canyon. This figure of speech, which to them meant "you go out the same way you go in," suggests the sense of awe and trepidation that the canyon inspired in their minds.

According to their beliefs, unseen spirits sometimes hurled stones down from the canyon walls, and the moody god Kinesava was apt to start mysterious fires—lightning—on heights no human could reach. The evil Wynopits, moreover, caused the canyon's river to rise suddenly in flash floods that killed unlucky Paiutes. Clearly the canyon was not a place for lingering. Today the memory of their legends still lives: the unpredictable Kinesava and the coyote-god Sinawava are commemorated in the names of a mountain and a beautiful natural temple in the depths of the canyon.

One thing remains certain: people of all nationalities and origins find the canyons of Zion at once fascinating and inspirational. In modern times it has fallen to European explorers and settlers to map and call the world's attention to the area's spectacular array of natural features. Two Spanish priests, Fathers Vélez de Escalante and Domínguez, explored the southern reaches of present-day Utah in 1776. Although they did not discover Zion Canyon, they did cross the Virgin River some 20 miles downstream. They or later Spaniards may have been the first to call it Río Virgen, in honor of the Virgin Mary.

More secular explorers, 16 mountain men in search of beaver pelts, roamed through the area under the leadership of Jedediah Smith in 1826. They also found the river, which they named the Adams for President John Quincy Adams, but probably missed the canyon. On a later trip, however, the Americans began to call the stream the Virgin River, possibly because they had learned of the previous Spanish name or perhaps because they wanted to honor one of their companions, Thomas Virgin, who had been wounded by Indians. Or it may simply have been that the coincidence of names appealed to the mountain men's sense of humor.

The first American definitely known to have entered Zion Canyon was a Mormon, Nephi Johnson, who had been sent by his leader, Brigham Young, to explore the upper Virgin River valley for potential farm sites in 1858. By 1860, small Mormon settlements, along with their orchards and cotton fields, were sprouting beside the Virgin, and by 1863 crops were being cultivated on the floor of Zion Canyon itself.

One of the pioneering farmers was Isaac Behunin, a longtime Mormon who had suffered great persecution before joining Brigham Young on his flight to the wilderness of Utah in 1846–47. It was amid the steep and protecting canyon walls along the Virgin River that Isaac Behunin finally found a place of peace and refuge, and so it seemed natural for him to call it Zion.

Other names more particular to the Mormon faith dot the map of the park. Mount Moroni is named for the angel who, it is believed, revealed the Book of Mormon on golden tablets to the founder of the religion, Joseph Smith. The brilliant red cliffs of the Kolob Terrace are named for the star in Mormon literature that shines brightly near the seat of God.

The intrepid explorer of the Colorado Plateau, Maj. John Wesley Powell, took in the sights of Zion in 1871. Other government explorers followed and made the glory of the place known to the American public by way of eloquent words and spectacular photographs. One of them, Clarence E. Dutton, named the East and West temples in an 1882 report. But natural barriers of desert and mountain prevented all but a few hardy tourists from visiting Zion until well into the 20th century.

One early visitor was a Methodist minister, Frederick Vining Fisher, who was also an avid traveler and photographer. Having heard of Zion's glories, he prevailed upon local Mormons to guide him into the canyon in 1916. Overwhelmed by the impact of the place, he began applying religious names to prominent features on every hand. The Three Patriarchs, the Organ, and the Great White Throne firmly established the tradition of strewing inspirational titles across the map of Zion.

That Zion touches a universal spirituality in mankind is demonstrated by the fact that Paiute and preacher, Mormon farmer and government explorer, all independently perceived a divine presence in the place. Given their common cultural heritage, Mormon and Methodist could be expected to have had such a reaction to the stupendous architecture of Zion. But Paiutes had no temples or altars in their religion. So it must be more than massive monoliths that accounts for the mood of the place.

Perhaps it is the constantly changing play of light on the colors of rock and leaf in the frequently shadowed depths of the canyon. Or maybe it is the lush streamside vegetation that contrasts so vividly with the surrounding desert. Drops of water that drip like tears from seemingly solid rock contribute to the mysterious aura of Zion, as do the undulating contours of petrified dunes that now stand revealed in natural sandstone sculptures. The list could go on infinitely and never total the reasons or completely explain the secret essence of Zion. Such is the nature of this majestic place that so clearly transcends the frail and transient handiwork of man.

Our Special Alaskan Parks

"If you are old, go by all means; but if you are young, stay away until you grow older. . . . It is not well to dull one's capacity for enjoyment by seeing the finest first."
Henry Gannett, *U.S. Geological Survey*

The very mention of Alaska has a curious effect on people: eyes become glazed with a faraway look as thoughts turn to this land of infinite beauty and purity, for Alaska is, in truth, the last frontier, the American wilderness, the place where it is possible to step back in time and see a world that is still young and fresh. It is also a world that is overwhelmingly vast—far grander in scale than most first-time visitors had ever imagined. A flight from the state capital of Juneau, on the southern Panhandle, to the village of Barrow on the Arctic Ocean—about equal to the distance from New York City to Miami Beach—passes over wave upon wave of snowcapped peaks, icebound valleys, untamed rivers, great forests, and immense tundra plains. Whatever your preference in landforms, in fact, Alaska seems to have them all—and many of the finest examples of these landscapes have been preserved in seven special Alaskan national parks.

Bay of the vanishing glaciers

Among the grandest of Alaska's grand features is its seacoast. Ragged, jagged, indented with uncounted bays and fjords and inlets, it is longer than the coastlines of all of the lower 48 states combined. And one special spot on that coast, Glacier Bay National Park, offers the opportunity to look at the land as it must have appeared when the world was emerging from the frigid grip of the Ice Age.

The towering glaciers of Glacier Bay, easily approached by excursion boat, are formidable to behold. But the park offers simpler pleasures too—finding brightly colored paintbrushes, for example, resplendent in full bloom.

In 1794, when British explorer George Vancouver sailed along Alaska's southeast coast, Glacier Bay did not exist—or, at least, not as we know it today. What Vancouver found was not an inlet, but a solid wall of gleaming blue ice that completely blocked the present entrance to the bay. Hundreds of feet high, it groaned and cracked with sharp explosions as huge blocks fell into the sea and drifted off as icebergs. Vancouver did not know at the time that the immense glacier filling the bay was in retreat; were he able to repeat his journey today, he would find that where mountains of ice once blocked his passage, he could now sail more than 65 miles into a large and lovely fjord.

And along the way he would find that remarkable changes have taken place as the ice has retreated: near the mouth of the bay the land is now covered with a lush rain forest of hemlock and spruce. Farther inland the vegetation becomes shorter and sparser until, at the heads of the many arms of the bay, glaciers are still calving icebergs, and the land, only recently laid bare of ice, is all but devoid of life.

Aside from lichens, those hardy pioneers that are able to survive even on bare rock, the first plant to gain a foothold in the gravelly debris left behind by the glaciers is yellow dryas, a low-growing species with lovely, delicate flowers. Though only inches high, it spreads rapidly and soon covers the ground with dense mats of greenery. Simple as it may seem, dryas performs an important soil-building chore; fungi growing among its roots convert nitrogen from the air into solid nitrogen compounds that aid in the growth of other plants; and the dryas plants themselves, when they die,

333

contribute organic material that further enriches the sterile glacial soil.

Alders, treelike shrubs that grow in dense, virtually impenetrable thickets, eventually move in and crowd out the dryas, which cannot survive in the shade of the taller shrubs. Black cottonwoods, in turn, crowd out the alders by overshadowing them, and are themselves finally replaced by thick, luxuriant forests of spruce and hemlock. From beginning to end, this 200-year-long process of one life-form replacing another—succession—can be seen along the shores of Glacier Bay.

Plants are also plentiful in the waters of the bay, although most of them are invisible. Every spring and summer, microscopic algae begin to multiply at a fantastic rate, as do the krill (small shrimplike creatures) and other minute drifting animals that feed on the algae. Fish populations soar and the fish in turn attract seals and other predators.

One of the largest populations of harbor seals along the Pacific coast, for example, is found in Glacier Bay and its inlets, where they are a common sight basking and sleeping on small icebergs afloat in the frigid water. With a thick layer of fat beneath its skin, a seal is well insulated against the cold and spends hours at a time drifting lazily on the ice. In other coastal areas harbor seals give birth on dry land—rocky shores and isolated beaches. But here, where beaches are few and the coastline is often steep and blocked with ice, the seals have come up with a different solution: the pups are born each spring right out on the many icebergs drifting about in the bay.

This arrangement offers protection against such predators as wolves and bears, but the floating islands are not without hazards of their own. Killer whales also are attracted to Glacier Bay. Reaching lengths of 30 feet, the streamlined creatures slip easily and rapidly through the water in pursuit of fish, the mainstay of their diet. But when the opportunity arises, they gladly settle for a meal of seal. Traveling in groups of up to a dozen, killer whales sometimes bump into small icebergs, dumping hapless seals and pups into the water where they become easy targets.

Glacier Bay also is the summer home of humpbacked whales, so named for the prominent hump on their backs. Like many other whales, they are wide-ranging creatures that travel long distances across the world's

Adrip with dangling tree mosses, the Sitka spruces in a Glacier Bay forest rise from ground cushioned with masses of more moss. Damp winds from the Pacific supply the abundant rainfall needed to nurture such rampant growth.

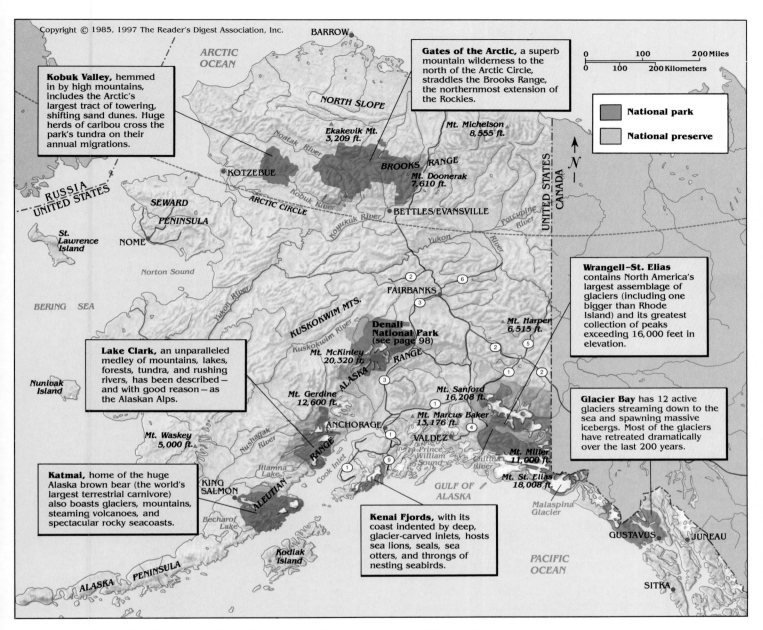

BARROW

ARCTIC OCEAN

NORTH SLOPE

Kobuk Valley, hemmed in by high mountains, includes the Arctic's largest tract of towering, shifting sand dunes. Huge herds of caribou cross the park's tundra on their annual migrations.

Gates of the Arctic, a superb mountain wilderness to the north of the Arctic Circle, straddles the Brooks Range, the northernmost extension of the Rockies.

Ekakevik Mt. 3,209 ft.

Mt. Michelson 8,555 ft.

BROOKS RANGE

Mt. Doonerak 7,610 ft.

Noatak River

KOTZEBUE

Kobuk River

ARCTIC CIRCLE

Koyukuk River

BETTLES/EVANSVILLE

Porcupine River

UNITED STATES / CANADA

N

| | National park |
| | National preserve |

0   100   200 Miles
0   100   200 Kilometers

RUSSIA
UNITED STATES

SEWARD PENINSULA

St. Lawrence Island

NOME

Norton Sound

Yukon River

Yukon

Wrangell–St. Elias contains North America's largest assemblage of glaciers (including one bigger than Rhode Island) and its greatest collection of peaks exceeding 16,000 feet in elevation.

BERING SEA

Yukon River

FAIRBANKS

KUSKOKWIM MTS.

Kuskokwim River

Mt. Harper 6,515 ft.

Lake Clark, an unparalleled medley of mountains, lakes, forests, tundra, and rushing rivers, has been described — and with good reason — as the Alaskan Alps.

Denali National Park (see page 98)

Mt. McKinley 20,320 ft.

ALASKA RANGE

Nunivak Island

Mt. Gerdine 12,600 ft.

Mt. Sanford 16,208 ft.

Glacier Bay has 12 active glaciers streaming down to the sea and spawning massive icebergs. Most of the glaciers have retreated dramatically over the last 200 years.

Mt. Waskey 5,000 ft.

Nushagak River

ANCHORAGE

Mt. Marcus Baker 13,176 ft.

VALDEZ

Chitina River

Mt. Miller 11,000 ft.

Iliamna Lake

ALEUTIAN RANGE

Cook Inlet

Prince William Sound

Mt. St. Elias 18,008 ft.

Malaspina Glacier

Katmai, home of the huge Alaska brown bear (the world's largest terrestrial carnivore) also boasts glaciers, mountains, steaming volcanoes, and spectacular rocky seacoasts.

KING SALMON

Becharof Lake

GULF OF ALASKA

GUSTAVUS

JUNEAU

Kodiak Island

Kenai Fjords, with its coast indented by deep, glacier-carved inlets, hosts sea lions, seals, sea otters, and throngs of nesting seabirds.

PACIFIC OCEAN

ALASKA PENINSULA

SITKA

---

oceans. In the Pacific, hundreds of these graceful mammals migrate more than 3,000 miles from their winter home off Hawaii to their summer one in Alaska. The calves are born in Hawaiian waters and make the long journey to Alaska with the parents.

Among the largest of all mammals, humpbacks can reach lengths of 50 feet and weigh 45 tons. Surprisingly, the primary food for such titans consists of some of the smallest of marine creatures—the diminutive krill, which they scoop up in huge mouthfuls of water and filter through fine, hairlike "teeth" called baleen. As long as the bloom of krill and plankton remains, so too do the humpbacks, plying the waters of Glacier Bay throughout the summer months. When not feeding, the gentle giants can often be seen lolling quietly near the surface. At times they even seem playful, leaping a full third or more of their body length out of the water, then crashing back in great explosions of spray.

A seaside sanctuary

Like Glacier Bay, Kenai Fjords National Park has the look of a world in flux—raw, rough, jagged around the edges. Not much time has elapsed here since the end of the Ice Age; erosion by the sea has not yet softened the contours of the rocks. Instead the coast is notched with steep-walled fjords, deep glacier-carved valleys that have been flooded by the ocean.

High above the fjords, atop the Kenai Mountains, is the Harding Icefield, a 700-square-mile remnant of the ice sheet that covered most of south-central Alaska 10,000 years ago. The icy fingers of 34 separate glaciers spill down in all directions from the center of the field, a dazzling plain of ice and snow. Nunataks, the tops of ice-buried mountains, protrude above the white expanse, some rising more than 2,000 feet above it. In places where howling winds have piled the snow into dunelike drifts, the field has the appearance of a frozen

Streaming endlessly down to the sea, the many glaciers at Kenai Fjords radiate from the Harding Icefield, a small mountaintop remnant of the much larger ice cap that smothered the entire region at the time of the last ice age.

Sahara. Despite the hostility of the ice cap, however, life clings to its edges. The same moisture-laden sea winds that dump snow on the heights also nurture a zone of luxuriant rain forest on the lower slopes.

Offshore, numerous islands are the focal points of life at Kenai Fjords. Birds of many kinds—kittiwakes, murres, cormorants, and others—nest by the thousands on their rocky cliffs. One of them, Matushka Island, is a prime nesting area for horned puffins, whose brilliant red and yellow beaks give rise to their nickname, "sea parrots." Chunky birds with stubby wings, the puffins are far from graceful fliers—it takes much flapping and running on the water for them to become airborne. Their ungainly wings, however, serve a dual purpose: when diving for fish, the birds "fly" as they swim underwater, using their wings for locomotion.

The group of islands called the Chiswells is home to a colony of Steller sea lions. These barren rocks jutting out of the ocean are a noisy place, especially in June when the pups are born: grunts, roars, bellows, and squeals echo across the water as if in competition with the crashing of the surf. Largest of the eared seals— bulls may weigh a ton or more—the Steller sea lions are a cantankerous lot; fights between bulls defending harems are common. When not fighting, the clumsy creatures flop awkwardly across the rocks to plunge into the sea, where they are instantly transformed into graceful swimmers in their pursuit of fish.

Sea otters, sleek and graceful creatures of the sea, also inhabit these cold northern waters, especially where kelp is plentiful. The playful, intelligent animals are well-known for their trait of mooring themselves with strands of the giant seaweed as they doze on the open water. A talented tool-user, it also has the good sense to bring along a rock when it returns to the surface from a dive for clams and other shellfish: lolling on its back, it uses the rock as an anvil for breaking open the hard shells to get at the tasty morsels inside. Though they once were hunted almost to extinction for the sake of their lustrous fur, sea otters are becoming quite numerous once again in Alaskan waters, where their return is welcomed by all who have ever witnessed their delightful antics.

Land of the big bears

Spring comes slowly to Katmai National Park. April arrives and the days grow gradually longer, but still it seems like the midst of winter. Snow lies deep in the forests and on the mountainsides; rivers are still frozen, cold, and seemingly lifeless. Here and there a line of tracks marks the meanderings of a wolverine or a snowshoe hare across the otherwise unbroken blanket of white, but there is little else to hint of changes about to come, of the new season that is about to begin.

One of the first signs of life is the emergence of Katmai's big Alaska brown bears from their winter dens, usually caves they had excavated in hillsides the previous fall. The bears do not truly hibernate; they sleep deeply and, like insomniacs, awaken from time to time. Occasionally they even venture out briefly into the cold winter darkness. But by April spring is in the air and the time has come to shake off the winter slumber once and for all. Stirring to life, the bears poke their massive heads out of their dens, sniff the air, and slowly amble out, blinking at the brightness of the new season.

If the bear is a female, she is likely to be followed by two cubs that were born during the winter. Though proportionately a little longer of leg and somewhat clumsy compared to the adult with its sure, fluid movements, the youngsters are miniature replicas of their mother. Given time, however, they will match their parents in stature: standing up to 10 feet tall on their hind legs, males of these behemoth bears can weigh as much as 1,500 pounds.

Though the bears have made their home here since the last ice age, the Katmai region was largely unknown until June 1912, when the world suddenly became aware of its existence. In one of the most violent eruptions of recent history, the area was racked by an explosion that was heard hundreds of miles away. The land raged with fire as a whole new volcano, christened Novarupta, formed within a matter of days and the summit of nearby Mount Katmai collapsed into its own vast magma chamber. All along the coast, daylight was transformed into gloomy darkness by ashfalls that continued for days.

Few, if any, people witnessed these incredible events, and three years passed before any organized attempt was made to explore the extent of the catastrophe. In 1915 an expedition led by Dr. Robert Griggs found a land completely devastated, still smoking and spewing out volcanic ash. Hampered by ash that melting snow had turned to mud, Griggs was unable to get beyond Katmai Valley, near the coast. In 1916 he returned, this time pushing farther inland and climbing Mount Katmai to look down into its caldera at a newly formed lake.

Pressing onward, the party descended into a valley beyond the mountain and there made their most amazing discovery: a lifeless moonscape, a valley filled to depths of hundreds of feet with pumice and ash, and smoldering with huge vents of steam—hundreds of them, even thousands. Thus was discovered the Valley of Ten Thousand Smokes.

Though Katmai's thermal activity diminished in the decades following Griggs's discovery—practically no steam vents remain active in the valley today—the scars of the cataclysm are as impressive as ever. Streams flowing down from nearby mountains have sliced deeply into the ash deposits, carving out spectacular gorges. A few plants dot the devastated valley, but the look of the place is one of utter desolation, the aftermath of a catastrophe that might have occurred just yesterday.

Horned puffins, comical pigeon-sized seabirds, are quite common at Kenai Fjords. In summer the park's coastal cliffs and crags are aswarm with hundreds of thousands of nesting puffins and other seabirds.

Lolling on offshore rocks and sea stacks, Steller sea lions bask in the sun at Kenai Fjords. These are females, each up to 9 feet long and weighing as much as 600 pounds. They usually give birth to a single pup in early summer. Nurtured by mother's milk that is extremely rich in fat, the pups grow rapidly and are weaned when they are about three months old.

A wilderness spectacular

Visitors who fly in from Anchorage—a popular way of approaching Lake Clark—feel a sense of anticipation as they near the dazzling white peaks of the Chigmit Mountains, which lie at the heart of the park. Occasional puffs of steam issue from the summits of two of the more prominent peaks, Redoubt Volcano and Iliamna Volcano, hinting at their internal fires. Yet volcanoes are only one facet of Lake Clark's beauty, for of all the Alaskan parks, this one alone is the gem complete. Larger than the state of Connecticut, it encompasses gigantic glaciers, jagged unnamed peaks, scores of unexplored valleys, and tundra plains inhabited by caribou. Here too are rugged and lonely seacoasts, lake after glittering lake, and rivers wild enough to challenge the hardiest of white water enthusiasts.

The most spectacular part of the flight into the park begins as the plane enters Lake Clark Pass. The pass is relatively low—slightly over 1,000 feet in elevation—and hemmed in on both sides by jagged snowcapped mountains that tower above the airplane. Gleaming blue glaciers spill down the slopes; waterfalls, creating intensely colorful rainbows in their spray, plunge hundreds of feet down smooth granite walls, and farther on whole hillsides are ablaze with the glow of fireweed. Finally the plane rounds a last bend in the pass, and you get your first look at Lake Clark, some 50 miles long but nowhere more than 5 miles wide. Its characteristic color is light blue, the result of flour-fine particles of glacial debris suspended in its water, but the color changes with the moods of the weather. Sometimes it is a deep, ominous blue-black as winds rake its surface into whitecaps; at other times, in early morning calm, it is an almost colorless gray.

At its southern end, the short but powerful Newhalen River connects Lake Clark to nearby Iliamna Lake, and there it is possible to watch one of nature's grand spectacles, the annual salmon migration. The waters of the Newhalen are clear—so clear, in fact, that even from a plane you can spot the migrating salmon, which sometimes color the river red from bank to bank. In peak years as many as 9 million fish fight their way upstream from Iliamna Lake to Lake Clark and its shallow spawning tributaries.

The show begins in late June when, with uncanny timing, most of the fish arrive off the coast of Alaska within a three-week period from points thousands of miles away in the Pacific. Using a finely tuned chemical sensing system, the fish swim to Iliamna Lake and then on to the very places where they were spawned. The obstacles are enormous. Numerous falls and rapids must be negotiated, and in shallower streams the fish become easy prey for bears, which return each summer to favored spots that they know will be choked with salmon. Like humans, each bear seems to develop its own style of fishing. Some use great finesse, stationing themselves in the shallows where a single swipe of a paw lofts a salmon out of the water and onto a nearby stream bank. Others are less refined: they charge into the stream like runaway locomotives, crashing through the water and swatting at anything that moves—but eventually they, too, emerge with dinner flopping in their jaws.

The fish that survive the onslaught of the bears stake out nesting sites on the gravel beds of various streams flowing into Lake Clark. Using her tail, the female scoops a shallow depression in the gravel and deposits eggs, which are immediately fertilized by the male. The adult salmon, having fasted for weeks during their homeward journey, then weaken rapidly and die, affording additional feasts for bears and birds alike.

In Katmai's Valley of Ten Thousand Smokes, the Ukak River has carved a sheer-walled gorge through 100 feet of volcanic ash deposited there by a devastating eruption in 1912. Farther upstream the gorge is nearly 400 feet deep.

Taking a break on a fishing expedition, an Alaska brown bear waits watchfully while her cub settles down for a *snooze. The bears, a local race of the more familiar grizzly, find safe sanctuary in the wilds of Katmai.*

The eggs hatch during the winter months, and the alevins, or hatchlings, remain in the gravel for protection, deriving nourishment from the yolk sacs attached to their undersides. At this stage they bear little resemblance to fish; huge, bulging eyes dominate their thin, almost transparent bodies, and the bulbous egg sacs impede their movements. By spring, however, the alevins transform into inch-long fry, miniature versions of the adults, and remain in Lake Clark for up to two seasons before migrating downstream to the open sea. There they range over wide areas—up to 2,000 miles a year for the next two to three years. And then they, like their parents before them, respond to the mysterious instinct that lures them home once more to complete their destinies in the streams of Lake Clark.

The biggest park
Whether it be Lake Clark or Katmai or Glacier Bay or Denali or any one of hundreds of places in Alaska, mountains dominate the land. And not just mountains, but stupendous, mind-boggling peaks. In Wrangell–St. Elias National Park, for example, the mighty Wrangell, Chugach, and St. Elias ranges join to pitch and toss in a sea of towering peaks and massive glaciers. Tallest of all is Mount St. Elias, rising 18,008 feet above sea level— and with the sea a mere 25 miles away. This is, indeed, the North American equivalent of the Himalayas, a topography bold and rugged and wild enough to excite any mountaineer.

Such is the setting for our largest park. With an area of more than 12 million acres, it is almost a third again as large as Switzerland and so spacious that more than 5 Yellowstones could fit into it with room to spare. But

unlike our first national park, this is an area largely unexplored, even today. Many of its peaks are still unscaled, and there are valleys where few, if any, humans have ever left their footprints—all this making it truly a park for the adventurous.

One of the easier routes to the rugged interior is via the Chitina River valley. Here are located the little towns of McCarthy and Kennecott, tiny dots on the map with a combined population of less than two dozen

Impelled by the urge to spawn, salmon by the millions overcome seemingly insuperable obstacles as they make their way upstream each spring in hundreds of Alaskan rivers. This one is leaping its way up Katmai's Idavain Falls.

The warm glow of a sunset in July burnishes the stately peaks that stand guard over the mirrorlike expanse of lovely Lake Clark, the

year-round residents. They were not always so sparsely populated. Shortly after the turn of the century, rich copper deposits were discovered nearby, and a 90-mile-long railroad was built into the valley. Beginning in 1911, the copper was mined and smelted in the newborn town of Kennecott; McCarthy was established when gold was found in the region as well, and for more than two decades the area boomed. But by 1938 the depletion of high-grade ores and other problems forced the closing of the mines. Today the red and white

painted buildings of the two towns keep a lonely vigil over the groaning ice of a nearby glacier.

A few miles east of McCarthy on a tributary of the Chitina River is Chitistone Canyon, a popular destination for wildlife enthusiasts. Sliced deeply into the mountains, the canyon has walls that tower 2,000 feet or more above the Chitistone River. And on the craggy walls of the canyon live both Dall sheep and mountain goats. An estimated 16,000 Dall sheep live in the park, perhaps the largest concentration in all Alaska. Their

crown jewel of one of Alaska's most scenic parklands.

and even run at speeds of up to 20 miles an hour. Feeding on sparse grasses and sedges that grow on broader ledges and benches, they venture only occasionally—and with great caution—to the valley floors to feast on more luxuriant vegetation.

Even mountain goats are unable to survive in the land farther up the Chitina River valley. The river is born at the confluence of the Logan and Chitina glaciers, a massive collision of ice marking the entry into the high and barren interior world of ice and rock that makes this park one of our most spectacular. The peaks themselves—uncounted numbers over 10,000 feet and many over 16,000—have enormous influence on the weather of the region. Moisture-laden winds sweeping in from the Gulf of Alaska are raised and chilled, releasing their moisture as snow; hundreds of inches falls each year and most of it remains unmelted, giving rise to the park's immense glaciers. The Malaspina Glacier alone is bigger than Rhode Island.

Fortunately there are more accessible areas as well. The northern end of the park, for example, borders the Copper River valley, and the forested lowlands are dotted with lakes. The combination of forest, bog, lake, and tundra affords ideal living conditions for hosts of birds and mammals. Moose are especially abundant, seeking out ponds where they can wade into water and browse for hours at a time on waterlilies and other plants. The ponds are also useful to moose during the peak of the insect season; they often submerge up to their heads to avoid the pests.

The boreal owl, a species rare in the lower 48 states, thrives here as well, although it is rarely seen. Roosting by day in spruce trees, it awakens at dusk and becomes instantly alert, scanning the forest floor for any sign of movement. Once it spots a vole or a mouse—its principal prey—the owl lifts off its perch and swoops silently down to snatch its victim in razor-sharp talons.

Ospreys, found along forested river courses, are equally effective hunters, though fish, rather than rodents, are their primary food. The big graceful hawks sometimes hover effortlessly over the water for minutes at a time, waiting for fish to rise to the surface. Then, with folded wings, they dive, pull up abruptly, and more often than not, fly off with a fish flopping in their talons. Occasionally, too, they come up with an especially large salmon or whitefish—a catch that calls for a great deal of labored beating of waterlogged wings to get airborne again. Such are the sights and signs of life that make for memorable moments in this vast wilderness wonderland.

A bridge to the past

Sand dunes anywhere—ever-shifting, moving, sometimes burying entire towns and forests—always seem to capture the imagination. But dune fields north of the Arctic Circle must surely be the most unexpected of all. Yet Kobuk Valley National Park has them, and in plenty. There, south of a bend in the Kobuk River, are 25 square

brilliant white coats make them easy to spot, and their abundance increases the chance of seeing them.

Mountain goats, on the other hand, are elusive and less frequently seen. More closely related to chamois than to domestic goats, these cliff-dwelling acrobats are one of nature's curiosities. To escape the threat of predators such as wolves, they spend much of their lives on towering cliffs and crags, some of which might give pause to the most skillful mountaineer. They clamber fearlessly along narrow ledges and outcroppings, miles of the Great Kobuk Sand Dunes, dazzling mountains of gold up to 100 feet high, and off in another corner of the park are the Little Kobuk Sand Dunes, covering another 5 square miles. Formed of sand blown in from mountains well to the north, the dunes are not new features: studies indicate that they predate the last ice sheet (which, curiously, left this area free of glaciation) and are more than 33,000 years old.

The Kobuk Valley itself is broad and gentle, hemmed in by mountains on both the north and the south. At its center is the Kobuk River, meandering lazily westward toward the sea. Aside from the dune fields, this is not a place of great scenic spectacle. But it offers something else that is rare and special: a glimpse into Eskimo life both past and present.

This is the land of the Kuuvangmiit—People of the Kobuk—whose ancestors made their homes here for thousands of years. With a few concessions to modern technology, the Kuuvangmiit today live much as their forebears did. In the long daylight hours of summer they catch fish in the river, split them, and hang them over wooden racks to sun-dry in the traditional way, and every fall they hunt moose and caribou for their winter's meat supply. It is a yearly cycle that

has gone on without interruption for a long, long time.

Just how long becomes apparent on a visit to one of the park's unique treasures, Onion Portage, where the Kobuk River flows in a broad bend around some low bluffs. Here, for uncounted centuries, vast herds of Arctic caribou have passed each autumn on their annual southward migrations. And here also the Eskimo hunters came to replenish their larders for the winter.

Arctic archeology is still in its infancy, and the significance of Onion Portage as an early human site has been recognized only in recent decades. But long and patient excavations have now shown that humans have lived there almost without interruption for more than 9,500 years—to the time of the last major ice age. The artifacts they left behind reveal that peoples of some seven different cultures awaited the comings and goings of the caribou at Onion Portage, the most important archeological site in the Far North.

Perhaps even more exciting is the possibility of future discoveries, for the Kobuk region may well hold answers to the puzzle of man's migration from Asia to North America. Several times in the last million years, a land connection—Beringia or the so-called Bering Land Bridge—existed between North America and Siberia.

Sending up a wall of seething foam and spray, ice crashes to the sea from the face of the Hubbard Glacier, one of many *in Wrangell–St. Elias National Park. The vast and rugged mountain wilderness is the largest of all our national parks.*

More than 1,000 miles wide, it emerged during periods of glaciation when so much of the world's water supply was tied up in ice sheets that sea levels dropped drastically—in some cases by hundreds of feet.

Because the Kobuk area remained free of glaciation, migration of Asiatic animals was relatively easy, and some 30,000 years ago the region became populated with mammoths and the ancestors of modern horses, pronghorns, and bison. It was probably sometime between 25,000 and 30,000 years ago that the first nomadic hunters also trekked eastward from Siberia. They were no doubt unwitting pioneers, hunters following game herds across the wind-whipped plains of Beringia. And it was probably chance that led them so far east as to enter what is now Alaska. Establishing only temporary encampments, they moved when the game moved, and perhaps even retraced their route back to Asia several times.

It seems likely that these early North Americans passed through the Kobuk Valley, since the region was free of glaciation. In addition, an ice-free route extended eastward to the Mackenzie River valley of northern Canada, and from there another glacier-free corridor led southward to the interior of North America—quite possibly serving as a route by which the lower part of the continent was peopled.

By about 9,000 years ago Beringia had once more disappeared beneath the black and frigid sea, but by then the Kobuk Valley was well populated. Some of those who lived here, such as the Denbigh people who inhabited the valley about 5,000 years ago, were extraordinary craftsmen. Even more impressive were the Ipiutak people who lived in Kobuk Valley about 2,000 years ago and transformed pieces of walrus ivory into exquisitely carved tools and weapons. It seems curious that a people who lived in such a hostile climate, at times near the very edge of survival, would take the time to produce objects that were not only utilitarian, but beautiful as well. Today a strong sense of that ancient heritage persists in the Kobuk Valley, where the soft lilt of the Eskimo language can still be heard along the riverbanks.

Far Northern frontier

Spread across northern Alaska, beyond the Arctic Circle, is the 600-mile-long Brooks Range, an austere barrier that separates the interior lowlands of the Yukon River basin from Alaska's North Slope. And in the heart of the great mountain range is Gates of the Arctic National Park, a mysterious land with a haunting, timeless beauty, a place that is at once bleak and savage, yet at the same time pure and sweet and rich in life.

In reality, the park encompasses two distinct worlds. The southern slopes are covered with taiga—a scraggly forest made up of trees growing at their northernmost limit on earth. Composed mainly of black spruce, it is a forest clinging to the ragged edge of survival: the trees, sparse and widely spaced, are spindly—often only 10 to

The caterpillar of a swallowtail butterfly etches the sand with a stitchlike trail as it traverses a dune, not on a balmy southern seashore but in Arctic Alaska. Driven by the wind, the dunes at Kobuk Valley are slowly but surely advancing on the doomed forest in their path.

The granitic cliffs and spires of the brooding Arrigetch Peaks are but one face of Gates of the Arctic. In addition to the awesome mountains of the Brooks Range, the park includes extensive tracts of pristine Arctic tundra.

15 feet tall—and growth is so slow that trees only 3 inches in diameter may be 300 years old.

North of the Brooks Range, in contrast, is the treeless Arctic tundra. To many that word suggests vast hostile plains swept by seemingly perpetual winds, and in fact this is a land of severe extremes. For nine months of the year the tundra is locked beneath the icy grip of winter. Snow usually begins to fall in October and remains on the ground until May, and temperatures plummet to nearly 70°F below zero. Then the tundra is indeed a demanding habitat.

But in June a miracle begins. Gradually the hours of sunlight increase each day until, by about June 21, the summer solstice, the sun remains above the horizon for 24 hours a day. Warmed by continuous sunlight—temperatures approach 80° F—the tundra explodes with life. There is a sudden rush of blooming and bearing of fruits and seeds, for in the brief Arctic summer, plants and animals must complete their life cycles quickly before winter sets in again.

Melting snow supplies life-giving moisture, and though the amount of annual precipitation may be small, little of it evaporates. In addition, the entire region is underlain by permafrost, permanently frozen ground up to 2,000 feet thick. In most places it begins only a few inches beneath the surface, and so prevents meltwater from seeping into the ground. As a result, the tundra becomes a soggy world each spring, with bogs and ponds and pools of water everywhere.

The most common tundra plants are low-growing grasses and sedges that form tight, tough carpets clinging tenaciously to the thin layer of soil. Fighting for available space are other ground-hugging species: in some places there are carpets of creamy white reindeer moss, while elsewhere stunted willows—diminutive forms of the familiar trees—grow in spreading tangles. And everywhere there are flowers—the white, tufted stalks of Arctic cottongrass that warn of boggy ground, along with more colorful species such as mountain avens, buttercups, moss campion, lupines, and others, all of them dwarfed relatives of the more familiar plants found elsewhere.

Dwarf willow, growing only inches high, is one of the common plants of the soggy, boggy Arctic tundra.

All these plants support a surprising variety of animal life, from insects and ground squirrels to throngs of waterfowl and other birds. Among the most conspicuous are the magnificently antlered caribou, which spend their summers on the plains of the North Slope. The young are born there, and within days the spindly-legged calves are able to keep up with the adults on their travels. That is vital, for the caribou are restless wanderers by necessity: the big deer must be constantly on the move to new feeding grounds to avoid overgrazing their food supply. In summer they travel in small bands of 20 to 100 individuals, but fall triggers an internal urge and the deer begin to mass into herds that sometimes number in the thousands. Slowly they begin the trek southward, over well-used passes in the Brooks Range, to their forested wintering grounds hundreds of miles away.

Lemmings, too, sometimes migrate, though for different reasons. The little rodents, active throughout the year, feed voraciously on the tundra plants, tunneling beneath the snow to get at their food in winter. Their numbers vary greatly from year to year in periodic boom and bust cycles. During population explosions the stress of sheer numbers sometimes sets off mass migrations, with thousands of lemmings scurrying across the tundra in search of greener pastures, and so giving rise to the myth of mass suicide.

During peak years, the lemmings are a bonanza for such predators as wolves and foxes. Even grizzly bears supplement their root and berry diet with the small rodents when they can. But one bird in particular, the snowy owl, is especially closely linked to lemmings. Year-round residents of the Far North, they are so dependent on lemmings as a food supply that in years when lemming populations collapse, the great white birds often migrate all the way south to the lower 48 states, far from their normal home, in search of other kinds of rodents.

Late August marks the beginning of autumn in the Brooks Range. The signs are everywhere, from the flocks of birds winging south, to the plumpness of the bears, secure for winter with their layers of stored fat. The tundra soon becomes a blaze of color. Across the plains and in sweeping mountain valleys, the land is burnished with a lovely golden hue, accented here and there with red and ocher and yellow. The low angle of the sun lends additional warmth to the colors, for the days are rapidly becoming shorter now as the noonday sun sinks lower in the sky with each passing day. Too soon, in mid-November, the day comes when the sun does not rise at all, and a suffused glow on the horizon is all that remains of daylight. By then the jagged peaks of the Brooks Range are coated with snow, temperatures are dropping rapidly, and the tundra is relapsing into the long night of winter.

To many, Gates of the Arctic National Park represents the ultimate in Alaska's—and all America's—wilderness. For the adventurous, there is the exciting knowledge that what lies beyond the next ridge or mountain is not civilization, but another valley, peaceful and beautiful, where perhaps no other human has ever set foot. Here too is a sense of spaciousness, in this place where one grizzly bear requires a hundred square miles in which to earn a living and caribou may migrate more than 1,200 miles in a single season. "In wildness," wrote Thoreau, "is the preservation of the world." And in our own Alaskan parks as in perhaps no others, we can still find that feeling of wildness and freedom and grand and glorious open space so necessary to nurture the spirit and cleanse the soul.

On the treeless tundra, the majestic snowy owl has little choice but to nest on the ground. This one is raising her wings in a threatening gesture as she defends her young and her unhatched eggs. The big birds lay clutches of as many as eight eggs, and begin to incubate as soon as the first egg is laid. As a result, the firstborn chick is nearly fully grown by the time the last egg hatches.

Index
*Page numbers in **bold** type refer to illustrations.*

A

Abbey, Edward, 63, 146
Abnaki Indians, 17
Absaroka Range, 310, **312**
Acadia National Park, 13, 16–23
Adams, John Quincy, 331
Aetosaurs, 235
Agarics, fly, **240**
Agate Bridge, 233
Agate House, 235
Agaves, **81,** 157
Ahwahneechee Indians, 320
Akialoas, 171
Alaska, 98–105, 332–345
Alaska, Gulf of, 341
Alaska Range, 98
Alders, 334
Aleut Indians, 89
Alevins, 339
Algae, 18, 48, 285–286, 309, 334.
    See also Kelp; Moss, Irish;
    Rockweeds.
Allamandas, **287**
All-American Man, 66
Alligators, 15, **112,** 114, 115
Altar of Sacrifice, 324
Amakihis, **173**
Amanitas, **229**
    Amanita muscaria (fly agarics),
    240
American Bison Society, 274
American Samoa, National Park
    of, 15
Anacapa, **82,** 83, 84, 88
Anasazi, 131, 202–207, 235, 331
Anchorage, Alaska, 338
Anemones, sea, 243
Angel Arch, 65
Angels Landing, 324
Anhingas (snakebirds), 111, 112,
    113
Anoles, 285, **287**
Antigua, 284
Ants, carpenter, 220
Apache Indians, 40, 157
Apapanes, 171–172, **173**
Appalachian Range, 265
Appalachian Trail, 266
Aragonite
    crystals, **77, 298**
    trees, 79
Araucarioxylon arizonicum, 234
Arbutuses, trailing, 266
Archelons, **35**
Arches, 24–31, **85,** 330
Arches National Park, 14, 24–31,
    74
Arch Rock, 84, **85**
Arctic Circle, 341, 343
Arizona, 126–135, 232–237,
    256–257
Arkansas, 174–177
Arnicas, **93**
Arrigetch Peaks, **344**
Artist Point, **308**
Artist's Palette, 96
Aspens, **61,** 94, 292
    quaking, 182, **251,** 255, 310
Asters, tansy, 252, **253**
Atlatls, 202

Audubon, John James, **11,** 106
Avalanches, 230–231
Azaleas
    pink, **268**
    western, 241
    wild, 266

B

Baculites, **35**
Badger Creek, 130
Badgers, 14, **75**
Badlands, 32–37, 272–279
Badlands National Monument, 36
Badlands National Park, 14, 32–37
Bad River, 33, 34
Badwater, 96, **97**
Baker River, 217–218
Bald Hills, 245
Balds, 150
Baleen, 335
Bar Harbor, Maine, 18
Bar Island, 18
Barnacles, 22, **87,**
    acorn, 243
Barrow, Alaska, 333
Basalt, 308
Basketmakers, 201
Bass Harbor Head Lighthouse, **16**
Basslets, fairy (royal grammas),
    52, **53**
Bat Cave, 79–80, **79**
Bathhouse Row, 174, **175, 177**
Bats, 15, 79–81, **195,** 199, 281
    Mexican free-tailed, 79–80, **79**
Bead-rubies, **229**
Beans, 202
Beargrass, 15, **119,** 124
Bears
    Alaska brown, 336, 338, **339**
    black, **151,** 152, 220, 266, 267,
        269, 310, 322–323
    grizzly, 14, 102, 123
Beartooth Range, 310
Beavers, 17, **140,** 144, **181,** 184,
    292–293, **292**
Beavers, mountain, 242
Beehive Geyser, 304
Beetles, wood-boring, 260
Behunin, Isaac, 331
Bemelmans, Ludwig, 38
Bentonite, 275
Beringia (Bering Land Bridge),
    342–343
Big Beaver Valley, 218
Big Bend National Park, 15, 38–47
Big Foot, 37
Big Foot Pass, 34
Bigfork Chert, 176
Big Meadows, 266
Big Room, 81
Birches, 292
    paper, **181,** 182, 296–297
Biscayne Bay, **48**
Biscayne National Park, 14, 48–55
Bishop, Stephen, 196
Bison, 14, 33, 36, 37, 273–275, 278,
    278, 297–298, **302**
Bison Flats, 297
Blackbeard, (Edward Teach), 50,
    284

Blackbirds, red-winged, **320**
Blackbrush, 31, 65
Black Caesar, 50
Blackfoot Indians, 142, 143
Black Hills, 33, 296, 299
Bladderworts, 110
Blake, William, 281
Bloodroots, 265–266
Blueberries, bog, **98**
Bluebirds, mountain, **295**
Bluebonnets, Big Bend, 42–43, **45**
Blue Glacier, 231
Blue Hill Bay, **16**
Blue Mesa, **234**
Blue Ridge Mountains, 13,
    264–271
Boars, European wild, 152
Bobcats, **136,** 261, **308**
Bogachiel River, 224
Boneyard, 81
Book of Mormon, 331
Boquillas Canyon, 42
Borax, 97
Boxfish, spiny (bridled burrfish),
    52, **53**
Boxwork, 299, **299**
Bridalveil Fall, 316
Bridger, Jim, 142
Brooks, Mount, **104–105**
Brooks Range, 343, **344,** 345
Bryce, Ebenezer, 61
Bryce Canyon National Park,
    56–61
Bullfrogs, **20,** 21
Bumpass, Kendall, 190
Bumpass Hell, 190
Buntings, snow, 102
Burrfish, bridled (spiny boxfish),
    52, **53**
Burroughs, John, 70
Bush Key, 106
Buttercups
    alpine, 252, **252**
    snow, 247–251
Butterfield, John, 158
Butterfield Line, 158
Butterflies
    California sister, **321**
    common blue, **141**
    fulvia checkerspot, **127**
    monarch, 270
    tiger swallowtail, **247, 269**
    zebra, **112**
Butterflyfish, foureye, **282**
Byron, George Gordon, Lord, 195

C

Cacti, 43, **45, 47,** 67, **81,** 256, **256,**
    257, **257, 273,** 297, 298,
    327–328
Cades Cove, 152
Cadillac Mountain, 15, **18,** 23
Calcite, 78–79, 299
Calderas, 95, 305–308
California, 82–89, 96–97, 186–187,
    188–193, 238–245, 258–263
California, Gulf of, 63
Calypso orchids, 183

Candlelilla, 46
Canyonlands National Park, 14,
    62–69
Capitol Reef National Park, 14,
    70–75
Cardinal flowers, 267
Caribbean Sea, 281
Caribou, 14, 102, 103, 342, 345
Caribs, 284
Carlsbad Caverns National Park,
    13, 76–81
Carmel Formation, 74
Carson, Rachel, 17, 83
Cascade Pass, **218**
Cascade Range, 14, 91, 93, **93,**
    216–221
Cataract Canyon, 68–69, **69**
Caterpillars, **343**
Cathedral Rocks, **322**
Cathedral Valley, **73,** 74–75
Cather, Willa, 201
Catlin, George, 10, **11**
Cats, saber-toothed, 35
Cattle, 39, 275, 279
Cave of Life, 236
Cave pearls, **78,** 79
Caves, 76–81, 146, 194–199,
    294–299
Cedars
    incense, 320
    salt (tamarisks), 66
Century plants, 39, 43, **44**
Champlain, Samuel de, 17
Champosaurus, **35**
Channel Islands National Park,
    14, 82–89
Chanterelles, **228**
Chaos Crags, 190
Chaos Jumbles, 190
Chapin Mesa, **202,** 204
Charlottesville, Va., 267
Chats, yellow-breasted, 299
Cheatgrass, 31
Checkerboard Mesa, **327**
Checkerspots, fulvia, **127**
Chesler Park, 67
Cheyenne River, 33, 34
Chickarees (Douglas' squirrels),
    191, 220, **229,** 260, **261**
Chigmit Mountains, 338
Chihuahuan desert, 38, 39, 42, 156
Chinle Formation, 73, 235
Chipewyan, Fort, 289
Chipmunks, lodgepole, 191
Chippewa Indians, 289
Chisos Basin, 47
Chisos Mountains, 38, **45,** 47
Chiswell Islands, 336
Chitina Glacier, 341
Chitina River, 339, 341
Chitistone Canyon, 340
Chitistone River, 340
Chollas, **45**
Chuckwallas, 134
Chugach Range, 339
Chumash Indians, 88, 89
Cinder Cone, **189,** 190
Claret cups, **47**
Clark, Lake, 338–339, **340**
Clark, William, 124
Claron Formation, 58, 60, 61

Cliff Palace, 201, **205,** 206
Cliffroses, 31
Clouds, mountain wave, 311
Clover, dwarf, 252, **252**
Coconuts, 173
Cohab Canyon, 75
Colorado, 200–207, 246–255
Colorado Desert, 186–187
Colorado Plateau, 27, 58, 67, 69, 72, 235, 329, 331
Colorado River, 26, 63, **63,** 66, 68, **68,** 69, 127–128, **131,** 132, 235
Colter, John, 142
Coltsfoot, 265
Columbia Crest, 211
Columbines
    blue, 252, **252**
    crimson, **220**
    wild, **269**
Columbus, Christopher, 281, 284
Comanche Indians, 40
Comanche War Trail, 40
Conchs, queen, 287
Confluence, The, 63, 69
Congress, U.S., 12
Continental Divide (Great Divide), 122, 247, 254, 255
Cook, Charles W., 11
Cook, Dr. Frederick, 100
Copper, 340
Copper River valley, 341
Coral reefs, 15, 48–54, 55, 107, **280, 282–283,** 285–287
Corals, 48–49, 54, 55, 107, **280,** 282, 285–286
    brain, 49, 55, 107, **282,** 286
    elkhorn, 49, **283,** 286
    fire, **50**
    pillar, 286
    staghorn, 49, 107, **282,** 286
    star, **283**
Corbett, "Gentleman Jim," 176
Coreopsis, **86,** 88
Corn, 201
Cottonwicks, 52, **53**
Cottonwoods, 66, **71,** 225, **279**
    black, 334
Cottonwood Springs, 187
Cougars. *See* Mountain lions.
Cowlitz Glacier, **212**
Coyotes, **57,** 309
Crabs
    Atlantic rock, 21, **21**
    hermit, 285
Cranberries, lowbush, **98**
Crane, Stephen, 176
Cranes, sandhill, 309
Crater Hill, 299
Crater Lake National Park, 13, 15, 90–95
Cratework, 299
Crayfish,199, **199**
Creosote bushes, 46
Crickets, 199
Crinoids, orange, **50**
Croakers, 52
Crocodiles, 117
Crowther, Patricia, 196
Cryptobiotic soil, 63–65
Curlews, long-billed, 244
Custer, Henry, 217
Cypresses, **110,** 114

D

Dagger Flat, **38**
Dark Angel, 26
Dark Hollow Falls, 267
Daturas (jimsonweed), 75, 328
Deadman's Cay, 284
Death Valley National Park, 96–97
Deemer, Jesse, 40
Deer, 14
    black-tailed, **214,** 220, 241, 245
    mule, 31, 39–40, **44,** 60, **133,** 146, 202, 220, 278, 320–321
    white-tailed, 278
Delicate Arch, 24, **28–29**
Denali (Mt. McKinley) National Park, 14, 98–105
Denbigh people, 343
Denmark, 284
De Soto, Hernando, 176
Developmental Pueblo, 203
Devil's Den, 81
Devil's Hole, 97
Devil's Lane, 67
Diablo, Mount, 89
Dillon Pass, 33, 34
Dippers (water ouzels), 123, **215** 217, 263
Dogwoods, 266
    Pacific, 320
Doll House, 69
Doll's Theater, **78**
Dolphins, 287
Domínguez, Father, 331
Dominica, 284
Dorr, George B., 13
Douglas, Marjorie Stoneman, 109
Dream Lake, **248–249**
Dryads, 125
    yellow, 333–334
Dry Tortugas National Park, 106–107
Duck on the Rock, 26
Dutton, Clarence E., 57, 331

E

Eagle Rock, 26
Eagles
    bald, **17**
    golden, **46, 315**
East Temple, 324, 331
Echo River, 196–197, 198
Eels, moray, 50, **282,** 287
Egrets, snowy, **109**
Einstein, Albert, 127
El Capitan (California), 315, **322**
El Capitán (Texas), **154,** 155, **159**
Elk, 14, 144, 145, **145,** 297, **301,** 309
    Roosevelt, 14, 226–230, **229,** 245
Elkhorn Ranch, 278
Elliott Key, 50
Elms, American, 296
Emerald Mile, 241
Emerald Pools, **328**
Emmons Glacier, 215
Emory Peak, 47
Entelodonts, 35, **35**
Entrada Sandstone, 26–30, 74

Epsomite needles, 78–79
Eskimos, 342, 343
Everglades National Park, 14, 108–117
Excelsior Geyser, 304
Exfoliation, 316
Explorers' Club of New York, 100

F

Falcons, prairie, 274
Fern Canyon, **243**
Ferns
    lady, **228**
    maidenhair, **229,** 241
    sword, **229,** 241
Ferris, Joe, 273–274, 278
Figs, strangler, 115–116
Finches, gray-crowned rosy, 323
Fins (rock formations), 30
Firehole River, 301, **301,** 304, 309
Fires, 14, 116–117, 180, 184–185
Fireweeds, **93**
Fireworms, 107
Firs
    Douglas, 220, 226, 255
    Shasta red, 94
    subalpine, 94, 247, 254, 310
Fisher, Frederick Vining, 331
Fishers, 263
Fitzpatrick, Thomas "Broken Hand," 142
Fjords, 17, 335
Flattops Village, 235
Flint Ridge system, 196
Florida, 48–55, 106–107 108–117
Florida Keys, 55, 106
Flowstone, **76,** 79, 81
Folsom, David E., 11
Forbidden Peak, 217
Forest and Stream, 13
Forget-me-nots, alpine, 252, **252**
Fort Jefferson, 106–107, **107**
49 Palms Oasis, 187
Fossil reefs, 155–156
Fossils, 34–36, 233–235
Fountain Paint Pot, 309
Fowey, H.M.S., 50
Foxes
    gray, **134, 268**
    kit, 237
    red, **181,** 208
Fremont, John, 186
Fremont people, 74
Fremont River, 75
Frogs. *See* Bullfrogs; Treefrogs.
Frostwork, **298**
Frozen Niagara, 198, **198**
Fumaroles, **189,** 190, **305,** 309
Fungi, **223, 228, 229**
Furnace Creek, 96, 97

G

Gaige, Frederick M., 41
Gallatin Range, 310
Gallinules, purple, **114**
Gambusias (mosquitofish), 41–42, 114
Gannett, Henry, 333
Garden Key 106, **107**

Garfield Peak, 92
Garibaldis, **87**
Gars, 114
Gates of the Arctic National Park, 343–345
Gaywings, **185**
Geckos, Texas banded, **45**
General Grant National Park, 12
General Grant sequoia (Nation's Christmas Tree), **260**
General Sherman sequoia, 260
Geological Survey, U.S., 33, 333
Geraniums, wild, **143**
Geyserite (sinter), 302, 309
Geysers, 11, 14, **300,** 301–304, **305,** 308
Ghost Dance, 37
Giant Dome, 81
Giant Forest, 260
Giant Stairway, 316
Glacier Bay, 15, **332,** 333–335
Glacier Bay National Park, 332–335
Glacier National Park, 13, 118–125
Glacier Point, 14
Glaciers, 17, 98, 100–101, 120–122, **122,** 211–213, 215, 313, 321, 333, **336,** 341
Glass, Hugh, 142–143
Glenn Spring, 40, 46
Goats, mountain, **124,** 125, 221, 340–341
Gobies, sharknose, **282–283**
Gold, 340
Gophers, pocket, 221
Gorgonians, 286
    common, **282**
Grammas, royal (fairy basslets), 52, **53**
Grand Canyon National Park, **10,** 12, 13, 15, 126–135
Grand Canyon of the Tuolumne, 323
Grand Canyon of the Yellowstone, **10,** 11, **308,** 313
Grand Portage, 290, 293
Grand Prismatic Spring, **304**
Grand River, 69
Grand Staircase, 58, **58,** 60
Grand Teton National Park, 13, 14, 136–145
Grand View Point, 63
Grapes, Oregon, **141**
Grass, stipa, 65
Grasshoppers, **116**
Great Basin National Park, 146–147
Great Divide (Continental Divide), 122, **246,** 254, 255
Great Fountain Geyser, 304
Great Kobuk Sand Dunes, 342
Great Plains, 10, 156, 295, 297, 305
Great Smoky Mountains National Park, 13, 15, 148–153
Great Sonoran Desert, 186
Great Unconformity, 132
Great White Throne, 324, 331
Greenland, 240
Green Lake, 81
Green River (Kentucky), 197, **197**
Green River (Utah), **62, 68,** 69
Griggs, Dr. Robert, 337
Grinnell, George Bird, 13
Grinnell Lake, 15, **119**

Grizzly Giant sequoia, 321
Gros Ventres Indians, 142
Grotto Geyser, 304
Grouse, 309
    blue, **193**
    ruffed, **231**
Grunts, 52
    French, **283**
Guadalupe Hidalgo, Treaty of
    (1848), 40
Guadalupe Mountains, 77, 78,
    155–159
Guadalupe Mountains National
    Park, 14, 154–159
Guadalupe Peak, 155, **159**
Guadeloupe, 284
Gulf Stream, 48
Gulls, **86**
    Bonaparte's, 102
    herring, 21, **21,** 22
    mew, 102
    western, 85
Gypsum, 195, 198, **198**

H

Haleakala National Park, 160–165
Half Dome, **314,** 315–316
Hallett Peak, **248–249**
"Hamburger Rocks," **73**
Hammocks, 115, 116
Hance Rapids, 134
Harding Icefield, 335–336, **336**
Hares, snowshoe, **217, 221, 228**
Harper, Walter, 100
Harris, Jodie P., 40
Havasu Canyon, 135, **135**
Havasu Creek, 135, **135**
Havasu Falls, 135, **135**
Havasupai Indians, 128, 135
Hawaii (state), 160–165, 166–173
Hawaii Volcanoes National Park,
    15, 166–173
Hawks
    broad-winged, 270
    marsh, **140**
    sharp-shinned, **147**
Hayden, Ferdinand V., 11–12, 36
Hayden Valley, **302,** 312
Helictites, 78
Hemlocks, **193,** 267
    western, 225
Hepaticas, 265
Herons
    great blue, **140**
    green, **20,** 21
Hetch Hetchy Valley, 323
Hewitt, Bob, 72
Hickories, shagbark, **268**
Hidden Lake, 120, **122**
Hidden Valley, 186
High Sierra, 263, **321,** 323
Historic Pratt Lodge, 156
Hoh Glacier, 231
Hoh River, 224
Holley, Robert A., 77
Honeycreepers, 171–172
Hoodoos, **31,** 59, 61, **61**
Hopi Indians, 132, 204, 236
Horses, 35, **35**
Horseshoe Canyon, 67, **67**
Hot pools, 309
Hot spots, 162, 169
Hot springs, 174–176, **305**

Hot Springs National Park,
    174–177
Hualalai, 167
Hualapai Indians, 128
Hubbard Glacier, **342**
Huber Wash, 329
Hummingbirds, lucifer, 44
Hunter, Mount, 100
Hyacinths, water, **110**
Hyaenodon horridus, 35
Hydromagnesite balloons, 79

I

Ibises, white, **112**
Ice ages, 17, 120, 149, 261, 329,
    333, 342
Iceberg Rock, 81
Icebergs, 333, 334
Ice worms, 213
Idaho, 300–313
Idavain Falls, 339
Iiwis, 171–172
Iliamna Lake, 338
Iliamna Volcano, 338
Ipiutak people, 343
Irish moss, 22
Isaiah, 324
Ishi, 192–193
Isle Royale National Park, 14,
    178–185

J

Jackknife fish, 52, **52**
Jackrabbits, **38,** 146
    black-tailed, **44**
Jackson, William Henry, 12, **13**
Jackson Hole, 136, **136,** 139, 142,
    143, 144, 145
Jaegers, long-tailed, 103
Javelinas (collared peccaries), 40
Jays, Steller's, 242, **242**
Jefferson, Thomas, 176, 267
Jewelweed, **149**
Jimsonweed (daturas), 75, 328
Johnson, Albert, 97
Johnson, Nephi, 331
Johnson, Robert Underwood, 12
Joshua Tree National Park,
    186–187
Juncos, **228**
Juneau, Alaska, 333
Junipers, 30–31, **63,** 133–134,
    133, 134, 146
    Rocky Mountain, 278, **279,** 296
    Sierra, 323
    Utah, 201

K

Kabetogama Lake, 289
Kabetogama Peninsula, 289
Kaibab Plateau, 58, 128–130, 132
Kangaroo rats, **44,** 46, **236,** 237
Karstens, Harry P., 100
Karsten's Ridge, 100
Katmai, Mount, 337
Katmai National Park, 336–337,
    338, 339
Katydids, **268**
Kauai, 162

Kautz Glacier, 215
Kayenta, 74
Kelp, 84, **87,** 224
Kenai Fjords, 335–336, **336, 337**
Kenai Fjords National Park,
    335–336
Kenai Mountains, 335
Kennecott, Alaska, 339–340
Kentucky, 194–199
Kephart, Horace, 149
Kern Canyon, 261
Kilauea, **166, 169,** 170
Kingfishers, belted, **140**
Kinglets, **228**
Kings Canyon National Park, 12,
    258–263
King's Palace, 81
Kings River, 261
Kipahulu Valley, 165
Kipuka, 172–173
Kipuka Puaulu, 173
Kite, Everglades, 110
Kivas, 204, 206, 207, **207**
Koas, 172, **172**
Kobuk River, 341, 342
Kobuk Valley National Park,
    341–343
Kohala, 167
Kolob Arch, 26, 330
Kolob Terrace, 331
Krill, 334, 335
Krummholz, 230, 247
Kuuvangmiit people, 342

L

Ladies' tresses, white, **178**
Ladybugs, 270
Lady's slippers, yellow, 15, **178**
Lafayette National Park, 13
Lake Clark National Park, 338,
    340–341
Lake Clark Pass, 338
Lake of the Clouds, **80**
Land of Standing Rocks, 65, **66,**
    69
Landscape Arch, 24–26, **26**
Langhorne, Maj. George T., 40
La Pérouse, Jean-François de
    Galaup, count de, 163
Larks, horned, **223**
Larkspurs, **143**
Lassen, Peter, 190
Lassen Volcanic National Park, 13,
    188–193
Laurel, mountain, 266, **268**
Lechugilla Cave, 81
Lechuguilla Cave, 39–40, **45**
Lehman Caves, 146
Lemmings, 345
Lesser Antilles, 281, 284
Lewis and Clark expedition, 142,
    143
Liberty Cap, **211**
Lichens, 310, 333
Lignite, 275–276, **275**
Lilies
    mariposa, 36
    sego, **63,** 328
    spider, **55**
    wood, 252, **253**
Lily pads (plants). *See* Waterlilies.
Lily pads (rocks), **78**
Limberlost, 267

Limestone, 49, 78–79, 81, 109, 130,
    131, 155–156, 196–198,
    196, 299
Limpkins, 110
Little Colorado River, 131–132
Little Kobuk Sand Dunes, 342
Little Missouri, Dakota Territory,
    273
Little Missouri National Grass-
    land, 278
Little Missouri River, **272,** 273,
    275, 278
Lizards, 65
    anole, 285, **287**
    chuckwalla, 134
    collared, 31, **66**
    Texas banded gecko, **45**
"Lob pines," 290
Lobsters, spiny, 51, 287
Logan Glacier, 341
London, Jack, 161
Longfellow, Henry Wadsworth, 48,
    223
Long House, 201, **206**
Longs Peak, **255**
Loons, 179, 291, **291**
López de Cárdenas, García, 128
Lorimer, George Horace, 13
Louisiana Purchase (1803), 176
Lupines, **22, 143,** 144, 146
Lyell, Mount, 323
Lythrodynastes, 235

M

Mackenzie River, 343
Madrones, Pacific, 226
Magic Mountain, **218**
Magma, 305, 337
Maine, 16–23
Malaspina Glacier, 341
Maltese Cross Ranch, 273, 275
Mamey Peak, 284
Mammoth Cave National Park,
    194–199
Mammoth Hot Springs, **12,**
    306–307
Mammoths, 89
Manatees, **51**
Mangroves, 48, **54,** 55, 117
Manzanitas, 94, 191, **192**
Maples
    bigleaf, 225
    vine, 225, **229,** 242
Marble Gorge, 127, 130, 131, 132
Marching Men, 26
Marias Pass, 120
Marigolds, marsh, **185**
Mariscal Canyon, 42
Marmots
    hoary, 124, 221
    yellow-bellied, 92, **93,** 251
Marquesas Islands, 173
Martens, 92
    pine, **261,** 263
Masefield, John, 295
Mather, Steve, 14
Matushka Island, 336
Mauna Kea, 167
Mauna Loa, 167–169
Mazama, Mount, **94,** 94–95
Maze, The, 65, **66,** 69
McCarthy, Alaska, 339–340
McDonald, Alvin, 296

McDonald, Lake, 120
McDonald Creek, 123
McDonald Valley, 122, 123
McKinley, Mount (Denali), 98–100, **99, 105**
McKittrick, Felix, 156
McKittrick Canyon, 156, **158**
Merced River, 315, 316
Mergansers, common, **141**
Merriam Cone, 95
Mesa Verde National Park, 13, 200–207
Mescalero Apache Indians, 40, 157
Mesohippus, 35, **35**
Mesquite, 46
Metamynodons, **35**
Metoposaurs, 235
Michelanglo, 24
Michener, James, 167
Michigan, 178–185
Millard Ridge, 34
Millipedes, **229**
Mills, Enos, 13
Minerva Terrace, **12**
Miniconjou Sioux Indians, 37
Mink, **140**
Minnesota, 289–293
Miohippus, 35
Mirror Lake, 320
Missouri Stockmen's Association, 279
Mistletoe, 321
Modified Basketmaker Period, 201
Moenkopi Formation, 73
Mogollon people, 235
Mojave Desert, 186
Mongooses, 285
Monkey flowers, 94, **143, 309, 328**
Montana, 118–125, 300–313
Monticello, 267
Montreal, Canada, 289
Montserrat, 284
Moose, 103, **141,** 178–179, 180, 183–185, **184, 302,** 341
Moran, Thomas, **10,** 12, 13
Mores, marquis de, 275, 279
Mormon, Book of, 331
Mormons, 75, 328, 331
Morning glories, beach, **245**
Moroni, Mount, 331
Morrison Formation, 75
Mosquitofish (gambusias), 41, 114
Moss, Irish, 22
Moss, Spanish, 115
Moss, tree, **334**
Moths, yucca, 157
Mountain lions, 31, **155,** 157–158, 220, **330**
Mountain mahogany, 146
Mount Desert Island, 17–18
Mount McKinley (Denali) National Park, 14, 98–105
Mount Rainier National Park, 12, 208–215
Mudd, Samuel, 106–107
Mud pots, 190, 309, 313
Mug House, 207
Muir, John, **10,** 11, 12, 119, 233, 247, 256, 260, 315
Muldrow Glacier, 100–101
Mule deer. *See* Deer.
Mule ears, **143,** 144
Muley Twist Canyon, **73**
Mummy Lake, 204
Murrelets, marbled, 242–243

Mushrooms, **193, 240**
Muskrats, 21, **21**

N

National Park Service, 3, 14
Natural Bridge, **60**
Nautiluses, chambered, **157**
Navajo Indians, 70, 233, 331
Navajo Sandstone, 74, 327, **327,** 329, 330
Needles district, 65, 67
Nenes, 164, **164**
Nettles, rock, **47**
Nevada, 96–97
Nevada Fall, 316
Never Summer Range, **246**
Newfound Gap, 15
Newhalen River, 338
New Mexico, 76–81
Newport Cove, 18
Nisqually Glacier, 215
Norbeck Pass, 34
Norman Island, 284
North Carolina, 148–153
North Cascades National Park, 14, 216–221
North Dakota, 272–279
Northern Pacific Railroad, **12,** 275
North Rim, Grand Canyon, 127, **131,** 132, 133
North Slope, Alaska, 343, 345
Novarupta, 337
Nunataks, 335
"Nurse logs," 225
Nutcrackers, Clark's, **258,** 263

O

Oahu, 162
Oak, poison, 242
Oak Creek, 47
Oaks
  bur, 296
  California black, 320
  northern red, **268**
Obsidian, 308
Obsidian Cliff, 308
Ocotillos, 43–46
Octopuses, 51, **281,** 287
Ofu, 15
Ohelo, 173
Ohia lehuas, 164, **168,** 172
Old Faithful, 14, **300,** 301–304, 308
Old Faithful Inn, 14
Old Rhodes Key, 50
Oligocene period, 33, 34, 35
Olympic Mountains, 231
Olympic National Park, 14, 222–231
Olympic Peninsula, 226
Olympic rain forest, 224–226, **228**
Olympus, Mount, 231
Onion Portage, 342
Opossums, **266**
Orchids, 15, 94, **178,** 183
Orchis, showy, **268**
Oregon, 90–95
Oreodonts, 35, **35**
Organ, The, **324,** 331
Orioles, Scott's, 157
Ormsby, Waterman, 158–159

Ospreys, 341
Otter Cove, **18**
Otters
  river, **20,** 21
  sea, 336
Ouzels, water (dippers), 123, **215,** 217, 263
Overhanging Rock, **13**
Owls
  boreal, 341
  burrowing, **37**
  great horned, **91**
  snowy, 345, **345**
  spotted, 220
Oystercatchers, black, **224**

P

Pacific Flyway, 244
Pacific Plate, 188–189
Packrats, 237
Pahayokee, 109, 114
Pahoehoe, **168,** 170
Paintbrushes, **143,** 221, 252, **333**
Painted Cave, 89
Painted Desert, 233, 235, **237**
Painted Dunes, 188, 190
Paiute Indians, 57–58, 59, 61, 128, 146, 233, 331
Palikea Stream, 165
Paliku, 164
Palmettos, saw, **116,** 117
Palms, paurotis, **116**
Panamint City, 97
Panamint Mountains, 96
Papalas, 173
Parade of Elephants, 26
Paradise Ice Caves, 212
Paria River, 58–59
Parrotfish, 107, 286
  stoplight, 52, **52, 283**
Parsnips, cow, **320**
Pasqueflowers, western, **93**
Paunsaugunt Plateau, 58–60, **60**
Peas, prairie golden, **33**
Peccaries, collared (javelinas), 40
Pelicans
  brown, 55, **85,** 88, **112,** 244
  white, 310, 312
Penstemons, 36, 252, **253**
Periwinkles, 18–22
Permafrost, 344
Petrels, 15, 164–165
Petrified dunes, **327,** 329
Petrified Forest National Park, 12, 13, 232–237
Petrified forests, 233–237, 305
Petrified wood, **233, 234, 311,** 329
Petroglyphs, **27, 70,** 74, 173, 236, 285, 331
Phytosaurs, 235
Pictographs, 66, **67,** 74
Piedmont Plateau, 265
Pigeon River, 290
Pikas, **103,** 125, 191, 251, 310
Pine Canyon, **47**
Pinery, 158–159
Pines, 117, 309
  bristlecone, 96, 147
  limber, 247
  lodgepole, 14, 94, 254, 310
  pinyon, 30, 60–61, 133–134, **133,** 146, 201

ponderosa, 60, 93, 133, 255, 296, **328**
  Torrey, 89
  white, 290
  whitebark, 94, 310
Pine Spring Canyon, 158, 159
Pink Cliffs, **56–57,** 58, 61
Pinnipeds, 86, 87
Pirates, 48, 50, 287
Pitcher plants, northern, **293**
Pit houses, 204, 235
Pit rooms, 203
Placerias, 235
Plantations, **286**
Poison oak, 242
Polynesians, 173
Polyps, coral, 48–49, 285–286, 287
Polyps, gorgonian, 286
Ponce de León, Juan, 106
Poppies, Arctic, **103**
Porcupines, 30, **144**
Porpoises, harbor, 22
Post Office, The, 299
Pottery, **201,** 202, 204, 207
Powell, John Wesley, 10, **10,** 69, 130, 331
Powell, Lake, 69, 132
Prairie dogs, 36–37, **37,** 278, **296,** 297, 298
Pratt, Wallace, 156
Pratt, William, 13
Prickly pears, **45, 81, 273,** 297, 298
Primroses, evening, **27**
Prince's plumes, 72–73
Pronghorns, 36, 39–40, 278, 297, **297,** 298
Protoceras, 35, **35**
Ptarmigan, 103
  white-tailed, 125, **125**
Pterosaur, Texas, **46,** 47
Pueblos (buildings), 203–207, 235–236
Pueblos (people), 40, 204
Puerco Pueblo, 235–236
Puerco River, 235–236
Puffballs, giant, 270
Puffins, horned, 336, **337**
Puget Sound, 208, 218
Pumas. *See* Mountain lions.
Pumice Desert, 95
Pumpkin Mountain, 217
Pupfish, Devil's Hole, 96–97

Q

Quail
  Gambel's, **324**
  scaled, **44**
Queen's Chamber, 81
Queens Garden, 61
Queen Victoria (Whistler's Mother), **25,** 26
Queets River, 224
Quinault River, 224

R

Rabbits, 202. *See also* Jackrabbits.
Raccoons, **113,** 177, 245
Rainbow Falls, **148**
Rain forests, 15, 224–226, 333, 336

Rainy Lake, 289, 290, 293
Rainier, Mount, 208–215, **209, 211**
Rapids, **10**, 68–69
Rats
  kangaroo, **44**, 46, **236**, 237
  wood-, 237
Rattlesnakes, black-tailed, **45**
Ravens, 92, 271
Redbuds, 266
Redoubt Volcano, 338
Redwall Cliffs, 130, 134, **135**
Redwood National Park, 14,
  238–245
Redwoods, 14, 238–241, **239, 241**
  coast, 239–240, 245
  dawn, 240
  sierra (giant sequoias), 12, 13,
    15, 240, 256–259
Reef Bay, 284, 285, 287
Reef Bay Trail, 284
Rhinoceroses, 35
Rhododendrons, 150–151, **150,**
  241
Rhyolite, 308
Ribbon Fall, 316
Rincon Mountain District, 256–257
Rincon Range, 256
Ring of Fire, 168, 188
Ringtails, **24**, 31, 75
Río Conchos, 42
Rio Grande, 38, 40–42, **42**
Rio Grande Wild and Scenic River,
  42
Riverside Geyser, 304
Riverside Walk, 330
Roadrunners, 43, **43**
Rock beauties, 52, **53**
Rockefeller, John D., Jr., 14
Rock nettles, **47**
Rock of Ages, 81
Rockweeds, 22
Rocky Mountain National Park,
  246–255
Rocky Mountains, 13, 15, 58, 72,
  120, 139, 235, 246–255
Roosevelt, Theodore, 12, 226,
  245, 273–279
Rosebay, California, 241
Roses, **22**
Ross Lake, 217
Royal Arch, 316

S

Sagebrush, 146, 275, **279**
Sage Creek Wilderness Area,
  33, 36
Saguaro National Park, 256–257
St. Croix, U.S. Virgin Islands,
  281
St. Elias, Mount, 339
St. Elias Range, 339
St. John, U.S. Virgin Islands,
  280–287
St. Kitts, 284
St. Thomas, U.S. Virgin Islands,
  281
Salamanders
  marbled, **153**
  pygmy, **153**
  red, **153**
Salmon, 338–339, **339**
  kokanee, 123
Salt, 27

Salt Creek, 65–66, 67, 68
Salt Creek Canyon, 66
Salt domes, 67–68
Saltpeter, 195
Salt Valley, 27–28
Sand divers, **283**
Sand dunes, 31, 88, **89**, 341–342,
  343
Sanderlings, 244
Sandpipers, spotted, **140**
San Miguel Island, 83, 86–87, **88,**
  89
Santa Barbara Island, 83, 85
Santa Cruz Island, 83, **86,** 89
Santa Elena Canyon, 42, **42**
Santa Monica Mountains, 84
Santarosae, 84
Santa Rosa Island, 83, 88–89
Saturday Evening Post, The, 13
Saw grass, 15, 109
Schilderia, 234
Schoodic Peninsula, 17
Scoria, 278
  badlands, **274**
Scorpions, **44**
Scott, Mount, 92
Scott, Walter, 97
Scotty's Castle, 97
Sea anemones, 243
Sea cabbages, **225**
Sea fans, **283**
Sea hares, 54
Sea lions
  California, 86–87
  Steller, 87, 336, **337**
Seals, 86–87
  elephant, **83,** 87
  Guadalupe fur, 87
  harbor, **20**, 21, 87, 243, **244**, 334
Sea stacks, **85**, 223, 224
Sea urchins, 54, **225**, 287
  long-spined, **282**
Selenium, 72–73
Sentinel Falls, 316
Sequoia National Park, 12, 14,
  258–263, 321
Sequoias, giant (sierra redwoods),
  12, 13, 240, 258–260, 321
  General Grant (Nation's
    Christmas Tree), **258**
  General Sherman, 258, 259
  Grizzly Giant, 321
Sergeant majors, **282**
Sharks, hammerhead, 54
Sheep
  bighorn, 37, 124–125, 134, 146,
    187, **255**
  Dall, 14, 102, **102,** 340–341
Sheep Rock, 26
Shelley, Percy Bysshe, 186
Shenandoah National Park, 13, 14,
  15, 264–271
Shenandoah Valley, 265
Shooting stars, 146, 252, **252**
Shoshone Indians, 97, 142, 146
Shrews, 242
  water, 263
Shrimps, 54
  banded coral, **283**
  cleaner, 51
  fairy, 43, 72, 287
Shuksan, Mount, 217, **221**
Sierra del Carmen, **39**
Sierra Nevada, **10**, 11, 258, 260,
  261, 263, 315

Silica, 302, 305, 329
Silverswords, **161,** 163–164
Sinagua people, 235
Sinkholes, 34, 197
Sinter (geyserite), 302, 309
Sioux Indians, 33, 37, 273, 289
Skagit River, 217, 218
Skyline Arch, 26
Skyline Drive, 266
Slugs, 225
  banana, **289**
Smith, Jedediah, 34, 142, 331
Smith, Joseph, 331
Snails
  apple, 110
  striped forest, **268**
  tree, 116, **117**
  Zion, 327
Snakebirds (anhingas), 111, 112,
  113
Snake River, 136–139, 144
Snakes, 65
  black-tailed rattle-, **45**
Snappers, yellowtail, **283**
Snow Creek Falls, 316
Snowdrift Avenue, **298**
Snow plants, **190,** 191
Soda Butte Creek, **312**
Soda Straw Forest, 78
Sol Duc Falls, **230**
Solitude, Lake, 146
Somes Sound, 17
Sonoran Desert, 256
Sotols, 39
Sourdough Mountain, 217
"Sourdoughs," 100
South Dakota, 32–37, 294–299
South Rim, Grand Canyon, 127,
  127, 132, 133
South Snake Range, 146, 147
Spanish Bottom, **69**
Spanish moss, 115
Specimen Ridge, 305, 310
Sperry Glacier, 122
Spiders, jumping, **113**
Spiderworts, Virginia, **268**
Sponges, 54–55, **225,** 286
  purple vase, **283**
Spoonbills, roseate, **113,** 117
Spring beauties, big-rooted, 252
  253
Springfish, 199
Spruces
  black, 343–344
  Colorado blue, 255
  Engelmann, 247, 254, 310
  red, 22
  Sitka, 225, **228, 334**
Squash, 201, 202
Squirrelfish, **283**
Squirrels
  Abert, 133, 255
  Belding's ground, 323
  Douglas' (chickarees), 220,
    229, 259, **259**
  flying, 191
  Kaibab, **132,** 133
  red, **11,** 254–255
Stalactites, 78, 79, 197
Stalagmites, 79, 81, 197
Starfish, (sea stars), 21, **21**, 22,
  87, 225
Steel, William Gladstone, 13
Stevens, Hazard, 208–210
Stingrays, 54, 287

Stipa grass, 65
Stony Man Mountain, 15
Storks, wood, 114–115
Stuck, the Rev. Hudson, 98, 100
Sublett, Rolth, 80
Succession, biological, 180–182,
  218, 220, 333–334
Sulfide Creek, 217–218
Sulfide Glacier, 217
Sulfur, **169,** 190, 309
Sullivan, John L., 176
Summerville Formation, 75
Supai Group, 130
Superior, Lake, 178, 180, 290
Surgeonfish, 51
Swallowtails, tiger, **247, 269**
Swans, trumpeter, 14, **139,** 144

T

Tahoma Glacier, 215
Tainos, 284
Tall Trees Grove, 241
Tamaracks, 22
Tamarisks (salt cedars), 66
Tanagers, western, **131**
Tangs, blue, **283**
Tapestry Wall, **74**
Tatoosh Range, **211**
Tatum, Robert, 100
Tau, 15
Tehama, Mount, 189
Telescope Peak, **97**
Temple of the Sun, **76**
Tenaya Creek, 316
Tennessee, 148–153
Tennyson, Alfred, Lord, 33
Terns
  Arctic, 102–103
  roddy, 106
  sooty, 106
Terrapins, diamondback, 117
Teton Range, 136–145, **137,** 310
Texas, 38–47, 154–159
Theodore Roosevelt National
  Park, 14, 272–279
Thoreau, Henry David, 24, 91, 345
Thor's Hammer, 59
Three Gossips, 26, **31**
Three Patriarchs, 331
Thunder Hole, 17–18
Tide pools, 223–224
Tidewater, 265
Titanotheres, 34–35, **35**
Toads
  spadefoot, 43, 72
  western, **140**
  Yosemite, 323
Toroweap Overlook, **131**
Tower Falls, 308
Tower of Babel, **25**
Tower Ruin, 66
Treefrogs, **112, 229, 287**
  canyon, **30**
Tree moss, **334**
Tree snails, 116, **117**
Trilliums, 241, 265
  large white, **271**
Troglobites, 199
Troglophiles, 199
Trogloxenes, 199
Tropic birds, white-tailed, **164**
Trunk Bay, **284**
Trunkfish, smooth, **282**

Tucson Mountain District, 257
Tulip trees, **265**, 266–267, **269**
Tundra, **99**, 101–103
    alpine, 247–251, 310
    Arctic, 344, **344, 345**
Tuolumne Meadows, 323
Tuolumne River, 323
Turkeys, 177, 204
Turkey tails, **229**
Turtles, 34, **35**, 110–111
    eastern box, **269**
    Florida redbelly, **113**
    green, 15
    hawksbill, 15, **282**
    See also Terrapins.
Tutuila, 15
Twain, Mark, 323
Twin Buttes, 309
Twin Domes, 81

Vélez de Escalante, Father, 331
Verbenas, sand, **245**
Vernal Fall, 316
Violets, **140**
    common blue, **269**
    yellow, 252, **253**
Virgin, Thomas, 331
Virginia, 264–271
Virgin Islands, U.S., 280–287
Virgin Islands National Park, 280–287
Virgin River, 324, 329, 331
    North Fork, 324, 328–329
Vishnu Schist, 132, 134, 135
Visitors' Guide, 8–9
Volcanic rock pinnacles, **96**
Volcanoes, 94–95, 188–193, 208–215, 281, 304–308, 329–330, 336–338
Voyageurs National Park, 14, 288–293
Vultures, turkey, **268**

Weeden, Robert B., 178
Weeping Rock, 327
West Island, 88
West Temple, 331
West Thumb, 308
Whales
    gray, 84, 243
    humpbacked, 287, 334–335
    killer, 334
Whale's Mouth, 81
Wharton, Joseph, 208
Wheeler Peak, 147, **147**
Whelks, dog, 21, **21**, 22
Whistler's Mother, (Queen Victoria), **25**, 26
White, Jim, 80
White Glacier, 231
White River, 33, 34
Whitney, Mount, 263
Wickersham, James, 100
Willows, **279**
    dwarf, 344, **344**
Wilson, Woodrow, 40
Wilson Canyon, 186
Wind Cave National Park, 13, 14, 294–299
Window, The, 47
Winfield, Scott, 88
Wingate, Benjamin, 74
Wingate Sandstone, 73–74, **74**
Witch hazel, 267–270
Wizard Cone, 95
Wizard Island, 90, 92, 95
Wolfe, Thomas, 301
Wolverines, 263
Wolves, 123, 178, 179–180, **182,** 183, 185, 292
Woodcocks, 23, 266, **271**
Woodland stars, **140**
Woodpeckers
    acorn, 320
    pileated, 220, **269, 289**

Woodrats, white-throated, 237
Woodworthia, 234
Worms, ice, 213
Wounded Knee Creek, 37
Wrangell Range, 339
Wrangell – St. Elias National Park, 339–341, **342**
Wrasses, bluehead, **283**
Wrens
    cactus, **45**
    winter, **229**
Wright, Cedric, 239
Wyoming, 136–147, 300–313

Y

Yellowstone Caldera, 309, 310
Yellowstone Lake, 308, 310–311
Yellowstone National Park, 11, 12, 14, 15, 300–313
Yellowstone Park Act (1872), 12
Yellowstone River, **302**, 312–313
Yews, American, 184
Yosemite, Lake, 316
Yosemite Falls, 316, **318–319**
Yosemite National Park, 11, 12, 14, 15, 314–323
Yosemite Valley, **315**, 316, 320
Young, Brigham, 331
Yuccas, 36, **38, 44,** 60, **81,** 157, 186 201, 202, 204, 297

Z

Zion Canyon, 324–331, **325**
Zion Narrows, 327, **329**, 330
Zion National Park, 26, 324–331
Zumwalt Meadow, 261

U

U'aus, 164–165
Ubehebe, 96
Ukak River, **338**
Upheaval Dome, 67–68
Uranium, 73
Utah, 24–31, 56–75, 324–331
Ute Indians, **27**

V

Valley of Ten Thousand Smokes, 337, **338**
Valley of the Vapors, 176, 177
Vampire Peak, 34
Vancouver, George, 163, 333
Vanilla leaf, **229**
Van Trump, P. B., 208–210
Vaughan, Henry, 265

W

Wahaula Heiau, 173
Wall, The, 34, **36**, 37
Warblers
    chestnut-sided, **268**
    Colima, 47
    Wilson's, **312**
    yellow, **140**
Washburn, Henry, 11
Washburn, Mount, 309
Washington, 208–215, 216–221, 222–231
Waterlilies, **291**
Waterpocket Fold, 72, **72**
Waterpockets, **75**
Weasels, long-tailed, 261, **313**

Acknowledgments and Credits

The editors appreciate the assistance of writers Durward L. Allen, Ruth W. Armstrong, William A. Bake, Conger Beasley, Jr., Greg Beaumont, Charles L. Cadieux, Hugh Crandall, Donna Dannen, Kent Dannen, Barbara Decker, Robert Decker, Roy Hayes, John F. Hoffman, Celia M. Hunter, Sandra L. Keith, Ruth E. Kirk, Anne LaBastille, Darwin Lambert, Allan May, Ben Moffett, Boyd Norton, Jack Rudloe, Bill Thomas, Connie Toops, Gilbert Wenger, and Donald Young.

Special contributions were also made by Donald L. Baars (Colorado Plateau geology) and Natalie Goldstein (archival picture material, "The Story of Our National Parks").

The editors acknowledge with gratitude the many contributions made by individuals in the National Park Service to the success of this book. Duncan Morrow, Chief Media Information Officer, was extraordinarily helpful as liaison.

Art

George Buctel: 64, 72, 84, 157 *left*, 250, 285
John Dawson: 44–45, 140-141, 228–229, 268–269, 282-283
Donnelley Cartographic Services: 59, 101, 128, 129, 138, 163, 180-181 (map only), 203, 219, 260, 267, 303, 317, 326
Geosystems: 6-7, 19, 41, 111, 121, 171, 210, 227, 250, 262, 285, 290, 335
Howard Friedman: 35, 46, 162, 196, 305 *right*
Vic Kalin: 205 (superimposed on photograph by Josef Muench)
National Park Service: 95, 122
Frank Schwartz: 58

Photographs

1 Alan D. Carey. 2-3 (Mt. Rainier National Park) David Muench. 10 National Park Service. 11 *left* The Granger Collection, New York; *right* The New York Public Library. 12 Montana Historical Society, Helena. 13 Denver Public Library, Western History Dept. 14 Santa Fe Industries, Inc. 15 Bryan Harry/National Park Service. 16 Kent & Donna Dannen. 17 Jeff Foott. 18 Glenn Van Nimwegen. 20 *top left* Bill Perry; *middle left* Kent & Donna Dannen; *top right* M. Stouffer/Animals Animals; *bottom* Leonard Lee Rue III/Animals Animals. 21 *top left* Jeff Rotman; *bottom left* Harry Engels/Bruce Coleman Inc.; *middle right* Manuel Rodriguez; *top & bottom right* Don & Pat Valenti. 22 *top* Hans Wendler; *bottom* Kent & Donna Dannen. 23 Glenn Van Nimwegen. 24 *left* Stephen J. Krasemann/DRK Photo. 24-25 Jeff Gnass. 26 Frank L. Mendonca. 27 *top* Glenn Van Nimwegen; *bottom* Tom Algire. 28-29 Tom & Pat Leeson. 30 Stephen Trimble. 31 Stephen Trimble. 32 Jeff Gnass. 33 Charles Palek/Earth Scenes. 36 Ed Cooper. 37 *left* John Gerlach/Animals Animals; *right* David C. Fritts/Animals Animals. 38 *left* Tom & Pat Leeson. 38-39 David Muench. 42 Jeff Gnass. 43 M. P. L. Fogden/Bruce Coleman Inc. 47 *left* David Muench; *right* Jim Bones. 48 *left* Douglas Faulkner/Sally Faulkner Collection. 48-49 James A. Kern. 50 Douglas Faulkner/Sally Faulkner Collection. 51 Jeff Foott. 52 *top* Douglas Faulkner/Sally Faulkner Collection; *bottom* Alex Kerstitch. 53 *top right* Alex Kerstitch; *remainder* Douglas Faulkner/Sally Faulkner Collection. 54 David Muench. 55 James A. Kern. 56-57 Bob Clemenz. 57 *right* Pat Powell. 60 Bob Clemenz. 61 *left* Josef Muench; *right* Glenn Van

Nimwegen. 62 David Muench. 63 Bill Ratcliffe. 66 *left* Wardene Weisser/Bruce Coleman Inc.; *right* Josef Muench. 67 David Muench. 68-69 Douglas Faulkner. 70 *left* Stephen Trimble. 70-71 David Muench. 73 *left* Josef Muench; *right* Stephen Trimble. 74 David Muench. 75 *top* Larry Rice; *bottom* Tom & Pat Leeson. 76 David Muench. 77 Stephen Fleming. 78 *left* Ed Cooper; remainder Bill Ratcliffe. 79 Robert & Linda Mitchell. 80 National Park Service. 81 David Muench. 82-83 Frans Lanting. 83 *right* Frans Lanting. 85 *top* Wild Shots Co. Photo/R. A. Clevenger; *bottom* Frans Lanting. 86 Frans Lanting. 87 Peter Arnold, Inc./Photos Bob Evans. 88 Tom Bean. 89 F. G. Hochberg. 90-91 David Muench. 91 *right* Leonard Lee Rue III. 93 *left* Philip Hyde; *top right* Don & Pat Valenti; *lower right* Connie Toops. 94 National Park Service. 96 Tom & Pat Leeson. 97 Pat O'Hara. 98 *left* Johnny Johnson. 98-99 Johnny Johnson. 100 Galen Rowell. 102 Craig Blacklock. 103 *top* Ed Cooper; *bottom* Craig Blacklock. 104-105 Rick McIntyre. 106 Connie Toops. 107 *top* Russ Finley; *bottom* Kent & Donna Dannen. 108 David Muench. 109 Caulion Singletary. 110 David Muench. 112 *top* Patti Murray/Animals Animals; *middle left* & *bottom right* Glenn Van Nimwegen; *center* James A. Kern; *bottom left* Stuart L. Craig/Bruce Coleman Inc. 113 *top right* Caulion Singletary; *middle left* Clyde L. Walker; *bottom left to right* Rod Planck, Jeff Foott, Laura Riley/Bruce Coleman Inc. 114 Stan Osolinski. 115 M. P. Kahl. 116 *top* Glenn Van Nimwegen; *bottom* Patricia Caulfield. 117 Glenn Van Nimwegen. 118-119 Ed Cooper. 119 *right* David Muench. 122 *left* National Park Service; *right* Ed Cooper. 123 Bob & Ira Spring. 124 Bill McRae. 125 *left* Charles G. Summers/Tom Stack & Associates; *right* Paul J. Oresky. 126-127 Manuel Rodriguez. 127 *right* E. S. Ross. 131 *left* Joseph Van Wormer/Bruce Coleman Inc.; *right* Josef Muench. 132 Joseph G. Hall. 133 Tom Bean. 134 Diane Allen. 135 David Muench. 136 *left* Erwin A. Bauer. 136-137 Tom Bean. 139 Jeff Foott. 143 David Muench. 144 Steven C. Kaufman. 145 Alan D. Carey. 146 Patti Murray/Animals Animals. 147 Jeff Gnass. 148 Pat O'Hara. 149 Connie Toops. 150 Sonja Bullaty & Angelo Lomeo. 151 Sonja Bullaty & Angelo Lomeo. 153 *center* Tom Blagden, Jr.; *top inset* John W. Netherton, Jr./Cumberland Valley Photographic Workshops; *lower inset* Jeff Foott. 154 Jeff Gnass. 155 Pat Powell. 157 *right* Steve Elmore. 158 Jim Bones. 159 David Muench. 160 David Muench. 161 Werner Stoy/Camera Hawaii. 164 *top* Sandy Sprunt/Photo Researchers; *bottom* Leonard Lee Rue III/Bruce Coleman Inc. 165 David Muench. 166 H. Armstrong Roberts. 167 Larry Ulrich. 168 David Muench. 169 David Cavagnaro. 172 David Muench. 173 Paul Banko/Hawaii Environmental Technology. 174 *left* Hot Springs National Park. 174-175 NPS Photo/Robert Mitchell. 176 Courtesy of the Arkansas History Commission, all rights reserved. 177 Hot Springs National Park. 178 *left* Tom Algire. 178-179 David Muench. 181 *top left* David Muench; *top right* Craig Blacklock. 182 *left* Jim Brandenburg/Frozen Images; *right* Rolf O. Peterson. 184 Rolf O. Peterson. 185 *left* David Muench; *right* Rolf O. Peterson. 186 Tom & Pat Leeson. 187 Tom Bean. 188 *left* Gerald A. Corsi. 188-189 Robert McKenzie. 190 George Elich. 191 Philip Hyde. 192 Josef Muench. 193 *top* David Cavagnaro; *bottom* Tom & Pat Leeson. 194 David Muench. 195 Kent & Donna Dannen. 197 David Muench. 198 *left*

Russ Kinne/Photo Researchers; *right* Kent & Donna Dannen. 199 Thomas C. Barr, Jr. 200 David Muench. 201 David Hiser/Aspen. 202 David Hiser/Aspen. 205 Josef Muench. 206 David Hiser/Aspen. 207 David Muench. 208 *left* Rolf O. Peterson. 208-209 Ed Cooper. 211 *left* Bob & Ira Spring; *right* Ruth & Louis Kirk. 212-213 Kirkendall/Spring. 214 Tom & Pat Leeson. 215 Charles A. Mauzy. 216 Bob & Ira Spring. 217 Pat Powell. 218 Diane Allen. 220 Hans Wendler. 221 David Muench. 222 David Muench. 223 Bob Clemenz. 224 *top* Ruth & Louis Kirk; *bottom* Tom & Pat Leeson. 225 Glenn Van Nimwegen. 230 David Muench. 231 Tom & Pat Leeson. 232 Larry Ulrich. 233 Stephen Trimble. 234 *left* Susan Brock; *right* Ed Cooper. 236 Allan Roberts. 237 Willard Clay. 238 Josef Muench. 239 Larry Ulrich. 240 Larry Ulrich. 241 Ed Cooper. 242 William J. Jahoda/Photo Researchers. 243 Connie Toops. 244 *upper* Larry Ulrich; *bottom* Joe & Carol McDonald/Animals Animals. 245 Charles A. Mauzy. 246 Don & Pat Valenti. 247 Kent & Donna Dannen. 248-249 Tom Algire. 251 Jeff Foott. 252 t*op left* & *bottom right* Kent & Donna Dannen; *top right* Manuel Rodriguez; *remainder* Jeff Foott. 253 *top left* Jeff Foott; *remainder* Kent & Donna Dannen. 254 David Muench. 255 Pat Powell. 256 Pat O'Hara. 257 David Muench. 258 *left* Jeff Foott. 258-259 Bob Clemenz. 260 Josef Muench. 261 *top* Leonard Lee Rue III/Animals Animals; bottom Bob & Clara Calhoun/Bruce Coleman Inc. 264 Willard Clay. 265 William Bake. 266 Jeff Foott. 270 David Muench. 271 Joe McDonald/Bruce Coleman Inc. 272 David Muench. 273 Greg Beaumont. 274 *left* Jeff Gnass; right Greg Beaumont. 275 Wilford Miller. 276-277 David Muench. 278 Jeff Gnass. 279 Glenn Van Nimwegen. 280 George Marler. 281 George Marler. 284 Russ Kinne/Photo Researchers. 286 George Marler. 287 George Marler. 288 David Muench. 289 Rolf O. Peterson. 291 *top* J. Arnold Bolz; *bottom* Rolf O. Peterson. 292 *top* Ed Cooper; *lower left* Wolfgang Bayer/Bruce Coleman Inc. 293 A. Limont/Bruce Coleman Inc. 294-295 John Shaw/Tom Stack & Associates. 295 *right* Greg Beaumont. 296 Jim Brandenburg. 297 Jeff Gnass. 298 National Park Service. 299 Ed Cooper. 300 Connie Toops. 301 Kent & Donna Dannen. 302 Steven Fuller. 304 Paul Chesley/Aspen. 305 *left* Daniel J. Cox. 306-307 David Muench. 308 *left* Ernest Wilkinson/Animals Animals; *right* Willard Clay. 310 Alan D. Carey. 311 Larry Ulrich. 312 *left* Daniel J. Cox; *right* Josef Muench. 313 Daniel J. Cox. 314 David Muench. 315 Gary R. Zahm/Bruce Coleman Inc. 318-319 Manuel Rodriguez. 320 Mary Lou Baer. 321 *top* Pat O'Hara; *lower left* E. S. Ross. 322 *left* David Muench/Image Bank; *right* Ed Cooper. 323 John Gerlach. 324 *left* G. C. Kelley. 324-325 Gerald A. Corsi. 327 David Muench. 328 *top* David Muench; bottom Manuel Rodriguez. 329 Gerald A. Corsi. 330 Wolfgang Bayer/Bruce Coleman Inc. 332 Tom Bean. 333 Art Wolfe/AlaskaPhoto. 334 Kent & Donna Dannen. 336 Steven C. Kaufman. 337 *left* Kent & Donna Dannen; *right* Stephen J. Krasemann/DRK Photo. 338 Dale M. Brown. 339 *top* Steven C. Kaufman; *bottom* Will Troyer/AlaskaPhoto. 340-341 Nancy Simmerman/AlaskaPhoto. 342 Tom Bean. 343 *top* Stephen J. Krasemann/DRK Photo; *bottom* Gil Mull/AlaskaPhoto. 344 *top* John & Margaret Ibbotson/AlaskaPhoto; *bottom* Stephen J. Krasemann/ DRK Photo. 345 Steven C. Kaufman.